Readings in **TWENTIETH CENTURY AMERICAN HISTORY**

edited by

DONALD R. McCOY and

RAYMOND G. O'CONNOR

The University of Kansas

THE MACMILLAN COMPANY, NEW YORK

COLLIER-MACMILLAN LTD., LONDON

First Printing

Library of Congress catalog card number: 62-16672

The Macmillan Company, New York
Collier-Macmillan Canada, Ltd., Galt, Ontario
Divisions of The Crowell-Collier Publishing Company

Printed in the United States of America

ACKNOWLEDGMENTS

The editors wish to express their appreciation for use of
the following copyrighted material:

Oliver Wendell Homes, Jr., "The Path of Law," *Harvard
Law Review, X* (1897), pp. 468-478. Copyright (1897)
by The Harvard Law Review Association. Used by permission.

Copyright ©, 1907, *Pragmatism, A New Name for Some
Old Ways of Thinking* by William James. Reprinted by
permission of Paul R. Reynolds and Son, 599 Fifth Avenue, New York 17, N.Y.

Reprinted with the permission of Charles Scribner's Sons
from THEODORE ROOSEVELT: AN AUTOBIOGRAPHY, p. 357,
by Theodore Roosevelt. Copyright 1913 Charles Scribner's
Sons; renewal copyright 1941 Edith K. Carrow Roosevelt.

Reprinted with the permission of Charles Scribner's Sons
from "Radicalism" by George Soule from AMERICA NOW,
pp. 259-263, edited by Harold E. Stearns.

To Vivian and Sally

a word to the reader

SINCE World War II, the study of the recent history of the United States has grown increasingly popular. Textbooks on the period have multiplied as have books dealing with many of its specialized facets. Until now, though, no book of readings and documents designed specifically for students of recent American history has been published.

The present volume was compiled and edited specifically to complement the textbooks and teaching patterns used in recent American history courses, and to encompass the interests of general readers. The book is meant to be usable rather than comprehensive. Yet it includes a range of material sufficiently broad to acquaint the reader with the complexities, the main channels, and the eddies, of twentieth century United States history. The readings embrace diplomatic, economic, and political affairs, as well as intellectual and social trends. Documents, articles, and books—many of which are relatively inaccessible to students and general readers—have been drawn on in preparing this book. The views of government, parties and interest groups, politicians and statesmen, scholars and thinkers, commentators and editors are used to illuminate dominant trends, turning points, and influential new ideas.

While the selections do not and can not reflect our views on specific events and ideas, our main objective has been to document the conflicts and contrasts of recent American history, not only to reflect the past but to tell what contemporaries wrote and said about it. We hope that the result will be found instructive and interesting, that it will generate your interest in becoming more intimately acquainted with the past.

Donald R. McCoy
Raymond G. O'Connor

contents

III   The Progressive Era   71

IV   The United States: Great World Power   111

V World War I and World Peace 151

VI The Mixture As Before? 183

IX The Way Back (1933–1940)   301

XII World War II (1941–1945)   413

XIII Leader Of The Free World (1946–1961)   457

XVI Our Generation and Our Future   587

the nineteenth century heritage

NINETEENTH century America left much to the twentieth century. Not only did it pass on most of the gifts of the eighteenth century like Individualism, Freedom, Constitutionalism, Republicanism, and Destiny, but it added a bequest of its own, a bequest even more revolutionary than that of the eighteenth century. The nation's size had more than tripled and its population increased fourteen-fold. Technology, manufacturing, commerce, and finance had transformed the land from an agricultural society to the world's greatest industrial producer. This development had made possible standards of living virtually undreamed of in 1800.

Yet the nineteenth century also passed on problems. The economic changes required disturbing adjustments from an unusually adaptable people. The new economic system smashed some of the better restraints of the old system and presented additional temptations to the venturesome. The erosion of social patterns, the increasing concentration of wealth and power, the loss of homogeneity, the developing barriers between social classes and groups, the sharper human competition for success, all contributed to unrest in the land. The assertion that this should be tolerated because it resulted from the relentless natural laws of the accumulation of wealth and competition could not calm the trouble. Nor could the teaching that reliability, persistence, obedience, and skill would make life worth while and reward probable.

The social critics of the last quarter of the nineteenth century reflected the turmoil of the times. Charges were made that the pursuit of self-interest was numbing sensitivity to suffering and injustice. The economic system was often pictured as permitting inequitable distribution of wealth, wasting human and natural resources, and encouraging the follies of conspicuous consumption and monetarily based standards of appraising beauty and ethics. The rich, it appeared, had too much of everything; the poor had not enough of anything. Life was hard for the lower half of society. Speculation, price gouging, hard money policies, and the fierce, unstable competition of the market place made the life of the worker, the farmer, and the small businessman precarious.

The myriad of solutions proposed for these problems added to the twentieth century's inheritance. Charles Sheldon asked "What would Jesus do?" and found in Him answers not only to the economic questions of the time but to the moral issues. Henry George demanded common ownership of land. Lester Ward advocated the development of a new political system, Sociocracy, where a society ruled by the gambles of individuals would yield to a society consciously acting in the interests of all society. The Populists prescribed a large-scale program of government regulation and ownership. Even the major party platforms did not avoid controversy, with the Republicans, for example, offering a mixture of defenses for tariff protectionism and hard money with demands for tariff reciprocity, voting reforms, and increased rights for women.

The nineteenth century died peacefully, but it left its resources and problems, its analyses and prescriptions as a complicated heritage for the twentieth century.

1

The Watershed of the Nineties

☆ *As the nineteenth century approached its end, new ideas and new forces were emerging that presaged the creation of a new America. Professor Commager, in the following selection, portrays the juxtaposition of the old and the new.** ☆

The decade of the nineties is the watershed of American history. As with all watersheds the topography is blurred, but in the perspective of half a century the grand outlines emerge clearly. On the one side lies an America predominantly agricultural; concerned with domestic problems; conforming, intellectually at least, to the political, economic, and moral principles inherited from the seventeenth and eighteenth centuries—an America still in the making, physically and socially; an America on the whole self-confident, self-contained, self-reliant, and conscious of its unique character and of a unique destiny. On the other side lies the modern America, predominantly urban and industrial; inextricably involved in world economy and politics; troubled with the problems that had long been thought peculiar to the Old World; experiencing profound changes in population, social institutions, economy, and technology; and trying to accommodate its traditional institutions and habits of thought to conditions new and in part alien.

The process of adjustment was, to be

sure, nothing novel in American experience. No people of modern times had ampler experience in adaptation or had proved more adaptable. Instability had characterized American society from the time the first settlers landed along the banks of the James and on the shores of Cape Cod down to the passing of the frontier almost three centuries later. The up-rooting from the Old World—a phenomenon which persisted for three centuries—was the first and perhaps the most profound wrench, and as each successive generation pulled up stakes and moved west, the process of transplanting and accommodation to new physical and social conditions was repeated. Never had that process been more violent or complex than during the generation after the Civil War—a generation which saw the expansion of settlement from the Missouri to the Pacific, the disruption of the plantation system and the redistribution of white and Negro population in the South, a revolution in agriculture, the rise of the modern industrial city, and the coming of the new immigration.

Yet throughout the nineteenth century this process of adjustment, for all the disorder with which it was attended, took

* From Henry Steele Commager, *The American Mind*, pp. 41-43. Copyright, 1950, by Yale University Press, New Haven. Used by permission.

But now—? right gone—?

place within an economic and social framework that was reasonably stable and a political and moral framework that was almost entirely so. Thus the institutions of property, family, school, church, and state, although subjected to continuous buffetings, were never seriously challenged. Thus, though men had to find new techniques of government, the fundamental practices of democracy were everywhere taken for granted. Thus the ethical standards to which men conformed were rarely questioned. In short, to the nineteenth-century American the cosmic scheme was familiar, the cosmic laws were regular. Even the processes of disintegration and reintegration followed a familiar pattern.

Certainly, though there was a continuous breaking up and reshaping of communities and even of institutions, there was no progressive deterioration from frontier to frontier or from country to city. Quite the contrary. The heritage of the past which pioneers took with them into the wilderness or which countryfolk brought to the cities, though it might be temporarily dissipated, was never lost, and the various processes of adaptation were material rather than moral. The traditions of western civilization were, after all, unbroken, and the American traditions, planted in the seventeenth and eighteenth centuries on the eastern seaboard, flourished without embarrassment over the whole continental expanse throughout the nineteenth century. If American society never achieved stability, (neither did it suffer from stagnation or decay.) If some of the amenities and even the achievements of civilization were sacrificed to change, something too was gained in new opportunities for the demonstration of energy, ingenuity, and independence.

With the closing years of the nineteenth century, this familiar pattern was distorted, and the rhythm of change became impetuous and erratic. Change itself became qualitative as well as quantitative. As a result, the demands made upon the integrity of the American character and the resourcefulness of the American mind at the end of the century were more complex and imperative than at any time in a hundred years. It was not only that Americans had to adjust themselves to changes in economy and society more abrupt and pervasive than ever before. It was rather that for the first time in their national experience they were confronted with a challenge to their philosophical assumptions. They were not unaccustomed to profound alterations in their physical surroundings; they were unprepared for the crumbling of their cosmic scheme. They were now to be required not only to articulate their economy to a new technology and adjust their society to new ways of life—that was a familiar task—but to make their politics and morals conform to new scientific and philosophical precepts. Under the impact of these new forces, the note of confidence which had long characterized the American accent gave way to doubt, self-assurance to bewilderment, and resolution to confusion.

2

Wealth

☆ *Andrew Carnegie (1835-1919), came to the United States in
1848. Beginning his career as a bobbin boy at $1.20 a week, he be-
came an outstanding figure in American industrial development and
one of the wealthiest men in the country. His words here reveal his
concern for the useful application of wealth.** ☆

To-day the world obtains commodities
of excellent quality at prices which even
the generation preceding this would have
deemed incredible. In the commercial
world similar causes have produced similar results, and the race is benefited thereby. The poor enjoy what the rich could
not before afford. What were the luxuries
have become the necessaries of life. The
laborer has now more comforts than the
farmer had a few generations ago. The
farmer has more luxuries than the landlord had, and is more richly clad and better housed. The landlord has books and
pictures rarer, and appointments more
artistic, than the King could then obtain.
The price we pay for this salutary
change is, no doubt, great. We assemble
thousands of operatives in the factory, in
the mine, and in the counting-house, of
whom the employer can know little or
nothing, and to whom the employer is
little better than a myth. All intercourse
between them is at an end. Rigid Castes
are formed, and, as usual, mutual ignorance breeds mutual distrust. Each Caste

* From Andrew Carnegie, "Wealth," *North American Review*, CXLVIII (June 1889), pp. 654-657,
661-662.

is without sympathy for the other, and
ready to credit anything disparaging in
regard to it. Under the law of competition,
the employer of thousands is forced into
the strictest economies, among which the
rates paid to labor figure prominently,
and often there is friction between the
employer and the employed, between capital and labor, between rich and poor.
Human society loses homogeneity.
The price which society pays for the
law of competition, like the price it pays
for cheap comforts and luxuries, is also
great; but the advantages of this law are
also greater still, for it is to this law that
we owe our wonderful material development, which brings improved conditions
in its train. But, whether the law be be-
nign or not, we must say of it, as we say
of the change in the conditions of men to
which we have referred: It is here; we
cannot evade it; no substitutes for it have
been found; and while the law may be
sometimes hard for the individual, it is
best for the race, because it insures the
survival of the fittest in every department. We accept and welcome, therefore,
as conditions to which we must accommodate ourselves, great inequality of en-

vironment, the concentration of business, industrial and commercial, in the hands of a few, and the law of competition between these, as being not only beneficial, but essential for the future progress of the race. Having accepted these, it follows that there must be great scope for the exercise of special ability in the merchant and in the manufacturer who has to conduct affairs upon a great scale. That this talent for organization and management is rare among men is proved by the fact that it invariably secures for its possessor enormous rewards, no matter where or under what laws or conditions. The experienced in affairs always rate the MAN whose services can be obtained as a partner as not only the first consideration, but such as to render the question of his capital scarcely worth considering, for such men soon create capital; while, without the special talent required, capital soon takes wings. Such men become interested in firms or corporations using millions; and estimating only simple interest to be made upon the capital invested, it is inevitable that their income must exceed their expenditures, and that they must accumulate wealth. Nor is there any middle ground which such men can occupy, because the great manufacturing or commercial concern which does not earn at least interest upon its capital soon becomes bankrupt. It must either go forward or fall behind: to stand still is impossible. It is a condition essential for its successful operation that it should be thus far profitable, and even that, in addition to interest on capital, it should make profit. It is a law, as certain as any of the others named, that men possessed of this peculiar talent for affairs, under the free play of economic forces, must, of necessity, soon be in receipt of more revenue than can be judiciously expended upon themselves; and this law is as beneficial for the race as the others.

Objections to the foundations upon which society is based are not in order, because the condition of the race is better with these than it has been with any others which have been tried. Of the effect of any new substitutes proposed we cannot be sure. The Socialist or Anarchist who seeks to overturn present conditions is to be regarded as attacking the foundation upon which civilization itself rests, for civilization took its start from the day that the capable, industrious workman said to his incompetent and lazy fellow, "If thou dost not sow, thou shalt not reap," and thus ended primitive Communism by separating the drones from the bees. One who studies this subject will soon be brought face to face with the conclusion that upon the sacredness of property civilization itself depends—the right of the laborer to his hundred dollars in the savings bank, and equally the legal right of the millionaire to his millions. To those who propose to substitute Communism for this intense Individualism the answer, therefore, is: The race has tried that. All progress from that barbarous day to the present time has resulted from its displacement. Not evil, but good, has come to the race from the accumulation of wealth by those who have the ability and energy that produce it. But even if we admit for a moment that it might be better for the race to discard its present foundation, Individualism,—that it is a nobler ideal that man should labor, not for himself alone, but in and for a brotherhood of his fellows, and share with them all in common, realizing Swedenborg's idea of Heaven, where, as he says, the angels derive their happiness, not from laboring for self, but for each other,—even admit all this, and a sufficient answer is, This is not evolution, but revolution. It necessitates the changing of human nature itself—a work of aeons, even if it were good to change it, which we cannot know. It is not practicable in our day or in our age. Even if desirable theoretically, it belongs to another and long-succeeding sociological stratum. Our duty is with what is practicable now; with the next step possible in our day and generation. It is criminal to waste our energies in endeavoring to uproot, when all we can profitably or possibly accomplish is to bend the universal tree of humanity a little in the direction most favorable to the production of good fruit under existing circumstances. We might as well urge the destruction of the highest existing type of man because he failed to reach our ideal as to favor the destruction of Individualism, Private Property, the Law of Accumulation of Wealth, and the Law of Competition; for these are the highest results of human experience, the soil in which society so far has produced the best fruit. Unequally or unjustly, perhaps, as these laws sometimes operate, and imperfect as they appear to the Idealist, they are, nevertheless, like the highest type of man, the best and most valuable of all that humanity has yet accomplished. . . .

This, then, is held to be the duty of the man of Wealth: First, to set an example of modest, unostentatious living, shunning display or extravagance; to provide moderately for the legitimate wants of those dependent upon him; and after doing so to consider all surplus revenues which come to him simply as trust funds, which he is called upon to administer, and strictly bound as a matter of duty to administer in the manner which, in his judgment, is best calculated to produce the most beneficial results for the community —the man of wealth thus becoming the mere agent and trustee for his poorer brethren, bringing to their service his superior wisdom, experience, and ability to administer, doing for them better than they would or could do for themselves.

3

A Message to Garcia

☆ *Elbert Hubbard (1856-1915) wrote extensively on the relation-ship between character and success. His most popular effort, originally published in 1899 and reproduced below, reached a circulation in the tens of millions. His name became a byword for initiative, duty, and perseverance.** ☆

In all this Cuban business there is one man stands out on the horizon of my memory like Mars at perihelion.

When war broke out between Spain and the United States, it was very necessary to communicate quickly with the leader of the Insurgents. Garcia was somewhere in the mountain fastnesses of Cuba—no one knew where. No mail or telegraph message could reach him. The President must secure his co-operation, and quickly.

What to do!

Someone said to the President, "There is a fellow by the name of Rowan will find Garcia for you, if anybody can."

Rowan was sent for and given a letter to be delivered to Garcia. How the "fellow by the name of Rowan" took the letter, sealed it up in an oilskin pouch, strapped it over his heart, in four days landed by night off the coast of Cuba from an open boat, disappeared into the jungle, and in three weeks came out on the other side of the Island, having traversed a hostile country on foot, and delivered his letter to Garcia—are things I have no special

* From Elbert Hubbard, *A Message to Garcia,* pp. 9-16. Copyright, 1916, by The House of Hub-bard, East Aurora, New York. Used by permission.

desire now to tell in detail. The point that I wish to make is this: McKinley gave Rowan a letter to be delivered to Garcia; Rowan took the letter and did not ask, "Where is he at?"

By the Eternal! there is a man whose form should be cast in deathless bronze and the statue placed in every college of the land. It is not book-learning young men need, nor instruction about this and that, but a stiffening of the vertebrae which will cause them to be loyal to a trust, to act promptly, concentrate their energies: do the thing—"Carry a message to Garcia."

General Garcia is dead now, but there are other Garcias. No man who has en-deavored to carry out an enterprise where many hands were needed, but has been well-nigh appalled at times by the imbe-cility of the average man—the inability or unwillingness to concentrate on a thing and do it.

Slipshod assistance, foolish inattention, dowdy indifference, and half-hearted work seem the rule; and no man suc-ceeds, unless by hook or crook or threat he forces or bribes other men to assist him; or mayhap, God in His goodness performs a miracle, and sends him an Angel of Light for an assistant.

You, reader, put this matter to a test: You are sitting now in your office—six clerks are within call. Summon any one and make this request: "Please look in the encyclopedia and make a brief memorandum for me concerning the life of Correggio."

Will the clerk quietly say, "Yes, sir," and go do the task?

On your life he will not. He will look at you out of a fishy eye and ask one or more of the following questions:

Who was he?

Which encyclopedia?

Where is the encyclopedia?

Was I hired for that?

Don't you mean Bismarck?

What's the matter with Charlie doing it?

Is he dead?

Is there any hurry?

Sha'n't I bring you the book and let you look it up yourself?

What do you want to know for?

And I will lay you ten to one that after you have answered the questions, and explained how to find the information, and why you want it, the clerk will go off and get one of the other clerks to help him try to find Garcia—and then come back and tell you there is no such man. Of course I may lose my bet, but according to the Law of Average I will not.

Now, if you are wise, you will not bother to explain to your "assistant" that Correggio is indexed under the C's, not in the K's, but you will smile very sweetly and say, "Never mind," and go look it up yourself. And this incapacity for independent action, this moral stupidity, this infirmity of the will, this unwillingness to cheerfully catch hold and lift—these are the things that put pure Socialism so far into the future. If men will not act for themselves, what will they do when the benefit of their effort is for all?

A first mate with knotted club seems necessary; and the dread of getting "the bounce" Saturday night holds many a worker to his place. Advertise for a stenographer, and nine out of ten who apply can neither spell nor punctuate—and do not think it necessary to.

Can such a one write a letter to Garcia?

"You see that bookkeeper," said the foreman to me in a large factory.

"Yes; what about him?"

"Well, he's a fine accountant, but if I'd send him up town on an errand, he might accomplish the errand all right, and on the other hand, might stop at four saloons on the way, and when he got to Main Street would forget what he had been sent for."

Can such a man be entrusted to carry a message to Garcia?

We have recently been hearing much maudlin sympathy expressed for the "down-trodden denizens of the sweatshop" and the "homeless wanderer searching for honest employment," and with it all often go many hard words for the men in power.

Nothing is said about the employer who grows old before his time in a vain attempt to get frowsy ne'er-do-wells to do intelligent work; and his long, patient striving after "help" that does nothing but loaf when his back is turned. In every store and factory there is a constant weeding-out process going on. The employer is constantly sending away "help" that have shown their incapacity to further the interests of the business, and others are being taken on. No matter how good times are, this sorting continues: only, if times are hard and work is scarce, the sorting is done finer—but out and forever out the incompetent and unworthy go. It is the survival of the fittest. Self-interest prompts every employer to keep the best—those who can carry a message to Garcia.

I know one man of really brilliant parts who has not the ability to manage a business of his own, and yet who is absolutely worthless to anyone else, because he carries with him constantly the insane suspicion that his employer is oppressing, or intending to oppress, him. He cannot give orders, and he will not receive them. Should a message be given him to take to Garcia, his answer would probably be, "Take it yourself!"

Tonight this man walks the streets looking for work, the wind whistling through his threadbare coat. No one who knows him dare employ him, for he is a regular firebrand of discontent. He is impervious to reason, and the only thing that can impress him is the toe of a thick-soled Number Nine boot.

Of course, I know that one so morally deformed is no less to be pitied than a physical cripple; but in our pitying let us drop a tear, too, for the men who are striving to carry on a great enterprise, whose working hours are not limited by the whistle, and whose hair is fast turning white through the struggle to hold in line dowdy indifference, slipshod imbecility, and the heartless ingratitude which, but for their enterprise, would be both hungry and homeless.

Have I put the matter too strongly? Possibly I have; but when all the world has gone a-slumming I wish to speak a word of sympathy for the man who succeeds—the man who, against great odds, has directed the efforts of others, and having succeeded, finds there's nothing in it: nothing but bare board and clothes. I have carried a dinner-pail and worked for day's wages, and I have also been an employer of labor, and I know there is something to be said on both sides. There is no excellence, per se, in poverty; rags are no recommendation; and all employers are not rapacious and high-handed, any more than all poor men are virtuous. My heart goes out to the man who does his work when the "boss" is away, as well as when he is at home. And the man who, when given a letter for Garcia, quietly takes the missive, without asking any idiotic questions, and with no lurking intention of chucking it into the nearest sewer, or of doing aught else but deliver it, never gets "laid off," nor has to go on a strike for higher wages. Civilization is one long, anxious search for just such individuals. Anything such a man asks shall be granted. He is wanted in every city, town and village—in every office, shop, store and factory. The world cries out for such; he is needed and needed badly—the man who can "Carry a Message to Garcia."

4

Looking Backward

☆ *Edward Bellamy (1850-1898). His novel,* Looking Backward, 2000-1887, *was published in 1888 and became an immediate success. The following allegory, drawn from the book, depicted what he considered to be the absurdities of society in his day.** ☆

By way of attempting to give the reader some general impression of the way people lived together [in the latter part of the nineteenth century], and especially of the relations of the rich and poor to one another, perhaps I cannot do better than to compare society as it then was to a prodigious coach which the masses of humanity were harnessed to and dragged toilsomely along a very hilly and sandy road. The driver was hunger, and permitted no lagging, though the pace was necessarily very slow. Despite the difficulty of drawing the coach at all along so hard a road, the top was covered with passengers who never got down, even at the steepest ascents. These seats on top were very breezy and comfortable. Well up out of the dust, their occupants could enjoy the scenery at their leisure, or critically discuss the merits of the straining team. Naturally such places were in great demand and the competition for them was keen, every one seeking as the first end in life to secure a seat on the coach for himself and to leave it to his child after him. By the rule of the coach a man could

* From Edward Bellamy, *Looking Backward, 2000-1887,* pp. 10-12. Published by Houghton Mifflin Company, Boston, 1926.

leave his seat to whom he wished, but on the other hand there were many accidents by which it might at any time be wholly lost. For all that they were so easy, the seats were very insecure, and at every sudden jolt of the coach persons were slipping out of them and falling to the ground, where they were instantly compelled to take hold of the rope and help to drag the coach on which they had before ridden so pleasantly. It was naturally regarded as a terrible misfortune to lose one's seat, and the apprehension that this might happen to them or their friends was a constant cloud upon the happiness of those who rode.

But did they think only of themselves? you ask. Was not their very luxury rendered intolerable to them by comparison with the lot of their brothers and sisters in the harness, and the knowledge that their own weight added to their toil? Had they no compassion for fellow beings from whom fortune only distinguished them? Oh, yes; commiseration was frequently expressed by those who rode for those who had to pull the coach, especially when the vehicle came to a bad place in the road, as it was constantly doing, or to a particularly steep hill. At such times, the desperate straining of the team, their agonized leaping and plunging under the pitiless lashing of hunger, the many who fainted at the rope and were trampled in the mire, made a very distressing spectacle, which often called forth highly creditable displays of feeling on the top of the coach. At such times the passengers would call down encouragingly to the toilers of the rope, exhorting them to patience, and holding out hopes of possible compensation in another world for the hardness of their lot, while others contributed to buy salves and liniments for the crippled and injured. It was agreed that it was a great pity that the coach should be so hard to pull, and there was a sense of general relief when the specially bad piece of road was gotten over.

This relief was not, indeed, wholly on account of the team, for there was always some danger at these bad places of a general overturn in which all would lose their seats.

It must in truth be admitted that the main effect of the spectacle of the misery of the toilers at the rope was to enhance the passengers' sense of the value of their seats upon the coach, and to cause them to hold on to them more desperately than before. If the passengers could only have felt assured that neither they nor their friends would ever fall from the top, it is probable that, beyond contributing to the funds for liniments and bandages, they would have troubled themselves extremely little about those who dragged the coach.

5

The New Leisure Class

☆ *Thorstein Veblen (1857-1929), economist and writer, was one of the most trenchant critics of the prevailing pecuniary values. His caustic and ironic style is well reflected in the following extracts from* The Theory of the Leisure Class.* ☆

With the exception of the instinct of self-preservation, the propensity for emulation is probably the strongest and most alert and persistent of the economic motives proper. In an industrial community this propensity for emulation expresses itself in pecuniary emulation; and this, so far as regards the Western civilized communities of the present, is virtually equivalent to saying that it expresses itself in some form of conspicuous waste. The need of conspicuous waste, therefore, stands ready to absorb any increase in the community's industrial efficiency or output of goods, after the most elementary physical wants have been provided for. Where this result does not follow, under modern conditions, the reason for the discrepancy is commonly to be sought in a rate of increase in the individual's wealth too rapid for the habit of expenditure to keep abreast of it; or it may be that the individual in question defers the conspicuous consumption of the increment to a later date—ordinarily with a view to heightening the spectacular effect of the aggregate expenditure

* From *The Theory of the Leisure Class* by Thorstein Veblen, 1899, pp. 110-112, 130-133. All rights reserved. Reprinted by permission of The Viking Press, Inc.

contemplated. As increased industrial efficiency makes it possible to procure the means of livelihood with less labour, the energies of the industrious members of the community are bent to the compassing of a higher result in conspicuous expenditure, rather than slackened to a more comfortable pace. The strain is not lightened as industrial efficiency increases and makes a lighter strain possible, but the increment of output is turned to use to meet this want, which is indefinitely expansible, after the manner commonly imputed in economic theory to higher or spiritual wants. It is owing chiefly to the presence of this element in the standard of living that J. S. Mill was able to say that "hitherto it is questionable if all the mechanical inventions yet made have lightened the day's toil of any human being."

The accepted standard of expenditure in the community or in the class to which a person belongs largely determines what his standard of living will be. It does this directly by commending itself to his common sense as right and good, through his habitually contemplating it and assimilating the scheme of life in which it belongs; but it does so also indirectly through popular insistence on conformity to the accepted scale of expenditure as a matter of propriety, under pain of disesteem and ostracism. To accept and practise the standard of living which is in vogue is both agreeable and expedient, commonly to the point of being indispensable to personal comfort and to success in life. The standard of living of any class, so far as concerns the element of conspicuous waste, is commonly as high as the earning capacity of the class will permit—with a constant tendency to go higher. The effect upon the serious activities of men is therefore to direct them with great singleness of purpose to the largest possible acquisition of wealth, and to discountenance work that brings no pecuniary gain. At the same time the effect on consumption is to concentrate it upon the lines which are most patent to the observers whose good opinion is sought; while the inclinations and aptitudes whose exercise does not involve a honorific expenditure of time or substance tend to fall into abeyance through disuse. . . .

The generalisation for which the discussion so far affords ground is that any valuable object in order to appeal to our sense of beauty must conform to the requirements of beauty and of expensiveness both. But this is not all. Beyond this the canon of expensiveness also affects our tastes in such a way as to inextricably blend the marks of expensiveness, in our appreciation, with the beautiful features of the object, and to subsume the resultant effect under the head of an appreciation of beauty simply. The marks of expensiveness come to be accepted as beautiful features of the expensive articles. They are pleasing as being marks of honorific costliness, and the pleasure which they afford on this score blends with that afforded by the beautiful form and colour of the object; so that we often declare that an article of apparel, for instance, is "perfectly lovely," when pretty much all that an analysis of the aesthetic value of the article would leave ground for is the declaration that it is pecuniarily honorific.

This blending and confusion of the elements of expensiveness and of beauty is, perhaps, best exemplified in articles of dress and of household furniture. The code of reputability in matters of dress decides what shapes, colours, materials, and general effects in human apparel are for the time to be accepted as suitable; and departures from the code are offensive to our taste, supposedly as being departures from aesthetic truth. The approval with which we look upon fashionable attire is by no means to be accounted pure make-believe. We readily, and for the most part with utter sincerity, find those things pleasing that are in vogue. Shaggy dress-stuffs and pronounced colour effects, for instance, offend us at times when the vogue is goods of a high, glossy finish and neutral colours. A fancy bonnet of this year's model unquestionably appeals to our sensibilities to-day much more forcibly than an equally fancy bonnet of the model of last year; although when viewed in the perspective of a quarter of a century, it would, I apprehend, be a matter of the utmost difficulty to award the palm for intrinsic beauty to the one rather than to the other of these structures. So, again, it may be remarked that, considered simply in their physical juxtaposition with the human form, the high gloss of a gentleman's hat or of a patent-leather shoe has no more of intrinsic beauty than a similarly high gloss on a threadbare sleeve; and yet there is no question but that all well-bred people (in the Occidental civilised communities) instinctively and unaffectedly cleave to the one as a phenomenon of great beauty, and eschew the other as offensive to every sense to which it can appeal. It is extremely doubtful if any one could be induced to wear such a contrivance as the high hat of civilised society, except for some urgent reason based on other than aesthetic grounds.

By further habituation to an appreciative perception of the marks of expensiveness in goods, and by habitually identifying beauty with reputability, it comes about that a beautiful article which is not expensive is accounted not beautiful. In this way it has happened, for instance, that some beautiful flowers pass conventionally for offensive weeds; others that can be cultivated with relative ease are accepted and admired by the lower middle class, who can afford no more expensive luxuries of this kind; but these varieties are rejected as vulgar by those people who are better able to pay for expensive flowers and who are educated to a higher schedule of pecuniary beauty in the florist's products; while still other flowers, of no greater intrinsic beauty than these, are cultivated at great cost and call out much admiration from flower-lovers whose tastes have been matured under the critical guidance of a polite environment.

The same variation in matters of taste, from one class of society to another, is visible also as regards many other kinds of consumable goods, as, for example, is the case with furniture, houses, parks, and gardens. This diversity of views as to what is beautiful in these various classes of goods is not a diversity of the norm according to which the unsophisticated sense of the beautiful works. It is not a constitutional difference of endowments in the aesthetic respect, but rather a difference in the code of reputability which specifies what objects properly lie within the scope of honorific consumption for the class to which the critic belongs. It is a difference in the traditions of propriety with respect to the kinds of things which may, without derogation to the consumer, be consumed under the head of objects of taste and art. With a certain allowance for variations to be accounted for on other grounds, these traditions are determined, more or less rigidly, by the pecuniary plane of life of the class.

6

Wealth Against Commonwealth

☆ *Henry Demarest Lloyd (1847-1903) was a crusading newspaper man and a precursor of the muckrakers. In his outspoken style, Lloyd brought out the apparent conflict between the practices of business entrepreneurs and the best interests of the nation.** ☆

Nature is rich; but everywhere man, the heir of nature, is poor. Never in this happy country or elsewhere—except in the Land of Miracle, where "they did all eat and were filled"—has there been enough of anything for the people. Never since time began have all the sons and daughters of men been all warm, and all filled, and all shod and roofed. Never yet have all the virgins, wise or foolish, been able to fill their lamps with oil.

The world, enriched by thousands of generations of toilers and thinkers, has reached a fertility which can give every human being a plenty undreamed of even in the Utopias. But between this plenty ripening on the boughs of our civilization and the people hungering for it step the "cornerers," the syndicates, trusts, combinations, with the cry of "over-production"—too much of everything. Holding back the riches of earth, sea, and sky from their fellows who famish and freeze in the dark, they declare to them that there is too much light and warmth and food. They assert the right, for their private profit, to regulate the consump-

tion by the people of the necessaries of life, and to control production, not by the needs of humanity, but by the desires of a few for dividends. The coal syndicate thinks there is too much coal. There is too much iron, too much lumber, too much flour—for this or that syndicate.

The majority have never been able to buy enough of anything; but this minority have too much of everything to sell.

Liberty produces wealth, and wealth destroys liberty. "The splendid empire of Charles V.," says Motley, "was erected upon the grave of liberty." Our bignesses —cities, factories, monopolies, fortunes, which are our empires, are the obesities of an age gluttonous beyond its powers of digestion. Mankind are crowding upon each other in the centres, and struggling to keep each other out of the feast set by the new sciences and the new fellowships. Our size has got beyond both our science and our conscience. The vision of the railroad stockholder is not far-sighted enough to see into the office of the General Manager; the people cannot reach across even a ward of a city to rule their rulers; Captains of Industry "do not know" whether the men in the ranks are dying from lack of food and shelter; we cannot clean our

* From Henry Demarest Lloyd, *Wealth Against Commonwealth*, pp. 1-2, 463-466. Published by Harper and Brothers, New York, 1894.

cities nor our politics; the locomotive has more man-power than all the ballot-boxes, and mill-wheels wear out the hearts of workers unable to keep up beating time to their whirl. If mankind had gone on pursuing the ideals of the fighter, the time would necessarily have come when there would have been only a few, then only one, and then none left. This is what we are witnessing in the world of livelihoods. Our ideals of livelihood are ideals of mutual deglutition. We are rapidly reaching the stage where in each province only a few are left; that is the key to our times. Beyond the deep is another deep. This era is but a passing phase in the evolution of industrial Caesars, and these Caesars will be of a new type—corporate Caesars. . . .

(A BILL OF PARTICULARS)

Yet, strange to say, these successful men did not discover the oil, nor how to "strike" it. They were not the lucky owners of oil lands. As late as 1888 they produced only 200 barrels a day—about 1 in every 3000—"an infinitesimal amount," their president said. They did not invent any of the processes of refining. They did not devise the pipe line, and they did all they could to prevent the building of the first pipe line to the seaboard, and to cripple the successful experiment of piping refined oil. They own all the important refineries, and yet they have built very few. They did not project the tank-car system, which came before them, and have used their irresistible power to prevent its general use on the railroads, and successfully. They were not the first to enter the field in any department. They did not have as great capital or skill as their competitors. They began their career in the wrong place—at Cleveland—out of the way of the wells and the principal markets, necessitating several hundred miles more of transportation for all of their product that was marketed in the East or Europe. They had no process of refining oil which others had not, and no legitimate advantages over others. They did not even invent the rebate. They made oil poor and scarce and dear.

The power to chalk down daily on the black-board of the New York Produce Exchange the price at which people in two hemispheres shall buy their light has followed these strokes of "cheapness":

1. Freight rates to the general public have been increased, often to double and more what is paid by a favored few.

2. The construction has been resisted of new lines of transportation by rail,

3. And pipe. This has been done by litigation, by influence, by violence, even to the threatened use of cannon, and by legislation, as in Ohio and Pennsylvania, to prevent the right of eminent domain from being given by "free pipe-line bills" to the people generally.

4. The cost of pipeage has been raised.

5. Rivers and canals have been closed.

6. Oil has been made to run to waste on the ground.

7. The outflow of oil from the earth has been shut down.

8. The outflow of human energy that sought to turn it to human use has been shut down by restricting the manufacture by the combination and by others, by contract, dismantling, and explosion.

9. High fees have been maintained for inspection, and the inspectors have been brought into equivocal relations with the monopoly.

10. The general use of tank-cars and tank-steamers has been prevented.

11. The people have been excluded from the free and equal use of the docks, storehouses, and other terminal facilities of the railroads in the great harbors of export.

12. Inventors and their better processes have been smothered.

13. Men have been paid more for spying than they could earn by working.

14. "Killing delay" has been created in the administration of justice.

[As a result,] All are poorer—oil-producers, land-owners, all labor, all the railroads, all the refiners, merchants, all the consumers of oil—the whole people. Less oil has flowed, less light shone, and there has been less happiness and virtue. . . .

When the trust's secretary was asked for the proper name of the combination, his reply was: "The Lord only knows; I don't." "An indescribable thing," he said again.

"Do you understand the practical work of refining as a refiner?" he was asked.

"I do not. . . . I have not been inside a refinery in ten years."

"Two mills a ton a mile for five hundred miles would be a dollar a ton?"

"I am not able to demonstrate that proposition."

"You have some arithmetical knowledge?"

"I cannot answer that question."

He could not state what proportion of the oil trade is now controlled by the trust. He had never looked into that question. He did not know who knows these things.

"You own the pipe line to New York?"

"Yes, sir."

"What does it cost you to do business on that pipe line?"

"I do not know anything about it. . . . I have never been in the oil regions but once in my life. . . . I am not a practical oilman. . . . For perhaps eight years I have given absolutely no attention to the details of our business."

Asked upon another occasion, before the Pennsylvania Legislature, about the accounts of the company when he was its secretary, he said:

"I am not familiar with the accounts."

"I am a clamorer for dividends. That is the only function I have," said another trustee.

7

How the Other Half Lives

☆ *Jacob August Riis (1849-1914) came to the United States when 21 years of age. As a reporter in New York City he became intimately acquainted with tenement conditions and the life of deprivation led by the lower classes, which he graphically portrayed in his writings.** ☆

It is estimated that at least one hundred and fifty thousand women and girls earn their own living in New York; but there is reason to believe that this estimate falls far short of the truth when sufficient account is taken of the large number who are not wholly dependent upon their own labor, while contributing by it to the family's earnings. These alone constitute a large class of the women wage-earners, and it is characteristic of the situation that the very fact that some need not starve on their wages condemns the rest to that fate. The pay they are willing to accept all have to take. What the "everlasting law of supply and demand," that serves as such a convenient gag for public indignation, has to do with it, one learns from observation all along the road of inquiry into these real woman's wrongs. To take the case of the sales women for illustration: The investigation of the Working Women's Society disclosed the fact that wages averaged from $2 to $4.50 a week were reduced by excessive fines, "the employers placing a value upon time lost

* From Jacob A. Riis, *How the Other Half Lives, Studies Among the Tenements of New York*, pp. 235-238. Published by Charles Scribner's Sons, New York, 1890, 1922.

that is not given to services rendered." A little girl, who received two dollars a week, made cash-sales amounting to $167 in a single day, while the receipts of a fifteen-dollar male clerk in the same department footed up only $125; yet for some trivial mistake the girl was fined sixty cents out of her two dollars. The practice prevailed in some stores of dividing the fines between the superintendent and the time-keeper at the end of the year. In one instance they amounted to $3,000, and "the superintendent was heard to charge the time-keeper with not being strict enough in his duties." One of the causes for fine in a certain large store was sitting down. The law requiring seats for saleswomen, generally ignored, was obeyed faithfully in this establishment. The seats were there, but the girls were fined when found using them.

Cash-girls receiving $1.75 a week for work that at certain seasons lengthened their day to sixteen hours were sometimes required to pay for their aprons. A common cause for discharge from stores in which, on account of the oppressive heat and lack of ventilation, "girls fainted day after day and came out looking like corpses," was too long service. No other fault was found with the discharged saleswomen than that they had been long enough in the employ of the firm to justly expect an increase of salary. The reason was even given with brutal frankness, in some instances.

These facts give a slight idea of the hardships and the poor pay of a business that notoriously absorbs child-labor. The girls are sent to the store before they have fairly entered their teens, because the money they can earn there is needed for the support of the family. If the boys will not work, if the street tempts them from home, among the girls at least there must be no drones. To keep their places they are told to lie about their age and to say that they are over fourteen. The precaution is usually superfluous. The Women's Investigating Committee found the majority of the children employed in the stores to be under age, but heard only in a single instance of the truant officers calling. In that case they came once a year and sent the youngest children home; but in a month's time they were all back in their places, and were not again disturbed. When it comes to the factories, where hard bodily labor is added to long hours, stifling rooms, and starvation wages, matters are even worse. The Legislature has passed laws to prevent the employment of children, as it has forbidden saloon-keepers to sell them beer, and it has provided means of enforcing its mandate, so efficient, that the very number of factories in New York is *guessed* at as in the neighborhood of twelve thousand. Up till this summer, a single inspector was charged with the duty of keeping the run of them all, and of seeing to it that the law was respected by the owners.

Sixty cents is put as the average day's earnings of the 150,000, but into this computation enters the stylish "cashier's" two dollars a day, as well as the thirty cents of the poor little girl who pulls threads in an East Side factory, and, if anything, the average is probably too high. Such as it is, however, it represents board, rent, clothing, and "pleasure" to this army of workers. Here is the case of a woman employed in the manufacturing department of a Broadway house. It stands for a hundred like her own. She averages three dollars a week. Pays $1.50 for her room; for breakfast she has a cup of coffee; lunch she cannot afford. One meal a day is her allowance. This woman is young, she is pretty. She has "the world before her." Is it anything less than a miracle if she is guilty of nothing worse than the "early and improvident marriage," against which moralists exclaim as one of the prolific causes of the distress of the poor. . .?

8

The Farmer's Woes

☆ *Agrarian unrest, which was frequent after the Civil War, reached its peak during the Panic of 1893. Professor Walker's article describes the farmer's plight with an objectivity which was rare during this time of crisis.** ☆

The widespread movement among the farmers to-day is their effort to adapt themselves and their occupation to the ever-changing environment, so that they shall be once more masters of the situation, receiving their due share of the product of American industry and exerting their due influence in the formation and development of national character. As a result of his industry the farmer has made food and the raw material of our factories produced from the soil more and more plenty, of better quality and cheaper. Here we find an efficient cause of his pecuniary embarrassment; the supply of agricultural products has been increased beyond the demand, with the consequent fall of price. If the surplus of agricultural products was matched by a corresponding surplus of gold, of personal services, of means of transportation, and of the comforts, conveniences, and luxuries of life, such universal plenty would enrich all, beggaring none. But with over-production in agriculture, and monopolies of coal, of telephones, of electric railroads and of other essentials of

modern civilization, the farmer finds himself at a great disadvantage.

Farmers have been content in the past to confine their labors to the production of wealth, leaving to others the control of those conditions which determine the distribution of this wealth. At last, however, they have awakened to the fact that the problems of distribution have not been successfully solved. They believe that they get too little for the product of their labor and others too much, that they must bear heavy burdens of society while they are at the same time practically debarred from the enjoyment of the advantages of the progressive culture of modern life. When in this discussion we speak of the farmer, it must be borne in mind that we refer to the average farmer, who tills on his own account his own or another's farm. We do not refer to those who derive a large share of their income from other sources than their farms, nor do we mean the farmer of exceptional ability or those whose opportunities have been remarkably fortunate. An investigation, carried on for a number of years, upon different lines, based upon statistics official and unofficial, as well as upon other reliable sources of informa-

* From C. S. Walker, "The Farmer's Movement," *Annals of the American Academy of Political and Social Science*, IV (1893-1894), pp. 790-792.

tion, shows that the average farmer, east and west, north and south, receives a lower remuneration for manual labor and for labor of superintendence than the average man in any other of the great classes of bread-winners, much less than those, who have not carefully considered the matter will think possible.

Because of this comparative decadence the farmer has for years demanded equal taxation, in order that the farmer's thousand dollars invested in his farm shall bear no more burdens than the thousand dollars of other men. But the statesman has confessed that he has not been able to remedy the evils of unjust taxation. He even acknowledges that they are growing worse.

The farmer has been content to refer questions of finance to the banker. Every autumn the farmers of America have hundreds of millions of dollars worth of crops which makes a demand for millions of currency. The supply of money at that season is inadequate to meet the demand. Hence, the price of crops falls relatively and the price of money advances. Year after year the farmer has been forced to sell in a glutted market and buy in times of scarcity. He demands a system of finance that shall make the supply of money at all times equal to the demand. He wants an elastic currency that shall do the money work of the nation with justice to both buyer and seller, to both creditor and debtor. But the bankers appear to confess that they cannot produce a medium of exchange and a standard of deferred payment that is capable of meeting the exigencies.

The farmer demands cheap transportation *between the farm and the market;* and he is met with the reply that the rates from the elevator of the middleman to the ship of the foreigner were never before so low as now, but this proves of little benefit to the farmer. When the farmer insists that modern masters of transportation might devise a system of cheap transportation from the country station to the city, he is told that the intricacies of the modern railroad system are too great and it cannot be done; to attempt it would bankrupt the roads. Moreover, when the farmers themselves, or their friends, organize an electric railroad to carry themselves and their freight at reasonable prices from the farmhouse to the city, the great railroad corporations oppose them at every point, going even to the extent of waging open war against the selectmen of the country town who lawfully attempt to lay the rails of the electric road across the track of the steam railroad.

The farmer turns to the politician and asks of him that his party shall champion the cause of the farmer and see to it that the government guarantee to the agricultural classes their rights and promote their interests equally with those of other citizens. But the farmer finds the politician more abundant in promises than prolific in efficient action.

Finally, the farmer has, in his emergency, turned to the scholar and asked of him a fair statement of the problem and a clear solution, based upon historic and economic grounds. But the scholar has been too preoccupied and prejudiced to give the question that painstaking investigation and careful and impartial decision which alone can make his answer of much practical value to the hard-pressed agriculturist.

Thus has experience taught the farmer that the solution of the problem of the future of American agriculture and of the American agriculturist depends upon himself. . . .

9

A Christian View

Special note

☆ *Charles M. Sheldon (1857-1946), a Congregational minister, be-came concerned with the disparity between Christian principles and the behavior of professed Christians. His novel,* In His Steps *(1896), asserts that though difficult, it is imperative to practice the precepts of Christianity in daily living.** ☆

He had taken for his theme the story of the young man who came to Jesus asking what he must do to obtain eternal life. Jesus had tested him. "Sell all that thou hast and give to the poor, and thou shalt have treasure in heaven; and come follow me." But the young man was not willing to suffer to that extent. If following Jesus meant suffering in that way, he was not willing. He would like to follow Jesus, but not if he had to give so much.

"Is it true," continued Henry Maxwell, and his fine, thoughtful face glowed with a passion of appeal that stirred the people as they had seldom been stirred, "is it true that the church of to-day, the church that is called after Christ's own name, would refuse to follow Him at the expense of suffering, of physical loss, of tempo-rary gain? The statement was made at a large gathering in the Settlement last week by a leader of workingmen that it was hopeless to look to the church for any reform or redemption of society. On what was that statement based? Plainly on the assumption that the church contains for

* From Charles M. Sheldon, *In His Steps*, pp. 235-239. Authorized edition published by Grosset and Dunlap, Inc., New York, 1935.

the most part men and women who think more of their own ease and luxury than of the sufferings and needs and sins of hu-manity. How far is that true? Are the Christians of America ready to have their discipleship tested? How about the men who possess large wealth? Are they ready to take that wealth and use it as Jesus would? How about the men and women of great talent? Are they ready to conse-crate that talent to humanity as Jesus un-doubtedly would do?

"Is it not true that the call has come in this age for a new exhibition of Christian discipleship? You who live in this great sinful city must know that better than I do. Is it possible you can go your ways careless or thoughtless of the awful con-dition of men and women and children who are dying, body and soul, for need of Christian help? Is it not a matter of con-cern to you personally that the saloon kills its thousands more surely than war? Is it not a matter of personal suffering in some form for you that thousands of able-bodied, willing men tramp the streets of this city and all cities, crying for work and drifting into crime and suicide be-cause they cannot find it? Can you say that this is none of your business? Let each man look after himself? Would it not be true, think you, that if every Christian in America did as Jesus would do, society itself, the business world, yes, the very political system under which our commercial and governmental activity is carried on, would be so changed that human suffering would be reduced to a minimum?

"What would be the result if all the church members of this city tried to do as Jesus would do? It is not possible to say in detail what the effect would be. But it is easy to say, and it is true, that instantly the human problem would begin to find an adequate answer.

"What is the test of Christian discipleship? Is it not the same as in Christ's own time? Have our surroundings modified or changed the test? If Jesus were here today would He not call some of the members of this very church to do just what He commanded the young man, and ask them to give up their wealth and literally follow Him? I believe He would do that if He felt certain that any church member thought more of his possessions than of the Saviour. The test would be the same to-day as then. I believe Jesus would demand—He does demand now—as close a following, as much suffering, as great self-denial as when He lived in person on the earth and said, 'Except a man renounce all that he hath he cannot be my disciple.' That is, unless he is willing to do it for my sake, he cannot be my disciple.

"What would be the result if in this city every church member should begin to do as Jesus would do? It is not easy to go into details of the result. But we all know that certain things would be impossible that are now practiced by church members. What would Jesus do in the matter of wealth? How would He spend it? What principle would regulate His use of money? Would He be likely to live in great luxury and spend ten times as much

on personal adornment and entertainment as He spent to relieve the needs of suffering humanity? How would Jesus be governed in the making of money? Would He take rentals from saloons and other disreputable property, or even from tenement property that was so constructed that the inmates had no such things as a home and no such possibility as privacy or cleanliness?

"What would Jesus do about the great army of unemployed and desperate who tramp the streets and curse the church, or are indifferent to it, lost in the bitter struggle for the bread that tastes bitter when it is earned on account of the desperate conflict to get it? Would Jesus care nothing for them? Would He go His way in comparative ease and comfort? Would He say that it was none of His business? Would He excuse Himself from all responsibility to remove the causes of such a condition?

"What would Jesus do in the center of a civilization that hurries so fast after money that the very girls employed in great business houses are not paid enough to keep soul and body together without fearful temptations so great that scores of them fall and are swept over the great boiling abyss; where the demands of trade sacrifice hundreds of lads in a business that ignores all Christian duties toward them in the way of education and moral training and personal affection? Would Jesus, if He were here to-day as a part of our age and commercial industry, feel nothing, do nothing, say nothing, in the face of these facts which every business man knows?

"What would Jesus do? Is not that what the disciple ought to do? Is he not commanded to follow in His steps? How much is the Christianity of the age suffering for Him? Is it denying itself at the cost of ease, comfort, luxury, elegance of living? What does the age need more than personal sacrifice? Does the church do its duty in following Jesus when it gives a little money to establish missions or relieve extreme cases of want? Is it any sacrifice for a man who is worth ten million dollars simply to give ten thousand dollars for some benevolent work? Is he not giving something that cost him practically nothing so far as any personal suffering goes? Is it true that the Christian disciples to-day in most of our churches are living soft, easy, selfish lives, very far from any sacrifice that can be called sacrifice? What would Jesus do?"

10

Progress and Poverty

☆ *Henry George (1839-1897), economist and reformer, advocated control of unearned profits and a more equitable distribution of wealth in his classic analysis of American economic problems,* Progress and Poverty *(1879).** ☆

We have now seen that while advancing population tends to advance rent, so all the causes that in a progressive state of society operate to increase the productive power of labour, tend, also, to advance rent, and not to advance wages or interest. The increased production of wealth goes ultimately to the owners of land in increased rent; and, although, as improvement goes on, advantages may accrue to individuals not landholders, which concentrate in their hands considerable portions of the increased produce, yet there is in all this improvement nothing which tends to increase the general return, either to labour or to capital.

But there is a cause, not yet adverted to, which must be taken into consideration to fully explain the influence of material progress upon the distribution of wealth.

That cause is the confident expectation of the future enhancement of land values, which arises in all progressive countries from the steady increase of rent, and which leads to speculation, or the holding of land for a higher price

* From Henry George, *Progress and Poverty,* pp. 180-184, 233-234. Published by Kegan Paul, Trench and Company, London, 1884.

than it would then otherwise bring.

We have hitherto assumed, as is generally assumed in elucidations of the theory of rent, that the actual margin of cultivation always coincides with what may be termed the necessary margin of cultivation—that is to say, we have assumed that cultivation extends to less productive points only as it becomes necessary from the fact that natural opportunities are at the more productive points fully utilized.

This, probably, is the case in stationary or very slowly progressing communities, but in rapidly progressing communities, where the swift and steady increase of rent gives confidence to calculations of further increase, it is not the case. In such communities, the confident expectation of increased prices produces, to a greater or less extent, the effects of a combination among landholders, and tends to the withholding of land from use, in expectation of higher prices, thus forcing the margin of cultivation farther than required by the necessities of production.

This cause must operate to some extent in all progressive communities, though in such countries as England, where the tenant system prevails in agriculture, it may be shown more in the selling price of land than in the agricultural margin of cultivation, or actual rent. But in communities like the United States, where the user of land generally prefers, if he can, to own it, and where there is a great extent of land to overrun, it operates with enormous power.

The immense area over which the population of the United States is scattered shows this. The man who sets out from the Eastern seaboard in search of the margin of cultivation, where he may obtain land without paying rent, must, like the man who swam the river to get a drink, pass for long distances through half-tilled farms, and traverse vast areas of virgin soil, before he reaches the point where land can be had free of rent—*i.e.* by homestead entry or pre-emption. He (and, with him, the margin of cultivation) is forced so much farther than he otherwise need have gone, by the speculation which is holding these unused lands in expectation of increased value in the future. And when he settles, he will, in his turn, take up, if he can, more land than he can use, in the belief that it will soon become available; and so those who follow him are again forced farther on than the necessities of production require, carrying the margin of cultivation to still less productive because still more remote, points.

The same thing may be seen in every rapidly growing city. If the land of superior quality as to location were always fully used before land of inferior quality were resorted to, no vacant lots would be left as a city extended, nor would we find miserable shanties in the midst of costly buildings. These lots, some of them extremely valuable, are withheld from use, or from the full use to which they might be put, because their owners, not being able or not wishing to improve them, prefer, in expectation of the advance of land values, to hold them for a higher rate than could now be obtained from those willing to improve them. And, in consequence of this land being withheld from use, or from the full use of which it is capable, the margin of the city is pushed away so much farther from the centre.

But when we reach the limits of the growing city—the actual margin of building, which corresponds to the margin of cultivation in agriculture—we shall not find the land purchasable at its value for agricultural purposes, as it would be were rent determined simply by present requirements; but we shall find that for a long distance beyond the city, land bears a speculative value, based upon the belief that it will be required in the future for urban purposes, and that to reach the point at which land can be purchased at a price not based upon urban rent, we must go very far beyond the actual margin of urban use.

Or, to take another case of a different kind, instances similar to which may doubtless be found in every locality. There is in Marin County, within easy access of San Francisco, a fine belt of redwood timber. Naturally, this would be first used, before resorting for the supply of the San Francisco market to timber lands at a much greater distance. But it yet remains uncut, and lumber procured many miles beyond is daily hauled past it on the railroad, because its owner prefers to hold for the greater price it will bring in the future. Thus, by the withholding from use of this body of timber, the margin of production of redwood is forced so much farther up and down the Coast Range. That mineral land, when reduced to private ownership, is frequently withheld from use while poorer deposits are worked, is well known, and in new states it is common to find individuals who are called "land poor"—that is, who remain poor, sometimes almost to deprivation, because they insist on holding land, which they themselves cannot use, at prices at which no one else can profitably use it. . . .

The influence of speculation in land in increasing rent is a great fact which cannot be ignored in any complete theory of the distribution of wealth in progressive countries. It is the force, evolved by material progress, which tends constantly to increase rent in a greater ratio than progress increases production, and thus constantly tends, as material progress goes on and productive power increases, to reduce wages, not merely relatively, but absolutely. It is this expansive force which, operating with great power in new countries, brings to them, seemingly long before their time, the social diseases of older countries; produces "tramps" on virgin acres, and breeds paupers on half-tilled soil.

In short, the general and steady advance in land values in a progressive community necessarily produces that additional tendency to advance which is seen in the case of commodities when any general and continuous cause operates to increase their price. As, during the rapid depreciation of currency which marked the latter days of the Southern Confederacy, the fact that whatever was bought one day could be sold for a higher price the next, operated to carry up the prices of commodites even faster than the depreciation of the currency, so does the steady increase of land values, which material progress produces, operate to still further accelerate the increase. We see this secondary cause operating in full force in those manias of land speculation which mark the growth of new communities; but though these are the abnormal and occasional manifestations, it is undeniable that the cause steadily operates, with greater, or less intensity, in all progressive societies.

The cause which limits speculation in commodities, the tendency of increasing price to draw forth additional supplies, cannot limit the speculative advance in land values, as land is a fixed quantity, which human agency can neither increase nor diminish; but there is nevertheless a limit to the price of land, in the minimum required by labour and capital as the condition of engaging in production. If it were possible to continuously reduce wages until zero were reached, it would be possible to continuously increase rent until it swallowed up the whole produce. But as wages cannot be permanently reduced below the point at which labourers will consent to work and reproduce, nor interest below the point at which capital will be devoted to production, there is a limit which restrains the speculative advance of rent. Hence, speculation cannot have the same scope to advance rent in countries where wages and interest are already near the minimum, as in countries where they are considerably above it. Yet that there is in all progressive countries a constant tendency in the speculative advance of rent to overpass the limit where production would cease, is, I think, shown by recurring seasons of industrial paralysis. . . .

There is but one way to remove an evil—and that is, to remove its cause. Poverty deepens as wealth increases, and wages are forced down while productive power grows, because land, which is the source of all wealth and the field of all labour, is monopolized. To extirpate poverty, to make wages what justice commands they should be, the full earnings of the labourer, we must therefore substitute for the individual ownership of land a common ownership. Nothing else will go to the cause of the evil—in nothing else is there the slightest hope.

This, then, is the remedy for the unjust and unequal distribution of wealth apparent in modern civilisation, and for all the evils which flow from it:

We must make land common property.

We have reached this conclusion by an examination in which every step has been proved and secured. In the chain of reasoning no link is wanting and no link is weak. Deduction and induction have brought us to the same truth—that the unequal ownership of land necessitates the unequal distribution of wealth. And as in the nature of things unequal ownership of land is inseparable from the recognition of individual property in land, it necessarily follows that the only remedy for the unjust distribution of wealth is in making land common property.

11

Sociocracy

☆ *Lester Frank Ward (1841-1913), sociologist, saw society as being disrupted by the competition of individual interests. He was an early American advocate of a cooperative society which would be operated in the interest of all.* *   ☆

The individual has reigned long enough. The day has come for society to take its affairs into its own hands and shape its own destinies. The individual has acted as best he could. He has acted in the only way he could. With a consciousness, will, and intellect of his own he could do nothing else than pursue his natural ends. He should not be denounced nor called any names. He should not even be blamed. Nay, he should be praised, and even *imitated*. Society should learn its great lesson from him, should follow the path he has so clearly laid out that leads to success. It should imagine itself an individual, with all the interests of an individual, and becoming fully *conscious* of these interests it should pursue them with the same indomitable *will* with which the individual pursues his interests. Not only this, it must be guided, as he is guided, by the social *intellect,* armed with all the knowledge that all individuals combined, with so great labor, zeal, and talent have placed in its possession, constituting the social intelligence.

Sociocracy will differ from all other

* From Lester F. Ward, *The Psychic Factors of Civilization*, pp. 323-327. Published by Ginn and Company, Boston, 1892, 1906.

forms of government that have been devised, and yet that difference will not be so radical as to require a revolution. Just as absolute monarchy passed imperceptibly into limited monarchy, and this, in many states without even a change of name has passed into more or less pure democracy, so democracy is capable of passing as smoothly into sociocracy, and without taking on this unfamiliar name or changing that by which it is now known. For, though paradoxical, democracy, which is now the weakest of all forms of government, at least in the control of its own internal elements, is capable of becoming the strongest. Indeed, none of the other forms of government would be capable of passing directly into a government by society. Democracy is a phase through which they must first pass on any route that leads to the ultimate social stage which all governments must eventually attain if they persist.

How then, it may be asked, do democracy and sociocracy differ? How does society differ from the people? If the phrase "the people" really meant the people, the difference would be less. But that shibboleth of democratic states, where it means anything at all that can be described or defined, stands simply for the majority of qualified electors, no matter how small that majority may be. There is a sense in which the action of a majority may be looked upon as the action of society. At least, there is no denying the right of the majority to act for society, for to do this would involve either the denial of the right of government to act at all, or the admission of the right of a minority to act for society. But a majority acting for society is a different thing from society acting for itself, even though, as must always be the case, it acts through an agency chosen by its members. All democratic governments are largely party governments. The electors range themselves on one side or the other of some party line, the winning side considers itself the state as much as Louis the Fourteenth did. The losing party usually then regards the government as something alien to it and hostile, like an invader, and thinks of nothing but to gain strength enough to overthrow it at the next opportunity. While various issues are always brought forward and defended or attacked, it is obvious to the looker-on that the contestants care nothing for these, and merely use them to gain an advantage and win an election.

From the standpoint of society this is child's play. A very slight awakening of the social consciousness will banish it and substitute something more business-like. Once get rid of this puerile gaming spirit and have attention drawn to the real interests of society, and it will be seen that upon nearly all important questions all parties and all citizens are agreed, and that there is no need of this partisan strain upon the public energies. This is clearly shown at every change in the party complexion of the government. The victorious party which has been denouncing the government merely because it was in the hands of its political opponents boasts that it is going to revolution-

ize the country in the interest of good government, but the moment it comes into power and feels the weight of national responsibility it finds that it has little to do but carry out the laws in the same way that its predecessors had been doing.

There is a vast difference between all this outward show of partisanship and advocacy of so-called principles, and attention to the real interests and necessary business of the nation, which latter is what the government must do. It is a social duty. The pressure which is brought to enforce it is the power of the social will. But in the factitious excitement of partisan struggles where professional politicians and demagogues on the one hand, and the agents of plutocracy on the other, are shouting discordantly in the ears of the people, the real interests of society are, temporarily at least, lost sight of, clouded and obscured, and men lose their grasp on the real issues, forget even their own best interests, which, however selfish, would be a far safer guide, and the general result usually is that these are neglected and nations continue in the hands of mere politicians who are easily managed by the shrewd representatives of wealth.

Sociocracy will change all this. Irrelevant issues will be laid aside. The important objects upon which all but an interested few are agreed will receive their proper degree of attention, and measures will be considered in a non-partisan spirit with the sole purpose of securing these objects. Take as an illustration the postal telegraph question. No one, not a stockholder in an existing telegraph company, would prefer to pay twenty-five cents for a message if he could send it for ten cents. Where is the room for discussing a question of this nature? What society wants is the cheapest possible system. It wants to know with certainty whether a national postal telegraph system would secure this universally desired object. It is to be expected that the agents of the present telegraph companies would try to show that it would not succeed. This is according to the known laws of psychology as set forth in this work. But why be influenced by the interests of such a small number of persons, however worthy, when all the rest of mankind are interested in the opposite solution? The investigation should be a disinterested and strictly scientific one, and should actually settle the question in one way or the other. If it was found to be a real benefit, the system should be adopted. There are to-day a great number of these strictly social questions before the American people, questions which concern every citizen in the country, and whose solution would doubtless profoundly affect the state of civilization attainable on this continent. Not only is it impossible to secure this, but it is impossible to secure an investigation of them on their real merits. The same is true of other countries, and in general the prevailing democracies of the world are incompetent to deal with problems of social welfare.

The more extreme and important case referred to a few pages back may make the distinction still more clear. It was shown, and is known to all political economists, that the prices of most of the staple commodities consumed by mankind have no necessary relation to the cost of producing them and placing them in the hands of the consumer. It is always the highest price that the consumer will pay rather than do without. Let us suppose that price to be on an average double what it would cost to produce, transport, exchange, and deliver the goods, allowing in each of these transactions a fair compensation for all services rendered. Is there any member of society who would prefer to pay two dollars for what is thus fairly worth only one? Is there any sane ground for arguing such a question? Certainly not. The individual cannot correct this state of things. No democracy can correct it. But a government that really represented the interests of society would no more tolerate it than an individual would tolerate a continual extortion of money on the part of another without an equivalent.

And so it would be throughout. Society would inquire in a business way without fear, favor, or bias, into everything that concerned its welfare, and if it found obstacles it would remove them, and if it found opportunities it would improve them. In a word, society would do under the same circumstances just what an intelligent individual would do. It would further, in all possible ways, its own interests.

12

The People's Party

☆ In 1891 the People's—or Populist—party was formed by dissenting farmer and labor groups, chiefly from the West and South. The party achieved considerable success in the national and state elections of 1892 and 1894. The Populist platform planks constituted the first truly national reform program since the Civil War.* ☆

FINANCE

1. We demand a national money, safe and sound, issued by the general government only, without the intervention of banks of issue, to be a full legal tender for all debts, public and private; a just, equitable, and efficient means of distribution direct to the people and through the lawful disbursements of the government.

2. We demand the free and unrestricted coinage of silver and gold at the present legal ratio of sixteen to one, without waiting for the consent of foreign nations.

3. We demand that the volume of circulating medium be speedily increased to an amount sufficient to meet the demands of business and population and to restore the just level of prices of labor and production.

4. We denounce the sale of bonds and the increase of the interest-bearing debt made by the present administration as unnecessary and without authority of law, and demand that no more bonds be issued except by specific act of Congress.

5. We demand such legislation as will prevent the demonetization of the lawful money of the United States by private contract.

6. We demand that the government, in payment of its obligations, shall use its option as to the kind of lawful money in which they are to be paid, and we denounce the present and preceding administrations for surrendering this option to the holders of government obligations.

7. We demand a graduated income tax, to the end that aggregated wealth shall bear its just proportion of taxation; and we regard the recent decision of the Supreme Court relative to the income tax law as a misinterpretation of the Constitution, and an invasion of the rightful powers of Congress over the subject of taxation.

8. We demand that postal savings banks be established by the government for the safe deposit of the savings of the people and to facilitate exchange.

* From People's Party Platform of 1896, in Edward Stanwood, *A History of the Presidency from 1788 to 1897*, pp. 551-554. Published by Houghton Mifflin Company, Boston, 1898.

TRANSPORTATION

1. Transportation being a means of exchange and a public necessity, government should own and operate the railroads in the interests of the people and on a non-partisan basis, to the end that all may be accorded the same treatment in transportation, and that the tyranny and political power now exercised by the great railroad corporations, which result in the impairment, if not the destruction, of the political rights and personal liberties of the citizen, may be destroyed. Such ownership is to be accomplished gradually, in a manner consistent with sound public policy.

2. The interest of the United States in the public highways, built with public moneys, and the proceeds of extensive grants of land to the Pacific railroads should never be alienated, mortgaged, or sold, but guarded and protected for the general welfare as provided by the laws organizing such railroads. The foreclosure of existing liens of the United States on these roads should at once follow default in the payment thereof by the debtor-companies; and at the foreclosure sales of said roads the government shall purchase the same if it become necessary to protect its interests therein, or if they can be purchased at a reasonable price; and the government shall operate said railroads as public highways for the benefit of the whole people, and not in the interest of the few, under suitable provisions for protection of life and property, giving to all transportation interests equal privileges and equal rates for fares and freight.

3. We denounce the present infamous schemes for refunding these debts, and demand that the laws now applicable thereto be executed and administered according to their true intent and spirit.

4. The telegraph, like the post-office system, being a necessity for the transmission of news, should be owned and operated by the government in the interest of the people.

LAND

1. The true policy demands that national and state legislation shall be such as will ultimately enable every prudent and industrious citizen to secure a home, and therefore the lands should not be monopolized for speculative purposes. All lands now held by railroads and other corporations in excess of their actual needs should by lawful means be reclaimed by the government and held for actual settlers only, and subject to the right of every human being to acquire a home upon the soil, and private land monopoly, as well as alien ownership, should be prohibited.

2. We condemn the frauds by which the land grants to the Pacific railroad companies have, through the connivance of the interior department, robbed multitudes of actual *bona fide* settlers of their homes and miners of their claims, and we demand legislation by Congress which will enforce the exemption of mineral land from such grants after as well as before the patent.

We demand that *bona fide* settlers on all public lands be granted free homes as provided in the national homestead law, and that no exception be made in the case of Indian reservations when opened for settlement, and that all lands not now patented come under this demand.

DIRECT LEGISLATION

We favor a system of direct legislation through the initiative and *referendum* under proper constitutional safeguards.

GENERAL PROPOSITIONS

1. We demand the election of Presi-

dent, Vice-President, and United States senators by a direct vote of the people.

2. We tender to the patriotic people of Cuba our deepest sympathy in their heroic struggle for political freedom and independence, and we believe the time has come when the United States, the great republic of the world, should recognize that Cuba is and of right ought to be, a free and independent state.

3. We favor home rule in the Territories and the District of Columbia, and the early admission of Territories as States.

4. All public salaries should be made to correspond to the price of labor and its products.

5. In times of great industrial depression, idle labor should be employed on public works as far as practicable.

6. The arbitrary course of the courts in assuming to imprison citizens for indirect contempt, and ruling by injunction, should be prevented by proper legislation.

7. We favor just pensions for our disabled Union soldiers.

8. Believing that the elective franchise and an untrammeled ballot are essential to a government of, for, and by the people, the People's party condemn the wholesale system of disfranchisement adopted in some of the States, as unrepublican and undemocratic, and we declare it to be the duty of the several state legislatures to take such action as will secure a full, free, and fair ballot and an honest count.

9. While the foregoing propositions constitute the platform upon which our party stands, and for the vindication of which its organization will be maintained, we recognize that the great and pressing issue of the present campaign upon which the present presidential election will turn is the financial question, and upon this great and specific issue between the parties we cordially invite the aid and cooperation of all organizations and citizens agreeing with us upon this vital question.

13

The Burden of Gold

☆ *William Jennings Bryan (1860-1925) won national acclaim by his eloquent advocacy of the free coinage of silver as a solution to the financial distresses which he attributed to the gold standard. As the Democratic presidential candidate in 1896, Bryan made bimetalism the foremost issue of the campaign. His typical approach to this issue was contained in his 1896 Madison Square Garden address.* ☆

The farmers are opposed to the gold standard because they have felt its effects. Since they sell at wholesale and buy at retail they have lost more than they have gained by falling prices, and, besides this, they have found that certain fixed charges have not fallen at all. Taxes have not been perceptibly decreased, although it requires more of farm products now than formerly to secure the money with which to pay taxes. Debts have not fallen. The farmer who owed $1,000 is still compelled to pay $1,000, although it may be twice as difficult as formerly to obtain the dollars with which to pay the debt. Railroad rates have not been reduced to keep pace with falling prices, and besides these items there are many more. The farmer has thus found it more and more difficult to live. Has he not a just complaint against the gold standard?

The wage earners have been injured by a gold standard, and have expressed themselves upon the subject with great emphasis. In February, 1895, a petition

asking for the immediate restoration of the free and unlimited coinage of gold and silver at 16 to 1 was signed by the representatives of all, or nearly all, the leading labor organizations and presented to Congress. Wage-earners know that while a gold standard raises the purchasing power of the dollar, it also makes it more difficult to obtain possession of the dollar; they know that employment is less permanent, loss of work more probable, and re-employment less certain. A gold standard encourages the hoarding of money, because money is rising; it also discourages enterprise and paralyzes industry. On the other hand, the restoration of bimetallism will discourage hoarding, because, when prices are steady or rising, money cannot afford to lie idle in the bank vaults. The farmers and wage-earners together constitute a considerable majority of the people of the country. Why should their interests be ignored in considering financial legislation? A monetary system which is pecuniarily advantageous to a few syndicates has far less to commend it than a system which would give hope and en-

* From William Jennings Bryan, *The First Battle, A Story of the Campaign of 1896*, pp. 322-323. Published by W. B. Conkey Company, Chicago, 1896.

couragement to those who create the nation's wealth.

Our opponents have made a special appeal to those who hold fire and life insurance policies, but these policy holders know that, since the total premiums received exceed the total losses paid, a rising standard must be of more benefit to the companies than to the policy holders.

Much solicitude has been expressed by our opponents for the depositors in savings banks. They constantly parade before these depositors the advantages of a gold standard, but these appeals will be in vain, because savings bank depositors know that under a gold standard there is increasing danger that they will lose their deposits because of the inability of the banks to collect their assets; and they still further know that, if the gold standard is to continue indefinitely, they may be compelled to withdraw their deposits in order to pay living expenses.

It is only necessary to note the increasing number of failures in order to know that a gold standard is ruinous to merchants and manufacturers. These business men do not make their profits from the people from whom they borrow money, but from the people to whom they sell their goods. If the people cannot buy, retailers cannot sell, and, if retailers cannot sell, wholesale merchants and manufacturers must go into bankruptcy.

Those who hold, as a permanent investment, the stock of railroads and of other enterprises—I do not include those who speculate in stocks or use stock holdings as a means of obtaining an inside advantage in construction contracts—are injured by a gold standard. The rising dollar destroys the earning power of these enterprises without reducing their liabilities, and, as dividends cannot be paid until salaries and fixed charges have been satisfied, the stockholders must bear the burden of hard times.

Salaries in business occupations depend upon business conditions, and the gold standard both lessens the amount and threatens the permanency of such salaries.

Official salaries, except the salaries of those who hold office for life, must, in the long run, be adjusted to the conditions of those who pay the taxes, and if the present financial policy continues we must expect the contest between the taxpayer and the taxeater to increase in bitterness.

The professional classes—in the main—derive their support from the producing classes, and can only enjoy prosperity when there is prosperity among those who create wealth.

14

The Republican Party

☆ *The Republican and Democratic parties were beset by internal confusion and dissension which reflected the conflicts in American society in the 1890's. The Republican platform of 1896 represented an attempt—successful at the polls—to harmonize a variety of national interests.* * ☆

We renew and emphasize our allegiance to the policy of protection as the bulwark of American industrial independence and the foundation of American development and prosperity. This true American policy taxes foreign products and encourages home industry; it puts the burden of revenue on foreign goods; it secures the American market for the American producer; it upholds the American standard of wages for the American workingman; it puts the factory by the side of the farm, and makes the American farmer less dependent on foreign demand and price; it diffuses general thrift, and founds the strength of all on the strength of each. In its reasonable application it is just, fair, and impartial, equally opposed to foreign control and domestic monopoly, to sectional discrimination and individual favoritism.

We denounce the present Democratic tariff as sectional, injurious to the public credit, and destructive to business enterprise. We demand such an equitable tariff on foreign imports which come into

* From Republican Party Platform of 1896, in Edward Stanwood, *A History of the Presidency from 1788 to 1897*, pp. 533-537. Published by Houghton Mifflin Company, Boston, 1898.

competition with American products as will not only furnish adequate revenue for the necessary expenses of the government, but will protect American labor from degradation to the wage level of other lands. We are not pledged to any particular schedules. The question of rates is a practical question, to be governed by the conditions of the time and of production; the ruling and uncompromising principle is the protection and development of American labor and industry. The country demands a right settlement, and then it wants rest.

We believe the repeal of the reciprocity arrangements negotiated by the last Republican administration was a national calamity, and we demand their renewal and extension on such terms as will equalize our trade with other nations, remove the restrictions which now obstruct the sale of American products in the ports of other countries, and secure enlarged markets for the products of our farms, forests, and factories. . . .

To all our products—to those of the mine and the fields, as well as those of the shop and factory; to hemp, to wool, the product of the great industry of sheep husbandry, as well as to the finished woollens of the mills—we promise the most ample protection.

We favor restoring the early American policy of discriminating duties for the upbuilding of our merchant marine and the protection of our shipping in the foreign carrying trade, so that American ships—the product of American labor, employed in American shipyards, sailing under the stars and stripes, and manned, officered, and owned by Americans—may regain the carrying of our foreign commerce.

The Republican party is unreservedly for sound money. It caused the enactment of the law providing for the resumption of specie payments in 1879; since then every dollar has been as good as gold. We are unalterably opposed to every measure calculated to debase our currency or impair the credit of our country. We are, therefore, opposed to the free coinage of silver, except by international agreement with the leading commercial nations of the world, which we pledge ourselves to promote, and until such agreement can be obtained the existing gold standard must be preserved. All our silver and paper currency must be maintained at parity with gold, and we favor all measures designed to maintain inviolably the obligations of the United States and all our money, whether coin or paper, at the present standard, the standard of the most enlightened nations of the earth.

The veterans of the Union armies deserve and should receive fair treatment and generous recognition. Whenever practicable they should be given the preference in the matter of employment, and they are entitled to the enactment of such laws as are best calculated to secure the fulfilment of the pledges made to them in the dark days of the country's peril. We denounce the practice in the Pension Bureau, so recklessly and unjustly carried on by the present administration, of reducing pensions and arbitrarily dropping names from the rolls, as deserving the severest condemnation of the American people.

Our foreign policy should be at all times firm, vigorous, and dignified, and all our interests in the Western hemisphere carefully watched and guarded. The Hawaiian islands should be controlled by the United States, and no foreign power should be permitted to interfere with them; the Nicaragua Canal should be built, owned and operated by the United States; and by the purchase of the Danish islands we should secure a proper and much-needed naval station in the West Indies.

The massacres in Armenia have aroused the deep sympathy and just indignation of the American people, and we believe that the United States should exercise all the influence it can properly exert to bring these atrocities to an end. In Turkey, American residents have been exposed to the gravest dangers and American property destroyed. There and everywhere American citizens and American property must be absolutely protected at all hazards and at any cost.

We reassert the Monroe doctrine in its full extent, and we reaffirm the right of the United States to give the doctrine effect by responding to the appeal of any American State for friendly intervention in case of European encroachment. We have not interfered and shall not interfere with the existing possessions of any European power in this hemisphere, but those possessions must not on any pretext be extended. We hopefully look forward to the eventual withdrawal of the European powers from this hemisphere, and to the ultimate union of all English-speaking parts of the continent by the free consent of its inhabitants.

From the hour of achieving their own independence, the people of the United

States have regarded with sympathy the struggles of other American people to free themselves from European domination. We watch with deep and abiding interest the heroic battle of the Cuban patriots against cruelty and oppression, and our best hopes go out for the full success of their determined contest for liberty.

The government of Spain, having lost control of Cuba, and being unable to protect the property or lives of resident American citizens, or to comply with its treaty obligations, we believe that the government of the United States should actively use its influence and good offices to restore peace and give independence to the island.

The peace and security of the republic and the maintenance of its rightful influence among the nations of the earth demand a naval power commensurate with its position and responsibility. We therefore favor the continued enlargement of the navy and a complete system of harbor and seacoast defences.

For the protection of the quality of our American citizenship and of the wages of our workingmen against the fatal competition of low-priced labor, we demand that the immigration laws be thoroughly enforced, and so extended as to exclude from entrance to the United States those who can neither read nor write.

The civil-service law was placed on the statute book by the Republican party, which has always sustained it, and we renew our repeated declarations that it shall be thoroughly and honestly enforced and extended wherever practicable.

We demand that every citizen of the United States shall be allowed to cast one free and unrestricted ballot, and that such ballot shall be counted and returned as cast.

We proclaim our unqualified condemnation of the uncivilized and barbarous practice, well known as lynching, or killing of human beings suspected or charged with crime, without process of law.

We favor the creation of a national Board of Arbitration to settle and adjust differences which may arise between employers and employees engaged in interstate commerce.

We believe in an immediate return to the free-homestead policy of the Republican party, and urge the passage by Congress of a satisfactory free-homestead measure such as has already passed the House, and is now pending in the Senate. . . .

We sympathize with all wise and legitimate efforts to lessen and prevent the evils of intemperance and promote morality.

The Republican party is mindful of the rights and interests of women. Protection of American industries includes equal opportunities, equal pay for equal work, and protection to the home. We favor the admission of women to wider spheres of usefulness, and welcome their cooperation in rescuing the country from Democratic and Populist mismanagement and misrule.

II

the twentieth century mind

THE MOST influential pattern of thought during the first half of the twentieth century had many names, Experimentalism, Instrumentalism, Pragmatism. It was not new for it had been earlier propounded, in rudimentary forms, by men like C. S. Pierce and had been slowly advanced in the closing years of the old century.

Experimentation, skepticism, adaptation, and an emphasis on change characterized the emerging pattern of thought. It was blunt in its assault on competing ways of thinking and doing things. It jeered at absolutes and abstractions. It hooted at thought based on *a priori* assumptions. It claimed to have no dogmas or doctrines except its hostility to dogma and doctrine. It exalted facts, action, and power. It sought to use ideas not as ritual jargon but as social instruments. Ideas were tools to be tested against life for their results and their practicality.

Conditions at the turn of the century were favorable for pragmatism to come to prominence. Its influence was seen in many fields. With John Dewey, it called into question the traditional recitative method of education and proposed a practical form of education that would develop man as a cooperative social being. With Oliver Wendell Homes, Jr., habit and precedent in the law were questioned as to whether they really served justice. And later, the questions were augmented by energetic efforts to adapt the law to the great changes in human institutions.

The pragmatic temper thrashed about with broader ideas, always wrestling with consequences. It could see value in social conflict, but, as with William James, it could exhort man to use his intelligence—as a moderating force—to understand himself and his enemies. While pragmatism was only a method, it was not forbidden the advocacy of sweeping generalizations. Brooks Adams used it to explain the cultural aridity and stagnation he saw in Western society. His brother, Henry Adams, in reviewing the developments of his lifetime, marveled at the consequences of the new forces, from the ocean steamer and the telegraph in his youth to radium and the automobile in his later years. Men and societies were jostled by these new forces, which commanded drastic changes in ways of living and thinking. Aspects of pragmatism were also reflected in fictional literature in the rising naturalist school of writers. Authors like Frank Norris abandoned polite stories of interesting predicaments of men and women for outspoken tales of the harsh tests awaiting man in his environment.

All this heralded an altered pattern of American thinking. Though pragmatism did not destroy *a priori* thinking or the concern with absolutes and abstractions, it made room for itself as the predominant twentieth century way of thought not only in opposition to them but ironically sometimes in combination with them. Few Americans in the new century could resist the emphasis on the practical testing of their intelligence, through science and experimentation, against the forces of environment.

1

Pragmatism

☆ *William James (1842-1910), psychologist and philosopher, elaborated on the ideas of Charles S. Pierce and is generally credited with bringing pragmatism as a philosophy into full flower.** ☆

Pragmatism represents a perfectly familiar attitude in philosophy, the empiricist attitude, but it represents it, as it seems to me, both in a more radical and in a less objectionable form than it has ever yet assumed. A pragmatist turns his back resolutely and once for all upon a lot of inveterate habits dear to professional philosophers. He turns away from abstraction and insufficiency, from verbal solutions, from bad *a priori* reasons, from fixed principles, closed systems, and pretended absolutes and origins. He turns towards concreteness and adequacy, towards facts, towards action and towards power. That means the empiricist temper regnant and the rationalist temper sincerely given up. It means the open air and possibilities of nature, as against dogma, artificiality, and the pretence of finality in truth.

At the same time it does not stand for any special results. It is a method only. But the general triumph of that method would mean an enormous change in what I called in my last lecture the 'temperament' of philosophy. Teachers of the ultra-

* From William James, *Pragmatism, A New Name for Some Old Ways of Thinking*, pp. 51-63. Published by Longmans, Green and Company, New York, 1907, 1931. Used by permission of Paul R. Reynolds and Son.

rationalistic type would be frozen out, much as the courtier type is frozen out in republics, as the ultramontane type of priest is frozen out in protestant lands. Science and metaphysics would come much nearer together, would in fact work absolutely hand in hand.

Metaphysics has usually followed a very primitive kind of quest. You know how men have always hankered after unlawful magic, and you know what a great part in magic *words* have always played. If you have his name, or the formula of incantation that binds him, you can control the spirit, genie, afrite, or whatever the power may be. Solomon knew the names of all the spirits, and having their names, he held them subject to his will. So the universe has always appeared to the natural mind as a kind of enigma, of which the key must be sought in the shape of some illuminating or power-bringing word or name. That word names the universe's *principle,* and to possess it is after a fashion to possess the universe itself. 'God,' 'Matter,' 'Reason,' 'the Absolute,' 'Energy,' are so many solving names. You can rest when you have them. You are at the end of your metaphysical quest.

But if you follow the pragmatic method,

you cannot look on any such word as closing your quest. You must bring out of each word its practical cash-value, set it at work within the stream of your experience. It appears less as a solution, then, than as a program for more work, and more particularly as an indication of the ways in which existing realities may be *changed*.

Theories thus become instruments, not answers to enigmas, in which we can rest. We don't lie back upon them, we move forward, and, on occasion, make nature over again by their aid. Pragmatism unstiffens all our theories, limbers them up and sets each one at work. Being nothing essentially new, it harmonizes with many ancient philosophic tendencies. It agrees with nominalism for instance, in always appealing to particulars; with utilitarianism in emphasizing practical aspects; with positivism in its disdain for verbal solutions, useless questions and metaphysical abstractions.

All these, you see, are *anti-intellectualist* tendencies. Against rationalism as a pretension and a method pragmatism is fully armed and militant. But, at the outset, at least, it stands for no particular results. It has no dogmas, and no doctrines save its method. As the young Italian pragmatist Papini has well said, it lies in the midst of our theories, like a corridor in a hotel. Innumerable chambers open out of it. In one you may find a man writing an atheistic volume; in the next some one on his knees praying for faith and strength; in a third a chemist investigating a body's properties. In a fourth a system of idealistic metaphysics is being excogitated; in a fifth the impossibility of metaphysics is being shown. But they all own the corridor, and all must pass through it if they want a practicable way of getting into or out of their respective rooms.

No particular results then, so far, but only an attitude of orientation, is what

the pragmatic method means. *The attitude of looking away from first things, principles, 'categories,' supposed necessities; and of looking towards last things, fruits, consequences, facts.*

So much for the pragmatic method. . . !

One of the most successfully cultivated branches of philosophy in our time is what is called inductive logic, the study of the conditions under which our sciences have evolved. Writers on this subject have begun to show a singular unanimity as to what the laws of nature and elements of fact mean, when formulated by mathematicians, physicists and chemists. When the first mathematical, logical, and natural uniformities, the first *laws,* were discovered, men were so carried away by the clearness, beauty and simplification that resulted, that they believed themselves to have deciphered authentically the eternal thoughts of the Almighty. His mind also thundered and reverberated in syllogisms. He also thought in conic sections, squares and roots and ratios, and geometrized like Euclid. He made Kepler's laws for the planets to follow; he made velocity increase proportionally to the time in falling bodies; he made the law of the sines for light to obey when refracted; he established the classes, orders, families and genera of plants and animals, and fixed the distances between them. He thought the archetypes of all things, and devised their variations; and when we rediscover any one of these his wondrous institutions, we seize his mind in its very literal intention.

But as the sciences have developed farther, the notion has gained ground that most, perhaps all, of our laws are only approximations. The laws themselves, moreover, have grown so numerous that there is no counting them; and so many rival formulations are proposed in all the branches of science that investigators have become accustomed to the notion that no theory is absolutely a transcript of reality, but that any one of them may from some point of view be useful. Their great use is to summarize old facts and to lead to new ones. They are only a man-made language, a conceptual shorthand, as some one calls them, in which we write our reports of nature; and languages, as is well know, tolerate much choice of expression and many dialects.

Thus human arbitrariness has driven divine necessity from scientific logic. . . .

Riding now on the front of this wave of scientific logic Messrs. Schiller and Dewey appear with their pragmatistic account of what truth everywhere signifies. Everywhere, these teachers say, 'truth' in our ideas and beliefs means the same thing that it means in science. It means, they say, nothing but this, *that ideas (which themselves are but parts of our experience) become true just in so far as they help us to get into satisfactory relation with other parts of our experience,* to summarize them and get about among them by conceptual short-cuts instead of following the interminable succession of particular phenomena. Any idea upon which we can ride, so to speak; any idea that will carry us prosperously from any one part of our experience to any other part, linking things satisfactorily, working securely, simplifying, saving labor; is true for just so much, true in so far forth, true *instrumentally.* . . .

Messrs. Dewey, Schiller and their allies, in reaching this general conception of all truth, have only followed the example of geologists, biologists and philologists. In the establishment of these other sciences, the successful stroke was always to take some simple process actually observable in operation—as denudation by weather, say, or variation from parental type, or change, of dialect by incorporation of new words and pronunciations—and then to generalize it, making it apply to all times, and produce great results by summating its effects through the ages.

The observable process which Schiller and Dewey particularly singled out for generalization is the familiar one by which any individual settles into *new opinions.* The process here is always the same. The individual has a stock of old opinions already, but he meets a new experience that puts them to a strain. Somebody contradicts them; or in a reflective moment he discovers that they contradict each other; or he hears of facts with which they are incompatible; or desires arise in him which they cease to satisfy. The result is an inward trouble to which his mind till then had been a stranger, and from which he seeks to escape by modifying his previous mass of opinions. He saves as much of it as he can, for in this matter of belief we are all extreme conservatives. So he tries to change first this opinion, and then that (for they resist change very variously), until at last some new idea comes up which he can graft upon the ancient stock with a minimum of disturbance of the latter, some idea that mediates between the stock and the new experience and runs them into one another most felicitiously and expediently.

This new idea is then adopted as the true one. It preserves the older stock of truths with a minimum of modification, stretching them just enough to make them admit the novelty, but conceiving that in ways as familiar as the case leaves possible. An *outrée* explanation, violating all our preconceptions, would never pass for a true account of a novelty. We should scratch round industriously till we found something less excentric. The most violent revolutions in an individual's beliefs leave most of his old order standing. Time and space, cause and effect, nature and history, and one's own biography remain untouched. New truth is always a go-between, a smoother-over of transitions. It marries old opinion to new fact so as ever to show a minimum of jolt, a maximum of continuity. We hold a theory true just in proportion to its success in solving this 'problem of maxima and minima.' But success in solving this problem is eminently a matter of approximation. We say this theory solves it on the whole more satisfactorily than that theory; but that means more satisfactorily to ourselves, and individuals will emphasize their points of satisfaction differently. To a certain degree, therefore, everything here is plastic.

The point I now urge you to observe particularly is the part played by the older truths. Failure to take account of it is the source of much of the unjust criticism levelled against pragmatism. Their influence is absolutely controlling. Loyalty to them is the first principle—in most cases it is the only principle; for by far the most usual way of handling phenomena so novel that they would make for a serious rearrangement of our preconception is to ignore them altogether, or to abuse those who bear witness for them.

You doubtless wish examples of this process of truth's growth, and the only trouble is their superabundance. The simplest case of new truth is of course the mere numerical addition of new kinds of facts, or of new single facts of old kinds, to our experience—an addition that in-

follows day, and its contents are simply added. The new contents themselves are added. The new contents themselves are not true, they simply *come* and *are*. Truth is *what we say about* them, and when we say that they have come, truth is satisfied by the plain additive formula.

But often the day's contents oblige a rearrangement. If I should now utter piercing shrieks and act like a maniac on this platform, it would make many of you revise your ideas as to the probable worth of my philosophy. 'Radium' came the other day as part of the day's content, and seemed for a moment to contradict our ideas of the whole order of nature, that order having come to be identified with what is called the conservation of energy. The mere sight of radium paying heat away indefinitely out of its own pocket seemed to violate that conservation. What to think? If the radiations from it were nothing but an escape of unsuspected 'potential' energy, pre-existent inside of the atoms, the principle of conservation would be saved. The discovery of 'helium' as the radiation's outcome, opened a way to this belief. So Ramsay's view is generally held to be true, because, although it extends our old ideas of energy, it causes a minimum of alteration in their nature.

2

The New Education

☆ *John Dewey (1859-1952), in his long career, applied the philosophy of pragmatism to almost every facet of human activity. He is best known for his advocacy of the adjustment of education to the needs of society.** ☆

... we find that one of the most striking tendencies at present is toward the introduction of so-called manual training, shop-work, and the household arts—sewing and cooking.

This has not been done "on purpose," with a full consciousness that the school must now supply that factor of training formerly taken care of in the home, but rather by instinct, by experimenting and finding that such work takes a vital hold of pupils and gives them something which was not to be got in any other way. Consciousness of its real import is still so weak that the work is often done in a half-hearted, confused, and unrelated way. The reasons assigned to justify it are painfully inadequate or sometimes even positively wrong.

If we were to cross-examine even those who are most favorably disposed to the introduction of this work into our school system, we should, I imagine, generally find the main reasons to be that such work engages the full spontaneous interest and attention of the children. It keeps them alert and active, instead of passive and

*Reprinted from *The School and Society* by John Dewey, pp. 22-28, 124-125, by permission of The University of Chicago Press. Copyright by John Dewey, 1899.

perceptive; it makes them more useful, more capable, and hence more inclined to be helpful at home; it prepares them to some extent for the practical duties of later life—the girls to be more efficient house managers, if not actually cooks and sempstresses; the boys (were our educational system only adequately rounded out into trade schools) for their future vocations. I do not underestimate these reasons. Of those indicated by the changed attitude of the children I shall indeed have something to say in my next talk, when speaking directly of the relationship of the school to the child, not to society. But the point of view is, upon the whole, unnecessarily narrow. We must conceive of work in wood and metal, of weaving, sewing, and cooking, as methods, not as distinct studies of life on its active and social sides. We must conceive of them in their social significance, as types of the processes by which society keeps itself going, as agencies for bringing home to the child some of the primal necessities of community life, and as the ways in which these have been met by the growing insight and ingenuity of man; in short, as instrumentalities through which the school itself shall be made a genuine form of active community life, instead of a place set apart in which to learn lessons.

A society is a number of people held together because they are working along common lines, in a common spirit, and with reference to common aims. The common needs and aims demand a growing interchange of thought and growing unity of sympathetic feeling. The radical reason that the present school cannot organize itself as a natural social unit is because just this element of common and productive activity is absent. Upon the playground, in game and sport, social organization takes place spontaneously and inevitably. There is something to do, some activity to be carried on, requiring natural divisions of labor, selection of leaders and followers, mutual coöperation and emulation. In the schoolroom the motive and the cement of social organization are alike wanting. Upon the ethical side, the tragic weakness of the present school is that it endeavors to prepare future members of the social order in a medium in which the conditions of the social spirit are eminently wanting.

The difference that appears when occupations are made the articulating centers of school life is not easy to describe in words; it is a difference in motive, of spirit and atmosphere. As one enters a busy workshop in which a group of children are actively engaged in the preparation of food, the psychological difference, the change from more or less passive and inert recipiency and restraint to one of buoyant outgoing energy, is so obvious as fairly to strike one in the face. Indeed, to those whose image of the school is rigidly set the change is sure to give a shock. But the change in the social attitude is equally marked. The mere absorption of facts and truths is so exclusively individual an affair that it tends very naturally to pass into selfishness. There is no obvious social motive for the acquirement of mere learning, there is no

clear social gain in success thereat. Indeed, almost the only measure for success is a competitive one, in the bad sense of that term—a comparison of results in the recitation or in the examination to see which child has succeeded in getting ahead of others in storing up, in accumulating the maximum of information. So thoroughly is this the prevalent atmosphere that for one child to help another in his task has become a school crime. Where the school work consists in simply learning lessons, mutual assistance, instead of being the most natural form of cooperation and association, becomes a clandestine effort to relieve one's neighbor of his proper duties. Where active work is going on all this is changed. Helping others, instead of being a form of charity which impoverishes the recipient, is simply an aid in setting free the powers and furthering the impulse of the one helped. A spirit of free communication, of interchange of ideas, suggestions, results, both successes and failures of previous experiences, becomes the dominating note of the recitation. So far as emulation enters in, it is in the comparison of individuals, not with regard to the quantity of information personally absorbed, but with reference to the quality of work done—the genuine community standard of value. In an informal but all the more pervasive way, the school life organizes itself on a social basis.

Within this organization is found the principle of school discipline or order. Of course, order is simply a thing which is relative to an end. If you have the end in view of forty or fifty children learning certain set lessons, to be recited to a teacher, your discipline must be devoted to securing that result. But if the end in view is the development of a spirit of social coöperation and community life, discipline must grow out of and be relative to this. There is little order of the first sort where things are in process of construction; there is a certain disorder in any busy workshop; there is not silence; persons are not engaged in maintaining certain fixed physical postures; their arms are not folded; they are not holding their books thus and so. They are doing a variety of things, and there is the confusion, the bustle, that results from activity. But out of occupation, out of doing things that are to produce results, and out of doing these in a social and coöperative way, there is born a discipline of its own kind and type. Our whole conception of school discipline changes when we get this point of view. In critical moments we all realize that the only discipline that stands by us, the only training that becomes intuition, is that got through life itself. That we learn from experience, and from books or the sayings of others *only* in their vital relation to experience, are not mere phrases. But the school has been so set apart, so isolated from the ordinary conditions and motives of life, that the place where children are sent for discipline is the one place in the world where it is most difficult to get experience—the mother of all discipline worth the name. It is only where a narrow and fixed image of traditional school discipline dominates, that one is in any danger of overlooking that deeper and infinitely wider discipline that comes from having a part to do in constructive work, in contributing to a result which, social in spirit, is none the less obvious and tangible in form—and hence in a form with reference to which responsibility may be exacted and accurate judgment passed.

The great thing to keep in mind, then, regarding the introduction into the school of various forms of active occupation, is that through them the entire spirit of the school is renewed. It has a chance to affiliate itself with life, to become the child's habitat, where he learns through directed living, instead of being only a place to learn lessons having an abstract and remote reference to some possible living to be done in the future. It gets a chance to be a miniature community, an embryonic society. This is the fundamental fact, and from this arise continuous and orderly sources of instruction. Under the industrial *régime* described, the child, after all, shared in the work, not for the sake of the sharing, but for the sake of the product. The educational results secured were real, yet incidental and dependent. But in the school the typical occupations followed are freed from all economic stress. The aim is not the economic value of the products, but the development of social power and insight. It is this liberation from narrow utilities and openness to the possibilities of the human spirit that makes these practical activities in the school allies of art and centers of science and history. . . .

•[Shifting to] the moral side, that of so-called discipline and order, where the work of the University Elementary School has perhaps suffered most from misunderstanding and misrepresentation, I shall say only that our ideal has been, and continues to be, that of the best form of family life, rather than that of a rigid graded school. In the latter, the large number of children under the care of a single teacher, and the very limited number of modes of activity open to the pupils, have made necessary certain fixed and somewhat external forms of "keeping order." It would be very stupid to copy these, under the changed conditions of our school, its small groups permitting and requiring the most intimate personal acquaintance of child and teacher, and its great variety of forms of work, with their differing adaptations to the needs of different children. If we have permitted to our children more than the usual amount of freedom, it has not been in order to relax or decrease real discipline, but because under our particular conditions larger and less artificial responsibilities could thus be required of the children, and their entire development of body and spirit be more harmonious and complete. And I am confident that the parents who have intrusted their children to us for any length of time will agree in saying that, while the children like, or love, to come to school, yet work, and not amusement, has been the spirit and teaching of the school; and that this freedom has been granted under such conditions of intelligent and sympathetic oversight as to be a means of upbuilding and strengthening character.

3

Sociological Jurisprudence

☆ *Oliver Wendell Holmes, Jr. (1841-1935), served as Chief Justice of the Massachusetts Supreme Court and Associate Justice of the United States Supreme Court. Concluding as a result of his historical studies that "the life of the law has not been logic; it has been experience," Holmes was in the forefront of those jurists who argued against immutable principles in law.** ☆

. . . let us consider the present condition of the law as a subject for study, and the ideal toward which it tends. We still are far from the point of view which I desire to see reached. No one has reached it or can reach it as yet. We are only at the beginning of a philosophical reaction, and of a reconsideration of the worth of doctrines which for the most part still are taken for granted without any deliberate, conscious, and systematic questioning of their grounds. The development of our law has gone on for nearly a thousand years, like the development of a plant, each generation taking the inevitable next step, mind, like matter, simply obeying a law of spontaneous growth. It is perfectly natural and right that it should have been so. Imitation is a necessity of human nature, as has been illustrated by a remarkable French writer, M. Tarde, in an admirable book, "Les Lois de l'Imitation." Most of the things we do, we do for no better reason than that our fathers have done them or that our neigh-

* From Oliver Wendell Holmes, Jr., "The Path of the Law," *Harvard Law Review*, X (1897), pp. 468-478. Copyright (1897) by The Harvard Law Review Association. Used by permission.

bors do them, and the same is true of a larger part than we suspect of what we think. The reason is a good one, because our short life gives us no time for a better, but it is not the best. It does not follow, because we all are compelled to take on faith at second hand most of the rules on which we base our action and our thought, that each of us may not try to set some corner of his world in the order of reason, or that all of us collectively should not aspire to carry reason as far as it will go throughout the whole domain. In regard to the law, it is true, no doubt, that an evolutionist will hesitate to affirm universal validity for his social ideals, or for the principles which he thinks should be embodied in legislation. He is content if he can prove them best for here and now. He may be ready to admit that he knows nothing about an absolute best in the cosmos, and even that he knows next to nothing about a permanent best for men. Still it is true that a body of law is more rational and more civilized when every rule it contains is referred articulately and definitely to an end which it subserves, and when the grounds for desiring that end are stated or are ready to be stated in words. . . .

Far more fundamental questions still await a better answer than that we do as our fathers have done. What have we better than a blind guess to show that the criminal law in its present form does more good than harm? I do not stop to refer to the effect which it has had in degrading prisoners and in plunging them further into crime, or to the question whether fine and imprisonment do not fall more heavily on a criminal's wife and children than on himself. I have in mind more far-reaching questions. Does punishment deter? Do we deal with criminals on proper principles? A modern school of Continental criminalists plumes itself on the formula, first suggested, it is said, by Gall, that we must consider the criminal rather than the crime. The formula does not carry us very far, but the inquiries which have been started look toward an answer of my questions based on science for the first time. If the typical criminal is a degenerate, bound to swindle or to murder by as deep seated an organic necessity as that which makes the rattlesnake bite, it is idle to talk of deterring him by the classical method of imprisonment. He must be got rid of; he cannot be improved, or frightened out of his structural reaction. If, on the other hand, crime, like normal human conduct, is mainly a matter of imitation, punishment fairly may be expected to help to keep it out of fashion. The study of criminals has been thought by some well known men of science to sustain the former hypothesis. The statistics of the relative increase of crime in crowded places like large cities, where example has the greatest chance to work, and in less populated parts, where the contagion spreads more slowly, have been used with great force in favor of the latter view. But there is weighty authority for the belief that,

however this may be, "not the nature of the crime, but the dangerousness of the criminal, constitutes the only reasonable legal criterion to guide the inevitable social reaction against the criminal."

The impediments to rational generalization, which I illustrated from the law of mercy, are shown in the other branches of the law, as well as in that of crime. Take the law of tort or civil liability for damages apart from contract and the like. Is there any general theory of such liability, or are the cases in which it exists simply to be enumerated, and to be explained each on its special ground, as is easy to believe from the fact that the right of action for certain well known classes of wrongs like trespass or slander has its special history for each class? I think that there is a general theory to be discovered, although resting in tendency rather than established and accepted. I think that the law regards the infliction of temporal damage by a responsible person as actionable, if under the circumstances known to him the danger of his act is manifest according to common experience, or according to his own experience if it is more than common, except in cases where upon special grounds of policy the law refuses to protect the plaintiff or grants a privilege to the defendant. I think that commonly malice, intent, and negligence mean only that the danger was manifest to a greater or less degree, under the circumstances known to the actor, although in some cases of privilege malice may mean an actual malevolent motive, and such a motive may take away a permission knowingly to inflict harm, which otherwise would be granted on this or that ground of dominant public good. But when I stated my view to a very eminent English judge the other day, he said: "You are discussing what the law ought to be; as the law is, you must show a right. A man is not liable for negligence unless he is subject to a duty." If our difference was more than a difference in words, or with regard to the proportion between the exceptions and the rule, then, in his opinion, liability for an act cannot be referred to the manifest tendency of the act to cause temporal damage in general as a sufficient explanation, but must be referred to the special nature of the damage, or must be derived from some special circumstances outside of the tendency of the act, for which no generalized explanation exists. I think that such a view is wrong, but it is familiar, and I dare say generally is accepted in England.

Everywhere the basis of principle is tradition, to such an extent that we even are in danger of making the role of history more important than it is. . . .

Since I wrote this discourse I have come on a very good example of the way in which tradition not only overrides rational policy, but overrides it after first having been misunderstood and having been given a new and broader scope than it had when it had a meaning. It is the settled law of England that a material alteration of a written contract by a party avoids it as against him. The doctrine is contrary to the general tendency of the law. We do not tell a jury that if a man ever has lied in one particular he is to be presumed to lie in all. Even if a man has tried to defraud, it seems no sufficient reason for preventing him from proving the truth. Objections of like nature in general go to the weight, not to the admissibility, of evidence. Moreover, this rule is irrespective of fraud, and is not confined to evidence. It is not merely that you cannot use the writing, but that the contract is at an end. What does this mean? The existence of a written contract depends on the fact that the offerer and offeree have interchanged their written expressions, not on the continued existence of those expressions. But in the case of a bond the primitive notion was differ-

ent. The contract was inseparable from the parchment. If a stranger destroyed it, or tore off the seal, or altered it, the obligee could not recover, however free from fault, because the defendant's contract, this is, the actual tangible bond which he had sealed, could not be produced in the form in which it bound him. About a hundred years ago Lord Kenyon undertook to use his reason on this tradition, as he sometimes did to the detriment of the law, and, not understanding it, said he could see no reason why what was true of a bond should not be true of other contracts. His decision happened to be right, as it concerned a promissory note, where again the common law regarded the contract as inseparable from the paper on which it was written, but the reasoning was general, and soon was extended to other written contracts, and various absurd and unreal grounds of policy were invented to account for the enlarged rule.

I trust that no one will understand me to be speaking with disrespect of the law, because I criticise it so freely. I venerate the law, and especially our system of law, as one of the vastest products of the human mind. No one knows better than I do the countless number of great intellects that have spent themselves in making some addition or improvement, the greatest of which is trifling when compared with the mighty whole. It has the final title to respect that it exists, that it is not a Hegelian dream, but a part of the lives of men. But one may criticise even what one reveres. Law is the business to which my life is devoted, and I should show less than devotion if I did not do what in me lies to improve it, and, when I perceive what seems to me the ideal of its future, if I hesitated to point it out and to press toward it with all my heart.

Perhaps I have said enough to show the part which the study of history necessarily plays in the intelligent study of the law as it is today. . . . We must beware of the pitfall of antiquarianism, and must remember that for our purposes our only interest in the past is for the light it throws upon the present. I look forward to a time when the part played by history in the explanation of dogma shall be very small, and instead of ingenious research we shall spend our energy on a study of the ends sought to be attained and the reasons for desiring them. As a step toward that ideal it seems to me that every lawyer ought to seek an understanding of economics. The present divorce between the schools of political economy and law seems to me an evidence of how much progress in philosophical study still remains to be made. In the present state or political economy, indeed, we come again upon history on a larger scale, but there we are called on to consider and weigh the ends of legislation, the means of attaining them, and the cost. We learn that for everything we have to give up something else, and we are taught to set the advantage we gain against the other advantage we lose, and to know what we are doing when we elect.

There is another study which sometimes is under-valued by the practical minded, for which I wish to say a good word, although I think a good deal of pretty poor stuff goes under that name. I mean the study of what is called jurisprudence. Jurisprudence, as I look at it, is simply law in its most generalized part. Every effort to reduce a case to a rule is an effort of jurisprudence, although the name as used in English is confined to the broadest rules and most fundamental conceptions. One mark of a great lawyer is that he sees the application of the broadest rules. There is a story of a Vermont justice of the peace before whom a suit was brought by one farmer against another for breaking a churn. The justice took time to consider, and then said that he had looked through the statutes and could find nothing about churns, and gave judgment for the defendant. The same state of mind is shown in all our common digests and textbooks. Applications of rudimentary rules of contract or tort are tucked away under the head of Railroads or Telegraphs or go to swell treatises on historical subdivisions, such as Shipping or Equity, or are gathered under an arbitrary title which is thought likely to appeal to the practical mind, such as Mercantile Law. If a man goes into law it pays to be a master of it, and to be a master of it means to look straight through all the dramatic incidents and to discern the true basis of prophecy. Therefore, it is well to have an accurate notion of what you mean by law, by a right, by a duty, by malice, intent, and negligence, by ownership, by possession, and so forth. I have in my mind cases in which the highest courts seem to me to have floundered because they had no clear ideas on some of these themes. . . .

The advice of the elders to young men is very apt to be as unreal as a list of the hundred best books. . . . The way to gain a liberal view of your subject is not to read something else, but to get to the bottom of the subject itself. The means of doing that are, in the first place, to follow the existing body of dogma into its highest generalizations by the help of jurisprudence; next, to discover from history how it has come to be what it is; and, finally, so far as you can, to consider the ends which the several rules seek to accomplish, the reasons why those ends are desired, what is given up to gain them, and whether they are worth the price. . . .

Theory is the most important part of the dogma of the law, as the architect is the most important man who takes part in the building of a house. The most important improvements of the last twenty-five years are improvements in theory. It is not to be feared as unpractical, for, to the competent, it simply means going to the bottom of the subject. For the incompetent, it sometimes is true, as has been said, that an interest in general ideas means an absence of particular knowledge. I remember in army days reading of a youth who, being examined for the lowest grade and being asked a question about squadron drill, answered that he never had considered the evolutions of less than ten thousand men. But the weak and foolish must be left to their folly. The danger is that the able and practical minded should look with indifference or distrust upon ideas the connection of which with their business is remote. I heard a story, the other day, of a man who had a valet to whom he paid high wages, subject to deduction for faults. One of his deductions was, "For lack of imagination, five dollars." The lack is not confined to valets. The object of ambition, power, generally presents itself nowadays in the form of money alone. Money is the most immediate form, and is a proper object of desire. "The fortune," said Rachel, "is the measure of the intelligence." That is a good text to waken people out of a fool's paradise. But, as Hegel says, "It

is in the end not the appetite, but the opinion, which has to be satisfied." To an imagination of any scope the most far-reaching form of power is not money, it is the command of ideas. If you want great examples read Mr. Leslie Stephen's "History of English Thought in the Eighteenth Century," and see how a hundred years after his death the abstract speculations of Descartes had become a practical force controlling the conduct of men. Read the works of the great German jurists, and see how much more the world is governed to-day by Kant than by Bonaparte. We cannot all be Descartes or Kant, but we all want happiness. And happiness, I am sure from having known many successful men, cannot be won simply by being counsel for great corporations and having an income of fifty thousand dollars. An intellect great enough to win the prize needs other food beside success. The remoter and more general aspects of the law are those which give it universal interest. It is through them that you not only become a great master in your calling, but connect your subject with the universe and catch an echo of the infinite, a glimpse of its unfathomable process.

4

Some New Law

☆ *One of the great questions at the turn of the century was how to justify legally the regulation of labor in industrial establishments. A partial answer was given in Muller v. Oregon, decided by the Supreme Court on February 24, 1908. In this case, Muller, a laundry operator, appealed a fine for violation of a state law forbidding labor by females for more than ten hours a day. The decision was not only important for upholding a form of social legislation but for its cognizance of non-legal data and its reflection of the contemporary status of women.** ☆

MR. JUSTICE BREWER delivered the opinion of the court. . . .

The single question is the constitutionality of the statute under which the defendant was convicted so far as it affects the work of a female in a laundry. That it does not conflict with any provisions of the state constitution is settled by the decision of the Supreme Court of the State. The contentions of the defendant, now plaintiff in error, are thus stated in his brief:

"(1) Because the statute attempts to prevent persons, *sui juris,* from making their own contracts, and thus violates the provisions of the Fourteenth Amendment, as follows:

" 'No State shall make or enforce any law which shall abridge the privileges or immunities of citizens of the United States; nor shall any State deprive any person of life, liberty, or property, without due process of law: nor deny to any

person within its jurisdiction the equal protection of the laws.'

"(2) Because the statute does not apply equally to all persons similarly situated, and is class legislation.

"(3) The statute is not a valid exercise of the police power. The kinds of work proscribed are not unlawful, nor are they declared to be immoral or dangerous to the public health; nor can such a law be sustained on the ground that it is designed to protect women on account of their sex. There is no necessary or reasonable connection between the limitation prescribed by the act and the public health, safety or welfare."

It is the law of Oregon that women, whether married or single, have equal contractual and personal rights with men. As said by Chief Justice Wolverton, in *First National Bank* v. *Leonard,* 36 Oregon, 390, 396, after a review of the various statutes of the State upon the subject:

"We may therefore say with perfect confidence that, with these three sections

* From 208 U.S. 416.

upon the statute book, the wife can deal, not only with her separate property, acquired from whatever source, in the same manner as her husband can with property belonging to him, but that she may make contracts and incur liabilities, and the same may be enforced against her, the same as if she were a *femme sole*. There is now no residuum of civil disability resting upon her which is not recognized as existing against the husband. The current runs steadily and strongly in the direction of the emancipation of the wife, and the policy, as disclosed by all recent legislation upon the subject in this State, is to place her upon the same footing as if she were a *femme sole,* not only with respect to her separate property, but as it affects her right to make binding contracts; and the most natural corollary to the situation is that the remedies for the enforcement of liabilities incurred are made co-extensive and co-equal with such enlarged conditions."

It thus appears that, putting to one side the elective franchise, in the matter of personal and contractual rights they stand on the same plane as the other sex. Their rights in these respects can no more be infringed than the equal rights of their brothers. We held in *Lochner* v. *New York,* 198 U. S. 45, that a law providing that no laborer shall be required or permitted to work in a bakery more than sixty hours in a week or ten hours in a day was not as to men a legitimate exercise of the police power of the State, but an unreasonable, unnecessary and arbitrary interference with the right and liberty of the individual to contract in relation to his labor, and as such was in conflict with, and void under, the Federal Constitution. That decision is invoked by plaintiff in error as decisive of the question before us. But this assumes that the difference between the sexes does not justify a different rule respecting a restriction of the hours of labor.

In patent cases counsel are apt to open the argument with a discussion of the state of the art. It may not be amiss, in the present case, before examining the constitutional question, to notice the course of legislation as well as expressions of opinion from other than judicial sources. In the brief filed by Mr. Louis D. Brandeis, for the defendant in error, is a very copious collection of all these matters, an epitome of which is found in the margin.[1] . . .

The legislation and opinions referred to in the margin may not be, technically speaking, authorities, and in them is little or no discussion of the constitutional question presented to us for determination, yet they are significant of a widespread belief that women's physical structure, and the functions she performs in consequence thereof, justify special legislation restricting or qualifying the conditions under which she should be permitted to toil. Constitutional questions, it is true, are not settled by even a consensus of present public opinion, for it is the peculiar value of a written constitution that it places in unchanging form limitations upon legislative action, and thus gives a permanence and stability to popular government

---

[1] The following legislation of the States impose restrictions in some form or another upon the hours of labor that may be required of women: [Then follow citations from the laws of nineteen states]. . . .

In foreign legislation Mr. Brandeis calls attention to [the statutes of seven foreign nations]. . . .

Then follow extracts from over ninety reports of committees, bureaus of statistics, commissioners of hygiene, inspectors of factories, both in this country and in Europe, to the effect that long hours of labor are dangerous for women, primarily because of their special physical organization. The matter is discussed in these reports in different aspects, but all agree as to the danger. It would of course take too much space to give these reports in detail. Following them are extracts from similar reports discussing the general benefits of short hours from an economic aspect of the question. In many of these reports individual instances are given tending to support the general conclusion. Perhaps the general scope and character of all these reports may be summed up in what an inspector for Hanover says: "The reasons for the reduction of the working day to ten hours—(a) the physical organization of women, (b) her maternal functions, (c) the rearing and education of the children, (d) the maintenance of the home—are all so important and so far reaching that the need for such reduction need hardly be discussed."

which otherwise would be lacking. At the same time, when a question of fact is debated and debatable, and the extent to which a special constitutional limitation goes is affected by the truth in respect to that fact, a widespread and long continued belief concerning it is worthy of consideration. We take judicial cognizance of all matters of general knowledge.

It is undoubtedly true, as more than once declared by this court, that the general right to contract in relations to one's business is part of the liberty of the individual, protected by the Fourteenth Amendment to the Federal Constitution; yet it is equally well settled that this liberty is not absolute and extending to all contracts, and that a State may, without conflicting with the provisions of the Fourteenth Amendment, restrict in many respects the individual's power of contract. . . .

That woman's physical structure and the performance of maternal functions place her at a disadvantage in the struggle for subsistence is obvious. This is especially true when the burdens of motherhood are upon her. Even when they are not, by abundant testimony of the medical fraternity continuance for a long time on her feet at work, repeating this from day to day, tends to injurious effects upon the body, and as healthy mothers are essential to vigorous offspring, the physical well-being of woman becomes an object of public interest and care in order to preserve the strength and vigor of the race.

Still again, history discloses the fact that woman has always been dependent upon man. He established his control at the outset by superior physical strength, and this control in various forms, with diminishing intensity, has continued to the present. As minors, though not to the same extent, she has been looked upon in the courts as needing especial care that her rights may be preserved. Education

was long denied her, and while now the doors of the school room are opened and her opportunities for acquiring knowledge are great, yet even with that and the consequent increase of capacity for business affairs it is still true that in the struggle for subsistence she is not an equal competitor with her brother. Though limitations upon personal and contractual rights may be removed by legislation, there is that in her disposition and habits of life which will operate against a full assertion of those rights. She will still be where some legislation to protect her seems necessary to secure a real equality of right. Doubtless there are individual exceptions, and there are many respects in which she has an advantage over him; but looking at it from the viewpoint of the effort to maintain an independent position in life, she is not upon an equality. Differentiated by these matters from the other sex, she is properly placed in a class by herself and legislation designed for her protection may be sustained, even when like legislation is not necessary for men and could not be sustained. It is impossible to close one's eyes to the fact that she still looks to her brother and depends upon him. Even though all restrictions on political, personal and contractual rights were taken away, and she stood, so far as statutes are concerned, upon an absolutely equal plane with him, it would still be true that she is so constituted that she will rest upon and look to him for protection; that her physical structure and a proper discharge of her maternal functions—having in view not merely her own health, but the well-being of the race— justify legislation to protect her from the greed as well as the passion of man. The limitations which this statute places upon her contractual powers, upon her right to agree with her employer as to the time she shall labor, are not imposed solely for her benefit, but also largely for the benefit of all. Many words cannot make this plainer. The two sexes differ in structure of body, in the functions to be performed by each, in the amount of physical strength, in the capacity for long-continued labor, particularly when done standing, the influence of vigorous health upon the future well-being of the race, the self-reliance which enables one to assert full rights, and in the capacity to maintain the struggle for subsistence. This difference justifies a difference in legislation and upholds that which is designed to compensate for some of the burdens which rest upon her.

We have not referred in this discussion to the denial of the elective franchise in the State of Oregon, for while it may disclose a lack of political equality in all things with her brother, that is not of itself decisive. The reason runs deeper, and rests in the inherent difference between the two sexes, and in the different functions in life which they perform.

For these reasons, and without questioning in any respect the decision in *Lochner v. New York,* we are of the opinion that it cannot be adjudged that the act in question is in conflict with the Federal Constitution, so far as it respects the work of a female in a laundry, and the judgment of the Supreme Court of Oregon is

Affirmed.

5

Reflections on Life's Ideals

☆ One of the continuing concerns of American thought has been the need for sympathetic comprehension of social and personal situations. William James, in the following excerpt, reflected on the compensations of understanding.* ☆

We are suffering to-day in America from what is called the labor-question; and, when you go out into the world, you will each and all of you be caught up in its perplexities. I use the brief term labor-question to cover all sorts of anarchistic discontents and socialistic projects, and the conservative resistances which they provoke. So far as this conflict is unhealthy and regrettable,—and I think it is so only to a limited extent,—the unhealthiness consists solely in the fact that one-half of our fellow-countrymen remain entirely blind to the internal significance of the lives of the other half. They miss the joys and sorrows, they fail to feel the moral virtue, and they do not guess the presence of the intellectual ideals. They are at cross-purposes all along the line, regarding each other as they might regard a set of dangerously gesticulating automata, or, if they seek to get at the inner motivation, making the most horrible mistakes. Often all that the poor man can think of in the rich man is a cowardly greediness for safety, luxury,

* From William James, *Talks to Teachers on Psychology: and to Students on Some of Life's Ideals,* pp. 297-301. Published by Henry Holt and Company, New York, 1906. Copyright, 1899, 1900, by William James. Used by permission of Holt, Rinehart and Winston, Inc.

and effeminacy, and a boundless affectation. What he is, is not a human being, but a pocket-book, a bank-account. And a similar greediness, turned by disappointment into envy, is all that many rich men can see in the state of mind of the dissatisfied poor. And, if the rich man begins to do the sentimental act over the poor man, what senseless blunders does he make, pitying him for just those very duties and those very immunities which, rightly taken, are the condition of his most abiding and characteristic joys! Each, in short, ignores the fact that happiness and unhappiness and significance are a vital mystery; each pins them absolutely on some ridiculous feature of the external situation; and everybody remains outside of everybody else's sight.

Society has, with all this, undoubtedly got to pass toward some newer and better equilibrium, and the distribution of wealth has doubtless slowly got to change: such changes have always happened, and will happen to the end of time. But if, after all that I have said, any of you expect that they will make any *genuine vital difference* on a large scale, to the lives of our descendants, you will have missed the significance of my entire lecture. The solid meaning of life is always the same eternal thing,—the marriage, namely, of some unhabitual ideal, however special, with some fidelity, courage, and endurance; with some man's or woman's pains. —And, whatever or wherever life may be, there will always be the chance for that marriage to take place.

Fitz-James Stephen wrote many years ago words to this effect more eloquent than any I can speak: "The 'Great Eastern,' or some of her successors," he said, "will perhaps defy the roll of the Atlantic, and cross the seas without allowing their passengers to feel that they have left the firm land. The voyage from the cradle to the grave may come to be performed with similar facility. Progress and science may perhaps enable untold millions to live and die without a care, without a pang, without an anxiety. They will have a pleasant passage and plenty of brilliant conversation. They will wonder that men ever believed at all in clanging fights and blazing towns and sinking ships and praying hands; and, when they come to the end of their course, they will go their way, and the place thereof will know them no more. But it seems unlikely that they will have such a knowledge of the great ocean on which they sail, with its storms and wrecks, its currents and icebergs, its huge waves and mighty winds, as those who battled with it for years together in the little craft, which, if they had few other merits, brought those who navigated them full into the presence of time and eternity, their maker and themselves, and forced them to have some definite view

of their relations to them and to each other."

In this solid and tridimensional sense, so to call it, those philosophers are right who contend that the world is a standing thing, with no progress, no real history. The changing conditions of history touch only the surface of the show. The altered equilibriums and redistributions only diversify our opportunities and open chances to us for new ideals. But, with each new ideal that comes into life, the chance for a life based on some old ideal will vanish; and he would needs be a presumptuous calculator who should with confidence say that the total sum of significances is positively and absolutely greater at any one epoch than at any other of the world.

I am speaking broadly, I know, and omitting to consider certain qualifications in which I myself believe. But one can only make one point in one lecture, and I shall be well content if I have brought my point home to you this evening in even a slight degree. *There are compensations:* and no outward changes of condition in life can keep the nightingale of its eternal meaning from singing in all sorts of different men's hearts. That is the main fact to remember. If we could not only admit it with our lips, but really and truly believe it, how our convulsive insistencies, how our antipathies and dreads of each other, would soften down! If the poor and the rich could look at each other in this way, *sub specie aeternatis,* how gentle would grow their disputes! What tolerance and good humor, what willingness to live and let live, would come into the world!

6

Civilization and Decay

☆ Brooks Adams (1848-1927), historian, descendant from Presidents John Adams and John Quincy Adams, viewed society as being in a state of disintegration. He sought to find scientific formulas leading to the revitalization of civilization.* ☆

The theory proposed is based upon the accepted scientific principle that the law of force and energy is of universal application in nature, and that animal life is one of the outlets through which solar energy is dissipated.

Starting from this fundamental proposition, the first deduction is, that, as human societies are forms of animal life, these societies must differ among themselves in energy, in proportion as nature has endowed them, more or less abundantly, with energetic material.

Thought is one of the manifestations of human energy, and among the earlier and simpler phases of thought, two stand conspicuous—Fear and Greed. Fear, which, by stimulating the imagination, creates a belief in an invisible world, and ultimately develops a priesthood; and Greed, which dissipates energy in war and trade.

Probably the velocity of the social movement of any community is proportionate to its energy and mass, and its centralization is proportionate to its velocity; therefore, as human movement is accelerated, societies centralize. In the earlier stages of concentration, fear ap-

pears to be the channel through which energy finds the readiest outlet; accordingly, in primitive and scattered communities, the imagination is vivid, and the mental types produced are religious, military, artistic. As consolidation advances, fear yields to greed, and the economic organism tends to supersede the emotional and martial.

Whenever a race is so richly endowed with the energetic material that it does not expend all its energy in the daily struggle for life, the surplus may be stored in the shape of wealth; and this stock of stored energy may be transferred from community to community, either by conquest, or by superiority in economic competition.

However large may be the store of energy accumulated by conquest, a race must, sooner or later, reach the limit of its martial energy, when it must enter on the phase of economic competition. But, as the economic organism radically differs from the emotional and martial, the effect of economic competition has been, perhaps invariably, to dissipate the energy amassed by war.

When surplus energy has accumulated in such bulk as to preponderate over pro-

* From Brooks Adams, *The Law of Civilization and Decay*, pp. viii-xi, 383. Published by The Macmillan Company, New York, 1896.

ductive energy, it becomes the controlling social force. Thenceforward, capital is autocratic, and energy vents itself through those organisms best fitted to give expression to the power of capital. In this last stage of consolidation, the economic, and, perhaps, the scientific intellect is propagated, while the imagination fades, and the emotional, the martial, and the artistic types of manhood decay. When a social velocity has been attained at which the waste of energetic material is so great that the martial and imaginative stocks fail to reproduce themselves, intensifying competition appears to generate two extreme economic types,—the usurer in his most formidable aspect, and the peasant whose nervous system is best adapted to thrive on scanty nutriment. At length a point must be reached when pressure can go no further, and then, perhaps, one of two results may follow: A stationary period may supervene, which may last until ended by war, by exhaustion, or by both combined, as seems to have been the case with the Eastern Empire; or, as in the Western, disintegration may set in, the civilized population may perish, and a reversion may take place to a primitive form of organism.

The evidence, however, seems to point to the conclusion that, when a highly centralized society disintegrates, under the pressure of economic competition, it is because the energy of the race has been exhausted. Consequently, the survivors of such a community lack the power necessary for renewed concentration, and must probably remain inert until supplied with fresh energetic material by the infusion of barbarian blood. . . .

No poetry can bloom in the arid modern soil, the drama has died, and the patrons of art are no longer even conscious of shame at profaning the most sacred of ideals. The ecstatic dream, which some twelfth-century monk cut into the stones of the sanctuary hallowed by the presence of his God, is reproduced to bedizen a warehouse; or the plan of an abbey, which Saint Hugh may have consecrated, is adapted to a railway station.

Decade by decade, for some four hundred years, these phenomena have grown more sharply marked in Europe, and, as consolidation apparently nears its climax, art seems to presage approaching disintegration. The architecture, the sculpture, and the coinage of London at the close of the nineteenth century, when compared with those of the Paris of St. Louis, recall the Rome of Caracalla as contrasted with the Athens of Pericles, save that we lack the stream of barbarian blood which made the Middle Age.

7

The Law of Acceleration

☆ *Henry Adams (1838-1918), the older brother of Brooks Adams, through his confessed inability to adjust to change, proclaimed the challenge of adaptability to man in the machine age.** ☆

A law of acceleration, definite and constant as any law of mechanics, cannot be supposed to relax its energy to suit the convenience of man. No one is likely to suggest a theory that man's convenience had been consulted by Nature at any time, or that Nature has consulted the convenience of any of her creations, except perhaps the *Terebratula*. In every age man has bitterly and justly complained that Nature hurried and hustled him, for inertia almost invariably has ended in tragedy. Resistance is its law, and resistance to superior mass is futile and fatal.

Fifty years ago, science took for granted that the rate of acceleration could not last. The world forgets quickly, but even today the habit remains of founding statistics on the faith that consumption will continue nearly stationary. Two generations with John Stuart Mill, talked of this stationary period, which was to follow the explosion of new power. All the men who were elderly in the forties died in this faith, and other men grew old

* The selection from Henry Adams, *The Education of Henry Adams, An Autobiography,* 1918, pp. 493-498, is reprinted by permission of and arrangement with Houghton Mifflin Company, the authorized publishers. Copyright, 1918, Massachusetts Historical Society.

nursing the same conviction, and happy in it; while science, for fifty years, permitted, or encouraged, society to think that force would prove to be limited in supply. This mental inertia of science lasted through the eighties before showing signs of breaking up; and nothing short of radium fairly wakened men to the fact, long since evident, that force was inexhaustible. Even then the scientific authorities vehemently resisted.

Nothing so revolutionary had happened since the year 300. Thought had more than once been upset, but never caught and whirled about in the vortex of infinite forces. Power leaped from every atom, and enough of it to supply the stellar universe showed itself running to waste at every pore of matter. Man could no longer hold it off. Forces grasped his wrists and flung him about as though he had hold of a live wire or a runaway automobile; which was very nearly the exact truth for the purposes of an elderly and timid single gentleman in Paris, who never drove down the Champs Élysées without expecting an accident, and commonly witnessing one; or found himself in the neighborhood of an official without calculating the chances of a bomb. So long as the rates of progress held good, these bombs would double in force and number every ten years.

Impossibilities no longer stood in the way. One's life had fattened on impossibilities. Before the boy was six years old, he had seen four impossibilities made actual—the ocean-steamer, the railway, the electric telegraph, and the Daguerreotype; nor could he ever learn which of the four had most hurried others to come. He had seen the coal-output of the United States grow from nothing to three hundred million tons or more. What was far more serious, he had seen the number of minds, engaged in pursuing force—the truest measure of its attraction—increase from a few scores or hundreds, in 1838, to many thousands in 1905, trained to sharpness never before reached, and armed with instruments amounting to new senses of indefinite power and accuracy, while they chased force into hiding–places where Nature herself had never know it to be, making analyses that contradicted being, and syntheses that endangered the elements. No one could say that the social mind now failed to respond to new force, even when the new force annoyed it horribly. Every day Nature violently revolted, causing so-called accidents with enormous destruction of property and life, while plainly laughing at man, who helplessly groaned and shrieked and shuddered, but never for a single instant could stop. The railways alone approached the carnage of war; automobiles and fire-arms ravaged society, until an earthquake became almost a nervous relaxation. An immense volume of force had detached itself from the unknown universe of energy, while still vaster reservoirs, supposed to be infinite, steadily revealed themselves, attracting mankind with more compulsive course than all the Pontic Seas or Gods or Gold that ever existed, and feeling still less of retiring ebb.

In 1850, science would have smiled at such a romance as this, but, in 1900, as far as history could learn, few men of science thought it a laughing matter. If a perplexed but laborious follower could venture to guess their drift, it seemed in their minds a toss-up between anarchy and order. Unless they should be more honest with themselves in the future than ever they were in the past, they would be more astonished than their followers when they reached the end. If Karl Pearson's notions of the universe were sound, men like Galileo, Descartes, Leibnitz, and Newton should have stopped the progress of science before 1700, supposing them to have been honest in the religious convictions they expressed. In 1900 they were plainly forced back on faith in a unity unproved and an order they had themselves disproved. They had reduced their universe to a series of relations to themselves. They had reduced themselves to motion in a universe of motions with an acceleration, in their own case, of vertiginous violence. With the correctness of their science, history had no right to meddle, since their science now lay in a plane where scarcely one or two hundred minds in the world could follow its mathematical processes; but bombs educate vigorously, and even wireless telegraphy or airships might require the reconstruction of society. If any analogy whatever existed between the human mind, on one side, and the laws of motion, on the other, the mind had already entered a field of attraction so violent that it must immediately pass beyond, into new equilibrium, like the Comet of Newton, to suffer dissipation altogether, like meteoroids in the earth's atmosphere. If it behaved like an explosive, it must rapidly recover equilibrium; if it behaved like a vegetable, it must reach its limits of growth; and even if it acted like the earlier creations of energy—the saurians and sharks—it must have nearly reached the limits of its expansion. If science were to go on doubling or quadrupling its complexities every ten years, even mathematics would soon succumb. An average mind had succumbed already in 1850; it could no longer understand the problem in 1900.

Fortunately, a student of history had no responsibility for the problem; he took it as science gave it, and waited only to be taught. With science or with society, he had no quarrel and claimed no share of authority. He had never been able to acquire knowledge, still less to impart it; and if he had, at times, felt serious differences with the American of the nineteenth century, he felt none with the American of the twentieth. For this new creation, born since 1900, a historian asked no longer to be teacher or even friend; he asked only to be a pupil, and promised to be docile, for once, even though trodden under foot; for he could see that the new American—the child of incalculable coal-power, chemical power, electric power, and radiating energy, as well as of new forces yet undetermined— must be a sort of God compared with any former creation of nature. At the rate of progress since 1800, every American who lived into the year 2000 would know how to control unlimited power. He would think in complexities unimaginable to an earlier mind. He would deal with problems altogether beyond the range of earlier society. To him the nineteenth century would stand on the same plane with the fourth—equally childlike—and he would only wonder how both of them, knowing so little, and so weak in force, should have done so much. Perhaps even he might go back, in 1964, to sit with Gibbon on the steps of Ara Coeli.

Meanwhile he was getting education. With that, a teacher who had failed to educate even the generation of 1870, dared not interfere. The new forces would educate. History saw few lessons in the past that would be useful in the future; but

one, at least, it did see. The attempt of the American of 1800 to educate the American of 1900 had not often been surpassed for folly; and since 1800 the forces and their complications had increased a thousand times or more. The attempt of the American of 1900 to educate the American of 2000, must be even blinder than that of the Congressman of 1800, except so far as he had learned his ignorance. During a million or two of years, every generation in turn had toiled with endless agony to attain and apply power, all the while betraying the deepest alarm and horror at the power they created. The teacher of 1900, if foolhardy, might stimulate; if foolish, might resist; if intelligent, might balance, as wise and foolish have often tried to do from the beginning; but the forces would continue to educate, and the mind would continue to react. All the teacher could hope was to teach it reaction.

Even there his difficulty was extreme. The most elementary books of science betrayed the inadequacy of old implements of thought. Chapter after chapter closed with phrases such as one never met in older literature: "The cause of this phenomenon is not understood"; "science no longer ventures to explain causes"; "the first step towards a causal explanation still remains to be taken"; "opinions are very much divided"; "in spite of the contradictions involved"; "science gets on only by adopting different theories, sometimes contradictory." Evidently the new American would need to think in contradictions, and instead of Kant's famous four antinomies, the new universe would know no law that could not be proved by its anti-law.

To educate—one's self to begin with— had been the effort of one's life for sixty years; and the difficulties of education had gone on doubling with the coal-output, until the prospect of waiting another ten years, in order to face a seventh doubling of complexities, allured one's imagination but slightly. The law of acceleration was definite, and did not require ten years more study except to show whether it held good. No scheme could be suggested to the new American, and no fault needed to be found, or complaint made; but the next great influx of new forces seemed near at hand, and its style of education promised to be violently coercive. The movement from unity into multiplicity, between 1200 and 1900, was unbroken in sequence, and rapid in acceleration. Prolonged one generation longer, it would require a new social mind. As though thought were common salt in indefinite solution it must enter a new phase subject to new laws. Thus far, since five or ten thousand years, the mind had successfully reacted, and nothing yet proved that it would fail to react —but it would need to jump.

8

Naturalism in Literature

☆ *Frank Norris (1870-1902) was one of the writers of a new school of literature which emphasized the rigorous challenges of environment to man and depicted in a starkly realistic manner the failure of men to meet these challenges.** ☆

McTeague had lost his ambition. He did not care to better his situation. All he wanted was a warm place to sleep and three good meals a day. At the first—at the very first—he had chafed at his idleness and had spent the days with his wife in their one narrow room, walking back and forth with the restlessness of a caged brute, or sitting motionless for hours, watching Trina at her work, feeling a dull glow of shame at the idea that she was supporting him. This feeling had worn off quickly, however, Trina's work was only hard when she chose to make it so, and as a rule she supported their misfortunes with a silent fortitude.

Then, wearied at his inaction and feeling the need of movement and exercise, McTeague would light his pipe and take a turn upon the great avenue one block above Polk Street. A gang of laborers were digging the foundations for a large brownstone house, and McTeague found interest and amusement in leaning over the barrier that surrounded the excavations and watching the progress of the work. He came to see it every afternoon;

by and by he even got to know the foreman who superintended the job, and the two had long talks together. Then McTeague would return to Polk Street and find Heise in the back room of the harness shop, and occasionally the day ended with some half dozen drinks of whiskey at Joe Frenna's saloon.

It was curious to note the effect of the alcohol upon the dentist. It did not make him drunk, it made him vicious. So far from being stupefied, he became, after the fourth glass, active, alert, quick-witted, even talkative; a certain wickedness stirred in him then; he was intractable, mean; and when he had drunk a little more heavily than usual, he found a certain pleasure in annoying and exasperating Trina, even in abusing and hurting her.

It had begun on the evening of Thanksgiving Day, when Heise had taken McTeague out to dinner with him. The dentist on this occasion had drunk very freely. He and Heise had returned to Polk Street towards ten o'clock, and Heise at once suggested a couple of drinks at Frenna's.

"All right, all right," said McTeague. "Drinks, that's the word. I'll go home and get some money and meet you at Joe's."

* From Frank Norris, *McTeague, A Story of San Francisco*, pp. 304-310. Published by Doubleday, McClure and Company, New York, 1899.

Trina was awakened by her husband pinching her arm.

"Oh, Mac," she cried, jumping up in bed with a little scream, "how you hurt! Oh, that hurt me dreadfully."

"Give me a little money," answered the dentist, grinning, and pinching her again.

"I haven't a cent. There's not a—oh, *Mac,* will you stop? I won't have you pinch me that way."

"Hurry up," answered her husband, calmly, nipping the flesh of her shoulder between his thumb and finger. "Heise's waiting for me." Trina wrenched from him with a sharp intake of breath, frowning with pain, and caressing her shoulder. "Mac, you've no idea how that hurts. Mac, *stop!*"

"Give me some money, then."

In the end Trina had to comply. She gave him half a dollar from her dress pocket, protesting that it was the only piece of money she had.

"One more, just for luck," said McTeague, pinching her again; "and another."

"How can you—how *can* you hurt a woman so!" exclaimed Trina, beginning to cry with the pain.

"Ah, now, *cry,*" retorted the dentist. "That's right, *cry.* I never saw such a little fool." He went out, slamming the door in disgust.

But McTeague never became a drunkard in the generally received sense of the term. He did not drink to excess more than two or three times in a month, and never upon any occasion did he become maudlin or staggering. Perhaps his nerves were naturally too dull to admit of any excitation; perhaps he did not really care for the whiskey, and only drank because Heise and the other men at Frenna's did. Trina could often reproach him with drinking too much; she never could say that he was drunk. The alcohol had its effect for all that. It roused the man, or rather the brute in the man, and now not only roused it, but goaded it to evil. McTeague's nature changed. It was not only the alcohol, it was idleness and a general throwing off of the good influence his wife had had over him in the days of their prosperity. McTeague disliked Trina. She was a perpetual irritation to him. She annoyed him because she was so small, so prettily made, so invariably correct and precise. Her avarice incessantly harassed him. Her industry was a constant reproach to him. She seemed to flaunt her work defiantly in his face. It was the red flag in the eyes of the bull. One time when she had just come back from Frenna's and had been sitting in the chair near her, silently watching her at her work, he exclaimed all of a sudden:

"Stop working. Stop it, I tell you. Put 'em away. Put 'em all away, or I'll pinch you."

"But why—why?" Trina protested.

The dentist cuffed her ears. "I won't have you work." He took her knife and her paint-pots away, and made her sit idly in the window the rest of the afternoon.

It was, however, only when his wits had been stirred with alcohol that the dentist was brutal to his wife. At other times, say three weeks of every month, she was merely an incumbrance to him. They often quarrelled about Trina's money, her savings. The dentist was bent upon having at least a part of them. What he would do with the money once he had it, he did not precisely know. He would spend it in royal fashion, no doubt, feasting continually, buying himself wonderful clothes. The miner's idea of money quickly gained and lavishly squandered, persisted in his mind. As for Trina, the more her husband stormed, the tighter she drew the strings of the little chamois-skin bag that she hid at the bottom of her trunk underneath her bridal dress. Her five thousand dollars invested in Uncle Oelbermann's business was a glittering, splendid dream which came to her almost every hour of the day as a solace and a compensation for all her unhappiness.

At times, when she knew that McTeague was far from home, she would lock her door, open her trunk, and pile all her little hoard on her table. By now it was four hundred and seven dollars and fifty cents. Trina would play with this money by the hour, piling it, and re-piling it, or gathering it all into one heap, and drawing back to the farthest corner of the room to note the effect, her head on one side. She polished the gold pieces with a mixture of soap and ashes until they shone, wiping them carefully on her apron. Or, again, she would draw the heap lovingly toward her and bury her face in it, delighted at the smell of it and the feel of the smooth, cool metal on her cheeks. She even put the smaller gold pieces in her mouth, and jingled them there. She loved her money with an intensity that she could hardly express. She would plunge her small fingers into the pile with little murmurs of affection, her long, narrow eyes half closed and shining, her breath coming in long sighs.

"Ah, the dear money, the dear money," she would whisper. "I love you so! All mine, every penny of it. No one shall ever, ever get you. How I've worked for you! How I've slaved and saved for you! And I'm going to get more; I'm going to get more, more, more; a little every day."

She was still looking for cheaper quarters. Whenever she could spare a moment from her work, she would put on her hat and range up and down the entire neighborhood from Sutter to Sacramento Streets, going into all the alleys and bystreets, her head in the air, looking for the "rooms-to-let" sign. But she was in despair. All the cheaper tenements were occupied. She could find no room more reasonable than the one she and the dentist now occupied.

As time went on, McTeague's idleness became habitual. He drank no more whiskey than at first, but his dislike for Trina increased with every day of their poverty, with every day of Trina's persistent stinginess. At times—fortunately rare —he was more than ever brutal to her. He would box her ears or hit her a great blow with the back of a hairbrush, or even with his closed fist. His old-time affection for his "little woman," unable to stand the test of privation, had lapsed by degrees, and what little of it was left was changed, distorted, and made monstrous by the alcohol.

The people about the house and the clerks at the provision stores often remarked that Trina's finger-tips were swollen and the nails purple as though they had been shut in a door. Indeed, this was the explanation she gave. The fact of the matter was that McTeague, when he had been drinking used to bite them, crunching and grinding them with his immense teeth, always ingenious enough to remember which were the sorest. Sometimes he extorted money from her by this means, but as often as not he did it for his own satisfaction.

And in some strange, inexplicable way this brutality made Trina all the more affectionate; aroused in her a morbid, unwholesome love of submission, a strange, unnatural pleasure in yielding, in surrendering herself to the will of an irresistible, virile power.

Trina's emotions had narrowed with the narrowing of her daily life. They reduced themselves at last to but two, her passion for her money and her perverted love for her husband when he was brutal. She was a strange woman during these days.

III

the progressive era

T HE PROGRESSIVE era was the public response to the
deficiencies of rapidly emerging industrialism in the United
States. Industrialism had brought with it great disparities
between the practices and the ideals of the nation. It subjected
old methods of business, government, and agriculture to tremendous stress and showed their inability to provide a balance
between the essential interest of economic development and the
interests of the nation.

The onset of the twentieth century was accompanied by a
gathering of the forces of protest and reform to try to strike this
balance. Many factors stimulated this congregation of reform
elements. Corporate development was greatly accentuated in
the first decade of the century revealing even more clearly the
actual and potential dangers of unregulated enterprise. Moreover, the conviction was growing among the people that the
new industrialism could, if forced to, provide all Americans with
greater benefits. The social justice movements of the churches
were also beginning to have an impact with their demands for
an economic system that was not antagonistic to Christian
teachings. "Muckraking" and "yellow journalism" gave
national publicity to corrupt government, irresponsible business,
and their "looting" of the people. Even government agencies
produced reports which, if better founded in fact, were often
no less shocking or indignant. Of prime importance to the rise
of progressivism was the development of political leaders like
Robert M. La Follette and Theodore Roosevelt to manage the
forces of protest and reform. Withal the "campaign against
privilege" was on, the Progressive era begun.

Progressivism was not doctrinaire. It accommodated many
different positions. The reform of political agencies was paramount to some and for others tariff revision or beating off
encroachments on the public domain or monetary reform was
foremost. Differences of approach also developed. President
Roosevelt asserted that public officials must meet social problems

aggressively, doing anything not expressly forbidden by the Constitution or law. In contrast, William Howard Taft contended
that action could be taken only when reasonably connected to
a specific grant of power. For Roosevelt and Taft, despite their
many differences, the object was regulation of evil. President
Wilson, though, viewed it less as a matter or regulation than of
the creation of conditions to eliminate privilege and to provide
for free competition and economic flexibility. To the Socialists
these were sham disagreements: capitalism was impervious to
reform; it must be replaced by an economic system based on
production for use rather than production for profit. Despite
these diverse positions, a most important trend was established
during the Progressive era. That trend was the development of
government power to regulate, to forbid, and to establish new
public programs in what was considered to be the broad national
interest.

1

The Curious Insurgents

☆ *William Allen White (1868-1944) for over half a century chronicled the passing scene as editor of the Emporia* Gazette. *Achieving nationwide prominence for his frank and penetrating editorials, he became a leader in the Bull Moose and Republican parties.** ☆

That curious insurgence in American politics which afterwards was known as the progressive movement was working in both of the parties in the United States in that first decade of the new century, which may well be called the Roosevelt decade. Bryan had appeared in American politics. In the last decade of the old century he had taken the leadership of the Democratic party away from the old silk stockings, and given it to the Populists. They, their heirs and assigns controlled the Democratic party except in its convention of 1904. For a dozen years following 1901, Theodore Roosevelt led the progressive movement in the Republican party. His leadership was challenged by that of Robert M. La Follette, first governor and then United States Senator from Wisconsin. La Follette represented the left wing of Republican insurgents, and an intransigent left wing it was. Roosevelt and La Follette wanted, on the whole, about the same things, but they were poles apart in their methods. Roosevelt would make a noisy fight, and in the end would compromise when he had gone

* From *The Autobiography of William Allen White*, pp. 427-430. Copyright 1946 by The Macmillan Company, and used with their permission.

as far as he could. La Follette never compromised. He would prefer to dramatize his cause in failure and take it up later rather than to surrender one jot or tittle of his original bill of contention. La Follette was bitter in his controversies. He was merciless in his attacks. In all my life I have never seen a braver man in politics. Moreover, he made his bravery count. He had come up from the ranks in Wisconsin politics, when those ranks were organized against him. When he came to the Senate, he had a long line of Wisconsin achievements in his baggage, which afterwards went into the platforms and statutes of other states. And the principles for which La Follette fought were known later as the Roosevelt policies.

But that decade which climaxed in 1912 was a time of tremendous change in our national life, particularly as it affected our national attitudes. The American people were melting down old heroes and recasting the mold in which heroes were made. Newspapers, magazines, books—every representative outlet for public opinion in the United States was turned definitely away from the scoundrels who had in the last third or quarter of the old century cast themselves in monumental brass as heroes. The muckrakers were melting it down. The people were questioning the way every rich man got his money. They were ready to believe— and too often they were justified in the belief—that he was a scamp who had pinched pennies out of the teacups of the poor by various shenanigans, who was distributing his largess to divert attention from his rascality.

Reform was in the air. In forging new weapons of democracy in the state legislatures and in the Congress, the people were setting out on a crusade. And I was wearing the crusader's armor. A sudden new interest in the under dog was manifest in the land. He was not exalted, but universally the people began to understand what slums were, what sweatshops were, what exploited labor was, what absentee landlordism had become in our urban life, what railroad rates were doing to the farmer and to the consumer. Two-cent railroad fares were demanded in the states. Anti-pass laws were being adopted state by state. Railroad regulation was everywhere an issue—on the stump, in the legislature, in Congress. The protective tariff, as a principle, began to irk the Republican leaders of reform, chiefly because it was regarded as the bulwark of "economic privilege"— and those two words were beginning to be common. Roosevelt was coining bitter phrases. La Follette and Bryan in the white heat of their indignation were melting rhetorical maledictions to hurl at the beneficiaries of privilege.

But the point of it all, as I look back upon it now after nearly forty years, is that the leaders—even Bryan, Roosevelt, La Follette—even the state leaders who grew up in more than half the American commonwealths—were the product of their times. If it had not been they who rode at the head of the procession in the red sash and gilded epaulet of political powers, others would have come along,

for it was a people's movement. The mercy that permeated their hearts, their yearning for justice which sent them to the newsstands and bookstores buying by tons newspapers, books and magazines that told them how to be intelligently just and fair in their political aspirations—all published, edited and written by men who took the coloring of their environment— sprang from a widening sense of duty, rather than of rights, moving in the hearts of the American people in that decade.

I did not know at the time how completely I was a product of my environment. If I was a young cocksure reactionary in the nineties, it was because my kind and class were that, and I fear sadly that I must confess that unconsciously I took the protective intellectual, political and social color of my time in the first decade. So we all went together down the road of reform to progress, Bryan, La Follette, Roosevelt; scores of leaders in scores of states—little Bryans, little La Follettes, little Roosevelts appeared in scores of statehouses and countless city halls. They were not conscious hypocrites. Perhaps I had better say "we" than they. We were the people. What the people felt about the vast injustice that had come with the settlement of a continent, we, their servants—teachers, city councilors, legislators, governors, publishers, editors, writers, representatives in Congress and senators—all made a part of our creed and so carried the banner of their cause. Of course demagogues came, many of them, who did not know intellectually nor care emotionally—political paranoiacs who whanged away and did probably more harm than good. But taking it by and large, the representatives of the progressive movement in that first glamorous vigorous decade when America turned the corner from conservatism were the product of the aspiration of the people. They were leaders who were led. Some way, into the hearts of the dominant middle class of this country, had come a sense that their civilization needed recasting, that their government had fallen into the hands of self-seekers, that a new relation should be established between the haves and the have-nots, not primarily because the have-nots were loyal, humble, worthy and oppressed—Heaven knows we knew that the under dog had fleas, mange and a bad disposition—but rather because we felt that to bathe and feed the under dog would release the burden of injustice on our own conscience. We should do it even unto the least of these. We were not maudlin, as I recollect it. We were joyous, eager, happily determined to make life more fair and lovely for ourselves by doing such approximate justice as we could to those who obviously were living in the swamps, morasses, deserts, and wildernesses of this world. It was not religious—at least not pious—this progressive movement. It was profoundly spiritual. And the insurgents, who were later called progressives, had the crusaders' ardor, and felt for one another the crusaders' fellowship. They sang songs, carried banners, marched in parades, created heroes out of their own ideals. It was an evangelical uprising without an accredited Messiah. Because I wrote books and magazine articles, had my newspaper and sometimes went around making progressive speeches, I was probably in the list of the first hundred leaders who were thrown into the public eye by this evangelical demonstration. I was one of perhaps fifty Republicans who had the confidence of Roosevelt and La Follette.

I fear I have painted too smooth a picture. All this social and political change did not appear automatically in American politics; the spirit of change did not wave a wand and say, "let there be light." In every state, indeed in every county and city across the land, these progressive leaders in both parties rose only after bitter struggle. They were the product of more than a lively contest. Sometimes the contests were combats. The conservatives did not give up control of the party organization in the northern states, at least, without bloody battle. And it was not all black or all white. The battles were in gray areas. Demagogues on both sides clamored for leadership. The conservatives spent money and the progressives spent time, energy and sometimes trickery. One side was as good as the other morally.

2

The Social Gospel

☆ *Walter Rauschenbusch (1861-1918), Baptist minister and profes-*
sor of church history at the Rochester Theological Seminary, urged
that Christian principles be applied to the economic and social prob-
lems of modern life. He contended that the church must denounce
*the existing world and change it, or surrender its holy mission.** ☆

The gospel, to have full power over an age, must be the highest expression of the moral and religious truths held by that age. If it lags behind and deals in outgrown conceptions of life and duty, it will lose power over the ablest minds and the young men first, and gradually over all. In our thought to-day the social problems irresistibly take the lead. If the Church has no live and bold thought on this dominant question of modern life, its teaching authority on all other questions will dwindle and be despised. It cannot afford to have young men sniff the air as in a stuffy room when they enter the sphere of religious thought. When the world is in travail with a higher ideal of justice, the Church dare not ignore it if it would retain its moral leadership. On the other hand, if the Church does incorporate the new social terms in its synthesis of truth, they are certain to throw new light on all the older elements of its teaching. The conception of race sin and race salvation become comprehensible once more to those who have made the

idea of social solidarity in good and evil a part of their thought. The law of sacrifice loses its arbitrary and mechanical aspect when we understand the vital union of all humanity. Individualistic Christianity has almost lost sight of the great idea of the kingdom of God, which was the inspiration and centre of the thought of Jesus. Social Christianity would once more enable us to understand the purpose and thought of Jesus and take the veil from our eyes when we read the synoptic gospels.

The social crisis offers a great opportunity for the infusion of new life and power into the religious thought of the Church. It also offers the chance for progress in its life. When the broader social outlook widens the purpose of a Christian man beyond the increase of his church, he lifts up his eyes and sees that there are others who are at work for humanity besides his denomination. Common work for social welfare is the best common ground for the various religious bodies and the best training school for practical Christian unity. The strong movement for Christian union in our country has been largely prompted by the realization of so-

* From *Christianity and the Social Crisis* by Walter Rauschenbusch, pp. 339-342. Copyright 1907 by The Macmillan Company, and used with their permission.

cial needs, and is led by men who have felt the attraction of the kingdom of God as something greater than any denomination and as the common object of all. Thus the divisions which were caused in the past by differences in dogma and church polity may perhaps be healed by unity of interest in social salvation.

As we have seen, the industrial and commercial life to-day is dominated by principles antagonistic to the fundamental principles of Christianity, and it is so difficult to live a Christian life in the midst of it that few men even try. If production could be organized on a basis of cooperative fraternity; if distribution could at least approximately be determined by justice; if all men could be conscious than their labor contributed to the welfare of all and that their personal well-being was dependent on the prosperity of the Commonwealth; if predatory business and parasitic wealth ceased and all men lived only by their labor; if the luxury of unearned wealth no longer made us all feverish with covetousness and a simpler life became the fashion; if our time and strength were not used up either in getting a bare living or in amassing unusable wealth and we had more leisure for the higher pursuits of the mind and the soul—then there might be a chance to live such a life of gentleness and brotherly kindness and tranquillity of heart as Jesus desired for men. It may be that the cooperative Commonwealth would give us the first chance in history to live a really Christian life without retiring from the world, and would make the Sermon on the mount a philosophy of life feasible for all who care to try.

This is the stake of the Church in the social crisis. If society continues to disintegrate and decay, the Church will be carried down with it. If the Church can rally such moral forces that injustice will be overcome and fresh red blood will course in a sounder social organism, it will itself rise to higher liberty and life. Doing the will of God it will have new visions of God. With a new message will come a new authority. If the salt lose its saltness, it will be trodden under foot. If the Church fulfils its prophetic functions, it may bear the prophet's reproach for a time, but it will have the prophet's vindication thereafter.

The conviction has always been embedded in the heart of the Church that "the world"—society as it is—is evil and some time is to make way for a true human society in which the spirit of Jesus Christ shall rule. For fifteen hundred years those who desired to live a truly Christian life withdrew from the evil world to live a life apart. But the principle of such an ascetic departure from the world is dead in modern life. There are only two other possibilities. The Church must either condemn the world and seek to change it, or tolerate the world and conform to it. In the latter case it surrenders its holiness and its mission. The other possibility has never yet been tried with full faith on a large scale. All the leadings of God in contemporary history and all the promptings of Christ's spirit in our hearts urge us to make the trial. On this choice is staked the future of the Church.

3

The Shame of the Cities

☆ *Lincoln Steffens (1866-1936) typified the crusading journalists of the first decade of the twentieth century, known as "muckrakers." In his vivid portrayals of urban corruption, he alerted the public to the need for reform.** ☆

[Do] the people want good government? Tammany says they don't. Are the people honest? Are the people better than Tammany? Are they better than the merchant and the politician? Isn't our corrupt government, after all, representative. . .?

No, the contemned methods of our despised politics are the master methods of our braggart business, and the corruption that shocks us in public affairs we practice ourselves in our private concerns. There is no essential difference between the pull that gets your wife into society or for your book a favorable review, and that which gets a heeler into office, a thief out of jail, and a rich man's son on the board of directors of a corporation; none between the corruption of a labor union, a bank, and a political machine; none between a dummy director of a trust and the caucus-bound member of a legislature; none between a labor boss like Sam Parks, a boss of banks like John D. Rockefeller, a boss of railroads like J. P. Morgan, and a political boss like Matthew S. Quay. The boss is not a po-

* From Lincoln Steffens, *The Shame of the Cities*, pp. 9-14. Published by McClure, Phillips and Company, New York, 1904.

litical, he is an American institution, the product of a freed people that have not the spirit to be free.

And it's all a moral weakness; a weakness right where we think we are strongest. Oh, we are good—on Sunday, and we are "fearfully patriotic" on the Fourth of July. But the bribe we pay to the janitor to prefer our interests to the landlord's, is the little brother of the bribe passed to the alderman to sell a city street, and the father of the air-brake stock assigned to the president of a railroad to have this life-saving invention adopted on his road. And as for graft, railroad passes, saloon and bawdy-house blackmail, and watered stock, all these belong to the same family. We are pathetically proud of our democratic institutions and our republican form of government, of our grand Constitution and our just laws. We are a free and sovereign people, we govern ourselves and the government is ours. But that is the point. We are responsible, not our leaders, since we follow them. We *let* them divert our loyalty from the United States to some "party"; we *let* them boss the party and turn our municipal democracies into autocracies and our republican nation into a plutocracy. We cheat our government and we let our leaders loot it, and we let them wheedle and bribe our sovereignty from us. True, they pass for us strict laws, but we are content to let them pass also bad laws, giving away public property in exchange; and our good, and often impossible, laws we allow to be used for oppression and blackmail. And what can we say? We break our own laws and rob our own government, the lady at the custom-house, the lyncher with his rope, and the captain of industry with his bribe and his rebate. The spirit of graft and of lawlessness is the American spirit.

And this shall not be said? Not plainly? William Travers Jerome, the fearless District Attorney of New York, says, "You can say anything you think to the American people. If you are honest with yourself you may be honest with them, and they will forgive not only your candor, but your mistakes." This is the opinion, and the experience too, of an honest man and a hopeful democrat. Who says the other things? Who says "Hush," and "What's the use?" and "ALL's well," when all is rotten? It is the grafter; the coward, too, but the grafter inspires the coward. The doctrine of "addition, division, and silence" is the doctrine of graft. "Don't hurt the party," "Spare the fair fame of the city," are boodle yells. The Fourth of July oration is the "front" of graft. There is no patriotism in it, but

treason. It is part of the game. The grafters call for cheers for the flag, "prosperity," and "the party," just as a highwayman commands "hands up," and while we are waving and shouting, they float the flag from the nation to the party, turn both into graft factories, and prosperity into a speculative boom to make "weak hands," as the Wall Street phrase has it, hold the watered stock while the strong hands keep the property. "Blame us, blame anybody, but praise the people," this, the politician's advice, is not the counsel of respect for the people, but of contempt. By just such palavering as courtiers play upon the degenerate intellects of weak kings, the bosses, political, financial, and industrial, are befuddling and befooling our sovereign American citizenship; and—likewise—they are corrupting it.

And it is corruptible, this citizenship. "I know what Parks is doing," said a New York union workman, "but what do I care. He has raised my wages. Let him have his graft!" And the Philadelphia merchant says the same thing: "The party leaders may be getting more than they should out of the city, but that doesn't hurt me. It may raise taxes a little, but I can stand that. The party keeps up the protective tariff. If that were cut down, my business would be ruined. So long as the party stands pat on that, I stand pat on the party."

4

The Treason of the Senate

☆ *David Graham Phillips (1867-1911) used his articles and novels as a means of social protest. His propensity to deal with more shocking themes of personal and civic corruption reached a peak in a series of articles called "The Treason of the Senate."* ☆

The sole source of Aldrich's power over the senators is "the interests"—the sole source, but quite sufficient to make him permanent and undisputed boss. Many of the senators, as we shall in due time and in detail note, are, like Depew and Platt, the direct agents of the various state or sectional subdivisions of "the interests," and these senators constitute about two-thirds of the entire Senate. Of the remainder several know that if they should oppose "the interests" they would lose their seats; several others are silent because they feel that to speak out would be useless; a few do speak out, but are careful not to infringe upon the rigid rule of "senatorial courtesy," which thus effectually protects the unblushing corruptionists, the obsequious servants of corruption, and likewise the many traitors to party as well as the people, from having disagreeable truths dinged into their ears. Tillman will "pitchfork" a president, but not a senator, and not the Senate in any but the most useless, futile way—this, though none knows better than he how the rights and the property of the people are

* From David Graham Phillips, "Aldrich, the Head of It All," *Cosmopolitan Magazine*, XL (April, 1906), pp. 632-634.

trafficked in by his colleagues of both parties, with a few exceptions. There are a few other honest men from the South and from the West, as many of the few honest Republicans as honest Democrats. Yet party allegiance and "senatorial courtesy" make them abettors of treason, allies of Aldrich and Gorman. . . .

The greatest single hold of "the interests" is the fact that they are the "campaign contributors"—the men who supply the money for "keeping the party together," and for "getting out the vote." Did you ever think where the millions for watchers, spellbinders, halls, processions, posters, pamphlets, that are spent in national, state and local campaigns come from? Who pays the big election expenses of your congressman, of the men you send to the legislature to elect senators? Do you imagine those who foot those huge bills are fools? Don't you know that they make sure of getting their money back, with interest, compound upon compound? Your candidates get most of the money for their campaigns from the party committees; and the central party committee is the national committee with which congressional and state and local committees are affiliated. The bulk of the money for the "political trust" comes from "the interests." "The interests" will give only to the "political trust." And that means Aldrich and his Democratic (!) lieutenant, Gorman of Maryland, leader of the minority in the Senate. Aldrich, then, is the head of the "political trust" and Gorman is his right-hand man. When you speak of the Republican party, of the Democratic party, of the "good of the party," of the "best interests of the party," of "wise party policy," you mean what Aldrich and Gorman, acting for their clients, deem wise and proper and "Republican" or "Democratic."

To relate the treason in detail would mean taking up bill after bill and going through it, line by line, word by word, and showing how this interpolation there or that excision yonder meant millions on millions more to this or that interest, millions on millions less for the people as merchants, wage or salary earners, consumers; how the killing of this measure meant immunity to looters all along the line; how the alteration of the wording of that other "trifling" resolution gave a quarter of a cent a pound on every one of hundreds of millions of pounds of some necessary of life to a certain small group of men; how this innocent looking little measure safeguarded the railway barons in looting the whole American people by excessive charges and rebates. Few among the masses have the patience to listen to these dull matters—and, so, the interests" and their agents have prosperity and honor instead of justice and jail.

No railway legislation that was not either helpful to or harmless against "the interests"; no legislation on the subject of corporations that would interfere with "the interests," which use the corporate form to simplify and systematize their stealing; no legislation on the tariff question unless it secured to "the interests" full and free license to loot; no investigations of wholesale robbery or of any of the evils resulting from it—there you have in a few words the whole story of the Senate's treason under Aldrich's leadership, and of why property is concentrating in the hands of the few and the little children of the masses are being sent to toil in the darkness of mines, in the dreariness and unhealthfulness of factories instead of being sent to school; and why the great middle class—the old-fashioned Americans, the people with the incomes of from two thousand to fifteen thousand a year—is being swiftly crushed into dependence and the repulsive miseries of "genteel poverty." The heavy and ever heavier taxes of "the interests" are swelling rents, swelling the prices of food, clothing, fuel, all the necessities and all the necessary comforts. And the Senate both forbids the lifting of those taxes and levies fresh taxes for its master.

5

Monopoly Profits

☆ *The United States Bureau of Corporations was established in 1903. In carrying out its mission to investigate corporate operations, the Bureau added official documentation to charges of business indifference to consumer interests.** ☆

The obnoxious character of the Standard's price policy and methods is . . . made clear by the present report. The Standard has repeatedly asserted that combination, as illustrated by its own history, is a great benefit to the public, in reducing costs and consequently prices. It may readily be that in some industries combination has had these beneficial results. It is probable that the Standard, by reason of its undoubtedly great efficiency, could, had it been content with reasonable profits, have made prices to consumers lower than would have been possible for smaller concerns, and thus have maintained its great proportion of the business by wholly fair and legitimate means.

The Standard is, however, a most conspicuous example of precisely the opposite—of a combination which maintains a substantial monopoly, not by superiority of service and by charging reasonable prices, but by unfair methods of destroying competition; a combination which then uses the power thus unfairly gained to oppress the public through highly extortionate prices. It has raised prices in-

* From United States Bureau of Corporations, *Report of the Commissioner of Corporations on the Petroleum Industry*, Part II, Washington, 1907, pp. xliv-xlv.

stead of lowering them. It has pocketed all the advantages of its economies instead of sharing them with the public, and has added still further monopoly profits by charging more than smaller and less economical concerns could sell for if the Standard allowed them the chance.

Some of the unfair and illegal means by which the Standard has been able to do this have been proved in the reports already published by this Bureau: namely, railroad discriminations, wide-reaching in extent and enormous in degree; failure to perform the duties of a common carrier in pipe-line transportation, and unjust methods of destroying competition in that business; and price discrimination of the most flagrant character. In the present report the following facts are established: The Standard has not reduced margins during the period in which it has been responsible for the prices of oil. During the last eight years covered by this report (1898 to 1905) it has raised both prices and margins. Its domination has not been acquired or maintained by its superior efficiency, but rather by unfair competition and by methods economically and morally unjustifiable. The Standard has superior efficiency in running its own business; it has an equal efficiency in destroying the business of competitors. It keeps for itself the profits of the first and adds to these the monopoly profits secured by the second. Its profits are far above the highest possible standard of a reasonable commercial return, and have been steadily increasing. Finally, the history of this great industry is a history of the persistent use of the worst industrial methods, the exaction of exorbitant prices from the consumer, and the securing of excessive profits for the small group of men who over a long series of years have thus dominated the business.

6

The "Money Trust"

☆ *A subcommittee of the House Committee on Banking and Currency, under Representative Arsène Pujo, conducted hearings in 1912-1913 on the concentration of financial and banking resources. The devious methods employed by financiers to effect the enormous concentration of wealth, publicized by the Pujo Committee, shocked the nation and led to remedial legislation.** ☆

That in recent years concentration of control of the banking resources and consequently of credit by the groups to which we will refer has grown apace in the city of New York is defended by some witnesses and regretted by others, but acknowledged by all to be a fact.

As appears from statistics compiled by accountants for the committee, in 1911, of the total resources of the banks and trust companies in New York City, the 20 largest held 42.97 per cent; in 1906, the 20 largest held 38.24 per cent of the total; in 1901, 34.97 per cent. . . .

This increased concentration of control of money and credit has been effected principally as follows:

First, through consolidations of competitive or potentially competitive banks and trust companies, which consolidations in turn have recently been brought under sympathetic management.

Second, through the same powerful interests becoming large stockholders in potentially competitive banks and trust companies. This is the simplest way of

* From *House Report* #1593, 62nd Congress, 3rd session, pp. 86-97.

acquiring control, but since it requires the largest investment of capital, it is the least used, although the recent investments in that direction for that apparent purpose amount to tens of millions of dollars in present market values.

Third, through the confederation of potentially competitive banks and trust companies by means of the system of interlocking directorates.

Fourth, through the influence which the more powerful banking houses, banks, and trust companies have secured in the management of insurance companies, railroads, producing and trading corporations, and public utility corporations, by means of stockholdings, voting trusts, fiscal agency contracts, or representation upon their boards of directors, or through supplying the money requirements of railway, industrial, and public utilities corporations and thereby being enabled to participate in the determination of their financial and business policies.

Fifth, through partnership or joint account arrangements between a few of the leading banking houses, banks, and trust companies in the purchase of security issues of the great interstate corporations, accompanied by understandings of recent growth—sometimes called "banking ethics"—which have had the effect of effectually destroying competition between such banking houses, banks, and trust companies in the struggle for business or in the purchase and sale of large issues of such securities. . . .

It is a fair deduction from the testimony that the most active agents in forwarding and bringing about the concentration of control of money and credit through one or another of the processes above described have been and are—

J. P. Morgan & Co.
First National Bank of New York
National City Bank of New York
Lee, Higginson & Co., of Boston and New York
Kidder, Peabody & Co., of Boston and New York
Kuhn, Loeb & Co. . . .

Summary of Directorships Held by These Members of the Group. . . . shows the combined directorships in the more important enterprises held by Morgan & Co., the First National Bank, the National City Bank, and the Bankers and Guaranty Trust Cos., which latter two . . . are absolutely controlled by Morgan & Co. through voting trusts. It appears there that firm members or directors of these institutions together hold:

One hundred and eighteen directorships in 34 banks and trust companies having total resources of $2,679,000,000 and total deposits of $1,983,000,000.

Thirty directorships in 10 insurance companies having total assets of $2,293,-000,000.

One hundred and five directorships in 32 transportation systems having a total capitalization of $11,784,000,000 and a total mileage (excluding express companies and steamship lines) of 150,200.

Sixty-three directorships in 24 producing and trading corporations having a total capitalization of $3,339,000,000.

Twenty-five directorships in 12 public utility corporations having a total capitalization of $2,150,000,000.

In all, 341 directorships in 112 corporations having aggregate resources or capitalization of $22,245,000,000.

The members of the firm of J. P. Morgan & Co. hold 72 directorships in 47 of the greater corporations: George F. Baker, chairman of the board, F. L. Hine, president, and George F. Baker, Jr., and C. D. Norton, vice-presidents, of the First National Bank of New York, hold 46 directorships in 37 of the greater corporations; and James Stillman, chairman of the board, Frank A. Vanderlip, president, and Samuel McRoberts, J. T. Talbert, W. A. Simonson, vice-presidents of the National City Bank of New York, hold 32 directorships in 26 of the greater corporations; making in all for these members of the group 150 directorships in 110 of the greater corporations. . . .

7

The New Nationalism

☆ *Theodore Roosevelt (1858-1919) succeeded to the presidency on the death of William McKinley, September 14, 1901, and won the presidential election of 1904. Roosevelt, in his aggressive manner, advocated the use of government power to rectify the inequities and injustices of a competitive industrial society. In his initial message to Congress in 1901 he revealed a concern for the harmonizing of corporate enterprise and civic obligations, a first step in developing a program for the national regulation of big business. Roosevelt also called for vigorous action to conserve the natural resources of the nation, and toward the end of his administration he urged government protection of individuals—employees, consumers, and stockholders —against injury by organized economic power.* ☆

(a) I DID GREATLY BROADEN THE USE OF EXECUTIVE POWER*

The most important factor in getting the right spirit in my Administration, next to the insistence upon courage, honesty, and a genuine democracy of desire to serve the plain people, was my insistence upon the theory that the executive power was limited only by specific restrictions and prohibitions appearing in the Constitution or imposed by the Congress under its Constitutional powers. My view was that every executive officer, and above all every executive officer in high position, was a steward of the people bound actively and affirmatively to do all he could for the people, and not to content himself with negative merit of keeping

* Reprinted with the permission of Charles Scribner's Sons from *Theodore Roosevelt: An Autobiography*, p. 357. Copyright 1913 Charles Scribner's Sons; renewal copyright 1941 Edith K. Carrow Roosevelt.

his talents undamaged in a napkin. I declined to adopt the view that what was imperatively necessary for the Nation could not be done by the President unless he could find some specific authorization to do it. My belief was that it was not only his right but his duty to do anything that the needs of the Nation demanded unless such action was forbidden by the Constitution or by the laws. Under this interpretation of executive power I did and caused to be done many things not previously done by the President and heads of departments. I did not usurp power, but I did greatly broaden the use of executive power. In other words, I acted for the public welfare, I acted for the common well-being of all our people, whenever and in whatever manner was necessary, unless prevented by direct constitutional or legislative prohibition. I did not care a rap for the mere form and show of power; I cared immensely for the use that could be made of the substance.

(b) CORPORATE RESPONSIBILITY*

The tremendous and highly complex industrial development which went on with ever accelerated rapidity during the latter half of the nineteenth century brings us face to face, at the beginning of the twentieth, with very serious social problems. The old laws, and the old customs which had almost the binding force of law, were once quite sufficient to regulate the accumulation and distribution of wealth. Since the industrial changes which have so enormously increased the productive power of mankind, they are no longer sufficient.

The growth of cities has gone on beyond comparison faster than the growth of the country, and the upbuilding of the great industrial centers has meant a startling increase, not merely in the aggregate of wealth, but in the number of very large individual, and especially of very large corporate, fortunes. The creation of these great corporate fortunes has not been due to the tariff nor to any other governmental action, but to natural causes in the business world, operating in other countries as they operate in our own.

The process has aroused much antagonism, a great part of which is wholly without warrant. . . .

The captains of industry who have driven the railway systems across this continent, who have built up our commerce, who have developed our manufactures, have on the whole done great good to our people. Without them the material development of which we are so justly proud could never have taken place.

* Theodore Roosevelt, first annual message to Senate and House of Representatives, December 3, 1901. From *A Compilation of the Messages and Papers of the Presidents*, XIV, pp. 6645-6649. Published by Bureau of National Literature, Inc., New York.

Moreover, we should recognize the immense importance of this material development of leaving as unhampered as is compatible with the public good the strong and forceful men upon whom the success of business operations inevitably rests. The slightest study of business conditions will satisfy anyone capable of forming a judgment that the personal equation is the most important factor in a business operation; that the business ability of the man at the head of any business concern, big or little, is usually the factor which fixes the gulf between striking success and hopeless failure.

An additional reason for caution in dealing with corporations is to be found in the international commercial conditions of to-day. The same business conditions which have produced the great aggregations of corporate and individual wealth have made them very potent factors in international commercial competition. Business concerns which have the largest means at their disposal and are managed by the ablest men are naturally those which take the lead in the strife for commercial supremacy among the nations of the world. America has only just begun to assume that commanding position in the international business world which we believe will more and more be hers. It is of the utmost importance that this position be not jeoparded, especially at a time when the overflowing abundance of our own natural resources and the skill, business energy, and mechanical aptitude of our people make foreign markets essential. Under such conditions it would be most unwise to cramp or to fetter the youthful strength of our Nation.

Moreover, it can not too often be pointed out that to strike with ignorant violence at the interests of one set of men almost inevitably endangers the interests of all. The fundamental rule in our national life—the rule which underlies all others—is that, on the whole, and in the

long run, we shall go up or down together.
. . . It surely ought not to be necessary to
enter into any proof of this statement; the
memory of the lean years which began in
1893 is still vivid, and we can contrast
which is now closing. Disaster to great
which is now closing. Disaster to great
business enterprises can never have its
effects limited to the men at the top. It
spreads throughout, and while it is bad
for everybody, it is worst for those farthest down. The capitalist may be shorn
of his luxuries; but the wageworker may
be deprived of even bare necessities.

The mechanism of modern business is
so delicate that extreme care must be
taken not to interfere with it in a spirit of
rashness or ignorance. Many of those who
have made it their vocation to denounce
the great industrial combinations which
are popularly, although with technical in-
accuracy, known as "trusts," appeal
especially to hatred and fear. These are
precisely the two emotions, particularly
when combined with ignorance, which unfit men for the exercise of cool and steady
judgment. In facing new industrial conditions, the whole history of the world
shows that legislation will generally be
both unwise and ineffective unless undertaken after calm inquiry and with sober
self-restraint. . . .

All this is true; and yet it is also true
that there are real and grave evils, one
of the chief being over-capitalization because of its many baleful consequences;
and a resolute and practical effort must
be made to correct these evils.

There is a widespread conviction in the
minds of the American people that the
great corporations known as trusts are in
certain of their features and tendencies
hurtful to the general welfare. . . . It is
based upon sincere conviction that combination and concentration should be, not
prohibited, but supervised and within
reasonable limits controlled; and in my
judgment this conviction is right.

It is no limitation upon property rights
or freedom of contract to require that
when men receive from Government the
privilege of doing business under corporate form, which frees them from individual responsibility, and enables them
to call into their enterprises the capital
of the public, they shall do so upon absolutely truthful representations as to the
value of the property in which the capital
is to be invested. Corporations engaged
in interstate commerce should be regulated if they are found to exercise a license working to the public injury. It
should be as much the aim of those who
seek for social betterment to rid the business world of crimes of cunning as to rid
the entire body politic of crimes of violence. Great corporations exist only because they are created and safeguarded
by our institutions; and it is therefore our
right and our duty to see that they work
in harmony with these institutions.

The first essential in determining how
to deal with the great industrial combinations is knowledge of the facts—publicity.
In the interest of the public, the Government should have the right to inspect and
examine the workings of the great corporations engaged in interstate business.
Publicity is the only sure remedy which
we can now invoke. What further remedies are needed in the way of governmental regulation, or taxation, can only be
determined after publicity has been obtained, by process of law, and in the
course of administration. The first requisite is knowledge, full and complete—
knowledge which may be made public to
the world. . . .

The large corporations, commonly
called trusts, though organized in one
State, always do business in many States,
often doing very little business in the
State where they are incorporated. There
is utter lack of uniformity in the State
laws about them; and as no State has any
exclusive interest in or power over their

acts, it has in practice proved impossible to get adequate regulation through State action. Therefore, in the interest of the whole people, the Nation should, without interfering with the power of the States in the matter itself, also assume power of supervision and regulation over all corporations doing an interstate business. This is especially true where the corporation derives a portion of its wealth from the existence of some monopolistic element or tendency in its business. There would be no hardship in such supervision; banks are subject to it, and in their case it is now accepted as a simple matter of course. Indeed, it is probable that supervision of corporations by the National Government need not go so far as is now the case with the supervision exercised over them by so conservative a State as Massachusetts, in order to produce excellent results.

When the Constitution was adopted, at the end of the eighteenth century, no human wisdom could foretell the sweeping changes, alike in industrial and political conditions, which were to take place by the beginning of the twentieth century. At that time it was accepted as a matter of course that the several States were the proper authorities to regulate, so far as was then necessary, the comparatively insignificant and strictly localized corporate bodies of the day. The conditions are now wholly different and wholly different action is called for. I believe that a law can be framed which will enable the National Government to exercise control along the lines above indicated; profiting by the experience gained through the passage and administration of the Interstate-Commerce Act. If, however, the judgment of the Congress is that it lacks the constitutional power to pass such an act, then a constitutional amendment should be submitted to confer the power.

(c) CONSERVATION OF NATURAL RESOURCES *

The conservation of our natural resources and their proper use constitute the fundamental problem which underlies almost every other problem of our National life. We must maintain for our civilization the adequate material basis without which that civilization cannot exist. We must show foresight, we must look ahead. As a nation we not only enjoy a wonderful measure of present prosperity but if this prosperity is used aright it is an earnest of future success such as no other nation will have. The reward of foresight for this Nation is great and easily foretold. But there must be the look ahead, there must be a realization of the fact that to waste, to destroy, our natural resources, to skin and exhaust the land instead of using it so as to increase its usefulness, will result in undermining in the days of our children the very prosperity which we ought by right to hand down to them amplified and developed. For the last few years, through several agencies, the Government has been endeavoring to get our people to look ahead and to substitute a planned and orderly development of our resources in place of a haphazard striving for immediate profit. Our great river systems should be developed as National water highways, the Mississippi, with its tributaries, standing first in importance, and the Columbia second, although there are many others of importance on the Pacific, the Atlantic and the Gulf slopes. The National Government should undertake this work, and I hope a beginning will be made in the present Congress; and the greatest of all our rivers, the Mississippi, should receive espe-

* Theodore Roosevelt, seventh annual message to Senate and House of Representatives, December 3, 1907. From *A Compilation of the Messages and Papers of the Presidents,* XIV, pp. 7094-7098. Published by Bureau of National Literature, Inc., New York.

cial attention. From the Great Lakes to the mouth of the Mississippi there should be a deep waterway, with deep waterways leading from it to the East and the West. Such a waterway would practically mean the extension of our coast line into the very heart of our country. It would be of incalculable benefit to our people. If begun at once it can be carried through in time appreciably to relieve the congestion of our great freight-carrying lines of railroads. The work should be systematically and continuously carried forward in accordance with some well-conceived plan. The main streams should be improved to the highest point of efficiency before the improvement of the branches is attempted; and the work should be kept free from every taint of recklessness or jobbery. The inland waterways which lie just back of the whole eastern and southern coasts should likewise be developed. Moreover, the development of our waterways involves many other important water problems, all of which should be considered as part of the same general scheme. The Government dams should be used to produce hundreds of thousands of horsepower as an incident to improving navigation; for the annual value of the unused water-power of the United States perhaps exceeds the annual value of the products of all our mines. As an incident to creating the deep waterways down the Mississippi, the Government should build along its whole lower length levees which taken together with the control of the headwaters, will at once and forever put a complete stop to all threat of floods in the immensely fertile Delta region. The territory lying adjacent to the Mississippi along its lower course will thereby become one of the most prosperous and populous, as it already is one of the most fertile, farming regions in all the world. I have appointed an Inland Waterways Commission to study and outline a comprehensive scheme of development along all the lines indicated. Later I shall lay its report before the Congress.

Irrigation should be far more extensively developed than at present, not only in the States of the Great Plains and the Rocky Mountains, but in many others, as, for instance, in large portions of the South Atlantic and Gulf States, where it should go hand in hand with the reclamation of swamp land. The Federal Government should seriously devote itself to this task, realizing that utilization of waterways and water-power, forestry, irrigation, and the reclamation of lands threatened with overflow, are all interdependent parts of the same problem. The work of the Reclamation Service in developing the larger opportunities of the western half of our country for irrigation is more important than almost any other movement. The constant purpose of the Government in connection with the Reclamation Service has been to use the water resources of the public lands for the ultimate greatest good of the greatest number; in other words, to put upon the land permanent home-makers, to use and develop it for themselves and for their children and children's children. . . .

The effort of the Government to deal with the public land has been based upon the same principle as that of the Reclamation Service. The land law system which was designed to meet the needs of the fertile and well-watered regions of the Middle West has largely broken down when applied to the dryer regions of the Great Plains, the mountains, and much of the Pacific slope, where a farm of 160 acres is inadequate for self-support. In these regions the system lent itself to fraud, and much land passed out of the hands of the Government without passing into the hands of the home-maker. The Department of the Interior and the Department of Justice joined in prosecuting the offenders against the law; and they have accomplished much, while where the administration of the law has been defective it has been changed. But the laws themselves are defective. Three years ago a public lands commission was appointed to scrutinize the law, and defects, and recommend a remedy. Their examination specifically showed the existence of great fraud upon the public domain, and their recommendations for changes in the law were made with the design of conserving the natural resources of every part of the public lands by putting it to its best use. Especial attention was called to the prevention of settlement by the passage of great areas of public land into the hands of a few men, and to the enormous waste caused by unrestricted grazing upon the open range. The recommendations of the Public Lands Commission are sound, for they are especially in the interest of the actual home-maker; and where the small home-maker can not at present utilize the land they provide that the Government shall keep control of it so that it may not be monopolized by a few men. The Congress has not yet acted upon these recommendations; but they are so just and proper, so essential to our National welfare, that I feel confident, if the Congress will take time to consider them, that they will ultimately be adopted.

Some such legislation as that proposed is essential in order to preserve the great stretches of public grazing land which are unfit for cultivation under present methods and are valuable only for the forage which they supply. These stretches amount in all to some 300,000,000 acres, and are open to the free grazing of cattle, sheep, horses and goats, without restriction. Such a system, or lack of system, means that the range is not so much used as wasted by abuse. As the West settles the range becomes more and more overgrazed. Much of it can not be used to advantage unless it is fenced, for fencing is the only way by which to keep in check the owners of nomad flocks which roam hither and thither, utterly destroying the pastures and leaving a waste behind so that their presence is incompatible with the presence of home-makers. The existing fences are all illegal. Some of them represent the improper exclusion of actual settlers, actual home-makers, from territory which is usurped by great cattle companies. Some of them represent what is in itself a proper effort to use the range for those upon the land, and to prevent its use by nomadic outsiders. All these fences, those that are hurtful and those that are beneficial, are alike illegal and must come down. But it is an outrage that the law should necessitate such action on the part of the Administration. The unlawful fencing of public lands for private grazing must be stopped, but the necessity which occasioned it must be provided for. The Federal Government should have control of the range, whether by permit or lease, as local necessities may determine. Such control could secure the great benefit of legitimate fencing, while at the same time securing and promoting the settlement of the country. In some places it may be that the tracts of range adjacent to the homesteads of actual settlers should be allotted to them severally or in common for the summer grazing of their stock. Elsewhere it may be that a lease system would serve the purpose; the leases to be temporary and subject to the rights of settlement, and the amount charged being large enough merely to permit of the efficient and beneficial control of the range by the Government, and of the payment to the county of the equivalent of what it would otherwise receive in taxes. The destruction of the public range will continue until some such laws as these are enacted. Fully to prevent the fraud in the public lands which, through the joint action of the Interior Department and the Department of Justice, we have been endeavoring to prevent, there must be further legislation, and especially a sufficient appropriation to permit the Department of the Interior to examine certain classes of entries on the ground before they pass into private ownership. The Government should part with its title only to the actual home-maker, not to the profit-maker who does not care to make a home. Our prime object is to secure the rights and guard the interests of the small ranchman, the man who plows and pitches hay for himself. It is this small ranchman, this actual settler and home-maker, who in the long run is most hurt by permitting thefts of the public land in whatever form.

Optimism is a good characteristic, but if carried to an excess it becomes foolishness. We are prone to speak of the resources of this country as inexhaustible; this is not so. The mineral wealth of the country, the coal, iron, oil, gas, and the like, does not reproduce itself, and therefore is certain to be exhausted ultimately; and wastefulness in dealing with it to-day means that our descendants will feel the exhaustion a generation or two before they otherwise would. But there are certain other forms of waste which could be entirely stopped—the waste of soil by washing, for instance, which is among the most dangerous of all wastes now in progress in the United States, is easily preventable, so that this present enormous loss of fertility is entirely unnecessary. The preservation or replacement of the forests is one of the most important means of preventing this loss. We have made a beginning in forest preservation, but it is only a beginning. At present lumbering is the fourth greatest industry in the United States; and yet, so rapid has been the rate of exhaustion of timber in the United States in the past, and so rapidly is the remainder being exhausted, that the country is unquestionably on the verge of a timber famine which will be felt in every household in the land. There has already **been** a rise in the price of lumber, but

there is certain to be a more rapid and heavier rise in the future. The present annual consumption of lumber is certainly three times as great as the annual growth; and if the consumption and growth continue unchanged, practically all our lumber will be exhausted in another generation, while long before the limit to complete exhaustion is reached the growing scarcity will make itself felt in many blighting ways upon our National welfare. About 20 per cent of our forested territory is now reserved in National forests; but these do not include the most valuable timber lands, and in any event the proportion is too small to expect that the reserves can accomplish more than a mitigation of the trouble which is ahead for the nation. . . .

(d) PROTECTION OF THE INDIVIDUAL *

I . . . very urgently advise that a comprehensive act be passed providing for compensation by the Government to all employees injured in the Government service. Under the present law an injured workman in the employment of the Government has no remedy, and the entire burden of the accident falls on the helpless man, his wife, and his young children. This is an outrage. It is a matter of humiliation to the Nation that there should not be on our statute books provision to meet and partially to atone for cruel misfortune when it comes upon a man through no fault of his own while faithfully serving the public. In no other prominent industrial country in the world could such gross injustice occur; for almost all civilized nations have enacted legislation embodying the complete recognition of the principle which places the entire trade risk for industrial accidents (excluding, of course,

* Theodore Roosevelt, special message to Senate and House of Representatives, January 31, 1908. From *A Compilation of the Messages and Papers of the Presidents,* XV, pp. 7126-7132. Published by Bureau of National Literature, Inc., New York.

accidents due to willful misconduct by the employee) on the industry as represented by the employer, which in this case is the Government. In all these countries the principle applies to the Government just as much as to the private employer. Under no circumstances should the injured employee or his surviving dependents be required to bring suit against the Government, nor should there be the requirement that in order to insure recovery negligence in some form on the part of the Government should be shown. Our proposition is not to confer a right of action upon the Government employee, but to secure him suitable provision against injuries received in the course of his employment. The burden of the trade risk should be placed upon the Government. Exactly as the working man is entitled to his wages, so he should be entitled to indemnity for the injuries sustained in the natural course of his labor. The rates of compensation and the regulations for its payment should be specified in the law, and the machinery for determining the amount to be paid should in each case be provided in such manner that the employee is properly represented without expense to him. In other words, the compensation should be paid automatically. . . .

The same broad principle which should apply to the Government should ultimately be made applicable to all private employers. Where the Nation has the power it should enact laws to this effect. Where the States alone have the power they should enact the laws. It is to be observed that an employers' liability law does not really mean mulcting employers in damages. It merely throws upon the employer the burden of accident insurance against injuries which are sure to occur. It requires him either to bear or to distribute through insurance the loss which can readily be borne when distributed, but which, if undistributed, bears with frightful hardship upon the unfortunate victim of accident. In theory, if wages were always freely and fairly adjusted, they would always include an allowance as against the risk of injury, just as certainly as the rate of interest for money includes an allowance for insurance against the risk of loss. In theory, if employees were all experienced business men, they would employ that part of their wages which is received because of the risk of injury to secure accident insurance. But as a matter of fact it is not practical to expect that this will be done by the great body of employees. An employers' liability law makes it certain that it will be done, in effect, by the employer, and it will ultimately impose no real additional burden upon him. . . .

I again call your attention to the need of some action in connection with the abuse of injunctions in labor cases. . . . I should consider it most unwise to abolish the use of the process of injunction. It is necessary in order that the courts may maintain their own dignity and in order that they may in effective manner check disorder and violence. The judge who uses it cautiously and conservatively, but who, when the need arises, uses it fearlessly, confers the greatest service upon our people, and his preeminent usefulness as a public servant should be heartily recognized. But there is no question in my mind that it has sometimes been used heedlessly and unjustly, and that some of the injunctions issued inflict grave and occasionally irreparable wrong upon those enjoined.

It is all wrong to use the injunction to prevent the entirely proper and legitimate actions of labor organizations in their struggle for industrial betterment, or under the guise of protecting property rights unwarrantably to invade the fundamental rights of the individual. It is futile to concede, as we all do, the right and the necessity of organized effort on the part of wage-earners and yet by injunctive process to forbid peaceable action to accomplish the lawful objects for which they are organized and upon which their success depends. The fact that the punishment for the violation of an injunction must, to make the order effective, necessarily be summary and without the intervention of a jury makes its issuance in doubtful cases a dangerous practice, and in itself furnishes a reason why the process should be surrounded with safeguards to protect individuals against being enjoined from exercising their proper rights. Reasonable notice should be given the adverse party.

This matter is daily becoming of graver importance and I can not too urgently recommend that the Congress give careful consideration to the subject. If some way of remedying the abuses is not found the feeling of indignation against them among large numbers of our citizens will tend to grow so extreme as to produce a revolt against the whole use of the process of injunction. The ultra-conservatives who object to cutting out the abuses will do well to remember that if the popular feeling does become strong many of those upon whom they rely to defend them will be the first to turn against them. Men of property can not afford to trust to anything save the spirit of justice and fair play; for those very public men who, while it is to their interest, defend all the abuses committed by capital and pose as the champions of conservatism, will, the moment they think their interest changes, take the lead in just such a matter as this and pander to what they esteem popular feeling by endeavoring, for instance, effectively to destroy the power of the courts in matters of injunction; and will even seek to render nugatory the power to punish for contempt, upon which power the very existence of the orderly administration of justice depends.

. . . there should . . . be . . . action on laws better to secure control over the great business concerns engaged in interstate commerce, and especially over the great common carriers. The Interstate Commerce Commission should be empowered to pass upon any rate or practice on its own initiative. Moreover, it should be provided that whenever the Commission has reason to believe that a proposed advance in a rate ought not to be made without investigation, it should have authority to issue an order prohibiting the advance pending examination by the Commission.

I would not be understood as expressing an opinion that any or even a majority of these advances are improper. Many of the rates in this country have been abnormally low. The operating expenses of our railroads, notably the wages paid railroad employees, have greatly increased. These and other causes may in any given case justify an advance in rates, and if so the advance should be permitted and approved. But there may be, and doubtless are, cases where this is not true; and our law should be so framed that the Government, as the representative of the whole people, can protect the individual against unlawful exaction for the use of these public highways. The Interstate Commerce Commission should be provided with the means to make a physical valuation of any road as to which it deems this valuation necessary. In some form the Federal Government should exercise supervision over the financial operations of our interstate railroads. In no other way can justice be done between the private owners of those properties and the public which pay their charges. When once an inflated capitalization has gone upon the market and has become fixed in value, its existence must be recognized. As a practical matter it is then often absolutely necessary to take account of the thousands of innocent stockholders who have purchased their stock in good faith. The usual result of such inflation is therefore to impose upon the public an unnecessary but everlasting tax, while the innocent purchasers of the stock are also harmed and only a few speculators are benefited. Such wrongs when once accomplished can with difficulty be undone; but they can be prevented with safety and with justice. When combinations of interstate railways must obtain Government sanction; when it is no longer possible for an interstate railway to issue stock or bonds, save in the manner approved by the Federal Government; when that Government makes sure that the proceeds of every stock and bond issue go into the improvement of the property and not the enrichment of some individual or syndicate; when, whenever it becomes material for guidance in the regulative action of the Government, the physical value of one of these properties is determined and made known—there will be eliminated from railroad securities that element of uncertainty which lends to them their speculative quality and which has contributed much to the financial stress of the recent past.

I think that the Federal Government must also assume a certain measure of control over the physical operation of railways in the handling of interstate traffic. The Commission now has authority to establish through routes and joint rates. In order to make this provision effective and in order to promote in times of necessity the proper movement of traffic, I think it must also have authority to determine the conditions upon which cars shall be interchanged between different interstate railways. It is also probable that the Commission should have authority, in particular instances, to determine the schedule upon which perishable commodities shall be moved. . . .

In reference to the Sherman antitrust law, I repeat the recommendations made in my message at the opening of the present Congress, as well as in my message to the previous Congress. The attempt in this law to provide in sweeping terms against all combinations of whatever character, if technically in restraint of trade as such restraint has been defined by the courts, must necessarily be either futile or mischievous, and sometimes both. The present law makes some combinations illegal, although they may be useful to the country. On the other hand, as to some huge combinations which are both noxious and illegal, even if the action undertaken against them under the law by the Government is successful, the result may be to work but a minimum benefit to the public. Even though the combination be broken up and a small measure of reform thereby produced, the real good aimed at can not be obtained, for such real good can come only by a thorough and continuing supervision over the acts of the combination in all its parts, so as to prevent stock watering, improper forms of competition, and, in short, wrongdoing generally. The law should correct that portion of the Sherman Act which prohibits all combinations of the character above described, whether they be reasonable or unreasonable; but this should be done only as a part of a general scheme to provide for this effective and thoroughgoing supervision by the National Government of all the operations of the big interstate business concerns. . . .

I do not know whether it is possible, but if possible, it is certainly desirable, that in connection with measures to restrain stock watering and overcapitalization there should be measures taken to prevent at least the grosser forms of gambling in securities and commodities, such as making large sales of what men do not possess and "cornering" the market. Legitimate purchases of commodities and of stocks and securities for investment have no connection whatever with purchases of stocks or other securities or commodities on a margin for speculative and gambling purposes. There is no moral difference between gambling at cards or in lotteries or on the race track and gambling in the stock market. . . .

Superficially it may seem that the laws, the passage of which I herein again advocate—for I have repeatedly advocated them before—are not connected. But in reality they are connected. Each and every one of these laws, if enacted, would represent part of the campaign against privilege, part of the campaign to make the class of great property holders realize that property has its duties no less than its rights. When the courts guarantee to the employer, as they should, the rights of the employer, and to property the rights of property, they should no less emphati-cally make it evident that they will exact from property and from the employer the duties which should necessarily accompany these rights; and hitherto our laws have failed in precisely this point of enforcing the performance of duty by the man of property toward the man who works for him, by the man of great wealth, especially if he uses that wealth in corporate form, toward the investor, the wageworker, and the general public. The permanent failure of the man of property to fulfill his obligations would ultimately assure the wresting from him of the privileges which he is entitled to enjoy only if he recognizes the obligations accompanying them. Those who assume or share the responsibility for this failure are rendering but a poor service to the cause which they believe they champion. . . .

8

Moderate Progressivism

☆ *William Howard Taft (1857-1930) was personally selected by Roosevelt to continue his program. President Taft soon demonstrated that while he agreed with his predecessor's goals he disapproved of his method.* ☆

(a) TAFT'S CONCEPT OF THE PRESIDENCY *

The true view of the Executive functions is, as I conceive it, that the President can exercise no power which cannot be fairly and reasonably traced to some specific grant of power or justly implied and included within such express grant as proper and necessary to its exercise. Such specific grant must be either in the Federal Constitution or in an act of Congress passed in pursuance thereof. There is no undefined residuum of power which he can exercise because it seems to him to be in the public interest. . . . The grants of Executive power are necessarily in general terms in order not to embarrass the Executive within the field of action plainly marked for him, but his jurisdiction must be justified and vindicated by affirmative constitutional or statutory provision, or it does not exist. . . .

I may add that Mr. Roosevelt, by way of illustrating his meaning as to differing usefulness of Presidents, divides the Presidents into two classes, and designates them as "Lincoln Presidents" and

* From William Howard Taft, *Our Chief Magistrate and His Powers*, pp. 139-145. Copyright, 1916, by Columbia University Press, New York. Used by permission.

"Buchanan Presidents." In order to fully illustrate his division of Presidents on their merits, he places himself in the Lincoln class of Presidents, and me in the Buchanan class. The identification of Mr. Roosevelt with Mr. Lincoln might otherwise have escaped notice, because there are many differences between the two, presumably superficial, which would give the impartial student of history a different impression. It suggests a story which a friend of mine told of his little daughter Mary. As he came walking home after a business day, she ran out from the house to greet him, all aglow with the importance of what she wished to tell him. She said, "Papa, I am the best scholar in the class." The father's heart throbbed with pleasure as he inquired, "Why, Mary, you surprise me. When did the teacher tell you? This afternoon?" "Oh, no," Mary's reply was, "the teacher didn't tell me—I just noticed it myself."

My judgment is that the view of Mr. Garfield and Mr. Roosevelt ascribing an undefined residuum of power to the President is an unsafe doctrine and that it might lead under emergencies to results of an arbitrary character, doing irremediable injustice to private right. The mainspring of such a view is that the Executive is charged with responsibility for the welfare of all the people in a general way, that he is to play the part of a Universal Providence and set all things right, and that anything that in his judgment will help the people he ought to do, unless he is expressly forbidden not to do it. The wide field of action that this would give to the Executive one can hardly limit.

(b) THE TARIFF ISSUE *

I am bound to say that I think the Payne tariff bill is the best tariff bill that the Republican party ever passed; that in it the party has conceded the necessity for following the changed conditions and reducing tariff rates accordingly. This is a substantial achievement in the direction of lower tariffs and downward revision, and it ought to be a accepted as such. Critics of the bill utterly ignore the very tremendous cuts that have been made in the iron schedule, which heretofore has been subject to criticism in all tariff bills. From iron ore, which was cut 75 per cent; to all the other items as low as 20 per cent, with an average of something like 40 or 50 per cent, that schedule has been reduced so that the danger of increasing prices through a monopoly of the business is very much lessened, and that was the chief purpose of revising the tariff downward under Republican protective principles. The severe critics of the bill pass this reduction in the metal schedule with a sneer, and say that the cut did not hurt the iron interests of the country. Well, of course it did not hurt them. It was not

* William Howard Taft, address on the tariff law of 1909 at Winona, Minnesota, September 17, 1909. From *A Compilation of the Messages and Papers of the Presidents,* XV, pp. 7403, 7406-7408. Published by Bureau of National Literature, Inc., New York.

expected to hurt them. It was expected only to reduce excessive rates, so that business should still be conducted at a profit, and the very character of the criticism is an indication of the general injustice of the attitude of those who make it, in assuming that it was the promise of the Republican party to hurt the industries of the country by the reductions which they were to make in the tariff, whereas it expressly indicated as plainly as possible in the platform that all of the industries were to be protected against injury by foreign competition, and the promise only went to the reduction of excessive rates beyond what was necessary to protect them. . . .

Of course, if I had vetoed the bill I would have received the applause of many Republicans who may be called low-tariff Republicans, and who think deeply on that subject, and of all the Democracy. Our friends the Democrats would have applauded, and then laughed in their sleeve at the condition in which the party would have been left; but, more than this, and waiving considerations of party, where would the country have been had the bill been vetoed, or been lost by a vote? It would have left the question of the revision of the tariff open for further discussion during the next session. It would have suspended the settlement of all our business down to a known basis upon which prosperity could proceed and investments be made, and it would have held up the coming of prosperity to this country certainly for a year and probably longer. These are the reasons why I signed it.

But there are additional reasons why the bill ought not to have been beaten. It contained provisions of the utmost importance in the interest of this country in dealing with foreign countries and in the supplying of a deficit which under the Dingley bill seemed inevitable. There has been a disposition in some foreign countries taking advantage of greater elasticity in their systems of imposing tariffs and of making regulations to exclude our products and exercise against us undue discrimination. Against these things we have been helpless, because it required an act of Congress to meet the difficulties. It is now proposed by what is called the maximum and minimum clause, to enable the President to allow to come into operation a maximum or penalizing increase of duties over the normal or minimum duties whenever in his opinion the conduct of the foreign countries has been unduly discriminatory against the United States. . . .

Second. We have imposed an excise tax upon corporations measured by 1 per cent upon the net income of all corporations except fraternal and charitable corporations after exempting $5,000. This, it is thought, will raise an income of 26 to 30 millions of dollars, will supply the deficit which otherwise might arise without it, and will bring under federal supervision more or less all the corporations of the country. The inquisitorial provisions of the act are mild but effective, and certainly we may look not only for a revenue but for some most interesting statistics and the means of obtaining supervision over corporate methods that has heretofore not obtained.

Then, we have finally done justice to the Philippines. We have introduced free trade between the Philippines and the United States, and we have limited the amount of sugar and the amount of tobacco and cigars that can be introduced from the Philippines to such an extent as shall greatly profit the Philippines and yet in no way disturb the products of the United States or interfere with those engaged in the tobacco or sugar interests here. . . .

Now, there is another provision in the new tariff bill that I regard as of the utmost importance. It is a provision which appropriates $75,000 for the President to employ persons to assist him in the execution of the maximum and minimum tariff clause and in the administration of the tariff law. Under that authority, I conceive that the President has the right to appoint a board, as I have appointed it, who shall associate with themselves, and have under their control, a number of experts who shall address themselves, first, to the operation of foreign tariffs upon the exports of the United States, and then to the operation of the United States tariff upon imports and exports. . . .

I think it is utterly useless, as I think it would be greatly distressing to business, to talk of another revision of the tariff during the present Congress. I should think that it would certainly take the rest of this administration to accumulate the data upon which a new and proper revision of the tariff might be had. By that time the whole Republican party can express itself again in respect to the matter and bring to bear upon its Representatives in Congress that sort of public opinion which shall result in solid party action. I am glad to see that a number of those who thought it their duty to vote against the bill insist that they are still Republicans and intend to carry on their battle in favor of lower duties and a lower revision within the lines of the party. That is their right and, in their view of things, is their duty.

It is vastly better that they should seek action of the party than that they should break off from it and seek to organize another party, which would probably not result in accomplishing anything more than merely defeating our party and inviting in the opposing party, which does not believe, or says that it does not believe, in protection. I think that we ought to give the present bill a chance. After it has been operating for two or three years, we can tell much more accurately than we can to-day its effect upon the industries of the country and the necessity for any amendment in its provisions.

9

The Socialist Solution

☆ *Eugene Victor Debs (1855-1926), socialist and labor leader, ran for the presidency in 1900, 1904, 1908, 1912, and 1920. While serving a term in Atlanta penitentiary for sedition, he received more than 900,000 votes as Socialist candidate in 1920. Debs was the foremost spokesman for socialism in the United States for a generation.** ☆

For the first time in fifty years, or since the Civil War, a great moral question cleaves the political atmosphere of this nation.

Socialism indicts capitalism at the bar of civilization and challenges its political spokesmen of whatever name or brand to defend it.

The political struggle now on in this nation is a struggle to the death; either capitalism, with its gorgeous wealth and power for its successful devotees and owners, and its brutal, degrading struggle for existence for its workers, will write "*esto perpetua*" upon the scroll of Time and this civilization will enter eclipse and decline, as have the civilizations of every previous age, or else capitalism will surrender the scepter of power to socialism and the race will progress to heights undreamed and establish a civilization as far in advance of capitalism in its beneficence to mankind as capitalism is in advance of savagery.

The fundamental difference between the Socialist political organization of this

and every other nation of earth and all other political organizations is in its *economic program*.

In this nation the politicians or statesmen of the Roosevelt, Taft, Wilson type, who are the chosen or self-appointed spokesmen for their respective political organizations, may have widely different convictions or opinions upon *political* issues, such as direct legislation, recall of public officials, including the judiciary, direct election of Senators, etc., *but upon economic questions affecting the present social order they are at one. They represent the capitalist system and they stand or fall with capitalism.*

The Socialist party and its chosen spokesmen, on the other hand, challenge the right of capitalism to longer exist, and they boldly proclaim the program of socialism as the legitimate successor of the present order.

Again, socialism appeals to the world's workers upon the lines of their *class interests*. The Socialist nominees make no pretense of attempting to serve *both* capitalists and workers. That is a political sophistry which socalism leaves a monopoly in the hands of

* From Eugene V. Debs, "The Socialist Party's Appeal," *The Independent*, LXXIII (October 24, 1912), pp. 950-952.

the political spokesmen for capitalism.

Socialism counts among the world's workers all those who labor with hand or brain in the production of life's necessities and luxuries. The services of a general manager of a great railway system, or the superintendent of a great department store, are quite as essential to modern civilization as are the section hand of the one or the delivery boy of the other, and the program of socialism appeals to the self-interest of every man and woman so employed. With the interests of the *owners* of the great machines of modern production and distribution the Socialists have no concern, *except to abolish that ownership and vest it in the public, thru legislation, municipal, State and national.*

Capitalism is founded upon production for *profit.* Socialism is postulated upon production for *use.* Whenever the owners of the world's machinery of production and distribution fail for any reason to realize profit, it is in their power to cease production or distribution and the world's workers may starve. Again, if the owners of the world's machinery of production and distribution permit it to be operated, they dictate the terms upon which the world's workers may use that machinery. In other words, the only function of the modern capitalist is to *own* that which his brother man must *use.* The worker has naught but his labor power, of hand or brain, to sell, and if he must sell his labor power upon terms dictated by another, *he is a slave.*

He who controls my bread controls my head, and so the contest between modern capitalism and socialism resolves itself into the age-old question of human slavery.

Upon this question the political forces of this nation and the world are cleaving.

Deny it as they may, confuse it as they will, the spokesmen for the existing order are being slowly but surely driven to an admission of the Socialist indictment of capitalism.

The so-called progressive programs of the Democrats under Bryan and Wilson and the Republicans under Roosevelt are merely so many apologies for the crimes of capitalism. The standpat capitalists under the leadership of President Taft offer few apologies, but boldly take their stand for the existing order as it is.

The deplorable poverty of millions upon millions of workers in high tariff America, and a like condition existing in the ranks of the workers in free trade England, save the Socialists the necessity for wasting time upon this hoary but oft resurrected "issue" of capitalism. Whether under high or low tariff, in America or elsewhere, the worker and producer is exploited at the door of the factory or farm to the point of mere existence.

With the owners of the machinery of production and distribution in possession of *both the machinery and its product,* it matters little to them or to the workers whether wages be high or low, since thru manipulation of prices under capitalism the capitalists readily reduce the purchasing power of the workers' wages to the point of *subsistence, and that is the point at which the world's workers always will exist under modern capitalism.*

The present high cost of living can never be reduced without throwing capitalism into helpless bankruptcy; present prices are necessary in order to pay interest and dividends upon the monstrous capitalization of this age. The monumental capitalization, so huge in the aggregate as to stagger human imagination, represents the investments and the incomes of the owners of this nation. No capitalist politician, statesman or party dares lift a finger to reduce it, and it will continue to increase until the coming of socialism unless the entire machinery of capitalism breaks down previous to that time, bringing with it universal bankruptcy and a complete readjustment of our social and industrial system under capitalism. Such an eventuation is a possibility, but not a probability.

Control of corporations and the enforcement of the penal clauses of capitalist anti-trust legislation, by capitalist politicians, are twin frauds in the program of capitalism's efforts to fool the people.

The corporate wealth of this nation controls the capitalist government of this nation and will to the end of capitalism. Corporate wealth is the result of economic and industrial evolution. Until *corporate wealth* is supplanted by *common wealth* in the ownership of this nation, it will continue to write our laws and to enforce them or not, as best pleases its owners.

If it were possible to imprison the trust owners of this nation, it would have exactly the same effect upon economic evolution which has produced the trusts as the imprisonment of Galileo had upon the turning of the planets in their orbits.

But the Socialist wastes little time in expatiating upon these fleeting fantasies of the capitalist politicians. He realizes that the issues which divide the capitalist political camps are merely quarrels between rival groups of capitalists over the division of the spoils which they have expropriated from the workers. He is no more interested in the outcome of these political quarrels than he would be in the result of a quarrel between two hold-up men who had robbed him of his purse and who had fallen out over a division of its contents.

The Socialist contents himself with sticking to his political text. The monumental corruption, the hypocrisy and the shams of capitalist politics he sets down as one of the counts in his indictment of capitalism. Beside it he places the inexcusable impoverishment of his brother workers, the prostitution of his sisters, the destruction of his wife and children in the mines and sweatshops of capitalism.

The Socialist calls upon his brother worker to join him in the overthrow of capitalism thru capturing the powers of government and legally transferring the ownership of the world from capitalism to socialism.

He points out the staggering burden of militarism, the colossal fraud of capitalist courts, the indescribable corruption of capitalist business, the cant, the chicanery and the hypocrisy of capitalist society, and he urges his brother worker to join him in the struggle to usher in a better day.

For the first time in the world's history a subject class has it in its own power to accomplish its own emancipation without an appeal to brute force.

This is the appeal which socialism makes to the workers of this nation and the world.

It invites them to seize political power in the name of the working class, and to legally write their own economic emancipation proclamation.

Under this invitation the nations of the earth, including our own, are seething with political revolt.

It is the sure precursor of mighty changes, political, social and economic, thruout the world.

10

The New Freedom

☆ *Woodrow Wilson (1856-1924), educator and scholar, was elected president in 1912 and reelected in 1916. He believed that government must go beyond the policing of human affairs to create new conditions which would make life tolerable in a highly complex modern society. Upon taking office, Wilson called Congress together in special session to begin government action to "quicken enterprise and keep independent energy alive."* ☆

(a) THE NEW SOCIETY*

There is one great basic fact which underlies all the questions that are discussed on the political platform at the present moment. That singular fact is that nothing is done in this country as it was done twenty years ago.

We are in the presence of a new organization of society. Our life has broken away from the past. The life of America is not the life that it was twenty years ago; it is not the life that it was ten years ago. We have changed our economic conditions, absolutely, from top to bottom; and, with our economic society, the organization of our life. The old political formulas do not fit the present problems; they read now like documents taken out of a forgotten age. The older cries sound as if they belonged to a past age which men have almost forgotten. Things which used to be put into the party platforms of ten years ago would

* From Woodrow Wilson, *The New Freedom*, pp. 3-7, 19-20, 30-31. Copyright, 1913, 1933, by Doubleday, Doran and Company, Inc., New York. Used by permission of Edith Bolling Wilson.

sound antiquated if put into a platform now. We are facing the necessity of fitting a new social organization, as we did once fit the old organization, to the happiness and prosperity of the great body of citizens; for we are conscious that the new order of society has not been made to fit and provide the convenience or prosperity of the average man. The life of the nation has grown infinitely varied. It does not centre now upon questions of governmental structure or of the distribution of governmental powers. It centres upon questions of the very structure and operation of society itself, of which government is only the instrument. Our development has run so fast and so far along the lines sketched in the earlier day of constitutional definition, has so crossed and interlaced those lines, has piled upon them such novel structures of trust and combination, has elaborated within them a life so manifold, so full of forces which transcend the boundaries of the country itself and fill the eyes of the world, that a new nation seems to have been created which the old formulas do not fit or afford a vital interpretation of.

We have come upon a very different age from any that preceded us. We have come upon an age when we do not do business in the way in which we used to do business,—when we do not carry on any of the operations of manufacture, sale, transportation, or communication as men used to carry them on. There is a sense in which in our day the individual has been submerged. In most parts of our country men work, not for themselves, not as partners in the old way in which they used to work, but generally as employees,—in a higher or lower grade,— of great corporations. There was a time when corporations played a very minor part in our business affairs, but now they play the chief part, and most men are the servants of corporations.

You know what happens when you are the servant of a corporation. You have in no instance access to the men who are really determining the policy of the corporation. If the corporation is doing the things that it ought not to do, you really have no voice in the matter and must obey the orders, and you have oftentimes with deep mortification to co-operate in the doing of things which you know are against the public interest. Your individuality is swallowed up in the individuality and purpose of a great organization.

It is true that, while most men are thus submerged in the corporation, a few, a very few, are exalted to a power which as individuals they could never have wielded. Through the great organizations of which they are the heads, a few are enabled to play a part unprecedented by anything in history in the control of the business operations of the country and in the determination of the happiness of great numbers of people.

Yesterday, and ever since history be-

gan, men were related to one another as individuals. To be sure there were the family, the Church, and the State, institutions which associated men in certain wide circles of relationship. But in the ordinary concerns of life, in the ordinary work, in the daily round, men dealt freely and directly with one another. To-day, the every-day relationships of men are largely with great impersonal concerns, with organizations, not with other individual men. . . .

We used to think in the old-fashioned days when life was very simple that all that government had to do was to put on a policeman's uniform, and say, "Now don't anybody hurt anybody else." We used to say that the ideal of government was for every man to be left alone and not interfered with, except when he interfered with somebody else; and that the best government was the government that did as little governing as possible. That was the idea that obtained in Jefferson's time. But we are coming now to realize that life is so complicated that we are not dealing with the old conditions, and that the law has to step in and create new conditions under which we may live, the conditions which will make it tolerable for us to live. . . .

We stand in the presence of a revolution—not a bloody revolution; America is not given to the spilling of blood—but a silent revolution, whereby America will insist upon recovering in practice those ideals which she has always professed, upon securing a government devoted to the general interest and not to special interests.

We are upon the eve of a great reconstruction. It calls for creative statesmanship as no age has done since that great age in which we set up the government under which we live, that government which was the admiration of the world until it suffered wrongs to grow up under it which have made many of our own compatriots question the freedom of our institutions and preach revolution against them. I do not fear revolution. I have unshaken faith in the power of America to keep its self-possession. Revolution will come in peaceful guise, as it came when we put aside the crude government of the Confederation and created the great Federal Union which governs individuals, not States, and which has been these hundred and thirty years our vehicle of progress. Some radical changes we must make in our law and practice. Some reconstructions we must push forward, which a new age and new circumstances impose upon us. But we can do it all in calm and sober fashion, like statesmen and patriots.

(b) "WE MUST ABOLISH PRIVILEGE" *

I am very glad indeed to have this opportunity to address the two Houses directly and to verify for myself the impression that the President of the United States is a person, not a mere department of the Government hailing Congress from some isolated island of jealous power, sending messages, not speaking naturally and with his own voice—that he is a human being trying to cooperate with other human beings in a common service. After this pleasant experience I shall feel quite normal in all our dealings with one another.

I have called the Congress together in extraordinary session because a duty was laid upon the party now in power at the recent elections which it ought to perform promptly, in order that the burden carried by the people under existing law may be lightened as soon as possible and in order, also, that the business interests of the country may not be kept too long in suspense as to what the fiscal changes

* Woodrow Wilson, address to Congress in special session, April 8, 1913. From *A Compilation of the Messages and Papers of the Presidents*, XVI, pp. 7871-7873. Published by Bureau of National Literature, Inc., New York.

are to be to which they will be required to adjust themselves. It is clear to the whole country that the tariff duties must be altered. They must be changed to meet the radical alteration in the conditions of our economic life which the country has witnessed within the last generation. While the whole face and method of our industrial and commercial life were being changed beyond recognition the tariff schedules have remained what they were before the change began or have moved in the direction they were given when no large circumstance of our industrial development was what it is to-day. Our task is to square them with the actual facts. The sooner that is done the sooner we shall escape from suffering from the facts and the sooner our men of business will be free to thrive by the law of nature (the nature of free business) instead of by the law of legislation and artificial arrangement.

We have seen tariff legislation wander very far afield in our day—very far indeed from the field in which our prosperity might have had a normal growth and stimulation. No one who looks the facts squarely in the face or knows anything that lies beneath the surface of action can fail to perceive the principles upon which recent tariff legislation has been based. We long ago passed beyond the modest notion of "protecting" the industries of the country and moved boldly forward to the idea that they were entitled to the direct patronage of the Government. For a long time—a time so long that the men now active in public policy hardly remember the conditions that preceded it—we have sought in our tariff schedules to give each group of manufacturers or producers what they themselves thought that they needed in order to maintain a practically exclusive market as against the rest of the world. Consciously or unconsciously, we have built up a set of privileges and exemptions from competition behind which it was easy by any, even the crudest, forms of combination to organize monopoly; until at last nothing is normal, nothing is obliged to stand the tests of efficiency and economy, in our world of big business, but everything thrives by concerted arrangement. Only new principles of action will save us from a final hard crystallization of monopoly and a complete loss of the influences that quicken enterprise and keep independent energy alive.

It is plain what those principles must be. We must abolish everything that bears even the semblance of privilege or of any kind of artificial advantage, and put our business men and producers under the stimulation of a constant necessity to be efficient, economical, and enterprising, masters of competitive supremacy, better workers and merchants than any in the world. Aside from the duties laid upon articles which we do not, and probably can not, produce, therefore, and the duties laid upon luxuries and merely for the sake of the revenues they yield, the object of the tariff duties henceforth laid must be effective competition, the whetting of American wits by contest with the wits of the rest of the world.

It would be unwise to move toward this end headlong, with reckless haste, or with strokes that cut at the very roots of what has grown up amongst us by long process and at our own invitation. It does not alter a thing to upset it and break it and deprive it of a chance to change. It destroys it. We must make changes in our fiscal laws, in our fiscal system, whose object is development, a more free and wholesome development, not revolution or upset or confusion. We must build up trade, especially foreign trade. We need the outlet and the enlarged field of energy more than we ever did before. We must build up industry as well, and must adopt free-

dom in the place of artificial stimulation only so far as it will build, not pull down. In dealing with the tariff the method by which this may be done will be a matter of judgment, exercised item by item. To some not accustomed to the excitements and responsibilities of greater freedom our methods may in some respects and at some points seem heroic, but remedies may be heroic and yet be remedies. It is our business to make sure that they are genuine remedies. Our object is clear. If our motive is above just challenge and only an occasional error of judgment is chargeable against us, we shall be fortunate.

We are called upon to render the country a great service in more matters than one. Our responsibility should be met and our methods should be thorough, as thorough as moderate and well considered, based upon the facts as they are, and not worked out as if we were beginners. We are to deal with the facts of our own day, with the facts of no other, and to make laws which square with those facts. It is best, indeed it is necessary, to begin with the tariff. I will urge nothing upon you now at the opening of your session which can obscure that first object or divert our energies from that clearly defined duty. At a later time I may take the liberty of calling your attention to reforms which should press close upon the heels of the tariff changes, if not accompany them, of which the chief is the reform of our banking and currency laws; but just now I refrain. For the present, I put these matters on one side and think only of this one thing—of the changes in our fiscal system which may best serve to open once more the free channels of prosperity to a great people whom we would serve to the utmost and throughout both rank and file.

11

Monetary Reform

☆   *One of the first fruits of the Wilson administration was the enactment of the Federal Reserve Act in 1913, which effected long overdue reforms in the country's monetary system. This act was designed to adjust the flow of the nation's currency to meet the requirements of a commercial society.* *   ☆

Experience had shown that the system of accumulating and impounding reserves for the national banks of the reserve cities, as well as those of the country banks, in the three "central reserve" cities of New York, Chicago, and St. Louis worked badly. The funds of the banks throughout the country were stored up and concentrated in these three cities. The banks in these cities, especially in New York, had become accustomed to lending largely in Wall Street on demand, on bond and stock collateral, the reserve balances which these banks held for other banks, and upon which they usually paid the depositing banks 2 per cent per annum interest. Periodically, or in the crop-moving season, when the country banks had to withdraw their deposits from the centers, the national banks in the large cities would call in these loans on bonds and stocks, money rates would advance, and stocks decline. This process went on from year to year.

When there was sudden strain and need, as in 1893 and 1907, the banks

* From *Annual Report of the Comptroller of the Currency to the First Session of the Sixty-fourth Congress of the United States,* December 6, 1915, Washington, 1916, pp. 2-4.

throughout the country having or anticipating a demand from their customers for money would seek to draw in their balances from New York and the other large cities. The New York banks, however, at these times unable to meet the demands upon them, would suspend currency shipments and resort to the usual remedy of issuing clearing-house certificates for protection until normal conditions should be resumed, and the banks in other large cities thereupon generally would be forced to follow the lead set by the New York banks, would hold onto the money of their correspondents, and issue clearing-house certificates, while currency was being bought and sold at a premium of 2 to 5 per cent.

AIMS OF FEDERAL RESERVE SYSTEM

The Federal Reserve System has been designed to correct these and other evil and dangerous conditions and to furnish to the banks and to the people of the country new and additional banking and financial facilities by providing:

First. A currency or circulating medium which will not only pass without question at its face value in every part of the country, but which will expand when necessary to meet legitimate demands of increasing business, and which will also contract at the proper time when no longer required and when its continuance in circulation would threaten or promote inflation.

Second. An improved system for the management and handling of the bank reserves, whereby these reserves become readily and easily available to meet demands for increased money and credit and where the proper utilization of that portion of the bank reserves not held in the vaults of the respective individual banks may be made available as a means of relief and to prevent the financial crisis or market panics from which the country has suffered so often when the country banks have tried to bring home their reserves to meet the wants of their customers.

Third. A clearing or collection system by which the checks on national banks and other banks which are members of the Federal Reserve System, drawn on solvent banks by solvent drawers, may be cashed or collected at par in every part of the country, without the burden and expense of the exchange and collection charges which have been a material expense and a serious drawback to business operations.

Fourth. The Federal reserve banks furnish through their capital, their large deposits, and their note-issuing power the facilities by which all members of the system, in any emergency, may rediscount their eligible paper and obtain funds to meet any sudden or unexpected demands. These reserve banks also provide their member banks in ordinary times with money and credit to enable them to meet the legitimate demands of customers for increased accommodations when the member banks themselves have not the needed funds.

Fifth. The Federal Reserve System, by providing a source from which all well-managed banks at all times may secure funds to meet any emergency, makes unnecessary the carrying by member banks of the reserves formerly required for national banks. By the reduction in reserve requirements provided by the act the loanable funds of the national banks upon the inauguration of the Federal Reserve System were increased immediately, through the release of reserves, by an amount figured at considerably more than $400,000,000.

The other direct advantages provided by the Federal reserve act are (a) the opportunity given to national banks under certain conditions to lend money on improved, unincumbered farm property; (b) the power conferred on national banks to establish branches in foreign countries; (c) the establishment and authorization of bank acceptances; (d) the provisions for open-market operations by Federal reserve banks; and, finally (e) the adoption of the new method for the compensation of bank examiners, which insures a more thorough and systematic examination of national banks than was possible under the antiquated fee system.

12

The Farmer and the State

☆ *Woodrow Wilson took pride in the accomplishments of his administration in providing for "the betterment of rural life," as indicated in his letter of August 11, 1916, to Congressman Asbury F. Lever. Wilson's farm program advanced the Progressive Movement beyond regulation and control to direct government subsidization of the agriculturalist.* ☆

The record, legislative as well as administrative, is a remarkable one. It speaks for itself and needs only to be set forth.

1. Appreciation of the importance of agriculture has been shown through greatly and intelligently increased appropriations for its support.

2. Particular pains have been taken to foster production by every promising means, and careful thought has been given especially to the matter of increasing the meat supply of the Nation.

3. Greatly increased provision has been made, through the enactment of the cooperative agricultural extension act, for conveying agricultural information to farmers and for inducing them to apply it. This piece of legislation is one of the most significant and far-reaching measures for the education of adults ever adopted by any Government. It provides for cooperation between the States and the Federal Government. This is a highly important and significant principle. When the act is in full operation there will be

* From *Congressional Record,* 64th Congress, 1st session, appn., pp. 1762-1763.

expended annually under its terms, from Federal and State sources alone, a total of over $8,600,000 in the direct education of the farmer; and this amount is being and will be increasingly supplemented by contributions from local sources. It will permit the placing in each of the 2,850 rural counties of the Nation two farm demonstrators and specialists, who will assist the demonstrators in the more difficult problems confronting them.

4. Systematic provision for the first time has been made for the solution of problems in that important half of agriculture which concerns distribution marketing, rural finance, and rural organization.

5. Provision was made promptly for the creation of an Office of Markets and Rural Organization, and the appropriations for this office, including those for enforcing new laws designed to promote better marketing, have been increased to $1,200,000. The more difficult problems of marketing are being investigated and plans are in operation for furnishing assistance to producers of perishables through a market news service. A simi-

lar service for live-stock interests will be inaugurated during the year.

6. The problem of securing the uniform grading of staple crops, of regulating dealings and traffic in them, of developing a better system of warehouses, and of providing more available collateral for farm loans has been successfully dealt with.

7. Under the cotton-futures act standards for cotton have been established, the operations of the future exchanges have been put under supervision, and the sale of cotton has been placed on a firmer basis.

8. The United States grain-standards act will secure uniformity in the grading of grain, enable the farmer to obtain fairer prices for his product, and afford him an incentive to raise better grades of grain.

9. The United States warehouse act will enable the Department of Agriculture to license bonded warehouses in the various States. It will lead to the development of better storage facilities for staple crops and will make possible the issuance of reliable warehouse receipts which will be widely and easily negotiable.

10. Of no less importance for agriculture and for the national development is the Federal aid road act. This measure will conduce to the establishment of more effective highway machinery in each State, strongly influence the development of good road building along right lines, stimulate larger production and better marketing, promote a fuller and more attractive rural life, add greatly to the convenience and economic welfare of all the people, and strengthen the national foundations. The act embodies sound principles of road legislation and will safeguard the expenditure of the funds arising under the act not only, but will also result in the more efficient use of the large additional sums made available by States and localities.

11. The Federal reserve act benefits the farmer, as it does all the other people of the Nation, by guaranteeing better banking, safeguarding the credit structure of the country, and preventing panics. It takes particular note of the special needs of the farmer by making larger provision for loans through national banks on farm mortgages and by giving farm paper a maturity period of six months.

12. It was essential, however, that banking machinery be devised which would reach intimately into the rural districts, that it should operate on terms suited to the farmer's needs, and should be under sympathetic management. The need was for machinery which would introduce business methods into farm finance, bring order out of chaos, reduce the cost of handling farm loans, place upon the market mortgages which would be a safe investment for private funds, attract into agricultural operations a fair share of the capital of the Nation, and lead to a reduction of interest. These needs and these ideals have been met by the enactment of the Federal farm-loan act.

IV

united states: great world power

A S EARLY as 1890, farsighted observers, like Captain Alfred Thayer Mahan, saw indications of change in American foreign policy. They saw in the development of the nation's industrial capacity a growing need to secure distant markets. They urged that the United States prepare to go out into the world of events and opportunities.

The emergence of the United States as a great world power came by the end of the century. With the annexation of Hawaii, and of the Philippines, Guam, and Puerto Rico, an American empire was begun. A new world opened to Americans who saw in these possessions incalculable economic advantages and the opportunity to play the part of "trustee, under God, of the civilization of the world." To Brooks Adams, the ramifications of American expansion were clear. The United States had been caught up in trends which offered world economic supremacy. The nation was reaching out for that supremacy, though to achieve it, and to retain it, great changes were necessary in the attitudes and organization of the nation. Others who foresaw important changes in American life as a result of expansion were not convinced that such changes or expansion itself were of value to the United States. Like William Graham Sumner, they warned that our military victory over Spain was not a victory at all; it was a conquest of the United States by the decadent ideas and methods of imperialist Spain.

Despite such warnings, the country had decided to pursue the task of being a world power. Much time was given to defining the relationships of the continental United States to its possessions, for the salutary "development of . . . the American empire." Yet the nation was realistic in appraising the value of empire. The primary goal, from the beginning, was not the acquisition of territorial possessions or even of protectorates but rather American economic expansion. This was seen in the attempt of Secretary of State John Hay to secure equal trading privileges for the United States in China, and in Theodore Roosevelt's Corollary to the Monroe Doctrine to stimulate order in neighboring countries to eliminate pretexts for foreign intervention and to facilitate American trade. President Taft gave a name to it—"Dollar Diplomacy." Even though some of his key projects failed and though President Wilson initially repudiated the idea, "Dollar Diplomacy" continued to be an important part of American foreign relations. Exports, imports, and investments abroad, aided by American diplomatic efforts, mounted year after year.

One important sidelight of American foreign policy between the Spanish War and World War I was the zeal of the government and the people for peace, world peace. While armed force was used occasionally as an instrument of foreign policy, it was a distasteful instrument. The expansion of the United States was accompanied by actions for peace which led to the intense efforts to establish an international system of arbitration or conciliation treaties to eliminate the bases of war. Even the military interventions of the United States were justified by reasons of insuring peace and stability in the areas affected and of securing to the nation the right to peaceful trade abroad.

1

Looking Outward

☆ *Alfred Thayer Mahan (1840-1914), naval officer and historian, popularized through his writings the significance of sea power in national development. The following selection, from an essay originally published in 1890, stresses the role which Mahan thought sea power should play in the future of the United States.** ☆

Indications are not wanting of an approaching change in the thoughts and policy of Americans as to their relations with the world outside their own borders. For the past quarter of a century, the predominant idea, which has asserted itself successfully at the polls and shaped the course of the government, has been to preserve the home market for the home industries. The employer and the workman alike have been taught to look at the various economical measures proposed from this point of view, to regard with hostility any step favoring the intrusion of the foreign producer upon their own domain, and rather to demand increasingly rigorous measures of exclusion than to acquiesce in any loosening of the chain that binds the consumer to them. The inevitable consequence has followed, as in all cases when the mind or the eye is exclusively fixed in one direction, that the danger of loss or the prospect of advantage in another quarter has been overlooked; and although the abounding resources of the country have

* From A. T. Mahan, "The United States Looking Outward," *The Interest of America in Sea Power, Present and Future,* pp. 3-6, 13-16, 26. Published by Little, Brown and Company, Boston, 1898.

maintained the exports at a high figure, this flattering result has been due more to the superabundant bounty of Nature than to the demand of other nations for our protected manufactures.

For nearly the lifetime of a generation, therefore, American industries have been thus protected, until the practice has assumed the force of a tradition, and is clothed in the mail of conservatism. In their mutual relations, these industries resemble the activities of a modern iron-clad that has heavy armor, but inferior engines and guns; mighty for defence, weak for offence. Within, the home market is secured; but outside, beyond the broad seas, there are the markets of the world, that can be entered and controlled only by a vigorous contest, to which the habit of trusting to protection by statute does not conduce. . . .

To affirm the importance of distant markets, and the relation to them of our own immense powers of production, implies logically the recognition of the link that joins the products and the markets,— that is, the carrying trade; the three together constituting that chain of maritime power to which Great Britain owes her wealth and greatness. Further, is it too much to say that, as two of these links, the shipping and the markets, are exterior to our own borders, the acknowledgment of them carries with it a view of the relations of the United States to the world radically distinct from the simple idea of self-sufficingness? We shall not follow far this line of thought before there will dawn the realization of America's unique position, facing the older worlds of the East and West, her shores washed by the oceans which touch the one or the other, but which are common to her alone. . . .

Despite a certain great original superiority conferred by our geographical nearness and immense resources,—due, in other words, to our natural advantages, and not to our intelligent preparations,—the United States is woefully unready, not only in fact but in purpose, to assert . . . a weight of influence proportioned to the extent of her interests. We have not the navy, and, what is worse, we are not willing to have the navy, that will weigh seriously in any disputes with those nations whose interests will conflict . . . with our own. We have not, and we are not anxious to provide, the defence of the seaboard which will leave the navy free for its work at sea. We have not, but many other powers have, positions, either within or on the borders of the Caribbean, which not only possess great natural advantages for the control of that sea, but have received and are receiving that artificial strength of fortification and armament which will make them practically inexpugnable. On the contrary, we have not on the Gulf of Mexico even the beginning of a navy yard which could serve as the base of our operations. Let me not be misunderstood. I am not regretting that we have not the means to meet on terms of equality the great navies of the Old World. I recognize, what few at least say, that, despite its great

surplus revenue, this country is poor in proportion to its length of seaboard and its exposed points. That which I deplore, and which is a sober, just, and reasonable cause of deep national concern, is that the nation neither has nor cares to have its sea frontier so defended, and its navy of such power, as shall suffice, with the advantages of our position, to weigh seriously when inevitable discussions arise, —such as we have recently had about Samoa and Bering Sea, and which may at any moment come up about the Caribbean Sea or the canal. Is the United States, for instance, prepared to allow Germany to acquire the Dutch stronghold of Curaçao, fronting the Atlantic outlet of both the proposed canals of Panama and Nicaragua? Is she prepared to acquiesce in any foreign power purchasing from Haiti a naval station on the Windward Passage, through which pass our steamer routes to the Isthmus? Would she acquiesce in a foreign protectorate over the Sandwich Islands, that great central station of the Pacific, equidistant from San Francisco, Samoa, and the Marquesas, and an important post on our lines of communication with both Australia and China? Or will it be maintained that any one of these questions, supposing it to arise, is so exclusively one-sided, the arguments of policy and right so exclusively with us, that the other party will at once yield his eager wish, and gracefully withdraw? Was it so at Samoa? Is it so as regards Bering Sea? The motto seen on so many ancient cannon, *Ultima ratio regum,* is not without its message to republics. . . .

To provide [adequate defense], three things are needful: First, protection of the chief harbors, by fortifications and coast-defence ships, which gives defensive strength, provides security to the community within, and supplies the bases necessary to all military operations. Secondly, naval force, the arm of offensive power, which alone enables a country to extend its influence outward. Thirdly, it should be an inviolable resolution of our national policy, that no foreign state should henceforth acquire a coaling position within three thousand miles of San Francisco,—a distance which includes the Hawaiian and Galapagos islands and the coast of Central America. For fuel is the life of modern naval war; it is the food of the ship; without it the modern monsters of the deep die of inanition. Around it, therefore, cluster some of the most important considerations of naval strategy. In the Caribbean and in the Atlantic we are confronted with many a foreign coal depot, bidding us to stand to our arms, even as Carthage bade Rome; but let us not acquiesce in an addition to our dangers, a further diversion of our strength, by being forestalled in the North Pacific.

2

New Empire

☆ *Brooks Adams perceived the position of the United States as the growing center of world commerce, and anticipated the need for a reorientation of American ways of life to take advantage of its new opportunities.** ☆

The United Kingdom, the supposed seat of energy, of capital, and of empire, engaged in a petty broil with 50,000 farmers, with undisputed control of the sea, and a fortified base adjoining the enemy's frontier, not only failed to concentrate her forces in the field as rapidly and effectively as the Japanese, but with prostrated trade had to rely on France and the United States for financial support, and upon her colonies for men. She could not fill her ranks from her own citizens. Mark also the content of the British public with their military performance. Throughout the war they made no serious effort to improve, and since the peace they exult as in an heroic victory. He who reads the letters of Symmachus may observe the same complacency on the eve of the sack of Rome. Inertia pervades all English society. The system of education is admittedly defective because controlled by the clergy, who are a conservative class, and yet the hold of the clergy upon the schools is unshaken. The relative decline in the purchasing power of England may be gauged by a single

* From Brooks Adams, *The New Empire,* pp. 207-211. Published by The Macmillan Company, New York, 1902.

example. A generation ago the United Kingdom bought two-thirds of the total American cotton crop. She now buys less than a quarter.

In industry the same phenomenon appears. As lately as 1866 she manufactured 48.7 per cent of the pig iron of the world. In 1901 only 19.2. Gold mining is, perhaps, the occupation which most excites the British imagination, and yet the British cannot work their own property. "The great mining magnates of South Africa, having the whole world before them to choose from, have preferred American mining engineers, and as the mining industry in South Africa has proved to be so marvellous a success, it is hardly necessary to add that the result has justified the selection."

Such instances might be multiplied, but these suffice. Each man can ponder the history of the last fifty years, and judge for himself whether the facts show that Great Britain apparently lies in the wake, and Japan in the path, of the advancing social cyclone.

The world seems agreed that the United States is likely to achieve, if indeed she has not already achieved, an economic supremacy. The vortex of the cyclone is near New York. No such activity prevails elsewhere; nowhere are undertakings so gigantic, nowhere is administration so perfect; nowhere are such masses of capital centralized in single hands. And as the United States becomes an imperial market, she stretches out along the trade-routes which lead from foreign countries to her heart, as every empire has stretched out from the days of Sargon to our own. The West Indies drift toward us, the Republic of Mexico hardly longer has an independent life, and the city of Mexico is an American town. With the completion of the Panama Canal all Central America will become a part of our system. We have expanded into Asia, we have attracted the fragments of the Spanish dominions, and reaching out into China we have checked the advance of Russia and Germany, in territory which, until yesterday, had been supposed to be beyond our sphere. We are penetrating into Europe, and Great Britain especially is gradually assuming the position of a dependency, which must rely on us as the base from which she draws her food in peace, and without which she could not stand in war.

Supposing the movement of the next fifty years only to equal that of the last, instead of undergoing a prodigious acceleration, the United States will outweigh any single empire, if not all empires combined. The whole world will pay her tribute. Commerce will flow to her both from east and west, and the order which has existed from the dawn of time will be reversed.

But if commerce, instead of flowing from east to west, as heretofore, changes its direction, trade-routes must be displaced, and the political organisms which rest upon those routes must lose their foundation. Russia, for example, could hardly continue to exist in her present form if the commerce of Siberia were to flow toward America instead of toward the Baltic. Yet if Russia should disintegrate she would disintegrate because of causes so widespread and deep-working that they would affect Great Britain with equal energy; for the inference to be drawn from human experience is that the rise of a new dominant market indicates the recentralization of trade-routes, and with trade-routes, of empires. Such changes, should they occur, would clearly alter the whole complexion of civilization. Speculation concerning their character, or the time of their advent, would be futile, as history offers no precedent by which we can measure the effects to be anticipated from an alteration so radical as the reversal of the direction of the channel of trade. It may, however, be permissible to draw certain inferences regarding the present.

Society is now moving with intense velocity, and masses are gathering bulk with proportionate rapidity. There is some reason also to surmise that the equilibrium is correspondingly delicate and unstable. If so apparently slight a cause as a fall in prices for a decade has sufficed to propel the seat of empire across the Atlantic, an equally slight derangement of the administrative functions of the United States might force it to cross the Pacific. The metallic resources of China are not inferior to ours, and distance offers daily less impediment to the migration of capital. Prudence, therefore, would dictate the adoption of measures to minimize the likelihood of sudden shocks. As Nature increases the velocity of movement, she augments her demands on human adaptability. She allowed our ancestors a century to become habituated to innovations which we must accept forthwith. Those who fail to keep the pace are discarded. Conversely, those who, other things being equal, first reach an adjustment, retain or improve a relative advantage. Under such circumstances but one precaution can be taken against the chances of the future. That intellectual quality can be strengthened on which falls the severest strain, so that our descendants may be prepared to meet any eventuality. The young can be trained to adaptability. The methods are perfectly understood; the difficulty lies in application. Success in the future promises, largely, to turn on the power of rapid generalization, for administration is only the practical side of generalization. It is the faculty of reducing details to an intelligent order. The masses generated in modern life exercise this faculty in its highest form.

On its theoretical side generalization necessitates the maintenance of an open mind. It is inconsistent with subserviency to *a priori* dogmas. Nothing is permitted to stand as fixed, and the individual is trained to hold the judgment in suspense, subject to new evidence. Such a temper of the mind tends to reduce the friction of adjustment.

If the New Empire should develop, it must be an enormous complex mass, to be administered only by means of a cheap, elastic, and simple machinery; an old and clumsy mechanism must, sooner or later, collapse, and in sinking may involve a civilization. If these deductions are sound, there is but one great boon which the passing generation can confer upon its successors: it can aid them to ameliorate that servitude to tradition which has so often retarded submission to the inevitable until too late.

3

Spain the Victor?

☆ *William Graham Sumner (1840-1910), pioneer social scientist, scornfully rejected the notion that the United States had become a great nation by defeating bankrupt and impotent Spain. He saw the expansion of the United States as a radical change from past American practices and ideals, a change representing a decline of true American greatness.* ☆*

During the last year the public has been familiarized with descriptions of Spain and of Spanish methods of doing things until the name of Spain has become a symbol for a certain well-defined set of notions and policies. On the other hand, the name of the United States has always been, for all of us, a symbol for a state of things, a set of ideas and traditions, a group of views about social and political affairs. Spain was the first, for a long time the greatest, of the modern imperialistic states. The United States, by its historical origin, its traditions, and its principles, is the chief representative of the revolt and reaction against that kind of a state. . . . We have beaten Spain in a military conflict, but we are submitting to be conquered by her on the field of ideas and policies. . . .

There is not a civilized nation which does not talk about its civilizing mission just as grandly as we do. . . . [yet] the most important thing which we shall inherit from the Spaniards will be the task

of suppressing rebellions. If the United States takes out of the hands of Spain her mission, on the ground that Spain is not executing it well, and if this nation in its turn attempts to be school-mistress to others, it will shrivel up into the same vanity and self-conceit of which Spain now presents an example. To read our current literature one would think that we were already well on the way to it. Now, the great reason why all these enterprises which begin by saying to somebody else, We know what is good for you better than you know yourself and we are going to make you do it, are false and wrong is that they violate liberty; or, to turn the same statement into other words, the reason why liberty, of which we Americans talk so much, is a good thing is that it means leaving people to live out their own lives in their own way, while we do the same. If we believe in liberty, as an American principle, why do we not stand by it . . .?

The doctrine that we are to take away from other nations any possessions of theirs which we think that we could manage better than they are managing

* From William Graham Sumner, "The Conquest of the United States By Spain" [1898] *War and Other Essays,* pp. 297-334 *passim.* Copyright, 1911, Yale University Press, New Haven. Used by permission.

them, or that we are to take in hand any countries which we do not think capable of self-government, is one which will lead us very far. With that doctrine in the background, our politicians will have no trouble to find a war ready for us the next time that they come around to the point where they think that it is time for us to have another. We are told that we must have a big army hereafter. What for; unless we propose to do again by and by what we have just done? In that case our neighbors have reason to ask themselves whom we will attack next. They must begin to arm, too, and by our act the whole western world is plunged into the distress under which the eastern world is groaning. Here is another point in regard to which the conservative elements in the country are making a great mistake to allow all this militarism and imperialism to go on without protest. It will be established as a rule that, whenever political ascendency is threatened, it can be established again by a little war, filling the minds of the people with glory and diverting their attention from their own interests. Hard-headed old Benjamin Franklin hit the point when, referring back to the days of Marlborough, he talked about the "pest of glory." The thirst for glory is an epidemic which robs a people of their judgment, seduces their vanity, cheats them of their interests, and corrupts their consciences. . . .

The United States is in a protected situation. It is easy to have equality where land is abundant and where the population is small. It is easy to have prosperity where a few men have a great continent to exploit. It is easy to have liberty when you have no dangerous neighbors and when the struggle for existence is easy. There are no severe penalties, under such circumstances, for political mistakes. Democracy is not then a thing to be nursed and defended, as it is in an old country like France. It is rooted and founded in the economic circumstances of the country. The orators and constitution-makers do not make democracy. They are made by it. This protected position, however, is sure to pass away. . . .

Now what will hasten the day when our present advantages will wear out and when we shall come down to the conditions of the older and densely populated nations? The answer is: war, debt, taxation, diplomacy, a grand governmental system, pomp, glory, a big army and navy, lavish expenditures, political jobbery—in a word, imperialism. In the old days the democratic masses of this country, who knew little about our modern doctrines of social philosophy, had a sound instinct on these matters, and it is no small ground of political disquietude to see it decline. They resisted every appeal to their vanity in the way of pomp and glory which they knew must be paid for. They dreaded a public debt and a standing army. They were narrow-minded and went too far with these notions, but they were, at least, right, if they wanted to strengthen democracy.

The great foe of democracy now and in the near future is plutocracy. Every year that passes brings out this antagonism more distinctly. It is to be the social war of the twentieth century. In that war militarism, expansion and imperialism will all favor plutocracy. In the first place, war and expansion will favor jobbery, both in the dependencies and at home. In the second place, they will take away the attention of the people from what the plutocrats are doing. In the third place, they will cause large expenditures of the people's money, the return for which will not go into the treasury, but into the hands of a few schemers. In the fourth place, they will call for a large public debt and taxes, and these things especially tend to make men unequal, because any social burdens bear more heavily on the weak than on the strong, and so make the weak weaker and the strong stronger. Therefore expansion and imperialism are a grand onslaught on democracy.

The point which I have tried to make in this lecture is that expansion and imperialism are at war with the best traditions, principles, and interests of the American people, and that they will plunge us into a network of difficult problems and political perils, which we might have avoided, while they offer us no corresponding advantage in return. . . .

Another answer which the imperialists make is that Americans can do anything. They say that they do not shrink from responsibilities. . . . [Yet,] the Americans in Connecticut cannot abolish the rotten borough system. . . , Americans cannot reform the pension list. Its abuses are rooted in the methods of democratic self-government, and no one dares to touch them. . . . Americans cannot disentangle their currency from the confusion into which it was thrown by the Civil War, and they cannot put it on a simple, sure, and sound basis which would give stability to the business of the country. . . . Americans cannot assure the suffrage to negroes throughout the United States; they have tried it for thirty years and now, contemporaneously with this war with Spain, it has been finally demonstrated that it is a failure. . . . Worse still, Americans cannot assure life, liberty, and the pursuit of happiness to negroes inside of the United States. When the negro postmaster's house was set on fire in the night in South Carolina, and not only he, but his wife and children, were murdered as they came out, and when, moreover, this incident passed without legal investigation or punishment, it was a bad omen for the extension of liberty, etc., to Malays and Tagals by simply setting over them the American flag. . . . Therefore prudence demands that we look ahead to see what we are about to do, and that we gauge the means at our disposal, if we do not

want to bring calamity on ourselves and our children. We see that the peculiarities of our system of government set limitations on us. We cannot do things which a great centralized monarchy could do. The very blessings and special advantages which we enjoy, as compared with others, bring disabilities with them. That is the great fundamental cause of what I have tried to show throughout this lecture, that we cannot govern dependencies consistently with our political system, and that, if we try it, the State which our fathers founded will suffer a reaction which will transform it into another empire just after the fashion of all the old ones. . . .

And yet this scheme of a republic which our fathers formed was a glorious dream which demands more than a word of respect and affection before it passes away. . . . They could not, it is true, strip their minds of the ideas which they had inherited, but in time, as they lived on in the new world, they sifted and selected these ideas, retaining what they chose. Of the old-world institutions also they selected and adopted what they chose and threw aside the rest. It was a grand opportunity to be thus able to strip off all the follies and errors which they had inherited, so far as they chose to do so. They had unlimited land with no feudal restrictions to hinder them in the use of it. Their idea was that they would never allow any of the social and political abuses of the old world to grow up here. There should be no manors, no barons, no ranks, no prelates, no idle classes, no paupers, no disinherited ones except the vicious. There were to be no armies except a militia, which would have no functions but those of police. They would have no court and no pomp; no orders, or ribbons, or decorations, or titles. They would have no public debt. They repudiated with scorn the notion that a public debt is a public blessing; if debt was incurred in war it was to be paid in peace and not entailed on posterity. There was to be no grand diplomacy, because they intended to mind their own business and not be involved in any of the intrigues to which European statesmen were accustomed. There was to be no balance of power and no "reason of state" to cost the life and happiness of citizens. . . . Our fathers would have economical government, even if grand people called it a parsimonious one, and taxes should be no greater than were absolutely necessary to pay for such a government. The citizen was to keep all the rest of his earnings and use them as he thought best for the happiness of himself and his family; he was, above all, to be insured peace and quiet while he pursued his honest industry and obeyed the laws. No adventurous policies of conquest or ambition, such as, in the belief of our fathers, kings and nobles had forced, for their own advantage, on European states, would ever be undertaken by a free democratic republic. Therefore the citizen here would never be forced to leave his family or to give his sons to shed blood for glory and to leave widows and orphans in misery for nothing. Justice and law were to reign in the midst of simplicity, and a government which had little to do was to offer little field for ambition. In a society where industry, frugality, and prudence were honored, it was believed that the vices of wealth would never flourish.

We know that these beliefs, hopes, and intentions have been only partially fulfilled. We know that, as time has gone on and we have grown numerous and rich, some of these things have proved impossible ideals, incompatible with a large and flourishing society, but it is by virtue of this conception of a commonwealth that the United States has stood for something unique and grand in the history of mankind and that its people have been happy. It is by virtue of these ideals that we have been "isolated," isolated in a position which the other nations of the earth have observed in silent envy; and yet there are people who are boasting of their patriotism, because they say that we have taken our place now amongst the nations of the earth by virtue of this war. My patriotism is of the kind which is outraged by the notion that the United States never was a great nation until in a petty three months' campaign it knocked to pieces a poor, decrepit, bankrupt old state like Spain. To hold such an opinion as that is to abandon all American standards, to put shame and scorn on all that our ancestors tried to build up here, and to go over to the standards of which Spain is a representative.

4

America's Destiny

☆ Albert J. Beveridge (1862-1927) was United States senator from Indiana, 1899 to 1911. In a speech to the Senate, January 9, 1900, Senator Beveridge maintained that it was our duty—to ourselves and to the Filipinos—to retain and develop the Philippine Islands.* ☆

Mr. President, the times call for candor. The Philippines are ours forever, "territory belonging to the United States," as the Constitution calls them. And just beyond the Philippines are China's illimitable markets. We will not retreat from either. We will not repudiate our duty in the archipelago. We will not abandon our opportunity in the Orient. We will not renounce our part in the mission of our race, trustee, under God, of the civilization of the world. And we will move forward to our work, not howling out regrets like slaves whipped to their burdens, but with gratitude for a task worthy of our strength, and thanksgiving to Almighty God that He has marked us as His chosen people, henceforth to lead in the regeneration of the world.

This island empire is the last land left in all the oceans. If it should prove a mistake to abandon it, the blunder once made would be irretrievable. If it proves a mistake to hold it, the error can be corrected when we will. Every other progressive nation stands ready to relieve us.

But to hold it will be no mistake. Our largest trade henceforth must be with Asia. The Pacific is our ocean. More and more Europe will manufacture the most it needs, secure from its colonies the most it consumes. Where shall we turn for consumers of our surplus? Geography answers the question. China is our natural customer. She is nearer to us than to England, Germany, or Russia, the commercial powers of the present and the future. They have moved nearer to China by securing permanent bases on her borders. The Philippines give us a base at the door of all the East.

Lines of navigation from our ports to the Orient and Australia; from the Isthmian Canal to Asia; from all Oriental ports to Australia, converge at and separate from the Philippines. They are a self-supporting, dividend-paying fleet, permanently anchored at a spot selected by the strategy of Providence, commanding the Pacific. And the Pacific is the ocean of the commerce of the future. Most future wars will be conflicts for commerce. The power that rules the Pacific, therefore, is the power that rules the world. And, with the Philippines, that power is and will forever be the American Republic. . . .

* From *Congressional Record*, 56th Congress, 1st session, pp. 704-712.

Nothing is so natural as trade with one's neighbors. The Philippines make us the nearest neighbors of all the East. Nothing is more natural than to trade with those you know. This is the philosophy of all advertising. The Philippines bring us permanently face to face with the most sought-for customers of the world. National prestige, national propinquity, these and commercial activity are the elements of commercial success. The Philippines give the first; the character of the American people supply the last. It is a providential conjunction of all the elements of trade, of duty, and of power. If we are willing to go to war rather than let England have a few feet of frozen Alaska, which affords no market and commands none, what should we not do rather than let England, Germany, Russia, or Japan have all the Philippines? And no man on the spot can fail to see that this would be their fate if we retired. . . .

Here, then, Senators, is the situation. Two years ago there was no land in all the world which we could occupy for any purpose. Our commerce was daily turning toward the Orient, and geography and trade developments made necessary our commercial empire over the Pacific. And in that ocean we had no commercial, naval, or military base. To-day we have one of the three great ocean possessions of the globe, located at the most commanding commercial, naval, and military points in the eastern seas, within hail of India, shoulder to shoulder with China, richer in its own resources than any equal body of land on the entire globe, and peopled by a race which civilization demands shall be improved. Shall we abandon it? That man little knows the common people of the Republic, little understands the instincts of our race, who thinks we will not hold it fast and hold it forever, administering just government by simplest methods. We may trick up devices to shift

our burden and lessen our opportunity; they will avail us nothing but delay. We may tangle conditions by applying academic arrangements of self-government to a crude situation; their failure will drive us to our duty in the end. . . .

But, Senators, it would be better to abandon this combined garden and Gibralter of the Pacific, and count our blood and treasure already spent a profitable loss, than to apply any academic arrangement of self-government to these children. They are not capable of self-government. How could they be? They are not of a self-governing race. They are Orientals, Malays, instructed by Spaniards in the latter's worst estate.

They know nothing of practical government except as they have witnessed the weak, corrupt, cruel, and capricious rule of Spain. What magic will anyone employ to dissolve in their minds and characters those impressions of governors and governed which three centuries of misrule have created? What alchemy will change the oriental quality of their blood and set the self-governing currents of the American pouring through their Malay veins? How shall they, in the twinkling of an eye, be exalted to the heights of self-governing peoples which required a thousand years for us to reach, Anglo-Saxon though we are . . . ?

The Declaration of Independence does not forbid us to do our part in the regeneration of the world. If it did, the Declaration would be wrong, just as the Articles of Confederation, drafted by the very same men who signed the Declaration, was found to be wrong. The Declaration has no application to the present situation. It was written by self-governing men for self-governing men. . . .

Senators in opposition are estopped from denying our constitutional power to govern the Philippines as circumstances may demand, for such power is admitted in the case of Florida, Louisiana, Alaska.

How, then, is it denied in the Philippines? Is there a geographical interpretation to the Constitution? Do degrees of longitude fix constitutional limitations? Does a thousand miles of ocean diminish constitutional power more than a thousand miles of land . . . ?

No; the oceans are not limitations of the power which the Constitution expressly gives Congress to govern all territory the nation may acquire. The Constitution declares that "Congress shall have power to dispose of and make all needful rules and regulations respecting the territory belonging to the United States." Not the Northwest Territory only; not Louisiana or Florida only; not territory on this continent only, but any territory anywhere belonging to the nation. The founders of the nation were not provincial. Theirs was the geography of the world. They were soldiers as well as landsmen, and they knew that where our ships should go our flag might follow. They had the logic of progress, and they knew that the Republic they were planting must, in obedience to the laws of our expanding race, necessarily develop into the greater Republic which the world beholds to-day, and into the still mightier Republic which the world will finally acknowledge as the arbiter, under God, of the destinies of mankind. And so our fathers wrote into the Constitution these words of growth, of expansion, of empire, if you will, unlimited by geography or climate or by anything but the vitality and possibilities of the American people: "Congress shall have power to dispose of and make all needful rules and regulations respecting the territory belonging to the United States. . . ."

Mr. President, this question is deeper than any question of party politics; deeper than any question of the isolated policy of our country even; deeper even than any question of constitutional power. It is elemental. It is racial. God has not been preparing the English-speaking and Teutonic peoples for a thousand years for nothing but vain and idle self-contemplation and self-admiration. No! He has made us the master organizers of the world to establish system where chaos reigns. He has given us the spirit of progress to overwhelm the forces of reaction throughout the earth. He has made us adepts in government that we may administer government among savage and senile peoples. Were it not for such a force as this the world would relapse into barbarism and night. And of all our race He has marked the American people as His chosen nation to finally lead in the regeneration of the world. This is the divine mission of America, and it holds for us all the profit, all the glory, all the happiness possible to man. We are trustees of the world's progress, guardians of its righteous peace. The judgment of the Master is upon us: "Ye have been faithful over a few things; I will make you ruler over many things."

What shall history say of us? Shall it say that we renounced that holy trust, left the savage to his base condition, the wilderness to the reign of waste, deserted duty, abandoned glory, forgot our sordid profit even, because we feared our strength and read the charter of our powers with the doubter's eye and the quibbler's mind? Shall it say that, called by events to captain and command the proudest, ablest, purest race of history in history's noblest work, we declined that great commission? Our fathers would not have had it so. No! They founded no paralytic government, incapable of the simplest acts of administration. They planted no sluggard people, passive while the world's work calls them. They established no reactionary nation. They unfurled no retreating flag. . . .

Mr. President and Senators, adopt the resolution offered, that peace may quickly come and that we may begin our saving, regenerating, and uplifting work .... Reject it, and the world, history, and the American people will know where to forever fix the awful responsibility for the consequences that will surely follow such failure to do our manifest duty. How dare we delay when our soldiers' blood is flowing?

5

Benevolent Interventionism

☆ *The Army Appropriation Act of March 2, 1901, provided for the independence of Cuba and American responsibility to maintain that independence. This provision of the act, known as the Platt Amendment, was later incorporated in the Cuban Constitution and was confirmed in a treaty between the two nations signed May 22, 1903.** ☆

Provided further, That in fulfillment of the declaration contained in the joint resolution approved April twentieth, eighteen hundred and ninety-eight, entitled, "For the recognition of the independence of the people of Cuba, demanding that the Government of Spain relinquish its authority and government in the island of Cuba, and to withdraw its land and naval forces from Cuba and Cuban waters, and directing the President of the United States to use the land and naval forces of the United States to carry these resolutions into effect," the President is hereby authorized to "leave the government and control of the island of Cuba to its people" so soon as a government shall have been established in said island under a constitution which, either as a part thereof or in an ordinance appended thereto, shall define the future relations of the United States with Cuba, substantially as follows:

I. That the government of Cuba shall never enter into any treaty or other compact with any foreign power or powers

which will impair or tend to impair the independence of Cuba, nor in any manner authorize or permit any foreign power or powers to obtain by colonization or for military or naval purposes or otherwise, lodgment in or control over any portion of said island.

II. That said government shall not assume or contract any public debt, to pay the interest upon which, and to make reasonable sinking fund provision for the ultimate discharge of which, the ordinary revenues of the island, after defraying the current expenses of government shall be inadequate.

III. That the government of Cuba consents that the United States may exercise the right to intervene for the preservation of Cuban independence, the maintenance of a government adequate for the protection of life, property, and individual liberty, and for discharging the obligations with respect to Cuba imposed by the treaty of Paris on the United States, now to be assumed and undertaken by the government of Cuba.

IV. That all Acts of the United States in Cuba during its military occupancy

* From William M. Malloy, *Treaties, Conventions, International Acts, Protocols and Agreements Between the United States of America and Other Powers 1776-1909*, I, Washington, 1910, pp. 362-363.

thereof are ratified and validated, and all lawful rights acquired thereunder shall be maintained and protected.

V. That the government of Cuba will execute, and as far as necessary extend, the plans already devised or other plans to be mutually agreed upon, for the sanitation of the cities of the island, to the end that a recurrence of epidemic and infectious diseases may be prevented thereby assuring protection to the people and commerce of Cuba, as well as to the commerce of the southern ports of the United States and the people residing therein.

VI. That the Isle of Pines shall be omitted from the proposed constitutional boundaries of Cuba, the title thereto being left to future adjustment by treaty.

VII. That to enable the United States to maintain the independence of Cuba, and to protect the people thereof, as well as for its own defense, the government of Cuba will sell or lease to the United States lands necessary for coaling or naval stations at certain specified points to be agreed upon with the President of the United States.

VIII. That by way of further assurance the government of Cuba will embody the foregoing provisions in a permanent treaty with the United States.

6

Colonial Administration

☆ *The Foracker Act of 1900 provided a form of government for recently ceded Puerto Rico which differed considerably from the traditional American forms of territorial administration. The constitutionality of the Foracker Act was upheld by the Supreme Court in Downes v. Bidwell, 1901, on the grounds that overseas territories presented problems quite different from those previously encountered in American expansion. The opinion of the Court and Justice John Marshall Harlan's dissent are excerpted below.** ☆

MR. JUSTICE BROWN announced the conclusion and judgment of the court . . . :

We are also of opinion that the power to acquire territory by treaty implies, not only the power to govern such territory, but to prescribe upon what terms the United States will receive its inhabitants, and what their status shall be in what Chief Justice Marshall termed the "American empire." There seems to be no middle ground between this position and the doctrine that if their inhabitants do not become, immediately upon annexation, citizens of the United States, their children thereafter born, whether savages or civilized, are such, and entitled to all the rights, privileges, and immunities of citizens. If such be their status, the consequences will be extremely serious. Indeed, it is doubtful if Congress would ever assent to the annexation of territory upon the condition that its inhabitants, however foreign they may be to our habits, traditions, and modes of life, shall become at once citizens of the United States. . . .

* From 182 U.S. 244.

It is obvious that in the annexation of outlying and distant possessions grave questions will arise from differences of race, habits, laws, and customs of the people, and from differences of soil, climate, and production, which may require action on the part of Congress that would be quite unnecessary in the annexation of contiguous territory inhabited only by people of the same race, or by scattered bodies of native Indians.

We suggest, without intending to decide, that there may be a distinction between certain natural rights enforced in the Constitution by prohibitions against interference with them, and what may be termed artificial or remedial rights which are peculiar to our own system of jurisprudence. Of the former class are the rights to one's own religious opinions and to a public expression of them, or, as sometimes said, to worship God according to the dictates of one's own conscience; the right to personal liberty and individual property; to freedom of speech and of the press; to free access to courts of justice, to due process of law, and to an equal protection of the laws; to immunities from unreasonable searches and seizures, as well as cruel and unusual punishments; and to such other immunities as are indispensable to a free government. Of the latter class are the rights to citizenship, to suffrage (Minor v. Happersett, 21 Wall. 162, 22 L. ed. 627), and to the particular methods of procedure pointed out in the Constitution, which are peculiar to Anglo-Saxon jurisprudence, and some of which have already been held by the states to be unnecessary to the proper protection of individuals.

Whatever may be finally decided by the American people as to the status of these islands and their inhabitants,—whether they shall be introduced into the sisterhood of states or be permitted to form independent governments,—it does not follow that in the meantime, awaiting that decision, the people are in the matter of personal rights unprotected by the provisions of our Constitution and subject to the merely arbitrary control of Congress. Even if regarded as aliens, they are entitled under the principles of the Constitution to be protected in life, liberty, and property. This has been frequently held by this court in respect to the Chinese, even when aliens, not possessed of the political rights of citizens of the United States. . . .

We do not desire, however, to anticipate the difficulties which would naturally arise in this connection, but merely to disclaim any intention to hold that the inhabitants of these territories are subject to an unrestrained power on the part of Congress to deal with them upon the theory that they have no rights which it is bound to respect. . . .

Patriotic and intelligent men may differ widely as to the desirableness of this or that acquisition, but this is solely a political question. We can only consider this aspect of the case so far as to say that no construction of the Constitution should be adopted which would prevent Congress from considering each case upon its merits, unless the language of the instrument imperatively demand it. A false step at this time might be fatal to the development of what Chief Justice Marshall called the American empire. Choice in some cases, the natural gravitation of small bodies towards large ones in others, the result of a successful war in still others, may bring about conditions which would render the annexation of distant possessions desirable. If those possessions are inhabited by alien races, differing from us in religion, customs, laws, methods of taxation, and modes of thought, the administration of government and justice, according to Anglo-Saxon principles, may for a time be impossible; and the question at once arises whether large concessions ought not to be made for a time, that ultimately our own theories may be carried out, and the blessings of a free government under the Constitution extended to them. We decline to hold that there is anything in the Constitution to forbid such action.

We are therefore of opinion that the island of Porto Rico is a territory appurtenant and belonging to the United States, but not a part of the United States within the revenue clauses of the Constitution; that the Foraker act is constitutional, so far as it imposes duties upon imports from such island, and that the plaintiff cannot recover back the duties exacted in this case.

The judgment of the Circuit Court is therefore affirmed. . . .

MR. JUSTICE HARLAN, dissenting . . . :
I reject altogether the theory that Congress, in its discretion, can exclude the Constitution from a domestic territory of the United States, acquired, and which could only have been acquired, in virtue

of the Constitution. I cannot agree that it is a domestic territory of the United States for the purpose of preventing the application of the tariff act imposing duties upon imports from foreign countries, but not a part of the United States for the purpose of enforcing the constitutional requirement that *all* duties, imposts, and excises imposed by Congress "shall be uniform throughout the United States." How Porto Rico can be a domestic territory of the United States, as distinctly held in De Lima *v.* Bidwell, and yet, as is now held, not embraced by the words "throughout the United States," is more than I can understand. . . .

It would seem, according to the theories of some, that even if Porto Rico is in and of the United States for many important purposes, it is yet not a part of this country with the privilege of protesting against a rule of taxation which Congress is expressly forbidden by the Constitution from adopting as to any part of the "United States." And this result comes from the failure of Congress to use the word "incorporate" in the Foraker act, although by the same act all power exercised by the civil government in Porto Rico is by authority of the United States, and although this court has been given jurisdiction by writ of error or appeal to re-examine the final judgments of the district court of the United States established by Congress for that territory. Suppose Congress had passed this act: *"Be it enacted by the Senate and House of Representatives in Congress assembled,* That Porto Rico be and is hereby incorporated into the United States as a territory," would such a statute have enlarged the scope or effect of the Foraker act? Would such a statute have accomplished more than the Foraker act has done? Indeed, would not such legislation have been regarded as most extraordinary as well as unnecessary?

I am constrained to say that this idea of "incorporation" has some occult meaning which my mind does not apprehend. It is enveloped in some mystery which I am unable to unravel.

In my opinion Porto Rico became, at least after the ratification of the treaty with Spain, a part of and subject to the jurisdiction of the United States in respect of all its territory and people, and that Congress could not thereafter impose any duty, impost, or excise with respect to that island and its inhabitants which departed from the rule of uniformity established by the Constitution.

7

The Open Door

☆ *The scramble for concessions and privileges in China by the great powers alarmed the United States. John Hay formulated a three-point proposal to guarantee equal commercial and other privileges to all foreign parties in China. This proposal was communicated to Germany, Russia, Great Britain, France, Italy, and Japan.** ☆

At the time when the Government of the United States was informed by that of Germany that it had leased from His Majesty the Emperor of China the port of Kiao-chao and the adjacent territory in the province of Shantung, assurances given to the ambassador of the United States at Berlin by the Imperial German minister for foreign affairs that the rights and privileges insured by treaties with China to citizens of the United States would not thereby suffer or be in anywise impaired within the area over which Germany had thus obtained control.

More recently, however, the British Government recognized by a formal agreement with Germany the exclusive right of the latter country to enjoy in said leased area and the contiguous "sphere of influence or interest" certain privileges, more especially those relating to railroads and mining enterprises; but, as the exact nature and extent of the rights thus recognized have not been clearly defined, it is possible that serious conflicts of interest may at any time arise, not

only between British and German subjects within said area, but that the interests of our citizens may also be jeopardized thereby.

Earnestly desirous to remove any cause of irritation and to insure at the same time to the commerce of all nations in China the undoubted benefits which should accrue from a formal recognition by the various powers claiming "spheres of interest" that they shall enjoy perfect equality of treatment for their commerce and navigation within such "spheres," the Government of the United States would be pleased to see His German Majesty's Government give formal assurances and lend its cooperation in securing like assurances from the other interested powers that each within its respective sphere of whatever influence—

First. Will in no way interfere with any treaty port or any vested interest within any so-called "sphere of interest" or leased territory it may have in China.

Second. That the Chinese treaty tariff of the time being shall apply to all merchandise landed or shipped to all such ports as are within said "sphere of interest" (unless they be "free ports"), no

* From William M. Malloy, *Treaties, Conventions, International Acts, Protocols and Agreements Between the United States of America and Other Powers 1776-1909*, I, Washington, 1910, pp. 246-247.

matter to what nationality it may belong, and that duties so leviable shall be collected by the Chinese Government.

Third. That it will levy no higher harbor dues on vessels of another nationality frequenting any port in such "sphere" than shall be levied on vessels of its own nationality, and no higher railroad charges over lines built, controlled, or operated within its "sphere" on merchandise belonging to citizens or subjects of other nationalities transported through such "sphere" than shall be levied on similar merchandise belonging to its own nationals transported over equal distances.

8

The Roosevelt Corollary

☆ *Theodore Roosevelt's foreign policy was often as aggressive as his domestic policy. This was exemplified in 1904 when he freely interpreted the Monroe Doctrine as justifying United States intervention in the internal affairs of Latin American nations in order to protect them from European incursions.* * ☆

It is not true that the United States feels any land hunger or entertains any projects as regards the other nations of the Western Hemisphere save such as are for their welfare. All that this country desires is to see the neighboring countries stable, orderly, and prosperous. Any country whose people conduct themselves well can count upon our hearty friendship. If a nation shows that it knows how to act with reasonable efficiency and decency in social and political matters, if it keeps order and pays its obligations, it need fear no interference from the United States. Chronic wrongdoing, or an impotence which results in a general loosening of the ties of civilized society, may in America, as elsewhere, ultimately require intervention by some civilized nation, and in the Western Hemisphere the adherence of the United States to the Monroe Doctrine may force the United States, however reluctantly, in flagrant cases of such wrongdoing or impotence, to the exercise of an international police power. If every country washed by the Caribbean Sea would show the progress in stable and just civi-

* From *Papers Relating to the Foreign Relations of The United States with The Annual Message of The President Transmitted to Congress December 6, 1904*, Washington, 1905, pp. xli-xlii.

lization which with the aid of the Platt amendment Cuba has shown since our troops left the island, and which so many of the republics in both Americas are constantly and brilliantly showing, all question of interference by this Nation with their affairs would be at an end. Our interests and those of our southern neighbors are in reality identical. They have great natural riches, and if within their borders the reign of law and justice obtains, prosperity is sure to come to them. While they thus obey the primary laws of civilized society they may rest assured that they will be treated by us in a spirit of cordial and helpful sympathy. We would interfere with them only in the last resort, and then only if it became evident that their inability or unwillingness to do justice at home and abroad had violated the rights of the United States or had invited foreign aggression to the detriment of the entire body of American nations. It is a mere truism to say that every nation, whether in America or anywhere else, which desires to maintain its freedom, its independence, must ultimately realize that the right of such independence can not be separated from the responsibility of making good use of it.

9

Root-Takahira Agreement

☆ *At the conclusion of her war with Russia in 1904-1905, Japan emerged as the most likely threat to American policies in the Far East. Both nations, in an effort to maintain the status quo and protect their special interests, concluded an agreement. This agreement was contained in messages between Ambassador K. Takahira and Secretary of State Elihu Root on November 30, 1908.* ☆

SIR: The exchange of views between us, which has taken place at the several interviews which I have recently had the honor of holding with you, has shown that Japan and the United States holding important outlying insular possessions in the region of the Pacific Ocean, the Governments of the two countries are animated by a common aim, policy, and intention in that region.

Believing that a frank avowal of that aim, policy, and intention would not only tend to strengthen the relations of friendship and good neighborhood, which have immemorially existed between Japan and the United States, but would materially contribute to the preservation of the general peace, the Imperial Government have authorized me to present to you an outline of their understanding of that common aim, policy, and intention:

1. It is the wish of the two Governments to encourage the free and peaceful development of their commerce on the Pacific Ocean.

2. The policy of both Governments, un-

influenced by any aggressive tendencies, is directed to the maintenance of the existing status quo in the region above mentioned and to the defense of the principle of equal opportunity for commerce and industry in China.

3. They are accordingly firmly resolved reciprocally to respect the territorial possessions belonging to each other in said region.

4. They are also determined to preserve the common interest of all powers in China by supporting by all pacific means at their disposal the independence and integrity of China and the principle of equal opportunity for commerce and industry of all nations in that Empire.

5. Should any event occur threatening the status quo as above described or the principle of equal opportunity as above defined, it remains for the two Governments to communicate with each other in order to arrive at an understanding as to what measures they may consider it useful to take.

If the foregoing outline accords with the view of the Government of the United States, I shall be gratified to receive your confirmation.

* From *Papers Relating to the Foreign Relations of The United States with The Annual Message of The President Transmitted to Congress December 8, 1908,* Washington, 1912, pp. 510-512.

I take this opportunity to renew to your excellency the assurance of my highest consideration.

K. TAKAHIRA

EXCELLENCY: I have the honor to acknowledge the receipt of your note of today setting forth the result of the exchange of views between us in our recent interviews defining the understanding of the two Governments in regard to their policy in the region of the Pacific Ocean.

It is a pleasure to inform you that this expression of mutual understanding is welcome to the Government of the United States as appropriate to the happy relations of the two countries and as the occasion for a concise mutual affirmation of that accordant policy respecting the Far East which the two Governments have so frequently declared in the past.

I am happy to be able to confirm to your excellency, on behalf of the United States, the declaration of the two Governments. . . .

ELIHU ROOT

10

Involvement in Europe

☆ *Though the United States had carefully avoided involvement in the political affairs of Europe during the nineteenth century, Theodore Roosevelt agreed to American participation in a conference devoted solely to the reconciliation of conflicting European interests in Morocco. His wish to avert an international war, which might jeopardize American security, was gratified in the Algeciras Convention of 1906. The reservations, reproduced below, were added to the Convention by the Senate to state its interpretation that no violation of traditional American policies had been done by United States participation in the Algeciras conference.* ☆

The said General Act and Additional Protocol were signed by the Plenipotentiaries of the United States of America under reservation of the following declaration:

The Government of the United States of America, having no political interest in Morocco and no desire or purpose having animated it to take part in this conference other than to secure for all peoples the widest equality of trade and privilege with Morocco and to facilitate the institution of reforms in that country tending to insure complete cordiality of intercourse without and stability of administration within for the common good, declares that, in acquiescing in the regulations and declarations of the conference, in becoming a signatory to the General Act of Algeciras and to the Additional Protocol, subject to ratification according to consti-

* From William M. Malloy, *Treaties, Conventions, International Acts, Portocols and Agreements Between the United States of America and Other Powers*, II, Washington, 1910, pp. 2182-2183.

tutional procedure, and in accepting the application of those regulations and declarations to American citizens and interests in Morocco, it does so without assuming obligation or responsbility for the enforcement thereof.

IN EXECUTIVE SESSION, SENATE OF THE UNITED STATES

Resolved (*two-thirds of the Senators present concurring therein*), That the Senate advise and consent to the ratification of the general act and an additional protocol, signed on April 7, 1906, by the delegates of the powers represented at the conference which met at Algeciras, Spain, to consider Moroccan affairs.

Resolved further, That the Senate, as a part of this act of ratification, understands that the participation of the United States in the Algeciras conference and in the formation and adoption of the general act and protocol which resulted therefrom, was with the sole purpose of preserving and increasing its commerce in Morocco, the protection as to life, liberty, and property of its citizens residing or traveling therein, and of aiding by its friendly offices and efforts, in removing friction and controversy which seemed to menace the peace between powers signatory with the United States to the treaty of 1880, all of which are on terms of amity with this Government; and without purpose to depart from the traditional American foreign policy which forbids participation by the United States in the settlement of political questions which are entirely European in their scope.

11

Dollar Diplomacy

☆ *An explicit affirmation of the commercial theme in American diplomacy was contained in President Taft's message to Congress of December 3, 1912. This "dollar diplomacy" provided for the use of statesmanship to yield commercial benefits, and in the employment of trade and investment to enhance American political prestige. President Wilson, however, in a public statement of 1913, repudiated American government support of investment activity in China as jeopardizing Chinese independence.* ☆

(a) WILLIAM HOWARD TAFT*

In China the policy of encouraging financial investment to enable that country to help itself has had the result of giving new life and practical application to the open-door policy. The consistent purpose of the present administration has been to encourage the use of American capital in the development of China by the promotion of those essential reforms to which China is pledged by treaties with the United States and other powers. The hypothecation to foreign bankers in connection with certain industrial enterprises, such as the Hukuang railways, of the national revenues upon which these reforms depended, led the Department of State early in the administration to demand for American citizens participation in such enterprises, in order that the United States might have equal rights and an

equal voice in all questions pertaining to the disposition of the public revenues concerned. The same policy of promoting international accord among the powers having similar treaty rights as ourselves in the matters of reform, which could not be put into practical effect without the common consent of all, was likewise adopted in the case of the loan desired by China for the reform of its currency. The principle of international cooperation in matters of common interest upon which our policy had already been based in all of the above instances has admittedly been a great factor in that concert of the powers which has been so happily conspicuous during the perilous period of transition through which the great Chinese nation has been passing.

In Central America the aim has been to help such countries as Nicaragua and Honduras to help themselves. They are the immediate beneficiaries. The national benefit to the United States is two-fold.

* Message to Congress, December 3, 1912. From *A Compilation of the Messages and Papers of the Presidents*, XVI, pp. 7772-7774, 7778, 7789-7790. Published by Bureau of National Literature, Inc., New York.

First, it is obvious that the Monroe doctrine is more vital in the neighborhood of the Panama Canal and the zone of the Caribbean than anywhere else. There, too, the maintenance of that doctrine falls most heavily upon the United States. It is therefore essential that the countries within that sphere shall be removed from the jeopardy involved by heavy foreign debt and chaotic national finances and from the ever-present danger of international complications due to disorder at home. Hence the United States has been glad to encourage and support American bankers who were willing to lend a helping hand to the financial rehabilitation of such countries because this financial rehabilitation and the protection of their customhouses from being the prey of would-be dictators would remove at one stroke the menace of foreign creditors and the menace of revolutionary disorder.

The second advantage of the United States is one affecting chiefly all the southern and Gulf ports and the business and industry of the South. The Republics of Central America and the Caribbean possess great natural wealth. They need only a measure of stability and the means of financial regeneration to enter upon an era of peace and prosperity, bringing profit and happiness to themselves and at the same time creating conditions sure to lead to a flourishing interchange of trade with this country.

I wish to call your especial attention to the recent occurrences in Nicaragua, for I believe the terrible events recorded there during the revolution of the past summer—the useless loss of life, the devastation of property, the bombardment of defenseless cities, the killing and wounding of women and children, the torturing of noncombatants to exact contributions, and the suffering of thousands of human beings—might have been averted had the Department of State, through approval of the loan convention by the Senate, been permitted to carry out its now well-developed policy of encouraging the extending of financial aid to weak Central American States with the primary objects of avoiding just such revolutions by assisting those Republics to rehabilitate their finances, to establish their currency on a stable basis, to remove the customhouses from the danger of revolutions by arranging for their secure administration, and to establish reliable banks.

During this last revolution in Nicaragua, the Government of that Republic having admitted its inability to protect American life and property against acts of sheer lawlessness on the part of the malcontents, and having requested this Government to assume that office, it became necessary to land over 2,000 marines and bluejackets in Nicaragua. Owing to their presence the constituted Government of Nicaragua was free to devote its attention wholly to its internal troubles, and was thus enabled to stamp out the rebellion in a short space of time. When the Red Cross supplies sent to Granada had been exhausted, 8,000 persons having been given food in one day upon the arrival of the American forces, our men supplied other unfortunate, needy Nicaraguans from their own haversacks. I wish to congratulate the officers and men of the United States navy and Marine Corps who took part in reestablishing order in Nicaragua upon their splendid conduct, and to record with sorrow the death of seven American marines and bluejackets. Since the reestablishment of peace and order, elections have been held amid conditions of quiet and tranquility. Nearly all the American marines have now been withdrawn. The country should soon be on the road to recovery. The only apparent danger now threatening Nicaragua arises from the shortage of funds. Although American bankers have already rendered assistance, they may naturally be loath to advance a loan adequate to set the country upon its feet without the support of some such convention as that of June, 1911, upon which the Senate has not yet acted. . . .

As illustrating the commercial benefits of the Nation derived from the new diplomacy and its effectiveness upon the material as well as the more ideal side, it may be remarked that through direct official efforts alone there have been obtained in the course of this administration, contracts from foreign Governments involving an expenditure of $50,000,000 in the factories of the United States. Consideration of this fact and some reflection upon the necessary effects of a scientific tariff system and a foreign service alert and equipped to cooperate with the business men of America carry the conviction that the gratifying increase in the export trade of this country is, in substantial amount, due to our improved governmental methods of protecting and stimulating it. It is germane to these observations to remark that in the two years that have elapsed since the successful negotiation of our new treaty with Japan, which at the time seemed to present so many practical difficulties, our export trade to that country has increased at the rate of over $1,000,-000 a month. Our exports to Japan for the year ended June 30, 1910, were $21,959,-310, while for the year ended June 30, 1912, the exports were $53,478,046, a net increase in the sale of American products of nearly 150 per cent. . . .

It is not possible to make to the Congress a communication upon the present foreign relations of the United States so detailed as to convey an adequate impression of the enormous increase in the importance and activities of those relations. If this Government is really to preserve to the American people that free opportunity in foreign markets which will soon be indispensable to our prosperity, even greater efforts must be made. Otherwise the American merchant, manufacturer,

and exporter will find many a field in which American trade should logically predominate preempted through the more energetic efforts of other governments and other commercial nations.

There are many ways in which through hearty cooperation the legislative and executive branches of this Government can do much. The absolute essential is the spirit of united effort and singleness of purpose. I will allude only to a very few specific examples of action which ought then to result. America can not take its proper place in the most important fields for its commercial activity and enterprise unless we have a merchant marine. American commerce and enterprise can not be effectively fostered in those fields unless we have good American banks in the countries referred to. We need American newspapers in those countries and proper means for public information about them. We need to assure the permanency of a trained foreign service. We need legislation enabling the members of the foreign service to be systematically brought in direct contact with the industrial, manufacturing, and exporting interests of this country in order that American business men may enter the foreign field with a clear perception of the exact conditions to be dealt with and the officers themselves may prosecute their work with a clear idea of what American industrial and manufacturing interests require.

(b) WOODROW WILSON *

We are informed that at the request of the last Administration a certain group of American bankers undertook to participate in the loan now desired by the Government of China (approximately one hundred twenty-five million dollars). Our

* Public Statement, March 8, 1913. From John V. A. MacMurray, *Treaties and Agreements With and Concerning China, 1894-1914*, II, pp. 1021-1023. Published by The Carnegie Endowment for International Peace, Washington, 1921.

Government wished American bankers to participate along with the bankers of other nations, because it desired that the good-will of the United States toward China should be exhibited in this practical way, that American capital should have access to that great country, and that the United States should be in a position to share with the other powers any political responsibilities that might be associated with the development of the foreign relations of China in connection with her industrial and commercial enterprises. The present Administration has been asked by this group of bankers whether it would also request them to participate in the loan. The representatives of the bankers through whom the Administration was approached declared that they would continue to seek their share of the loan under the proposed agreements only if expressly requested to do so by the Government. The Administration has declined to make such request, because it did not approve the conditions of the loan or the implications of responsibility on its own part which it was plainly told would be involved in the request.

The conditions of the loan seem to us to touch very nearly the administrative independence of China itself, and this Administration does not feel that it ought, even by implication, to be a party to those conditions. The responsibility on its part which would be implied in requesting the bankers to undertake the loan might conceivably go the length in some unhappy contingency of forcible interference in the financial, and even the political, affairs of that great Oriental State, just now awakening to a consciousness of its power and of its obligations to its people. The conditions include not only the pledging of particular taxes, some of them antiquated and burdensome, to secure the loan but also the administration of those taxes by foreign agents. The responsibility on the part of our Government implied in the encouragement of a loan thus secured and administered is plain enough and is obnoxious to the principles upon which the Government of our people rests.

12

Efforts Toward World Peace

☆ *The United States, during the Roosevelt and Taft administrations, strived earnestly to achieve world peace by treaties providing for the settlement of disputes between nations by arbitration. Similar efforts were made during the Wilson administration.* ☆

(a) ARBITRATION TREATY BETWEEN THE UNITED STATES AND AUSTRIA-HUNGARY *

Article I. Differences which may arise of a legal nature, or relating to the interpretation of treaties existing between the High Contracting Parties, and which it may not have been possible to settle by diplomacy, shall be referred to the Permanent Court of Arbitration established at The Hague by the Convention of the 29th July, 1899; provided, nevertheless, that they do not affect the vital interests, the independence, or the honor of the High Contracting Parties, and do not concern the interests of third Parties.

Article II. In each individual case the High Contracting Parties, before appealing to the Permanent Court of Arbitration, shall conclude a special Agreement defining clearly the matter in dispute,

---

* January 15, 1909. From *Papers Relating to the Foreign Relations of The United States with The Annual Message of The President Transmitted to Congress December 7, 1909*, Washington, 1914, pp. 33-34.

the scope of the powers of the Arbitrators, and the periods to be fixed for the formation of the Arbitral Tribunal and the several stages of the procedure.

It is understood that such special agreements on the part of the United States will be made by the President of the United States by and with the advice and consent of the Senate thereof.

Such agreements shall be binding only when confirmed by the governments of the High Contracting Parties by an exchange of notes.

Article III. The present Convention shall be ratified by the High Contracting Parties, and the ratifications shall be exchanged as soon as possible at Washington.

The present Convention shall remain in force for five years from the fifteenth day after the date of the exchange of the ratifications.

(b) IDENTIC TREATY SIGNED WITH GREAT BRITAIN AND FRANCE*

Article I. All differences hereafter arising between the High Contracting Parties, which it has not been possible to adjust by diplomacy, relating to international matters in which the High Contracting Parties are concerned by virtue of a claim of right made by one against the other under treaty or otherwise, and which are justiciable in their nature by reason of being susceptible of decision by the application of the principles of law or equity, shall be submitted to the Permanent Court of Arbitration established at The Hague by the Convention of October 18, 1907, or to some other arbitral tribunal, as [shall] may be decided in each case by special agreement, which special agreement shall provide for the organization of such tribunal if necessary, define the scope of the powers of the arbitrators, the question or questions at issue, and settle the terms of reference and the procedure thereunder. . . .

The special agreement in each case shall be made on the part of the United States by the President of the United States, by and with the advice and consent of the Senate thereof. . . .

Article II. The High Contracting Parties further agree to institute as occasion arises, and as hereinafter provided, a Joint High Commission of Inquiry to which, upon the request of either Party, shall be referred for impartial and conscientious investigation any controversy

between the Parties within the scope of Article I, before such controversy has been submitted to arbitration, and also any other controversy hereafter arising between them even if they are not agreed that it falls within the scope of Article I. . . .

Article III. . . . It is further agreed, however, that in cases in which the Parties disagree as to whether or not a difference is subject to arbitration under Article I of this Treaty, that question shall be submitted to the Joint High Commission of Inquiry; and if all or all but one of the members of the Commission agree and report that such difference is within the scope of Article I, it shall be referred to arbitration in accordance with the provisions of this Treaty.

[*Provided,* That the Senate advises and consents to the ratification of the said treaty with the understanding, to be made part of such ratification, that the treaty does not authorize the submission to arbitration of any question which affects the admission of aliens into the United States, or the admission of aliens to the educational institutions of the several States, or the territorial integrity of the several States or of the United States, or concerning the question of the alleged indebtedness or monied obligation of any State of the United States, or any question which depends upon or involves the maintenance of the traditional attitude of the United States concerning American questions, commonly described as the Monroe doctrine, or other purely governmental policy.]

* August 3, 1911. From *Senate Document* #476, 62nd Congress, 2nd session, pp. 2-6. The additions to the treaty by the Senate are included in the text in brackets.

13

Mexican Crisis

☆ *One of the most pressing problems of the Wilson administration was American relations with Mexico. No sooner had President Wilson announced a policy of non-intervention toward Latin American countries in 1913 than a series of incidents occurred that finally resulted in the dispatching of a large American expeditionary force to Mexico in 1916. The situation was reviewed by Secretary of State Robert Lansing in a letter to the Mexican Secretary of Foreign Relations of June 20, 1916.** ☆

SIR: I have read your communication, which was delivered to me on May 22, 1916, under instructions of the Chief Executive of the de facto government of Mexico, on the subject of the presence of American troops in Mexican territory, and I would be wanting in candor if I did not, before making answer to the allegations of fact and the conclusions reached by your Government, express the surprise and regret which have been caused this Government by the discourteous tone and temper of this last communication of the de facto Government of Mexico.

The Government of the United States has viewed with deep concern and increasing disappointment the progress of the revolution in Mexico. Continuous bloodshed and disorders have marked its progress. For three years the Mexican Republic has been torn with civil strife; the lives of Americans and other aliens have been sacrificed; vast properties developed by American capital and enter-

* From *Congressional Record*, 64th Congress, 2nd session, Appn., pp. 1270-1271, 1273.

prise have been destroyed or rendered nonproductive; bandits have been permitted to roam at will through the territory contiguous to the United States and to seize, without punishment or without effective attempt at punishment, the property of Americans, while the lives of citizens of the United States who ventured to remain in Mexican territory or to return there to protect their interests have been taken, and in some cases barbarously taken, and the murderers have neither been apprehended nor brought to justice. It would be difficult to find in the annals of the history of Mexico conditions more deplorable than those which have existed there during these recent years of civil war.

It would be tedious to recount instance after instance, outrage after outrage, atrocity after atrocity, to illustrate the true nature and extent of the widespread conditions of lawlessness and violence which have prevailed. During the past nine months in particular, the frontier of the United States along the lower Rio

Grande has been thrown into a state of constant apprehension and turmoil because of frequent and sudden incursions into American territory and depredations and murders on American soil by Mexican bandits, who have taken the lives and destroyed the property of American citizens, sometimes carrying American citizens across the international boundary with the booty seized. American garrisons have been attacked at night, American soldiers killed and their equipment and horses stolen; American ranches have been raided, property stolen and destroyed, and American trains wrecked and plundered. The attacks on Brownsville, Red House Ferry, Progreso Post Office, and Las Peladas, all occurring during September last, are typical. In these attacks on American territory, Carranzista adherents, and even Carranzista soldiers, took part in the looting, burning, and killing. Not only were these murders characterized by ruthless brutality, but uncivilized acts of mutilation were perpetrated. Representations were made to Gen. Carranza and he was emphatically requested to stop these reprehensible acts in a section which he has long claimed to be under the complete domination of his authority. Notwithstanding these representations and the promise of Gen. Nafarrete to prevent attacks along the international boundary, in the following month of October a passenger train was wrecked by bandits and several persons killed 7 miles north of Brownsville, and an attack was made upon United States troops at the same place several days later. Since these attacks leaders of the bandits well known both to Mexican civil and military authorities as well as to American officers have been enjoying with impunity the liberty of the towns of northern Mexico. So far has the indifference of the de facto Government to these atrocities gone that some of these leaders, as I am advised, have received not only the protection of that Government, but encouragement and aid as well.

Depredations upon American persons and property within Mexican jurisdiction have been still more numerous. This Government has repeatedly requested in the strongest terms that the de facto government safeguard the lives and homes of American citizens and furnish the protection which international obligation imposes to American interests in the northern States of Tamaulipas, Nuevo Leon, Coahuila, Chihuahua, and Sonora, and also in the States to the south. For example, on January 3 troops were requested to punish the bands of outlaws which looted the Cusi mining property, 80 miles west of Chihuahua, but no effective results came from this request. During the following week the bandit Villa, with his band of about 200 men, was operating without opposition between Rubio and Santa Ysabel, a fact well known to Carranzista authorities. Meanwhile a party of unfortunate Americans started by train from Chihuahua to visit the Cusi mines, after having received assurances from the Carranzista authorities in the State of Chihuahua that the country was safe and that a guard on the train was not necessary. The Americans held passports or safe conducts issued by authorities of the de facto government. On January 10 the train was stopped by Villa bandits and 18 of the American party were stripped of their clothing and shot in cold blood in what is now known as "the Santa Ysabel massacre." Gen. Carranza stated to the agent of the Department of State that he had issued orders for the immediate pursuit, capture, and punishment of those responsible for this atrocious crime, and appealed to this Government and to the American people to consider the difficulties of according protection along the railroad where the massacre occurred. Assurances were also given by Mr. Arredondo, presumably under instructions from the de facto government, that the murderers would be brought to justice and that steps would also be taken to remedy the lawless conditions existing in the State of Durango. It is true that Villa, Castro, and Lopez were publicly declared to be outlaws and subject to apprehension and execution, but so far as known only a single man personally connected with this massacre has been brought to justice by Mexican authorities. Within a month after this barbarous slaughter of inoffensive Americans it was notorious that Villa was operating within 20 miles of Cusihuiriachic, and publicly stated that his purpose was to destroy American lives and property. Despite repeated and insistent demands that military protection should be furnished to Americans, Villa openly carried on his operations, constantly approaching closer and closer to the border. He was not intercepted, nor were his movements impeded by troops of the de facto government, and no effectual attempt was made to frustrate his hostile designs against Americans. In fact, as I am informed, while Villa and his band were slowly moving toward the American frontier in the neighborhood of Columbus, N. Mex., not a single Mexican soldier was seen in his vicinity. Yet the Mexican authorities were fully cognizant of his movements, for on March 6, as Gen. Gavira publicly announced, he advised the American military authorities of the outlaw's approach to the border, so that they might be prepared to prevent him from crossing the boundary. Villa's unhindered activities culminated in the unprovoked and cold-blooded attack upon American soldiers and citizens in the town of Columbus on the night of March 9, the details of which do not need repetition here in order to refresh your memory with the heinousness of the crime. After murdering, burning, and plundering, Villa and his bandits, fleeing south, passed within sight of the Carranzista military post at Casas Grandes, and no effort was made to stop him by the officers and garrison of the de facto government stationed there.

In the face of these depredations, not only on American lives and property on Mexican soil but on American soldiers, citizens, and homes on American territory, the perpetrators of which Gen. Carranza was unable or possibly considered it inadvisable to apprehend and punish, the United States had no recourse other than to employ force to disperse the bands of Mexican outlaws who were with increasing boldness systematically raiding across the international boundary.

The marauders engaged in the attack on Columbus were driven back across the border by American Cavalry, and subsequently, as soon as a sufficient force to cope with the band could be collected, were pursued into Mexico in an effort to capture or destroy them. Without cooperation or assistance in the field on the part of the de facto government, despite repeated requests by the United States, and without apparent recognition on its part of the desirability of putting an end to these systematic raids, or of punishing the chief perpetrators of the crimes committed, because they menaced the good relations of the two countries, American forces pursued the lawless bands as far as Parral, where the pursuit was halted by the hostility of Mexicans, presumed to be loyal to the de facto government, who arrayed themselves on the side of outlawry and became in effect the protectors of Villa and his band.

In this manner and for these reasons have the American forces entered Mexican territory. Knowing fully the circumstances set forth the de facto government cannot be blind to the necessity which compelled this Government to act, and yet it has seen fit to recite groundless sentiments of hostility toward the expedition and to impute to this Government ulterior motives for the continued presence of American troops on Mexican soil. It is charged that these troops crossed the frontier without first obtaining the consent or permission of the de facto government. Obviously, as immediate action alone could avail, there was no opportunity to reach an agreement—other than that of March 10 to 13, now repudiated by Gen. Carranza—prior to the entrance of such an expedition into Mexico if the expedition was to be effective. Subsequent events and correspondence have demonstrated to the satisfaction of this Government that Gen. Carranza would not have entered into any agreement providing for an effective plan for the capture and destruction of the Villa bands. While the American troops were moving rapidly southward in pursuit of the raiders, it was the form and nature of the agreement that occupied the attention of Gen. Carranza rather than the practical object which it was to attain—the number of limitations that could be imposed upon the American forces to impede their progress rather than the obstacles that could be raised to prevent the escape of the outlaws. It was Gen. Carranza who suspended, through your note of April 12, all discussions and negotiations for an agreement along the lines of the protocols between the United States and Mexico concluded during the period 1882-1896, under which the two countries had so successfully restored peaceful conditions on their common boundary. It may be mentioned here that, notwithstanding the statement in your note that "the American Government gave no answer to the note of the 12th of April," this note was replied to on April 14, when the department instructed Mr. Rodgers by telegraph to deliver this Government's answer to Gen. Carranza. Shortly after this reply the conferences between Gens. Scott, Funston, and Obregon began at El Paso, during which they signed on May 2 a proj-

ect of a memorandum ad referendum regarding the withdrawal of American troops. As an indication of the alleged bad faith of the American Government, you state that though Gen. Scott declared in this memorandum that the destruction and dispersion of the Villa band "had been accomplished," yet American forces are not withdrawn from Mexico. It is only necessary to read the memorandum, which is in the English language, to ascertain that this is clearly a misstatement, for the memorandum states that "the American punitive expeditionary forces have destroyed or dispersed many of the lawless elements and bandits, * * * or have driven them far into the interior of the Republic of Mexico," and further, that the United States forces were then "carrying on a vigorous pursuit of such small numbers of bandits or lawless elements as may have escaped." The context of your note gives the impression that the object of the expedition being admittedly accomplished, the United States had agreed in the memorandum to begin the withdrawal of its troops.

The memorandum shows, however, that it was not alone on account of partial dispersion of the bandits that it was decided to begin the withdrawal of American forces, but equally on account of the assurances of the Mexican government that their forces were "at the present time being augmented and strengthened to such an extent that they will be able to prevent any disorders occurring in Mexico that would in any way endanger American territory," and that they would "continue to diligently pursue, capture, or destroy any lawless bands of bandits that may still exist or hereafter exist in the northern part of Mexico," and that it would "make a proper distribution of such of its forces as may be necessary to prevent the possibility of invasion of American territory from Mexico." It was because of these assurances and because of Gen. Scott's confidence that they would be carried out that he stated in the memorandum that the American forces would be "gradually withdrawn." It is to be noted that, while the American Government was willing to ratify this agreement, Gen. Carranza refused to do so, as Gen. Obregon stated, because, among other things, it imposed improper conditions upon the Mexican government.

Nothwithstanding the assurances in the memorandum, it is well known that the forces of the de facto government have not carried on a vigorous pursuit of the remaining bandits, and that no proper distribution of forces to prevent the invasion of American territory has been made .... I am reluctant to be forced to the conclusion which might be drawn from these circumstances that the de facto government, in spite of the crimes committed and the sinister designs of Villa and his followers, did not and does not now intend or desire that these outlaws should be captured, destroyed, or dispersed by American troops, or, at the request of this Government, by Mexican troops. . . .

The United States has not sought the duty which has been forced upon it of pursuing bandits who under fundamental principles of municipal and international law ought to be pursued and arrested and punished by Mexican authorities. Whenever Mexico will assume and effectively exercise that responsibility the United States, as it has many times before publicly declared, will be glad to have this obligation fulfilled by the de facto government of Mexico. If, on the contrary, the de facto government is pleased to ignore this obligation and to believe that "in case of a refusal to retire these troops there is no further recourse than to defend its territory by an appeal to arms," the Government of the United States would surely be lacking in sincerity and friendship if it did not frankly impress upon the de facto government that the execution of this threat will lead to the gravest consequences. While this Government would deeply regret such a result, it can not recede from its settled determination to maintain its national rights and to perform its full duty in preventing further invasions of the territory of the United States and in removing the peril which Americans along the international boundary have borne so long with patience and forbearance.

V

world war 1 and world peace

THE COMING of World War I had an immediate effect on the United States. The nation was shocked that civilized countries could so quickly go to war over obscure issues. Questions were raised about the economic impact of the war as over half of America's foreign trade was with the warring countries and their colonies. Moreover, conflicting sympathies were stirred in the United States whose population and culture were European in origin.

President Wilson tried to set the nation's policy and attitude as those of mediation and neutrality. Americans must think of the United States first, he contended, and strive for impartiality in thought and action. In these ways we could avoid being drawn into the war and could determine the effects of the war on the United States. Yet it was difficult for the nation to avoid entanglements and partiality. Both the Allied powers and the Central powers interferred with American citizens and trade abroad. This reached a high point in vexation in 1915 with the German submarine attack on the British ocean liner *Lusitania*. War-borne prosperity, based largely on Allied trade demands, also tended to lure the United States from the path of strict neutrality. And the United States became a prime target—and a ripe one—for Allied propaganda.

The resolve of the government for peace and neutrality was increasingly shaken as events proved that the United States was not its own master in determining the effect of the war on the nation. The pursuit of peace through neutrality slowly turned into the pursuit of peace through war as Americans first became convinced that foreign attack was possible and that "preparedness" for defense was necessary. Then followed the growth of opinion that the actions of the Central powers not only threatened our stability but endangered morality, jeopardized international law, and promoted needless slaughter. By 1917, large numbers of Americans saw the war as a battle by autocracies to crush nations of free peoples. With this in mind, and a number of German provocations at hand, President Wilson, on April 2, 1917, asked Congress for a declaration of war against Germany, asserting that only in this way could we protect freedom and achieve a true peace. After a spirited debate, the opponents of war were voted down, and the United States went to war with a fervor that surprised both its allies and enemies.

America's war aims were directed toward perpetual peace. In his war message, Wilson had called for a league for peace. By early 1918, the President announced his fourteen point program for the self-determination of nations and international peace with justice. At the Versailles Peace Conference which followed the war, Wilson vigorously pursued these aims but with only partial success. He returned to the United States, not completely satisfied with the Versailles Treaty, but determined to secure its ratification and to give effect to the portions of the treaty— especially the League of Nations—which might lead to world peace and justice. The President's arguments and influence were insufficient to overcome the strong opposition to the treaty which had developed in a nation returning to "Normalcy."

1

American Neutrality

☆ *With the coming of war in Europe in 1914, President Wilson declared, in a message of August 20 to the people, that America's policy would be based on neutrality in action and impartiality in thought.** ☆

MY FELLOW COUNTRYMEN: I suppose that every thoughtful man in America has asked himself, during these last troubled weeks, what influence the European war may exert upon the United States, and I take the liberty of addressing a few words to you in order to point out that it is entirely within our own choice what its effects upon us will be and to urge very earnestly upon you the sort of speech and conduct which will best safeguard the Nation against distress and disaster.

The effect of the war upon the United States will depend upon what American citizens say and do. Every man who really loves America will act and speak in the true spirit of neutrality, which is the spirit of impartiality and fairness and friendliness to all concerned. The spirit of the Nation in this critical matter will be determined largely by what individuals and society and those gathered in public meetings do and say, upon what newspapers and magazines contain, upon what ministers utter in their pulpits, and men proclaim as their opinions on the street.

The people of the United States are

* From *A Compilation of the Messages and Papers of the Presidents*, XVI, pp. 7978-7979. Published by Bureau of National Literature, Inc., New York.

drawn from many nations, and chiefly from the nations now at war. It is natural and inevitable that there should be the utmost variety of sympathy and desire among them with regard to the issues and circumstances of the conflict. Some will wish one nation, others another, to succeed in the momentous struggle. It will be easy to excite passion and difficult to allay it. Those responsible for exciting it will assume a heavy responsibility, responsibility for no less a thing than that the people of the United States, whose love of their country and whose loyalty to its Government should unite them as Americans all, bound in honor and affection to think first of her and her interests, may be divided in camps of hostile opinion, hot against each other, involved in the war itself in impulse and opinion if not in action.

Such divisions among us would be fatal to our peace of mind and might seriously stand in the way of the proper performance of our duty as the one great nation at peace, the one people holding itself ready to play a part of impartial mediation and speak the counsels of peace and accommodation, not as a partisan, but as a friend.

I venture, therefore, my fellow countrymen, to speak a solemn word of warning to you against that deepest, most subtle, most essential breach of neutrality which may spring out of partisanship, out of passionately taking sides. The United States must be neutral in fact as well as in name during these days that are to try men's souls. We must be impartial in thought, as well as in action, must put a curb upon our sentiments as well as upon every transaction that might be construed as a preference of one party to the struggle before another.

My thought is of America. I am speaking, I feel sure, the earnest wish and purpose of every thoughtful American that this great country of ours, which is, of course, the first in our thoughts and in our hearts, should show herself in this time of peculiar trial a Nation fit beyond others to exhibit the fine poise of undisturbed judgment, the dignity of self-control, the efficiency of dispassionate action; a Nation that neither sits in judgment upon others nor is disturbed in her own counsels and which keeps herself fit and free to do what is honest and disinterested and truly serviceable for the peace of the world.

2

The Lusitania

☆ *On May 7, 1915, the British transatlantic passenger liner* Lusitania *was sunk without warning by a German submarine with a loss of 1,198 lives, including 124 Americans. This and earlier incidents were viewed by the United States government and public as violations of the rules of war. Secretary of State William Jennings Bryan expressed the American position on the* Lusitania *sinking in a note of May 13, 1915.** ☆

The Secretary of State to the American Ambassador at Berlin:

Please call on the Minister of Foreign Affairs and after reading to him this communication leave with him a copy.

In view of recent acts of the German authorities in violation of American rights on the high seas, which culminated in the torpedoing and sinking of the British steamship Lusitania on May 7, 1915, by which over 100 American citizens lost their lives, it is clearly wise and desirable that the Government of the United States and the Imperial German Government should come to a clear and full understanding as to the grave situation which has resulted.

The sinking of the British passenger steamer Falaba by a German submarine on March 28, through which Leon C. Thrasher, an American citizen, was drowned; the attack on April 28 on the American vessel Cushing by a German aeroplane: the torpedoing on May 1 of the American vessel Gulflight by a German

* From *A Compilation of the Messages and Papers of the Presidents*, XVI, pp. 8062-8064. Published by Bureau of National Literature, Inc., New York.

submarine, as a result of which two or more American citizens met their death; and, finally the torpedoing and sinking of the steamship Lusitania, constitute a series of events which the Government of the United States has observed with growing concern, distress, and amazement. . . .

The Government of the United States has been apprised that the Imperial German Government considered themselves to be obliged by the extraordinary circumstances of the present war and the measures adopted by their adversaries in seeking to cut Germany off from all commerce, to adopt methods of retaliation which go much beyond the ordinary methods of warfare at sea, in the proclamation of a war zone from which they have warned neutral ships to keep away. This Government has already taken occasion to inform the Imperial German Government that it cannot admit the adoption of such measures or such a warning of danger to operate as in any degree an abbreviation of the rights of American shipmasters or of American citizens bound on lawful errands as passengers on merchant ships of belligerent nationality, and that it must hold the Imperial German Government to a strict accountability for any infringement of those rights, intentional or incidental. It does not understand the Imperial German Government to question those rights. It assumes, on the contrary, that the Imperial Government accept, as of course, the rule that the lives of non-combatants, whether they be of neutral citizenship or citizens of one of the nations at war, cannot lawfully or rightfully be put in jeopardy by the capture or destruction of an unarmed merchantman, and recognize also, as all other nations do, the obligation to take the usual precaution of visit and search to ascertain whether a suspected merchantman is in fact of belligerent nationality or is in fact carrying contraband of war under a neutral flag.

The Government of the United States, therefore, desires to call the attention of the Imperial German Government with the utmost earnestness to the fact that the objection to their present method of attack against the trade of their enemies lies in the practical impossibility of employing submarines in the destruction of commerce without disregarding those rules of fairness, reason, justice and humanity which all modern opinion regards as imperative. It is practically impossible for the officers of a submarine to visit a merchantman at sea and examine her papers and cargo. It is practically impossible for them to make a prize of her; and, if they cannot put a prize crew on board of her, they cannot sink her without leaving her crew and all on board of her to the mercy of the sea in her small boats. These facts it is understood the Imperial German Goverment frankly admit. We are informed that in the instances of which we have spoken time enough for even that poor measure of safety was not given, and in at least two of the cases cited not so much as a warning was re-

ceived. Manifestly, submarines cannot be used against merchantmen, as the last few weeks have shown, without an inevitable violation of many sacred principles of justice and humanity.

American citizens act within their indisputable rights in taking their ships and in traveling wherever their legitimate business calls them upon the high seas, and exercise those rights in what should be the well-justified confidence that their lives will not be endangered by acts done in clear violation of universally acknowledged international obligations, and certainly in the confidence that their own Government will sustain them in the exercise of their rights. . . .

Long acquainted as this Government has been with the character of the Imperial Government, and with the high principles of equity by which they have in the past been actuated and guided, the Government of the United States cannot believe that the commanders of the vessels which commited these acts of lawlessness did so except under a misapprehension of the orders issued by the Imperial German naval authorities. It takes it for granted that, at least within the practical possibilities of every such case, the commanders even of submarines were expected to do nothing that would involve the lives of non-combatants or the safety of neutral ships, even at the cost of failing of their object of capture or destruction. It confidently expects, therefore, that the Imperial German Government will disavow the acts of which the Government of the United States complains; that they will make reparation so far as reparation is possible for injuries which are without measure, and that they will take immediate steps to prevent the recurrence of anything so obviously subversive of the principles of warfare for which the Imperial German Government have in the past so wisely and so firmly contended. . . .

Expressions of regret and offers of

reparation in case of the destruction of neutral ships sunk by mistake, while they may satisfy international obligations, if no loss of life results, cannot justify or excuse a practice the natural and necessary effect of which is to subject neutral nations and neutral persons to new and immeasurable risks.

3

War and Finance

☆ *As the war progressed, the Allied powers increased their demands on American production for the materials of war. This posed a serious problem for the United States, for while these orders contributed greatly to American prosperity, Allied financial resources were at the point of exhaustion by the fall of 1915. Secretary of State Robert Lansing successfully urged that the Allied powers be permitted to float loans in the United States. The Secretary's position was criticized not only as a breech of neutrality but as an unwarranted diversion of funds needed for the development of domestic enterprise.* ☆

(a) ROBERT LANSING TO WOODROW WILSON*

MY DEAR MR. PRESIDENT: Doubtless Secretary McAdoo has discussed with you the necessity of floating government loans for the belligerent nations, which are purchasing such great quantities of goods in this country, in order to avoid a serious financial situation which will not only affect them but this country as well.

Briefly the situation, as I understand it, is this: Since December 1st, 1914, to June 30, 1915, our exports have exceeded our imports by nearly a billion dollars, and it is estimated that the excess will be from July 1st to December 31, 1915, a billion and three quarters. Thus for the year 1915 the excess will be approximately two and [a] half billions of dollars.

It is estimated that the European banks have about three and [a] half billions of dollars in gold in their vaults. To

*September 6, 1915. From *Foreign Relations of The United States, The Lansing Papers 1914-1920,* I, Washington, 1939, pp. 144-147.

withdraw any considerable amount would disastrously affect the credit of the European nations, and the consequence would be a general state of bankruptcy.

If the European countries cannot find means to pay for the excess of goods sold to them over those purchased from them, they will have to stop buying and our present export trade will shrink proportionately. The result would be restriction of outputs, industrial depression, idle capital and idle labor, numerous failures, financial demoralization, and general unrest and suffering among the laboring classes.

Probably a billion and three quarters of the excess of European purchases can be taken care of by the sale of American securities held in Europe and by the transfer of trade balances of oriental countries, but that will leave three quarters of a billion to be met in some other way. Furthermore, even if that is arranged, we will have to face a more serious situation in January, 1916, as the American securities held abroad will have been exhausted.

I believe that Secretary McAdoo is convinced and I agree with him that there is only one means of avoiding this situation which would so seriously affect economic conditions in this country, and that is the flotation of large bond issues by the belligerent governments. Our financial institutions have the money to loan and wish to do so. On account of the great balance of trade in our favor the proceeds of these loans would be expended here. The result would be a maintenance of the credit of the borrowing nations based on their gold reserve, a continuance of our commerce at its present volume and industrial activity with the consequent employment of capital and labor and national prosperity.

The difficulty is—and this is what Secretary McAdoo came to see me about—that the Government early in the war announced that it considered "war loans" to be contrary to "the true spirit of neutrality." A declaration to this effect was given to the press about August 15, 1914, by Secretary Bryan. The language is as follows: "In the judgment of this Government loans by American bankers to any foreign nation at war is inconsistent with the true spirit of neutrality."

In October, 1914, after a conference with you, I gave my "impressions" to certain New York bankers in reference to "credit loans," but the general statement remained unaffected. In drafting the letter of January 20, 1915, to Senator Stone I sought to leave out a broad statement and to explain merely the reasons for distinguishing between "general loans" and "credit loans." However, Mr. Bryan thought it well to repeat the August declaration. . . .

On March 31, 1915, another press statement was given out from the Department which reads as follows:

"The State Department has from time to time received information directly or indirectly to the effect that belligerent nations had arranged with Banks in the United States for credits in various sums. While loans to belligerents have been disapproved, this Government has not felt that it was justified in interposing objection to the credit arrangements which have been brought to its attention. It has neither approved these nor disapproved —it has simply taken no action in the premises and expressed no opinion."

Manifestly the Government has committed itself to the policy of discouraging general loans to belligerent governments. The practical reasons for the policy at the time we adopted it were sound, but basing it on the ground that loans are "inconsistent with the true spirit of neutrality" is now a source of embarrassment. This latter ground is as strong today as it was a year ago, while the practical reasons for discouraging loans have largely disappeared. We have more money than we can use. Popular sympathy has become crystallized in favor of one or another of the belligerents to such an extent that the purchase of bonds would in no way increase the bitterness of the partisanship or cause a possibly serious situation.

Now, on the other hand, we are face to face with what appears to be a critical economic situation, which can only be relieved apparently by the investment of American capital in foreign loans to be used in liquidating the enormous balance of trade in favor of the United States.

Can we afford to let a declaration as to our conception of "the true spirit of neutrality" made in the first days of the war stand in the way of our national interests which seem to be seriously threatened?

If we cannot afford to do this, how are we to explain away the declaration and maintain a semblance of consistency?

My opinion is that we ought to allow the

loans to be made for our own good, and I have been seeking some means of harmonizing our policy, so unconditionally announced, with the flotation of general loans. As yet I have found no solution to the problem.

Secretary McAdoo considers that the situation is becoming acute and that something should be done at once to avoid the disastrous results which will follow a continuance of the present policy.

(b) JOHN BRISBEN WALKER (NATIONAL CHAIRMAN, FRIENDS OF PEACE) TO ROBERT LANSING*

SIR: The newspapers today report Pierpont Morgan and other Americans as in treaty with the English Government through Baron Reading, its Lord Chief Justice, and Basil P. Blackett, C. B., Special Treasury Agent of the English Government to use one thousand millions of American money in aiding the cause of the allies.

These millions are badly needed in America for financing the agricultural interests, especially that of cotton, for the railways, for the building of good roads, et cetera. Jas. J. Hill says that twice that sum is needed to put American railways in proper condition.

* September 11, 1915. From *Foreign Relations of The United States, The Lansing Papers* 1914-1920, 1, Washington, 1939, p. 147.

The money which Mr. Morgan proposes to lend can only be obtained by making use of the United States Treasury Reserve, putting commercial paper upon the Government, and using the funds thus relieved; or else by deceiving the small investor into accepting a war loan which may yet fall to 48 cents on the dollar, as did our American war securities, under English manipulation, during the war of the rebellion.

May I ask you to telegraph this organization whether we have, or have not, laws on the statute books which, as construed by you, would prevent this flagrant breach of neutrality, in thus giving aid to the financially distressed allies, while committing a positive injustice against the American people?

4

Allied Propaganda

☆ *Though not a new weapon of war, propaganda was used most effectively by Great Britain and France to develop sympathy for their cause. The Germans were portrayed as being ruthless and inhuman waging war on civilian and soldier alike.** ☆

The British in 1916 developed several new media for propaganda. One innovation which held great promise, but which was not fully exploited, was the motion picture.... Numerous newsreels and feature length pictures were released in the United States and John Masefield reported that these "cinemas" had been effective. He suggested that "films of Stratford and of other places dear to Americans, such as the old Washington home with troops passing etc. might be shown...."

Cartoons, always popular with the public, were issued in great numbers. Raemakers, the Hollander, immortalized the atrocity stories, and other cartoonists of much less fame contributed their bit towards objectifying the Allies' cause. More dignified drawings were turned out by Muirhead Bone, who was the first of many official artists at the front appointed by Wellington House.

A tremendously important department of the American Ministry of Information was that which issued photographs.... This pictorial department of Wellington

* From H. C. Peterson, *Propaganda for War: The Campaign Against American Neutrality, 1914-1917,* pp. 238-247. Copyright, 1939, by The University of Oklahoma Press, Norman. Used by permission.

House supplied the American press very liberally with photographs. It issued "a monthly illustrated magazine called *The War Pictorial,* which was sent out every month in ... [a] bewildering variety of languages. ...." In his report of August 16, 1916, [Sir Gilbert] Parker was able to say that "pictures supplied by Wellington House to the American papers are conspicuous in the Sunday editions, and on front pages of papers of every locality." The following week he gave a tremendously long list of weeklies and dailies which carried photographs emanating from Wellington House.

Propagandists who issued photographic material found that they could use effectively the same technique which the writers of propaganda employed. Questionable and even false interpretations were given to pictures just as they were given to news stories. For instance a picture of marching German troops was captioned: "The Germans Retreat"; atrocity photographs which had been taken in 1905 were re-dated 1915, and given titles which placed the blame on Germans; a snapshot of a carpet beater was issued as a picture of a whip used in German prison camps; some interned

French and English prisoners lined up were said to be German workers in a bread line; a picture of a German soldier helping a wounded Russian was given the title: "German Ghoul Actually Caught in the Act of Robbing a Russian"; a pre-war picture of German cavalry officers with their trophies of competition was entitled "Three German Cavalrymen Loaded with Gold and Silver Loot;" a picture of three men happy to return home in Germany was captioned as men happy to become French prisoners of war. The British and French not only gave false titles to news pictures; they also doctored them. The French were especially competent in this branch of propaganda.

The propaganda appeals continued along much the lines as in the early days of the war. However, by this time an entirely different situation confronted the propagandists. In the first place, although American opinion had been won over almost completely to the side of Great Britain and France, a number of difficulties had to be taken into consideration. For instance, the Germans were not so generous in making blunders as they had been in 1914 and 1915. There were no more Louvains, Edith Cavells, or *Lusitanias*. The British also found it impossible to arouse any new indignation over German activities in the United States since the propaganda and sabotage work of the latter had been practically eliminated. Another thing which detracted from British effectiveness was the fact that improved radio facilities brought considerable German news to the American press, including "the radiograph transmission of the full reports of American correspondents in Berlin and on the German fronts. . . ."

The pity campaign or the attempt to exploit American sentimentality continued unabated. Advantage was taken of every opportunity to extract tears from American eyes over "poor ruined Bel-

gium," or heroic France. One of Parker's American agents recommended the "writing-up of Belgium and the devastated parts of France rather more particularly than . . . [had] been done." Perhaps as a result of this suggestion numerous articles and interviews tending to evoke sympathy appeared in the American press. Parker found these to be successful as late as 1917. He remarked that "any allusion to Belgium is assured of an instant response from American opinion."

In the field of atrocities, considerable new material was developed. Lord Bryce issued another excellent collection of stories, this time on Armenia. Parker was able to report that "The New York *Times,* Philadelphia *Public Ledger,* and the Chicago *Herald* . . . devoted much space to the advance sheets of 'these Armenian horror stories'." Unfortunately they did not have the cordial reception given to the earlier Bryce Report. In spite of the fact that Americans greeted the Armenian reports with apathy, they still maintained a strong interest in any stories of violence which might come out of Belgium or France. In the middle of 1916 Parker commented: "It is remarkable to notice how instant is the response in the United States to every fresh German atrocity." "It might have been expected . . . [that] German atrocities would have by this time become somewhat stale. But this is not the case. There seems to be no more certain appeal to the American public than through the medium of such atrocities." Even in 1917 it was stated that they "still hold a very prominent place in American public writing."

Air attacks upon defenseless cities continued to provide material for the pity propaganda. Sir Gilbert Parker noted that "air raids upon London . . . [were] supplying a most desirable tonic to American opinion." In this particular propaganda, as in that connected with gas, there occurred a somewhat changed attitude in cases where the efficiency of the Allies was comparable with that of the Germans. On June 26, 1916, the Corpus Christi procession at Carlsruhe in Germany was bombed by planes belonging to the Allies. Five women and sixty-five children were killed. A little later Munich was attacked. In these two cases the American press reacted quite satisfactorily, in some cases even complimenting the Allies. The New York *Herald's* headline stated: "Munich Bombed By Daring French Flier In Great Feat." Here the atrocity, when done by a French aviator, became a commendable action.

. . . In April, [1916,] Bonar Law gave an interview, at the instigation of Parker, on the danger of a German invasion of the United States. It will be remembered that this was the tenor of the motion picture "The Battle Cry of Peace." In May, Lord Cromer gave an interview entitled "England's Defeat, Our Defeat." In order to establish a belief in the identity of interests of Great Britain and the United States, John Masefield even suggested: "A big application of the idea of the Rhodes scholarships" along with public mark of thanks to Yale or Harvard for their sons who have served the Allies, might be of great value. He commented, "Some few scraps of autograph by famous English writers would be ample for the purpose."

Closely akin to the "our fight" arguments was the propaganda of democracy. The injection of this issue into World War propaganda was a brilliant maneuver. It created a facade behind which the real issues of the war could be hidden, and invalidated adverse criticism of the related propaganda. It was not only an appeal to the American belief in democracy; it was an exploitation of the age-old hatred of everything foreign—in this case a foreign type of government. Many Americans had the idea that history is the story of man's struggle for a voice in his own government, and when they were told that this was the issue in the World War, their interest and sympathy were immediately enlisted. . . .

The propaganda of the last year of neutrality was not colorful, nor was it new. Not much happened that could be sensationalized, and, after a year and a half of writing and talking about the war, very little that was original remained to be said. The major task of Parker and his legion of volunteer assistants in the United States was to maintain the advantages which had already been won. This was accomplished largely through repetition of the propaganda arguments devised at the beginning of the war. Incessant reiteration of these ideas until they became an integral part of American thought patterns made possible the final conversion of the American public from passive to active adherents of the Allies.

The resulting climate of opinion made it impossible for those Americans who desired to keep out of the war to express their views. Their warning cries were drowned out by the pro-Ally tub-thumping. Even the most timid isolationists were accused of being pro-German and immediately muzzled. On the other hand, those Americans who were expressing the fashionable pro-Ally sympathies were able to be violently partisan without encountering the slightest criticism. Anglophiles and Francophiles had all the fervor of religious converts and looked upon anyone who disagreed with them as utterly devoid of decency. Propaganda had thus created an intolerance in America comparable with that in any of the warring nations. This attitude of mind made possible and inevitable the American course of action in April, 1917.

5

The Call to Prepare

☆ *Many Americans, as World War I continued, became apprehensive that should war come the United States would be unprepared. President Wilson, in a speech in New York, November 5, 1915, assumed leadership of the movement to prepare the nation for any eventuality.** ☆

. . . we are asking ourselves at the present time what our duty is with regard to the armed force of the nation. Within a year we have witnessed what we did not believe possible—a great European conflict involving many of the greatest nations of the world. The influences of a great war are everywhere in the air. All Europe is embattled.

Force everywhere speaks out with a loud and imperious voice in a titanic struggle of governments, and from one end of our own dear country to the other men are asking one another what our own force is, how far we are prepared to maintain ourselves against any interference with our national action or development. . . .

We have it in mind to be prepared, not for war, but only for defense; and with the thought constantly in our minds that the principles we hold most dear can be achieved by the slow processes of history only in the kindly and wholesome atmosphere of peace, and not by the use of hostile force. The mission of America in

* From *A Compilation of the Messages and Papers of the Presidents*, XVI, pp. 8081-8086. Published by Bureau of National Literature, Inc., New York.

the world is essentially a mission of peace and good will among men. She has become the home and asylum of men of all creeds and races. Within her hospitable borders they have found homes and congenial associations and freedom and a wide and cordial welcome, and they have become part of the bone and sinew and spirit of America itself. America has been made up out of the nations of the world and is the friend of the nations of the world.

But we feel justified in preparing ourselves to vindicate our right to independent and unmolested action by making the force that is in us ready for assertion. . . . .

It is with this idea, with this conception in mind that the plan had been made which it will be my privilege to lay before the Congress at its next session.

That plan calls for only such an increase in the regular army of the United States as experience has proved to be required for the performance of the necessary duties of the army in the Philippines, in Hawaii, in Porto Rico, upon the borders of the United States, at the coast fortifications and at the military posts of the interior.

For the rest, it calls for the training within the next three years of a force of 400,000 citizen soldiers to be raised in annual contingents of 133,000, who would be asked to enlist for three years with the colors and three years on furlough, but who, during their three years of enlistment with the colors, would not be organized as a standing force, but would be expected merely to undergo intensive training for a very brief period of each year.

Their training would take place in immediate association with the organized units of the regular army. It would have no touch of the amateur about it, neither would it exact of the volunteers more than they could give in any one year from their civilian pursuits. . . .

Moreover, it has been American policy time out of mind to look to the Navy as the first and chief line of defense. The Navy of the United States is already a very great and efficient force. Not rapidly, but slowly, with careful attention, our naval force has been developed until the Navy of the United States stands recognized as one of the most efficient and notable of the modern time.

All that is needed in order to bring it to a point of extraordinary force and efficiency as compared with the other navies of the world is that we should hasten our peace in the policy we have long been pursuing, and that chief of all we should have a definite policy of development, not made from year to year but looking well into the future and planning for a definite consummation.

We can and should profit in all that we do by the experience and example that have been made obvious to us by the military and naval events of the actual present. It is not merely a matter of building battleships and cruisers and submarines, but also a matter of making sure that we shall have the adequate equipment of men and munitions and supplies for the vessels we build and intend to build.

Part of our problem is the problem of what I may call the mobilization of the resources of the nation at the proper time if it should ever be necessary to mobilize them for national defense. We shall study efficiency and adequate equipment as carefully as we shall study the number and size of our ships, and I believe that the plans already in part made public by the Navy Department are plans which the whole nation can approve with rational enthusiasm. . . .

The only thing within our own borders that has given us grave concern in recent months has been that voices have been raised in America professing to be the voices of Americans which were not indeed and in truth American, but which spoke alien sympathies, which came from men who loved other countries better than they loved America, men who were partisans of other causes than that of America and had forgotten that their chief and only allegiance was to the great government under which they live.

These voices have not been many, but they have been very loud and very clamorous. They have proceeded from a few who were bitter and who were grievously misled. America has not opened its doors in vain to men and women out of other nations. The vast majority of those who have come to take advantage of her hospitality have united their spirits with hers as well as their fortunes.

These men who speak alien sympathies are not their spokesmen, but are the spokesmen of small groups whom it is high time that the nation should call to a reckoning. The chief thing necessary in America in order that she should let all the world know that she is prepared to maintain her own great position is that the real voice of the nation should sound forth unmistakably and in majestic volume in the deep unison of a common, unhesitating national feeling. I do not doubt that upon the first occasion, upon the first opportunity, upon the first definite challenge, that voice will speak forth in tones which no man can doubt and with commands which no man dare gainsay or resist.

6

The Declaration of War

☆ *The German announcement of the resumption of unrestricted submarine warfare in January, 1917, was soon followed by the sinking of American merchant vessels. President Wilson called Congress into a special session beginning April 2, and asked for a declaration of war against the Imperial German Government. After four days of debate, Congress resolved that a state of war existed between the United States and Germany.* ☆

(a) WOODROW WILSON*

GENTLEMEN OF THE CONGRESS: I have called the Congress into extraordinary session, because there are serious, very serious, choices of policy to be made, and made immediately which it was neither right nor constitutionally permissible that I should assume the responsibility of making.

On the third of February last, I officially laid before you the extraordinary announcement of the Imperial German Government that on and after the first day of February it was its purpose to put aside all restraints of law or of humanity and use its submarines to sink every vessel that sought to approach either the ports of Great Britain and Ireland or the western coast of Europe or any of the ports controlled by the enemies of Germany within the Mediterranean. That had seemed to be the object of the German submarine warfare earlier in the

* War message to Congress, April 2, 1917. From *A Compilation of the Messages and Papers of the Presidents*, XVII, pp. 8226-8233. Published by Bureau of National Literature, Inc., New York.

war; but since April of last year the Imperial Government had somewhat restrained the commanders of its undersea craft, in conformity with its promise then given to us that passenger boats should not be sunk, and that due warning would be given to all other vessels which its submarines might seek to destroy, when no resistance was offered or escape attempted, and care taken that their crews were given at least a fair chance to save their lives in their open boats. The precautions taken were meager and haphazard enough, as was proved in distressing instance after instance in the progress of the cruel and unmanly business, but a certain degree of restraint was observed.

The new policy has swept every restriction aside. Vessels of every kind, whatever their flag, their character, their cargo, their destination, their errand, have been ruthlessly sent to the bottom without warning and without thought of help or mercy for those on board—the vessels of friendly neutrals along with those of belligerents. Even hospital ships and ships carrying relief to the sorely bereaved and stricken people of Belgium, though the latter were provided with safe conduct through the proscribed areas by the German Government itself, and were distinguished by unmistakable marks of identity, have been sunk with the same reckless lack of compassion or of principle.

I was for a little while unable to believe that such things would in fact be done by any government that had hitherto subscribed to the humane practices of civilized nations. International law had its origin in the attempt to set up some law which would be respected and observed upon the seas, where no nation had right of dominion and where lay the free highways of the world. By painful stage after stage has that law been built up, with meager enough results, indeed, after all was accomplished that could be accomplished, but always with a clear view, at least, of what the heart and conscience of mankind demanded.

This minimum of right the German Government has swept aside under the plea of retaliation and necessity, and because it had no weapons which it could use at sea except these which it is impossible to employ as it is employing them without throwing to the winds all scruples of humanity or of respect for the understandings that were supposed to underlie the intercourse of the world.

I am not now thinking of the loss of property involved, immense and serious as that is, but only of the wanton and wholesale destruction of the lives of noncombatants, men, women and children, engaged in pursuits which have always, even in the darkest period of modern history, been deemed innocent and legitimate. Property can be paid for; the lives of peaceful and innocent people cannot be.

The present German submarine warfare against commerce is a warfare against mankind. It is a war against all nations. American ships have been sunk, American lives taken in ways which it has stirred us very deeply to learn of, but the ships and people of other neutral and friendly nations have been sunk and overwhelmed in the waters in the same way. There has been no discrimination. The challenge is to all mankind. Each nation must decide for itself how it will meet it. The choice we make for ourselves must be made with a moderation of counsel and a temperateness of judgment befitting our character and our motives as a nation. . . .

There is one choice we cannot make, we are incapable of making—we will not choose the path of submission and suffer the most sacred rights of our nation and our people to be ignored or violated. The wrongs against which we now array ourselves are no common wrongs; they cut to the very roots of human life.

With a profound sense of the solemn and even tragical character of the step I am taking and of the grave responsibilities which it involves, but in unhesitating obedience to what I deem my constitutional duty, I advise that the Congress declare the recent course of the Imperial German Government to be, in fact, nothing less than war against the Government and people of the United States; that it formally accept the status of belligerent which has thus been thrust upon it; and that it take immediate steps not only to put the country in a more thorough state of defense, but also to exert all its power and employ all its resources to bring the Government of the German Empire to terms and end the war. . . .

While we do these things, these deeply momentous things, let us be very clear, and make very clear to all the world what our motives and our objects are. My own thought has not been driven from its habitual and normal course by the unhappy events of the last two months, and I do not believe that the thought of the nation has been altered or clouded by them.

I have exactly the same things in mind now that I had in mind when I addressed the Senate on the 22d of January last; the same that I had in mind when I addressed the Congress on the 3d of February and on the 26th of February. Our object now, as then, is to vindicate the principles of peace and justice in the life of the world as against selfish and autocratic power and to set up among the really free and self-governed peoples of the world such a concert of purpose and of action as will henceforth insure the observance of those principles.

Neutrality is no longer feasible or desirable where the peace of the world is involved and the freedom of its peoples, and the menace to that peace and freedom lies in the existence of autocratic governments backed by organized force which is controlled wholly by their will, not by the will of their people. We have seen the last of neutrality in such circumstances.

We are at the beginning of an age where it will be insisted that the same standards of conduct and of responsibility for wrong done shall be observed among nations and their governments that are observed among the individual citizens of civilized states. . . .

A steadfast concert for peace can never be maintained except by a partnership of democratic nations. No autocratic government could be trusted to keep faith within it or observe its covenants. It must be a league of honor, a partnership of opinion. Intrigue would eat its vitals away; the plottings of inner circles who could plan what they would and render account to no one would be a corruption seated at its very heart. Only free peoples can hold their purpose and their honor steady to a common end and prefer the interests of mankind to any narrow interest of their own.

Does not every American feel that assurance has been added to our hope for the future peace of the world by the wonderful and heartening things that have been happening within the last few weeks in Russia?

Russia was known by those who knew her best to have been always in fact democratic at heart, in all the vital habits of her thought, in all the intimate relationships of her people that spoke their natural instinct, their habitual attitude toward life.

The autocracy that crowned the summit of her political structure, long as it had stood and terrible as was the reality of its power, was not in fact Russian in origin, character or purpose; and now it has been shaken off and the great generous Russian people have been added in all their native majesty and might to the forces that are fighting for a freedom in the world, for justice and for peace. Here is a fit partner for a league of honor.

One of the things that has served to convince us that the Prussian autocracy was not and could never be our friend is that from the very outset of the present war it has filled our unsuspecting communities and even our offices of government with spies and set criminal intrigues everywhere afoot against our national unity of council, our peace within and without, our industries and our commerce.

Indeed, it is now evident that its spies were here even before the war began; and it unhappily is not a matter of conjecture, but a fact proved in our courts of justice, that the intrigues which have more than once come perilously near to disturbing the peace and dislocating the industries of the country been carried on at the instigation, with the support, and even under the personal direction of offical agents of the Imperial Government accredited to the Government of the United States.

Even in checking these things and trying to extirpate them, we have sought to put the most generous interpretation possible upon them because we knew that their source lay, not in any hostile feeling or purpose of the German people toward us (who were, no doubt, as ignorant of them as we ourselves were), but only in the selfish designs of a government that did what it pleased and told its people nothing. But they have played their part in serving to convince us at long last that that government entertains no real friendship for us and means to act against our peace and security at its convenience. That it means to stir up enemies against us at our very doors, the intercepted note to the German Minister at Mexico City is eloquent evidence.

We are accepting this challenge of hostile purpose because we know that in such a government, following such methods, we can never have a friend; and that in the presence of its organized power always lying in wait to accomplish we know not what purpose, there can be no assured security for the democratic governments of the world.

We are now about to accept gauge of battle with this natural foe to liberty and shall, if necessary, spend the whole force of the nation to check and nullify its pretentions and end its power. We are glad, now that we see the facts with no veil of false pretense about them, to fight thus for the ultimate peace of the world and for the liberation of its peoples, the German peoples included; for the rights of nations great and small and the privilege of men everywhere to choose their way of life and of obedience. The world must be made safe for democracy. Its peace must be planted upon the tested foundations of political liberty.

We have no selfish ends to serve. We desire no conquest, no dominion. We seek no indemnities for ourselves, no material compensation for the sacrifices we shall freely make. We are but one of the champions of the rights of mankind. We shall be satisfied when those rights have been made as secure as the faith and the freedom of the nations can make them.

Just because we fight without rancor and without selfish object, seeking nothing for ourselves but what we shall wish to share with all free peoples, we shall, I feel confident, conduct our operations as belligerents without passion and ourselves observe with proud punctilio the principles of right and of fair play we profess to be fighting for. . . .

We are, let me say again, the sincere friends of the German people, and shall desire nothing so much as the early reestablishment of intimate relations of mutual advantage between us—however hard it may be for them, for the time being, to believe that this is spoken from our hearts. We have borne with their present Government through all these bitter months because of that friendship—exercising a patience and forbearance which would otherwise have been impossible. We shall, happily, still have an opportunity to prove that friendship in our daily attitude and actions toward the millions of men and women of German birth and native sympathy who live among us and share our life, and we shall be proud to prove it toward all who are in fact loyal to their neighbors and to the Government in the hour of test. They are, most of them, as true and loyal Americans as if they had never known any other fealty or allegiance. They will be prompt to stand with us in rebuking and restraining the few who may be of a different mind and purpose.

If there should be disloyalty, it will be dealt with with a firm hand of stern repression; but if it lifts its head at all, it will lift it only here and there and without countenance, except from a lawless and malignant few.

It is a distressing and oppressive duty,

gentlemen of the Congress, which I have performed in thus addressing you. There are, it may be, many months of fiery trial and sacrifice ahead of us. It is a fearful thing to lead this great peaceful people into war, into the most terrible and disastrous of all wars, civilization itself seeming to be in the balance. But the right is more precious than peace, and we shall fight for the things which we have always carried nearest our hearts—for democracy, for the right of those who submit to authority to have a voice in their own governments, for the rights and liberties of small nations, for a universal domination of right by such a concert of free peoples as shall bring peace and safety to all nations and make the world itself at last free. To such a task we can dedicate our lives and our fortunes, everything that we are and everything that we have, with the pride of those who know that the day has come when America is privileged to spend her blood and her might for the principles that gave her birth and happiness and the peace which she has treasured. God helping her, she can do no other.

(b) SENATOR GEORGE W. NORRIS*

There are a great many American citizens who feel that we owe it as a duty to humanity to take part in this war. Many instances of cruelty and inhumanity can be found on both sides. Men are often biased in their judgement on account of their sympathy and their interests. To my mind, what we ought to have maintained from the beginning was the strictest neutrality. If we had done this I do not believe we would have been on the verge of war at the present time. We had a right as a nation, if we desired, to cease at any time to be neutral. We had

a technical right to respect the English war zone and to disregard the German war zone, but we could not do that and be neutral. I have no quarrel to find with the man who does not desire our country to remain neutral. While many such people are moved by selfish motives and hopes of gain, I have no doubt but that in a great many instances, through what I believe to be a misunderstanding of the real condition, there are many honest, patriotic citizens who think we ought to engage in this war and who are behind the President in his demand that we should declare war against Germany. I think such people err in judgment and to a great extent have been misled as to the real history and the true facts by the almost unanimous demand of the great combination of wealth that has a direct financial interest in our participation in the war. We have loaned many hundreds of millions of dollars to the allies in this controversy. While such action was legal and countenanced by international law, there is no doubt in my mind but the enormous amount of money loaned to the allies in this country has been instrumental in bringing about a public sentiment in favor of our country taking a course that would make every bond worth a hundred cents on the dollar and making the payment of every debt certain and sure. Through this instrumentality and also through the instrumentality of others who have not only made millions out of the war in the manufacture of munitions, etc., and who would expect to make millions more if our country can be drawn into the catastrophe, a large number of the great newspapers and news agencies of the country have been controlled and enlisted in the greatest propaganda that the world has ever known, to manufacture sentiment in favor of war. It is now demanded that the American citizens shall be used as insurance policies to guaran-

*Speech against war, April 4, 1917. From *Congressional Record*, 65th Congress, 1st session, pp. 213-214.

tee the safe delivery of munitions of war to belligerent nations. The enormous profits of munition manufacturers, stockbrokers, and bond dealers must be still further increased by our entrance into the war. This has brought us to the present moment, when Congress, urged by the President and backed by the artificial sentiment, is about to declare war and engulf our country in the greatest holocaust that the world has ever known.

In showing the position of the bondholder and the stockbroker I desire to read an extract from a letter written by a member of the New York Stock Exchange to his customers. This writer says:

"Regarding the war as inevitable, Wall Street believes that it would be preferable to this uncertainty about the actual date of its commencement. Canada and Japan are at war, and are more prosperous than ever before. The popular view is that stocks would have a quick, clear, sharp reaction immediately upon outbreak of hostilities, and that then they would enjoy an old-fashioned bull market such as followed the outbreak of war with Spain in 1898. The advent of peace would force a readjustment of commodity prices and would probably mean a postponement of new enterprises. As peace negotiations would be long drawn out, the period of waiting and uncertainty for business would be long. If the United States does not go to war it is nevertheless good opinion that the preparedness program will compensate in good measure for the loss of the stimulus of actual war."

Here we have the Wall Street view. Here we have the man representing the class of people who will be made prosperous should we become entangled in the present war, who have already made millions of dollars, and who will make many hundreds of millions more if we get into the war. Here we have the cold-blooded proposition that war brings prosperity to that class of people who are within the viewpoint of this writer. He expresses the view, undoubtedly, of Wall Street, and of thousands of men elsewhere, who see only dollars coming to them through the handling of stocks and bonds that will be necessary in case of war. "Canada and Japan," he says, "are at war, and are more prosperous than ever before."

To whom does the war bring prosperity? Not to the soldier who for the munificent compensation of $16 per month shoulders his musket and goes into the trench, there to shed his blood and to die if necessary; not to the broken-hearted widow who waits for the return of the mangled body of her husband; not to the mother who weeps at the death of her brave boy; not to the little children who shiver with cold; not to the babe who suffers from hunger; nor to the millions of mothers and daughters who carry broken hearts to their graves. War brings no prosperity to the great mass of common and patriotic citizens. It increases the cost of living of those who toil and those who already must strain every effort to keep soul and body together. War brings prosperity to the stock gambler on Wall Street—to those who are already in possession of more wealth than can be realized or enjoyed. Again this writer says that if we can not get war, "it is nevertheless good opinion that the preparedness program will compensate in good measure for the loss of the stimulus of actual war." That is, if we can not get war, let us go as far in that direction as possible. If we can not get war, let us cry for additional ships, additional guns, additional munitions, and everything else that will have a tendency to bring us as near as possible to the verge of war. And if war comes do such men as these shoulder the musket and go into the trenches?

Their object in having war and in preparing for war is to make money. Human suffering and the sacrifice of human life are necessary, but Wall Street considers only the dollars and the cents. The men who do the fighting, the people who make the sacrifices, are the ones who will not be counted in the measure of this great prosperity that he depicts. The stock brokers would not, of course, go to war, because the very object they have in bringing on the war is profit, and therefore they must remain in their Wall Street offices in order to share in that great prosperity which they say war will bring. The volunteer officer, even the drafting officer, will not find them. They will be concealed in their palatial offices on Wall Street, sitting behind mahogany desks, covered up with clipped coupons —coupons soiled with the sweat of honest toil, coupons stained with mothers' tears, coupons dyed in the lifeblood of their fellow men.

We are taking a step today that is fraught with untold danger. We are going into war upon the command of gold. We are going to run the risk of sacrificing millions of our countrymen's lives in order that other countrymen may coin their lifeblood into money. And even if we do not cross the Atlantic and go into the trenches, we are going to pile up a debt that the toiling masses that shall come many generations after us will have to pay. Unborn millions will bend their backs in toil in order to pay for the terrible step we are now about to take. We are about to do the bidding of wealth's terrible mandate. By our act we will make millions of our countrymen suffer, and the consequences of it may well be that millions of our brethren must shed their lifeblood, millions of broken-hearted women must weep, millions of children must suffer with cold, and millions of babes must die from hunger, and all because we want to preserve the commercial right of American citizens to deliver munitions of war to belligerent nations.

7

The Cost of the War

☆ *Federal government expenditures had not significantly increased before the war, but the cost of the war—over $35,000,000,000—was three times the amount of expenditures during the first century of the federal government's operation. Due to the method of financing the war, the national debt increased from $1,225,000,000 in 1916 to $25,484,000,000 in 1919.* ☆

The total expenditures of the Government, exclusive of the principal of the public debt and postal disbursements from postal revenues, for the war period from April 6, 1917, to October 31, 1919, amounted to $35,413,000,000, according to statistics compiled on the basis of the daily Treasury statements. Of that great total covering the disbursements for two years and seven months, $11,280,000,000, or nearly 32 per cent, was met out of tax receipts and other revenues than borrowed money, although the amount of taxes does not include the December 15, 1919, installment of income and profits taxes for the fiscal year 1919, nor any part of such taxes for the fiscal year 1920.

The above calculation includes capital outlays as well as expenditures that have been permanently absorbed. No deduc-

* From *Annual Report of the Secretary of the Treasury on the State of the Finance for the Fiscal Year Ended June 30, 1919,* Washington, 1920, pp. 25-26.

tion is made for loans to the Allies, or for other investments, such as ships, stock of the War Finance Corporation, bonds of the Federal land banks, etc. Foreign loans on October 31, 1919, aggregated $9,406,000,000, and if that amount is deducted from the total expenditures, the disbursements for the purposes of the American Government during the war period under consideration were $26,007,-000,000. And on that basis, the proportion met out of tax receipts and revenues other than borrowed money was over 43 per cent.

If it is assumed that the expenses of the Government on a peace basis would have been at the rate of $1,000,000,000 a year, or $2,583,000,000 for the two years and seven months mentioned, the estimate of the gross cost of the war to October 31, 1919, would be $32,830,000,-000, inclusive of loans to foreign Governments, or $23,424,000,000 exclusive of such loans.

8

Wilson's Fourteen Points

☆ *The achievement of a permanent peace with justice became Wilson's primary reason for fighting the war. In a message to Congress, January 8, 1918, he presented the nation's war aims which provided, in his words, "the only possible program" for peace.** ☆

Not once, but again and again, we have laid our whole thought and purpose before the world, not in general terms only, but each time with sufficient definition to make it clear what sort of definite terms of settlement must necessarily spring out of them. Within the last week Mr. Lloyd George has spoken with admirable candor and in admirable spirit for the people and Government of Great Britain. There is no confusion of counsel among the adversaries of the Central Powers, no uncertainty of principle, no vagueness of detail. The only secrecy of counsel, the only lack of fearless frankness, the only failure to make definite statement of the objects of the war, lie with Germany and her allies. The issues of life and death hang upon these definitions. No statesman who has the least conception of his responsibility ought for a moment to permit himself to continue this tragical and appalling outpouring of blood and treasure unless he is sure beyond a peradventure that the objects of the vital sacrifice are part and parcel of the very life of society and that the people for

* From *A Compilation of the Messages and Papers of the Presidents*, XVII, pp. 8422-8426. Published by Bureau of National Literature, Inc., New York.

whom he speaks think them right and imperative as he does. . . .

It will be our wish and purpose that the processes of peace, when they are begun, shall be absolutely open, and that they shall involve and permit henceforth no secret understandings of any kind. The day of conquest and aggrandizement is gone by; so is also the day of secret covenants entered into in the interest of particular governments and likely at some unlooked-for moment to upset the peace of the world. It is this happy fact, now clear to the view of every public man whose thoughts do not still linger in an age that is dead and gone, which makes it possible for every nation whose purposes are consistent with justice and the peace of the world to avow now or at any other time the objects it has in view.

We entered this war because violations of right had occurred which touched us to the quick and made the life of our own people impossible unless they were corrected and the world secured once for all against their recurrence. What we demand in this war, therefore, is nothing peculiar to ourselves. It is that the world be made fit and safe to live in; and particularly that it be made safe for every peace-loving nation which, like our own, wishes to live its own life, determine its own institutions, be assured of justice and fair dealings by the other peoples of the world, as against force and selfish aggression. All the peoples of the world are in effect partners in this interest, and for our own part we see very clearly that unless justice be done to others it will not be done to us.

The program of the world's peace, therefore, is our program, and that program, the only possible program, as we see it, is this:

I.—Open covenants of peace, openly arrived at, after which there shall be no private international understandings of any kind, but diplomacy shall proceed always frankly and in the public view.

II.—Absolute freedom of navigation upon the seas, outside territorial waters, alike in peace and in war, except as the seas may be closed in whole or in part by international action for the enforcement of international covenants.

III.—The removal, so far as possible, of all economic barriers and the establishment of an equality of trade conditions among all the nations consenting to the peace and associating themselves for its maintenance.

IV.—Adequate guarantees given and taken that national armaments will be reduced to the lowest point consistent with domestic safety.

V.—Free, open-minded, and absolutely impartial adjustment of all colonial claims, based upon a strict observance of the principle that in determining all such questions of sovereignty the interests of the population concerned must have equal weight with the equitable claims of the Government whose title is to be determined.

VI.—The evacuation of all Russian territory and such a settlement of all questions affecting Russia as will secure the best and freest cooperation of the other nations of the world in obtaining for her an unhampered and unembarrassed opportunity for the independent determination of her own political development and national policy, and assure her of a sincere welcome into the society of free nations under institutions of her own choosing; and, more than a welcome, assistance also of every kind that she may need and may herself desire. The treatment accorded Russia by her sister nations in the months to come will be the acid test of their good-will, of their comprehension of her needs as distinguished from their own interests, and of their intelligent and unselfish sympathy.

VII.—Belgium, the whole world will agree, must be evacuated and restored, without any attempt to limit the sovereignty which she enjoys in common with all other free nations. No other single act will serve as this will serve to restore confidence among the nations in the laws which they have themselves set and determined for the government of their relations with one another. Without this healing act the whole structure and validity of international law is forever impaired.

VIII.—All French territory should be freed and the invaded portions restored, and the wrong done to France by Prussia in 1871 in the matter of Alsace-Lorraine, which has unsettled the peace of the world for nearly fifty years, should be righted, in order that peace may once more be made secure in the interest of all.

IX.—A readjustment of the frontiers of Italy should be effected along clearly recognizable lines of nationality.

X.—The peoples of Austria-Hungary, whose place among the nations we wish to see safeguarded and assured, should be accorded the freest opportunity of autonomous development.

XI.—Rumania, Serbia, and Montenegro should be evacuated; occupied territories restored; Serbia accorded free and secure access to the sea; and the relations of the several Balkan States to one another determined by friendly counsel along historically established lines of allegiance and nationality; and international guarantees of the political and economic independence and territorial integrity of the several Balkan States should be entered into.

XII.—The Turkish portions of the present Ottoman Empire should be assured a secure sovereignty, but the other nationalities which are now under Turkish rule should be assured an undoubted security of life and an absolutely unmolested opportunity of autonomous development, and the Dardanelles should be permanently opened as a free passage to the ships and commerce of all nations under international guarantees.

XIII.—An independent Polish State should be erected which should include the territories inhabited by indisputably Polish populations, which should be assured a free and secure access to the sea, and whose political and economic independence and territorial integrity should be guaranteed by international covenant.

XIV.—A general association of nations must be formed under specific covenants for the purpose of affording mutual guarantees of political independence and territorial integrity to great and small states alike.

In regard to these essential rectifications of wrong and assertions of right, we feel ourselves to be intimate partners of all the governments and peoples associated together against the imperialists. We cannot be separated in interest or divided in purpose. We stand together until the end.

For such arrangements and covenants we are willing to fight and to continue to fight until they are achieved; but only because we wish the right to prevail and desire a just and stable peace, such as can be secured only by removing the chief provocations to war, which this program does remove. We have no jealousy of German greatness, and there is nothing in this program that impairs it. We grudge her no achievement or distinction of learning or of pacific enterprise such as have made her record very bright and very enviable. We do not wish to injure her or to block in any way her legitimate influence or power. We do not wish to fight her either with arms or with hostile arrangements of trade, if she is willing to associate herself with us and the other peace-loving nations of the world in covenants of justice and law and fair dealing. We wish her to only accept a place of equality among the peoples of the world—the new world in which we now live—instead of a place of mastery. . . .

We have spoken, now, surely, in terms too concrete to admit of any further doubt or question. An evident principle runs through the whole program I have outlined. It is the principle of justice to all peoples and nationalities, and their right to live on equal terms of liberty and safety with one another, whether they be strong or weak. Unless this principle be made its foundation, no part of the structure of international justice can stand. The people of the United States could act upon no other principle, and to the vindication of this principle they are ready to devote their lives, their honor, and everything that they possess. The moral climax of this, the culminating and final war for human liberty, has come, and they are ready to put their own strength, their own highest purpose, their own integrity and devotion to the test.

9

Debate on the League of Nations

☆ *President Wilson was not completely satisfied with the results of the Versailles Peace Conference of 1919. He was convinced, however, that the resulting Treaty, and especially its provisions for the League of Nations, offered the best hope for enduring peace. The President fought arduously but unsuccessfully for Senate approval of the Treaty.* ☆

(a) DEFENSE OF THE VERSAILLES TREATY*

. . . this treaty was not intended merely to end this war; it was intended to prevent any similar war.

I wonder if some of the opponents of the League of Nations have forgotten the promises we made our people before we went to that peace table. We had taken by processes of law the flower of our youth from every countryside, from every household, and we told those mothers and fathers and sisters and wives and sweethearts that we were taking those men to fight a war which would end business of that sort, and if we do not end it, if we do not do the best that human concert of action can do to end it, we are of all men the most unfaithful—the most unfaithful to the loving hearts who suffered in this war, the most unfaithful to those households bowed in grief, yet lifted with the feeling that the lad laid down his life for a great thing—among other things in

order that other lads might not have to do the same thing.

That is what the League of Nations is for, to end this war justly, and it is not merely to serve notice on Governments which would contemplate the same thing which Germany contemplated, that they will do so at their peril, but also concerning the combination of power which will prove to them that they will do it at their peril. It is idle to say the world will combine against you because it may not, but it is persuasive to say the world is combined against you and will remain combined against any who attempt the same things that you attempted.

The League of Nations is the only thing that can prevent the recurrence of this dreadful catastrophe and redeem our promises. And the character of the League is based upon the experience of this very war. . . .

Now look what else is in the treaty. This treaty is unique in the history of mankind because the centre of it is the redemption of weak nations. There never was a con-

* Woodrow Wilson, address in Columbus, Ohio, September 4, 1919. From *A Compilation of the Messages and Papers of the Presidents*, XVII, pp. 8786-8789, 8792-8793. Published by Bureau of National Literature, Inc., New York.

gress of nations before that considered the rights of those who could not enforce their rights. There never was a congress of nations before that did not seek to effect some balance of power brought about by means of serving the strength and interest of the strongest powers concerned, whereas this treaty builds up nations that never could have won their freedom in any other way. It builds them up by gift, by largess, not by obligation; builds them up because of the conviction of the men who wrote the treaty that the rights of people transcended the rights of Governments, because of the conviction of the men who wrote that treaty that the fertile source of war is wrong; that the Austro-Hungarian Empire, for example, was held together by military force and consisted of peoples who did not want to live together; who did not have the spirit of nationality as toward each other; who were constantly chafing at the bonds that held them.

Hungary, though a willing partner of Austria, was willing to be her partner because she could share Austria's strength for accomplishing her own ambitions, and her own ambitions were to hold under her the Jugo-Slavic peoples that lay to the south of her; Bohemia, an unhappy partner—a partner by duress, beating in all her veins the strongest national impulse that was to be found anywhere in Europe; and north of that, pitiful Poland, a great nation divided up among the great powers of Europe, torn asunder—kinship disregarded, natural ties treated with contempt and an obligatory division among sovereigns imposed upon her, a part of her given to Russia, a part of her given to Austria, and a part of her given to Germany, and great bodies of Polish people never permitted to have the normal intercourse with their kinsmen for fear that that fine instinct of the heart should assert itself which binds families together. Poland could never have won her in-

dependence. Bohemia never could have broken away from the Austro-Hungarian combination. The Slavic peoples to the south, running down into the great Balkan peninsula, had again and again tried to assert their nationality and their independence, and had as often been crushed, not by the immediate power they were fighting, but by the combined power of Europe.

The old alliances, the old balances of power, were meant to see to it that no little nation asserted its rights to the disturbance of the peace of Europe, and every time an assertion of rights was attempted it was suppressed by combined influence and force. And this treaty tears away all that and says these people have a right to live their own lives under the governments which they themselves choose to set up. That is the American principle and I was glad to fight for it, and when strategic consideration was urged I said (not I alone, but it was a matter of common counsel) that strategic conditions were not in our thoughts; that we were not now arranging for future wars, but were giving people what belonged to them.

My fellow-citizens, I do not think there is any man alive who has a more tender sympathy for the great people of Italy than I have, and a very stern duty was presented to us when we had to consider some of the claims of Italy on the Adriatic, because strategically, from the point of view of future wars, Italy needed a military foothold on the other side of the Adriatic, but her people did not live there except in little spots. It was a Slavic people, and I had to say to my Italian friends: "Everywhere else in this treaty we have given territory to the people who lived on it, and I do not think that it is for the advantage of Italy, and I am sure it is not for the advantage of the world, to give Italy territory where other people live."

I felt the force of the argument for what they wanted, and it was the old argument that had always prevailed, namely, that they needed it from a military point of view, and I have no doubt that if there is no League of Nations they will need it from a military point of view. But if there is a League of Nations they will not need it from a military point of view. If there is no League of Nations the military point of view will prevail in every instance and peace will be brought into contempt, but if there is a League of Nations Italy need not fear the fact that the shores on the other side of the Adriatic tower above her sandy shores on her side of the sea, because there will be no threatening guns there, and the nations of the world will have concerted not merely to see that the Slavic peoples have their rights but that the Italian people have their rights as well. I would rather have everybody on my side than be armed to the teeth; and every settlement that is right, every settlement that is based upon the principles I have alluded to, is a safe settlement because the sympathy of mankind will be behind it.

Some gentlemen have feared with regard to the League of Nations that we will be obliged to do things we don't want to do. If the treaty were wrong, that might be so; but if the treaty is right, we will wish to preserve right. I think I know the heart of this great people, whom I for the time being have the high honor to represent, better than some other men that I hear talk. . . .

If I were to state what seems to me to be the central idea of this treaty it would be this (it is almost a discovery in international conventions):—"Nations do not consist of their Government, but consist of their people."

That is a rudimentary idea; it seems to go without saying to us in America; but, my fellow-citizens, it was never the leading idea in any other international congress that I ever heard of, that is to say international congress made up of the representatives of Government. They were always thinking of national policy, of national advantages, of the rivalries of trade, of the advantages of territorial conquest.

There is nothing of that in this treaty. You will notice that even the territories which are taken away from Germany, like her colonies, are not given to anybody. There isn't a single act of annexation in this treaty. But territories inhabited by people not yet able to govern themselves, either because of economic or other circumstances or the stage of their development, are put under the care of powers who are to act as trustees—trustees responsible in the forum of the world, at the bar of the League of Nations, and the terms upon which they are to exercise their trusteeship are outlined. They are not to use those people by way of profit and to fight their wars for them; they are not to permit any form of slavery among them or of enforced labor. They are to see to it that there are humane conditions of labor with regard not only to the women and children, but to the men, also. They are to establish no fortifications; they are to regulate the liquor and opium traffic; they are to see to it, in other words, that the lives of the people whose care they assume—not sovereignty over whom they assume, but whose care they assume—are kept clean and safe and wholesome. There again the principle of the treaty comes out, that the object of the arrangement is the welfare of the people who live there and not the advantages of the Government which is the trustee.

It goes beyond that, and it seeks to gather under the common supervision of the League of Nations the various instrumentalities by which the world has been trying to check the evils that were in some places debasing men, like the opium traffic, like the traffic—for it was a traffic—

in men, women, and children; like the traffic in other dangerous drugs; like the traffic in arms among uncivilized peoples, who could use arms only for their detriment; for sanitation; for the work of the Red Cross.

Why, those clauses, my fellow-citizens, draw the hearts of the world into league; draw the noble impulses of the world together and make a poem of them.

(b) DENUNCIATION OF THE TREATY*

Look upon the scene as it is now presented. Behold the task we are to assume, and then contemplate the method by which we are to deal with this task. Is the method such as to address itself to a Government "conceived in liberty and dedicated to the proposition that all men are created equal"? When this league, this combination, is formed four great powers representing the dominant people will rule one-half of the inhabitants of the globe as subject peoples—rule by force, and we shall be a party to the rule of force. There is no other way by which you can keep people in subjection. You must either give them independence, recognize their rights as nations to live their own life and to set up their own form of government, or you must deny them these things by force. That is the scheme, the method proposed by the league. It proposes no other. We will in time become inured to its inhuman precepts and its soulless methods, strange as this doctrine now seems to a free people. If we stay with our contract, we will come in time to declare with our associates that force—force, the creed of the Prussian military oligarchy—is after all the true foundation upon which must rest all stable governments. Korea, despoiled and bleeding at every pore; India, sweltering in ignorance and burdened with in-

human taxes after more than one hundred years of dominant rule; Egypt, trapped and robbed of her birthright; Ireland, with 700 years of sacrifice for independence—this is the task, this is the atmosphere, and this is the creed in and under which we are to keep alive our belief in the moral purposes and self-governing capacity of the people, a belief without which the Republic must disintegrate and die. The maxim of liberty will soon give way to the rule of blood and iron. We have been pleading here for our Constitution. Conform this league, it has been said, to the technical terms of our charter, and all will be well. But I declare to you that we must go further and conform to those sentiments and passions for justice and freedom which are essential to the existence of democracy. . . .

Sir, we are told that this treaty means peace. Even so, I would not pay the price. Would you purchase peace at the cost of any part of our independence? We could have had peace in 1776—the price was high, but we could have had it. James Otis, Sam Adams, Hancock, and Warren were surrounded by those who urged peace and British rule. All through that long and trying struggle, particularly when the clouds of adversity lowered upon the cause, there was a cry of peace— let us have peace. We could have had peace in 1860; Lincoln was counseled by men of great influence and accredited wisdom to let our brothers—and, thank Heaven, they are brothers—depart in peace. But the tender, loving Lincoln, bending under the fearful weight of impending civil war, an apostle of peace, refused to pay the price, and a reunited country will praise his name forevermore —bless it because he refused peace at the price of national honor and national integrity. Peace upon any other basis than national independence, peace purchased at the cost of any part of our national integrity, is fit only for slaves, and even

* Senator William E. Borah, address on the floor of the Senate, November 19, 1919. From *Congressional Record*, 66th Congress, 1st session, pp. 8783-8784.

when purchased at such a price it is a delusion, for it can not last.

But your treaty does not mean peace —far, very far, from it. If we are to judge the future by the past it means war. Is there any guaranty of peace other than the guaranty which comes of the control of the war-making power by the people? Yet what great rule of democracy does the treaty leave unassailed? The people in whose keeping alone you can safely lodge the power of peace or war nowhere, at no time and in no place, have any voice in this scheme for world peace. Autocracy which has bathed the world in blood for centuries reigns supreme. Democracy is everywhere excluded. This, you say, means peace.

Can you hope for peace when love of country is disregarded in your scheme, when the spirit of nationality is rejected, even scoffed at? Yet what law of that moving and mysterious force does your treaty not deny? With a ruthlessness unparalleled your treaty in a dozen instances runs counter to the divine law of nationality. Peoples who speak the same language, kneel at the same ancestral tombs, moved by the same traditions, animated by a common hope, are torn asunder, broken in pieces, divided, and parceled out to antagonistic nations. And this you call justice. This, you cry, means peace. Peoples who have dreamed of independence, struggled and been patient, sacrificed and been hopeful, peoples who were told that through this peace conference they should realize the aspirations of centuries, have again had their hopes dashed to earth. One of the most striking and commanding figures in this war, soldier and statesman, turned away from the peace table at Versailles declaring to the world, "The promise of the new life, the victory of the great humane ideals for which the peoples have shed their blood and their treasure without stint, the fulfillment of their aspirations toward a new international order and a fairer and better world, are not written into the treaty." No; your treaty means injustice. It means slavery. It means war. And to all this you ask this Republic to become a party. You ask it to abandon the creed under which it has grown to power and accept the creed of autocracy, the creed of repression and force.

VI

the mixture as before?

IMPORTANT antagonisms and confusions in American society came dramatically to the surface during the immediate post-World War I period. New problems and opportunities were profoundly altering the nation's character and attitudes, and these changes were having their effect on old problems. Urbanization and industrialism were still disrupting old patterns and converting the simple into the complex. Twenty years of reform had not stopped their inroads. The war also had a great impact on American life. Old ties and ways of life had been loosened; the status of whole layers of society had been changed; and new fears and expectations had been unleashed.

The antagonisms of the post-war period were expressed in many ways. Large-scale race riots erupted in many areas, reflecting the conflicts resulting from mass migrations of Negroes from the farm to the city and from the South to the North in response to new economic opportunities. Encouraged by the rise of international Bolshevism, wartime political conformism was perpetuated in bitterly hostile attitudes toward left-wing groups. And a revived movement—the Ku Klux Klan—swept the nation, enrolling hundreds of thousands, perhaps millions of citizens in a crusade to intimidate racial and religious minorities, immigrants, and those of unorthodox political persuasions.

While antagonism plagued American social movements, national thought was in confusion. Older ideas of morality were vigorously asserted. Pragmatism increased its influence, as did science. Cynicism also became a force in some circles. The disorder in American thought was encouraged by—and perhaps reflected in—disillusion with past idealisms, relaxed moral standards, and increased lawlessness and ballyhoo. (To many, Chicago became not just the name of a city but a way of life.) Cynics were encouraged in their disillusionment to challenge all standards; moralists were prodded to more fervent proclamations of standards by the transgressions of a new generation. Pragmatism, science, and cynicism worked to subject all

American actions and ideas to greater scrutiny. Americans were assured that they were too compulsive, too addicted to their work habits to enjoy life. They were urged to recognize the social basis of morals and to strive for a scientific set of moral standards. They were told of their increasing propensities for crowd action and for spectatorship rather than participation. They were reproved for their emphases, as one European observer saw it, on quantity rather than quality, on mechanization and standardization rather than uniqueness, and on interest in things and practicality rather than in people and ideas. They were even advised that our civilization was effete and decadent, a lost cause soon to be overwhelmed by barbarism. These messages were varied and confusing but their significance was not. American life had changed rapidly and meaning had to be found for it.

1

Racial Conflict

☆ *The movement of Negroes to the cities to take advantage of new economic opportunities was accelerated by the war. The closer contact between Negroes and urban whites accompanied by keen competion for jobs, housing, and status, resulted in violent conflict between the races in a number of communities between 1918 and 1921. The riots in the nation's capital in 1919 first focused attention on this problem.* ☆

(a) "SERVICE MEN BEAT NEGROES IN RACE RIOT AT CAPITAL"*

Police reserves were called out last night because of rioting in the Centre Market district, Seventh and Pennsylvania Avenue, in the very heart of the city, to quell soldiers, sailors, marines, and civilians who made attacks on negroes in retaliation for attacks on white women in Washington during the past month.

Several hundred soldiers, sailors, and marines participated in the rioting, along with more than a thousand civilians. Negroes were hauled from street cars and from automobiles. The Provost Guard was called out, and at 10:20 the police reserves.

Half a dozen arrests were made. Among those taken into custody were a sailor and a soldier. They were charged with disorderly conduct.

ATTACK NEAR WHITE HOUSE

Reports were received by the police of

* From *The New York Times*, July 21, 1919. Used by permission.

attacks late at night on negroes in several parts of the city, and the belief was expressed that these were the result of organized action.

Late at night several negroes were attacked by soldiers and marines at Fifteenth Street and New York Avenue Northwest, near the Riggs National Bank and within a stone's throw of the White House. Three negroes beaten here were taken to the Third Precinct Police Station. . . .

At 1 o'clock this morning a riot call was sent in to police headquarters from Ninth Street and New York Avenue. All available reserves were sent there in patrol wagons under command of Captain Flaherty.

It was reported that from 200 to 250 soldiers, sailors, and marines were engaged in an attack there on negroes.

A second riot call was sent in from Tenth and L Streets, N.W., at 1:05 A.M. A patrol wagon loaded with policemen was sent out. This place is about three blocks from Ninth Street and New York Avenue.

The group of soldiers responsible for most of the attacks moved into the Second Precinct, where they attacked negroes near the American League baseball park and drew the reserves of that precinct into action. At 2:15 o'clock the city was quiet, but reserves were still on duty.

A late report puts the number of negroes taken to the Emergency Hospital from various parts of the city at fifteen. One of the men who was attacked in the Seventh Street riot had his collarbone broken. A number of negroes who were brought bruised and bleeding into police stations were badly frightened and refused to go to their homes except under police escort.

Policeman Hellmuth, who arrested a soldier near Seventh Street and Pennsylvania Avenue, N. W., shortly after 11 o'clock, was threatened by a large crowd of soldiers, sailors, and civilians. He fought off the crowd, but finally was forced to draw his revolver and fire into the air. He managed to hold his prisoner until the patrol wagon arrived.

A number of disturbances were caused by civilians who, when a crowd of soldiers and sailors collected, pointed to any negro who might be passing and yelled, "There he goes!" Such outcries generally were followed by an attack upon the negro by some of the sailors and soldiers.

All of the policemen who reported off duty at midnight were ordered to sections where the attacks had occurred, with instructions to remain on duty until further orders.

The rioting was a repetition of disorders late Saturday night and early Sunday morning, when two hundred soldiers, sailors, and marines bent on lynching a negro in connection with an attack on a

*From *The New York Times*, July 22, 1919. Used by permission.

white woman in Southwest Washington forced the police to call out the reserves.

(b) "RACE RIOTS IN WASHINGTON"*

Race rioting was resumed with renewed violence in this city last night after a day of comparative quiet, and the disorder was still unchecked early this morning, when crowds were out in the streets, and police and armed soldiers, marines, and mounted cavalrymen were busy answering riot calls and trying to stop the clashes between whites and negroes.

A canvass of the police precincts and hospitals at 8 o'clock this morning showed four persons known dead as a result of wounds and fully seventy wounded taken to hospitals. Five of the latter are in such a precarious condition that their deaths were expected. . . .

Hundreds had been arrested for disorderly conduct or carrying concealed weapons, and in some parts of the city the rioters were from time to time beyond control.

Negroes are apparently touring the city in organized bands, many armed with revolvers, razors and loaded clubs. Some are even said to have rifles. Many of the negroes are defiant and do not hesitate to insult and attack white men and women.

In expectation of further trouble last night two troops of cavalry and detachments of infantry were ordered out late in the day to reinforce the police, but apparently these forces are not sufficient to cope with the situation. There is talk that military law may be put into effect at least in some districts where the race riots have been most violent. . . .

The race riots are the most serious with which Washington officials have had to cope in years, and large numbers of soldiers, mounted and on foot, and marines are being called to police the city.

The cavalrymen are carrying revolvers, also carbines and sabres.

The riots have taken place in spite of precautions taken by the civil and military authorities and the evidence is growing that the negroes are organized to avenge attacks made upon some of their number by soldiers and sailors within the last seventy-two hours. . . .

The scene at Seventh and Ninth Streets, Northwest, from Pennsylvania Avenue to L Street, where most of the rioting occurred, up to 10 o'clock was a picturesque one.

Small bands of negroes were walking up and down the streets in defiant mood and not a few of the negroes had their hands on hip pockets. They were being watched by the cavalry which patrolled the streets.

The infantry were patrolling also with rifles over their shoulders, ever watchful for riot calls. At times the streets were all but deserted of civilians in the district where the early rioting took place, but at intervals crowds came from moving picture theatres and strolled about, apparently showing little concern until a volley of revolver shots sent them scurrying in every direction for cover.

There were not a few officers in the crowds and even women appeared, most of them with escorts. It was evident that the seriousness of the situation was not realized by them.

It was not until after nightfall that things began to move in the second precinct at the North. Thence night attacks by negroes spread all over the city. They were especially serious in the second, eighth, and sixth precincts, and then spread into the downtown precinct, where the principal Government offices are situated.

Seventh Street northward from the old Patent Office Building at G Street, to the baseball grounds, was crowded after 9 o'clock with negroes whom the police and military forces found it difficult to disperse. East of Seventh Street and north of New York Avenue, especially along M and N Streets, eastward from Sixth Street, there are many negro centres.

The negroes in this region became active after 10 o'clock. Groups of fifty to 100 men moved around the neighborhood bent on retaliation, many of them firing shots.

2

Organized Bigotry

☆ *The Ku Klux Klan, formed in 1915 ostensibly in the image of the post-Civil War Ku Klux Klan, appealed to those who believed that American ideals and practices were being threatened by "non-assimilable" groups. Rapidly increasing its membership after World War I, the Klan in many parts of the country came to employ violent and terroristic methods.** ☆

One finds on every page of Klan literature an insistent, imperative, and even intolerant demand for like-mindedness. It is, of course, the beliefs and traditions of the old native American stock that are to provide the basis for this like-mindedness. The Catholic is free to entertain his own ideas in religion but he must feel, think, and act in terms of pure and unadulterated Americanism. The foreign-born member of the community is tolerated only on the presupposition that he learns the American tongue, adopts the American dress and conventionalities, in a word assimilates as quickly and thoroughly as possible the traditions of the old American stock. The eternal quarrel of the Klan with the Jew and the Negro is that mental and physical differences seem to have conspired to place them in groups entirely to themselves so that it becomes to all intents and purposes impossible for them to attain with anything like completeness this like-mindedness synonymous with one hundred per

* From *The Ku Klux Klan, A Study of the American Mind* by John Moffatt Mecklin, pp. 109-110, 121-123, 107-109. Copyright, 1924, by Harcourt, Brace & World, Inc. and reprinted with their permission.

cent Americanism. The Negro is granted a place in American society only upon his willingness to accept a subordinate position, for one hundred per cent Americanism means white supremacy. The Jew is tolerated largely because native Americanism cannot help itself. The Jew is disliked because of the amazing tenacity with which he resists absolute Americanization, a dislike that is not unmingled with fear; the Negro is disliked because he is considered essentially an alien and unassimilable element in society. . . .

The Klan, though organized in 1915, owes its marvellous growth to the disturbed post-war conditions. The war, with its hymns of hate, its stories of poison gas and human carnage, its secret spyings upon fellow Americans, its accounts of Belgian atrocities, its imprisonment of radicals, its fearful tales of Bolshevist designs upon American institutions, had opened up the fountains of the great deep of national feeling. After the armistice these hates kindled by the war and to which the nation had become habituated during years of bloodshed were suddenly set adrift because stripped of the objects and the ends around which they had been organized by the experience of the war. As a nation we have cultivated a taste for the cruel, the brutal, the intolerant, and the un-Christian that demanded gratification. Here was an unparalleled opportunity for the Klan "salesmen of hate." The Klan offered just what the war-torn distraught emotions of the nation demanded.

The Klan has literally battened upon the irrational fear psychology that followed on the heels of the war. The Klan's first move in the South was to capitalize the white's fear of the Negro owing to the Negro's new ambitions created by his fight for democracy and the increased demands for his labor. To-day, for various reasons, the Negro is a negligible quantity in the Klan issue South or North. The center of the fear psychology has been shifted even in the South from the Negro to the Catholic, the Jew, and the foreigner. What keeps the Klan alive in the face of powerful opposition and its patent incompatibility with the principles of true Americanism is undoubtedly a widespread distrust of all things foreign. . . .

The Klan makes a powerful appeal to the petty impotence of the small-town mind. A close observer of the Klan from Texas makes the following suggestive remark: "There is a great 'inferiority complex' on the part of the Klan membership—due in part to lack of education— Dallas and Fort Worth (where the Klan is especially strong) being largely populated by men and women reared in obscure towns and country places where public schools are short-termed and scarce." Here we have a curious sidelight upon the psychology of the average man of native American stock who fills

the ranks of the Klan. He is tossed about in the hurly-burly of our industrial and so-called democratic society. Under the stress and strain of social competition he is made to realize his essential mediocrity. Yet according to traditional democratic doctrine he is born free and the equal of his fellow who is outdistancing him in the race. Here is a large and powerful organization offering to solace his sense of defeat by dubbing him a knight of the Invisible Empire for the small sum of ten dollars. Surely knighthood was never offered at such a bargain! He joins. He becomes the chosen conservator of American ideals, the keeper of the morals of the community. He receives the label of approved "one hundred per cent Americanism." The Klan slogan printed on the outside of its literature is "an urgent call for men." This flatters the pride of the man suffering from the sense of mediocrity and defeat. It stimulates his latent idealism. It offers fantastic possibilities for his dwarfed and starved personality. Membership in a vast mysterious empire that "sees all and hears all" means a sort of mystic glorification of his petty self. It identifies his own weak incompetent will with the omnipotent and universal will of a great organization. The appeal is irresistible. There are of course others who see in this secret and powerful organization opportunities for gratifying individual ambition. Strong but unscrupulous men have availed themselves of the Klan to attain their selfish ends. On the whole, however, the high-minded and independent members of the community do not identify themselves with the Klan. It is a refuge for mediocre men, if not for weaklings, and for obvious reasons.

3

A Catholic as President?

☆ Religious intolerance was injected into the 1928 presidential campaign. For the first time in American history a Roman Catholic was nominated by a major political party as its candidate for president. While the Republican candidate, Herbert Hoover, deplored the injection of the religious issue into the campaign, many members of both parties believed that Alfred Smith's religion disqualified him for the presidency. Governor Smith discussed this matter in a letter to Charles C. Marshall in The Atlantic Monthly.* ☆

—I—

Your first proposition is that Catholics believe that other religions should, in the United States, be tolerated only as a matter of favor and that there should be an established church. You may find some dream of an ideal of a Catholic State, having no relation whatever to actuality, somewhere described. But, voicing the best Catholic thought on this subject, Dr. John A. Ryan, Professor of Moral Theology at the Catholic University of America, writes in *The State and the Church* of the encyclical of Pope Leo XIII, quoted by you:—

'In practice, however, the foregoing propositions have full application only to the completely Catholic State. . . . The propositions of Pope Pius IX condemning the toleration of non-Catholic sects do not now, says Father Pohle, "apply even to Spain or the South American republics,

* From "Catholic and Patriot: Governor Smith Replies," *The Atlantic Monthly*, CXXXIX (May, 1927), pp. 724-728.

to say nothing of countries possessing a greatly mixed population." He lays down the following general rule: "When several religions have firmly established themselves and taken root in the same territory, nothing else remains for the State than to exercise tolerance towards them all, or, as conditions exist to-day, to make complete religious liberty for individual and religions bodies a principle of government." '

That is good Americanism and good Catholicism. And Father Pohle, one of the great writers of the Catholic Church says further:—

'If religious freedom has been accepted and sworn to as a fundamental law in a constitution, the obligation to show this tolerance is binding in conscience.'

The American prelates of our Church stoutly defend our constitutional declaration of equality of all religions before the law. Cardinal O'Connell has said: 'Thus to every American citizen has come the blessed inheritance of civil, political, and religious liberty safeguarded by the American Constitution . . . the right to worship God according to the dictates of his conscience. . . .'

—II—

I come now to the speculation with which theorists have played for generations as to the respective functions of Church and State. You claim that the Roman Catholic Church holds that, if conflict arises, the Church must prevail over the State. You write as though there were some Catholic authority or tribunal to decide with respect to such conflict. Of course there is no such thing. As Dr. Ryan writes: 'The Catholic doctrine concedes, nay, maintains, that the State is coordinate with the Church and equally independent and supreme in its own distinct sphere. . . .'

What is this conflict about which you talk? It may exist in some lands which do not guarantee religious freedom. But in the wildest dreams of your imagination you cannot conjure up a possible conflict between religious principle and political duty in the United States, except on the unthinkable hypothesis that some law were to be passed which violated the common morality of all God-fearing men. And if you can conjure up such a conflict, how would a Protestant resolve it? Obviously by the dictates of his conscience. That is exactly what a Catholic would do. There is no ecclesiastical tribunal which would have the slightest claim upon the obedience of Catholic communicants in the resolution of such a conflict. As Cardinal Gibbons said of the supposition that 'the Pope were to issue commands in purely civil matters':—

'He would be offending not only against civil society, but against God, and violating an authority as truly from God as his own. Any Catholic who clearly recognized this would not be bound to obey the Pope; or rather his conscience would

bind him absolutely to disobey, because with Catholics conscience is the supreme law which under no circumstances can we ever lawfully disobey. . . .'

It is a well-known fact that I have made all of my appointments to public office on the basis of merit and have never asked any man about his religious belief. In the first month of this year there gathered in the Capitol at Albany the first Governor's cabinet that ever sat in this State. It was composed, under my appointment, of two Catholics, thirteen Protestants, and one Jew. The man closest to me in the administration of the government of the State of New York is he who bears the title of Assistant to the Governor. He had been connected with the Governor's office for thirty years, in subordinate capacities, until I promoted him to the position which makes him the sharer with me of my every thought and hope and ambition in the administration of the State. He is a Protestant, a Republican, and a thirty-second-degree Mason. In my public life I have exemplified that complete separation of Church from State which is the faith of American Catholics to-day.

—III—

I next come to education. You admit that the Supreme Court guaranteed to Catholics the right to maintain their parochial schools; and you ask me whether they would have so ruled if it had been shown that children in parochial schools were taught that the State should show discrimination between religions, that Protestants should be recognized only as a matter of favor, that they should be intolerant to non-Catholics, and that the laws of the State could be flouted on the ground of the imaginary conflict. My summary answer is: I and all my children went to a parochial school. I never heard of any such stuff being taught or of anybody who claimed that it was. That any group of Catholics would teach it is unthinkable.

—IV—

You next challenge the action of the Rota in annulling the Marlborough marriage. You suggest that the Rota by annulling the marriage (where the civil courts recognized it, but granted only a divorce) is interfering with the civil jurisdiction. That might be so if anybody claimed that the decree of the Rota had any effect under the laws of America, or any other nation of the world. But you must know that it has no such effect and that nobody claims it has. The decree merely defined the status of the parties as communicants of the Church. Your Church refuses to recognize the ecclesiastical validity of divorces granted by the civil tribunals. Your Church has its tribunals to administer its laws for the government of its members as communicants of your Church. But their decrees have no bearing upon the status of your members as citizens of the United States. There is no difference in that respect between your tribunals and the Rota.

—V—

Finally you come to Mexico. By inference from the brief of a distinguished lawyer you intimate that it is the purpose of organized Catholics to seek intervention by the United States. . . . the Pastoral Letter of the Catholic Episcopate of the United States in unmistakable words disclaimed any such intention. I do not see how, with complete candor, you could write to me about Mexico without quoting the following from that Pastoral Letter:—

'What, therefore, we have written is no call on the faithful here or elsewhere to purely human action. It is no interposition of our influence either as Bishops or as citizens to reach those who possess political power anywhere on earth, and least of all in our own country, to the end that they should intervene with armed force in the internal affairs of Mexico for the protection of the Church. Our duty is done when, by telling the story, we sound a warning to Christian civilization that its foundations are again being attacked and undermined. For the rest, God will bring His will to pass in His own good time and in His own good way.'

My personal attitude, wholly consistent with that of my Church, is that I believe in peace on earth, good will to men, and that no country has a right to interfere in the internal affairs of any other country. I recognize the right of no church to ask armed intervention by this country in the affairs of another, merely for the defense of the rights of a church. But I do recognize the propriety of Church action to request the good offices of this country to help the oppressed of any land, as those good offices have been so often used for the protection of Protestant missionaries in the Orient and the persecuted Jews of eastern Europe.

—VI—

I summarize my creed as an American Catholic. I believe in the worship of God according to the faith and practice of the Roman Catholic Church. I recognize no power in the institutions of my Church to interfere with the operations of the Constitution of the United States or the enforcement of the law of the land. I believe in absolute freedom of conscience for all men and in equality of all churches, all sects, and all beliefs before the law as a matter of right and not as a matter of favor. I believe in the absolute separation of Church and State and in the strict enforcement of the provisions of the Constitution that Congress shall make no law respecting an establishment of religion or prohibiting the free exercise thereof. I believe that no tribunal of any church has any power to make any decree of any force in the law of the land, other than to establish the status of its own communicants within its own church. I believe in the support of the public school as one of the corner stones of American liberty. I believe in the right of every parent to choose whether his child shall be educated in the public school or in a religious school supported by those of his own faith. I believe in the principle of noninterference by this country in the internal affairs of other nations and that we should stand steadfastly against any such interference by whomsoever it may be urged. And I believe in the common brotherhood of man under the common fatherhood of God.

4

Anti-Radicalism

☆ *Bigotry in the post-World War I era was also directed against political dissenters. During this period of the "great Red scare," state and federal governmental officials undertook to discredit and intimidate left-wing political action. One of the prime incidents in this episode was the refusal in 1920 to seat five socialists elected to the lower house of the New York State Legislature. The fears which contributed to the "great Red Scare" of 1919-1920 continued throughout the 1920's and were best publicized during the long drawn-out Sacco-Vanzetti case.* ☆

(a) AN ORDEAL OF THE SOCIALISTS*

"Imagine a defendant brought into court on a charge of larceny," said Morris Hillquit, summing up toward the end of the trial of the five Socialist Assemblymen at Albany, "the District Attorney trying him for forgery, the judge submitting the case to the jury upon the theory of arson, and the jury bringing in a verdict of assault and battery. That is practically what you are confronted with."

Thaddeus C. Sweet, Speaker; Simon L. Adler, Republican floor leader; Louis M. Martin, chairman of the Judiciary Committee; Charles D. Newton, Attorney General; Martin Conboy, special counsel for the prosecution—each of them made an attempt at formulating the charges against the Socialists. The results varied. The evidence varied too.

The drama began in the Assembly on

* From Lewis S. Gannett, "The Socialists' Trial at Albany: A Summary," *The Nation,* CX (March 20, 1920), pp. 361-362.

January 7. Speaker Sweet called upon the Sergeant-at-Arms to produce the five Socialists before the bar. "You are seeking seats in this body," the Speaker began, "after having been elected on a platform that is absolutely inimical to the best interests of the State of New York and of the United States. . . . You . . . are bound to act subject to instructions received from an Executive Committee which may be made up in whole or in part of aliens or alien enemies." He quoted from the Socialist platform of 1917, which declared in substance that the only war worth fighting was the class war, and from the resolution passed at the emergency convention last September, which declared solidarity with the organized workers of Russia. Speaker Sweet then read parts of the Communist Manifesto of the Moscow Internationale as an interpretation of the American resolution.

Mr. Adler, Republican floor leader,

followed, reading a resolution denying seats in the Assembly to the five Socialists, "pending the determination of their qualification and eligibility to their respective seats," by a Judiciary Committee, yet to be appointed. This resolution recited that:

(1) The five Assemblymen were members of the Socialist Party of America;

(2) That party had declared "its adherence to and solidarity with the revolutionary forces of Soviet Russia," and was pledged to the furtherance of the international socialist revolution;

(3) It had thereby endorsed the principles of the Communist Internationale, which was pledged to the violent overthrow of all organized governments;

(4) The Assemblymen had agreed on joining to be guided by the constitution and platform of the Socialist party;

(5) If they did not carry out the instructions of the dues-paying members of the party, they were subject to suspension from the party;

(6) The Executive Committee, which might give them such instructions, might be made up of aliens or alien enemies;

(7) The party had declared that only the class struggle could justify taking up arms;

(8) The party had urged its members to refrain from taking any part in the war;

(9) The party had been "convicted of a violation of the Espionage act of the United States."

The charges, obviously, were charges against the Socialist party, not against the individual Assemblymen who were members thereof; and it was chiefly on that ground that the New York City Bar Association protested against the proceedings and sent a committee, headed by Charles E. Hughes, to Albany "to safeguard and protect the principles of representative government which are involved in the proceedings now pending."

Senator Clayton R. Lusk said it would be unfortunate if an impression went out that the action against these men was due to the fact that they happened to be Socialists. Senator Lusk is chairman of the joint legislative committee to investigate seditious activities which gathered such of the evidence against the Assemblymen as had been gathered before their suspension, and which was generally credited by the Albany correspondents with a large share of responsibility for the trial.

Speaker Sweet, who had formulated the first indictment, also named the Judiciary Committee which was to try the Socialists. It consisted of thirteen lawyers, ten Republicans and three Democrats, the chairman being Louis M. Martin, vice-chairman of the Lusk Committee. Mr. Martin, in formulating the indictment for the third time, combined the Lusk and Sweet-Adler points of view. He declared that the five Socialists were members of a party which "called for and demanded the complete destruction of our form of government by the fomentation of industrial unrest, the bringing into play of force and violence and direct action by the masses," but he added that as individuals they had "by voice and vote in public and in private opposed every measure intended to aid the prosecution of the war to a successful conclusion and gave aid and comfort to the enemy." They were, he said, "engaged in a large and well-organized conspiracy to subvert the due administration of law and to destroy the right to hold and own private property honestly acquired, to weaken the family tie which they assert is the seed of capitalism, to destroy the influence of the church, and overturn the whole fabric of a constitutional form of government.

The evidence may be classified roughly in three groups: evidence regarding the individual Assemblymen, evidence regarding the Socialist party as a party, and evidence having to do with Socialist parties in other countries, with the Communist party in this country, and with various other members of the Socialist party of America.

An extraordinary variety of evidence of this third class was introduced. The complete testimony of the Russian Soviet Ambassador before the Lusk Committee and before the United States Senate Committee, the complete record of the Victor Berger trial, the court record of three Socialists convicted at Syracuse for distributing amnesty circulars, speeches by various present and former members of the Socialist party, articles from Socialist papers going back as far as 1912, the manifesto of an international group of communists with headquarters at Moscow, an account of the general strike at Winnipeg in western Canada, propaganda of the Communist and Communist Labor parties which seceded from, or were expelled from, the Socialist party—all these were read into the record. In any ordinary court such remote evidence would have been excluded. But John B. Stanchfield, attorney for the prosecution, justified its introduction by the statement that "Every declaration, every speech, every statement of every man who is affiliated with or belongs to that party, is bound by the speeches, the sentiments, the writings, the books, the publications of every other man affiliated with that association, whether they were present at the time when it was uttered or whether they were absent."

Morris Hillquit moved the exclusion of much of the evidence. "I am inclined to deny all your motions without further argument," Chairman Martin replied. "Not because I do not say that you have argued conclusively as to some of the evidence, but in this wide scope of evidence, I am carefully analyzing it. I have gone down through 515 pages, and, as I have carefully analyzed it, 92 pages of that are quite important. You are dealing with a lot of lawyers and we can fix that up."

Much of the evidence hinged upon the interpretation of words. Various declarations of the Socialist party referring to "mass action," the "general strike," and the "social revolution" were introduced, and the prosecution interpreted these as appeals to violence. The party had, in April, 1917, just as the United States was entering the war, pledged itself to "unyielding opposition to all legislation for military and industrial conscription, continuous efforts for the repeal of such laws, and support of all mass movements in opposition to conscription." Algernon Lee, director of the Rand School of Social Science, and long a leading member of the party, defined "mass action," as used by Socialists, to mean "strikes, activities of labor unions, carrying out political campaigns, holding mass meetings." Otto F. Branstetter, national secretary of the Socialist party, said that the general strike as a weapon had never been endorsed officially by the Socialist party, although "it admitted the possibility of a general strike, and under conditions which might possibly arise, as being even desirable." Morris Hillquit explained on the stand that "the term 'social revolution' in Socialist pamphlets and the party manifesto meant merely a change of economic development and the substitution of public for private ownership of all necessities. The word 'revolution' does not have for us the romantic significance of barricade fights or any other acts of violence that it has for most of our newspaper writers and schoolboys. We mean by it merely change or transition."

"Solidarity with the revolutionary workers of Russia in the support of the government of the Soviets," as pledged by the Socialist party in September, 1919, came in for a great deal of definition. Attorney General Newton read in this an intent to substitute the Russian Soviet form of government for the American; attorneys for the defense saw only an expression of the right of self-determination. The attitude of the Socialists during the war was also a topic of much controversy. The Socialists opposed the war before it began, but did not obstruct it, declared Algernon Lee. They were flagrantly disloyal, said the attorneys for the prosecution, and cited the convictions of Victor Berger and others. "We opposed the war because we regarded it wrong to enter this hideous, inhuman slaughter called war for a country four thousand miles away from the scene of conflict and not concerned in it. If similar conditions arise again I am sure we will take the same position," said Morris Hillquit. "It is only the arrant political coward who supinely submits to what he in good faith considers a crime."

(b) REFUSAL OF PARDON BY GOVERNOR ALVAN T. FULLER IN SACCO-VANZETTI CASE*

. . . the most vital question of all, is that of the guilt or innocence of the accused. In this connection I reviewed the Bridgewater attempted hold-up for which Vanzetti had previously been tried before another jury and found guilty. At this trial Vanzetti did not take the witness stand in his own defense. He waived the privilege of telling his own story to the jury, and did not subject himself to cross-examination.

Investigating this case, I talked to the counsel for Vanzetti at the Plymouth trial, the jurymen, the trial witnesses, new witnesses, present counsel and Vanzetti. I have talked with the Government witnesses who saw the Bridgewater hold-up and who identified Vanzetti, and I believe their testimony to be substantially correct.

I believe with the jury that Vanzetti was guilty and that his trial was fair. I found nothing unusual about this case except, as noted above, that Vanzetti did not testify. In the Bridgewater case, practically every one who witnessed the attempted hold-up and who could have identified the bandits identified Vanzetti.

The South Braintree crime was particularly brutal. The murder of the paymaster (Parmenter) and the guard (Berardelli) was not necessary to the robbery. The murders were accomplished first, the robbery afterward. The first shot laid Berardelli low in the roadway, and after Parmenter was shot, he dropped the money box in the road and ran across the street.

The money could then have been taken, but the murderers pursued Parmenter across the road and shot him again, and then returned and fired three more shots into Berardelli, four in all, leaving his lifeless form in the roadway.

The plan was evidently to kill the witnesses and terrorize the bystanders. The murderers escaped in an automobile driven by one of their confederates, the automobile being afterward located in the woods at Bridgewater, eighteen miles distant.

Vanzetti, when arrested on May 5, had in his hip-pocket a fully loaded revolver. Sacco had a loaded pistol tucked into the front of his trousers and twenty loose cartridges which fitted this pistol.

Upon being questioned by the police both men told what they afterward admitted was a tissue of lies. Sacco claimed to have been working at Kelly's shoe factory on April 15, the date of the South Braintree crime. Upon investigation, it was proven that he was not at work on that day.

He then claimed to have been at the

* From *The New York Times*, August 4, 1927.

Italian Consulate in Boston on that date, but the only confirmation of this claim is the memory of a former employee of the Consulate who made a deposition in Italy that Sacco among forty others was in the office that day. This employee had no memorandum to assist his memory.

As the result of my study of the record and my personal investigation of the case, including my interviews with a large number of witnesses, I believe, with the jury, that Sacco and Vanzetti were guilty and that the trial was fair.

This crime was committed seven years ago. For six years, through dilatory methods, one appeal after another, every possibility for delay has been utilized, all of which lends itself to attempts to frighten and coerce witnesses, to influence changes in testimony, to multiply by the very years of time elapsed the possibilities of error and confusion.

It might be said that by undertaking this investigation I have contributed to the elaborate consideration accorded these men. My answer is that there was a feeling on the part of some people that the various delays that had dragged this case through the courts for six years were evidence that a doubt existed as to the guilt of these two men.

The feeling was not justified. The persistent determined efforts of an attorney of extraordinary versatility and industry, the Judge's illness, the election efforts of three district attorneys, and dilatoriness on the part of most of those concerned are the principal causes of delay. The delays that have dragged this case out for six years are inexcusable.

This task of review has been a laborious one and I am proud to be associated in this public service with clear-eyed witnesses, unafraid to tell the truth, and with jurors who discharged their obligations in accordance with their convictions and their oaths.

As a result of my investigation I find no sufficient justification for Executive intervention.

I believe with the jury, that these men, Sacco and Vanzetti, were guilty and that they had a fair trial. I furthermore believe that there was no justifiable reason for giving them a new trial.

(c) STATEMENT OF BARTOLOMEW VANZETTI TO THE COURT BEFORE SENTENCING*

Yes. What I say is that I am innocent, not only of the Braintree crime, but also of the Bridgewater crime. That I am not only innocent of these two crimes, but in all my life I have never stole and I have never killed and I have never spilled blood. That is what I want to say. And it is not all. Not only am I innocent of these two crimes, not only in all my life I have never stole, never killed, never spilled blood, but I have struggled all my

life, since I began to reason, to eliminate crime from the earth.

Everybody that knows these two arms knows very well that I did not need to go in between the street and kill a man to take the money. I can live with my two arms and live well. But besides that, I can live even without work with my arm for other people. I have had plenty of chance to live independently and to live what the world conceives to be a higher life than not to gain our bread with the sweat of our brow. . . .

Now, I should say that I am not only innocent of all these things, not only have I never committed a real crime in my

* April 9, 1927. From *The Sacco-Vanzetti Case, Transcript of the Record of the Trial of Nicola Sacco and Bartolomeo Vanzetti in the Courts of Massachusetts and Subsequent Proceedings, 1920-1927, V*, pp. 4896-4899, 4904. Published by Henry Holt and Company, New York, 1929.

life—though some sins but not crimes—not only have I struggled all my life to eliminate crimes, the crimes that the official law and the official moral condemns, but also the crime that the official moral and the official law sanctions and sanctifies,—the exploitation and the oppression of the man by the man, and if there is a reason why I am here as a guilty man, if there is a reason why you in a few minutes can doom me, it is this reason and none else. . . .

Is it possible that only a few on the jury, only two or three men, who would condemn their mother for worldly honor and for earthly fortune; is it possible that they are right against what the world, the whole world has say it is wrong and that I know that it is wrong? If there is one that I should know it, if it is right or if it is wrong, it is I and this man. You see it is seven years that we are in jail. What we have suffered during these seven years no human tongue can say, and yet you see me before you, not trembling, you see me looking you in your eyes straight, not blushing, not changing color, not ashamed or in fear. . . .

We have proved that there could not have been another Judge on the face of the earth more prejudiced and more cruel than you have been against us. We have proven that. Still they refuse the new trial. We know, and you know in your heart, that you have been against us from the very beginning, before you see us. Before you see us you already know that we were radicals, that we were underdogs, that we were the enemy of the institution that you can believe in good faith in their goodness—I don't want to condemn that

—and that it was easy on the time of the first trial to get a verdict of guiltiness.

We know that you have spoke yourself and have spoke your hostility against us, and your despisement against us with friends of yours on the train, at the University Club of Boston, on the Golf Club of Worcester, Massachusetts. I am sure that if the people who know all what you say against us would have the civil courage to take the stand, maybe your Honor —I am sorry to say this because you are an old man, and I have an old father—but maybe you would be beside us in good justice at this time. . . .

Well, I have already say that I not only am not guilty of these two crimes, but I never commit a crime in my life—I have never steal and I have never kill and I have never spilt blood, and I have fought against the crime, and I have fought and I have sacrificed myself even to eliminate the crimes that the law and the church legitimate and sanctify.

This is what I say: I would not wish to a dog or to a snake, to the most low and misfortunate creature of the earth—I would not wish to any of them what I have had to suffer for the things that I am not guilty of. But my conviction is that I have suffered for things that I am guilty of. I am suffering because I am a radical and indeed I am a radical; I have suffered because I was an Italian, and indeed I am an Italian; I have suffered more for my family and for my beloved than for myself; but I am so convinced to be right that if you could execute me two times, and if I could be reborn two other times, I would live again to do what I have done already.

5

The Tinseled Twenties

☆ *Change in American social attitudes and behavior was accelerated by prosperity, encouraged by advertising, and exemplified by the automobile, the radio, and the motion picture. Lloyd Morris discusses some of these factors and their consequences in the following selection.* * ☆

The eighteenth amendment to the Constitution aroused no organized opposition. The Senate debated it for thirteen hours; the House, for only seven. The prospect of national sobriety infatuated the American conscience, pitched to the highest idealism suddenly collapsed. When the end all wars forever, to make the world safe for democracy. Then, after hostilities ceased and the last parades disbanded, idealism suddenly collapsed. When the prohibition amendment became effective, in 1920, Americans were tired of causes, surfeited with conscience. Did they care to follow Woodrow Wilson to those heights upon which there rests nothing but the pure light of the justice of God? They did not. Presently Wilson, broken and embittered, made way for genial, handsome Senator Harding. "Normalcy," the familiar dead level, was preferable to lonely, inaccessible heights. In the emotional reaction which that choice represented, a new dispensation began.

All at once, America was going on the greatest, gaudiest spree in history. The older generation was merely weary of

idealism. The young generation was truculently cynical. Heroism, and the sweetness of dying for exalted principles? Let John Dos Passos answer for them, in *Three Soldiers,* or E. E. Cummings, in *The Enormous Room;* both had been "over there." F. Scott Fitzgerald, recently of Princeton and the army, spoke for them too. The note was one of utter disenchantment; pride alone modulated tears into a febrile, heartbreaking laughter. *This Side of Paradise* announced the jazz age —the reign of the beautiful who thought themselves damned, the lost generation whose casual couplings were casually reported by Ernest Hemingway in *The Sun Also Rises.*

Gentlemen might prefer blondes, but youth declared its extreme disillusion: the older generation had pretty well ruined this world before passing it on to them. It had grown up to find all Gods dead, all wars fought, all faiths in man shaken. What remained—except, perhaps, the mystical gospel of the wisdom of the flesh expounded by D. H. Lawrence? Wasn't it worth a trial? In one's stride. Without pledges. If possible, burdened by no hope but the hope of a momentary oblivion. So, disappointment would be

* From *Postscript to Yesterday,* by Lloyd Morris, pp. 68-70. Copyright 1947 by Lloyd Morris. Reprinted by permission of Random House, Inc., and Nannine Joseph.

cheated of its opportunity. The new vocabulary of passion excluded sentiment: Edna St. Vincent Millay—her shining palace built upon the sand—wrote the bittersweet, skeptical love songs of a frightened generation.

Over the land, youth was convinced that life was lousy, but that sex might be swell. The word "neck" ceased to be a noun; abruptly became a verb; immediately lost all anatomical precision. Closed automobiles swiftly replaced the familiar old open car. In Muncie, Indiana, a judge of the juvenile court told the investigating Lynds that the family bus had become a house of prostitution on wheels. This new use was expedient, and prevalent. After a little, older folk picked up the trick from their juniors. Sheiks and their shebas flocked to the movies to see *Woman Who Give,* and *The Queen of Sin.* They sang and danced to, "Hot Lips" and "Baby, I Need Lovin'." Two and one half million literates emptied the newsstands of Bernarr McFadden's *True Stories.* In New York City's austere temple of classical music, Paul Whiteman offered the first performance of George Gershwin's "A Rhapsody in Blue." With *Black Oxen* Mrs. Gertrude Atherton, a novelist no longer young, aroused wistful hopes in her feminine contemporaries. The story revealed how, by means of a glandular operation, grandmothers might be rejuvenated, and thereafter raise the temperature of youthful sophisticates.

"Normalcy" was being ushered in by the ubiquitous wail of the saxophone. By petting parties and gate crashing. By drunken brawls in exclusive country clubs. By bootleggers and speakeasies; rumrunners, hijacking, bank robberies. By a procession of weeping women eleven blocks long which filed past the mortal remains of Rudolph Valentino. By the cosy extermination of new enterprisers whose disgruntled competitors took them "for a ride" or buried them alive in barrels filled with cement. The Federal government fostered a boom in padlocks. Jewelers did a brisk trade in hip flasks. These new accessories were usually made of silver; but one could likewise procure them in gold, sometimes encrusted with gems. For this was the coprosperity era of Harding, Coolidge and the luckless Hoover— who foresaw a national destiny of two automobiles in every garage, a fat chicken in every pot. Cooks, bootblacks, clerks, housewives, teachers, errand boys were plunging into the maelstrom of a runaway bull market in Wall Street.

An outstandingly successful advertising agent became the nation's favorite theologian. Were not the gospels obsolete? Bruce Barton unveiled *The Man Nobody Knows.* Barton knew, and told the world. In the new gospel according to Bruce, Jesus was an efficient executive who picked twelve men from the bottom ranks of business and forged them into an organization that conquered the world. His parables were the most successful advertisements of all time. He was, in short, the founder of modern business. There was another man whom nobody knew who, by the efforts of Barton's professional colleagues, achieved an almost equivalent celebrity. This was "Mr. Addison Sims of Seattle." He was the American whom everyone had met and promptly forgotten. But it was important to remember him; to be able to greet him by name, after years of oblivion. It was important if one wanted to be, like Jesus, an efficient executive—as who did not? Why it was important, except as a minor matter of courtesy, was a mystery understood only by copy writers for a memory course; but the mystery became an article of faith. When Dr. Charles W. Eliot, president-emeritus of Harvard, sternly rebuked America's "best people" for setting an example of lawlessness, few heeded him. The age of ballyhoo had invented its retort to all old-fashioned moralists: "Aw, you're nuts!"

6

The Gangsters

☆ *Crime and corruption had disrupted life in American cities for decades, but the 1920's saw skillful organization and administration of illegal activities on a scale previously unknown. It appeared to many that crime did pay as underworld lords such as Johnny Torrio and Alphonse Capone systematically exploited the flaws in America's moral makeup.** ☆

As an organizer and administrator of underworld affairs Johnny Torrio is unsurpassed in the annals of American crime; he was probably the nearest thing to a real master mind that this country has yet produced. He conducted his evil enterprises as if they had been legitimate business. In the morning he kissed his wife good-by and motored to his magnificently furnished offices on the second floor of the Four Deuces. There he bought and sold women, conferred with the managers of his brothels and gambling dens, issued instructions to his rum-runners and bootleggers, arranged for the corruption of police and city officials, and sent his gun squads out to slaughter rival gangsters who might be interfering with his schemes. But he never accompanied his killers on these forays, for Torrio himself was not a gunman; he once boasted proudly that he had never fired a pistol in his life. . . .

Already the foremost vicemonger in the United States, with an annual income

* Reprinted from *Gem of the Prairie* by Herbert Asbury, pp. 320-321, 324, 336-340, by permission of Alfred A. Knopf, Inc. Copyright 1940 by Alfred A. Knopf, Inc.

from prostitution of at least a hundred thousand dollars a year, Johnny Torrio began to organize the beer and liquor traffic of Chicago and Cook County in the late summer of 1920. He held long conferences with the leaders of the principal criminal gangs and persuaded them to abandon bank robbery, burglary, and banditry, for the time being at least, in favor of bootlegging and rum-running. He promised them riches beyond their wildest dreams, and more than made good his promises. He formed an alliance with Joseph Stenson, member of a well-known family and a wealthy brewer before prohibition, and took over the five breweries which, according to the Illinois Crime Survey, Stenson was operating in partnership with Terry Druggan and Frankie Lake, co-captains of the Valley gang and trusted henchman of Morris Eller, trustee of the Chicago Sanitary District and political boss of the Twentieth Ward. Utilizing Stenson's business experience and connections, Torrio acquired more breweries. Some were bought outright. Others were leased. A few remained in the hands of their original owners, while Torrio and his gangsters "fronted" for them—that is, assumed ownership and accepted responsibility in the event of trouble. . . .

The fortunes of Johnny Torrio reached their peak . . . in the late spring of 1924, [when] in partnership with Al Capone, he was running twenty-five large brothels scattered throughout Cook County, probably twice as many gambling-houses and immoral cabarets in the suburbs and in Chicago, and was operating or handling the output of sixty-five breweries. He also controlled several distilleries, and was running enormous quantities of hard liquor into Chicago from Canada and the Atlantic seaboard, using trucks and automobiles with secret compartments built into the top and floors. Most of Torrio's breweries were in operation for nearly ten years; many continued to manufacture beer even after they had been officially padlocked by the Federal government. Trucks belonging to Torrio and allied gang leaders, loaded with beer and whisky and guarded by armed gunmen, rumbled day and night through the streets of Chicago and Cook County, supplying at least three-fourths of the twenty thousand drinking places which came into existence after the dry amendment had gone into effect on January 16, 1920.

Except for an occasional attempt at hijacking by Spike O'Donnell and a few other independent gangsters, Torrio's liquor convoys were seldom molested; on the contrary, whenever a particularly valuable shipment was made, the criminal guards were frequently supplemented by detachments of uniformed policemen. For as the money rolled in, Torrio expanded to appalling proportions the system of corruption by which he had kept his brothels immune from interference. He gave liberally to campaign funds, and bought policemen, prohibition and enforcement agents, judges, politicians, and city and county officials as he needed them; hundreds openly received their bribes each week at a payoff station conveniently established in a downtown office building. It was not without reason that Torrio boasted: "I own the police." Many officials, of course, refused to "go along" with the gangsters. . . . But for all practical purposes Johnny Torrio dominated the political machines of Chicago and Cook County, and to a somewhat lesser degree the Federal enforcement agencies for those districts, throughout the first and second administrations of Mayor William Hale Thompson, just as Al Capone did during most of Thompson's third term. . . .

Torrio's payroll, exclusive of the huge sums disbursed for protection, was not less than thirty thousand dollars a week. The profits from his various criminal enterprises were never accurately computed, but evidence obtained by the authorities from time to time indicated that they totaled an enormous amount. . . . Federal investigators declared that from vice and gambling combined Torrio and Capone divided net earnings of two hundred thousand dollars a week. Ledgers seized in a raid on the gangsters' headquarters, transferred in 1923 from the Four Deuces to an elaborate suite of offices on Michigan Avenue, listed profits of three million dollars a year from whisky, beer, and wine. But these ledgers formed only a small part of the syndicate's bookkeeping system; the police estimated that the total annual profits from the manufacture and sale of liquor were at least thirty million dollars. Edwin A. Olson, United States District Attorney, told the newspapers that Torrio and Capone operated on a gross basis of seventy million dollars a year.

With the police demoralized and helpless and the whole machinery of law-enforcement in a condition of collapse, criminals who for years had lurked in the dark corners of the underworld came brazenly into the open. They took service under the captains of the gangs and so shared generously in the golden flood of prohibition, but at the same time they didn't neglect their own specialties. Banks all over Chicago were robbed in broad daylight by bandits who scorned to wear masks. Desk sergeants at police stations grew weary of recording holdups—from one hundred to two hundred were reported every night. Burglars marked out sections of the city as their own and embarked upon a course of systematic plundering, going from house to house night after night without hindrance. Fences accompanied thieves into stores and appraised stocks of merchandise before they were stolen. Pickpockets and confidence men flourished as they had not done since the first World's Fair. Payroll robberies were a weekly occurrence and necessitated the introduction of armored cars and armed guards for the delivery of money from banks to business houses. Automobiles were stolen by the thousands. Motorists were forced to the curb on busy streets and boldly robbed. Women who displayed jewelry in night clubs or at the theater were followed and held up. Wealthy women seldom left their homes unless accompanied by armed escorts.

Chicago seemed to be filled with gang-sters—gangsters slaughtering one another, two hundred and fifteen in four years; gangsters being killed by the police, one hundred and sixty in the same length of time; gangsters shooting up saloons for amusement; gangsters throwing bombs, called "pineapples"; gangsters improving their marksmanship on machine-gun ranges in sparsely settled districts; gangsters speeding in big automobiles, ignoring traffic laws; gangsters strutting in the Loop, holstered pistols scarcely concealed; gangsters giving orders to the police, to judges, to prosecutors, all sworn to uphold the law; gangsters calling on their friends and protectors at City Hall and the County Court House; gangsters dining in expensive restaurants and cafes; tuxedoed gangsters at the opera and the theater, their mink-coated, Paris-gowned wives or sweethearts on their arms; gangsters entertaining politicians and city officials at "Belshazzar feasts," some of which cost twenty-five thousand dollars; gangsters giving parties at which the guests playfully doused each other with champagne at twenty dollars a bottle, popping a thousand corks in a single evening; gangsters armed with shotguns, rifles, and machine-guns, convoying beer trucks; gangsters everywhere—except in jail.

7

The Noble Experiment

☆ *The crusade against the manufacture and sale of alcoholic beverages, led by the powerful Anti-Saloon League, resulted in the adoption of the 18th Amendment to the Constitution in 1919. The Volstead Act, passed later in 1919, attempted to provide for strict enforcement of prohibition. President Herbert Hoover comments on the problems encountered in administering this legislation.* * ☆

Prohibition cast a cloud over all our problems of law enforcement and was generally a constant worry. I should have been glad to have humanity forget all about strong alcoholic drinks. They are moral, physical, and economic curses to the race. But in the present stage of human progress, this vehicle of joy could not be generally suppressed by Federal law.

The first hard practical fault was in the concept of enforcement. The Federal law assumed that state and local officials would look after violations within the state, and that the Federal government would simply stop the interstate traffic. During the nine years of the law prior to my administration, the officials of the states most clamorous for national prohibition, including Iowa, Kansas, Ohio, Indiana, Alabama, and Georgia, steadily abandoned their responsibilities and loaded them upon the Federal government. Practically nowhere in the country

did the local police forces even take notice of violations, except as a basis of graft. The Federal government could not have come anywhere near enforcement with a police force of fewer than 250,000 men. In the meantime, the bootleg business had grown to such dimensions as to be able to corrupt or mislead the Federal enforcement officers all over the country.

However, under my oath of office, the very core of the Presidency was enforcement of the laws. I therefore gave prohibition enforcement the utmost organization that the Federal government could summon. We secured legislative authority to reorganize, consolidate, and greatly expand the Federal agencies. Under Mrs. Mabel Walker Willebrant's direction we certainly locked up or otherwise punished a horde of bootleggers. During my four years we increased the number of bootlegging citizens resident in Federal jails, or on parole, from an average of about 22,000 to about 53,000. These did not include the vast number of cases resulting in fines, padlockings, confiscations, and other suppression devices. The number of prohibition convictions rose to about 80,-

* From *The Memoirs of Herbert Hoover—The Cabinet and the Presidency*, pp. 275-278. Copyright 1951, 1952 by Herbert Hoover and used with permission of The Macmillan Company.

000 in 1932, and finally demonstrated the futility of the whole business.

However, prohibition was not the only law to be enforced. This was indicated by the steady increase of Federal convictions for other crimes from 9,600 in 1929 to 13,800 in 1932.

One of the notable triumphs in law enforcement was the conviction of Al Capone. This action represented much more than just sending a gangster to jail. In March, 1929, a committee of prominent Chicago citizens, under the leadership of Walter Strong, the publisher of the *Daily News,* and Judge Frank Loesch, president of the Chicago Crime Commission, called upon me to reveal the situation in that city. They gave chapter and verse for their statement that Chicago was in the hands of gangsters, that the police and the magistrates were completely under their control, that the governor of the state was futile, that the Federal government was the only force by which the city's ability to govern itself could be restored. At once I directed that all the Federal agencies concentrate upon Mr. Capone and his allies. Our authority was limited to violations of income-tax and prohibition laws. It was ironic that a man guilty of inciting hundreds of murders, in some of which he took a personal hand, had to be punished merely for failure to pay taxes on the money he had made by murder. The Attorney General set up a special Deputy Attorney General and equipped him with the best men from every bureau of investigation in the government. It required two years to assemble the evidence and conduct the trials, but in the end we restored the freedom of Chicago.

In the subsequent Presidential campaign Vice President Curtis informed me he had been approached by an important lawyer who said he was in a position to deliver the bootleg vote in the large cities if I would agree to pardon Capone. I asked the Vice President what answer he made.

He said: "I told him he really could think up a better joke than that."

THE WICKERSHAM COMMISSION

On May 28, 1929, I announced the appointment of a commission to investigate and recommend action upon the whole crime and prohibition question, under the chairmanship of former Attorney General George W. Wickersham.

The commission, in addition to Mr. Wickersham, consisted of former Secretary of War Newton D. Baker, United States Circuit Judge William S. Kenyon, United States District Judges Paul McCormick and William Grubb, former Chief Justice Kenneth Mackintosh of the Washington (State) Supreme Court, Dean Roscoe Pound of Harvard, Dr. Ada Comstock, President of Radcliffe College, and Messrs. Henry Anderson, Monte Lemann, and Frank Loesch. Rarely has a more impressive or open-minded commission been appointed.

This body made an exhaustive investigation of every phase of the problem. On the Prohibition Amendment it was mentally divided, and the recommendations were conflicting. On January 20, 1931, the commission brought in a preliminary report opposing repeal of the Amendment —and then made a long report demonstrating the futility of the law. Therefore, its investigations failed to prove of any great use so far as prohibition was concerned, although it made recommendations for other legal reforms that were of lasting value. My personal difficulty was something that did not appear upon the surface.

Former Secretary of State Elihu Root had once been my guest at the White House; and I had used the opportunity to describe the tremendous difficulty of this problem and seek his advice as to whether I should not at once recommend repeal. Without trying to quote his exact language, my note of the time indicates that his reply was as follows:

This amendment should never have been put in the Constitution. But it is there. You are under the most sacred of all oaths to uphold the Constitution. The Constitution does not contemplate any relation of the President to its amendment. You can veto any other form of legislative action but you do not have that power in relation to Constitutional amendments. That distinction was made for the definite purpose of holding alterations of the Constitution away from the President, who is solely an enforcement officer in this relation. Furthermore, this law expresses itself in criminal proceedings. If you were to recommend repeal you would be nullifying the Constitution because from that day no jury and no judge would convict. You must not do that. Your sacred duty is to enforce the law with every power you can exert. Daily the futility will become more evident, and the people will demand its repeal.

The Wickersham Commission had experienced this same difficulty. The nullification problem accounts partly for their indirect damnation of the law and, at the same time, their recommendation against repeal. There can be no doubt that the prohibition law brought economic benefits, but those benefits were more than offset by the spirit of corruption and defiance of law. Until about the winter of 1932, I was convinced that major public opinion was in favor of retaining the Amendment; but, as is often the case in American attitudes toward long contentious issues and impractical reforms, the country suddenly jelled against it. The whole question loomed up large in the 1932 Presidential campaign.

8

The Mores of the Twenties

☆ *The decade of the 1920's is frequently described as a period of revolt against conventional attitudes and behavior. Some evidence for this is presented by Hornell Hart, an eminent social scientist.** ☆

A study of interests and opinions reflected in leading magazines and allied sources in the United States since 1900, as presented in this chapter, indicates the following as the most outstanding trends:

1. *Religious sanctions have been largely displaced by scientific sanctions* in discussions published in leading magazines. Applied science has risen to a paramount position in the intellectual life reflected in periodicals of opinion. Discussions of education increased to about twice as much proportionate space in general periodicals in 1928 as in 1912.

Antagonistic criticism of the church, of ministers and of traditional creeds reached a maximum in 1925-1928 in general magazines, and still exceeds the volume of favorable comment. The leading part in antagonistic criticism has been taken by the periodicals circulating among the more highly educated part of the population; periodicals read by the great masses of the people reflect a growing lack of interest in rather than aggressive criticism of religion. Favorable dis-

* From Hornell Hart, "Changing Social Attitudes and Interests," in The President's Research Committee on Social Trends, *Recent Social Trends in the United States,* pp. 441-442. Copyright, 1933, by McGraw-Hill Book Company, New York. Used by permission.

cussions of God, of religion in relation to science and of the spiritual life reached a new high peak in 1925-1928. Analysis of short stories suggests that even this type of religion has definitely less grip on the public in 1932 than it had in 1900-1905.

2. *Sexual irregularities, easy divorce and sex freedom in general have recently been approved* to an extent entirely unprecedented in 1900-1905 in the channels studied. In magazine articles, challenges to traditional sex attitudes developed to a maximum between 1925 and 1928. In fiction, increased tolerance for violations of monogamistic sex mores on the part of heroines and heroes has been evident for all groups studied but especially for the "intellectual" periodicals. The wave of approval for sex freedom appears to have been closely associated with the decline of religious sanctions for sex conduct.

3. *Opposition to prohibition in magazines had increased by 1931* to five times the amount expressed in 1914. Opinions expressed about drinking had also shifted toward the "wet" side but not so extremely. Drinking by moving picture heroes and heroines is from two to seven times as frequent as for approved characters in short stories of various types.

4. *Discussion of economic and political institutions* has shown the following tendencies, among others: Increasing interest in social uplift and reform developed in the first two decades of the century. The World War was followed, in 1919-1921, by a wave of discussion of socialism, communism and other radical proposals, but the opposition expressed was overwhelming. Scientific management, industrial goodwill, low prices and high wages, service to the consumer and the like, became favorite slogans from 1915 to 1928. A new and unprecedented wave of discussion of unemployment and business conditions has developed during the present depression.

5. *In international relations,* the World War first intensified the agitation for military preparedness, then led to a wave of enthusiasm for international courts and international government and finally produced a new and growing demand for reduction of armaments.

9

A New Basis for Morals?

☆ As social behavior came under close scrutiny, John Dewey condemned abstract moral principles as a basis for conduct. His contention that rules of behavior should be consistent with the social conditions existent at any given time, won widespread acceptance.* ☆

It sounds academic to say that substantial bettering of social relations waits upon the growth of a scientific social psychology. For the term suggests something specialized and remote. But the formation of habits of belief, desire and judgment is going on at every instant under the influence of the conditions set by men's contact, intercourse and associations with one another. This is the fundamental fact in social life and in personal character. It is the fact about which traditional human science gives no enlightenment—a fact which this traditional science blurs and virtually denies. The enormous role played in popular morals by appeal to the supernatural and quasi-magical is in effect a desperate admission of the futility of our science. Consequently the whole matter of the formation of the pre-dispositions which effectively control human relationships is left to accident, to custom and immediate personal likings, resentments and ambitions. . . .

At present we not only have no assured means of forming character except crude devices of blame, praise, exhortation and

* From John Dewey, *Human Nature and Conduct*, pp. 323-329. Copyright, 1922, by Henry Holt and Company, New York. Used by permission of Holt, Rinehart and Winston, Inc.

punishment, but the very meaning of the general notions of moral inquiry is matter of doubt and dispute. The reason is that these notions are discussed in isolation from the concrete facts of the interactions of human beings with one another —an abstraction as fatal as was the old discussion of phlogiston, gravity and vital force apart from concrete correlations of changing events with one another. Take for example such a basic conception as that of Right involving the nature of authority in conduct. There is no need here to rehearse the multitude of contending views which give evidence that discussion of this matter is still in the realm of opinion. We content ourselves with pointing out that this notion is the last resort of the anti-empirical school in morals and that it proves the effect of neglect of social conditions.

In effect its adherents argue as follows: "Let us concede that concrete ideas about right and wrong and particular notions of what is obligatory have grown up within experience. But we cannot admit this about the idea of Right, of Obligation itself. Why does moral authority exist at all? Why is the claim of the Right recognized in conscience even by those who violate it in deed? Our opponents say that such and such a course is wise, expedient, better. But *why* act for the wise, or good, or better? Why not follow our own immediate devices if we are so inclined? There is only one answer: We have a moral nature, a conscience, call it what you will. And this nature responds directly in acknowledgment of the supreme authority of the Right over all claims of inclination and habit. We may not act in accordance with this acknowledgment, but we still know that the authority of the moral law, although not its power, is unquestionable. Men may differ indefinitely according to what their experience has been as to just *what* is Right, what its contents are. But they all spontaneously agree in recognizing the supremacy of the claims of whatever is thought of as Right. Otherwise there would be no such thing as morality, but merely calculations of how to satisfy desire."

Grant the foregoing argument, and all the apparatus of abstract moralism follows in its wake. A remote goal of perfection, ideals that are contrary in a wholesale way to what is actual, a free will of arbitrary choice; all of these conceptions band themselves together with that of a non-empirical authority of Right and a non-empirical conscience which acknowledges it. They constitute its ceremonial or formal train.

Why, indeed, acknowledge the authority of Right? That many persons do not acknowledge it in fact, in action, and that all persons ignore it at times, is assumed by the argument. Just what is the significance of an alleged recognition of a supremacy which is continually denied in fact? How much would be lost if it were dropped out, and we were left face to face with actual facts? If a man lived alone in the world there might be some sense in the question "Why be moral?" were it not for one thing: No such question would then arise. As it is, we live in a world where other persons live too. Our acts affect them. They perceive these effects, and react upon us in consequence. Because they are living beings they make demands upon us for certain things from us. They approve and condemn—not in abstract theory but in what they do to us. The answer to the question "Why not put your hand in the fire?" is the answer of fact. If you do your hand will be burnt. The answer to the question why acknowledge the right is of the same sort. For Right is only an abstract name for the multitude of concrete demands in action which others impress upon us, and of which we are obliged, if we would live, to take some account. Its authority is the exigency of their demands, the efficacy of their insistencies. There may be good ground for the contention that in theory the idea of the right is subordinate to that of the good, being a statement of the course proper to attain good. But in fact it signifies the totality of social pressures exercised upon us to induce us to think and desire in certain ways. Hence the right can in fact become the road to the good only as the elements that compose this unremitting pressure are enlightened, only as social relationships become themselves reasonable.

It will be retorted that all pressure is a non-moral affair partaking of force, not of right; that right must be ideal. Thus we are invited to enter again the circle in which the ideal has no force and social actualities no ideal quality. We refuse the invitation because social pressure is involved in our own lives, as much so as the air we breathe and the ground we walk upon. If we had desires, judgments, plans, in short a mind, apart from social connections, then the latter would be external and their action might be regarded as that of a non-moral force. But we live mentally as physically only *in* and *because* of our environment. Social pressure is but a name for the interactions which are always going on and in which we participate, living so far as we partake and dying so far as we do not. The pressure is not ideal but empirical, yet empirical here means only actual. It calls attention to the fact that considerations of right are claims originating not outside of life, but within it. They are "ideal" in precisely the degree in which we intelligently recognize and act upon them, just as colors and canvas become ideal when used in ways that give an added meaning to life.

Accordingly failure to recognize the authority of right means defect in effective apprehension of the realities of human association, not an arbitrary exercise of free will. This deficiency and perversion in apprehension indicates a defect in education—that is to say, in the operation of actual conditions, in the consequences upon desire and thought of existing interactions and interdependencies. It is false that every person has a consciousness of the supreme authority of right and then misconceives it or ignores it in action. One has such a sense of the claims of social relationships as those relationships enforce in one's desires and observations. The belief in a separate, ideal or transcendental, practically ineffectual Right is a reflex of the inadequacy with which existing institutions perform their educative office— their office in generating observation of social continuities. It is an endeavor to "rationalize" this defect. Like all rationalizations, it operates to divert attention from the real state of affairs. Thus it helps maintain the conditions which created it, standing in the way of effort to make our institutions more humane and equitable. A theoretical acknowledgment of the supreme authority of Right, of moral law, gets twisted into an effectual substitute for acts which would better the customs which now produce vague,

dull, halting and evasive observation of actual social ties. We are not caught in a circle; we traverse a spiral in which social customs generate some consciousness of interdependencies, and this consciousness is embodied in acts which in improving the environment generate new perceptions of social ties, and so on forever. The relationships, the interactions are forever there as fact, but they acquire meaning only in the desires, judgments and purposes they awaken.

We recur to our fundamental propositions. Morals is connected with actualities of existence, not with ideals, ends and obligations independent of concrete actualities. The facts upon which it depends are those which arise out of active connections of human beings with one another, the consequences of their mutually intertwined activities in the life of desire, belief, judgment, satisfaction and dissatisfaction. In this sense conduct and hence morals are social: they are not just things which *ought* to be social and which fail to come up to the scratch. But there are enormous differences of better and worse in the quality of what is social. Ideal morals begin with the perception of these differences. Human interaction and ties are there, are operative in any case. But they can be regulated, employed in an orderly way for good only as we know how to observe them. And they cannot be observed aright, they cannot be understood and utilized, when the mind is left to itself to work without the aid of science. For the natural unaided mind means precisely the habits of belief, thought and desire which have been accidentally generated and confirmed by social institutions or customs. But with all their admixture of accident and reasonableness we have at last reached a point where social conditions create a mind capable of scientific outlook and inquiry. To foster and develop this spirit is the social obligation of the present because it is its urgent need.

10

Contemporary Life

☆ *Some observers discerned certain American traits which appeared more clear in the 1920's. Among these were working hard at leisure, the rise of "spectatorship" in sports, the standardization of taste, and the synonymity of success, victory, and practicality.* ☆

(a) "ON AMERICAN LEISURE"*

The best test of the quality of a civilization is the quality of its leisure. Not what the citizens of a commonwealth do when they are obliged to do something by necessity, but what they do when they can do anything by choice, is the criterion of a people's life. One can tell much about a man by noting the objects and pastimes to which he spontaneously turns for joy. The same may be said of a nation. It was a suggestive comment of Maxim Gorky's on visiting Coney Island, "What an unhappy people it must be that turns for happiness here." The most serious criticism leveled against American civilization is not that its work is standardized and its business engulfing, but that its pleasures are mechanical and its leisure slavish. It is not that we have not time. Foreign observers are repeatedly astonished at the number of hours an ever-increasing number of Americans have to themselves. It is not time we lack, but leisure. . . .

* By Erwin Edman. The selections from Erwin Edman, *Adam, the Baby and the Man from Mars*, 1929, pp. 3-4, 6-9, 11-14, are reprinted by permission of and arrangement with Houghton Mifflin Company, the authorized publishers.

A number of years ago Professor Veblen in his "Theory of the Leisure Class" tried to point out how the traditions and interests of a leisure class had shaped our tastes and our morals. A quite plausible volume might be written on the thesis that the pursuit of leisure in our civilization is determined by our traditions of work; we carry the morals and ideals of an essentially industrial, essentially business civilization over into our play. Leisure—a quiet and emancipated absorption in things and doings for their own sake—has always seemed to us effeminate and exotic. We wish leisure for relief, for release, for escape; for instruction, enlightenment, or advancement. There is something immoral about moments that are good in themselves. There is probably no other country in the world where idleness is one of the deadly sins.

With us, therefore, leisure has been a melodramatic escape into self-improvement. We oscillate between night clubs and outlines of culture. Every one has at some time or other been present at a determinedly gay party. He has seen ordinarily quiet, intelligent people become wilfully noisy and stupid. He has seen men and women, separately delightful and entertaining, prance about loudly, screaming vulgarities, acting the "grown-up babies of the age." And his pain has been increased by a sense that none of these people cared to do the silly things they were doing. They drank more than they really wished to, and uttered hic-coughing nonsense that they themselves despised.

Every one, likewise, has listened to a group of people at dinner or afterwards, talk with obligatory boredom about the modish books and plays and ideas. Spontaneity, which is of the essence of any truly spiritual life, flies out of the conversation and out of the window, when "culture" becomes deliberate. We settle down as grimly to being serious as we settle down to being silly. Between the foolish and the funereal we have managed to find no middle course.

Of escapes from the pressure of an increasingly mechanized life to occasional outbursts of excitement or triviality there is much to be said. At least it may be said for them that they are natural, perhaps needful, refuges from a world whose tightly woven days would otherwise be unbearable. It is perhaps a sad commentary on the angular and constricted lives we lead that we should have to seek lurid or futile ways to peace. But it is not to be wondered at that, living in such a world of routine, we should plunge ever so often into the loud nonsense of inane parties, wallow in the absurd pathos and comedy of the screen, or fall enraptured victims to successive crazes of footless puzzles and dull games. We may be forgiven our excursions to musical comedies without wit or music, and conversational evenings without humanity or ideas. The contemporary citizen is vexed beyond his own realization by the humdrum unthrilling pressure of his days; he craves naturally now and then an opportunity to be trivial, irresponsible, and absurd. . . .

But while leisure has in one direction gone toward conventional amusement and stereotyped triviality, in another direction it has become a kind of elegant overtime work. The latest use we have found for leisure is to make it useful. Its usefulness, which might have been supposed to be that it was a good in itself, has been transformed into its possibility as a means of systematic self-improvement. Correspondence courses, outlines of knowledge, scrapbooks of learning—agencies not always disinterested—have been trying to teach us what we might do with our unharnessed moments if only we would harness them. A little less carousal and a little less bridge, and we might become heirs to all of Western culture, or experts in philosophy or French. There is a revealing irrelevance in the reasons assigned for turning the casual moments of our lives to the pursuit of knowledge. It is not that knowledge will render us self-possessed and whole, that it will give wings to our imagination and give a larger, clearer, and sweeter horizon to our lives. It is that knowledge, or a smattering of it, will make us successful or respected, that a veneer of garbled French will reveal our breeding, or a parade of the names of philosophers testify to our intellectual curiosity. There is possibly no clearer index to the remoteness of a native American culture than the eager indiscriminate voracity with which Americans gobble up tabloid versions of fields of expert knowledge. Far from meaning that we have turned to the love of wisdom, it means that we have turned our idle hours into the hurried business of getting short cuts to knowledge. Outlines simply are a way of applying efficiency to culture as well as to business. Their very essence is to say that here is all philosophy or history or literature for those who have not the patience or sympathy to explore any corner of any of them with disinterested delight. Worst of all, they have taken from leisure its saving essence—the sense of doing some lovely thing for its own lovable sake.

There are aristocratic pessimists in our midst who hold that leisure in the sense of a fine spontaneous use of free time is increasingly impossible in America. They point to the facts cited in the foregoing and to other equally distressing social habits. The omnipresence of the automobile is not simply a temptation to literal speed, but has come to be a symbol for speed in spiritual matters as well. The only excitement in any activity, even in the pursuit of truth, is the excitement of going fast. It is for that reason, they insist, that there is no country where ideas become popular so fast as in America, no country where, half-learned, they are so quickly outmoded and forgotten. A book is the book of a month or at most a season, and the rapid-transit reader comes to forswear books for the reviews of them, and forswear reviews for excerpts from them in a synthetic magazine.

It is pointed out again, and with justice, that the multiplication of physical luxuries and physical distractions is a constant intruder upon that collectedness of spirit in which alone leisure can come to being. Serenity and integrity are menaced as much by the telephone as by any single invention of the last century. Long quiet waves of time have become almost impossible in evenings shattered by radios, by movies, and by the constant seduction and noise of the automobile. Speculation begins in a dreaming fantasy; meditation in reverie. In our contemporary urban world one almost never has a chance to achieve that half-drowsy detachment in which fantasy and reverie begin. We are kept too wide-awake ever to be really at peace or in thought. Finally, in a country where there is still a glamorous sense of unlimited opportunity, the desire for first place makes almost impossible that freedom and detachment, which leaves one free to follow an impulse for its own self-rewarding delight.

(b) "RECREATION AND LEISURE TIME ACTIVITIES"*

Evidence of the popularity of games, played by both professional and amateur teams, can be found in the increasing size of grand stands and stadia, the large amount of space given to sports by newspapers, and the broadcasting of games play by play over nationwide networks of radio stations. Every city has its athletes whose prowess is a matter of local pride and concern. Following the fortunes of favorite teams and players is an important leisure time pursuit for large numbers of people.

Among athletic sports which are popular public spectacles, college football has

outstanding public support. The whole nation demands information concerning victories and defeats of better known teams, and the accomplishments of the more successful players also receive wide publicity. During the past few years, in spite of record breaking crowds at some of the games, considerable discussion has arisen concerning the future of college football and its possible decline in public favor. Critics are pointing to the fact that students in general seem less excited than formerly over the outcome of games, and that the public quickly loses interest in teams which fall below championship caliber.

In order to get facts that would throw light on this situation, an effort was made to secure records of football attendance and receipts for the past ten years from the leading colleges and universities.

* By J. F. Steiner. From J. F. Steiner, "Recreation and Leisure Time Activities," in The President's Research Committee on Social Trends, *Recent Social Trends in the United States*, pp. 929-931. Copyright, 1933, by McGraw-Hill Book Company, New York. Used by permission.

There was a commendable willingness to cooperate in this study but unfortunately few institutions have satisfactory records on football attendance over a period of years. The 49 institutions replying reported that attendance more than doubled between 1921 and 1930, the increase being 119 percent. Football receipts, as reported by 65 institutions, grew from $2,-696,345 to $8,363,674, a gain of 210 percent. Both attendance and receipts increased with considerable regularity during the first nine years of this period, with a sharp falling off in 1930, the decline over the preceding year amounting to 6 percent in the case of admissions and 9 percent in receipts. While only a small number of institutions supplied information on this phase of the study, the reliability of the results is strengthened by the fact that they included a large number of the leading universities long prominent in football history. Moreover, reports for a five year period, from 1926 to 1930, which were received from 88 institutions in the matter of attendance and from 102 institutions covering receipts, corroborate in a striking manner the results secured from the reports covering the ten year period. Available evidence, therefore, seems to indicate that college football is not on the wane unless the decline in attendance and receipts in 1930 represents a turning of the tide. The total attendance at all football games in 1930, estimated from reports received from 109 institutions, was approximately 10,300,000. The total receipts, computed in a similar way from data furnished by 129 institutions, could not have been less than $21,500,000. The average gross receipts per school in 1930 ranged from $5,565 for colleges of less than 500 students to $245,417 for universities of the largest size. Of the 129 institutions reporting receipts for 1930, 8 reported gross receipts in excess of $500,000 each and 33 reported receipts of more than $100,000. Since neither the curve of attendance nor the curve of receipts showed any tendency to flatten out previous to 1930, there is reason to assume that hard times rather than declining interest is responsible for the decreased size of the football crowds.

The spectacular increase in attendance at football games during the past decade has been accompanied by a wave of grand stand and stadium building far surpassing any previous development of this kind. According to reports from 135 institutions the seating facilities for football spectators increased from 929,523 in 1920 to 2,307,850 in 1930, a gain of 148 percent. These institutions reported 74 concrete stadia, 55 of which had been built since 1920. Only one of these college stadia in 1920 had a seating capacity of more than 70,000, while there were seven in this class in 1930.

(c) "THE AMERICANIZATION OF THE SOUL"*

As the first characteristic of the external image of America I laid stress on its different dimensions, on the massive, quantitative, gigantic nature of this world as compared with Europe. What we learned in school, but never quite realized, is here demonstrated by an object-lesson on the largest scale: America is not a country, like Germany, France, or San Marino, but a continent. Even an inhabitant of Berlin feels a little provincial when he realizes, on studying the timetable, that in crossing this country one's watch must repeatedly be set back, since when it is noon or midnight in New York, it is eleven o'clock in Chicago, ten

* By Richard Müller-Freienfels. From Richard Müller-Freienfels, The Mysteries of the Soul, pp. 245-247, 252-260. Copyright, 1929, by George Allen & Unwin Ltd., London. Used by permission.

o'clock in Denver, and nine o'clock in San Francisco. In America they will ask you on your arrival in New York: "I suppose you will take in the Yellowstone Park and California?"—as though a man traveling from London to Berlin were asked whether he would not include in his journey an excursion to Leningrad and to Egypt. Spatially considered, the distance from New York to San Francisco is much greater than the distance from London to Leningrad, but physically speaking the distance is trifling. No frontiers lie between them; the same language is spoken from the Atlantic to the Pacific; and there is no need to visit the money-changer. It is truly a continent that the traveler is crossing, but it is also a country, and *one* country of stupendous dimensions. Its provincial cities are larger than many European capitals; its lakes are small seas, wider in area than a European kingdom; its agricultural land is not divided up into small parcels, but the cornfields cover the plains like a shoreless ocean. Everything has other dimensions than with us: the coins are four or five times the size of European money, and compared with the newspapers, the great "dailies" of London, Paris, and Berlin seem small and insufficient. In short, we find that even in every day things of secondary importance other quantitative notions prevail. . . .

Quantity, in America, is not a fact, as with us; it is a value. To say that something is large, massive, gigantic, is in America not a mere statement of fact, but the highest commendation. It is true that this may be so in Europe, but here the contrary valuation obtains as well; here small and graceful and modest things have a special value, while mere bulk may be felt as a defect, and colossal things are often regarded as crude, vulgar, and unqualitative. All this the American can hardly understand. The idyllic frame of mind which sees positive value in small and restrained and limited things is un-American, and occurs only as a reaction against Americanism, while in many European peoples it is a positive characteristic. In America everything big is blindly accepted. Magnitude, in the purely external sense of largeness, sets the standard of value. . . .

The second chief characteristic of Americanism is the technicalization or mechanization of life. Not that we Western Europeans are deficient in technique, but nowhere is it so obtrusive as in America. In Europe it is a servant—at least, in theory—but in America it is the almost undisputed despot of life. The decisive point is not the existence, but the different valuation of technical methods and knowledge. In Europe—at least, in intellectual circles—such terms as "mechanical" or "machine-made" are employed as terms of censure, which are opposed to "organic" or "artistic." In the same way the word "technique" seems often to savor of the superficial, unintellectual, and inartistic. The average American sets an absolute and positive value on technique. In the American cities it is not only the finished wares that are displayed in the stores; if possible they are actually manufactured before the eyes of the passing crowd. You will see the pressing-machine at work in the shop-windows, stretching, folding, and pressing a suit of clothes in the course of a few minutes; cigar-makers will show anyone who cares to linger before their windows how cigars are made by hand and machine; or you may see—and this is quite an appetizing sight—how sweets and pastry are made and cooked by neat and pretty young women. Technique is not, as it should be in theory, a means to an end, but is becoming an end in itself. The clatter of machinery, which we find disturbing, is music to the true American ear. Only by the fact that he does not inwardly rebel against it can we explain the fact that the American's nerves do not suffer from noise like those of the European, who is distressed by these things because he inwardly protests against them.

In a purely external sense, the mechanization of life is conditioned by the size of the country. To be sure, we Europeans too have need of our railways, telegraphs, and telephones; but in America these are far more essential if the different parts of the Continent are to be connected. A vast network of railways covers the land; the telegraph and the telephone, both largely American inventions, have reached a high degree of development. The air-mail is a necessity, not a kind of sport, as with us. Above all, the motor-car is not a luxury, but an article of everyday utility, which is obvious from the shabby condition of most of the cars one sees. The majority of the railways, whether above or below ground, are single lines for one-way traffic, and there are separate tracks for the express trains. In the dwelling-houses people ascend to their apartments not by the stairs, but by elevators; in the large buildings there are frequently a dozen or more lifts at the inmates' disposal, and they may even be divided into express and local elevators. . . .

Everyone who has visited the United States will be able to recall similar characteristics, all of which go to prove the same thing, namely, that the whole of life has been mechanized in a far greater degree than with us. Psychologically speaking, all these traits may be referred to an intellectual attitude on the part of the American, which is not indeed unknown in Europe, but is found in a purer form in America, and this attitude may be described as the rationalization of the soul. By rationalization I mean the prevalence of practical thinking, of the concentration of the intellect on the practical, useful, and efficient, and the obverse of this attitude is the repression and suppression

of all that is merely agreeable, emotional, and irrational in the personality. This rationality, as a form of thinking and willing, expresses itself in constructions and instruments and machines which impress the purposeful will of humanity, with the aid of the inorganic forces of Nature, on the outer world. The machine is above all the typical creation and manifestation of the utilitarian and practical reason. It is pure practicality, embodied rationality.

Even organic and intellectual life are mechanized in accordance with the ideal of the rationally operating machine. A cow or a pig, which the German peasant will regard as a personality, and for which he often feels affection, is in America a machine for producing meat and leather. How should any personal relation to the animal be possible when animals are "produced" by the thousand? Even man himself is becoming mechanized, is considered solely with regard to his performance. What are the holders of the great athletic titles but machines for boxing, playing baseball, or running? And the workers in the factories? They too are machines, which indefatigably exercise the same function, a function rationally acquired, without any personal relation to the thing which they are making. How should the individual worker have any personal relation to his work when he is only one of thousands, who are all co-operating in a task which he cannot survey as a whole? Strictly speaking, the factory worker is not even a complete machine, but only a portion of a machine, with no more independence than a cog-wheel or driving belt. . . .

The mathematization and technicalization of life is connected inextricably with a further trait of Americanism—with the *typicalization,* or, to use the American expression, the *standardization* of life. . . .

All these clean-shaven men, all these girls, with their doll-like faces, which are generally painted, seem to have been produced somewhere in a Ford factory, not by the dozen but by the thousand. In no other country are the individuals reduced to such a dead-level as in the United States, and this appears all the more remarkable when we reflect that nowhere is there such a disorderly mixture of races and peoples as in this Eldorado of the needy and adventurous of all countries. And yet, surprisingly enough, after a few years as a rule, and certainly after a few generations, the immigrant, whether he was English, German, Russian, Syrian, or Greek, has become "an American." And this transformation affects even his features! We can understand that as regards his clothing and other externals he will do his best not to look a "greenhorn. . . ." And if this transformation affects the features, which would seem to be independent of the will, it is naturally far more perceptible in the bearing and behavior, in speech and accent, and in social manners.

As in the case of "quantification" and mechanization, so in that of typification we are confronted by a different valuation. In Europe, time out of mind, people have preferred to maintain a distance, and therefore a difference, between races and classes and other social groups, and even between individuals. Distance, uniqueness, and originality are European values, which are foreign to the American. His values are the very reverse of these: adherence to type, agreement, similarity. In the Middle Ages the classes were divided by dress, custom, and many other characteristics; there was no intercourse between them. Even in Europe time has brought many changes; even in Europe the bourgeois is victorious, and noblemen and peasants alike wear bourgeois clothes. Nevertheless, these differences persist, even though they may not be visible; the spirit of caste still survives; classes and professional groups still regard one another with disfavor; the educated man looks down on the man of the people, and the man of the people is resentful of education; the officer has a special standing, and so forth. In America these differences do not exist. There the only difference that counts is a man's quantitative achievement and success, which in the last resort is expressed in dollars. Here is a marshal's baton which everyone carries in his knapsack. It does not matter how he makes his way; whether he succeeds as a professor, or a merchant, or an artisan, there is only the one method of valuation. There are no insuperable barriers, such as that of noble birth. If a man fails in one calling, he adopts another. No one looks down on a man who fails as a professor and then becomes a hotel-keeper, provided he is successful. This lack of social discrimination impresses the newcomer. People treat one another with a peculiarly equilitarian politeness, which to us often seems an obtrusive cordiality, but which is an attribute of the type, not of the individual. The American sees in his neighbor not a certain Mr. M——— or Mrs. N———, but simply an impersonal being, with whom he can exchange opinions, or rather the usual phrases, concerning the weather or the last glove-fight.

11

An Effete Civilization?

☆ *Joseph Wood Krutch (1893-   ), essayist and critic, attacked the prevailing optimism of the 1920's on the grounds that civilized man's values had become so divorced from his nature that he was doomed to extinction.* * ☆

The decadent civilizations of the past were not saved by their philosophers but by the influx of simpler peoples who had centuries yet to live before their minds should be ripe for despair. Neither Socrates nor Plato could teach his compatriots any wisdom from which they could draw the strength to compete with the crude energy of their Roman neighbors, and even their thought inevitably declined soon after it had exhausted their vital energy. Nor could these Romans, who flourished longer for the very reason, perhaps, that they had slower and less subtle intellects, live forever; they too were compelled to give way in their time to barbarians innocent alike both of philosophy and of any possible need to call upon it.

The subhuman will to live which is all-sufficient for the animal may be replaced by faith, faith may be replaced by philosophy, and philosophy may attenuate itself until it becomes, like modern metaphysics, a mere game; but each of these developments marks a stage in a progressive enfeeblement of that will to live

for the gradual weakening of which it is the function of each to compensate. Vitality calls upon faith for aid, faith turns gradually to philosophy for support, and then philosophy, losing all confidence in its own conclusions, begins to babble of "beneficent fictions" instead of talking about Truth; but each is less confident than what went before and each is, by consequence, less easy to live by. Taken together, they represent the successive and increasingly desperate expedients by means of which man, the ambitious animal, endeavors to postpone the inevitable realization that living is merely a physiological process with only a physiological meaning and that it is most satisfactorily conducted by creatures who never feel the need to attempt to give it any other. But they are at best no more than expedients, and when the last has been exhausted there remains nothing except the possibility that the human species will be revitalized by some race or some class which is capable of beginning all over again.

Under the circumstances it is not strange that decadent civilizations are likely to think that the collapse of their culture is in reality the end of the human story. Perhaps some of the last of the old Roman intelligentsia realized that the future belonged to the barbarians from the north and that it belonged to them for the very reason that they were incapable of assimilating ancient thought, but even among the early Christian theologians there was a widespread belief that the end of Rome could mean nothing except the end of the world, and, for similar reasons, it is difficult for us to believe in the possibility of anything except either the continuation of modern culture or the extinction of human life. But a glance at history should make us hesitate before asserting that either one of these alternative possibilities is likely to become a reality. On the one hand all cultures have ultimately collapsed and human life has, on the other hand, always persisted—not because philosophers have arisen to solve its problems but because naiver creatures, incapable of understanding the problems and hence not feeling the need to solve them, have appeared somewhere upon the face of the globe.

If modern civilization is decadent then perhaps it will be rejuvenated, but not by the philosophers whose subtlest thoughts are only symptoms of the disease which they are endeavoring to combat. If the future belongs to anybody it belongs to those to whom it has always belonged, to those, that is to say, too absorbed in living to feel the need for thought, and they will come, as the barbarians have always come, absorbed in the processes of life for their own sake, eating without asking if it is worth while to eat, begetting children without asking why they should beget them, and conquering without asking for what purpose they conquer. . . .

Whence will the barbarians (and we may use that word, not as a term of contempt, but merely as a way of identifying these people animated by vitally simple thoughts) come? We are not surrounded as the Romans were by childlike savages, and we can hardly imagine the black tribes of Africa pushing in upon us. Have we, within the confines of our own cities, populations quite as little affected by modern thought as the Goths were affected by Greek philosophy, and hence quite capable either of carrying peaceably on as the aristocracy dies quietly off at the top or of arising sometime to overwhelm us? Has China, having died once, lain fallow long enough to have become once more primitive, or are the Russians indeed the new barbarians, even if they are such in a somewhat different sense than that implied in the sensational literature of anti-communist propaganda . . . ?

Some critics of communism have, to be sure, maintained that its tendencies were fundamentally anti-human and that, should it ever become established, it would so arrest the development of the humanistic spirit as to fix mankind forever in some changelessly efficient routine like that of an ant-hill. But even if this be true it does not alter the fact that its hopes are no hopes in which we can have any part, since we would be even more alien to such a society than to one which promised to recapitulate our own youth. The world may be rejuvenated in one way or another, but we will not. Skepticism has entered too deeply into our souls ever to be replaced by faith, and we can never forget the things which the new barbarians will never need to have known. This world in which an unresolvable discord is the fundamental fact is the world in which we must continue to live, and for us wisdom must consist, not in searching for a means of escape which does not exist, but in making such peace with it as we may. . . .

Leaving the future to those who have faith in it, we may survey our world and, if we bear in mind the facts just stated, we may permit ourselves to exclaim, a little rhetorically perhaps,

> Hail, horrors, hail,
> Infernal world! and thou profoundest hell,
> Receive thy new possessor.

If Humanism and Nature are fundamentally antithetical, if the human virtues have a definite limit set to their development, and if they may be cultivated only by a process which renders us progressively unfit to fulfill our biological duties, then we may at least permit ourselves a certain defiant satisfaction when we realize that we have made our choice and that we are resolved to abide by the consequences. Some small part of the tragic fallacy may be said indeed to be still valid for us, for if we cannot feel ourselves great as Shakespeare did, if we no longer believe in either our infinite capacities or our importance to the universe, we know at least that we have discovered the trick which has been played upon us and that whatever else we may be we are no longer dupes.

Rejuvenation may be offered to us at a certain price. Nature, issuing her last warning, may bid us embrace some new illusion before it is too late and accord ourselves once more with her. But we prefer rather to fail in our own way than to succeed in hers. Our human world may have no existence outside of our own desires, but those are more imperious than anything else we know, and we will cling to our own lost cause, choosing always rather to know than to be. Doubtless fresh people have still a long way to go with Nature before they are compelled to realize that they too have come to the parting of the ways, but though we may wish them well we do not envy them. If death for us and our kind is the inevitable result of our stubbornness then we can only say, "So be it." Ours is a lost cause and there is no place for us in the natural universe, but we are not, for all that, sorry to be human. We should rather die as men than live as animals.

VII

the nation's business is business

WHILE intellectual confusion was prominent and social antagonism frequent in American life in the 1920's, there was a clear emphasis on business in the nation's economics and politics. That emphasis was an integral part of the return to "Normalcy" which Warren G. Harding promised during the Presidential campaign of 1920. The idea that business made America great and would make it even greater was readily acceptable to most Americans.

The wartime prosperity had been followed, in 1920-1921, by a severe recession, and business asked the chance to show that it could bring back prosperity without government interference and the artificial stimulus of war. It was given that opportunity. Under Presidents Harding, Coolidge, and Hoover the policies of less government in business and more business in government were followed. Increased tariff protection was sought and received, and labor organizations were restrained. Taxes were reduced time after time on the theories that efficient government —one that did not meddle in the legitimate affairs of private enterprise—needed less money, and that the development of investments and consumer purchasing required more. Government operations also felt the influence of commercial ideals as centralized budgeting and independent auditing procedures were provided for the Federal government. Rigid economies and work efficiency in government were sought along with balanced budgets.

Yet the triumph of business brought problems. The farming sector of the economy did not make a full recovery from the 1920-1921 recession and agriculture's determination to secure government support was usually frustrated by those who stood as guardians against government intervention. Sometimes the emphasis on business seemed to encourage the unscrupulous to plunder the government's resources as in the case of the infamous Teapot Dome scandal. And the growth of commerce and industry caused concern. Men like Herbert Hoover conceded that our increasingly complex society demanded regulation. They urged voluntary regulation, motivated by loftier purposes than materialism, to set and to enforce ethical standards of business practice and thereby to reduce the need for government intervention. Others saw the corporation as an institution which might supersede the state as the dominant form of social organization and averred that business would have to take a broad statesmanlike approach to the needs of the community. Some, less impressed with private enterprise's accomplishments, argued that greater government control and even ownership were required in the nation's economy.

Despite its problems, business prospered and most of the American public shared in the prosperity. It appeared to one prominent American economist that an economic revolution was being achieved in the United States with wealth being more greatly diffused and class differences lessened. It was in the common interest to encourage this revolution. On the eve of the great depression, it was generally conceded that commerce and industry had succeeded in ameliorating evils. What remained was for business to improve itself so it could bring further prosperity without going astray down the road of corporate oligarchy and industrial plundering.

1

Economic Preface to the Twenties

☆ *Wartime prosperity continued until the spring of 1920 when sup-ply overtook demand and the United States found itself in a brief but severe recession. It was against this background that the vaunted prosperity of the 1920's developed.** ☆

The immediate effect in this country of the outbreak of the European war was a general paralysis of trade, industry, and finance. The suspension of business on the stock and other exchanges and the prompt declaration of moratoriums aided in securing stabilization, and the financial measures which were immediately put into effect by the Treasury Department were instrumental in preventing a commercial crisis and a financial crash. Confidence in the ability of this country to meet its obligations abroad, however vast they seemed at that time, was soon established; and before the expiration of 12 months, fear, stagnation, and confusion had given way to confidence and re-newed business activities; and by the latter part of 1915 the upward swing was well under way. The year 1916 was one of feverish activity, and our foreign trade, which in the year 1914 amounted to less than 4 billion dollars, nearly doubled, and amounted, for the calendar year 1916, to approximately 8 billion dollars. The balance of trade in our favor for 1916 ex-

* From *Annual Report of the Comptroller of the Currency to the Third Session of the Sixty-sixth Congress of the United States,* December 6, 1920, Washington, 1921, pp. 2-4, 7-8.

ceeded 3 billion dollars, and was approxi-mately *ten times* as great as the favorable balance of the year 1914.

With our declaration of war against Germany early in the year 1917, the business of this country—farming, manu-facturing, commercial, mining, and every-thing else—was given additional impetus. Commodity prices soared to unprece-dented heights, and were finally restrained only by Government mediation and price fixing. The prices, however, which pro-ducers and traders were allowed by the Government to charge yielded unprece-dented profits in well-nigh every branch of industry; and inflation was stimulated further by the importation in the years 1916 and 1917 of huge sums of gold from abroad. Our imports of gold in 1916 and 1917 amounted actually to $1,238,444,608, our exports to $527,676,-811, leaving a net excess of imports of gold over exports for the two years of $710,767,797, which, with the excess of imports over exports for the year 1915 provided a net surplus of gold imports for the three years of 1915, 1916 and 1917, of $1,131,296,469.

The urgent and unguarded buying of American products by the Allies in the early days of the war had driven the prices of our products to unprecedented figures; and it became difficult, subsequently when a more orderly system of buying was instituted, both for our own Government and for the Allies to return to anywhere near normal prices. It has been estimated that the profits and increments accruing to the people of this country during the last year of the war amounted, approximately, to 50 billions of dollars; and that the surplus income over and above the living expenses of the people despite the extravagant rate at which they were living, approximated 15 billion dollars for that year.

After the armistice, the demands for war materials of course ceased, but the cries from the impoverished countries of Europe for foods continued, and the demands for materials for reconstruction and rehabilitation developed rapidly.

The profits which South America, China and Japan had also realized in supplying the products of those respective countries to the Allies had brought about a condition of high prosperity and activity in all of those countries, and their peoples had acquired a taste for luxuries and for the products of other countries which we were called upon to supply in huge quantities.

The demands made upon the United States for steel and iron products, machinery, agricultural implements, fabrics, foods, automobiles, and specialities of all kinds gave to our business men visions of unchecked and limitless prosperity; and our exports of merchandise for the year 1919 following the war exceeded by nearly 1 billion dollars our total exports for the war year 1918. Imports into this country of merchandise from every quarter of the globe also broke all records, and amounted for the year 1919 to $3,904,000,000, nearly 1 billion dollars more than the maximum amount of imports ever before brought in.

TURN OF THE TIDE

The turning of the tide in the world delirium and inflation came in the spring of 1920, with the financial and industrial collapse which took place in the Empire of Japan. The Japanese had profited hugely from the supplies which they had furnished to the Allies, and from the operation of their merchant marine, the profits of which during the war were enormous. This great business had brought about the creation and flotation of numerous new financial, manufacturing, and trading corporations throughout Japan; and in the flotation of these companies a spirit of reckless speculation had been developed which pervaded every section of the population of that country—farmers, merchants, professional men, bankers, and public officials.

The efforts which were made primarily in this country to bring about an orderly deflation, and the curbing of reckless speculation, began to make themselves felt, not only here but in all the countries with which we had been dealing. The apparently insatiable demand which America had developed for such luxuries as silks had tremendously stimulated the silk industry of Japan. The prices of raw silk had advanced in the space of a year or two approximately 400 per cent, maximum prices having been reached in January and February of 1920.

A rather sudden curtailment or suspension of the American demand for silks had an immediate effect upon the Japanese market. The collapse in the prices of raw and manufactured silks was followed by the prostration of the Japanese market for cotton goods, which in recent years has become one of the great industries of that country. The closing down of numerous other industries followed in the wake of the financial panic, which had resulted in the suspension of some of the largest banks and business houses in the Empire, and an acute depression in business set in, and still continues. . . .

The deflation which . . . took place so precipitately in Japan has made headway in every country, civilized and uncivilized, from the Artic Ocean to the tropical jungles; and most of the products of human labor and human enterprise in nearly every country on the globe are now obtainable for a fraction of the prices which prevailed a year ago. . . .

SHRINKAGE ESTIMATED AT TWELVE TO EIGHTEEN BILLIONS

It is probable that the shrinkage in the past year in the market or salable value of the products of our fields and forests, of factories, mills, and mines, in this country alone, as compared with the high level from which they have descended, amounts to between twelve and eighteen billion dollars.

This melting away of property values is reflected, but only partially, in the decline which has taken place in the market value of the shares of industrial corporations listed on the New York Stock Exchange. A computation recently made shows that the depreciation which has taken place from the high prices of last year and this to the low prices of the current year in the stocks of industrial corporations alone listed on the New York Stock Exchange amounts to between three and four thousand million dollars. This is irrespective of the shrinkage which has occurred in the shares of many railroad corporations which have reached this year the lowest prices in their history.

A serious shrinkage of values was foreseen and predicted more than a year ago by those who studied conditions and considered the history of past wars. It has come faster and more violently than heretofore, presumably because more rapid communication and transportation expedite the succession of inevitable effect on cause. Thus far results have not only come more quickly than after our former severe wars, but have been less calamitous. There is every reason to believe that the same facts that hasten disaster will hasten recovery; and that the people of different countries and classes, being more intimately in touch with each other than ever before, will more promptly understand each other's rights and requirements and realize that it is to the interest of all to work together for fair readjustments.

The precipitate decline which has already been witnessed in so many leading commodities encourages the belief that in most cases we are near the bottom, the fall, in some instances, having been already excessive and abnormal and really not justified by actual conditions. Despite the tremendous decline in the prices of the raw materials for the articles upon which the cost of living is based—food, clothing, and the cost of shelter or housing—the private citizen is not yet receiving the full benefit of the drop; but he is required to pay a tax in the shape of middlemen's profits, which, in many cases, is inexcusable and unwarranted. We need not imagine that we have reached a firm and stable foundation until *excessive profits* are further deflated; until the private citizen is able to acquire, at the expenditure of $1 of his hard-earned money, something approximating the quantity and quality which that dollar commanded in prewar times.

2

Prescription for Normalcy

☆ *Warren Gamaliel Harding was elected president of the United States by a landslide in 1920. In his first major message to Congress, December 6, 1921, Harding called for legislation that would protect the domestic economy yet allow America to contribute to world reconstruction.* * ☆

There is before you the completion of the enactment of what has been termed a "permanent" tariff law, the word "permanent" being used to distinguish it from the emergency act which the Congress expedited early in the extraordinary session, and which is the law today. I can not too strongly urge an early completion of this necessary legislation. It is needed to stabilize our industry at home; it is essential to make more definite our trade relations abroad. More, it is vital to the preservation of many of our own industries which contribute so notably to the very lifeblood of our nation. There is now, and there always will be, a storm of conflicting opinion about any tariff revision. We can not go far wrong when we base our tariffs on the policy of preserving the productive activities which enhance employment and add to our national prosperity.

Again comes the reminder that we must not be unmindful of world conditions, that peoples are struggling for industrial rehabilitation and that we can not

dwell in industrial and commercial exclusion and at the same time do the just thing in aiding world reconstruction and readjustment. We do not seek a selfish aloofness, and we could not profit by it, were it possible. We recognize the necessity of buying wherever we sell, and the permanency of trade lies in its acceptable exchanges. In our pursuit of markets we must give as well as receive. We can not sell to others who do not produce, nor can we buy unless we produce at home. Sensible of every obligation of humanity, commerce and finance, linked as they are in the present world condition, it is not to be argued that we need destroy ourselves to be helpful to others. With all my heart I wish restoration to the peoples blighted by the awful World War, but the process of restoration does not lie in our acceptance of like conditions. It were better to remain on firm ground, strive for ample employment and high standards of wage at home, and point the way to balanced budgets, rigid economies, and resolute, efficient work as the necessary remedies to cure disaster.

Everything relating to trade. among

* From *A Compilation of the Messages and Papers of the Presidents*, XVIII, pp. 9023-9028, 9030-9031. Published by Bureau of National Literature, Inc., New York.

ourselves and among nations, has been expanded, excessive, inflated, abnormal, and there is a madness in finance which no American policy alone will cure. We are a creditor nation, not by normal processes, but made so by war. It is not an unworthy selfishness to seek to save ourselves, when the processes of that salvation are not only not denied to others, but commended to them. We seek to undermine for others no industry by which they subsist; we are obligated to permit the undermining of none of our own which make for employment and maintained activities.

Every contemplation, it little matters in which direction one turns, magnifies the difficulties of tariff legislation, but the necessity of the revision is magnified with it. Doubtless we are justified in seeking a more flexible policy than we have provided heretofore. I hope a way will be found to make for flexibility and elasticity, so that rates may be adjusted to meet unusual and changing conditions which can not be accurately anticipated. There are problems incident to unfair practices, and to exchanges which madness in money have made almost unsolvable. I know of no manner in which to effect this flexibility other than the extension of the powers of the Tariff Commission, so that it can adapt itself to a scientific and wholly just administration of the law.

I am not unmindful of the constitutional difficulties. These can be met by giving authority to the chief executive, who could proclaim additional duties to meet conditions which the Congress may designate. At this point I must disavow any desire to enlarge the Executive's powers or to add to the responsibilities of the office. They are already too large. If there were any other plan I would prefer it. . . .

Something more than tariff protection is required by American agriculture. To the farmer has come the earlier and the heavier burdens of readjustment. There is actual depression in our agricultural industry, while agricultural prosperity is absolutely essential to the general prosperity of the country. Congress has sought very earnestly to provide relief. It has promptly given such temporary relief as has been possible, but the call is insistent for the permanent solution. It is inevitable that large crops lower the prices and short crops advance them. No legislation can cure that fundamental law. But there must be some economic solution for the excessive variation in returns for agricultural production . . .

In the main the remedy lies in distribution and marketing. Every proper encouragement should be given to the cooperative marketing programs. These have proven very helpful to the cooperating communities in Europe. In Russia the cooperative community has become the recognized bulwark of law and order, and saved individualism from engulfment in social paralysis. Ultimately they will be accredited with the salvation of the Russian state. There is the appeal for this experiment. Why not try it? No one challenges the right of the farmer to a larger share of the consumer's pay for his product, no one disputes that we can not live without the farmer. . . .

The right of Labor to organize is just as fundamental and necessary as is the right of Capital to organize. The right of Labor to negotiate, to deal with and solve its particular problems in an organized way, through its chosen agents, is just as essential as is the right of Capital to organize, to maintain corporations, to limit the liabilities of stockholders. Indeed, we have come to recognize that the limited liability of the citizen as a member of a labor organization closely parallels the limitation of liability of the citizen as a stockholder in a corporation for profit. Along this line of reasoning we shall make the greatest progress toward solution of our problem of Capital and Labor. In the case of the corporation which enjoys the privilege of limited liability of stockholders, particularly when engaged in the public service, it is recognized that the outside public has a large concern which must be protected; and so we provide regulations, restrictions, and in some cases detailed supervision. Likewise in the case of Labor organizations, we might well apply similar and equally well-defined principles of regulation and supervision in order to conserve the public's interests as affected by their operations.

Just as it is not desirable that a corporation shall be allowed to impose undue exactions upon the public, so it is not desirable that a Labor organization shall be permitted to exact unfair terms of employment or subject the public to actual distresses in order to enforce its terms. Finally, just as we are earnestly seeking for procedure whereby to adjust and settle political differences between nations without resort to war, so we may well look about for means to settle the differences between organized Capital and organized Labor without resort to those forms of warfare which we recognize under the name of strikes, lockouts, boycotts, and the like.

As we have great bodies of law carefully regulating the organization and operations of industrial and financial corporations, as we have treaties and compacts among nations which look to the settlement of differences without the necessity of conflict in arms, so we might well have plans of conference, of common counsel, of mediation, arbitration, and judicial determination in controversies between Labor and Capital. To accomplish this would involve the necessity to develop a thorough-going code of practice in dealing with such affairs. It might be well to frankly set forth the superior interest of the community as a whole to either the labor group or the capital group. With rights, privi-

leges, immunities, and modes of organization thus carefully defined, it should be possible to set up judicial or quasi-judicial tribunals for the consideration and determination of all disputes which menace the public welfare. In an industrial society such as ours the strike, the lockout, and the boycott are as much out of place and as disastrous in their results as is war or armed revolution in the domain of politics. . . .

While we are thinking of promoting the fortunes of our own people I am sure there is room in the sympathetic thought of America for fellow human beings who are suffering and dying of starvation in Russia. A severe drought in the valley of the Volga has plunged 15,000,000 people into grievous famine. Our voluntary agencies are exerting themselves to the utmost to save the lives of children in this area, but it is now evident that unless relief is afforded the loss of life will extend into many millions. America can not be deaf to such a call as that. We do not recognize the government of Russia, nor tolerate the propaganda which emanates therefrom, but we do not forget the traditions of Russian friendship. We may put aside our consideration of all international politics and fundamental differences in government. The big thing is the call of the suffering and the dying. Unreservedly I recommend the appropriation necessary to supply the American Relief Administration with 10,000,000 bushels of corn and 1,000,000 bushels of seed grains, not alone to halt the wave of death through starvation, but to enable spring planting in areas where the seed grains have been exhausted temporarily to stem starvation.

The American Relief Administration is directed in Russia by former officers of our own armies, and has fully demonstrated its ability to transport and distribute relief through American hands without hindrance or loss. The time has come to add the Government's support to the wonderful relief already wrought out of the generosity of the American private purse. I am not unaware that we have suffering and privation at home. When it exceeds the capacity for the relief within the states concerned, it will have Federal consideration. . . .

I think our tax problems, the tendency of wealth to seek nontaxable investment, and the menacing increase of public debt, federal, state and municipal—all justify a proposal to change the Constitution so as to end the issue of nontaxable bonds . . . . I suggest the consideration because the drift of wealth into nontaxable securities is hindering the flow of large capital to our industries, manufacturing, agricultural and carrying, until we are discouraging the very activities which make our wealth. . . .

3

Fiscal Responsibility

☆ *The growth of the national government had drastically outmoded decentralized methods of budgeting and auditing procedures. In 1921, the Harding administration secured the passage of the Budget and Accounting Act. This legislation was designed to secure a more orderly utilization of public money and a more efficient system of fiscal accountability.** ☆

CHAP. 18.—An Act to provide a national budget system and an independent audit of Government accounts, and for other purposes. . . .

SEC. 201. The President shall transmit to Congress on the first day of each regular session the budget, which shall set forth in summary and in detail:

(a) Estimates of the expenditures and appropriations necessary, in his judgment, for the support of the Government for the ensuing fiscal year; except that the estimates for such year for the legislative branch of the Government and the Supreme Court of the United States shall be transmitted to the President on or before October 15 of each year, and shall be included by him in the budget without revision;

(b) His estimates of the receipts of the Government during the ensuing fiscal year, under (1) laws existing at the time the budget is transmitted, and also (2) under the revenue proposals, if any, contained in the budget;

(c) The expenditures and receipts of the Government during the last completed fiscal year;

(d) Estimates of the expenditures and receipts of the Government during the fiscal year in progress;

(e) The amount of annual, permanent, or other appropriations, including balances of appropriations for prior fiscal years, available for expenditure during the fiscal year in progress, as of November 1 of such year;

(f) Balanced statements of (1) the condition of the Treasury at the end of the last completed fiscal year, (2) the estimated condition of the Treasury at the end of the fiscal year in progress, and (3) the estimated condition of the Treasury at the end of the ensuing fiscal year, if the financial proposals contained in the budget are adopted;

(g) All essential facts regarding the bonded and other indebtedness of the Government; and

(h) Such other financial statements and data as in his opinion are necessary or desirable in order to make known in all practicable detail the financial condition of the Government. . . .

* From 42 U.S. Stats. 20-27.

SEC. 207. There is hereby created in the Treasury Department a bureau to be known as the bureau of the budget. . . . The bureau, under such rules and regulations as the President may prescribe, shall prepare for him the budget, the alternative budget, and any supplemental or deficiency estimates, and to this end shall have authority to assemble, correlate, revise, reduce, or increase the estimates of the several departments or establishments. . . .

SEC. 209. The bureau, when directed by the President, shall make a detailed study of the departments and establishments for the purpose of enabling the President to determine what changes (with a view of securing greater economy and efficiency in the conduct of the public service) should be made in (1) the existing organization, activities, and methods of business of such departments or establishments, (2) the appropriations therefor, (3) the assignment of particular activities to particular services, or (4) the regrouping of services. . . .

SEC. 213. Under such regulations as the President may prescribe, (1) every department and establishment shall furnish to the bureau such information as the bureau may from time to time require, and (2) the director and the assistant director or any employee of the bureau when duly authorized shall, for the purpose of securing such information, have access to, and the right to examine, any books, documents, papers, or records of any such department or establishment.

SEC. 214. (a) The head of each department and establishment shall designate an official thereof as budget officer therefor, who, in each year under his direction and on or before a date fixed by him, shall prepare the departmental estimates.

(b) Such budget officer shall also prepare, under the direction of the head of the department or establishment, such supplemental and deficiency estimates as may be required for its work.

SEC. 215. The head of each department and establishment shall revise the departmental estimates and submit them to the bureau on or before September 15 of each year. In case of his failure so to do the President shall cause to be prepared such estimates and data as are necessary to enable him to include in the budget estimates and statements in respect to the work of such department or establishment.

SEC. 216. The departmental estimates and any supplemental or deficiency estimates submitted to the bureau by the head of any department or establishment shall be prepared and submitted in such form, manner, and detail as the President may prescribe. . . .

SEC. 301. There is created an establishment of the Government to be known as the general accounting office, which shall be independent of the executive departments and under the control and direction of the comptroller general of the United States. . . .

SEC. 304. . . . The balances certified by the comptroller general shall be final and conclusive upon the executive branch of the Government. . . .

SEC. 305. Section 236 of the revised statutes is amended to read as follows: "Sec. 236. All claims and demands whatever by the Government of the United States or against it, and all accounts whatever in which the Government of the United States is concerned, either as debtor or creditor, shall be settled and adjusted in the general accounting office. . . ."

SEC. 309. The comptroller general shall prescribe the forms, systems, and procedure for administrative appropriation and fund accounting in the several departments and establishments, and for the administrative examination of fiscal officers' accounts and claims against the United States. . . .

SEC. 312. (a) The comptroller general shall investigate, at the seat of government or elsewhere, all matters relating to the receipt, disbursement, and application of public funds, and shall make to the President when requested by him, and to Congress at the beginning of each regular session, a report in writing of the work of the general accounting office, containing recommendations concerning the legislation he may deem necessary to facilitate the prompt and accurate rendition and settlement of accounts and concerning such other matters relating to the receipt, disbursement, and application of public funds, as he may think advisable. In such regular report, or in special reports at any time when Congress is in session, he shall make recommendations looking to greater economy or efficiency in public expenditures.

(b) He shall make such investigations and reports as shall be ordered by either House of Congress or by any committee of either House having jurisdiction over revenue, appropriations, or expenditures. The comptroller general shall also, at the request of any such committee, direct assistants from his office to furnish the committee such aid and information as it may request.

(c) The comptroller general shall specially report to Congress every expenditure or contract made by any department or establishment in any year in violation of law.

(d) He shall submit to Congress reports upon the adequacy and effectiveness of the administrative examination of accounts and claims in the respective departments and establishments and upon the adequacy and effectiveness of departmental inspection of the offices and accounts of fiscal officers.

(e) He shall furnish such information relating to expenditures and accounting to the bureau of the budget as it may request from time to time.

SEC. 313. All departments and establishments shall furnish to the comptroller general such information regarding the powers, duties, activities, organization, financial transactions, and methods of business of their respective offices as he may from time to time require of them; and the comptroller general, or any of his assistants or employees, when duly authorized by him, shall for the purpose of securing such information have access to and the right to examine any books, documents, papers, or records of any such department or establishment. . . .

4

Corruption in Government

☆ The mild-mannered Harding was deceived by unscrupulous members of his official family, men more interested in personal profit than in public service. Their violation of the public trust reached its apogee in the Teapot Dome scandal.* ☆

In June 1920, still in the Wilson administration, Congress provided for the leasing of the United States Naval Reserves by the Secretary of the Navy, and in November 1920, two weeks after Harding's election, but before he was inaugurated, Edward L. Doheny, an oil baron, and J. Leo Stack, an oil promoter, of Denver, contracted to negotiate with the United States for a lease to develop offset wells along the boundary of Teapot Dome Reserve. It was highly important that a Secretary of the Interior should be appointed who would initiate for Doheny the preliminaries necessary to the leasing of those oil reserves. Albert Bacon Fall, of New Mexico, was selected by President Harding as Secretary of the Interior.

And two months after Albert Fall was sworn in as Secretary of the Interior, he sent to Edwin Denby, Secretary of the Navy, the outline of a letter for Denby to sign requesting the president to transfer all the Naval Reserve oil lands from the Navy Department to the Interior Department. Denby, two weeks later, wrote

* From William Allen White, *A Puritan in Babylon, The Story of Calvin Coolidge,* pp. 224-228. Copyright, 1938, by The Macmillan Company, New York. Used by permission of William L. White.

to President Harding requesting the transfer of those oil reserve lands from the Navy to the Interior Department. And less than a week later, the President signed the executive order transferring the control of the Naval Petroleum Reserves from the Navy Department to Fall's Department of the Interior. Fast work this.

Two months later a lease and contract for drilling offset wells in Reserve No. 1, at Elk Hills, California, were entered into between the government and the Pan American Petroleum & Transport Company. The lease was signed by Acting Secretary of the Interior Finney and by Vice President Danziger of Pan American. So much for Naval Oil Reserve No. 1.

Now before considering Reserve No. 2, we must detour to pick up a loose thread in the narrative but an important thread —a golden thread in truth! In November, 1921, arrrangements were made between Harry F. Sinclair, representing the Sinclair Consolidated Oil Company, H. M. Blackmer of the Midwest Oil Company, Robert W. Stewart of the Standard Oil Company of Indiana, and associates, to purchase 33,333,333 barrels of oil in the name of the Continental Trading Company, from A. E. Humphreys, in Texas, and his associates, at $1.50 per barrel. Sinclair and his group were to purchase the same amount of oil for the Continental Trading Company for $1.75 per barrel. Observe the profit of twenty-five cents a barrel. When the profits on this deal had amounted to three million dollars, the contract which had been signed and delivered in November, 1921, was closed out. The Continental Trading Company, chartered at Toronto under the laws of Canada, seems to have been organized for the purpose of accumulating a fund for political purposes. So much for the detour and that deal.

But Doheny, Sinclair, Stewart and Blackmer were fairly busy with other coordinated matters in those days. The last of November, 1921, a little less than nine months after Harding's inauguration and just a week after the Continental Trading Company had been organized, a little more than four months after Fall had leased Naval Oil Reserve No. 1 at Elk Hills, California, to Doheny, Doheny loaned Fall $100,000 and sent the money to Fall in a satchel which became famous later as "the little black bag." Doheny's son carried this apparently, surreptitiously to Fall. A few days less than a month after the "little black bag" had passed from Doheny to Fall, Harry Sinclair and his attorney, J. W. Zeveley, visited Secretary Fall at his ranch at Three Rivers, New Mexico, and negotiated for the Teapot Dome lease. And a little more than a month after Sinclair and his attorney had visited Fall at Three Rivers and had negotiated for the Teapot Dome Reserve, Harry Sinclair filed public application for the Teapot Dome Naval Reserve No. 3, with the Secretary of the Interior. While the lease was still pending, February 28, 1922, the Mammoth Oil Company was organized under the laws of Delaware, to exploit Teapot Dome. Ten or a dozen days later this Company paid

a million dollars to a subsidiary of the Midwest Oil Company, for the Teapot Dome contract. In March, a few weeks later, H. Foster Bain, Director of the Bureau of Mines, issued a memorandum showing the loss of government oil as a result of delayed government drilling and a week later Senator La Follette, having been told of what was going on, introduced a resolution to investigate the leasing of oil reserves. Captain John Halligan, of the United States Navy, wrote to the Secretary of the Navy, protesting against the private exploitation of Reserve No. 3, Teapot Dome. The newspapers were filling up with questions and revelations concerning the leases. The drift of public opinion was definitely against the negotiations. Less than a week after La Follette's resolution appeared, the contract for leasing Teapot Dome Naval Reserve No. 3 to the Mammoth Oil Company was executed and signed by Secretaries Denby and Fall, though the information was not made public at the time. The existence of the lease was even publicly denied. Three days after the contract was signed Director Bain, of the Bureau of Mines, innocently wrote to Senator Kendrick, of Wyoming, who was inquiring about these oil leases in his own state that "as yet no definite contracts have been made," though the leases for Teapot Dome and Elk Hills had been signed and delivered for nine months.

In the meantime, the Continental Trading Company in Canada bought $30,000 worth of Liberty Bonds, easily negotiable securities, almost as fluid as cash, but alas not quite so fluid for they were numbered. These bonds were bought for purposes of political intrigue, and two days later the Trading Company bought $200,000 more of this high-powered financial fluid to operate in politics. The next day the *Wall Street Journal* published the story of the lease of Teapot Dome and the Senate adopted a resolution offered by Senator Kendrick, asking Denby and Fall to advise the Senate if negotiations were in progress to lease national oil reserves. A few days later, the Canadian Continental Company's war chest was strengthened by another $50,-000 in Liberty Bonds. And April 25, Assistant Secretary Finney of the Interior Department, and Secretary Denby, of the Navy Department, wrote a letter in answer to the Kendrick resolution, explaining the oil leases. Senator Robert M. La Follette, the elder, in a Senate speech, demanded an investigation of the whole oil lease conspiracy. The next day the Senate after a bitter and fiery debate adopted the La Follette resolution. On May 10, Fall's son-in-law, M. T. Everhart, received from H. F. Sinclair, on Sinclair's private car in Washington, $198,000 of the Continental Trading Company's Liberty Bonds. A week later he received $35,000 more in Liberty Bonds from Sinclair's office in New York. May 29, Everhart left $90,000 of those Liberty Bonds with the First National Bank of Pueblo, Colorado, declaring they were the property of Secretary Fall, and delivered $140,000 in Liberty Bonds to the M. D. Thatcher estate in Pueblo. These bonds which later came to Fall were identified by their numerals as those purchased for the Continental Trading Company.

Agitation was beginning to interest the people. The smell of oil was over Washington. To calm the public, President Harding, always a good fellow, addressed to the Senate a letter which declared that the oil land leasing policy was submitted to him before its adoption and that the policy and acts under it "have at all times my entire approval." Of course Harding did not know about the Continental Trading Company's activity in Liberty Bonds, nor about Fall's deals with Doheny and Sinclair.

By the summer of 1922, the stench of these oil scandals was beginning to rise and among informed people it was known that the Secretary of the Interior had formed some kind of alliance with Doheny, Sinclair and certain elements of the Standard Oil that were interested in the main chance. December 11 of that year, the second lease of Reserve No. 1, at Elk Hills, California, was turned over to the Pan-American Oil Company and the lease was signed by Fall and Doheny. A few weeks later in early January, 1923, Fall, realizing that his day of usefulness to the oil companies was over, announced that he would resign from President Harding's Cabinet on March 4, after serving two years. That day, or about that time, Harry Sinclair, in his room in Washington, at the Wardman Park Hotel, handed $25,000 in cash to Fall's son-in-law as a loan to Fall, taking no note. When Fall retired from the Cabinet, after two years of service, he gave as a reason for his resignation "the pressure of private business interests," and when he resigned, President Harding announced that he had once offered Fall an appointment as Justice of the Supreme Court, a sadder commentary upon Harding than upon Fall. Fall had been out of the Cabinet less than a month when $70,000 of the $90,000 lot of Liberty Bonds turned over to the First National Bank of Pueblo in May the year before, were deposited with the Exchange Bank of Carrizozo, New Mexico to the credit of Albert Fall. After Fall's resignation Harry Sinclair gave Fall an additional $50,000 as a loan and $10,000 in cash for Fall's expenses for a trip to Russia on behalf of Sinclair and his oil interests.

5

Government and Business, 1924

☆ *There was a growing awareness among certain business leaders in the 1920's of the problems of population growth and the developing complexity of business and human affairs. They could perceive the need for increased regulation, but stressed the need for voluntary rather than governmental regulation. This viewpoint was well expressed by Secretary of Commerce Herbert Hoover. There were those, largely caught up in the 1924 LaFollette presidential candidacy, who strongly disagreed with this position.* ☆

(a) ADDRESS OF HERBERT HOOVER TO THE UNITED STATES CHAMBER OF COMMERCE*

The advancement of science and our increasing population require constantly new standards of conduct and breed an increasing multitude of new rules and regulations. The basic principles laid down in the Ten Commandments and the Sermon on the Mount are as applicable today as when they were declared, but they require a host of subsidiary clauses. The ten ways to evil in the time of Moses have increased to ten thousand now.

A whole host of rules and regulations are necessary to maintain human rights with this amazing transformation into an industrial era. Ten people in a whole country, with a plow apiece, did not elbow each other very much. But when we put 7,000,000 people in a county with the tools of electric, steam, thirty-floor buildings,

telephones, miscellaneous noises, streetcars, railways, motors, stock exchanges, and what not, then we do jostle each other in a multitude of directions. Thereupon our law-makers supply the demand by the ceaseless piling up of statutes.

Moreover, with increasing education our senses become more offended and our moral discriminations increase; for all of which we discover new things to remedy. In one of our states over 1000 laws and ordinances have been added in the last eight months. It is also true that a large part of them will sleep peacefully in the statute book.

The question we need to consider is whether these rules and regulations are to be developed solely by government or whether they cannot be in some large part developed out of voluntary forces in the nation. In other words, can the abuses which give rise to government in business be eliminated by the systematic

* May 7, 1924. From *Congressional Record*, 68th Congress, 1st session, pp. 8134-8136.

and voluntary action of commerce and industry itself . . .?

National character cannot be built by law. It is the sum of the moral fibre of its individuals. When abuses which rise from our growing system are cured by live individual conscience, by initiative in the creation of voluntary standards, then is the growth of moral perceptions fertilized in every individual character.

No one disputes the necessity for constantly new standards of conduct in relation to all these tools and inventions. Even our latest great invention—radio—has brought a host of new questions. No one disputes that much of these subsidiary additions to the Ten Commandments must be made by legislation. Our public utilities are wasteful and costly unless we give them a privilege more or less monopolistic. At once when we have business affected with monopoly we must have regulation by law. Much of even this phase might have been unnecessary had there been a higher degree of responsibility to the public, higher standards of business practice among those who dominated these agencies in years gone by. . . .

When legislation penetrates the business world it is because there is abuse somewhere. A great deal of this legislation is due rather to the inability of business hitherto to so organize as to correct abuses than to any lack of desire to have it done. Sometimes the abuses are more apparent than real, but anything is a handle for demagoguery. In the main, however, the public acts only when it has lost confidence in the ability or willingness of business to correct its own abuses.

Legislative action is always clumsy—it is incapable of adjustment to shifting needs. It often enough produces new economic currents more abusive than those intended to be cured. Government too often becomes the persecutor instead of the regulator.

The thing we all need to searchingly consider is the practical question of the method by which the business world can develop and enforce its own standards and thus stem the tide of governmental regulation. The cure does not lie in mere opposition. It lies in the correction of abuse. It lies in an adaptability to changing human outlook.

The problem of business ethics as a prevention of abuse is of two categories: those where the standard must be one of individual moral perceptions, and those where we must have a determination of standards of conduct for a whole group in order that there may be a basis for ethics.

The standards of honesty, of a sense of mutual obligation, and of service, were determined two thousand years ago. They may require at times to be recalled. And the responsibility for them increases infinitely in high places either in business or government, for there rests the high responsibility for leadership in fineness of moral perception. Their failure is a blow at the repute of business and at confidence in government itself.

The second field and the one which I am primarily discussing is the great area of indirect economic wrong and unethical practices that spring up under the pressures of competition and habit. There is also the great field of economic waste through destructive competition, through strikes, booms, and slumps, unemployment, through failure of our different industries to synchronize, and a hundred other causes which directly lower our productivity and employment. Waste may be abstractly unethical, but in any event it can only be remedied by economic action.

If we are to find solution to these collective issues outside of government regulation we must meet two practical problems:

First, there must be organization in such

form as can establish the standards of conduct in this vast complex of shifting invention, production, and use. There is no existing basis to check the failure of service or the sacrifice of public interest. Some one must determine such standards. They must be determined and held flexibly in tune with the intense technology of trade.

Second, there must be some sort of enforcement. There is the perpetual difficulty of a small minority who will not play the game. They too often bring disrepute upon the vast majority; they drive many others to adopt unfair competitive methods which all deplore; their abuses give rise to public indignation and clamor which breed legislative action.

I believe we now for the first time have the method at hand for voluntarily organized determination of standards and their adoption. I would go further; I believe we are in the presence of a new era in the organization of industry and commerce in which, if properly directed, lie forces pregnant with infinite possibilities of moral progress. I believe that we are, almost unnoticed, in the midst of a great revolution—or perhaps a better word, a transformation in the whole super-organization of our economic life. We are passing from a period of extremely individualistic action into a period of associational activities.

Practically our entire American working world is now organized into some form of economic association. We have trade associations and trade institutes embracing particular industries and occupations. We have chambers of commerce embracing representatives of different industries and commerce. We have the labor unions representing the different crafts. We have associations embracing all the different professions—law, engineering, medicine, banking, real estate, and what not. We have farmers' associations, and we have the enormous growth of farmers' co-operatives for actual dealing in commodities. Of indirect kin to this is the great increase in ownership of industries by their employees, and customers, and again we have a tremendous expansion of mutualized insurance and banking.

Associational activities are, I believe, driving upon a new road where the objectives can be made wholly and vitally of public interest. . . .

Three years of study and intimate contact with associations of economic groups whether in production, distribution, labor, or finance, convince me that there lies within them a great moving impulse toward betterment.

If these organizations accept as their primary purpose the lifting of standards, if they will co-operate together for voluntary enforcement of high standards, we shall have proceeded far along the road of the elimination of government from business. . . .

The test of our whole economic and social system is its capacity to cure its own abuses. New abuses and new relationships to the public interest will occur as long as we continue to progress. If we are to be wholly dependent upon government to cure these abuses we shall by this very method have created an enlarged and deadening abuse through the extension of bureaucracy and the clumsy and incapable handling of delicate economic forces. . . .

American business needs a lifting purpose greater than the struggle of materialism. Nor can it lie in some evanescent, emotional, dramatic crusade. It lies in the higher pitch of economic life, in a finer regard for the rights of others, a stronger devotion to obligations of citizenship that will assure an improved leadership in every community and the nation; it lies in the organization of the forces of our economic life so that they may produce happier individual lives, more secure in employment and comfort, wider in the possibilities of enjoyment of nature, larger in its opportunities of intellectual life.

(b) THE PROGRESSIVE PLATFORM OF 1924*

The great issue before the American people today is the control of government and industry by private monopoly.

For a generation the people have struggled patiently, in the face of repeated betrayals by successive administrations, to free themselves from this intolerable power which has been undermining representative government.

Through control of government, monopoly has steadily extended its absolute dominion to every basic industry.

In violation of law, monopoly has crushed competition, stifled private initiative and independent enterprise, and without fear of punishment now exacts extortionate profits upon every necessity of life consumed by the public.

The equality of opportunity proclaimed by the Declaration of Independence and asserted and defended by Jefferson and Lincoln as the heritage of every American citizen has been displaced by special privilege for the few, wrested from the government of the many.

That tyrannical power which the American people denied to a king, they will no longer endure from the monopoly system. The people know they cannot yield to any group the control of the economic life of the nation and preserve their political liberties. They know monopoly has its representatives in the halls of Congress, on the Federal bench, and in the executive departments; that these servile agents barter away the nation's natural resources, nullify acts of Congress by judicial veto and administrative favor, invade the people's rights by unlawful arrests and unconstitutional searches and sei-

zures, direct our foreign policy in the interests of predatory wealth, and make wars and conscript the sons of the common people to fight them. . . .

The present condition of American agriculture constitutes an emergency of the gravest character. The Department of Commerce report shows that during 1923 there was a steady and marked increase in dividends paid by the great industrial corporations. The same is true of the steam and electric railways and practically all other large corporations. On the other hand, the Secretary of Agriculture reports that in the fifteen principal wheat growing states more than 108,000 farmers since 1920 have lost their farms through foreclosure and bankruptcy; that more than 122,000 have surrendered their property without legal proceedings, and that nearly 375,000 have retained possession of their property only through the leniency of their creditors. . . .

Almost unlimited prosperity for the great corporations and ruin and bankruptcy for agriculture is the direct and logical result of the policies and legislation which deflated the farmer while extending almost unlimited credit to the great corporations; which protected with exorbitant tariffs the industrial magnates, but depressed the prices of the farmers' products by financial juggling while greatly increasing the cost of what he must buy; which guaranteed excessive freight rates to the railroads and put a premium on wasteful management while saddling an unwarranted burden onto the backs of the American farmer; which permitted gambling in the products of the farm by grain speculators to the great detriment of the farmer and to the great profit of the grain gambler.

* From Kirk H. Porter, *National Party Platforms*, pp. 516-522. Published by The Macmillan Company, New York, 1924.

A COVENANT WITH THE PEOPLE

Awakened by the dangers which menace their freedom and prosperity the American people still retain the right and courage to exercise their sovereign control over their government. In order to destroy the economic and political power of monopoly, which has come between the people and their government, we pledge ourselves to the following principles and policies:

1. We pledge a complete housecleaning in the Department of Justice, the Department of the Interior, and the other executive departments. We demand that the power of the Federal Government be used to crush private monopoly, not to foster it.

2. We pledge recovery of the navy's oil reserves and all other parts of the public domain which have been fraudulently or illegally leased, or otherwise wrongfully transferred, to the control of private interests. . . . We favor public ownership of the nation's water power and the creation and development of a national super-water-power system, including Muscle Shoals, to supply at actual cost light and power for the people and nitrate for the farmers, and strict public control and permanent conservation of all the nation's resources, including coal, iron and other ores, oil and timber lands, in the interest of the people.

3. We favor repeal of the Esch-Cummins railroad law and the fixing of railroad rates upon the basis of actual, prudent investment and cost of service. We pledge speedy enactment of the Howell-Barkley Bill for the adjustment of controversies between railroads and their employees, which was held up in the last Congress by joint action of reactionary leaders of the Democratic and Republican parties. We declare for public ownership of railroads with definite safeguards against bureaucratic control, as the only

final solution of the transportation problem.

4. We favor reduction of Federal taxes upon individual incomes and legitimate business, limiting tax exactions strictly to the requirements of the government administered with rigid economy, particularly by curtailment of the eight hundred million dollars now annually expended for the army and navy in preparation for future wars; by the recovery of the hundreds of millions of dollars stolen from the Treasury through fraudulent war contracts and the corrupt leasing of the public resources; and by diligent action to collect the accumulated interest upon the eleven billion dollars owing us by foreign governments.

We denounce the Mellon tax plan as a device to relieve multi-millionaires at the expense of other tax payers, and favor a taxation policy providing for immediate reductions upon moderate incomes, large increases in the inheritance tax rates upon large estates to prevent the indefinite accumulation by inheritance of great fortunes in a few hands; taxes upon excess profits to penalize profiteering, and complete publicity, under proper safeguards, of all Federal tax returns.

5. We favor submitting to the people, for their considerate judgment, a constitutional amendment providing that Congress may by enacting a statute make it effective over a judicial veto.

We favor such amendment to the constitution as may be necessary to provide for the election of all Federal Judges, without party designation, for fixed terms not exceeding ten years, by direct vote of the people.

6. We favor drastic reduction of the exorbitant duties on manufacturers provided in the Fordney-McCumber tariff legislation, the prohibiting of gambling by speculators and profiteers in agricultural products; the reconstruction of the Federal Reserve and Federal Farm Loan

Systems, so as to eliminate control by usurers, speculators and international financiers, and to make the credit of the nation available upon fair terms to all and without discrimination to business men, farmers and home-builders. We advocate the calling of a special session of Congress to pass legislation for the relief of American agriculture. We favor such further legislation as may be needful or helpful in promoting and protecting cooperative enterprises. We demand that the Interstate Commerce Commission proceed forthwith to reduce by an approximation to pre-war levels the present freight rates on agricultural products, including live stock, and upon the materials required upon American farms for agricultural purposes.

7. We favor abolition of the use of injunctions in labor disputes and declare for complete protection of the right of farmers and industrial workers to organize, bargain collectively through representatives of their own choosing, and conduct without hindrance cooperative enterprises.

We favor prompt ratification of the Child Labor amendment, and subsequent enactment of a Federal law to protect children in industry. . . .

11. Over and above constitutions and statutes and greater than all, is the su-

preme sovereignty of the people, and with them should rest the final decision of all great questions of national policy. We favor such amendments to the Federal Constitution as may be necessary to provide for the direct nomination and election of the President, to extend the initiative and referendum to the federal government, and to insure a popular referendum for or against war except in cases of actual invasion.

12. We denounce the mercenary system of foreign policy under recent administrations in the interests of financial imperialists, oil monopolists and international bankers, which has at times degraded our State Department from its high service as a strong and kindly intermediary of defenseless governments to a trading outpost for those interests and concession-seekers engaged in the exploitations of weaker nations, as contrary to the will of the American people, destructive of domestic development and provocative of war. We favor an active foreign policy to bring about a revision of the Versailles treaty in accordance with the terms of the armistice, and to promote firm treaty agreements with all nations to outlaw wars, abolish conscription, drastically reduce land, air and naval armaments, and guarantee public referendum on peace and war.

6

Tax Reduction

☆ *Over the years, and partly due to the costs of World War I, taxes had multiplied in number and amount. During the 1920's the Republican administrations in cooperation with the Congress made a number of downward revisions in federal taxes.** ☆

Once the 1924 election was over, a vigorous campaign was begun to repeal the gift and estate taxes and to lower drastically the surtaxes. That December Coolidge told Congress of the need for taxation "scientifically revised downward." An organization, first known as the American Bankers' League, later as the American Taxpayers' League, was formed to spread propaganda and to bring pressure on Congress. Early in the fall of 1925 the House Ways and Means Committee met in order to hear proposals for tax revision by Mellon, such experts as Professors Seligman and T. S. Adams, and the general public. Numerous Tax Clubs from Iowa, Texas, and other states, composed of newspapermen, bankers, and "political wire-pullers," appeared before the Committee, attempted to reach Congressmen, and tried to create a political backfire which would stampede Congress. Two conferences of state and federal representatives on inheritance and estate taxation were also held in February and November, 1925, at the instigation of the President.

* Reprinted from *American Taxation* by Sidney Ratner, pp. 424-427, 432-433. By permission of W. W. Norton & Company, Inc. Copyright 1942 by Sidney Ratner.

Although the first conference did not agree with Coolidge's proposal that the federal government retire from the estate tax field, the second was more amenable.

Mellon recommended reduction of the income tax rates to a maximum surtax of 20 per cent, and a normal tax of 5 per cent, the reduction and eventual repeal of the estate tax, and the immediate repeal of the gift tax and the excises on automobiles, admissions, and jewelry. He also advocated restricting the publicity of income tax returns and a constitutional amendment to abolish the tax exemption of government securities. The opposition to the second Mellon Tax Plan in Congress was very weak on most points, except on that of the estate tax. The Democratic party had been left divided and demoralized by the election and lacked vigorous leadership. The progressive wing of the Republican party had also suffered election losses and had been deprived of La Follette's dynamic leadership by his death in 1925. The consequence was that although William R. Green and John N. Garner fought hard for the estate and gift taxes the Republican machine, with the assistance of the Democratic leaders, was able to steamroller the administation revenue bill through Congress with unusual speed. Garner and Senator Simmons made their bargains with the Republicans and then used their influence to keep the Democratic party in line as supporters of the Republican bill.

The outstanding opponents of the measure were Representatives Rainer and Frear and Senator Norris. Others who contributed to the opposition were Cordell Hull and Fiorello La Guardia in the House and Couzens, Borah, King, and Robert La Follette, Jr., in the Senate. Couzens published in January and February, 1926, the full report of his extended investigation into the Bureau of Internal Revenue, and throughout the Senate debate presented facts indicative of fraud and ineffciency in the administration of the Bureau. Tax refunds were revealed which totaled $1,271 million since 1922. Large corporations and wealthy individuals were involved, among whom were various Mellon corporations. But these revelations failed to have much effect upon Congress or the general public because the dominant business interests were satisfied with Mellon's work as Secretary of the Treasury and the administration was able to make a plausible defense on the ground that most of the charges came from dissatisfied Bureau employees and Couzens's antagonism to Mellon.

Given such a background, it is no surprise that the revenue bill introduced into Congress on December 7, 1925, was passed in the House on December 18 by the overwhelming majority of 390 to 25 and in the Senate on February 12, 1926, by a vote of 58 to 19. The bill became law on February 26, 1926. Proof that big business was in control was the widespread approval of the new tax law by the press. The Republican newspapers and many conservative Democratic papers praised the law as a sound, businesslike, and intelligent tax measure. . . .

The Revenue Act of 1926 was distinguished by the greatly reduced burden on the rich, especially the very rich, through lower surtaxes on the high incomes, much diminished tax rates on large estates, and the repeal of the gift tax. The political support for this consideration for the wealthy was secured through the granting of smaller tax cuts to those in the lower brackets. An analysis of the Act will reveal that although the 1926 Revenue Act seemed to be in accord with what the majority of the electorate voted for in the 1924 election, not all of them clearly understood how that program would affect them practically.

The normal income tax rates were reduced from the 1924 rates of 2 per cent upon the first $4,000 of net taxable income, 4 per cent upon the next $4,000, and 6 per cent upon the amount over $8,000 to 1½ per cent, 3 per cent, and 5 per cent respectively. The personal exemptions were increased from $1,000 to $1,500 for single persons and from $2,500 to $3,500 for heads of families or married persons. These increases meant the complete exemption of about one third of 7,300,000 income tax payers of 1925 and was sharply opposed by Cordell Hull and a few others because the exemption made possible retention of the far heavier burdens of the protective tariff and various war-excise taxes. The 1924 deduction of $400 for each dependent was retained. The 25 per cent credit first allowed in 1924 on taxes on earned incomes was not only kept, but the maximum amount of net income upon which this credit was permitted was increased from $10,000 to $20,000. This provision was in line with progressive economic thought and was at the same time politically useful to the conservatives.

The minor favors given to the middle classes were greatly outweighed by those given the wealthy through changes in the surtax. The 1926 surtax rates on incomes of $26,000 and less followed the 1924 rate in beginning at 1 per cent upon net incomes over $10,000 and rising to 7 per cent on those in the $24,000—$26,000 bracket. But after that income level a gradually increasing reduction in the surtax rates, as compared with the 1924 rates, occurred. The result was that the maximum surtax rate became 20 per cent upon the net income in excess of $100,000. This was a sharp drop from the 1924 maximum of 40 per cent on the amount over $500,000. . . .

To compensate for the repeal of the 1924 corporation tax of $1 per $1,000 of capital, the tax on corporate net income was increased from 12½ per cent to 13 per cent for 1925 and to 13½ per cent for each year thereafter. But life insurance companies, which had not been subject to the capital stock tax, were to continue to pay only 12½ per cent upon their net income. The 1924 tax of 50 per cent on undistributed corporate surpluses was kept, but the tax was modified so as not to apply if all the stockholders included in their income tax returns their distributive shares of the corporation's net income for the taxable year, whether distributed or not. . . .

The Revenue Act of 1928 was the fourth in the series of post-first World War tax reductions. No radical changes in the 1926 Revenue Act were made except in form. The principal alterations occurred in the corporation tax and the excise taxes on automobiles, admissions, and dues. The normal tax and surtax rates on individual incomes remained the same as in the 1926 law. The normal rate was 1½ per cent on the first $4,000 of taxable net income, 3 per cent on the next $4,000, and 5 per cent on the amount over $8,000. The surtax began at 1 per cent upon net income in excess of $10,000 and gradually increased to 20 per cent upon net income in excess of $100,000. The personal exemptions were held to $1,500 for single persons, $3,500

for the head of the family or married person, and $400 for each dependent. But the 25 per cent tax credit on earned incomes was raised from $20,000 to $30,000.

The tax on corporate net income was reduced from 13½ per cent to 12 per cent, and the lower rate was made applicable to incomes of 1928 as well as those of succeeding years. To corporations of a net income of $25,000 or less a credit of $3,000, in contrast with the $2,000 credit of 1926, was given. Capital net gains were taxed the same as in 1926, and the option given affiliated corporations on filing consolidated returns was retained. Nor was any change made in the tax on undistributed corporate surpluses.

Against the advice of Mellon, but in response to the pressure from automobile manufacturers, Congress repealed the large revenue-yielding tax of 3 per cent upon the manufacturers' prices of passenger automobiles. Congress also granted large increases in the exemptions from taxes on admissions and dues and reduced drastically the taxes on wines. The amount of tax withheld at the source was increased in the case of certain "tax-free covenant" bonds owned by nonresident aliens, foreign corporations, and unknown holders.

The federal estate tax was kept at the same rates as in the 1926 law notwithstanding what William R. Green characterized as "the most extraordinary, highly financed propaganda for a selfish purpose . . . that has ever been known in the whole history of this country." Mellon and the conservative Republicans in Congress worked for the repeal of the estate tax, but were foiled by the progressive Republicans and Democrats. The nomination of Green to the Court of Claims by Coolidge early in the spring of 1928 was interpreted by many as a stratagem for securing the repeal of the tax at a later period. Among the administrative changes were provisions giving the Commissioner of Internal

Revenue the authority to close cases by agreement with the taxpayer and requiring that all refunds or credits on income, estate, or gift taxes in excess of $75,000 be referred to the Joint Committee on Internal Revenue Taxation before being paid to the taxpayers. . . .

The New York *Times* and the *Sun* praised the reduction of the corporation tax as giving a healthy stimulus to business. Yet despite the agreement of most Republicans and Democrats on the desirability of tax reduction, a minority group of liberal and radical dissenters persisted in arguing that the wiser policy was to pay off the national debt while the country was prosperous and thereby improve the national credit and reduce the rate of interest necessary to pay on all refunding. But their contentions could not prevail against those who felt that taxes were too heavy, that their reduction would aid business, promote general prosperity, and prevent the accumulation of large surpluses which would tempt Congress into extravagant expenditures. . . .

7

Agriculture in the Twenties

☆ *The farmer, plagued by overproduction and falling prices, generally failed to share in the prosperity of the 1920's. Agricultural agitation was rife and though Congress responded with legislation designed to alleviate the farmer's condition, the chief legislative objective, the McNary-Haugen plan, repeatedly failed to meet with presidential approval.* ☆

(a) FARM TROUBLE AND RELIEF*

The line-up of forces on farm relief from 1923 to 1926 was discouraging from the point of view of those who favored aggressive action to restore farm prices to equality with costs. The cooperative marketing associations, which had developed along commodity lines into strength and prominence in the years following the war, were generally hostile. They were unconvinced that, given Federal recognition and support, they could not do the job themselves. The South as a whole was indifferent, partly because its chief farm organizations were the cotton, tobacco, and rice cooperatives and partly because of traditional opposition to increased Federal powers and to extension or recognition of the protective-tariff principle.

The East and the industrial centers were inherently opposed. Even when prominent industrialists recognized the

* From Chester C. Davis, "The Development of Agricultural Policy Since the End of the World War," in United States Department of Agriculture, *Farmers in a Changing World*, Washington, 1940, pp. 304-305.

importance to national prosperity of restored farm buying power, they were violently critical of any specific method proposed to that end.

Agricultural colleges and economists were as a whole indifferent to the problem. During the early years their leadership was negative and their attitude scoffing.

Outside of Congress and a small group close to the Secretary in the Department of Agriculture, official Washington was solidly opposed to any but the most orthodox Government moves to strengthen agriculture.

The spearhead of the movement for positive Government action from 1923 to 1926, therefore, was made up in the first stages by individuals and special groups; State units of general farm organizations were next to fall in line, and after them the national farm associations—the American Farm Bureau Federation, the Farmers' Union, and the Grange.

Generally through those years the farm forces were disposed to divide all over the field as to details of procedure. The co-operatives went their own way, with the exception of Northwest wheat associations, who favored the surplus-disposal plan. Some farm leaders were for outright Government guaranty of fixed prices. There were lively debates over the surplus problem—even over the question whether in fact any surplus of farm products existed. Many farm leaders contended that there could be no overproduction if marketing were properly organized.

Secretary Wallace, in his annual report for 1922, summed up the opposite view in saying:

"Some contend that there is no such thing as overproduction of farm products and cannot be as long as there are people in the world who suffer for food and clothing. On the same line of reasoning it can be argued that the production of automobiles will be inadequate until every man and woman and every boy and girl of high-school age owns one. There is overproduction, so far as the producer is concerned, whenever the quantity produced cannot be marketed at a price which will cover all production costs and leave the producer enough to tempt him to continue production."

Small voices were raised but scarcely heard when they questioned the wisdom of a tariff policy which excluded from this country the means by which foreign buyers could pay for our exports, while at the same time we demanded and expected that our exports would be maintained. Meanwhile the policy of raising tariffs swept on to its culmination in the Tariff Act of 1929 without effective protest either from the pros or the antis in the farm-relief fight.

Both sides failed to recognize the fact that continued exports through these years were made possible by the extension of credit to foreign nations and buyers. The total volume of new foreign issues floated in the United States from 1919 to 1929, inclusive, amounted to $8,172,000,000, while the net outward movement of long-term capital during the period exceeded $6,000,000,000. The heaviest flotations of new issues during these years were $1,201,000,000 worth in 1928 and $1,111,000,000 worth in 1928.

Even the farm proposals for a protected domestic consumption at parity with non-agricultural prices, independent of the world price for the surplus, depended for effective operation on the willingness and ability of the world market to take all the surplus the United States produced.

There was failure to recognize the effect of our change from a debtor to a creditor nation. Our status as a nation in another sense had also changed. We at last were at the end of the pioneering period. We now had a preempted continent —the last of the good free land had been taken up, and we were face to face with the problem of a maturing nation. No longer was there a frontier to act as a shock absorber for dispossessed farmers and unemployed from industrial centers, with outside creditor nations ready to take our surplus production in payment on our debts to them.

(b) VETO MESSAGE OF PRESIDENT CALVIN COOLIDGE "RELATING TO THE AGRICULTURE SURPLUS CONTROL ACT"*

In its essentials the objectionable plan proposed here is the stimulation of the price of agricultural commodities and

*May 3, 1928. *Senate Document* #141, Misc. II, 70th Congress, 1st session, pp. 1-7.

products thereof by artificially controlling the surpluses so that there will be an apparent scarcity on the market. This is to be done by means of a board having supposedly adequate powers and adequate funds to accomplish such purpose through various agencies, governmental and private. The surpluses of the different selected commodities so accumulated by the board are then to be sold by export and otherwise directly or through such agencies at whatever loss is necessary in making the disposition. The fund to pay the losses and other costs while at first furnished by the Government is ultimately to be replaced and thereafter replenished from time to time by means of a tax or fee charged against the product. The theory is that the enhanced price of the commodity would enable the producer to pay the equalization fee and still reap a profit. . . .

A detailed analysis of all of the objections to the measure would involve a document of truly formidable proportions. However, its major weaknesses and perils may be summarized under six headings:

I. Its attempted price-fixing fallacy.

II. The tax characteristics of the equalization fee.

III. The widespread bureaucracy which it would set up.

IV. Its encouragement to profiteering and wasteful distribution by middlemen.

V. Its stimulation of overproduction.

VI. Its aid to our foreign agricultural competitors.

These topics by no means exhaust the list of fallacious and indeed dangerous aspects of the bill, but they afford ample ground for its emphatic rejection.

I. *Price fixing.*—This measure is as cruelly deceptive in its disguise as governmental price-fixing legislation and involves quite as unmistakably the impossible scheme of attempted governmental control of buying and selling of agricultural products through political agencies as any of the other so-called surplus control bills. . . . There is apparently no change in the import of the bill in the resolution to impose upon the farmer and upon the consumers of farm produce a regime of futile, delusive experiments with price fixing, with indirect governmental buying and selling, and with a nation-wide system of regulatory policing, intolerable espionage, and tax collection on a vast scale. . . .

II. *The equalization fee,* which is the kernel of this legislation, is a sales tax upon the entire community. It is in no sense a mere contribution to be made by the producers themselves, as has been represented by supporters of the measure. It can be assessed upon the commodities in transit to the consumer and its burdens can often unmistakably be passed on to him.

Furthermore, such a procedure would certainly involve an extraordinary relinquishment of the taxing power on the part of Congress, because the tax would not only be levied without recourse to legislative authority but its proceeds would be expended entirely without the usual safeguards of congressional control of appropriations. This would be a most dangerous nullification of one of the essential checks and balances which lie at the very foundation of our Government.

Incidentally, this taxation or fee would not be for purposes of revenue in the accepted sense but would simply yield a subsidy for the special benefit of particular groups of processors and exporters. . . .

III. *Widespread bureaucracy.*—A bureaucratic tyranny of unprecedented proportions would be let down upon the backs of the farm industry and its distributors throughout the Nation in connection with the enforcement of this measure. Thousands of contracts involving scores of different grades, quantities, and varieties of products would have to be signed by the board with the 4,400 millers, the 1,200 meat-packing plants, the 3,000 or more cotton and woolen mills, and the 2,700 canners. If this bill had been in operation in 1925 it would have involved collections upon an aggregate of over 16,000,000,000 units of wheat, corn, and cotton. . . .

IV. *Encouragement to profiteering and wasteful distribution by middlemen.*—As was pointed out in the veto last year, it seems almost incredible that the farmers of this country are being offered this scheme of legislative relief in which the only persons who are guaranteed to benefit are the exporters, packers, millers, canners, spinners, and other processors. Their profits are definitely assured. They have, in other words, no particular incentive toward careful operation, since each of them holding a contract, no matter how unscrupulous, wasteful, or inefficient his operations may have been, would be fully reimbursed for all of his losses. . . .

V. *Stimulation of overproduction.*— The bill runs counter to an economic law as well settled as the law of gravitation. Increased prices decrease consumption; they also increase production. These two conditions are the very ones that spell disaster to the whole program. The vaguely drawn clause in the measure to meet this obvious danger merely amounts to moral suasion and as a last resort the withdrawal of the equalization fee. Thus if 90 per cent of the growers of a given commodity heed the admonitions of the board and refrain from production, they will, nevertheless, be punished because of the evasions of the remaining 10 per cent who have ignored the board's requests. In other words, no farmer will be safe in directing his planning upon his individual judgment, for should the result be a stimulation of an increased yield the board will be likely to withdraw the support which encouraged the surpluses and allow the prices to collapse under the weight of that artificially created excess. The annals of the industrial and agricul-

tural world are replete with the catastrophes that have come in the wake of such attempted distortions of one of the most fundamental principles of commercial relations.

VI. *Aid to our foreign agricultural competitors.*—This measure continues, as did its predecessor, to give substantial aid to the foreign competitors of American agriculture and industry. It continues the amazing proposal to supply foreign workers with cheaper food than those of the United States, and this at the expense of the American farm industry, thereby encouraging both the foreign peasant, whose produce is not burdened with the costs of any equalization fees, and also affording through reduced food prices the means of cutting the wage rates paid by foreign manufacturers. The latter step would promptly impair the prosperity of our manufacturing population, which is by far the leading and most profitable market for our farm produce. . . .

By the inevitable stimulation of production the bill can only mean an increase of exportable surplus to be dumped in the world market. This in turn will bring about a constantly decreasing world price, which will soon reach so low a figure that a wholesale curtailment of production in this country with its attendant demoralization and heavy losses would be certain. Where is the advantage of dragging our farmers into such folly?

Furthermore, as the board undertakes to dump the steadily mounting surplus into foreign countries at the low-cost figures, it will come into direct conflict with the dumping and similar trade laws of many foreign lands which are interested in the maintenance of their own agricultural industries. We might, therefore, expect immediately a series of drastic, retaliatory discriminations on the part of these consumer countries. This will drive our surplus into narrower market channels and force even further price reductions with consequent increases in the burdens of the equalization tax.

Lastly, and most important, in connection with this aspect of the bill as an aid to our foreign competitors, the measure will inevitably devastate many of our important farm areas. For instance, the board is expected to obtain higher prices for the American farmer for corn by removing the surplus from the home market and dumping it over our borders at a lower level of prices. In other words, the hog grower in Ontario, Canada, may buy American corn at a very much lower level than the hog grower in the State of Ohio. Both being situated equally as to the European market for their pork products, we shall see immediately the migration of the Ohio hog industries across the border into Canada with consequent losses to our pork industry by this Canadian competition.

8

Economic Revolution

☆ As prosperity developed during the twenties there was a relaxation of tension between labor and capital. The increasing popular acceptance of capitalism as the vehicle of economic well-being was heralded by Professor Thomas Nixon Carver of Harvard University as an economic revolution. ☆

Forty years or more ago, it began to be fashionable to comment, on the one hand, upon the awful concentration of wealth in this country, and, on the other, upon the masses of poverty that were concentrated in the slums of our cities. A flood of ink was poured upon the subject, and lecturers made the ears of the public to tingle with horror at the evils of the so-called capitalist system. Some went so far as to say not only that the rich were growing richer and the poor poorer, but that this was the inevitable result of the capitalist system. Plutocracy and poverty were its twin offspring. The public was asked to choose between Capitalism with its hideous progeny and some other system, say socialism, with its difficulties. We were told positively that we had no other choice; that the modern world was between the devil of plutocracy and the deep sea of socialism.

In all of this discussion the facts were perverted and the underlying principles misstated, and yet there were certain

* From Thomas Nixon Carver, *The Present Economic Revolution in the United States*, pp. 3-14. Copyright, 1926, Little, Brown and Company, Boston. Used by permission of Margaret Carver Leighton.

large and visible facts that lent a semblance of color to the argument. If any one undertook to show that such results were not necessary products of the present economic system, the huge fortunes of our multimillionaires and the slums of our cities were pointed out to him as evidence to the contrary. Here was something that was difficult to explain; at least to the satisfaction of minds that were not trained to clear economic analysis.

The speeches that were written during the period from 1870 to 1910 are now out of date, and yet a considerable number of people who learned their speeches then are unable to stop. They are still repeating them with parrot-like persistency. Instead of the concentration of wealth, we are now witnessing its diffusion; but the old tirades against plutocracy are still repeated. Instead of low wages for the manual trades, we are now having high wages; and yet the old phraseology, including such terms as wage slavery, still has a certain vogue. Instead of the laborer being in a position of dependence, he is now rapidly attaining a position of independence. The apostles of discontent are being robbed of their thunder. . . .

—II—

The Great War produced a number of political revolutions in Europe. It has not yet produced an economic revolution. . . . The only economic revolution now under way is going on in the United States. It is a revolution that is to wipe out the distinction between laborers and capitalists by making laborers their own capitalists and by compelling most capitalists to become laborers of one kind or another, because not many of them will be able to live on the returns from capital alone. This is something new in the history of the world.

The labor movement in this country is so far in advance of that in any other country as to make comparison impossible. In European countries, including Great Britain, labor organizations and the more conspicuous labor leaders are still pursuing antiquated methods that are comparable to the attempt of a man to lift himself by his boot straps. Here they are using the solid ground of capital ownership and are actually lifting themselves into positions of well-being that amount to affluence in comparison with the conditions of European laborers. In European countries their organized, political activities are dominated by a psychology that was built up in a primitive and fighting stage of social development; here they are emerging from that stage and are beginning to think in constructive terms such as belong to a progressive and industrial stage. In European countries they are grasping at the shadow of political control, but never have and never will by that method put an ounce of the substance of economic prosperity into the hands of any laborer. In this country they have, with few exceptions, refused to be deceived by shadows and are rapidly gaining the real substance of prosperity.

Those minds that are still thinking in terms of the primitive tactics of class war will not understand a single syllable of the last paragraph. The labor movement in this country is passing out of the stage in which leadership concerned itself mainly with the immediate tactics of battle. It is passing into the stage where it is concerning itself with the higher strategy of labor. This higher strategy takes account of the permanent economic forces and puts laborers in a position where these forces work for them rather than against them. Instead of continuing to fight capital they are beginning to recognize its power and to use it as an implement for their own improvement. . . . They will understand a little more clearly what it is and what it does. Employers likewise who find it necessary to work harder than before, in order to make anything out of their capital, will be compelled to think a little more about the problems of their employees, and both employer and employee will be compelled to think more about the common enterprise in which they are engaged, from which each derives his income, and on whose growth and prosperity the welfare of both classes depends. This in itself should bring a greater degree of harmony between them, as surely as a greater degree of harmony comes to husband and wife when they think primarily of the things that unite them rather than of the things that divide them; or when producer and consumer think of their common interests rather than of their antagonisms. This will be a new thing in the modern world; and we are justified in calling it an economic revolution.

9

The Pleasing Prospect of 1928

☆ *President Calvin Coolidge, in one of his last messages to Congress, December 4, 1928, declared his satisfaction with the policies of his government which, he believed, had enabled the country to achieve "unexampled blessings."* ☆

No Congress of the United States ever assembled, on surveying the state of the Union, has met with a more pleasing prospect than that which appears at the present time. In the domestic field there is tranquility and contentment, harmonious relations between management and wage earner, freedom from industrial strife, and the highest record of years of prosperity. In the foreign field there is peace, the good will which comes from mutual understanding, and the knowledge that the problems which a short time ago appeared so ominous are yielding to the touch of manifest friendship. The great wealth created by our enterprise and industry, and saved by our economy, has had the widest distribution among our own people, and has gone out in a steady stream to serve the charity and the business of the world. The requirements of existence have passed beyond the standard of necessity into the region of luxury. Enlarging production is consumed by an increasing demand at home and an expanding commerce abroad. The country can regard the present with satisfaction

* From *Congressional Record*, 70th Congress, 2nd session, p. 20.

and anticipate the future with optimism.

The main source of these unexampled blessings lies in the integrity and character of the American people. They have had great faith, which they have supplemented with mighty works. They have been able to put trust in each other and trust in their Government. Their candor in dealing with foreign governments has commanded respect and confidence. Yet these remarkable powers would have been exerted almost in vain without the constant cooperation and careful administration of the Federal Government.

We have been coming into a period which may be fairly characterized as a conservation of our national resources. Wastefulness in public business and private enterprise has been displaced by constructive economy. This has been accomplished by bringing our domestic and foreign relations more and more under a reign of law. A rule of force has been giving way to a rule of reason. We have substituted for the vicious circle of increasing expenditures, increasing tax rates, and diminishing profits the charmed circle of diminishing expenditures, diminishing tax rates, and increasing profits.

10

The Modern Corporation

☆ *One of the most influential analyses of American corporate structure was made by Adolf Berle, Jr., and Gardiner C. Means. They transcended the usual investigation and discussion of the economic implications of business concentration to probe trenchantly the social meaning of the corporation.** ☆

Most fundamental to the new picture of economic life must be a new concept of business enterprise as concentrated in the corporate organization. In some measure a concept is already emerging. Over a decade ago, Walter Rathenau wrote concerning the German counterpart of our great corporation:

"No one is a permanent owner. The composition of the thousandfold complex which functions as lord of the undertaking is in a state of flux. . . . This condition of things signifies that ownership has been depersonalized. . . . The depersonalization of ownership simultaneously implies the objectification of the thing owned. The claims to ownership are subdivided in such a fashion, and are so mobile, that the enterprise assumes an independent life, as if it belonged to no one; it takes an objective existence, such as in earlier days was embodied only in state and church, in a municipal corporation, in the life of a guild or a religious order. . . . The depersonalization of ownership, the

* From *The Modern Corporation and Private Property* by Adolf A. Berle, Jr., and Gardiner C. Means, pp. 352-357. Copyright 1932 by The Macmillan Company, and used with their permission.

objectification of enterprise, the detachment of property from the possessor, leads to a point where the enterprise becomes transformed into an institution which resembles the state in character."

The institution here envisaged calls for analysis, not in terms of business enterprise but in terms of social organization. On the one hand, it involves a concentration of power in the economic field comparable to the concentration of religious power in the mediaeval church or of political power in the national state. On the other hand, it involves the interrelation of a wide diversity of economic interests, —those of the "owners" who supply capital, those of the workers who "create," those of the consumers who give value to the products of enterprise, and above all those of the control who wield power.

Such a great concentration of power and such a diversity of interest raise the long-fought issue of power and its regulation—of interest and its protection. A constant warfare has existed between the individuals wielding power, in whatever form, and the subjects of that power. Just as there is a continuous desire for power, so also there is a continuous desire to make that power the servant of the bulk of the individuals it affects. The long struggles for the reform of the Catholic Church and for the development of constitutional law in the states are phases of this phenomenon. Absolute power is useful in building the organization. More slow, but equally sure is the development of social pressure demanding that the power shall be used for the benefit of all concerned. This pressure, constant in ecclesiastical and political history, is already making its appearance in many guises in the economic field.

Observable throughout the world, and in varying degrees of intensity, is this insistence that power in economic organization shall be subjected to the same tests of public benefit which have been applied in their turn to power otherwise located. In its most extreme aspect this is exhibited in the communist movement, which in its purest form is an insistence that *all* of the powers and privileges of property, shall be used only in the common interest. In less extreme forms of socialist dogma, transfer of economic powers to the state for public service is demanded. In the strictly capitalist countries, and particularly in time of depression, demands are constantly put forward that the men controlling the great economic organisms be made to accept responsibility for the well-being of those who are subject to the organization, whether workers, investors, or consumers. In a sense the difference in all of these demands lies only in degree. In proportion as an economic organism grows in strength and its power is concentrated in a few hands, the possessor of power is more easily located, and the demand for responsible power becomes increasingly direct.

How will this demand be made effective? To answer this question would be to foresee the history of the next century. We can here only consider and appraise certain of the more important lines of possible development.

By tradition, a corporation "belongs" to its shareholders, or, in a wider sense, to its security holders, and theirs is the only interest to be recognized as the object of corporate activity. Following this tradition, and without regard for the changed character of ownership, it would be possible to apply in the interests of the *passive* property owner the doctrine of strict property rights. . . . By the application of this doctrine, the group in control of a corporation would be placed in a position of trusteeship in which it would be called on to operate or arrange for the operation of the corporation for the *sole* benefit of the security owners despite the fact that the latter have ceased to have power over or to accept responsibility for the *active* property in which they have an interest. Were this course followed, the bulk of American industry might soon be operated by trustees for the sole benefit of inactive and irresponsible security owners.

In direct opposition to the above doctrine of strict property rights is the view, apparently held by the great corporation lawyers and by certain students of the field, that corporate development has created a new set of relationships, giving to the groups in control powers which are absolute and not limited by any implied obligation with respect to their use. This logic leads to drastic conclusions. For instance, if, by reason of these new relationships, the men in control of a corporation can operate it in their own interests, and can divert a portion of the asset fund of income stream to their own uses, such is their privilege. Under this view, since the new powers have been acquired on a quasi-contractual basis, the security holders have agreed in advance to any losses which they may suffer by reason of such use. The result is, briefly, that the existence of the legal and economic relationships giving rise to these powers must be frankly recognized as a modification of the principle of private property.

If these were the only alternatives, the former would appear to be the lesser of two evils. Changed corporate relationships have unquestionably involved an essential alteration in the character of property. But such modifications have hitherto been brought about largely on the principle that might makes right. Choice between strengthening the rights of passive property owners, or leaving a set of uncurbed powers in the hands of control therefore resolves itself into a purely realistic evaluation of different results. We might elect the relative certainty and safety of a trust relationship in favor of a particular group within the corporation, accompanied by a possible diminution of enterprise. Or we may grant the controlling group free rein, with the corresponding danger of a corporate oligarchy coupled with the probability of an era of corporate plundering.

A third possibility exists, however. On the one hand, the owners of passive property, by surrendering control and responsibility over the active property, have surrendered the right that the corporation should be operated in their sole interest,—they have released the community from the obligation to protect them to the full extent implied in the doctrine of strict property rights. At the same time, the controlling groups, by means of the extension of corporate powers, have in their own interest broken the bars of tradition which require that the corporation be operated solely for the benefit of the owners of passive property. Eliminating the sole interest of the passive owner, however, does not necessarily lay a basis for the alternative claim that the new powers should be used in the interest of the controlling groups. The latter have not presented, in acts or words any acceptable defense of the proposition that these

powers should be so used. No tradition supports that proposition. The control groups have, rather, cleared the way for the claims of a group far wider than either the owners or the control. They have placed the community in a position to demand that the modern corporation serve not alone the owners or the control but all society.

This third alternative offers a wholly new concept of corporate activity. Neither the claims of ownership nor those of control can stand against the paramount interests of the community. The present claims of both contending parties now in the field have been weakened by the developments described in this book. It remains only for the claims of the community to be put foward with clarity and force. Rigid enforcement of property rights as a temporary protection against plundering by control would not stand in the way of the modification of these rights in the interest of other groups. When a convincing system of community obligations is worked out and is generally accepted, in that moment the passive property right of today must yield before the larger interests of society. Should the corporate leaders, for example, set forth a program comprising fair wages, security to employees, reasonable service to their public, and stabilization of business, all of which would divert a portion of the profits from the owners of passive property, and should the community generally accept such a scheme as a logical and human solution of industrial difficulties, the interests of passive property owners would have to give way. Courts would almost of necessity be forced to recognize the result, justifying it by whatever of the many legal theories they might choose. It is conceivable,—indeed it seems almost essential if the corporate system is to survive,—that the "control" of the great corporations should develop into a purely neutral technocracy, balancing a variety of claims by various groups in the community and assigning to each a portion of the income stream on the basis of public policy rather than private cupidity. . . .

In still larger view, the modern corporation may be regarded not simply as one form of social organization but potentially (if not yet actually) as the dominant institution of the modern world. In every age, the major concentration of power has been based upon the dominant interest of that age. The strong man has, in his time, striven to be cardinal or pope, prince or cabinet minister, bank president or partner in the House of Morgan. During the Middle Ages, the Church, exercising spiritual power, dominated Europe and gave to it a unity at a time when both political and economic power were diffused. With the rise of the modern state, political power, concentraetd into a few large units, challenged the spiritual interest as the strongest bond of human society. Out of the long struggle between church and state which followed, the state emerged victorious; nationalist politics superseded religion as the basis of the major unifying organization of the western world. Economic power still remained diffused.

The rise of the modern corporation has brought a concentration of economic power which can compete on equal terms with the modern state—economic power versus political power, each strong in its own field. The state seeks in some aspects to regulate the corporation, while the corporation, steadily becoming more powerful, makes every effort to avoid such regulation. Where its own interests are concerned, it even attempts to dominate the state. The future may see the economic organism, now typified by the corporation, not only on an equal plane with the state, but possibly even superseding it as the dominant form of social organization. The law of corporations, accordingly, might well be considered as a potential constitutional law for the new economic state, while business practice is increasingly assuming the aspect of economic statesmanship.

VIII

depression

I N OCTOBER, 1929, the stock market suffered virtual collapse. The plunge in stock and bond values signified the failure of the nation's business policies and heralded the coming of the Great Depression.

The depression had a disastrous effect on the country. At its depth one-third of America's workers were without jobs. Hundreds of thousands of farmers lost their farms and tens of thousands of businessmen closed their shops. Most of those who kept their jobs, their farms, and their businesses constantly worried that they too would lose their security. Millions were robbed of their savings and credit. Homes were lost and families broken up. Bitterness, fear, and lack of confidence were common during the long years of depression.

As the impact of the economic calamity increased, politicians, businessmen, labor leaders, and scholars frantically searched for its causes and for ways to stimulate recovery. The causes of depression were found to be many, intricate, and debatable. The world economy, as President Hoover pointed out, had been unstable. Speculative orgies inflated the American stock market, and the masters of managerial manipulation built shaky organizational structures. The relations of supply, demand, and prices were improperly administered. Business leaders had made too many mistakes while government failed to respond to economic crises. The search for economic recovery led to general agreement on certain objectives. Economic institutions must be strengthened, suffering prevented, production and demand balanced, planning undertaken, and national coordination and cooperation effected. Despite widespread acceptance of these goals, little agreement could be found on ways to achieve them. Socialists and other radicals saw this disagreement as proof that "We are facing a breakdown of the capitalist system."

The Federal government was cautious in acting on the depression emergency. At first, reliance was placed on trying to achieve public confidence by proclamation and business cooperation through conference. When this failed, government gradually turned to positive measures. By 1932, desperate attempts were being made to reduce unnecessary expenditures and sustain revenues to preserve the government's credit for future emergencies. Some relief and credit were provided to agriculture, business, the states, and homeowners. Efforts were made to bolster the nation's faltering banking system. Public works programs were implemented. The tariff was maintained and immigration cut. Even forms of relief to the unemployed were devised. While these measures constituted unprecedented economic action by the United States government, they were unsuccessful in stopping the spread of the depression.

It was against this background that the Presidential campaigns of 1932 were conducted. President Hoover asked for better legislative support and for more time to allow the government's policies to take effect. The Democratic nominee, Governor Franklin D. Roosevelt of New York, spoke of the need for "bold, persistent experimentation," and the use of stronger government action to put life back into the economy (even though he warned that government costs would have to be reduced). While Roosevelt gave little indication of the specific steps he would take if elected President, the majority of the American voters decided to take a chance on the man who promised to "try something."

1

Prelude to Crash

☆ *The phenomenal rise of stock market averages in the later twenties was accepted as an indication of an expanding economy. Despite occasional charges that stock prices were over-inflated, trading in the market continued its unprecedented acceleration. In October 1929, stock values broke drastically, signalling the onset of the Great Depression.* * ☆

On the first of January 1929, the Coolidge Bull Market was at least four years old. The *New York Times* average of the prices of twenty-five representative industrial stocks which had stood at 110 at the beginning of 1924 had eased up to 135 at the beginning of 1925. At the close of trading on January 2, 1929, it was at 338.35. Apart from mild setbacks notably in early 1926 and early 1928, this climb had been almost uninterrupted. There were very few months when the averages did not show an improvement on the month preceding. There had been, in short, a speculative upsurge of unparalleled magnitude and duration.

There were some reasons for thinking that 1929 might be different. For one thing, Mr. Hoover would replace President Coolidge in the White House in March and, in the narrow political spectrum of the day, that meant a marked shift to the left. Mr. Coolidge, as Mr.

* From John Kenneth Galbraith, "The Great Wall Street Crash," *Harper's Magazine*, CCIX (October, 1954), pp. 72-73, based on selections from John Kenneth Galbraith, *The Great Crash*, copyright 1955. The above material is reprinted by permission of an arrangement with Houghton Miflin Company and Hamish Hamilton Ltd., the authorized publishers.

Hoover himself has testified, knew nothing and cared less about the speculative orgy in which the country was indulging itself. (A few days before leaving office he assured the country that things were "absolutely sound" and that stocks were a good buy at current prices.) Moreover, the instrument through which Mr. Coolidge would have had to act was the Federal Reserve Board, and in his time the possibility of this body's initiating any drastic measures was remarkably slight. Its authority, constitutional and moral, was shared with the powerful Federal Reserve Bank of New York. The Chairman of the Board, one Daniel R. Crissinger, had become a central banker by grace of the doctrine, which had held sway a few years before, that what was good enough for Marion, Ohio, was good enough for the country. His colleagues, with one exception, have been described by Mr. Hoover, with his characteristic conservatism, as mediocrities.

In his memoirs, Mr. Hoover suggests that, by the beginning of 1929, the halting of the stock-market boom had become practically an obsession with him. This was a fairly well-kept secret, for the market hailed his election in November with the wildest advance to date, and a day or two before he took office in March there was a fine upsurge which was dubbed the "inaugural market." However, Mr. Hoover did know what was going on, and late in 1927 Crissinger had been replaced by Roy A. Young, a more substantial figure. There was now at least a chance that an effort might be made to restrain the speculation.

There remained, however, the problem of what could be done—and at what cost. Stocks, overwhelmingly, were being bought on margin. That meant that someone had to put up as a loan the part of the price which the purchaser wasn't paying. The task of the Federal Reserve was to get control of the funds that were being thus used to finance the speculative purchase of securities. But the rates on these broker's loans were high—through January 1929, for example, they averaged a shade under 7 per cent. Seven per cent with near-perfect safety and your money available on demand is a very decent return. Individuals and especially corporations were finding this an increasingly attractive outlet for surplus cash, and the Federal Reserve had no obvious way of checking this source of money for the market.

However, in many respects this was a detail. There was the much more inconvenient question of whether any control could be exercised which, if effective, wouldn't bring an awful smash. It is easy enough to burst a bubble. To incise it with a needle so that it subsides gradually is an operation of undoubted delicacy. Collapse and an ensuing depression would be unpleasant for, among others, those who were blamed for bringing them about. This was sensed if not seen.

Yet, there was the danger that if the bull market were allowed to go roaring along there would eventually be an even more violent crack-up. So early in 1929 the monetary authorities began debating the relative merits of sudden death and a slightly more horrible demise a little later on. Secretary Mellon was passionately for inaction; Governor Young and a part of his Board were for action although there was dispute on the particular controls to be invoked.

The issue was never decided, but the knowledge that the debate was going on began to be a source of uneasiness in Wall Street.

Meanwhile, there were more serious sources of uneasiness from within the market itself. In a market like that of 1929 there are three possible reasons why people buy stocks. One is for the old-fashioned purpose of sharing in the current income of an enterprise. Some eccentrics were undoubtedly so motivated in those days, although in the case of such a speculative favorite as Radio, which, adjusted for split-ups, reached 505 on September 3, 1929, up from 94½ in the preceding eighteen months, the desire for immediate income must have been fairly slight. The stock had never paid a dividend. Elsewhere the showing was better. A hundred dollars' worth of shares which provided an average return of $5.90 in 1921 paid $3.50 in 1929. Yields did not keep pace with market values, but neither, as some have suggested, did they vanish.

A second and far larger group of people were buying stocks because they had heard that the stock market was a place where people could get rich and they were righteously persuaded that their right to be rich was as good as the next person's. These were the innocent, although it was also their misfortune to believe—perhaps with some assistance from a customer's man—that they were really very wise. These buyers talked of the prospects for Steel, GM, United Corporation, and Blue Ridge with the familiarity of a friend and the unique certainty, not of one who knows, but of one who doesn't know that he doesn't know.

Finally, stocks were being bought by those who knew that a boom was on but who intended to get out—or even, at a high level of professionalism, to go short —before the crash came. As 1929 wore along, it was this group that became increasingly nervous. The market was making phenomenal advances; one couldn't get out while there were still such gains to be made. But whenever there was upsetting news the market dropped sharply on large volume. Some *were* getting out.

Thus, in February, when the Federal Reserve Board finally decided to issue a warning—"a member bank is not within its reasonable claims for rediscount facilities at the Federal Reserve Bank when it borrows for the purpose of making speculative loans"—prices broke sharply. There was a prompt recovery, but in the following month it became known that the Federal Reserve Board was meeting daily on its problems of suicide *versus* eventual disaster. The market broke again, and on March 26, 8,239,000 shares changed hands on the New York Stock Exchange. (Once in the early days of the bull market it had been said that men might live to see a five million-share day.) Prices fell precipitately, and call money rates that day went to 20 per cent, which meant that anyone who bought General Electric on margin paid at rate of 20 per cent per annum for that day to carry a security which was yielding 1.25 per cent.

There is a chance—no one will ever know—that the bubble might have been pricked then and there, but, in an act of historic arrogance, Charles E. Mitchell, Chairman of the Board of the National City Bank, put his bank behind the boom. "We feel that we have an obligation which is paramount to any Federal Reserve warning, or anything else, to avert . . . any dangerous crisis in the money market.'" The National City let it be known that it was loaning freely in the call market and had more to come if rates got unduly high, *i.e.*, much above 15 per cent. The market steadied and by the end of March 26 most of that day's losses had been recovered.

There were further breaks and more nervousness during the next two months. However, the Federal Reserve remained quiet and presumably undecided. In any case, it had met Mr. Mitchell on the field, Mr. Mitchell had spoken, and the field was Mitchell's. So there was a brief recovery of confidence, and prices started on their last great zoom. There was no summer lull in Wall Street that year. Each day the market went on to new highs. Not everyone was playing it as legend holds—the great majority of Americans were then as innocent of knowledge of how to buy a stock as they are today—but subsequent estimates of undoubted unreliability have suggested that as many as a million people were involved in the speculation. During that summer, practically all of them made money. Never, before or since, have so many people so suddenly got so wonderfully rich.

2

The Disaster of Unemployment

☆ *The most widespread hardship of the depression was unemployment with little hope of securing a job. As the number of jobless increased, it became apparent that sources of relief were inadequate.* * ☆

About 1,000,000 out of the city's [New York] 3,200,000 working population are unemployed. Last April 410,000 were estimated to be in dire want. Seven hundred and fifty thousand in 150,000 families were receiving emergency aid while 160,000 more in 32,000 families were waiting to receive aid not then available. Of these latter families—families which normally earn an average of $141.50 a month—the average income from all sources was $8.20. Of families receiving relief, the allowance has been anything from a box of groceries up to $60 a month. In general, New York relief, in the phrase of Mr. William Hodson, executive director of the New York Welfare Council, has been on "a disaster basis." And the effects have been disaster effects. It is impossible to estimate the number of deaths in the last year in which starvation was a contributing cause. But ninety-five persons suffering directly from starvation were admitted to the city hospitals in 1931, of whom twenty died; and 143 suffering from malnutrition, of whom twenty-five died. . . .

The situation in Philadelphia was de-

* From "No One Has Starved," *Fortune*, VI (September, 1932), pp. 22-24, 27-28. Used by permission.

scribed by its Community Council in July, 1932, as one of "slow starvation and progressive disintegration of family life. . . ." "Normal" unemployment in Philadelphia is 40,000 to 50,000. In April, 1931, 228,000 or 25.6 per cent of the city's normally employed were unemployed, and 122,000 or 13.7 per cent were on part time. Of the city's 445,000 families with employable workers, 210,000 had workers unemployed or on part time, about one in four had no worker employed on full time, and 12 per cent had *no* worker employed. Even the average person unemployed had been out of work for thirty-seven weeks and had had only a little over one week of casual or relief work during the period. By December, 1931, the number of unemployed had reached 238,000 with 43,000 families receiving relief and 56,000 families in which no one was at work. And by May, 1932, the total of unemployed was 298,000. In the following month the Governor of the state estimated that 250,000 persons in Philadelphia "faced actual starvation." Over the state at large the same conditions held. In June, 1931, 919,000 or 25 per cent of the normally employed in the state were unemployed, according to the "secret" report then submitted to the Governor, and the number had risen to 1,000,000 by December and to 1,250,000 in August, 1932. One hundred and fifty thousand children were in need of charity. Malnutrition had increased in forty-eight counties—27 per cent of school children being undernourished (216,000 out of a school population of 800,000). New patients in the tuberculosis clinics had doubled. And the general death rate and disease rate had risen. . . .

Unemployed in Chicago number somewhere between 660,000 and 700,000 or 40 per cent of its employable workers while the number for the state at large is about one in three of the gainfully employed. About 100,000 families have applied down to July for relief in Cook County. The minimum relief budget has been $2.40 per week for an adult and $1.50 per week for a child for food, with $22 to $23 per month to a family. But these figures have since been cut to $2.15 weekly for a man, $1.10 for a child. And persons demanding relief must be completely destitute to receive it. Rents are not paid by the relief agencies and housing is, in certain sections, unspeakably bad. Meanwhile the situation of city employees is tragic. Teachers in May, 1932, had had only five months cash for the last thirteen months, 3,177 of them had lost $2,367,000 in bank failures, 2,278 of them had lost $7,800,000 in lapsed policies, 805 had borrowed $232,000 from loan sharks at rates adding up to 42 per cent a year, and 759 had lost their homes. . . .

In Youngstown, due to the local optimism, no united relief was undertaken until January, 1931. Meantime homeless men slept in the garbage in the municipal incinerator to keep warm. In January an abandoned police station was made into a flophouse. Attempts of Communists to organize the flophouseholders failed and a bond issue was eventually floated. Men in desperate need get two days work a week. As ex-Mayor Heffernan puts it:

"If a man owned a small home, if a young couple possessed furniture, if a woman had a good coat or her husband a presentable suit, these things had to be sacrificed first. Not until they had drained every other resource was official charity able to do anything for them. . . ."

Obviously, however, urban figures give an incomplete picture of the whole industrial situation, for they do not include such areas as the industrial area of New Jersey. In Passaic County, for example, 23,749 persons, heads of families, representing 90,699 of the county's 300,000 population, have applied for relief. The authorities have been forced to pick 12,-171 families, about half, and give them relief amounting to about $9 a month per family. And in Patterson 8,500 of the registered 12,000 unemployed are without relief of any kind. Moreover, the situation in the textile areas of the state is complicated by the fact that certain employers have taken advantage of the necessity of their employees to reestablish sweatshop conditions. Under such circumstances the employed as well as the unemployed become a burden upon the community. But elsewhere in the textile mill towns even the pretense of a living wage has been dropped. North Carolina has 100,000 unemployed textile workers with another 100,000 on the payrolls of closed plants, most of whom are begging on the roads, having long ago exhausted their savings from the low wage paid them before the depression. And those employed on part time are hardly better off since the full-time wage now averages about $6.50. In Georgia, in the Piedmont Mill Village of Egan Park, fifteen families have banded together to keep alive on a total weekly income of $10. And similar stories come from other towns in the region. While some of the small steel towns are almost as badly off. At Donora, Pennsylvania, there were in March 277 regular workers out of a population of 13,900 while 2,500 others performed "made work" at $3.50 per week and 2,000 others "seem to have disappeared." It is hardly necessary to add that malnutrition, undernourishment, rickets, tuberculosis, and other diseases increase under such conditions. And that relief in these areas is badly organized or nonexistent.

The story of factory unemployment is, however, only part of the story. In *agriculture* and in *mining,* particularly soft-coal mining, the depression is not in its fourth year but in its eighth or tenth or twelfth. It is estimated that there is a destitute coal-mining population of 1,200,-000 souls dependent upon some 240,000 unemployed and distressed bituminous miners, most of whom live in six states in regions where coal mining is the only important enterprise, where merchants are bankrupt, banks closed, schools without funds, and once wealthy residents in actual want. And this situation is of many years' standing for even in the boom years of 1928 and 1929 the industry as a whole lost a total of $41,000,000. The American Friends Service Committee, which has worked with children in Kentucky, West Virginia, and Williamson and Franklin counties, Illinois, estimates that of the 500,000 soft-coal workers making a living in 1928 only 300,000 are now employed and on wages often as low as $8 a week. Over the entire area from 20 per cent to 99 per cent of the children are found to be underweight and the probability is that 20,000 children and 20,000 adults will shortly be in actual and pressing want. . . .

The difficulty with such facts is that in mass they cease to have meaning. And the reiteration of the statement that hundreds of thousands of people have faced or are facing starvation with inadequate doles to support them merely produces skepticism. "They haven't starved yet," remarks the reader. "They get along somehow."

It is true they get along somehow. But just how they get along is another matter. There were eleven days in Philadelphia last April when private funds had run out and public funds were not yet available. During that period, the relief organizations studied ninety-one families to see just how people get along under those circumstances. They found out. One woman borrowed fifty cents, bought stale bread at three and one-half cents a loaf, and the family lived on it for eleven days. Another put the last food order into soup stock and vegetables and made a soup. When a member of the family was hungry, he ate as little as he could. Another picked up spoiled vegetables along the docks and except for three foodless days, the family ate them. Another made a stew with her last food order, which she cooked over and over daily to keep it from spoiling. Another family lived on dandelions. Another on potatoes. Another had no food for two and one-half days. And one in ten of the women were pregnant and one in three of the children of nursing age. "And they got along." . . .

But the depression, along with its misery, has produced its social curiosities, not the least of which is the wandering population it has spilled upon the roads. Means of locomotion vary but the objective is always the same—somewhere else. No one has yet undertaken to estimate the number of hitchhikers whose thumbs jerk onward along the American pike, nor the number of spavined Fords dragging destitute families from town to town in search of a solvent relative or a generous friend. But the total migratory population of the country has been put at 600,000 to 1,000,000. The Pacific Coast, the Southwest, and the Atlantic South are the habitat of the larger groups. Los Angeles once had over 70,000 with a daily influx of 1,500 more while the state of California reported an increase of 311.8 per cent in the monthly average of meals served to homeless men in early 1931 as compared with early 1929. And 365 vagrant boys running from fourteen to twenty and including college students, high school students, and eighth-graders applied to the Salt Lake Salvation Army and the Salt Lake County Jail for shelter between May 15 and June 15, 1932. Many of them were homeless, destitute children of families broken up by unemployment. And save for the fact that almost all of them were traveling alone or with one companion, and that most of them wanted work, they suggested with an uncomfortable accuracy the vagrant children who haunted the Russian railway stations after the October Revolution.

The presence of these wandering groups is curious and significant. It has long been recognized that the population of the U.S. was becoming increasingly migratory in character. But it was not until the depression that the meaning of the phenomenon was made clear. When millions of people have no relation to the land and are able at the same time to find cheap transportation, the effect of an economic crisis is not to fix them in one place but to drive them elsewhere. And the consequence, as regards these groups, is a complete failure of local relief. The destitute familes of the Fords and the homeless men of the flat cars are entitled to relief in no city, as the history of the Bonus Expeditionary Force after its ouster from Washington makes clear. . . .

3

Voices of Protest

☆ *As prices continued to fall and unemployment spread, demands for government action to provide relief were vigorously pressed and occasionally erupted into violence. Two incidents in the summer of 1932, the Farm Strike and the routing of the Bonus Expeditionary Force, characterized the seriousness of the situation as desperate men faced uneasy officials.* ☆

(a) THE FARMERS STRIKE*

Standpat politicians in the Middle West, as well as farm creditors, have been quaking in their boots at the unexpected enthusiasm generated by the agrarian strike. While the farm-holiday project has made but little headway toward its major objective, the movement has spread like wildfire across the prairies, bringing into flame a rebellion that had been smoldering a long time. Henry A. Wallace, editor of *Wallace's Farmer,* views the crusade as a gesture which, without immediate import, may attain a far-reaching significance.

Torpedoes, tear gas, rotten eggs, brickbats, and planks spiked to puncture truck tires figure in this latest effort of corn-belt farmers to boost the prices of their products to the cost of production. Declaring a holiday on selling, thousands of farmers have been picketing the roads to "persuade" their neighbors to join in holding back produce for higher offers.

The movement began quietly but soon was dramatized by the dumping of several truckloads of milk on a road outside Sioux City, Iowa. The pickets allowed milk and cream for hospitals to enter, however, and they donated 2,200 gallons of milk to the unemployed. Suddenly realizing that 90 per cent of the shipments from nearby milk-producers had been cut off, Sioux City people began frantically to order milk shipped by train from Omaha and to have the blockade run by trucks bearing armed deputy sheriffs. This local milk war soon ended in a price compromise, but it gave impetus and publicity to the more widespread and more inclusive program of the National Farmers' Holiday Association with which it was not directly connected.

The holding back of produce in an attempt to force prices up has often been advocated in the corn belt; but it has seldom been tried, mainly because the farmers have not been united and because so few of them have had enough cash, credit, or storage facilities to withhold their pro-

* From the Wayne Gard, "The Farmers' Rebellion," *The Nation,* CXXXV (September 7, 1932), pp. 207-208. Used by permission.

duce for any long period. The current farm strike had its inception in agitation by Milo Reno, kingfish of the Iowa Farmers' Union, and by John Chalmers, a Boone County farmer who is vice-president of the union. At Boone last February, a local meeting drew one thousand farmers and led to the calling of a State meeting. This conclave was held in Des Moines in May, with about ten thousand present. Here the National Farmers' Holiday Association was born, with Reno as its temporary head.

A thirty-day holiday on farm selling was begun August 8 and later was extended indefinitely. Thus far, the strike has centered mainly about the Sioux City and Omaha markets, but lately it has spread into the Dakotas, Minnesota, Wisconsin, and Illinois. At the height of the Sioux City milk war, two thousand sunburned and overall-clad farmers were living in tent colonies along the nine trunk highways leading to that city. Some were armed with pitchforks for use on truck tires. But except for sporadic outbreaks the picketing has been peaceful, and truck drivers not amenable to argument have been allowed to pass on. On August 17, a crowd of 450 farmers, equipped with clubs and brickbats, tried to remove animals from stockyard pens in Sioux City and from trucks which had run the blockade, but this attempt was repulsed by deputy sheriffs and city policemen.

Skirmishes have taken place along some of the roads. At one point outside Sioux City, pickets stopped trucks by spreading across the pavement a section of threshing-machine belt studded with menacing spikes, but this weapon was later confiscated by deputy sheriffs. In other instances, roads were blocked with railroad ties, logs, boulders, or cables. A few windshields were shattered with rocks or clubs and one sheriff was overpowered, and his gun taken from him, after he had fired a shot to warn the pickets.

Yet, in spite of such incidents, resort to force has been exceptional. The usual method of stopping trucks has been for a mass of men to stand doggedly upon the highway, in the manner of Gandhi's followers, defying the truck-drivers to crash into them. Since the drivers do not want to be guilty of manslaughter, they always stop, though some—not influenced by the arguments of the pickets—later drive on. Some of the picket forces have included women. The two rules of the patrols are "no guns and no liquor."

The picket groups have been even more active by night than by day, since much of the rural trucking is habitually done at night. Many of the picket squads have been without recognized leaders. The men come and go as they wish, but many have been on duty almost continuously.

"I'll stay till corn pickin'," one farmer declared.

"Till corn pickin'?" said another. "What do you care about corn pickin'? No use doin' all that work the way things are now."

Cars and trucks other than those bearing farm produce to market are, of course, allowed to proceed without molestation. One truck-driver, headed for Sioux City, was allowed to pass unharmed when his load was found to consist of thirty one-gallon jugs of whiskey.

At Council Bluffs, fifty-five pickets, jailed on a charge of unlawful assembly, were released after a crowd of one thousand farmers had threatened to storm the jail, which had been surrounded by officers armed with machine guns. Preparations have been made for sending a unit of the Iowa National Guard to that city. One sheriff has boasted, "We are going to stop this picketing if we have to enlist 50,000 deputies to do it." The pickets, he declared, "are hoodlums just as much as are Chicago gangsters." Other sheriffs and deputies, however, have been more sympathetic with the strike, and some have conveniently looked the other way when trucks were turned back.

Thus far, the strike has affected prices only locally and sporadically. Hog receipts have been almost halved in Sioux City, and in some towns a shortage of vegetables has sent residents scampering to their own or their neighbors' gardens or has forced them to use more tinned food. But considered on a national scale, the farm holiday has neither reduced the available supply, nor raised the price, of any agricultural product. In fact, the prices of wheat and hogs have come down during much of the period in which the sellers' strike has been in progress. In the Sioux City milk fight, the farmers did effect a small gain. Whereas they had been receiving only 2 cents a quart for milk which retailed at 8 cents, the new agreement allows them 3.6 cents and will force consumers to pay 9 cents.

The enthusiasm of the farm-holiday leaders appears, however, to have gained new momentum. "It is a finish fight now," declared Milo Reno as his organization dispatched one hundred emissaries to carry the strike west to Montana and east to Ohio. Even some of New Jersey's potato-growers have joined the movement, which obviously is an effort not so much of radicalism as of desperation.

One of the strikers, who had just gone through a barrage of overripe eggs handled by blockade runners, explained the holiday movement in terms of his own experience:

"I own a farm near Boone. My share of the oats crop from twenty-four acres on this farm was $40. My taxes on this same land amounted to $44.16. Before prices took a jump, I could buy a 400-pound packing sow for 90 cents a hundred, or $3.60. At the same time, I went to a meat market and priced a 20-pound smoked ham. It was $3.20. I told them to go to hell; I'd buy a whole hog and cut off a ham."

(b) THE ROUTING OF THE BONUS EXPEDITIONARY FORCE*

But the actual significance of the B.E.F. is not a march for the bonus so much as it is a march of the unemployed. This was truly another Coxey's Army. These men came to Washington because they had nowhere else to go, nothing else to do, and were as willing to starve on the road as in the streets of the cities they once called home. When Mr. Hoover insisted that they leave Washington, he had no alternative to propose. In effect, he said to them: "You are breaking my heart; go away and starve somewhere else, out of my sight...." Mr. Hoover and the Republican party have clung to their archaic ideas of rugged individualism. Tear gas and cavalry sabres, property stolen and burned, the corpses of

    * From The Editors, "Bullets for the B.E.F.: Hoover Relief, New Style," *The New Republic*, LXXI (August 10, 1932), pp. 328-329. Used by permission.

the murdered William Hushka and Erie Carlson are the ironic epilogue to the era of rugged individualism so far as the ex-soldiers are concerned.

From the time that the veterans first encamped in Washington, all sensible people realized that the situation there was one which might end in catastrophe. President Hoover was warned, a hundred times, that this was the case and that, since he had chosen to take personal responsibility in the situation, he should act promptly and firmly to end the danger. But characteristically, for weeks he could not make up his mind to act at all. Then after waiting until Congress was no longer in session, so that he was free from the danger of investigation, he acted with inexcusable and wholly unnecessary violence. If you grant that the ex-soldiers should eventually have been removed from their rookeries on Pennsylvania Avenue, there was no reason for any such frantic haste as the authorities displayed at the end. There was no reason why the removal could not have been made piecemeal. It was absolutely outrageous that these men, many accompanied by their wives and children, should have been driven out without being given any place to go. Even if none of these things were true, and if it be conceded that, the police having proved themselves helpless, it was legitimate to call in the United States Army—an assumption which is open to the gravest question—it was unforgivably stupid and cruel to let the troops employ full military equipment, including tear-gas bombs. Any commander with an ounce of imagination, sense and humor would have sent in the police, without firearms, plus only infantry to whom had been issued no bombs, bayonets or ammunition. The ultimate purposes would have been served exactly as well, without the disgraceful scenes which culminated in two veterans' being killed; the public tension would have been ten times less and public sympathy in Washington would not be, as it appears to be today, strongly in favor of the veterans.

But whatever justification there may have been for clearing out the ex-soldiers from Pennsylvania Avenue, there is absolutely none for what followed at Anacostia. The land where the main body of the B.E.F. was encamped was not needed for any other purpose; the veterans were harming no one by staying there. The orders which sent the soldiers to Anacostia, routing men, women and children out of bed, drenching them with tear gas, ruthlessly burning their poor shelters and whatever personal property they could not carry on their backs, then driving all of them, cripples, babies, pregnant women, up a steep hill at the point of a bayonet— these were the orders of a furious child who has been thwarted and is raging for revenge. It is profoundly humiliating to every decent American that he must see his government thus persecuting and stealing from these hungry and ragged men whom, fourteen years ago, it did not hesitate to send into the trenches at the risk of death.

Having issued orders which killed two veterans, injured hundreds through tear-gas and other means, and turned thousands of them out upon the highways, President Hoover proceeded to attack the character of his victims. He issued a series of statements implying that the veterans were largely either criminals or Communists—two categories which in his mind are evidently identical. We do not know how many members of the B.E.F. had "criminal records," nor what those criminal records mean. Poverty, in America, is often enough to get one behind the bars. But we should be surprised if the proportion of genuine criminals among the veterans were much higher than in the population as a whole. Certainly no evidence to the contrary has been advanced.

In regard to the presence of Communists, Mr. Hoover seems to us to have reached his lowest point in connection with the whole affair. If the entire B.E.F. had been made up of Communists, this fact would reflect upon our civilization and not upon the individuals. But the testimony of dozens of observers who possess in varying degrees that spirit of scientific impartiality which is so utterly foreign to the great Anti-Engineer is that radicals in the B.E.F. constituted only an insignificant percentage; that the main body of the veterans, even suffering under stool-pigeon leadership and the advice of *agents provocateurs,* remained pathetically conservative and confident that they would be protected by that flag which they had once been asked to serve with their lives. When Mr. Hoover seizes the popular prejudice against radicalism and uses it to blacken the character of the bonus marchers, he acts in the spirit of a man who would quarrel with his wife about the household bills and, plunging out of doors in anger, would shout to the neighbors false accusations against her personal honor.

Mr. Hoover's tin-hatted soldiers burned the homes of the veterans, but they did not in any sense solve the problem. Today the remnants of the B.E.F. are strung along many miles of highway, in even more desperate plight than before the dispersal. As we write, physical violence is threatened at Johnstown, Pennsylvania, and is possible at several other places. Meanwhile, the sinister and concealed motives in the minds of some, at least, of the "respectable" leaders of the veterans are shown by the announcement of a plan for the remnants of the B.E.F. to be made the nucleus for an American Fascist organization, the "Khaki Shirts." There are just enough wealthy Americans who favor Fascism, and are willing to spend money to aid its cause here, to make such a movement extremely dangerous. Hardly less dangerous is the peril that thousands of veterans will become permanently pauperized, will drift along the highways begging for food and shelter.

The federal government has abdicated its responsibility in the case. Mr. Hoover's petulance and rage have first made the problem far worse, and then dumped it upon the states and cities. The way in which they carry their burden will be, in a very real sense, the answer to the charge that the old American spirit of pioneer neighborliness and response in emergency has rotted away with the years.

4

Origins of Depression

☆ *Numerous inquiries were made into the causes of the depression and the forces which perpetuated the economic collapse. The President and those sympathetic to the position in which he found himself, while conceding the importance of domestic factors, contended that the depression was prolonged by international economic dislocations stemming from the first World War. Many other observers disagreed with this view and emphasized the role of uncoordinated American business activity in bringing about the depression.* ☆

(a) PRESIDENT HOOVER'S ANALYSIS*

In the large sense the primary cause of the Great Depression was the war of 1914-1918. Without the war there would have been no depression of such dimensions. There might have been a normal cyclical recession; but, with the usual timing, even that readjustment probably would not have taken place at that particular period, nor would it have been a "Great Depression."

The Great Depression was a two-stage process of several phases. We had a normal recession due to domestic causes beginning with the stock-market slump in October, 1929, but we were on the way out of it when the European difficulties rose to hurricane force and struck us in April, 1931. Thus the *Great* Depression did not really begin in the United States until European collapse.

It has been asserted that the American

* From *The Memoirs of Herbert Hoover—The Great Depression 1929-1941*, pp. 2-4. Copyright 1952 by Herbert Hoover, and used with permission of The Macmillan Company.

stock-market slump pulled down the world. That was not the fact.

A study by the National Bureau of Economic Research states: "Several countries entered the phase of recession in 1927 and 1928, long before the date usually taken as marking the crisis in the United States, that of the Wall Street crash of October, 1929."

The report enumerates Bolivia, Australia, Germany, Brazil, India, and Bulgaria as having entered the depression phase before the American stock market crash.

The Report of the Agent General for Reparations Payments as to Germany states:

"A considerable increase has taken place since the beginning of 1929 in the number of business concerns in difficulties. Business failures during the first five months of the year were about 20 per cent more numerous than in the corresponding part of 1928. . . ."

German stock prices had fallen sharply by the summer of 1929.

Great Britain, Canada, Holland, Sweden, and Japan also had entered a business recession prior to the stock-market crash. On this Leonard P. Ayres, an eminent economist, states:

"Wholesale commodity prices had been falling in England and Canada since the beginning of 1925, and serious declines got under way in a long list of other countries in 1928 and early in 1929. The market prices of stocks turned down in Germany in the summer of 1928; in Great Britain and the Netherlands early in the spring of 1929, and in Sweden in the summer of that year. Industrial activity began to decline in Canada and in Italy in the spring of 1929, and in Japan in the summer of the same year."

France also had shown weakness prior to the slump in the United States. The French index of common-stock prices had dropped from 543 in January, to 491 in June.

Large areas of the world are not very sensitive to economic tides—such as China, Russia, Central Asia, and Central Africa. Eliminating these countries, the economic situation began to decline in more than four-fifths of the economically sensitive peoples of the world before it began in the United States.

We could not but be affected by the degenerative forces moving elsewhere in the world. Our immediate weak spot was the orgy of stock speculation which began to slump in October, 1929. The inflation which led to the orgy was a contributory cause of our own difficulties. Secondary causes arose from eight years of increasing productivity. By our energies in invention and enterprise, we had raised our per capita productivity to levels never hitherto known in the world. Various economic studies showed that in the twenties our productivity per person increased by over 30 per cent—a ratio without parallel. As a result of distortions in this advance, some readjustments were due. The depth of our recession during the first seventeen months did not constitute a major depression, and our internal strength enabled us to begin a strong convalescence during the first three months of 1931. Had no external influences struck us, it is certain that we should have passed out of the slump shortly.

(b) A CASE OF FINANCIAL MANIPULATION*

At the peak of their power, the Insulls were suzerain over a tremendous and far-flung system of power and light. Theirs was the third largest group of utility companies in the country, exceeded only in size by the Electric Bond and Share and the United Corporation. The main elements of the system consisted of five holding companies in each of which the Insulls owned a minority interest. These five holding companies in turn owned controlling interests in numerous subsidiaries

which were directly engaged in the business of marketing gas and electricity.

The largest of these holding companies was the Middle West Utilities Company which had assets of over $1,200,000,000 and no less than one hundred and eleven subsidiaries. The Commonwealth Edison Company, which was the second largest, had assets in excess of $450,000,000 and six subsidiary companies. The Midland United Company, the third in point of size, had assets of approximately $352,000,000 and thirty subsidiaries. The fourth company was the People's Gas, Light and Coke Company, whose assets exceeded $211,000,000, and which controlled eight

* From Ferdinand Pecora, *Wall Street Under Oath,* pp. 226-232. Copyright, 1939, by Ferdinand Pecora. Reprinted by permission of Simon and Schuster, Inc. and The Cresset Press.

subsidiaries. And finally there was the Public Service Company of Northern Illinois, with assets of $210,000,000, and but one subsidiary.

It will be seen that the combined assets of these five holding company groups aggregated well over $2,500,000,000. In 1930, at the height of its prosperity, this system was furnishing gas or electricity or both to more than 4,500,000 customers. It produced more than one eighth of the total electric power of the country.

Theoretically, a corporation belongs to the individuals who own its stock, and the law says that the owners of fifty-one per cent of this stock control the corporation. But the law must be considered an optimist in this regard. Not fifty-one per cent, but twenty per cent and often less, is sufficient to ensure effective working control. The great bulk of the stock of a huge modern corporation is held by so many thousands of relatively small stockholders scattered all over the country, who do not know each other and have no means of organizing, that the owners of a substantial corporate minority generally have no difficulty in running things to suit themselves.

This control by minority groups is much facilitated through the instrumentality of the holding company. One holding company adequately supplied with the public's funds, and itself controlled by a small group of minority stockholders, may in its turn control any number of operating companies by similar minority stock ownership. Other holding companies may be superimposed on the first holding company, as additional vehicles for borrowing or for the public sale of securities. In the end a vast and complicated structure is thus erected over which, with a comparatively small investment, large sums of public money are controlled. . . .

The control which the Insulls exercised over this system did not, however, seem to them to be very secure. The stocks of all these companies were listed on the Exchanges, hence anyone so disposed could purchase them; and so the Insulls might suddenly find an opposition group in control of what they regarded as their own holding companies. . . . It was necessary to acquire additional shares of these holding companies, enough to prevent the rival groups from getting a foothold therein. To do this, however, required money. And the Insulls, acting in accordance with the *mores* of the times, exemplified as we have seen by many distinguished men of that era, naturally determined to obtain this money from the great reservoir of wealth—the public. The thing to do was to organize a holding company—or, if you will, a superholding company—for the purpose of obtaining control of the five existing holding companies.

The new company was quickly formed and was called Insull Utility Investments (Incorporated). The total amount of securities issued by this company was approximately $150,000,000. Of this amount, the Insulls themselves contributed between $8,000,000 and $9,000,000 by transferring the stock owned by them in the other holding companies to this new corporation. The new corporation employed its funds, of course, in purchasing additional stock in the five holding companies which the Insulls dominated. The Insulls were thus, with the aid of the money contributed by the public, enabled to establish themselves more firmly in control of their utility empire.

Apparently, however, the danger which brought about the organization of Insull Utility Investments (Incorporated) still continued, for again the stock of the new company was listed on the Exchange and, as the Insulls owned only a minority of it, there was a real danger that competing groups might gain control of the whole pyramid by the simple process of acquiring a large block of the stock of the superholding company in the open market.

In order to forestall this unpleasant contingency, the Insulls again went to the public for a further contribution. This was in 1929, when they formed the Corporation Securities Company of Chicago. Again the Insulls acquired a minority interest in this new corporation by the exchange of securities and a comparatively small cash contribution. The new company also invested heavily in the securities of the Insull Utility Investments (Incorporated). The latter had in its portfolio securities of an aggregate market value of $285,000,000, and the Corporation Securities Company of Chicago had about $150,700,000 of similar securities.

The control by the Insulls and their associates of this vast system seemed now complete, although they did not own a majority of the stock of either of these top holding companies. Thus they owned only 46.9 per cent of the stock of the Corporation Securities Company of Chicago, and only 19.2 per cent of the stock of Insull Utility Investments (Incorporated). By causing the former corporation to acquire 25.7 per cent of the stock of the latter, and by causing the latter corporation to acquire 11.5 per cent of the stock of the former, the Insulls were able effectively to control both corporations, and through them, the entire pyramidic structure.

In all, by January 31, 1932, the Insulls had formed more than ninety-five holding companies and two hundred and fifty-five operating companies. The investment which the Insulls had made to secure the direction of this pyramid was something less than one million dollars. If we consider the market value of their holdings in March, 1930, it amounted to more than $100,000,000. This $100,000,000, in turn, now controlled $2,500,000,000. For every dollar that the Insulls originally invested, they now controlled $2,500 of the public's money.

(c) THE INFLEXIBILITY OF PRICES*

2. The whole trend of social development both in this country and abroad has been to recognize the failure of a complete laissez faire policy.

3. The basic cause for the failure of a laissez faire policy is to be found in the very same forces which have made possible a high standard of living for all, namely, the gradual, century-long shift from market to administrative coordination of economic activity which has resulted in modern industrial organization and modern technology. This shift to administration has brought a new type of competition and inflexible administered prices which disrupt the workings of the market.

4. A century ago the great bulk of economic activity in the United States was conducted on an atomistic basis by individuals or families—as is most of agriculture today—while the actions of the separate individuals were coordinated by the market. The individual produced for sale and his activity was geared to and in part controlled by flexible market prices. . . .

5. But gradually more and more of economic coordination has been accomplished administratively. Great numbers of individuals have been drawn into large factories or business organizations and their activities have come to be coordinated within the separate enterprises by administrative action. . . .

6. The shift from market to administrative coordination has gone so far that a major part of American economic activity is now carried on by great administrative units—our great corporations. More than half of all manufacturing activity is carried on by 200 big corporations. . . .

7. This development of administrative

* From Gardiner C. Means, "Industrial Prices and their Relative Inflexibility," *Senate Document* #13, 74th Congress, 1st session, pp. 9-12.

coordination has made possible tremendous increases in the efficiency of industrial production within single enterprises. The large number of workers brought into a single organization has allowed a high degree of subdivision of labor and the use of complicated series of machines so that the volume of production has been expanded way beyond the capacity of the same number of workers operating independently. . . .

8. But the very concentration of economic activity which brought increased productivity has by its nature destroyed the free market and disrupted the operations of the law of supply and demand in a great many industries and for the economy as a whole.

9. Evidence of this disruption is to be found in the administrative character and relative inflexibility of price in a great many industries and the fact that on the whole prices during the depression have tended to go down least where the drop in demand has been greatest.

10. The failure of prices to adjust is perfectly familiar to business men in nearly every industry. But the implications of this familiar fact for the economy as a whole have not been recognized.

11. In a large part of industry, the market is not equating supply and demand through a flexible price mechanism, but is bringing an adjustment of production to demand at administratively determined prices. . . .

12. The presence of administered prices, while it does not indicate monopoly, does mean that the number of concerns competing in the market has been reduced to the point that the individual concern has a significant power to choose within limits between changing its prices and changing its volume of production or sales. . . .

13. But this means that individuals have a direct power over industrial policy which they exercise in making business policy for their own enterprise. . . .

15. According to laissez faire principles, industrial policy was supposed to result from the interaction in the market of the business policies of a large number of independent units, no one of which had any significant power. . . .

16. Where the number of competing units in a particular industry have been reduced to a relatively small handful, industrial policy is no longer made wholly by the market but in part by individuals. . . .

17. But when the business man has the power to affect industrial policy, he almost necessarily makes wrong industrial decisions. The very position, experience and training of the business man which lead him to make the correct decisions on business policy tend to force him to make the wrong decisions on industrial policy in spite of the utmost public spirit which he, as an individual, may seek to exercise. . . .

18. The business man is expected to make business policy in a way to maximize the profits of his own enterprise. When he has the power to choose between lowering price and lowering production, good business policy frequently requires him in the presence of falling demand to hold price and curtail his production even though this means idle hands and idle machines . . . His interest dictates lowering price only when he is able to squeeze his costs, particularly his labor costs. . . .

19. The net effect of business control over industrial policy is, therefore, to aggravate any fluctuations in economic activity and prevent any necessary readjustments. An initial drop in demand would result, not in price readjustment, but in maintained prices and curtailment of production, thus throwing workers and machines out of employment, reducing money income and spending power, and further reducing demand. . . .

(d) CORPORATION STEWARDSHIP*

. . . the America of sixty years ago . . . has gone, but the political and economic ideas of that epoch still dominate our thoughts and actions. From a nation of small independent enterprises we have become largely a nation of employees. The masses of the people depend primarily not upon prices but upon wages and salaries for their prosperity while the organization of industry has grown ever more hierarchical.

These changes have been progressing for a long time in the fields of manufacturing, mining, and transportation. The million and a half workers on our railroads, most of them employed by fourteen great systems, can in no sense of the word be termed independent workmen. There is also great concentration in the field of manufacturing. For according to the 1923 *Census of Manufactures,* 71 per cent of the 8.8 million factory wage earners were employed in factories with over 100 employees, and no less than 38 per cent were in establishments with more than 500 workers. Nor does even this measure the full degree of concentration since it does not make allowance for the ownership by one company of many plants. When we consider that the United States Steel Corporation employs approximately 225,000 workers, the Bethlehem Steel Company 64,000, that the General Motors Company Corporation in 1929 employed 233,000, that there were 100,000 in the Detroit plants alone of the Ford Motor Company, and that there are huge numbers in the service of such companies as the International Harvester and General Electric, we can see how far the metal trades alone have departed from that primitive simplicity which Longfellow celebrated in his "Village Black-

* From Paul H. Douglas, *The Coming of a New Party,* pp. 5-10. Copyright, 1932, McGraw-Hill Book Company, New York. Used by permission.

smith." To these should be added the 192,000 employed by the Standard Oil Companies of New Jersey, New York, and Indiana, and the 60,000 and 58,000 respectively in the employ of Armour and Company and Swift and Company, and the hundreds of thousands in the service of the American Telephone and Telegraph Company, the Western Union Telegraph Company, and the Western Electric Company.

Professor Gardner C. Means of Columbia in his recent comprehensive study of the role of large corporations in American life found that the largest 200 non-financial corporations with gross assets of $80,-000,000 and over "controlled over 45 per cent of the assets of all non-financial corporations, received over 40 per cent of corporate income, controlled over 35 per cent of all business wealth and between 15 and 25 per cent of national wealth. Between 1909 and 1927, the assets of the 200 largest increased more than twice as fast as the assets of other non-financial corporations. They reinvested a larger proportion of their earnings, secured a larger proportion of new capital in the open market, and increased in size through mergers." Professor Means concluded that, "If recent rates of growth were to continue, 80 per cent of non-financial corporate wealth would be in the hands of 200 corporations by 1950." When we add to all this the fact that many of these companies are controlled by a common management and that there are strong communities of interest between many others, a still further idea is obtained of the degree to which concentration has gone. . . .

There are of course some, like Professor Carver of Harvard, who believe that concentration of production does not mean concentration of ownership and who claim that the workers by reason of their invested savings are in fact coming into the control of industry itself. But this is almost a grotesque misunderstanding. Some years ago, Dr. W. I. King startled the country by showing that according to the probate records of Massachusetts and Wisconsin, 2 per cent of the population apparently owned 60 per cent of the wealth. His study was attacked at the time as being unrepresentative, but a more recent investigation by the Federal Trade Commission over a wider field has shown that his figures underestimate rather than overestimate the degree of concentration which exists. According to this study the wealthiest 2 per cent possessed approximately 70 rather than 60 per cent of the total value of property probated.

Interestingly enough, if we take surplus income only into account we find on the basis of the estimated distribution worked out for 1918 by the National Bureau of Economic Research that approximately 70 per cent of all the income above the $2,000 point went also into the hands of 2 per cent of the income recipients.

The surplus available for investment as well as for luxuries is therefore in the possession of a relatively small class. It is this class which owns the mills, mines, railways, power companies, banks, and newspapers. Colleges, churches, and charities are largely dependent upon them for the donations which are needed for maintenance and expansion.

It is this class therefore which sets the tone and furnishes the standards for our society. As a people we tend to be predominantly in awe of men of large wealth and we in the main accept unquestioningly the tendency to make money the measuring stick for all values. For it is this small business group which after all fundamentally own the jobs by which urban workers, whether by hand or brain, must live. Such being the case, men are naturally chary of offending the sources of power which so largely control their destinies. Part of this fear is conscious, part is unconscious, but in its totality it operates to reduce not only significant social criticism but also any action designed to alter the balance of power. "He who is the bread-giver is the law-maker," remarked Harrington at the time of the Commonwealth, nearly three centuries ago. "And if a man feeds his people, they are become his fiefs." And what Harrington saw with wise insight to be the inevitable result of the concentration of landed property in the seventeenth century we now see to be the consequence of the concentration of industrial and commercial property in the twentieth. If we wish to find communities where men do not dare to speak their minds, we need not go to the villages of Hungary where almost the last open remnants of feudalism still exist. We need only go to textile towns in New England and the South, to mining communities in Pennsylvania, West Virginia, and Kentucky, and to factory cities of the East and Middle West to find a degree of industrial domination over the lives and social thinking of the community which is not greatly dissimilar to that feudal control which our ancestors planned to abolish when they founded free communities on free soil.

5

What Do We Do Now?

☆ *Toward the end of the second year of the depression even the most complacent despaired of the traditional method of dealing with economic crisis—waiting for it to run its course. Plans abounded for the economic reconstruction of the United States. The most representative elements emphasized planning and cooperative action by government, labor, and business in combatting the depression.* ☆

(a) ADDRESS BY HERBERT HOOVER TO THE INDIANA EDITORIAL ASSOCIATION*

We have many citizens insisting that we produce an advance 'plan' for the future development of the United States. They demand that we produce it right now. I presume the 'plan' idea is an infection from the slogan of the 'five-year plan' through which Russia is struggling to redeem herself from the ten years of starvation and misery.

I am able to propose an American plan to you. We plan to take care of twenty million increase in population in the next twenty years. We plan to build for them four million new and better homes, thousands of new and still more beautiful city buildings, thousands of factories; to increase the capacity of our railways; to add thousands of miles of highways and waterways; to install twenty-five million electrical horsepower; to grow twenty per cent more farm products. We plan to provide new parks, schools, colleges, and

* June 15, 1931. From *The New York Times*, June 16, 1931.

churches for this twenty million people. We plan more leisure for men and women and better opportunities for its enjoyment.

We not only plan to provide for all the new generation, but we shall, by scientific research and invention, lift the standard of living and security of life to the whole people. We plan to secure a greater diffusion of wealth, a decrease in poverty and a great reduction in crime. And this plan will be carried out if we just keep on giving the American people a chance. Its impulsive force is in the character and spirit of our people. They have already done a better job for one hundred and twenty million people than any other nation in all history.

Some groups believe this plan can only be carried out by a fundamental, a revolutionary, change of method. Other groups believe that any system must be the outgrowth of the character of our race, a natural outgrowth of our race, a natural outgrowth of our traditions; that we have established certain ideals, over one hundred and fifty years, upon which we must build rather than destroy.

If we analyze the ideas which have been put forward for handling our great national plan, they fall into two groups. The first is whether we shall go on with our American system, which holds that the major purpose of a state is to protect the people and to give them equality of opportunity; that the basis of all happiness is in development of the individual, that the sum of progress can only be gauged by the progress of the individual, that we should steadily build up cooperation among the people themselves to these ends.

The other idea is that we shall, directly or indirectly, regiment the population into a bureaucracy to serve the state, that we should use force instead of cooperation in plans and thereby direct every man as to what he may or may not do.

These ideas present themselves in practical questions which we have to meet. Shall we abandon the philosophy and creed of our people for one hundred and fifty years by turning to a creed foreign to our people? Shall we establish a dole from the Federal Treasury? Shall we undertake federal ownership and operation of public utilities instead of the rigorous regulation of them to prevent imposition? Shall we protect our people from the lower standards of living of foreign countries? Shall the Government, except in temporary national emergencies, enter upon business processes in competition with its citizens? Shall we regiment our people by an extension of the arm of bureaucracy into a multitude of affairs?

Our immediate and paramount task as a people is to rout the forces of economic disruption and pessimism that have swept upon us.

The exacting duty of Government in these times is by use of its agencies and its influence to strengthen our economic institutions; by inspiring cooperation in the community to sustain good-will and to keep our country free of disorder and conflict; by cooperation with the people to assure that the deserving shall not suffer; and by the conduct of government to strengthen the foundatons of a better and stronger national life. These have been the objectives of my administration in dealing with this the greatest crisis the world has ever known. I shall adhere to them.

(b) REPORT ON THE ECONOMIC SITUATION BY THE EXECUTIVE COUNCIL OF THE AMERICAN FEDERATION OF LABOR*

National Planning. Business depression is a very costly experience. No economic group escapes heavy losses. The social wastes to the nation and the economic wastes to industry amount to enormous totals of tangible and intangible values. It is quite obvious the technical ability to produce has far out-stripped our understanding of our economic structure. Our

distribution of the returns from production are not balanced. Increased profits have been monopolized by the few so that incomes of the masses—wage earners— have not increased sufficiently to provide buyers proportionate to the capacity of industry to produce. Instead of shortening the work-day as output per worker increased, industries have taken away jobs of some workers and compelled the rest to work the standard which was adjusted to an older technical equipment.

It is obvious that business has been following the wrong principles. Each group,

* October, 1931, From "Report on the Economic Situation by the Executive Council of the American Federation of Labor," Annual Convention of the American Federation of Labor, October, 1931. Used by permission of The American Federation of Labor and Congress of Industrial Organizations.

each industry, each company, has been advancing its interest against the other, often at the expense of the others. To control our business machine so that it will function regularly, we must learn how different parts work together so that we shall have a balance of forces and a balance in progress. Team-work is what we need and leadership for team-work. Team-work comes from organized intelligence and coordinated activity.

When industries were organized on a more limited scale with a smaller output, their dependence on wage-earner buying was not so obvious. Mass production, however, must be accompanied by mass buying. The principles of balance in industry are the key to sustained progress. Single companies or even industries cannot work out the principles of balance. Fact-finding and plans must be national in scope. While we have some vague information on the forces involved in balancing consumption, production, and distribution, we have not the facts necessary for control.

Balance is not a result that can be maintained by arbitrary decision; it comes through working with laws in the light of knowledge of the facts. The first step toward getting balance in our economic machine, is a coordinating group through which information of all elements and groups in production shall bring together the necessary information to reveal the interplay between economic forces and thus the facts that should guide all groups in their individual planning as well as in the development of policies for concerted action. To give all groups an understanding of how the national mechanism works so that each may understand how it fits into the whole operation is the first step in developing team-work. Nothing more definite should be imposed upon any national economic council that might be created by our Federal Government. We do not yet know enough to plan the agen-

cies or chart the functions of economic control. We do, however, know that national economic conferences will disclose the way. We have, therefore, repeatedly urged upon the President of the United States that he call a national economic conference to find a way forward. Such a conference would be a step toward planning on a national scale. We have everywhere throughout industry very successful attempts at planning by industrial undertakings, by industries, by unions, by communities, by states, and by geographic sections. But this is not adequate —there must be comprehensive planning by all the groups that affect each other. No one industry can prevent business depression—nor even all industries, unless they work together. . . .

Balance Worktime and Wages Against Increase in Productivity. Economic equilibrium depends on keeping a balanced relationship between economic forces. For instance, consuming power must keep pace with producing power, income from trade and industry must be so distributed that it will increase the capacity to buy in proportion as it increases the capacity to produce. When these factors are thrown out of balance, trade and industry can no longer function normally, and we are plunged into business depression.

It is the task of trade unions to see that the worker's side of the balance is kept up, and that workers advance proportionately with other groups. Wage-earners and small salaried workers with their families, form eighty-three per cent of the nation's population and receive fifty-four per cent of the national income. Almost the entire amount of this income is spent to buy industry's products and services or to pay rent, for there is little margin for savings. In recent years workers have received about $32,000,000,000 a year. The immensity of this sum and its huge influence as an economic force make it essential that workers' income advance proportionately with industry's producing power. Industry depends on workers buying; it is a severe handicap when workers' incomes do not keep pace.

(c) REPORT OF THE UNITED STATES CHAMBER OF COMMERCE COMMITTEE ON CONTINUITY OF BUSINESS AND EMPLOYMENT*

LONG TIME MEASURES

Your Committee has received innumerable suggestions designed to forestall or cure the evils of depression. In one form or another, many of these suggestions contemplate the adoption of devices to establish a better balance between production and consumption.

In principle, your Committee is in accord with this point of view. Only through a proper coordination of production and consumption can a sane, orderly, and progressive economic life be developed. A freedom of action which might have been justified in the relatively simple life of the last century cannot be tolerated today, because the unwise action of one individual may adversely affect the lives of thousands. We have left the period of extreme individualism and are living in a period in which national economy must be recognized as the controlling factor.

Under our form of industry a large part of the national income is distributed through the instrumentality of industry and business, the distribution being in the form of wages, salaries, rents, interest, and dividends. If, then, as is to be desired, industry is to pay out high wages to people working a reasonable number of hours and is to set up reserves in time of prosperity for unemployment benefits and to provide means to care for accidents, sickness, and old age, business must be on a sound basis, and production must be balanced with consumption.

* October 30, 1931. From *Planning Proposals of the Committee on Continuity of Business and Employment of the United States Chamber of Commerce,* "Referendum No. 58, On the Report of the Special Committee on Continuity of Business and Employment, Part II, October 30, 1931," pp. 10-14. Used by permission of the Chamber of Commerce of the United States of America.

Many producers would prefer to gauge their output to the consuming capacity and divide the volume of such production among the different units of industry on an equitable basis. But they hesitate to attempt this today because of ever-present risk of incurring penalties under anti-trust laws which, suitable as they may have been for economic conditions of another day, are not entirely in consonance with the present-day needs of industry.

It is not suggested that the present anti-trust laws be repealed, but it is suggested that they be amended to provide that

(a) Business concerns desiring to enter into contracts for the purpose of equalizing production to consumption and so carrying on business on a sound basis, may file such contracts with some governmental authority, the contracts to take effect and to remain effective unless the governmental authority having supervision finds on its own initiative or on complaint that such agreements are not in the public interest, in which event such agreements would be abrogated; and

(b) Business concerns that desire to combine may find out from some suitable governmental authority before the combination is made whether or not such combination is prohibited by the anti-trust laws. . . .

This Committee has considered carefully the feasibility of establishing a national economic council in the United States. It has reviewed the experience of

European countries and it has sounded out the opinion of leading business men and economists, the majority of whom favored the idea. Our own studies have led to the same conclusion, and we are in good agreement with those consulted in regard to the functions and scope of such a council.

The Council should be an advisory body as its name implies rather than an executive board with functions like those of the War Industries Board. The present depression is compelling evidence that our country is confronted with economic problems of the gravest importance. As yet there is not united or settled opinion as to how these problems should be met. An advisory council in dealing with them could perform a great national service, provided that it be so constituted that it would command respect by reason of the ability, integrity, and impartiality of its members, and so staffed that its recommendations could be based and supported with adequate analysis of conditions. A few illustrations will serve to indicate the range and character of the problems with which it might deal so as to help us decide what courses of action will best contribute to a sound economic life:

1. The tendency of productive capacity to outrun ability to buy.—How can our enormous ability to produce wealth be controlled and directed so as to be of the most use instead of being as it now is a menace to prosperity?

2. The levels of wages—How should they be determined and maintained so as to contribute to prosperity?

3. Foreign trade, both export and import—The extent to which it should be encouraged and the methods by which international debts, resulting from this trade or otherwise, can best be dealt with.

4. In what way and by what agencies can authoritative information and statistics be gathered and published so as to be the most useful guides to industry . . . ?

Industrial planning to regularize production and employment is recognized by business management as an essential phase of successful business operation. Wholly aside from humanitarian considerations, the value of a carefully planned schedule for future production and sales, based on anticipated demand within the industry as well as on reliable forecasts of general business conditions, has repeatedly been demonstrated in a wide variety of industries. . . .

Your Committee is deeply impressed with the possibilities to be realized from a comprehensive expansion of far-sighted company planning, though we do not intend to imply that herein may be found a panacea for all industrial ailments. Experience demonstrates that regularization programs cannot be applied to all industries or to all types of products; but, within the limitations imposed by such factors as changing styles and excessive costs, individual planning offers very definite promise to many branches of industry as a means of eliminating waste, curtailing excess production, anticipating seasonal fluctuations and maintaining a scheduled rate of production throughout the year.

There should be wide education as to the possibilities of company planning and we particularly recommend that trade associations study this subject for the benefit of their own industries. By constant emphasis and widespread publicity as to the type of company planning best adapted to their particular fields, these associations have abounding opportunities, not only to enhance the welfare of their own industries, but to contribute to the orderly and sustained progress of the nation.

Some trade associations have developed activities which materially assist concerns in their fields in their own planning for stability in operation and employment. Every trade association should undertake such activities, in order that the possibilities of planning may be utilized in each field in accordance with its conditions. These activities in the fields of production should include such relations with the fields of distribution that production may proceed with thorough understanding as to the requirements and preferences of ultimate consumers. Every producer needs for his own advantage the specialized suggestions and information distributors can give him as to markets and their extension.

6

Socialist Party Platform of 1932

☆ *Some groups, however, demanded that drastic steps be taken to eliminate defects in the economy. The Socialist Party platform represented the clearest statement of the ideas most commonly shared by radical groups.** ☆

We are facing a breakdown of the capitalist system. This situation the Socialist Party has long predicted. In the last campaign it warned the people of the increasing insecurity in American life and urged a program of action which, if adopted, would have saved millions from their present tragic plight.

To-day in every city of the United States jobless men and women by the thousands are fighting the grim battle against want and starvation while factories stand idle and food rots on the ground. Millions of wage earners and salaried workers are hunting in vain for jobs while other millions are only partly employed.

Unemployment and poverty are inevitable products of the present system. Under capitalism the few own our industries. The many do the work. The wage earners and farmers are compelled to give a large part of the product of their labor to the few. The many in the factories, mines, shops, offices, and on the farms obtain but a scanty income and are able to buy back only a part of the goods that can be produced in such abundance by our mass industries.

* From *Congressional Record*, 72nd Congress, 1st session, pp. 14702-14703.

Goods pile up. Factories close. Men and women are discharged. The Nation is thrown into a panic. In a country with natural resources, machinery, and trained labor sufficient to provide security and plenty for all, masses of people are destitute.

Capitalism spells not only widespread economic disaster but class strife. It likewise carries with it an ever-present threat of international war. The struggle of the capitalist class to find world markets and investment areas for their surplus goods and capital was a prime cause of the World War. It is to-day fostering those policies of militarism and imperialism which, if unchecked, lead to another world conflict.

From the poverty, insecurity, unemployment, the economic collapse, the wastes, and the wars of our present capitalistic order only the united efforts of workers and farmers, organized in unions and cooperatives and, above all, in a political party of their own, can save the Nation.

The Republican and Democratic Parties, both controlled by the great industrialists and financiers, have no plan or program to rescue us from the present collapse. In this crisis their chief purpose and desire has been to help the railroads, banks, insurance companies, and other capitalist interests.

The Socialist Party is to-day the one democratic party of the workers whose program would remove the causes of class struggles, class antagonisms, and social evils inherent in the capitalist system.

It proposes to transfer the principal industries of the country from private ownership and autocratic, cruelly inefficient management to social ownership and democratic control. Only by these means will it be possible to organize our industrial life on a basis of planned and steady operation, without periodic breakdowns and disastrous crises.

It proposes the following measures:

UNEMPLOYMENT AND LABOR

1. A Federal appropriation of $5,000,000,000 for immediate relief for those in need, to supplement State and local appropriations.

2. A Federal appropriation of $5,000,000,000 for public works and roads, reforestation, slum clearance, and decent homes for the workers, by Federal Government, States, and cities.

3. Legislation providing for the acquisition of land, buildings, and equipment necessary to put the unemployed to work producing food, fuel, and clothing and for the erection of houses for their own use.

4. The 6-hour day and the 5-day week without a reduction of wages.

5. A comprehensive and efficient system of free public employment agencies.

6. A compulsory system of unemployment compensation with adequate benefits, based on contributions by the Government and by employers.

7. Old-age pensions for men and women 60 years of age and over.

8. Health and maternity insurance.

9. Improved systems of workmen's compensation and accident insurance.

10. The abolition of child labor.

11. Government aid to farmers and small-home owners to protect them against mortgage foreclosures and a moratorium on sales for nonpayment of taxes by destitute farmers and unemployed workers.

12. Adequate minimum wage laws.

SOCIAL OWNERSHIP

1. Public ownership and democratic control of mines, forests, oil, and power resources; public utilities dealing with light and power, transportation and communication, and of all other basic industries.

2. The operation of these publicly owned industries by boards of administration on which the wageworker, the consumer, and the technician are adequately represented; the recognition in each industry of the principles of collective bargaining and civil service.

BANKING

Socialization of our credit and currency system and the establishment of a unified banking system, beginning with the complete governmental acquisition of the Federal reserve banks and the extension of the services of the postal savings banks to cover all departments of the banking business and the transference of this department of the post office to a Government-owned banking corporation. . . .

AGRICULTURE

Many of the foregoing measures for socializing the power, banking, and other industries, for raising living standards among the city workers, etc., would greatly benefit the farming population.

As special measures for agricultural upbuilding we propose:

1. The reduction of tax burdens by a

shift from taxes on farm property to taxes on incomes, inheritances, excess profits, and other similar forms of taxation.

2. Increased Federal and State subsidies to road building and educational and social services for rural communities.

3. The creation of a Federal marketing agency for the purchase and marketing of agricultural products.

4. The acquisition by bona fide cooperative societies and by governmental agencies of grain elevators, stockyards, packing houses, and warehouses and the conduct of these services on a nonprofit basis. The encouragement of farmers' cooperative societies and of consumers' cooperatives in the cities, with a view of eliminating the middleman.

5. The socialization of Federal land banks and the extension by these banks of long-term credit to farmers at low rates of interest.

6. Social insurance against losses due to adverse weather conditions.

7. The creation of national, regional, and State land utilization boards for the purpose of discovering the best uses of the farming land of the country, in view of the joint needs of agriculture, industry, recreation, water supply, reforestation, etc., and to prepare the way for agricultural planning on a national and, ultimately, on a world scale.

CONSTITUTIONAL CHANGES

1. Proportional representation.

2. Direct election of the President and Vice President.

3. The initiative and referendum.

4. An amendment to the Constitution to make constitutional amendments less cumbersome.

5. Abolition of the power of the Supreme Court to pass upon the constitutionality of legislation enacted by Congress.

6. The passage of the Socialist Party's proposed workers' rights amendment to the Constitution empowering Congress to establish national systems of unemployment, health and accident insurance and old age pensions, to abolish child labor, establish and take over enterprises in manufacture, commerce, transportation, banking, public utilities, and other business and industries to be owned and operated by the Government and, generally, for the social and economic welfare of the workers of the United States. . . .

INTERNATIONAL RELATIONS

While the Socialist Party is opposed to all war, it believes that there can be no permanent peace until socialism is established internationally. In the meanwhile, we will support all measures that promise to promote good will and friendship among the nations of the world, including:

1. The reduction of armaments, leading to the goal of total disarmament by international agreement, if possible; but, if that is not possible, by setting an example ourselves. Soldiers, sailors, and workers unemployed by reason of disarmament to be absorbed, where desired, in a program of public works, to be financed in part by the savings due to disarmament. The abolition of conscription, of military training camps, and the Reserve Officers' Training Corps.

2. The recognition of the Soviet Union and the encouragement of trade and industrial relations with that country.

3. The cancellation of war debts due from the allied governments as part of a program for wiping out war debts and reparations, provided that such cancellation does not release money for armaments but promotes disarmament.

4. The entrance of the United States into the World Court.

5. The entrance of the United States into the League of Nations under condi-

tions which will make it an effective instrument for world peace and renewed cooperation with the working-class parties abroad to the end that the league may be transformed from a league of imperialist powers to a democratic assemblage representative of the aspirations of the common people of the world.

6. The creation of international economic organizations on which labor is adequately represented, to deal with problems of raw material, investments, money, credit, tariffs, and living standards from the viewpoint of the welfare of the masses throughout the world.

7. The abandonment of every degree of military intervention by the United States in the affairs of other countries. The immediate withdrawal of military forces from Haiti and Nicaragua.

8. The withdrawal of United States military and naval forces from China and the relinquishment of American extraterritorial privileges.

9. The complete independence of the Philippines and the negotiation of treaties with other nations safeguarding the sovereignty of these islands.

10. Prohibition of the sales of munitions to foreign powers.

7

The Democratic Attack

☆ *Franklin D. Roosevelt, the personable governor of New York, was nominated for president by the Democratic Party in 1932. He advocated the use of government power to protect the people's interest by eliminating abuses from our economic system. Roosevelt also contended that the government had to operate on the basis of a fiscal policy that would not lead it into bankruptcy.* * ☆

(a) FRANKLIN D. ROOSEVELT ADDRESS AT ATLANTA, GEORGIA*

That which seems most important to me in the long run is the problem of controlling by adequate planning the creation and distribution of those products which our vast economic machine is capable of yielding. It is true that capital, whether public or private, is needed in the creation of new enterprise and that such capital gives employment.

But think carefully of the vast sums of capital or credit which in the past decade have been devoted to unjustified enterprises—to the development of unessentials and to the multiplying of many products far beyond the capacity of the Nation to absorb. . . .

No, our basic trouble was not an insufficiency of capital. It was an insufficient distribution of buying power coupled with an oversufficient speculation in production. While wages rose in many of our industries, they did not as a whole rise proportionately to the reward to capital, and at the same time the purchasing

* May 22, 1932. From *The New York Times*, May 23, 1932.

power of other great groups of our population was permitted to shrink. We accumulated such a superabundance of capital that our great bankers were vying with each other, some of them employing questionable methods, in their efforts to lend this capital at home and abroad.

I believe that we are at the threshold of a fundamental change in our popular economic thought, that in the future we are going to think less about the producer and more about the consumer. Do what we may have to do to inject life into our ailing economic order, we cannot make it endure for long unless we can bring about a wiser, more equitable distribution of the national income. . . .

The country needs and, unless I mistake its temper, the country demands bold, persistent experimentation. It is common sense to take a method and try it: If it fails, admit it frankly and try another. But above all, try something. The millions who are in want will not stand by silently forever while the things to satisfy their needs are within easy reach.

(b) FRANKLIN D. ROOSEVELT ADDRESS AT THE COMMONWEALTH CLUB, SAN FRANCISCO, CALIFORNIA*

A glance at the situation today only too clearly indicates that equality of opportunity as we have known it no longer exists. Our industrial plant is built; the problem just now is whether under existing conditions it is not overbuilt. Our last frontier has long since been reached, and there is practically no more free land. More than half of our people do not live on the farms or on lands and cannot derive a living by cultivating their own property. There is no safety valve in the form of a Western prairie to which those thrown out of work by the Eastern economic machines can go for a new start. We are not able to invite the immigration from Europe to share our endless plenty. We are now providing a drab living for our own people.

Our system of constantly rising tariffs has at last reacted against us to the point of closing our Canadian frontier on the north, our European markets on the east, many of our Latin-American markets to the south, and a goodly proportion of our Pacific markets on the west, through the retaliatory tariffs of those countries. It has forced many of our great industrial institutions which exported their surplus production to such countries, to establish plants in such countries, within the tariff walls. This has resulted in the reduction of the operation of their American plants, and opportunity for employment.

Just as freedom to farm has ceased, so also the opportunity in business has narrowed. It still is true that men can start small enterprises, trusting to native shrewdness and ability to keep abreast of competitors; but area after area has been preempted altogether by the great corporations, and even in the fields which

still have no great concerns, the small man starts under a handicap. The unfeeling statistics of the past three decades show that the independent business man is running a losing race. Perhaps he is forced to the wall; perhaps he cannot command credit; perhaps he is "squeezed out," in Mr. Wilson's words, by highly organized corporate competitors, as your corner grocery man can tell you. Recently a careful study was made of the concentration of business in the United States. It showed that our economic life was dominated by some six hundred odd corporations who controlled two-thirds of American industry. Ten million small business men divided the other third. More striking still, it appeared that if the process of concentration goes on at the same rate, at the end of another century we shall have all American industry controlled by a dozen corporations, and run by perhaps a hundred men. Put plainly, we are steering a steady course toward economic oligarchy, if we are not there already.

Clearly, all this calls for a re-appraisal of values. A mere builder of more industrial plants, a creator of more railroad systems, an organizer of more corporations, is as likely to be a danger as a help. The day of the great promoter or the financial Titan, to whom we granted anything if only he would build, or develop, is over. Our task now is not discovery or exploitation of natural resources, or necessarily producing more goods. It is the soberer, less dramatic business of administering resources and plants already in hand, of seeking to reestablish foreign markets for our surplus production, of meeting the problem of underconsumption, of adjusting production to consumption, of distributing wealth and products more equitably, of adapting existing eco-

* September 23, 1932. From *The New York Times*, September 24, 1932.

nomic organizations to the service of the people. The day of enlightened administration has come.

Just as in older times the central Government was first a haven of refuge, and then a threat, so now in a closer economic system the central and ambitious financial unit is no longer a servant of national desire, but a danger. I would draw the parallel one step farther. We did not think because national Government had become a threat in the 18th century that therefore we should abandon the principle of national Government. Nor today should we abandon the principle of strong economic units called corporations, merely because their power is susceptible of easy abuse. In other times we dealt with the problem of an unduly ambitious central Government by modifying it gradually into a constitutional democratic Government. So today we are modifying and controlling our economic units.

As I see it, the task of Government in its relation to business is to assist the development of an economic declaration of rights, and economic constitutional order. This is the common task of states-man and business man. It is the minimum requirement of a more permanently safe order of things.

Happily, the times indicate that to create such an order not only is the proper policy of Government, but it is the only line of safety for our economic structures as well. We know, now, that these economic units cannot exist unless prosperity is uniform, that is, unless purchasing power is well distributed throughout every group in the Nation. That is why even the most selfish of corporations for its own interest would be glad to see wages restored and unemployment ended and to bring the Western farmer back to his accustomed level of prosperity and to assure a permanent safety to both groups. That is why some enlightened industries themselves endeavor to limit the freedom of action of each man and business group within the industry in the common interest of all; why business men everywhere are asking a form of organization which will bring the scheme of things into balance, even though it may in some measure qualify the freedom of action of individual units within the business. . . .

(c) FRANKLIN D. ROOSEVELT ADDRESS AT PITTSBURGH, PENNSYL-VANIA*

One of these great problems—and a very vital one to my family and your family and to the whole community—is the financial problem of making both ends meet. I want to discuss this problem with you tonight. To do so sincerely I must tell the facts as they are and conceal nothing from you. It is not a pretty picture, but if we know that picture and face it we have nothing to fear. This country is the richest and most resourceful Nation in the world. It can and will meet successfully every problem which it faces;

but it can do so only through intelligent leadership working unselfishly for the good of all people. That it has not had such leadership in its financial affairs will become obvious from the facts I am going to relate to you tonight.

We all know that our own family credit depends in large part on the stability of the credit of the United States. And here, at least, is one field in which all business —big business and little business and family business and the individual's business—is at the mercy of our big Government down at Washington, D. C.

What I should like to do is to reduce, in so far as possible, the problem of our

* October 19, 1932. From *The New York Times*, October 20, 1932.

national finances to the terms of a family budget.

The credit of the family depends chiefly on whether that family is living within its income. And that is equally true of the Nation. If the Nation is living within its income, its credit is good. If, in some crises, it lives beyond its income for a year or two, it can usually borrow temporarily at reasonable rates. But if, like a spendthrift, it throws discretion to the winds, and is willing to make no sacrifice at all in spending; if it extends its taxing to the limit of the people's power to pay and continues to pile up deficits, then it is on the road to bankruptcy. . . .

The air is now surcharged with Republican death-bed repentance on the subject of economy, but it is too late. We must look deeper than these eleventh-hour pronouncements. You cannot go very far with any real Federal economy, without a complete change of concept of what are the proper functions and limits of the Federal Government itself.

Perhaps we can get some glimpse of the President's underlying philosophy about the Federal Government by going back and opening the volume of his 1928 speeches. He proposed, you remember, as he said, "a new thing in Government." He says that he "reorganized the Department of Commerce on a greater scale than has ever been attempted or achieved by any Government in the world." In his book, called *The New Day,* he says this: "A nation which is spending ninety billions a year can well afford a few hundred million for a workable program."

I could go on quoting for a good many minutes, but perhaps the point could be made clearer by recalling that the Department of Commerce went through even the heavy war strain, back in the days of the World War, on about 13 millions a year. When Secretary Hoover left it, it was spending 39 millions a year; and this year it is estimated that it will be spend-

ing 43 millions a year. And the Department of Commerce is now housed in that great marble building which is face-tiously called in Washington the "Temple of Fact Finding," which cost the people considerably more than the Capitol of the United States.

That little example, my friends, may explain the 50 percent increase in Government overhead in four years, 1927-1931, and I am sure that the whole group of quotations reveal why you can never expect any important economy from this Administration. It is committed to the idea that we ought to center control of everything in Washington as rapidly as possible—Federal control. That was the idea that increased the cost of Government by a billion dollars in four years. Ever since the days of Thomas Jefferson, that has been the exact reverse of the democratic concept, which is to permit Washington to take from the States nothing more than is necessary to keep abreast of the march of our changing economic situation.

In the latter philosophy, and not in the philosophy of Mr. Hoover—which I think is responsible for so much of our trouble —I shall approach the problem of carrying out the plain precept of our Party, which is to reduce the cost of current Federal Government operations by 25 percent.

Of course that means a complete realignment of the unprecedented bureaucracy that has assembled in Washington in the past four years. . . .

Now, I am going to disclose to you a definite personal conclusion which I reached the day after I was nominated in Chicago. Here it is: Before any man enters my Cabinet he must give me a two-fold pledge:

1. Absolute loyalty to the Democratic platform and especially to its economy plank.

2. Complete cooperation with me, look-

ing to economy and reorganization in his
Department.

I regard reduction in Federal spending
as one of the most important issues of this
campaign. In my opinion it is the most
direct and effective contribution that

Government can make to business.

In accordance with this fundamental
policy it is equally necessary to eliminate
from Federal budget-making during this
emergency all new items except such as
relate to direct relief of unemployment.

8

President Hoover's Defense

☆ *President Hoover waged a vigorous campaign in defense of his administration. In his address at Detroit, Michigan, October 22, 1932, he summarized the program, already partially accomplished, which he believed would lead to recovery.* ☆

You will recollect my recommendations to the Congress in my message of last December 8:

First. Drastic reduction in Government expenses.

Second. By this and an increase in revenues to balance the budget, thus to hold the impregnability of the credit of the Federal Government.

Third. The strengthening of the capital of the Federal Land Banks by $125,000,-000 in order to relieve the pressure upon farmers to repay their mortgages.

Fourth. Creation of the Reconstruction Finance Corporation with $2,000,000,000 of resources in order that, having maintained national credit, we should thrust the full resources of public credit behind the private credit system of the country in order to reestablish and maintain it in an unassailable position. That with the backing of Federal credit it should protect the depositors in savings banks, insurance policyholders, the lenders and borrowers in building and loan associations; that it should through existing agencies expand the funds available for loans to merchants, manufacturers,

* From *The New York Times,* October 23, 1932.

farmers, agricultural marketing associations; that it should protect the railways from receiverships in order that in turn the railroad securities in the insurance companies and savings banks might be protected and the employees of the railways—and a score of other services. . . .

Fifth. Extension of authority of the Federal Reserve Board to meet the danger to our gold standard and to expand credit in counteraction to the strangulation due to hoarding and foreign withdrawals.

Sixth. Creation of the Home Loan Discount Banks with resources of several hundred millions to give home owners a chance to hold their homes from foreclosure and to furnish credit to create new homes and to expand employment.

Seventh. An authority by which we could secure early liquidation of deposits in closed banks that we might relieve the distress on millions of depositors.

Eighth. Revision of our banking laws.

Ninth. Continuation of the public-works program of some $600,000,000 per annum to aid employment.

Later in the session of Congress I expanded these emergency recommendations to include:

Tenth. Authorities to the Reconstruction Finance Corporation to loan up to $300,000,000 to the states whose resources had been exhausted for relief of distress.

Eleventh. Loans by the Reconstruction Finance Corporation up to $1,500,000,-000 for the undertaking of great works which would add to employment and from their own earnings repay the outlay.

Twelfth. The erection of a new system of agricultural credit banks with indirect resources of $300,000,000.

Thirteenth. The extension of credits through the Reconstruction Corporation for movement of agricultural commodities. And may I add to these measures others which we have in motion to aid in this emergency.

Fourteenth. To maintain the protective tariff as the first safeguard of every manufacturer and every workman and every farmer in the United States. Never has this been so vital as in this emergency when twenty countries are suffering from depreciated currencies and their standards of living and wages are so low. The danger of flooding our markets with foreign goods was never greater than at this moment. A week ago in Cleveland I showed that wages in foreign countries would buy only from one-eighth to one-third as much bread and butter as could be bought by the wage in America today. In the face of these standards of living the Democratic Party proposes to lower tariffs. In this emergency as never before we require the preservation of our nonpartisan Tariff Commission, by which this flood can be prevented and through which, if tariffs should become too high, they can be lowered without all the disruption and log-rolling of congressional action. Our opponents propose to destroy this function.

Fifteenth. The prevention of immigration during this emergency except for relatives of those already resident in the United States. This is vital to hold for our people the jobs which they have.

Sixteenth. The mobilization and support of all private relief agencies as we have done over the past three years in order that we may have the fullest care and support given to those who are ill and in distress, and that we may maintain a sense of responsibility of every man to his neighbor.

Seventeenth. The mobilization of our businessmen, our labor and agricultural leaders to carry on their present cooperative activities and initiate new activities for increasing employment and aids to agriculture.

Eighteenth. The vigorous consummation of results from the World Economic Conference with a view to relieving the pressures from the outside and preventing recurrences of this distress in the future. The continuation of our negotiations for reduction of armament in order to reduce our own expense and to relieve the world of fear and political instability.

This is the constructive program proposed by the Republican Administration and largely adopted for relief of this emergency. . . .

Practically the only evidence of the attitude of the Democratic candidate upon this program is the sneer that it has been designed to help banks and corporations, that it has not helped the common man. He knows full well that the only purpose of helping an insurance company is to protect the policyholder. He knows full well that the only purpose in helping a bank is to protect the depositor and the borrower. He knows full well that the only purpose of helping a farm-mortgage company is to enable the farmer to hold his farm. He knows full well that the only purpose of helping the building and loan associations is to protect savings and homes. He knows full well that in sustaining the businessman it maintains the worker in his job. He knows full well that in loans to the states it protects the families in distress.

Millions of men and women are employed today because there has been restored to his employer the ability to borrow the money to buy raw materials and pay labor and thus keep his job. . . . Nothing has ever been devised in our history which has done more for those whom Mr. Coolidge has aptly called the common run of men and women.

IX

the way back (1933-1940)

RANKLIN Roosevelt took office during the depth of the depression. Promising the nation a "New Deal," his administration and the Congress rushed through a multitude of bills designed to bolster confidence, alleviate hardship and unemployment, and restore the economy. The Federal government acknowledged its responsibility for the material well-being of the people.

This responsibility was implemented in the most far-reaching early measures of the Roosevelt administration. The National Industrial Recovery Act authorized huge federal works programs, gave labor the right to organize and bargain collectively, and established the National Recovery Administration. The Civil Works Administration, under Harry Hopkins, sought to put 4,000,000 people to work on federal, state, and local projects. Coming under heavy criticism for the make-work nature of its projects, the C.W.A. and its successor agencies were vigorously defended as the feasible alternatives to the dole. Farmers, plagued by over-production and lowered prices since World War I, were given the Agricultural Adjustment Act. Calling for the curtailed production of farm produce, the establishment of parity prices for certain commodities, and the payment of direct subsidies for a reduction of acreage, the act became the subject of continued controversy.

The depression offered a fertile field for the growth of radical movements. Not only long-established Marxist societies but a variety of indigenous groups joined in the scramble for political power. Though radical agitation attracted a good deal of attention and gathered some strength in certain sections of the country, pro-labor legislation and ameliorated economic conditions by 1936 offset the appeal of extremist parties. The election campaign of 1936 developed into a bitter contest between the two major parties with the Republicans espousing a modified New Deal program and charging that Roosevelt had placed constitutional government in jeopardy.

Overwhelmingly reelected in 1936, Roosevelt launched an all-out attempt to reorganize the Supreme Court, which had invalidated certain prominent legislation. The ensuing bitter contest alienated many of the President's supporters and his proposal was defeated, though the Court began to temper its attitudes toward New Deal legislation.

Despite the political successes of the New Deal and the impact of its program, serious questions could be raised as to whether it grappled with the fundamental defects in the economy. Broadus Mitchell's appraisal discerned that the impetus for New Deal legislation was to be found in Herbert Hoover's measures to alleviate the depression, and that the policies espoused by Franklin Roosevelt had failed to restore prosperity. Though in 1939 a dream world could be visualized for 1960, not until 1940 with the influx of orders for the materials of war did the promise of industrial recovery come true.

1

The Blue Eagle

☆ *The new administration's foremost objective was to put people back to work. The principal legislative measure designed to accomplish this task was the National Industrial Recovery Act. This Act authorized the establishment of the National Recovery Administration to coordinate and direct the activities of business and labor in an effort to overcome the malfunctioning of the economy.** ☆

The law I have just signed was passed *to put people back to work*—to let them buy more of the products of farms and factories and start our business at a living rate again. This task is in two stages— first, to get many hundreds of thousands of the unemployed back on the pay roll by snowfall and second, to plan for a better future for the longer pull. While we shall not neglect the second, the first stage is an emergency job. It has the right of way.

The second part of the act gives employment by a vast program of public works. Our studies show that we should be able to hire many men at once and to step up to about a million new jobs by October 1, and a much greater number later. We must put at the head of our list those works which are fully ready to start now. Our first purpose is to create employment as fast as we can, but we should not pour money into unproved projects.

We have worked out our plans for ac-

* From "Statement by the President of the United States of America Outlining Policies of the National Recovery Administration," June 16, 1933, National Recovery Administration Bulletin No. 1.

tion. Some of it will start tomorrow. I am making available $400,000,000 for State roads under regulations which I have just signed, and I am told that the States will get this work under way at once. I have also just released over $200,000,000 for the Navy to start building ships under the London treaty.

In my inaugural I laid down the simple proposition that nobody is going to starve in this country. It seems to me to be equally plain that no business which depends for existence on paying less than living wages to its workers has any right to continue in this county. By "business" I mean the whole of commerce as well as the whole of industry; by workers I mean all workers—the white-collar class as well as the men in overalls; and by *living* wages I mean more than a bare subsistence level—I mean the wages of *decent* living.

Throughout industry, the change from starvation wages and starvation employment to living wages and sustained employment can, in large part, be made by an industrial covenant to which all employers shall subscribe. It is greatly to their interest to do this because decent living, widely spread among our 125,000,-000 people, eventually means the opening up to industry of the richest market which the world has known. It is the only way to utilize the so-called excess capacity of our industrial plants. This is the principle that makes this one of the most important laws that ever came from Congress because, before the passage of this act, no such industrial covenant was possible.

On this idea, the first part of the act proposes to our industry a great spontaneous cooperation to put millions of men back in their regular jobs this summer. The idea is simply for employers to hire more men to do the existing work by reducing the work-hours of each man's week and at the same time paying a living wage for the shorter week.

No employer and no group of less than all employers in a single trade could do this alone and continue to live in business competition. But if *all* employers in each trade now band themselves faithfully in these modern guilds—without exception —and agree to act together and at once, none will be hurt and millions of workers, so long deprived of the right to earn their bread in the sweat of their labor, can raise their heads again. The challenge of this law is whether we can sink selfish interest and present a solid front against a common peril.

It is a challenge to industry which has long insisted that, given the right to act in unison, it could do much for the general good which has hitherto been unlawful. From today it has that right.

Many good men voted this new charter with misgivings. I do not share these doubts. I had part in the great cooperation of 1917 and 1918 and it is my faith that we can count on our industry once more to join in our general purpose to lift this new threat and to do it without taking any advantage of the public trust which has

this day been reposed without stint in the good faith and high purpose of American business.

But industry is challenged in another way. It is not only the slackers within trade groups who may stand in the path of our common purpose. In a sense these groups compete with each other, and no single industry, and no separate cluster of industries, can do this job alone, for exactly the same reason that no single employer can do it alone. In other words, we can imagine such a thing as a *slacker industry*.

This law is also a challenge to labor. Workers, too, are here given a new charter of rights long sought and hitherto denied. But they know that the first move expected by the Nation is a great cooperation of all employers, by one single mass action, to improve the case of workers on a scale never attempted in any nation. Industries can do this only if they have the support of the whole public and especially of their own workers. This is not a law to foment discord and it will not be executed as such. This is a time for mutual confidence and help and we can safely rely on the sense of fair play among all Americans to assure every industry which now moves forward promptly in this united drive against depression that its workers will be with it to a man.

It is, further, a challenge to administration. We are relaxing some of the safeguards of the antitrust laws. The public must be protected against the abuses that led to their enactment, and to this end we are putting in place of old principles of unchecked competition some new Government controls. They must above all be impartial and just. Their purpose is to free business—not to shackle it—and no man who stands on the constructive forward-looking side of his industry has anything to fear from them. To such men the opportunities for individual initiative will open more amply than ever. Let me make it clear, however, that the antitrust laws still stand firmly against monopolies that restrain trade and price fixing which allows inordinate profits or unfairly high prices.

If we ask our trade groups to do that which exposes their business, as never before, to undermining by members who are unwilling to do their parts, we must guard those who play the game for the general good against those who may seek selfish gains from the unselfishness of others. We must protect them from the racketeers who invade organizations of both employers and workers. We are spending billions of dollars and if that spending is really to serve our ends it must be done quickly. We must see that our haste does not permit favoritism and graft. All this is a heavy load for any government and one that can be borne only if we have the patience, cooperation, and support of people everywhere.

Finally, this law is a challenge to our whole people. There is no power in America that can force against the public will such action as we require. But there is no group in America that can withstand the force of an aroused public opinion. This great cooperation can succeed only if those who bravely go forward to restore jobs have aggressive public support and those who lag are made to feel the full weight of public disapproval.

As to the machinery—the practical way of accomplishing what we are setting out to do, when a trade association has a code ready to submit and the association has qualified as truly representative, and after reasonable notice has been issued to all concerned, a public hearing will be held by the Administrator or a deputy. A Labor Advisory Board appointed by the Secretary of Labor will be responsible that every affected labor group, whether organized or unorganized, is fully and adequately represented in an advisory capacity and any interested labor group will be entitled to be heard through representatives of its own choosing. An Industrial Advisory Board appointed by the Secretary of Commerce will be responsible that every affected industrial group is fully and adequately represented in an advisory capacity and any interested industrial group will be entitled to be heard through representatives of its own choosing. A Consumers' Advisory Board will be responsible that the interests of the consuming public will be represented and every reasonable opportunity will be given to any group or class who may be affected directly or indirectly to present their views.

At the conclusion of these hearings and after the most careful scrutiny by a competent economic staff the Administrator will present the subject to me for my action under the law.

I am fully aware that wage increases will eventually raise costs, but I ask that managements give first consideration to the improvement of operating figures by greatly increased sales to be expected from the rising purchasing power of the public. That is good economics and good business. The aim of this whole effort is to restore our rich domestic market by raising its vast consuming capacity. If we now inflate prices as fast and as far as we increase wages, the whole project will be set at naught. We cannot hope for the full effect of this plan unless, in these first critical months, and, even at the expense of full initial profits, we defer price increases as long as possible. If we can thus start a strong sound upward spiral of business activity our industries will have little doubt of black-ink operations in the last quarter of this year. The pent-up demand of this people is very great and if we can release it on so broad a front, we need not fear a lagging recovery. There is greater danger of too much feverish speed.

In a few industries, there has been some forward buying at unduly depressed prices in recent weeks. Increased costs resulting from this Government-inspired movement may make it very hard for some manufacturers and jobbers to fulfill some of their present contracts without loss. It will be a part of this wide industrial cooperation for those having the benefit of these forward bargains (contracted before the law was passed) to take the initiative in revising them to absorb some share of the increase in their suppliers' costs, thus raised in the public interest. It is only in such a willing and considerate spirit, throughout the whole of industry, that we can hope to succeed.

Under title I of this act, I have appointed Hugh Johnson as Administrator of the NRA and a special Industrial Recovery Board under the chairmanship of the Secretary of Commerce. This organization is now prepared to receive proposed codes and to conduct prompt hearings looking toward their submission to me for approval. While acceptable proposals of no trade group will be delayed, it is my hope that the 10 major industries which control the bulk of industrial employment can submit their simple basic codes at once and that the country can look forward to the month of July as the beginning of our great national movement back to work.

During the coming 3 weeks title II relating to public works and construction projects will be temporarily conducted by Col. Donald H. Sawyer as Administrator and a special temporary board consisting of the Secretary of the Interior as chairman, the Secretary of Commerce, the Secretary of Agriculture, the Secretary of War, the Attorney General, the Secretary of Labor, and the Director of the Budget.

During the next 2 weeks the Administrator and this board will make a study of all projects already submitted or to be submitted and, as previously stated, certain allotments under the new law will be made immediately.

Between these twin efforts—public works and industrial reemployment, it is not too much to expect that a great many men and women can be taken from the ranks of the unemployed before winter comes. It is the most important attempt of this kind in history. As in the great crisis of the World War, it puts a whole people to the simple but vital test: *"Must we go on in many groping, disorganized, separate units to defeat or shall we move as one great team to victory?"*

2

Farm Relief

☆ One of the thorniest problems with which the Roosevelt Administration had to deal was that of increasing the purchasing power of
agriculture. Under the authority granted by the Agricultural Adjustment Act, the government sought to accomplish this by controlling
the laws of supply and demand. President Roosevelt commented on
the operation of the Act in an address of May 14, 1935.* ☆

Let us go back for a minute to that spring of 1933 when there was a huge carryover. Let us take some examples. There was a carryover of almost thirteen million bales of cotton and a price, because of that carryover, of six cents a pound. Henry Wallace insists it was six and a half cents a pound, but I know that I got only four and a half cents for my cotton. You and I know what six-cent cotton means to the purchasing power of the Cotton Belt. And you and I remember that there was a huge carryover of to-bacco and that the price of tobacco during the preceding six months was the lowest on record for a great many years. Wheat had a carryover of nearly four hundred million bushels and a price of thirty-five cents on the farm or less; corn, a price of fifteen cents a bushel on many farms —and I knew some farmers who sold it at nine cents; hogs, a price of three cents a pound.

You and I know what those figures meant in the way of purchasing power for forty million Americans.

* From *Vital Speeches*, I (May 20, 1935), pp. 522-523.

When we came down here to Washington that spring we were faced with three possible ways of meeting the situation. The first method that was suggested in-volved price fixing by Federal decree. We discarded that because the problem of overproduction was not solved thereby.

The second plan was to let farmers grow as much as they wanted of every-thing, and to have the Federal Govern-ment then step in, take from them that portion of their crop which represented what we called the exportable surplus and, in their name and on their behalf, dump this surplus on the other Nations of the world. We discarded that plan for a good many reasons and one was because the other Nations of the world had already taken steps to stop dumping. From that time on, with increasing frequency they were raising their tariffs, establishing quotas and clamping on embargoes against just that kind of proposition. And that is why we discarded that.

Therefore, we came to the third plan —a plan for the adjustment of totals in our major crops, so that from year to year production and consumption would be kept in reasonable balance with each other, to the end that reasonable prices would be paid to farmers for their crops and unwieldy surpluses would not depress our markets and upset the balance.

We are now at the beginning of the third year of carrying out this policy. You know the results thus far attained. You know the present price of cotton, of wheat, of tobacco, of corn, of hogs and of other farm products today. Further comment on the successful partial attainment of our objective up to this time is unnecessary on my part. You know.

I want, for a moment, to emphasize that word "adjustment." It is almost a forgotten word just as some of you, once upon a time, were forgotten men. As you know, a great many of the high and mighty, with special axes to grind, have been deliberately trying to mislead people who know nothing of farming by misrepresenting—no, why use a pussyfoot word?—by lying about the kind of farm program under which this Nation is operating today. . . .

I was speaking to you about that word adjustment. I think it is your duty and mine to continue to educate the people of this country to the fact that adjustment means not only adjustment downward but adjustment upward. If you and I agree on a correct figure for a normal carryover in a basic crop, it means that if we have a bumper crop one year we will, by mutual consent, reduce the next year's crop in order to even up that carryover. At the same time, if we get a short crop in a given year, you and I agree to increase the next year's crop to make up the shortage. That is exactly what we are doing in the case of wheat this year.

Yes, it is high time for you and for me to carry, by education, knowledge of the fact that not a single program of the A.A.A. contemplated the destruction of an acre of food crops in the United States, in spite of what you may read or what you

may have been told by people who have special axes to grind.

It is high time for you and for me to make clear that we are not plowing under cotton this year—that we did not plow it under in 1934 and that we only plowed some of it under in 1933 because the Agricultural Adjustment Act was passed by that Congress at that famous Special Session after a huge crop of cotton was already in the ground.

It is high time for us to repeat on every occasion that we have not wastefully destroyed food in any form. It is true that the Relief Administrator has purchased hundreds of thousands of tons of foodstuffs in order to feed the needy and hungry who have been on the relief rolls in every part of the United States.

The crocodile tears shed by the professional mourners of an old and obsolete order over the slaughter of little pigs and over other measures to reduce surplus agricultural inventories deceive very few thinking people in this country, and least of all the farmers themselves.

I have always supposed, ever since I was able to play around, that the acknowledged destiny of a pig is sausage, or ham, or bacon or pork. It was in those forms —as sausage, ham, bacon or pork—that millions of pigs were consumed by vast numbers of needy people who otherwise would have had to do without them.

Let me make one other point clear for the benefit of the millions in cities who have to buy meats. Last year the Nation suffered a drought of unparalleled intensity. If there had been no Government program, if the old order had obtained in 1933 and 1934, that drought on the cattle ranges of America and in the corn belt would have resulted in the marketing of thin cattle, immature hogs and the death of these animals on the range and on the farm, and if the old order had been in effect those years, we would have had a vastly greater shortage than we face today.

Our program—we can prove it—saved the lives of millions of head of livestock. They are still on the range, and other millions of heads are today canned and ready for this country to eat.

I think that you and I are agreed in seeking a continuance of a national policy which on the whole is proving successful. The memory of old conditions under which the product of a whole year's work often would not bring you the cost of transporting it to market is too fresh in your minds to let you be led astray by the solemn admonitions and specious lies of those who in the past profited most when your distress was greatest.

You remember and I remember that not so long ago the poor had less food to eat, and less clothes to wear, at a time when you had practically to give away your products. Then the surpluses were greater, and yet the poor were poorer than they are today when you farmers are getting a reasonable, although still an insufficient, price.

I have not the time to talk with you about many other policies of your Government which affect the farm population of the country. I have not the time, although I would like to do it, to go into the practical work of the Farm Credit Administration which, in all of its ramifications, has saved a million farms from foreclosure and has accomplished the first great reduction in exorbitant interest rates that this country has ever known. . . .

I want to thank you for your patience with us, your Government. I want to pledge to you not only our wholehearted cooperation as you go forward, but our continued deep interest in a problem that is not just a farmer's problem because, as I have said before, your prosperity is felt in every city home, in every bank and in every industry in the land.

3

Unemployment Relief

☆ *The unemployment relief programs of the administration were among the most sharply criticized New Deal measures. Harry Hopkins, in 1936, then administrator of the Works Progress Administration, aggressively defended those programs in one of his rare recorded public speeches.** ☆

I am getting sick and tired of these people on the W.P.A. and local relief rolls being called chiselers and cheats. It doesn't do any good to call these people names, because they are just like the rest of us. They don't drink any more than the rest of us, they don't lie any more, they're no lazier than the rest of us—they're pretty much a cross section of the American people. . . .

Now I want to say this, I have been at this thing for three and a half years. I have never been a public official before. I was brought up in that school of thought that believed that no one went on the public payroll except for political purposes or because he was incompetent or unless he had a job that he didn't work at. One of the most insidious things is the propaganda that something is wrong about one that works for the people. I have learned something in these three and a half years. I have taken a look at a lot of these public servants. I have seen these technical fellows working for three or four thou-

sand a year—not working seven hours a day but working fifteen hours a day. I have seen these fellows in the Army engineer corps. The motivation can't be money—they don't get very much. I have seen them work just as hard as any engineers in America and just as qualified and just as competent, and I have come to resent an attitude on the part of some people in America that you should never be part of this business of public service. I am proud of having worked for the Government. It has been a great experience for me. I have signed my name to about $6,000,000,000 in the last three and a half years. None of it has stuck to the fingers of our administrators. You might think some of it has been wasted. If it has been wasted it was in the interest of the unemployed. You might say we have made mistakes. I haven't a thing to apologize for about our so-called mistakes. If we have made mistakes we have made them in the interests of the people that were broke.

When this thing is all over and I am out of the Government the things I am going to regret are the things I have failed to do for the unemployed. I don't know

* From Robert E. Sherwood, *Roosevelt and Hopkins, An Intimate History,* pp. 83-85. Copyright, 1948, Harper and Brothers, New York. Used by permission.

whether you would have liked the job. Every night when you went home and after you got home and remembered there was a telegram you didn't answer, the fact that you failed to answer the telegram and the telephone call may have resulted in somebody not eating. That is the kind of a job I have had for the last three and a half years, and still have. When it is all over, the thing I am going to be proudest of are the people all over America, public officials, volunteers, paid workers, thousands of people of all political and religious faiths who joined in this enterprise of taking care of people in need. It has been a great thing. I am not ashamed of one of them and I hope when I am through they are not going to be ashamed of me, and as I go around this country and see the unemployment and see the people who are running this show of ours, I am tremendously proud of this country of ours and I am tremendously proud that I am a citizen of it. Thank you very much.

4

The Radical Movements

☆ *The activities of radical movements did not diminish with the implementation of the New Deal program. Some radical groups, like the Socialist and Communist parties during Roosevelt's early years in office, refused to accept the New Deal as a harbinger of fundamental change in American society. Others, like Upton Sinclair's End Poverty in California movement, the various farmer-labor and progressive political movements, often worked with the New Deal, but felt that its efforts were inadequate. Still others, like Senator Huey Long's Share-Our-Wealth movement and Father Charles E. Coughlin, initially cooperated with the administration but by 1934 and 1935 became bitterly critical. With Roosevelt's reelection in 1936 American radicalism found that its appeal had been greatly weakened by New Deal innovations. ☆*

(a) SENATOR HUEY P. LONG OF LOUISIANA, THE SHARE-OUR-WEALTH PROGRAM*

1. All personal fortunes over $3,000,-000 would be liquidated, yielding $170,-000,000,000 to be turned over to the United States Treasury.

2. From this fund, every family in the United States was to receive about $4,000 [or $5,000] to purchase a home, an automobile, and a radio. The estimated government expenditure for these services was $100,000,000,000.

3. All persons over sixty-five [or sixty] years of age were to receive pensions of $30 per month [or an adequate amount].

4. The minimum wage would be adjusted to provide a floor of $2,500 a year

per worker, resulting in, among other things, a permanent increase in the purchasing power of the benefited group.

5. Hours of labor would be limited to balance industrial production with consumption and enable the worker to enjoy some of the conveniences of life.

6. The government would purchase and store agricultural surpluses in order to balance agricultural production with demand "according to the laws of God."

7. Cash payment of veterans' bonuses would begin immediately.

8. From the remainder of the Treasury fund, boys of proven ability, as determined by intelligence tests, were to receive a college education at government expense.

* 1933-1934. From Donald R. McCoy, *Angry Voices, Left-of-Center Politics in the New Deal Era,* pp. 122-123. Published by University of Kansas Press, Lawrence, 1958. Used by permission.

(b) "THE NORTHWEST GOES LEFTISH"*

Since 1931 the leftward drift in the Pacific Northwest has been clearly indicated —particularly in Oregon and Washington. Progressive bills have been fought through state legislatures. Grange leaders have relentlessly defeated sales-tax proposals at the polls. Reactionary congressmen have been repudiated by their constituents. The unemployed have shown increasingly diminishing inclination to be satisfied with newspaper platitudes and commercial-club resolutions. The working class has raised its voice against the absentee ownership of many of the region's basic industries. (Such a situation prevailed in the longshoremen's strike.)

Most significant of all the recent events occurred recently in Oregon, where workers and grangers at last united to form a Farmer-Labor fusion with the ultimate purpose of "building a political party separate and distinct from the two older parties dominated by big business and the financiers." Oregon is essentially a rural commonwealth and there is an excellent chance that this initial venture will prove successful. It already has terrified the old party hacks.

The results of a straw poll taken by a newspaper in Clackamas County are illuminating. General Charles L. Martin and Joe Dunne, the candidates of the old parties, received a combined total of 876 votes. Slightly more than one thousand ballots were cast for Peter Zimmerman, a square-jawed granger who harvests a precarious living on a meager farm in the Willamette Valley. He has no campaign funds, but determined farmers and workers are selling their small personal belongings at public auction to send him around the state.

Zimmerman is the most extreme left-

winger ever to be within hearkening distance of a Pacific Northwest gubernatorial chair. The principal plank in his platform is the Grange Power Bill, pounded through the last state legislature, but sidetracked for referendum by a bloc of private utilities. If adopted by the people and administered by a governor of Zimmerman's views, the bill would embark Oregon upon the most ambitious plan of public ownership of electrical energy ever attempted in the nation. It provides for a bond issue to construct state-owned transmission lines from the great federal dam at Bonneville, on the Columbia River, to every section of the commonwealth.

Other issues on which Zimmerman is appealing to the harassed farmers and laborers of the state are shifting the tax burden to incomes and inheritances, establishment of a state-owned bank, repeal of Oregon's criminal-syndicalism law, unemployment insurance, old-age pensions and the assurance to workers that the National Guard will not be used as a strike-breaking agency. Zimmerman's power platform alone has aligned the press against him in virtually a solid front, but the influence of Upton Sinclair's Democratic party primary victory in California has more than made up for this opposition. Like Sinclair, Zimmerman once was identified with the Socialists, and in 1924 he supported La Follette. As a state senator he consistently advocated government ownership of industries vested with a public interest and he cast his vote against the criminal-syndicalism laws.

In Washington the Democrats recently nominated Lewis Schwellenbach to succeed Senator Clarence C. Dill. Schwellenbach, who was associated with Senator Homer Bone in the fight for public ownership, tore a leaf from Sinclair's notebook and ran on a platform to end poverty in Washington (E.P.I.W.). He is an odds-

* From Richard L. Neuberger, "The Northwest Goes Leftish," *The New Republic,* LXXX (November 7, 1934), p. 357. Used by permission.

on favorite to win the election from Reno Odlin, conservative Republican banker and former commander of the state American Legion.

This sort of use of the ballot-box was the prologue to the pronounced swing leftward now centering in Oregon. The longshoremen's strike provided the impetus. Whether a radical-progressive Governor in the Northwest can end the problem of poverty is dubious. That he can make his state a better place in which to settle and live is a certainty.

(c) THE COURSE OF RADICALISM*

It may throw some light ... to trace a little more precisely the course of radicalism in this country since 1929. The details are multifarious and confusing, but the general pattern is obvious enough. There are two main currents—first, the generalized, spontaneous impulse toward social change arising from the experience and background of multitudes of people, and expressing itself in terms of the native culture; second, the organized movements with conscious revolutionary aims, deriving their inspiration from intellectual formulations and their policies from foreign—or perhaps it would be less invidious to say from international —sources.

Of the first component, it is clear that we have had a demonstration hitherto unparalleled in American history. Our former major political overturns, such as the Revolution and the Civil War, moved large masses of people, it is true, but in each case the unrest and the formulation of issues were expressed mainly by the already existing leaders in wealth and prestige. It was the propertied classes, or at least an important section of them, who led the movement for American inde-

pendence, and it was the struggle between the Southern plantation owners and land speculators on the one hand and the Northern industrialists and capitalists on the other that formed the core of the conflict about slavery. This time, however, the protest that carried so much dead wood out in flood came most insistently from below, and found no solid economic interest among the bested institutions to champion it.

This is not to say that it had no forerunners or that the form of its expression was not determined by traditional forces. It was a little like the democratic uprising under Andrew Jackson. The 19th-century struggles against the railroads and the other big corporations, flowering first in the Populist and later in the Progressive moments, had blazed a rude trail in the same direction. Previous farmers' complaints against low prices for crops, leading to demand for monetary reform (or, in the disparaging terminology, for inflation), had been signposts for part of the program of the New Deal. The agitation for "parity prices" for farmers to be obtained by some offset against the benefits secured by industry under the protective tariff, which had begun under Coolidge and Hoover, was intensified and came to issue in the AAA. The century-old struggle for freedom in labor organization and collective bargaining surged up again and made its mark, first in the NRA and later in the Labor Relations Act. The cry of the underprivileged city workers for more consideration, hitherto expressed mainly through social workers and proponents of social legislation, had its first comprehensive answer in large-scale federal relief, in housing projects and in social security legislation. The protest against the money power and Wall Street, long a political tradition, was the prototype of the new banking legislation and security regulation. Finally, the dead hand of the Supreme Court, concerning

* Reprinted with the permission of Charles Scribner's Sons from "Radicalism" by George Soule from *America Now*, pp. 259-263, edited by Harold E. Stearns.

which complaints had been lodged for a generation at least, was pushed aside.

The phraseology in which this revolt was clothed, after it had been channelled into political action, was similar to that of a popular revolution. Democracy was supposed to be assuming control of the economic empire in order to use it for the general benefit. The enemies of reforms were identified as "economic royalists." What was done was spoken of as if it were a new social order in some genuine sense. This bombardment of words from the President and his cohorts was returned in good earnest from the other side. The population divided on class lines in its opinions and in its votes more completely than ever before. Above a certain income level it was difficult to find support of the President, difficult at times to find even anything but violent hatred. The press itself went over almost *en masse* to the opposition, while the majority of voters became more loyal to the New Deal, the more vocal the opposition grew.

All the fury, however, marked no fundamental change in the social order itself. The means of production were not expropriated; there was comparatively little advance even in mild socialization of particular industries. Taxes on incomes and profits were somewhat increased, but not so high as they had been after the War. No essential powers were taken from the hands of the traditional rulers of industry; they still decided to as great an extent as before how much to charge for their products, how much to produce, how and when to invest their money. Some policing of the financial markets was undertaken. There was an expansion of public enterprise, chiefly in fields where it involved no competition with private industry. Collective bargaining was made obligatory and union organization gained. But all were things that had occurred in other countries without anything approaching a revolutionary

crisis. There was, finally, little permanent alteration in the distribution of income. And the business cycle continued as usual; a sharp depression, with large unemployment, followed the major victories of the New Deal. Radical in its impetus, radical in some of its terminology, but only reformist in its outcome, the popular revolt itself fell far short of its assumed objective.

On the side of the theoretically conscious and organized radicals, there continued the usual divisions and shadings. The Socialists persisted as a political entity without becoming anything more than the agitational minority they had long been. Syndicalists and anarchists, once prominent in revolutionary circles, all but disappeared. The Communists were undoubtedly the greatest beneficiaries on the Left from the economic upheaval. They had behind them the prestige of Soviet Russia, which kept on increasing production and avoiding unemployment while the rest of the world was sinking further and further into the morass. They took their work seriously; to be a party member was more like being in a strict religious order than in a congregation whose religious duty is fulfilled by attending church—or the polls— once in a while. They worked zealously among the unemployed, the tenant farmers, every group where their influence might count. They stimulated the formation of countless committees and councils for all sorts of worthy purposes. Their new tactics emphasized, not so much preaching doctrine or talking revolution as organizing for immediate gains, such as unemployment relief. Nowhere was their advance in influence more striking than among the younger literary men and other intellectuals. The predicted social crisis was at last a reality; Marx and Lenin had the theory that seemed to fit it; the exponents of that theory were in power in one great country and were working lustily toward power in others. At last the lost generations had something solid to believe in, something that was at once unfamiliar enough, adventurous enough and demanding enough to engage their emotional energies.

As soon as the Communists began to take a larger and more active part in the common struggles, however, they faced the problem of doing something to neutralize the doctrinaire quality of their faith that had tended to separate them from the main currents of life and culture. They had long been making enemies of people who were willing to go at least part way with them; their influence had often been disruptive of genuine popular movements wherever it had been felt at all. Whether the failure of their former tactics in this country would have brought a change in policy is uncertain. But at this very moment the unexpected rise of the Nazis in Germany put international Communism on the defensive and led it to look for help. On the field of politics in every country this reorientation led first to the United Front with other groups on the Left, and later to the People's Front, in which the Communists attempted to work on friendly terms with merely democratic and progressive forces which were not revolutionary at all. On the field of diplomacy the new policy led to the effort of Soviet Russia to strengthen the League of Nations as a bulwark against Fascist aggressors and the efforts of Communists everywhere to win converts to the doctrine of "collective security." This program had, for them, the double advantage that if applied in time it might prevent war, and so restrict the growth of Fascism, while if it were unsuccessful in that declared aim it would serve the undeclared aim of ensuring that the Soviet Union, which would presumably be the main object of attack, would have powerful allies in the coming struggle.

So the American party, which had been bitterly attacking the inconsistencies and hesitancies of the New Deal and calling the Socialists social fascists, turned squarely about and became supporters of the Roosevelt administration nationally and of progressive candidates locally. It suppressed, at least for the time being, any hint of revolutionary aim for the sake of broadening its influence.

But in the meantime that influence was becoming undermined from another direction. The factions split off by internal quarrels—the Trotskyites and the Lovestonites—had been small and without importance. But the quarrels in the Soviet Union of which these factions were merely shadows loomed larger and larger through the long series of arrests, trials and executions of prominent revolutionaries which followed the Kiroff assassination. The prestige of the spiritual mother country received incalculable injury as a result of these startling events. Some believed the accused innocent and so either joined or gave vicarious assistance to the dissenting factions. Others, who believed the accused guilty, suffered a shock to their faith in the success, as a desirable form of political and cultural organization, of the Soviet system. The traditional doctrinaire virulence, now withdrawn from its disturbing impact on the external world, seemed to have broken out in an internal malady. All this came to a head at a time when the economic crisis which had given hope of a catastrophic change had been relieved, and when the Communists' domestic program was so watered down that it held promise of nothing more exciting than the New Deal itself. The inevitable result was a widespread loss of élan, especially among the recently converted intellectuals.

So it turned out that the conscious revolutionaries had almost no effect in changing or hastening the course of the native revolt. It went its way almost as if they had not existed. They did, through hard work, help to make it more effective in approaching some of its own goals. Such self-sacrificing zeal might have been sadly missed. But the goals themselves had little connection with the ultimate revolutionary goals of the radicals. When the social changes occurring as a result of the great depression and the New Deal are assessed, one stands out above all the others—the growth in numbers, power and status of organized labor. The C.I.O., the Wagner Labor Relations Act, the widespread acceptance of collective bargaining, the growing political power of the unions—all this is a real change in the balance of social forces, with implications for the future. Is it radical, however, either in its origin or in its results? Certainly it is not the outcome of the work of conscious revolutionaries, and trade union movements in other countries, once they have grown strong, have not been noted for their daring. One must regard this development, nevertheless, as a good way of dealing with reality, as a desirable next step. It is the nearest thing we can show to a growing-up of the American radical impulse.

5

A Socialist Speaks

☆ *While the appeal of radical attacks on the administration had considerably diminished by the time of the 1936 campaign, the Socialist party candidate, Norman Thomas, emerged as the most trenchant radical analyst of American political trends.* ☆

Whatever the New Deal was in character, it was at least possessed of a force and, in spite of its experimental qualities, a degree of inclusiveness which it no longer has. . . .

While Mr. Roosevelt's actions were prompted by the emergency, the evidence is clear and overwhelming that he never regarded his program as intended merely for emergency or for "recovery." Definitely he had in mind the idea of reform. His New Deal has not won a secure or solid "recovery" and in no basic sense has it got reform. Although Mr. Roosevelt may continue to refer to the New Deal, his further efforts, whatever they are, cannot be any mere and logical extension of the New Deal as it first acquired form. That period is definitely over, as definitely over as the Coolidge period itself. The consequences are with us, as are the consequences of all our social experiments.

The reasons which justify us in speaking of the New Deal in the past tense are clear and not far to seek. Three causes are responsible for its death.

* From *After the New Deal, What?* by Norman Thomas, pp. 8-9, 12-14. Copyright 1936 by Norman Thomas. Used with permission of The Macmillan Company.

First, there is the loss of that element of consent and cooperation of the business world in the processes of change on which Mr. Roosevelt largely depended in the initial stages of his New Deal. The United States Chamber of Commerce which early in 1933 might almost be said to have invited N.R.A., had pretty definitely turned against it before the Supreme Court of the United States killed it. The proof for this is strong, even though the Liberty League as late as April 1935 favored the extension of N.R.A. until April 1936. This opposition of big business to N.R.A. was the more surprising because on the whole it had' fared well under it. Thanks to N.R.A., it blocked compulsory 30-hour week legislation. It gained permission to disregard the Sherman anti-trust law. It made substantial gain in profits. Neither N.R.A. nor any other New Deal legislation affected the relative distribution of income adversely to business. . . .

The second cause of the death of the New Deal, and the one which bulks largest, was the action of the Supreme Court of the United States in reasserting its power as the final authority in our governmental system. This it did in a series of decisions, eight out of ten of which were adverse to the New Deal. Probably those declaring N.R.A., A.A.A., and the Guffey coal act completely unconstitutional were the most significant. So important is this power of the Court in American affairs that it must loom large in every discussion of our future. Here it is enough to point out that the Supreme Court decisions destroyed what President Roosevelt and the public regarded as two of the major pillars of his New Deal structure; namely, his plan for the regulation of business and his plan for the regulation of agriculture. To an imperfect degree partial substitutes for these measures have been found, or are being sought, which have still to run the gauntlet of the Supreme Court. None of them nor all of them together can do in a straightforward fashion what the President and his advisers proposed in the original legislation. The question before the American public is not merely whether the New Deal can find some way to do what the Court said it could not do—in most cases by a divided vote—but whether there is any constitutional authority under which the federal government can act legally and constructively in an economic emergency of the magnitude which Mr. Roosevelt faced. His own failure to face squarely the Constitutional impasse which he once recognized and propose a definite remedy for it may be good politics, but it is bad statesmanship. The Democratic Party's declaration that if the Court keeps on kicking its laws around it may seek a "clarifying" amendment is an evasion of the issue.

The third factor in the death of the New Deal is the plain fact that it did not perform its basic task, provided that basic task is conceived, as I think President Roosevelt rather vaguely conceived it, in terms of an effective control of our economic and social order, at least to the extent that it should be made to provide some security against the lowest depths of poverty and the worst effects of economic crisis. This it was not doing satisfactorily when the Supreme Court intervened.

The reforms of the New Deal, while by no means negligible, were largely superficial. Perhaps the greatest contribution it made toward what we call recovery was that it suggested hope, confidence, action. The American people in 1933 were a bit like a man who caught in a blizzard sits down to wait for death. Mr. Roosevelt made us start running, and in the process we engendered enough animal heat to escape freezing. It cannot be said that we got anywhere in particular, but for a few months by contrast with the Coolidge or Hoover epoch this New Deal looked like a revolution of a sort.

It was not a revolution which lasted or brought to men a sense of security. We still have an army of the unemployed greater than all the rest of the world. Even the middle-class beneficiaries of our present spotty and partial recovery are jittery about it. They aren't at all sure but that some morning they will awake and find it gone. How else can one explain the effusions of the Liberty League and some of the Republican statesmen? There have been no very fundamental changes in the structure of a profit-making society. None seems to be envisaged. Bitter as is the conflict between Republicans and Democrats, both tacitly—and fearfully—rest their hope of the future on the same thing; that is, that the present partial recovery can last for an indefinite time.

6

A Republican Speaks

☆ *Alfred M. Landon of Kansas, the only Republican governor reelected in 1934, was nominated to lead his party's attack on the New Deal in the 1936 campaign. The Republican approach was summarized in Governor Landon's Madison Square Garden speech on October 29, 1936.* * ☆

In direct defiance of the 1932 Democratic platform, which condemned the unsound policy of crop restriction, the triple A was enacted. The triple A restricted agricultural production by 36,000,000 acres.

This administration has rewarded scarcity and penalized plenty. Not only has it failed to correct the basic ills of agriculture, it has added to them. . . .

I know how this program dislocated our agricultural system. I know, for instance, that almost over night, it forced the southern farmer out of cotton into crops competing with the north and west. It led him into dairy farming and the raising of livestock. This affected not only the farmer of the north and west. It also affected the farmer of the south, who lost a large part of his cotton export market. . . .

Government has a moral obligation to help repair the damage caused to the farmer by this administration's destructive experiments. Farming, by its very nature, cannot readjust itself as rapidly as industry to the after effects of eco-

* From press release, "Alfred M. Landon, address at New York City, Madison Square Garden, October 29, 1936."

nomic planning. During the period of readjustment, and until foreign markets are reopened, the government must help the farmer.

We can do this without violating the Constitution. We can do this without imposing such burdens as the processing tax upon the consumer. We can do this within the limits of a balanced budget. . . .

The Republican Party also proposes a sound long-term program of conservation and land use. This is the only permanent solution of the farm problem and is essential to the preservation of the nation's land resources. We propose to stop muddling and meddling and to begin mending. And what does the President mean to do for agriculture? Is he going to continue the policy of scarcity?

The answer is: no one can be sure.

Now let us turn to industry. What was the basic declaration of the Democratic platform of 1932? It was that the antitrust laws—the laws protecting the little fellow from monopoly—should be strengthened and enforced.

And what did the administration do? It created the NRA. This law gives the sanction of government to private monopoly. It indorsed the vicious policy of price-fixing. It disregarded the interest of 130,000,000 Americans as consumers. It attempted to tell every business man, large and small, how to run his business.

The NRA was the direct opposite of the American system of free competition. It was an attempt to supplant American initiative with Washington dictation. And what happened? Monopolies prospered and a little New Jersey pants presser went to jail.

I am against private monopoly. I am against monopolistic practices. I am against monopoly of an all-powerful central government. And while I am President I intend to see that the anti-trust laws are strengthened and enforced without fear or favor.

I intend to see that government bureaucracy never again starts choking business. I intend to see that American initiative has a chance to give jobs to American workers. And I intend to broaden the market for American products by encouraging freer interchange of goods in world trade.

And what program does the President propose for industry? He pays tribute to free initiative at Chicago on a Wednesday and to planned economy at Detroit on a Thursday. One day the President's son says the NRA will be revived. The next day the President's son says it will not. When the President was asked about NRA last Tuesday in a press conference, he said: "You pay your money and you take your choice." What does he mean? The answer is: no one can be sure. . . .

In 1932 the President said 11,000,000 Americans were looking for work. Today, according to the American Federation of Labor, there are still 11,000,000 Americans looking for work. Yet the President boasts of recovery—in one city in terms of a baseball game and in another city in terms of a patient he has cured.

These fellow citizens of ours can and will be re-employed. There is no need for one-fifth of our working population to be condemned to live in an economic world apart. There is work to be done in this country—more than enough to give jobs to all the unemployed. This work will start just as soon as uncertainty in government policies is replaced by confidence.

There can be no confidence when the government is proud of spending more than it takes in. There can be no confidence when the government creates uncertainty about the value of money. There can be no confidence when the government threatens to control every detail of our economic life. There can be no confidence when the government proclaims that the way to have more is to produce less. In short, there can be no confidence while this administration remains in power.

As Chief Executive I intend to follow a course that will restore confidence. I intend to be open and above-board on the policies of my administration. I intend in the task of reconstruction to make use of the best talent available, irrespective of party. I intend to throw out all plans based on scarcity. I intend to put an end to this administration's policy of "try anything once." The time has come for a steady hand at the wheel. And how does the President propose to restore confidence? Another "Breathing-spell?"

The answer is: no one can be sure. . . .

The Democratic platform in 1932 condemned the "improper and excessive use of money in political activities." In defiance of this pledge we have had an outrageous use of public money for political purposes. Public funds appropriated for relief have been used in an attempt to buy the votes of our less fortunate citizens. But it will not do them any good. The votes of the American people are not for sale.

As chief executive I intend to see that relief is purged of politics. There is ample money in this country to take care of those in need. When I am President they will be taken care of. This is the plain will of the American people.

And what does the President propose to do about relief? How does he propose to free the victims of the depression from political exploitation?

The answer is: no one can be sure.

In a highly industrialized society we must provide for the protection of the aged. The present administration claims it has done this through its social security act. But the act does not give security. It is based upon a conception that is fundamentally wrong. It assumes that the American people are so improvident that they must be compelled to save by a paternal government.

Beginning next January 1st, workers, no matter how small their wages, will have their pay docked—they will have their pay docked for the purpose of building up a phantom reserve fund—a fund that any future congress can spend any time it sees fit and for any purpose it sees fit. . . .

The Republican Party proposes to replace this unworkable hodge-podge by a plan that is honest, fair and financially sound. We propose that the funds for security payments shall be provided as we go along. We propose that they shall be obtained from a direct and specific tax, widely distributed. We propose that all American citizens over 65 shall receive whatever additional income is necessary to keep them from need. . . .

And what does the President propose to do about [the payroll deductions]? Is he going to continue a plan that takes money from workers without any assurance that they will get back what they put in?

The answer is: no one can be sure.

Since the NRA was declared unconstitutional—there has been some improvement in business. Since then there has been no reduction in the total of government spending. In the year ending last June the federal government spent nearly nine billion dollars. This is an all-time peace-time high.

We will spend this year over 900 million dollars more for the ordinary routine expenditures of government than in 1934. And we will spend one and one-half billion dollars more for relief than in 1934.

Under this administration 75 new agencies have been created. Two hundred and fifty thousand additional employes have been foisted on the taxpayers. The federal pay roll has reached the staggering sum of one billion 500 million dollars a year. As I said at Chicago, any one at all familiar with what has been going on could almost count on the fingers of one hand foolish experiments the government could cut out and save at least a billion dollars any time it wanted to.

I pledge myself to put an end to extravagance and waste. I pledge myself to stop the policy that glorifies spending. I pledge myself to balance the budget. And what is the President going to do? Is he going to stop his policy of spending for spending's sake?

The answer is: no one can be sure.

I come finally to the underlying and fundamental issue of this campaign. This is the question of whether our American form of government is to be preserved. . . .

The President has been responsible for nine acts declared unconstitutional by the supreme court. He has publicly urged congress to pass a law, even though it had reasonable doubts as to its constitutionality. He has publicly belittled the supreme court of the United States. He has publicly suggested that the Constitution is an outworn document. He has retained in high office men outspoken in their contempt for the American form of government. He has sponsored laws which have deprived states of their constitutional rights. Every one of these actions—and the list is by no means complete—strikes at the heart of the American form of government.

Our Constitution is not a lifeless piece of paper. It is the underlying law of the land and the charter of the liberties of our people. The people, and they alone, gave it life. The people, and they alone, have the right to amend or destroy it. Until the people in their combined wisdom decide to make the change, it is the plain duty of the people's servants to keep within the Constitution. It is the plain meaning of the oath of office that they keep within the Constitution.

Our federal system allows great leeway. But if changes in our civilization make amendment to the Constitution desirable it should be amended. It has been amended in the past. It can be in the future.

I have already made my position clear on this question. I am on record that proper working conditions cannot be regulated by the states. I shall favor a constitutional amendment giving the states the necessary powers.

And what are the intentions of the President with respect to the Constitution.

Does he believe changes are required? If so, will an amendment be submitted to the people, or will he attempt to get around the Constitution by tampering with the supreme court?

The answer is: no one can be sure. . . .

Forty-eight hours from tonight, standing where I am standing, there will be a President of the United States. He will be seeking re-election.

A little more than forty-eight hours after he has spoken, the American people will be streaming to the polls. . . .

I leave a challenge with the President. I say to him: Mr. President, I am willing to trust the people. I am willing to stand up and say openly that I am against economic planning by the government. I am against the principles of the Agricultural Adjustment Act. I am against the concentration of power in the hands of the Chief Executive.

Tell us where you stand, Mr. President. Tell us not in generalities, but clearly so that no one can mistake your meaning. And tell us why you have evaded the issue until the eve of the election.

7

The President Answers

☆ *Franklin D. Roosevelt was renominated by acclamation in 1936. In his campaign speeches, represented by his Madison Square Garden address of October 31, 1936, the President emphasized the achievements of his administration, which, he contended, had greatly benefitted the nation.* * ☆

What was our hope in 1932? Above all other things the American people wanted peace. They wanted peace of mind instead of gnawing fear.

First, they sought escape from the personal terror which had stalked them for three years. They wanted the peace that comes from security in their homes: safety for their savings, permanence in their jobs, a fair profit from their enterprise.

Next, they wanted peace in the community, the peace that springs from the ability to meet the needs of community life: schools, playgrounds, parks, sanitation, highways—those things which are expected of solvent local government. They sought escape from disintegration and bankruptcy in local and state affairs.

They also sought peace within the Nation: protection of their currency, fairer wages, the ending of long hours of toil, the abolition of child labor, the elimination of wild-cat speculation, the safety of their children from kidnappers.

And, finally, they sought peace with other Nations—peace in a world of unrest.

* From *The New York Times*, November 1, 1936.

The Nation knows that I hate war, and I know that the Nation hates war.

I submit to you a record of peace; and on that record a well-founded expectation for future peace—peace for the individual, peace for the community, peace for the Nation, and peace with the world.

Tonight I call the roll—the roll of honor of those who stood with us in 1932 and stand with us today.

Written on it are the names of millions who never had a chance—men at starvation wages, women in sweatshops, children at looms.

Written on it are the names of those who despaired, young men and young women for whom opportunity had become a will-o'-the-wisp.

Written on it are the names of farmers whose acres yielded only bitterness, business men whose books were portents of disaster, home owners who were faced with eviction, frugal citizens whose savings were insecure.

Written there in large letters are the names of countless other Americans of all parties and all faiths, Americans who had eyes to see and hearts to understand, whose consciences were burdened because too many of their fellows were burdened, who looked on these things four years ago and said, "This can be changed. We will change it."

We still lead that army in 1936. They stood with us then because in 1932 they believed. They stand with us today because in 1936 they know. And with them stand millions of new recruits who have come to know.

Their hopes have become our record.

We have not come this far without a struggle and I assure you we cannot go further without a struggle.

For twelve years this Nation was afflicted with hear-nothing, see-nothing, do-nothing Government. The Nation looked to Government but the Government looked away. Nine mocking years with the golden calf and three long years of the scourge! Nine crazy years at the ticker and three long years in the breadlines! Nine mad years of mirage and three long years of despair! Powerful influences strive today to restore that kind of government with its doctrine that that Government is best which is most indifferent.

For nearly four years you have had an Administration which instead of twirling its thumbs has rolled up its sleeves. We will keep our sleeves rolled up.

We had to struggle with the old enemies of peace—business and financial monopoly, speculation, reckless banking, class antagonism, sectionalism, war profiteering.

They had begun to consider the Government of the United States as a mere appendage to their own affairs. We know now that Government by organized money is just as dangerous as Government by organized mob.

Never before in all our history have these forces been so united against one candidate as they stand today. They are unanimous in their hate for me—and I welcome their hatred.

I should like to have it said of my first Administration that in it the forces of selfishness and of lust for power met their match. I should like to have it said of my second Administration that in it these forces met their master. . . .

Only desperate men with their backs to the wall would descend so far below the level of decent citizenship as to foster the current pay-envelope campaign against America's working people. Only reckless men, heedless of consequences, would risk the disruption of the hope for a new peace between worker and employer by returning to the tactics of the labor spy.

Here is an amazing paradox! The very employers and politicians and publishers who talk most loudly of class antagonism and the destruction of the American system now undermine that system by this attempt to coerce the votes of the wage earners of this country. It is the 1936 version of the old threat to close down the factory or the office if a particular candidate does not win. It is an old strategy of tyrants to delude their victims into fighting their battles for them.

Every message in a pay envelope, even if it is the truth, is a command to vote according to the will of the employer. But this propaganda is worse—it is deceit.

They tell the worker his wage will be reduced by a contribution to some vague form of old-age insurance. They carefully conceal from him the fact that for every dollar of premium he pays for that insurance, the employer pays another dollar. That omission is deceit.

They carefully conceal from him the fact that under the federal law, he receives another insurance policy to help him if he loses his job, and that the premium of that policy is paid 100 percent by the employer and not one cent by the worker. They do not tell him that the insurance policy that is bought for him is far more favorable to him than any policy that any private insurance company could afford to issue. That omission is deceit.

They imply to him that he pays all the cost of both forms of insurance. They carefully conceal from him the fact that for every dollar put up by him his employer puts up three dollars—three for one. And that omission is deceit.

But they are guilty of more than deceit. When they imply that the reserves thus created against both these policies will be stolen by some future Congress, diverted to some wholly foreign purpose, they attack the integrity and honor of American Government itself. Those who suggest that, are already aliens to the spirit of American democracy. Let them emigrate and try their lot under some foreign flag in which they have more confidence. . . .

It is because I have sought to think in terms of the whole Nation that I am confident that today, just as four years ago, the people want more than promises.

Our vision for the future contains more than promises. This is our answer to those who, silent about their own plans, ask us to state our objectives.

Of course we will continue to seek to improve working conditions for the workers of America—to reduce hours over-long, to increase wages that spell starvation, to end the labor of children, to wipe out sweatshops. Of course we will continue every effort to end monopoly in business, to support collective bargaining, to stop unfair competition, to abolish dishonorable trade practices. For all these we have only just begun to fight.

Of course we will continue to work for cheaper electricity in the homes and on the farms of America, for better and cheaper transportation, for low interest rates, for sounder home financing, for better banking, for the regulation of security issues, for reciprocal trade among nations, for the wiping out of slums. For all these we have only just begun to fight.

Of course we will continue our efforts in behalf of the farmers of America. With their continued cooperation we will do all in our power to end the piling up of huge surpluses which spelled ruinous prices for their crops. We will persist in successful action for better land use, for reforestation, for the conservation of water all the way from its source to the sea, for drought and flood control, for better marketing facilities for farm commodities, for a definite reduction of farm tenancy, for encouragement of farmer cooperatives, for crop insurance and a stable food supply. For all these we have only just begun to fight.

Of course we will provide useful work for the needy unemployed; we prefer useful work to the pauperism of a dole.

Here and now I want to make myself clear about those who disparage their fellow citizens on the relief rolls. They say that those on relief are not merely jobless—that they are worthless. Their solution for the relief problem is to end relief—to purge the rolls by starvation. To use the language of the stock broker, our needy unemployed would be cared for when, as, and if some fairy godmother should happen on the scene.

You and I will continue to refuse to accept that estimate of our unemployed fellow Americans. Your Government is still on the same side of the street with the Good Samaritan and not with those who pass by on the other side.

Again—what of our objectives?

Of course we will continue our efforts for young men and women so that they may obtain an education and an opportunity to put it to use. Of course we will continue our help for the crippled, for the blind, for the mothers, our insurance for the unemployed, our security for the aged. Of course we will continue to protect the consumer against unnecessary price spreads, against the costs that are added by monopoly and speculation. We will continue our successful efforts to increase his purchasing power and to keep it constant.

For these things, too, and for a multitude of others like them, we have only just begun to fight.

8

The National Labor Policy

☆ *With the demise of the National Industrial Recovery Act in 1935, the Wagner-Connery Act was passed to protect the organizational rights of labor and to provide for the settlement of disputes between unions and management. Upheld by the Supreme Court in 1937, the effectiveness of the Act was tested that same year by serious labor conflicts.* ☆*

In brief terms, this Act provided that in industries which affected "the flow" of interstate commerce, if the workers wished to unionize and bargain collectively or act for purposes of mutual aid, they must be left free to do so in fact as well as in law. That is, employers must agree to bargain exclusively on such basic questions as wages, hours and conditions of employment, with that group which represented the free choice of the majority of the workers. The purposes behind this were at least two: (1) To reduce strikes waged to compel employers to deal collectively with the workers. This had been the primary cause in 18.8 per cent of the strikes between 1881 and 1905, while in 4.5 per cent it had been a contributory cause. From 1919 to 1934 inclusive, it was the primary cause in 24.5 per cent of the strikes. In 1933, it accounted for 29 per cent, and in 1934, according to a classification which was not precisely comparable, 46 per cent. (2) To strengthen unionism as an agency for improving the condition of the workers.

* From Paul H. Douglas, "American Labor Relations Acts," *The American Economic Review,* XXVII (December, 1937), pp. 740-749. Used by permission.

Collective bargaining was not, of course, to be forced upon the workers if they did not want it; but it was to be theirs if a majority actually desired it. . . .

But while the Act provided that the representatives of the majority were to have the exclusive right to represent the workers in such matters as wages, hours and other basic conditions of employment, individual employees and minority groups were, nevertheless, to have "right at any time to present grievances to the employer."

The principle of majority rule, in order to be effective, requires an agency and a method to determine who actually represents the choice of the majority. This power is given by the Act, as it was by the joint resolution of the preceding year, to the National Labor Relations Board. This body is given the power to decide in each case whether "the unit appropriate for the purposes of collective bargaining shall be the employer unit, craft unit, plant unit, or subdivision thereof." It is also authorized in case of a dispute as to where the real majority lies to hold a hearing on the matter and either to "take a secret ballot of employees, or utilize any other suitable method to ascertain such representatives." . . .

In addition to this, certain of the powers formerly possessed by employers which could be used by them to prevent their employees from unionizing and bargaining collectively, were declared to be "unfair labor practices," in which it was illegal for them to indulge and from which they could be restrained. As is well known, these unfair practices are five in number—namely, for an employer:

(1) To refuse to bargain collectively with the authorized representatives of his employees. This provision helps to transform the nominal right of the workers to collective bargaining into an effective right. For when the majority of the workers demanded such a right, it was made obligatory upon the employers in the included industries to accord it.

(2) "To interfere with, restrain or coerce employees" in the exercise of their right to unionize and bargain collectively.

(3) To encourage or discourage membership in any labor organization by "discrimination in regard to hire or tenure of employment or any term or condition of employment."

These two latter prohibitions struck at the employers' power to use his control over a worker's job as a means of preventing or deterring him from unionizing and trying to bargain collectively. They aimed to free the worker so that he could exercise his legal rights without the fear that he would, therefore, be subject to discrimination or discharge. An employer was, of course, still free to discharge workers on other grounds, provided that these were genuine and not fictitious reasons; but he could not do so for union membership or activity. These clauses also obviously outlawed the yellow-dog contract whether in an explicit or implicit form.

Closed-shop agreements made with bona fide labor organizations representing a majority of the employees were, however, exempted from the provision of the above prohibition, provided that the labor organization was not established, maintained, or assisted in any way by the employer.

(4) "To dominate or interfere with the formation of any labor organization or contribute financial or other support to it." This was to enable the workers to select their own representatives and to choose such type of organization as they deemed best. The employer was to keep his hands off. . . .

(5) "To discharge or otherwise discriminate against an employee because he had filed charges or given testimony under the Act." This prohibition was obviously needed if the Act was to be effective.

A previous crucial weakness in both the National Labor Board, which operated in connection with Section 7A of the NRA, and the first National Labor Relations Board, had been that they were virtually destitute of any effective means for enforcing their decisions. A big step toward meeting this difficulty was made by granting to the Labor Relations Board the same powers of issuing cease and desist orders (Sec. 10) which had been fairly successfully used by the Federal Trade Commission in connection with unfair trade practices. It could do so only after a complaint had been made to it and a hearing had been held before the Board or a representative of it. After reviewing the testimony and such further evidence or arguments as it adjudged proper, the Board could then issue its orders. If the employer was found guilty of an unfair labor practice, a cease and desist order could be issued against him. The Board could also require him to take certain affirmative actions. These would include the reinstatement of employees either with or without back pay as the Board might decide, who had been discharged or discriminated against in violation of the provisions of the Act. It might also, of course, order an election within an appropriate jurisdiction and certify a group as the chosen representative of the majority of the workers.

To lend effective strength to its decision, the Board could ask the federal Circuit Court of Appeals in the district in which the offense took place for an enforcing order. The Court was ordinarily to consider only objections which had been argued before the Board; and the Board's findings of fact, "if supported by evidence," were to be conclusive. Similarly, an aggrieved party had the right of equal recourse to the courts. In both cases, however, such resort to the courts was not to constitute a stay of the Board's order unless specifically ordered by the Court. If the rulings of the Court were disobeyed, the violators could be punished under the procedure of contempt of court. The Board was given full investigatory powers (Sec. 11), and anyone who resisted, impeded, or interfered with any member of the Board or one of its agents was liable to fine or imprisonment or both (Sec. 12). The Board itself was to consist of three members appointed by the President for overlapping terms of five years.

Two final features should be noted. The first was that it was expressly stated (Sec. 13) that the Act should not be construed in any way "so as to interfere or impede or diminish the right to strike." The second (Sec. 2) was that workers out on strike or locked out, and those discharged because of an unfair labor practice who had not obtained "regular and substantially equivalent employment," were still to be considered employees and hence could claim the protection of the Act.

For over a year and a half after the Board was set up, its decisions were ineffective because of a common belief that the Act would be declared unconstitutional and because large numbers of injunctions were obtained from the courts by employers which restrained the Board from putting its rulings into effect. After the favorable opinions by the Supreme Court in 1937, the Board was, however, able to obtain a respectable degree of compliance, while the volume of cases which poured in upon it enormously increased. . . .

Another issue which is given to the Board to settle is that of the unit appropriate to collective bargaining. This, as stated, may be on the basis of a common employer, a common craft, a common plant, or a subdivision thereof. This obviously gives to the Board the power of determining jurisdiction. It has naturally sought to avoid this issue wherever possible and to throw the determination in these instances back upon the independent labor movement. But in view of the struggle for supremacy between the A.F. of L. and the C.I.O., this issue cannot always be avoided. The Board has stated that in all such decisions as to the proper unit, it is guided by (1) the history of labor relations in the industry and between the employer and his employees, (2) the degree of common skill possessed, (3) functional coherence, (4) the degree of mutual interest between the employees, (5) the degree of uniformity of the wage, (6) the organization of the employer's business, (7) the form of self-organization among the workers, and (8) the eligibility to membership in a labor organization. The Board, however, states that "the precise weight to be given to any one of these factors cannot be mathematically stated"; and since several of these criteria may in specific cases be diametrically opposed, the conclusion seems clear that it has large discretionary powers concerning the much mooted question of craft versus industrial unionism, and that it can make its decisions according to its own beliefs in the desirability of one form of representation as compared with another—tempered by the realities of the relative distribution of the economic and political power as between the A.F. of L. and the C.I.O. This possibility was in fact foreseen by certain of the A.F. of L. leaders and accounted for certain reservations which they held concerning the Act. It is probable that the A.F. of L. would now like to amend the Act to provide explicitly as in the Railway Labor act that a majority of each craft must decide upon its own representation. This would prevent industrial unionism except where a majority of each craft agreed.

In dealing with the question of "restraint, interference, or coercion," the Board has ruled that espionage practised upon union activities by employers constituted such action. "Nothing," the Board has stated, "is more calculated to interfere with, restrain, and coerce employees in the exercise of their right to self-organization than such activity. Even where no discharges result, the information obtained by means of espionage is invaluable to the employer and can be used in a variety of ways to break a union." The "slugging" of union organizers, members, and officials, under general direction from the management also clearly constitutes coercion, as does the hiring of men to worm their way into union offices and then use their position to break up and weaken the organization.

A twilight zone of uncertainty, however, seems to exist as to how far employers may carry through general propaganda to deter their workers from associating themselves with an outside union. In general, the decisions seem to hold that employers or their representatives should not (1) threaten employees with reprisals for union membership or activity, or (2) put too much pressure upon them in individual interviews, or (3) unduly vilify unions or their leaders. In a recent case, the Board has approved an order directing an employer to desist from "carrying on propaganda by the publication of newspaper advertisements or otherwise against union activities" and "from in any manner inducing and causing citizens, civic bodies, or public officials and their supervisory employees to interfere with, restrain, or coerce their employees in the exercise of the rights guaranteed in Section 7 of the Act."

When a strike or lockout occurs, the workers involved must still be regarded as employees and must be reinstated by the employers if requested by the workers or their representatives. Nor could the employers, moreover, make their offer of re-employment conditional upon the striker's or locked-out worker's giving up membership in a union.

9

The Court Fight

☆ *In February of 1937, Roosevelt proposed a reorganization of the Federal judiciary. Bitter controversy arose over the provision to permit the President to appoint an additional justice, up to a total of six, for each member who declined to retire upon reaching the age of 70½. As a result of this opposition the President's court plan was emasculated in Congress.** ☆

Three principal arguments have been advanced in behalf of the President's plan to alter the personnel of the Supreme Court by act of Congress. First, it is said that the present court is obstructing orderly social progress by its practice of invalidating necessary measures enacted by the Administration. Second, it is claimed that in the last election the President received a virtual mandate to put an end to this situation, even though he did not propose or discuss his present method of doing it. Third, it is asserted that the President has chosen the wisest course of action available to him in the circumstances.

I

As for the first of these arguments, the argument that the court is blocking social progress, the record shows that eight laws enacted by the Roosevelt Administration have been held unconstitutional. These eight laws are:

1. A measure providing for the con-

* From The Editors, "The President's Plan," *The New York Times*, IV, February 14, 1937.

version of building and loan associations to Federal charters.

2. A measure which was never on the Administration's own program, but which was forced on it through a filibuster staged by Huey Long, providing for a moratorium on farm mortgages.

3. A measure which the President said was "crudely drawn" and which was signed by him only after "a difficult decision," providing for the payment of railway pensions.

4. An act, known as the Municipal Bankruptcy Act, of which practically no use was ever made.

5. A "hot oil" law for the petroleum industry, which dealt with a situation which is no longer present.

6. **The law creating NRA,** a statute held to be flagrantly unconstitutional by a unanimous Supreme Court, including its three stanch liberals, precisely at the time when Congress was preparing to discard the measure anyway.

7. AAA, which has been both defended and denounced at length, but which

was in any case a pre-drought measure for the prevention of farm surpluses which do not exist at present.

8. The Guffey Coal Act, which established a "little NRA" for the bituminous coal industry, with provisions which included wages-and-hours regulations.

In addition to these eight measures, there are two others which may be held unconstitutional at the present session of the court. One is the Public Utility Act of 1935, a measure whose "death sentence clause" has been criticized by many reasonable people as high-handed and confiscatory. The other is the Wagner Labor Relations Act, an admittedly partisan measure, drawn solely in the interest of a single group and of so little practical value that the Government itself made no use of it in the case of the most important labor controversy to arise since the passage of the act.

It must be said, of course, that this list does not include the New York Minimum Wage Law, a measure held to be unconstitutional in a regrettable 5-to-4 decision handed down last June. But this decision involved a State law, not an enactment of the Roosevelt Administration, and it is reasonable to believe that the normal process of change in the court's membership will alter its position on such State legislation at an early date. The switch of a single vote would be sufficient for this purpose.

Of the Roosevelt Administration's own program, it is fair to say that the eight measures which have been declared unconstitutional, and the two which may be held unconstitutional at the present session, are not the measures which have won the President the support of many thoughtful, middle-of-the-road progressives. Doubtless these measures have appealed to various "blocs" and factions.

But it is difficult to believe that, for the nation as a whole, they really represent the best work of the Roosevelt Administration—work to be placed on a par with such statesmanlike achievements as its foreign policy, its reciprocal trade agreements, its revision of the banking laws, its reorganization of the Federal Reserve System, its regulation of the Stock Exchanges, its control of the issuance of securities, its social security legislation, its brilliant handling of the bank panic.

It is still more difficult to believe that the social progress of the country has really been obstructed by the invalidation of a particular group of eight measures, some of which were forced on the Administration against its will, some of which dealt with situations no longer in existence, some of which were seldom used, and some of which achieved in the long run the intense unpopularity and the widespread disregard which characterized the last days of NRA.

II

The President apparently having reached a different conclusion, we come to the second argument: namely, the question of his "mandate."

Those who hold that he received a mandate in the last election for his present plan do not attempt to argue that the Democratic platform embodied the proposal he now offers, or to assert that the President himself so much as mentioned this plan on a single occasion during the entire course of his campaign. Rather, they rely upon one or the other of two deductions: either they say that the country must have known that the President would change the personnel of the Supreme Court in any case, in the event of his re-election, as rapidly as its present members died, retired or resigned, or else they say that the Republicans repeatedly charged that the President would do something of the kind that he has now done, and that they thereby made the issue for him.

So far as the first theory is concerned, the President has now shown that he is unwilling to wait for the present members of the court to die, retire or resign. As for the second theory, it must be said that a mandate achieved by the process of failing to reply to the accusation of an adversary is circuitously obtained.

One thing can be said with certainty: the President has no mandate for this plan from those who would have withheld their support from him in the last election had they known during the campaign that he would subsequently pursue this course.

III

The third argument in behalf of the President's proposal is that it represents the wisest and least dangerous course of action available to him in the present circumstances. From this opinion we dissent. The wisest course for Mr. Roosevelt to follow was the course which this newspaper ventured on more than one occasion to hope that he would follow during his second Administration. This course, as it seemed clearly to be indicated both by the needs of the occasion and by the President's own apparent recognition of these needs, was to consolidate as effectively as possible the gains of the recovery movement; to perfect the many

reforms and innovations already introduced, before risking new adventures; to rid the President's office of the vast, unhealthy "war powers" vested in it during the emergency of the depression, rather than to seek still further powers; to restore the normal processes of democratic government in this country, after the storm of 1929 to 1933, by decentralizing the heavily overcentralized authority of government and by strengthening once more the traditional American system of checks and balances.

That course was the wisest course for the President to pursue. It is not a course from which he was swerved by influences beyond his control. For it is difficult to believe that the present Congress could force on the President a major policy objectionable to him, by a two-thirds vote overriding a Presidential veto.

If, however, Mr. Roosevelt chose to propose a change in the Constitution or the court, a constitutional amendment giving the country an opportunity to express an opinion directly on the question would have been preferable to the plan which he has followed. There would have been certain inevitable dangers in any amendment which might have been proposed. But at least this method would have had the merit of meeting the issue squarely, without exposing the Administration to the charge that it has sought to solve a great constitutional question by resort to political cleverness.

10

The New Deal: An Appraisal

☆ *In the following selection, economic historian Broadus Mitchell observes that there was no sharp break between the methods of Hoover and Roosevelt in dealing with the depression. In viewing the flow of policy under the two presidents the experimental nature of government operations during the great economic crisis is highlighted.* * ☆

The Hoover treatment of the depression was founded on outmoded tenets, false optimism, and inertia. This approach was not due simply to Hoover's attachment to the sufficiency—almost the sacredness—of free economic forces. Time was a factor. The experience of business exuberance was so fresh. Coolidge had shown, or so it was felt, that government could coast while prosperity smiled all around. Hoover, so auspiciously placed in the driver's seat, had no need to use the engine, for the car gathered speed. The sudden blowout left all with a sense, mocking though it was, of continued forward motion.

Much that was later ascribed to Roosevelt daring was made possible by instructive observation of Hoover's failure. Roosevelt in his first campaign was not so far ahead of Hoover, in the seriousness of his apprehensions or the boldness of his proposals, as his later policies imply. Nor was Hoover's reaction to the depression all of a piece. Reluctantly but stead-

* From Broadus Mitchell, *Depression Decade, From New Era through New Deal, 1929-1941*, pp. 404-407. Copyright, 1947, by Rinehart and Company, New York. Used by permission of Holt, Rinehart and Winston, Inc.

ily, as forced by circumstances, he departed from his predilections, devising numerous government aids to recovery. As more or less developed, not a few of these were patterned after by the New Deal. Hoover's still waters ran deeper than he has been given credit for. Relative to the period and the party, Hoover was experimental and adaptable. The moratorium on intergovernmental debts was a courageous stroke. The Federal Farm Board plainly pointed to the more effectual curbing of agricultural surpluses. Federal relief to the states was small in amount but big in what it portended. The Reconstruction Finance Corporation was taken over bodily by the New Deal, expanded in function during the remaining depression years, and grew into even greater vigor in the war economy.

Still, Hoover never grasped the magnitude of the problem or summoned resources to meet it. His inhibitions while in office, if not proved then, spoke loud in his criticisms of his successor.

Roosevelt, called upon to lead just when the banking crisis had rapidly matured, lacked plans but possessed what was of greater immediate importance—a superb purpose. Confident of his own powers, he poured strength into the people. His inaugural assurance was a moral triumph, outweighing in influence the legislative improvisations of the next "hundred days." Someone has said that economic law is what a country decides it wants. The aphorism was illustrated then. Hearts beat again, minds went to work. There was a grandeur in the promise, albeit not always borne out in the performance.

Roosevelt's course falls, roughly, into four stages: (1) Intimate government participation in banking, currency management, industry, and agriculture. Erring bankers were reproached; the currency was cut loose from gold and controlled for national ends; industry and labor, through NRA, were drawn into a partnership with government which had collusive as well as merely cooperative features; staple crops were restricted when the AAA paid farmers not to produce. Other projects were included, such as more generous federal relief through CWA, FERA, and WPA. This effort, or combination of efforts, came to an end with the Banking Act of 1935 and the revolt of the Supreme Court when it invalidated NRA and AAA. The President's stigmatic "horse and buggy" outburst and his thwarted attempt suddenly to change the composition of the Court were expressions of disappointment followed by a change of tack.

(2) The next stage, 1935-1937, took the wind on a new quarter, but the sails of government were to be filled by the same breeze of higher prices at all costs. The NRA was a wreck and had to be abandoned, but the AAA was patched up and still served its turn, while fiscal freedom had been happily vouchsafed by liberal Supreme Court decisions covering currency powers. Though government was no longer allowed to be the partner of business, it could and must be the patron of business. The method was to support private enterprise, even superseding it where necessary, through robust spending and lending. This was the period of "pump priming," as it was fondly called, the instruments being RFC subventions, and vast public works including TVA and public housing.

This was the high tide of the New Deal in its recovery rather than its reform phase. Perhaps the administration lacked the courage of its convictions. Maybe the doubts which it developed were the results of the cries of those alarmed over deficits. More likely the New Dealers concluded from the gratifying business indexes that the spend-lend pump priming had turned the trick, that the depression was conquered, and that therefore the government could resign its efforts. Whatever be the case, expectations were premature. The "recession" or relapse of the autumn of 1937 was bitterly disappointing to New Dealers and, in the eyes of the critics, discredited the policies used.

(3) The President and his strategists, never committed to consistency, recovered poise faster than did the country. Refusing to resume their price-raising program, or to deprecate it as having been a mistaken policy on their part, they pretended innocence of the error, and sent up a hue and cry after the culprits, now designated as private concentrations of economic power which deserve to be exposed and prosecuted. One miscreant had donned tunic and badge of policeman, and pointed to the others—monopolies and all their cohorts—as the public enemies. This was the New Deal's nimblest shift of role. The solemn investigation by the Temporary National Economic Committee into the evil lapse of competition was the sequel. This third policy of the New Deal in attacking the depression was at length abandoned in mingled minor chagrin and major relief of mind.

(4) The passing embarrassment was

caused by the fact that chief inquisitors into the wickedness of price and production control scampered from the committee hearings to assume command [in 1941] of [the] O[ffice of] P[rice] A[dministra-tion] and Emergency Management. And a vast anxiety was overcome because to the benefits of the "arsenal of democracy" had been added America's full engagement in World War II.

11

A View of the Future

☆ *One of the most popular exhibits at the 1939 New York World's Fair was the Futurama display which depicted American life in 1960, in dramatic contrast to a society still blighted by the depression. The following selection is a report of that exhibit** ☆

On an early June afternoon in 1960, the trees of the U.S. are still green and the wheat yellow. The sun shines; night must fall; people are being born and eating and sleeping and dying. But the works of man are subtly or spectacularly different. The land is really greener than it was in 1939. Strip planting protects the valley fields against erosion. Federal laws forbid the wanton cutting of wooded hillsides. Dams and canals prevent freshets and floods. Men love their fields and gardens better and more wisely. Fewer acres, intensively and chemically cultivated, feed all the citizens of the U.S. More of the surface of the land is in forest and park.

These great parklands of America in that June of 1960 are full of a tanned and vigorous people who in 20 years have learned how to have fun. They camp in the forests and hike along the upcountry roads with their handsome wives and children. The college class of 1910 is out there hiking, half its members alive and very fit. They swarm into planetaria to see the cosmos. Great telescopes show them 100 times more than the men of 1939

saw in the sky. On the earth, these people do not care much for possessions. They are not attached to their own homes and home towns, because trains, express highways (and of course planes) get them across America in 24 hours. They have their choice of all America for their two-month vacations. Some own cars or trailers; some hire cars at their destinations. When they drive off, they get to the great parklands on giant express highways. . . .

The two-way [highway] skein . . . consists of four 50-m.p.h. lanes on the outer edges; two pairs of 75-m.p.h. lanes and in the center, two lanes for 100-m.p.h. express traffic. Cars change from lane to lane at specified intervals, on signal from spaced control towers which can stop and start all traffic by radio. Being out of its drivers' control, each car is safe against accident. When two such highways cross . . . the high-speed lanes go straight ahead; the low-speed make both left and right turns to get on the other highway. These are raised or depressed, taking less space than in the cloverleaf pattern of 1939's highway crossings. Notice that there is no bottleneck. All cars keep going at least 50 m.p.h. on all turns. The cars, built like raindrops, are powered by

* From "America in 1960," *Life*, VI (June 5, 1939), p. 81. Courtesy *Life;* copyright 1939 Time Inc.

rear engines that are probably improvements of the Diesel. Inside, they are air-conditioned. They cost as low as $200. Off the highway, the driver dawdles again at his own speed and risk.

The highways skirt the great cities. . . . But the happiest people live in one-factory farm-villages producing one small industrial item and their own farm produce.

Behind this visible America of 1960, hidden in the laboratories, are the inventors and engineers. By the spring of 1939 they had cracked nearly every frontier of progress and waited on unwieldy, cautious industry to feed their inventions to the people. Liquid air is by 1960 a potent, mobile source of power. Atomic energy is being used cautiously. Power is transmitted by radio beams, focused by gold reflectors. These great new powers make life in 1960 immensely easier. Such new alloys as heat-treated beryllium bronze give perfect service. Cures for cancer and infantile paralysis have extended man's life span and his wife's skin is still perfect at the age of 75. Architecture and plane construction have been revolutionized by light, noninflammable, strong plastics from soybeans. Houses are light, graceful, easily replaced. The Lanova Cell has made all gasoline motors Diesels. Electronic microscopes literally see everything.

On every front America in 1960 knows more about unleashing the best energies in its citizens. Nearly everyone is a high-school graduate. The talented get the best education in the world. More people are interested in life, the world, themselves and in making a better world. The people of 1939 are still very much alive, pitting their old prejudices and fears against the new world. Politics and emotion still slow progress. But these obstructions are treated with dwindling patience in 1960. America's appetite has been whettened by its widening realization of what somber, courageous planning can do.

12

War: A Spur to Recovery?

☆ *In 1939, the American industrial machine was still sputtering. The coming of war in Europe, however, in September of 1939, brought an influx of orders for war material which stimulated the American economy and offered hope of complete recovery from depression.** ☆

There never was a year in which business had less confidence, or in which industry moved faster.

The year 1940 opened and closed in gloom. Around Labor Day 1939, Business had begun to prepare for big orders. Assuming that World War II would resume where World War I had stopped, manufacturers started buying frantically from each other in order to be ready. The FRB production index headed straight up; then—when the export orders failed to materialize—it dived. So 1940 opened to the twinge of a familiar business headache: inventory trouble, just like stagnant 1938's.

Suddenly everything changed. First Finland, then the rest of Scandinavia was blocked off. The price of unbleached sudfite pulp in the U.S. jumped $6.60 a ton. Two months later, with Holland, Belgium and France gone, and Italy in, the U.S. had lost an export market (including Scandinavia) amounting to $568,000,000 in 1939. The stockmarket broke 35 points from May 1 to June 15, lay paralyzed with

fear. But the U.S. swung into the greatest production boom in its history.

The signal for it came not from Business, but from events. Within 15 days of France's fall, the Army & Navy began to dump orders of $41,000,000 a day in industry's lap. The important fact about these orders was that they were for capital goods. For the first time in more than a decade, industry's prime mover—capital-goods expansion—agitated the indexes again. The steel rate soared from 60 per cent of capacity (April) to 92 per cent in September. At 11:30 p.m., on Dec. 9, steelworkers finishing the second shift also finished an era. They cast the year's 60,835,000th ton of ingots, and thereby put 1940 ahead of the previous peak steel year of 1929. The FRB production index, its base broadened by FRB statisticians in August, touched its all-time high two months later, kept on going up. Confidence was not an issue; the only issue was production, and that fast.

There were three striking paradoxes of the 1940 boom:

1) For the first time in ten years, unemployment ceased to be U. S. Problem No. 1. Yet even this month there were still

some 8,000,000 unemployed. At the same time, many industries complained of a skilled-labor shortage. Perhaps, like Britain, the U. S. could not absorb all its unemployed because its industrial mobilization never would be complete.

2) Agriculture is the one sector of the U. S. economy that depends heavily on exports. Farm crops were also the chief U. S. export which, in 1940, the rest of the world could not buy. Many farm surpluses in 1940 were higher than ever; for farm prices, "parity" remained just a slogan. Yet farm income for the year was estimated at $9 billions, highest since 1937. Thanks were due less to the production boom than to Government aid of $1,300,-000,000.

3) Eeriest paradox of all was Wall Street. A capital-goods boom was under way with almost no help at all from private investment. The corporate securities markets did $1,666,805,000 of refundings during eleven months of 1940, but raised only $660,799,000 of new money. As the year ended, Wall Street, its best barometer, was huddled in the storm cellar with Confidence.

Reason for this was plain. Despite the production boom, nothing Business really wanted had been achieved. Taxes, far from easing, were made tougher by an excess-profits tax and likely to grow more so. Government spending was multiplied; the 76th Congress appropriated more than $17 billions. Interest rates on capital continued to fall. The National Labor Relations Board underwent a personnel shakeup, but Wagner Act modification was less likely than ever. Government regulation in general, previously little more than a list of "Don'ts," began to turn into positive control. Every well-editorialized reason why Business should hold back was more conspicuous than ever. Knowing the economic consequences of war, businessmen naturally disliked the defense boom. They were swept downstream almost against their will, steering as cautiously as they could. They ploughed their profits back into debt retirement or new plant, drove good bargains with the Government in answer to its demands for industrial expansion. When the boom ends, this caution may help Business to face a buyer's market with efficient plant, low overhead—may ease post-war adjustments. But the engine of industry did not speed up because of confidence burning within. It was sped up from without by the energy of wartime economy. Not moneymen but politicos had started it, and supplied the power to keep it going.

the illusion of peace (1920-1931)

AMERICAN participation in World War I had not produced the kind of world envisioned by Wilson, and Senate rejection of the Versailles Treaty heralded a reaction against involvement in European affairs. Disillusion over the crusade in Europe, increased naval competition, and tension in the Far East led to the Washington Conference on Limitation of Armaments in 1921. The delegates, greeted by a startling American proposal to destroy a number of vessels and establish a ratio of naval strength between the major powers, finally imposed limitations on capital ships and aircraft carriers, and provided for a maintenance of the status quo in the Far East through the Four-Power and Nine-Power treaties. Unfortunately, naval competition was soon resumed in auxiliary ships, namely, cruisers, destroyers, and submarines. The abortive Geneva Naval Conference of 1927 failed to settle the problem, though the Kellogg-Briand Pact of 1928, wherein the signatory nations renounced war as an instrument of national policy, furnished a basis for further negotiation on disarmament. At the London Naval Conference of 1930 agreement was reached among the United States, Great Britain, and Japan on a limitation of all naval vessels, but no one could forsee the effect of the treaty on subsequent Japanese activities.

The dislocations and settlements of World War I demanded a new affirmation of American foreign policy, and in 1923 Secretary of State Charles Evans Hughes delivered a comprehensive summation of the nation's aims in Europe, Latin America, and the Far East. Basing his position on the Monroe Doctrine, The Open Door, and the territorial integrity of China, Hughes clearly defined American responsibilities in terms of traditional policies. Yet the problems facing the country were not traditional. World War I had transformed the United States from a debtor to a creditor nation, and adjustments in American economic policies appeared necessary to enable foreign nations to pay their debts and continue trade. But the Hawley-Smoot

Act of 1930 raised duties even higher, stimulated retaliatory tariffs, and added to growing antagonism among nations. Another result of the war was the creation of a Communist regime in Russia, and Senator William E. Borah insisted that the estrangement of that huge country inhibited efforts toward peace and international understanding.

Under the guise of the Monroe Doctrine, and especially of the so-called Roosevelt Corollary, the United States government had continued to interfere in the internal affairs of certain Latin American nations. Hoover, however, was to begin a gradual shift from the principle of intervention to an acknowledgment of the sovereignty and integrity of Western Hemisphere nations. This retreat from paternalistic imperialism in favor of a Good Neighbor attitude marked another return to traditional American foreign policy.

1

Unregenerate Europe

☆ *The American reaction to World War I and the reconstruction that followed revealed a deep suspicion of the motives of European powers. Many people agreed that the United States should hold itself aloof from European affairs until it was given satisfactory evidence that those nations were willing to work for peace.** ☆

It is natural that pacifists and excited humanitarians should stress the evil consequences of the world war at this time. It is equally natural that foreign statesmen and public agencies should join them in keeping this phase of the European situation before us. It gives a tremendous momentum to the pacifist propaganda, and it relieves the governments and peoples of Europe of a large part of their responsibility for the present condition of their affairs.

But the American mind should clear itself on this point. No one will deny that the war is responsible directly for a vast wastage of life and property. But what needs recognition and emphasis at this moment, and from the very beginning of the conference, is that had common sense and self-control governed the policies of the governments and the sentiments of the peoples of Europe their affairs would not be tottering now on the rim of chaos.

On the contrary, were there wisdom and courage in the statesmanship of Europe, were there the same selfless devotion in chancelleries and parliaments as was ex-

* From The Editors, "Unregenerate Europe," *The Chicago Tribune*, November 13, 1921. Used by permission.

hibited on the battlefield, Europe would have been today well on the way to recovery.

The expenditures of the war and the intensification of long existing animosities and jealousies undoubtedly have complicated the problems of statecraft and of government. Undoubtedly the temporary depletion of man power and the temporary exhaustion of body and spirit among the war worn peoples were a burden which recovery has had to assume. Undoubtedly the wastage of wealth and diversion of productive agencies were a handicap to expeditious restoration.

But that these are chiefly responsible for the present state of Europe we do not admit and the future judgment of history, we are confident, will deny.

It is chiefly the folly which has been persistently demonstrated by governments and people since the war that is responsible for Europe's condition today. It is because the moment hostilities ceased and the enemy was disarmed, victors and vanquished turned their backs on the healing and constructive principles they had solemnly asserted from time to time when matters were going against them at the battle front, that the European nations almost without exception have been going down hill. There never in history has been a more perfect illustration of the ancient sarcasm: "When the devil is sick, the devil a monk would be; when the devil is well, the devil a monk is he."

If we wish to know why Europe is in the present state, we cannot do better than to draw a parallel between the assertions of purpose and principle of the allies and "associated" powers in 1916, '17, and '18, and what has actually happened since Nov. 11, 1918.

The war was a gigantic folly and waste. No one will deny that. But it was not so foolish nor so wasteful as the peace which has followed it. The European governments, those who come at our invitation and those who remain away, would have us believe they were mere victims of the war. They say nothing of what the war did for them. We might remind them that they profited as well as lost by the war. Many of them were freed from age long tyranny. They got rid of kaisers and saber clattering aristocracies. They were given freedom, and their present state shows how little they have known how to profit by it. They have been given new territories and new resources, and they have shown how little they deserve their good fortune. The last three years in Europe have been given not to sane efforts to heal wounds, remove hostilities, develop cooperation for the common economic restoration which is essential to the life of each. On the contrary, they have been marked by new wars and destruction, by new animosities and rivalries, by a refusal to face facts, make necessary sacrifices and compromises for financial and economic recovery, by greedy grabbing of territory and new adventures in the very imperialism which brought about the war.

It is well for Americans and their representatives to keep this in mind. The appeal to America's disinterestedness is unfairly fortified by the assumption that Europe is the innocent victim of one egotist's or one nation's ruthless ambition. We can take due account of the disastrous effects of the Prussian effort at dominance, but that should not overshadow the stubborn errors which began over again on the very threshold of peace, and which have made the peace more destructive than the war. When the European governments and peoples are ready to make a real peace, which cannot arrive until they give over the policies and attitudes that produced the world war, America will then not fail to give generous aid. But America would be foolish to contribute to the support of present methods or give any encouragement to the spirit which now prevails in the old world.

2

The Washington Conference 1921-1922

☆ *The Washington Conference on Limitation of Armaments met on November 12, 1921, to consider the limitation of naval armaments and problems concerning the Pacific and the Far East. The extent of agreements to reduce capital ships and aircraft carriers was probably greater than had been anticipated, although restrictions were not placed on other types of warships. Despite a desire to avoid involvement in European affairs, the United States demonstrated a willingness to cooperate in maintaining peace in the Far East.* ☆

(a) SECRETARY HUGHES' INITIAL PROPOSAL FOR NAVAL DISARMAMENT*

In the public discussions which have preceded the conference there have been apparently two competing views; one, that the consideration of armament should await the result of the discussion of Far Eastern questions, and another, that the latter discussion should be postponed until an agreement for limitation of armament has been reached. I am unable to find sufficient reason for adopting either of these extreme views. I think that it would be most unforunate if we should disappoint the hopes which have attached to this meeting by a postponement of the consideration of the first subject. The world looks to this conference to relieve humanity of the crushing burden created by competition in armament, and it is the view of the American Government that we should meet that expec-

* November 12, 1921. From *A Compliation of the Messages and Papers of the Presidents,* XVIII, pp. 9045, 9048-9049. Published by Bureau of National Literature, Inc., New York.

tation without any unnecessary delay. It is therefore proposed that the conference should proceed at once to consider the question of the limitation of armament. . . .

I am happy to say that I am at liberty to go beyond . . . general propositions, and on behalf of the American delegation, acting under the instructions of the President of the United States, to submit to you a concrete proposition for an agreement for the limitation of naval armament. . . .

In making the present proposal the United States is most solicitous to deal with the question upon an entirely reasonable and practicable basis, to the end that the just interests of all shall be adequately guarded and that national security and defense shall be maintained. Four general principles have been applied:

(1) That all capital-ship building programs, either actual or projected, should be abandoned;

(2) That further reduction should be made through the scrapping of certain of the older ships;

(3) That in general regard should be had to the existing naval strength of the Powers concerned;

(4) That the capital-ship tonnage should be used as the measurement of strength for navies and proportionate allowance of auxiliary combatant craft prescribed.

The principal features of the proposed agreement are as follows:

CAPITAL SHIPS
UNITED STATES

The United States is now completing its program of 1916 calling for ten new battleships and six battle cruisers. One battleship has been completed. The others are in various stages of construction; in some cases from 60 to over 80 per cent of the construction has been done. On these fifteen capital ships now being built over $330,000,000 have been spent. Still the United States is willing in the interest of an immediate limitation of naval armament to scrap all of these ships.

The United States proposes if this plan is accepted—

(1) To scrap all capital ships now under construction. This includes six battle cruisers and seven battleships on the ways and in course of building, and two battleships launched.

The total number of new capital ships thus to be scrapped is fifteen. The total tonnage of the new capital ships when completed would be 618,000 tons.

(2) To scrap all of the older battleships up to, but not including, the *Delaware* and *North Dakota*. The number of these old battleships to be scrapped is fifteen. Their total tonnage is 227,740 tons.

Thus the number of capital ships to be scrapped by the United States, if this plan is accepted, is thirty, with an ag-

gregate tonnage (including that of ships in construction, if completed) of 845,740 tons.

GREAT BRITAIN

The plan contemplates that Great Britain and Japan shall take action which is fairly commensurate with this action on the part of the United States.

It is proposed that Great Britain—

(1) Shall stop further construction on the four new Hoods, the new capital ships not laid down but upon which money has been spent. These four ships, if completed, would have tonnage displacement of 172,000 tons.

(2) Shall, in addition, scrap her predreadnaughts, second-line battleships, and first-line battleships up to, but not including, the *King George V class*.

These, with certain predreadnaughts which it is understood have already been scrapped, would amount to nineteen capital ships and a tonnage reduction of 411,-375 tons.

The total tonnage of ships thus to be scrapped by Great Britain (including the tonnage of the four Hoods, if completed) would be 583,375 tons.

JAPAN

It is proposed that Japan—

(1) Shall abandon her program of ships not yet laid down, viz., the *Kii, Owari, No. 7* and *No. 8* battleships, and *Nos. 5 6, 7,* and *8* battle cruisers.

It should be observed that this does not involve the stopping of construction, as the construction of none of these ships has been begun.

(2) Shall scrap three capital ships (the *Mutsu* launched, the *Tosa,* and *Kago* in course of building) and four battle cruisers (the *Amagi* and *Akagi* in course of building, and the *Atoga* and *Takao* not yet laid down, but for which certain material has been assembled).

The total number of new capital ships to be scrapped under this paragraph is seven. The total tonnage of these new capital ships when completed would be 289,100 tons.

(3) Shall scrap all predreadnaughts and battleships of the second line. This would include the scrapping of all ships up to, but not including, the *Settsu*; that is, the scrapping of ten older ships, with a total tonnage of 159,828 tons.

The total reduction of tonnage on vessels existing, laid down, or for which material has been assembled (taking the tonnage of the new ships when completed), would be 448,928 tons.

Thus, under this plan there would be immediately destroyed, of the navies of the three Powers, sixty-six capital fighting ships, built and building, with a total tonnage of 1,878,043.

It is proposed that it should be agreed by the United States, Great Britain and Japan that their navies, with respect to capital ships, within three months after the making of the agreement shall consist of certain ships designated in the proposal and numbering for the United States eighteen, for Great Britain twenty-two, for Japan ten.

The tonnage of these ships would be as follows: Of the United States, 500,650; of Great Britain, 604,450; of Japan, 299,700. In reaching this result, the age factor in the case of the respective navies has received appropriate consideration.

(b) NAVAL LIMITATION TREATY*

Article III. Subject to the provision of Article II, the Contracting Powers shall abandon their respective capital ship building programs, and no new capital ships shall be constructed or acquired by any of the Contracting Powers except

* February 6, 1922. From *Papers Relating to the Foreign Relations of The United States, 1922*, I, Washington, 1938, pp. 249-253.

replacement tonnage which may be constructed or acquired as specified in Chapter II, Part 3. . . .

Article IV. The total capital ship replacement tonnage of each of the Contracting Powers shall not exceed in standard displacement, for the United States, 525,000 tons (533,400 metric tons); for the British Empire 525,000 tons (533,400 metric tons); for France 175,000 tons (177,800 metric tons); for Italy 175,000 tons (177,800 metric tons); for Japan 315,000 tons (320,040 metric tons).

Article V. No capital ship exceeding 35,000 tons (35,560 metric tons) standard displacement shall be required by, or constructed by, for, or within the jurisdiction of, any of the Contracting Powers.

Article VI. No capital ship of any of the Contracting Powers shall carry a gun with a calibre in excess of 16 inches (406 millimetres).

Article VII. The total tonnage for aircraft carriers of each of the Contracting Powers shall not exceed in standard displacement, for the United States 135,000 tons (137,160 metric tons); for the British Empire 135,000 tons (137,160 metric tons); for France 60,000 tons (60,960 metric tons); for Italy 60,000 tons (60,960 metric tons); for Japan 81,000 tons (82,-296 metric tons). . . .

Article XI. No vessel of war exceeding 10,000 tons (10,160 metric tons) standard displacement, other than a capital ship or aircraft carrier, shall be acquired by, or constructed by, for, or within the jurisdiction of, any of the Contracting Powers. Vessels not specifically built as fighting ships nor taken in time of peace under government control for fighting purposes, which are employed on fleet duties or as troop transports or in some other way for the purpose of assisting in the prosecution of hostilities otherwise than as fighting ships, shall not be within the limitations of this Article. . . .

Article XIX. The United States, the

British Empire and Japan agree that the status quo at the time of the signing of the present Treaty, with regard to fortifications and naval bases, shall be maintained in their respective territories and possessions specified hereunder:

(1) The insular possessions which the United States now holds or may hereafter acquire in the Pacific Ocean, except (a) those adjacent to the coast of the United States, Alaska and the Panama Canal Zone, not including the Aleutian Islands, and (b) the Hawaiian Islands;

(2) Hongkong and the insular possessions which the British Empire now holds or may hereafter acquire in the Pacific Ocean, east of the meridian of 110° east longitude, except (a) those adjacent to the coast of Canada, (b) the Commonwealth of Australia and its Territories, and (c) New Zealand;

(3) The following insular territories and possessions of Japan in the Pacific Ocean, to wit: the Kurile Islands, the Bonin Islands, Anami-Oshima, the Loochoo Islands, Formosa and the Pescadores, and any insular territories or possessions in the Pacific Ocean which Japan may hereafter acquire.

The maintenance of the *status quo* under the foregoing provisions implies that no new fortifications or naval bases shall be established in the territories and possessions specified; that no measures shall be taken to increase the existing naval facilities for the repair and maintenance of naval forces, and that no increase shall be made in the coast defenses of the territories and possessions above specified. This restriction, however, does not preclude such repair and replacement of worn-out weapons and equipment as is customary in naval and military establishments in time of peace.

(c) TREATY BETWEEN THE UNITED STATES, GREAT BRITAIN, FRANCE AND JAPAN*

I. The High Contracting Parties agree as between themselves to respect their rights in relation to their insular possessions and insular dominions in the region of the Pacific Ocean.

If there should develop between any of the High Contracting Parties a controversy arising out of any Pacific question and involving their said rights which is not satisfactorily settled by diplomacy and is likely to affect the harmonious accord now happily subsisting between them, they shall invite the other High Contracting Parties to a joint conference to which the whole subject will be referred for consideration and adjustment.

II. If the said rights are threatened by the aggressive action of any other Power,

the High Contracting Parties shall communicate with one another fully and frankly in order to arrive at an understanding as to the most efficient measures to be taken, jointly or separately, to meet the exigencies of the particular situation.

III. This Treaty shall remain in force for ten years from the time it shall take effect, and after the expiration of said period it shall continue to be in force subject to the right of any of the High Contracting Parties to terminate it upon 12 months' notice.

IV. This Treaty shall be ratified as soon as possible in accordance with the constitutional methods of the High Contracting Parties and shall take effect on the deposit of ratifications, which shall take place at Washington, and thereupon the agreement between Great Britain and Japan, which was concluded at London on July 13, 1911, shall terminate. The

* December 13, 1921. From *Papers Relating to the Foreign Relations of The United States, 1922*, I, Washington, 1938, p. 35.

Government of the United States will transmit to all the signatory Powers a certified copy of the *proces-verbal* of the deposit of ratifications.

(d) TREATY BETWEEN THE UNITED STATES, GREAT BRITAIN, FRANCE, JAPAN, ITALY, BELGIUM, CHINA, THE NETHERLANDS, AND POR-TUGAL*

Article I. The Contracting Powers, other than China, agree:

(1) To respect the sovereignty, the independence, and the territorial and administrative integrity of China;

(2) To provide the fullest and most unembarrassed opportunity to China to develop and maintain for herself an effective and stable government;

(3) To use their influence for the purpose of effectually establishing and maintaining the principle of equal opportunity for the commerce and industry of all nations throughout the territory of China;

(4) To refrain from taking advantage of conditions in China in order to seek special rights or privileges which would abridge the rights of subjects or citizens of friendly States, and from countenancing action inimical to the security of such States.

Article II. The Contracting Powers agree not to enter into any treaty, agreement, arrangement or understanding, either with one another, or, individually or collectively, with any Power or Powers, which would infringe or impair the principles stated in Article I.

Article III. With a view to applying more effectually the principles of the Open Door or equality of opportunity in China for the trade and industry of all nations, the Contracting Powers, other than China, agree that they will not seek, nor support their respective nationals in seeking—

(a) any arrangement which might purport to establish in favor of their interests any general superiority of rights with respect to commercial or economic development in any designated region of China;

(b) any such monopoly or preference as would deprive the nationals of any other Power of the right of undertaking any legitimate trade or industry in China, or of participating with the Chinese Government, or with any local authority, in any category of public enterprise, or which by reason of its scope, duration or geographical extent is calculated to frustrate the practical application of the principle of equal opportunity.

It is understood that the foregoing stipulations of this Article are not to be so construed as to prohibit the acquisition of such properties or rights as may be necessary to the conduct of a particular commercial, industrial or financial undertaking or to the encouragement of invention and research.

China undertakes to be guided by the principles stated in the foregoing stipulations of this Article in dealing with applications for economic rights and privileges from Governments and nationals of all foreign countries, whether parties to the present Treaty or not.

Article IV. The Contracting Powers agree not to support any agreements by their respective nationals with each other designed to create Spheres of Influence or to provide for the enjoyment of mutually exclusive opportunities in designated parts of Chinese territory.

Article V. China agrees that, throughout the whole of the railways in China, she will not exercise or permit unfair discrimination of any kind. In particular there

* February 6, 1922. From *Papers Relating to the Foreign Relations of The United States, 1922*, I, Washington, 1938, pp. 278-280.

shall be no discrimination whatever, direct or indirect, in respect of charges or of facilities on the ground of the nationality of passengers or the countries from which or to which they are proceeding or the origin or ownership of goods or the country from which or to which they are consigned, or the nationality or ownership of the ship or other means of conveying such passengers or goods before or after their transport on the Chinese Railways.

The Contracting Powers, other than China, assume a corresponding obligation in respect of any of the aforesaid railways over which they or their nationals are in a position to exercise any control in virtue of any concession, special agreement or otherwise.

Article VI. The Contracting Powers, other than China, agree fully to respect China's rights as a neutral in time of war to which China is not a party; and China declares that when she is a neutral she will observe the obligations of neutrality.

Article VII. The Contracting Powers agree that, whenever a situation arises which in the opinion of any one of them involves the application of the stipulations of the present Treaty, and renders desirable discussion of such application, there shall be full and frank communication between the Contracting Powers concerned.

3

The Immigration Act of 1924

☆ *The curtailment of immigration had been a recurring issue for several generations. It became a major issue following World War I and led to the Emergency Quota Act in 1921 and permanent quota legislation in 1924.** ☆

It will undoubtedly be considered that the most important event in the immigration history of the fiscal year was the passage of the act of May 26, officially known as the "Immigration act of 1924." This legislation which supplants the so-called quota limit act of May 19, 1921, the latter having expired by limitation at the close of the fiscal year just ended, makes several very important changes not only in our immigration policy but also in the administrative machinery of the Immigration Service. Some of the more important changes in these respects will be briefly referred to.

It will be remembered that the quota limit act of May, 1921, provided that the number of aliens of any nationality admissable to the United States in any fiscal year should be limited to 3 per cent of the number of persons of such nationality who were resident in the United States according to the census of 1910, it being also provided that not more than 20 per cent of any annual quota could be admitted in any one month. Under the act

* From *Annual Report of the Commissioner General of Immigration to the Secretary of Labor—Fiscal Year Ended June 30, 1924*, Washington, 1924, pp. 24-26.

of 1924 the number of each nationality who may be admitted annually is limited to 2 per cent of the population of such nationality resident in the United States according to the cenus of 1890, and not more than 10 per cent of any annual quota may be admitted in any month except in cases where such quota is less than 300 for the entire year.

Under the act of May, 1921, the quota area was limited to Europe, the Near East, Africa, and Australasia. The countries of North and South America, with adjacent islands, and countries immigration from which was otherwise regulated, such as China, Japan, and countries within the Asiatic barred zone, were not within the scope of the quota law. Under the new act, however, immigration from the entire world, with the exception of the Dominion of Canada, Newfoundland, the Republic of Mexico, the Republic of Cuba the Republic of Haiti, the Dominican Republic, the Canal Zone, and independent countries of Central and South America, is subject to quota limitations. The various quotas established under the new law are shown in the following proclamation of the President, issued on the last day of the present fiscal year:

BY THE PRESIDENT OF THE
UNITED STATES OF AMERICA
A PROCLAMATION

Whereas it is provided in the act of Congress approved May 26, 1924, entitled "An act to limit the immigration of aliens into the United States, and for other purposes" that—

"The annual quota of any nationality shall be two per centum of the number of foreign-born individuals of such nationality resident in continental United States as determined by the United States census of 1890, but the minimum quota of any nationality shall be 100 (Sec. 11(a)).

"For the purposes of this Act nationality shall be determined by country by birth . . . (Sec. 12 (a)).

"The Secretary of State, the Secretary of Commerce, and the Secretary of Labor, jointly, shall, as soon as feasible after the enactment of this act, prepare a statement showing the number of individuals of the various nationalities resident in continental United States as determined by the United States census of 1890, which statement shall be the population basis for the purposes of subdivision (a) of Section 11 (Sec. 12 (b)).

"Such officials shall, jointly, report annually to the President the quota of each nationality under subdivision (a) of Section 11, together with the statements, estimates, and revisions provided for in this section. The President shall proclaim and make known the quotas so reported" (Sec. 12 (e)).

And whereas satisfactory evidence has been presented to me that the Secretary of State, the Secretary of Commerce, and the Secretary of Labor, pursuant to the authority conferred upon them in the act of Congress approved May 26, 1924, have made the statement and the quotas therein provided.

Now, therefore, I, Calvin Coolidge, President of the United States of America acting under and by virtue of the power in me vested by the aforesaid act of Congress, do hereby proclaim and make known that on and after July 1, 1924, and throughout the fiscal year 1924-1925, the quota of each nationality provided in said Act shall be as follows:

COUNTRY OR AREA OF BIRTH

	Quota 1924-1925
* Afghanistan	* 100
Albania	100
Andorra	100
Arabian peninsula	100
Armenia	124

	Quota 1924-1925
Australia, including Papua, Tasmania, and all islands appertaining to Australia	121
Austria	785
Belgium	512
* Bhutan	* 100
Bulgaria	100
Cameroon (proposed British mandate)	100
Cameroon (French mandate)	100
* China	* 100
Czechoslovakia	3,073
Danzig, Free City of	228
Denmark	2,789

	Quota 1924-1925
Egypt	100
Esthonia	124
Ethiopia (Abyssinia)	100
Finland	471
France	3,954
Germany	51,227
Great Britain and Northern Ireland	34,007
Greece	100
Hungary	473
Iceland	100
* India	* 100
Iraq (Mesopotamia)	100
Irish Free State	28,567
Italy, including Rhodes, Dodekanesia, and Castellorizzo	3,845
* Japan	* 100
Latvia	142
Liberia	100
Liechtenstein	100
Lithuania	344
Luxemburg	100
Monaco	100
Morocco (French and Spanish Zones and Tangier)	100
* Muscat (Oman)	* 100
Nauru (proposed British mandate)	100
* Nepal	* 100
Netherlands	1,648
* New Guinea, and other Pacific Islands (under proposed Australian mandate)	* 100
New Zealand (including appertaining islands)	100
Norway	6,453
Palestine (with Trans-Jordan, proposed British mandate)	100
Persia	100
Poland	5,982
Portugal	503
Ruanda and Urundi (Belgium mandate)	100
Rumania	603
Russia, European and Asiatic	2,248
Samoa, Western (proposed mandate of New Zealand)	100
San Marino	100
* Siam	* 100
South Africa, Union of	100
South West Africa (proposed mandate of Union of South Africa)	100
Spain	131
Sweden	9,561
Switzerland	2,081

Syria and The Lebanon (French mandate)	100
Tanganyika (proposed British mandate)	100
Togoland (proposed British mandate)	100
Togoland (French mandate)	100
Turkey	100
* Yap, and other Pacific islands (under Japanese mandate)	* 100
Yugoslavia	671

* For each of the countries indicated by an asterisk (*) is established a nominal quota according to the minimum fixed by law. These nominal quotas, as in the case of all quotas hereby established, are available only for persons born within the respective countries who are eligible to citizenship in the United States and admissible under the immigration laws of the United States.

4

The Outlawry of War

☆ *In April of 1927, French Foreign Minister Aristide Briand proposed an agreement renouncing war as an instrument of national policy. In June, Secretary of State Frank B. Kellogg responded to this overture, and soon a treaty was formulated to outlaw war. Ultimately, sixty-two nations signed this treaty.** ☆

Art. 1. The high contracting parties solemnly declare in the names of their respective peoples that they condemn recourse to war for the solution of international controversies, and renounce it as an instrument of national policy in their relations with one another.

Art. 2. The high contracting parties agree that the settlement or solution of all disputes or conflicts of whatever nature or of whatever origin they may be, which may arise among them, shall never be sought except by pacific means.

Art. 3. The present treaty shall be ratified by the high contracting parties

* From *The General Pact for the Renunciation of War*, Washington, 1928, pp. 1-3.

named in the preamble in accordance with their respective constitutional requirements, and shall take effect as between them as soon as all their several instruments of ratification shall have been deposited at Washington.

This treaty shall, when it has come into effect as prescribed in the preceding paragraph, remain open as long as may be necessary for adherence by all the other powers of the world. Every instrument evidencing the adherence of a power shall be deposited at Washington and the treaty shall immediately upon such deposit become effective as between the power thus adhering and the other powers parties hereto.

5

Further Naval Disarmament

☆ *The defects of the Naval Limitation Treaty of 1922 stimulated efforts to impose restrictions on auxiliary warships. Though these restrictions were effected at London in 1930, controversy over this treaty in the United States centered on the ratios with Japan. In the following selection Walter Lippman contended that the agreement was advantageous to the United States.* ☆*

The nature of the agreement with Japan can be most clearly stated by taking as a basis of discussion the position of the American and Japanese fleets on December 31, 1936, assuming the completion of ships now building, the scrapping of obsolete ships, and the absence of any new construction after the London Conference. The situation would be then as follows:

	United States	Japan	Ratio
Big cruisers	130,000	108,400	100:83.3
Small cruisers	70,500	81,455	86.6:100
Destroyers	14,653	86,405	16.9:100
Submarines	22,950	52,252	43.9:100

These figures show that in all classes not limited at Washington, Japan had been building far beyond any theoretical ratio of 60 percent. In terms of real modern ships she had actually surpassed America in every category except the big cruisers and there she had 83 percent. Japan did not, however, ask the right to maintain

* From Walter Lippmann, "The London Naval Conference: An American View," *Foreign Affairs*, VIII (July, 1930), pp. 508-509. Copyright, 1930, The Council on Foreign Relations, New York. Used by permission.

this relative position. She was willing to come down to 70 percent in big cruisers, and she was willing to let America surpass her in small cruisers and destroyers. She asked for parity in submarines.

It became evident that the Japanese were actuated by two motives: fear and pride. That they had a defensive fear rather than an aggressive purpose is shown by their willingness to accept definite inferiority not only in battleships but in big cruisers; that they are willing to spend relatively so much money to maintain a very powerful but a definitely inferior navy can be explained only on the ground that they feel isolated and in danger. That they insisted on different ratios in different categories rather than a single ratio throughout is partly due to a desire for extra strength in the smaller defensive ships and partly to a revolt of their pride against being rated as a generally inferior Power. Their insistence on having it said in the treaty (Article XXIII) that none of its provisions "shall prejudice the attitude" of anyone at the Conference of 1935 is almost certainly due to the same desire not to be rated once and for all.

After prolonged negotiations the Japanese were given very liberal concessions. The ratio agreed to for completed big cruisers by the next conference is 72 percent. If big cruisers laid down are included the ratio is 60 percent. One can take one's choice as to which figure is the more significant. The ratio agreed to in small cruisers is 70 percent. The ratio for destroyers is 71 percent. The ratio for submarines is parity.

In judging the concessions these percentages may easily be misleading. In the most important categories, the big cruis-, ers, the Japanese agreed to take a complete holiday, while we start to build 50,000 tons. This building of ours will reduce the Japanese ratio to 60 percent

before a new competition can begin. This is a great concession to America on a vital point. In the other categories the substantial fact is that Japan agrees to stand still or build very slowly while we may, if we wish, build tremendously. She does practically no submarine building, for example, while we may build 29,750 tons to attain parity with her. In small cruisers we may build nearly four tons to every one ton the Japanese build. In destroyers we may build seven tons to every one ton which Japan builds.

The substantial truth is that, having effected an enormous expansion since the Washington Conference, Japan is now going to take what amounts to a naval holiday. The total authorization up to 1936 for new construction in all categories including aircraft carrriers is 50,768 tons. Ours is nearly seven times as great: 346,811 tons.

Merely to scrutinize ratios and to ignore the realities of this agreement is a pedantic form of jingoism.

6

American Foreign Policy 1923

☆ *Though the United States had rejected membership in the League of Nations, Secretary Hughes, in an address on November 30, 1923, declared the nation's interest in international affairs and justified this interest as being consistent with historic American policies.* * ☆

Foreign policies are not built upon abstractions. They are the result of practical conceptions of national interest arising from some immediate exigency or standing out vividly in historical perspective. When long maintained, they express the hopes and fears, the aims of security or aggrandizement, which have become dominant in the national consciousness and thus transcend party divisions and make negligible such opposition as may come from particular groups. . . .

We are fortunate in our detachment from many difficulties and dangers which oppress the imagination of other peoples, but we should resist the tendency to indulge in self-praise. When we have a clear sense of our own interests, we are just as inflexible as others. The great advantage we have had is that, coming to independence in a world afflicted with the long rivalries of military powers, the traditions of conquest, and the dreams of empire, we sought simply the assurance of freedom, and our national instinct has been opposed to aggression and intervention. The Monroe Doctrine was the embodiment of this sentiment. Through

* From *The New York Times,* December 1, 1923.

the one hundred years since its announcement, despite the strife of parties and opposing convictions as to domestic issues, it has been a unifying principle, contributing not only to our security and peace but to our dignity and prestige as a power capable of thus asserting and maintaining a vigorous independent policy. . . .

The anxiety to escape the toils of European politics and intrigues was early manifested. . . . We were not isolated and could not be. The European powers were at our doors; their conflicts had embroiled the New World from the beginning. There was no thought of escaping constant dealings with these powers, whose rivalries menaced our peace, but upon what basis should these dealings be had? We had the choice of seeking the protection of alliances, or the more difficult course of maintaining independence. With splendid courage no less than with profound wisdom the fathers chose the latter course, at once conserving our safety and enhancing our influence. It was the choice of an infant nation, but of a nation conscious of the promise of its influence as a world power. . . .

As our paramount interest dictated abstention from participation in European politics, so it also required that the machinations of foreign Powers should not have increased opportunity here, and when the independence achieved by the Spanish colonies in this hemisphere was threatened by the imposing combination of European sovereigns, styled the Holy Alliance, this correlative policy found emphatic expression in Monroe's message.

... the Doctrine in its essentials ... may ... be summarized ... as being opposed (1) to any non-American action encroaching upon the political independence of American States under any guise, and (2) to the acquisition in any manner of the control of additional territory in this hemisphere by any non-American Power. . . .

In relation to the Pacific Ocean and the Far East we have developed the policies of (1) the Open Door, (2) the maintenance of the integrity of China, (3) co-operation with other Powers in the declaration of common principles, (4) co-operation with other Powers by conference and consultation in the interests of peace, (5) limitation of naval armament, and (6) the limitation of fortifications and naval bases. . . .

How do these policies in the region of the Pacific Ocean square with the Monroe Doctrine? Is there any inconsistency? Has our entrance into this region as a World Power of first rank led us to violate our traditions? Manifestly not. We fought the Spanish War to put an end to an intolerable nuisance at our very door, and to establish and make secure the independence of Cuba, not to override it. And as a consequence of victory in that war we acquired distant possessions, but not with the purpose of making these a basis for encroaching upon the territory or interfering with the political independence of the peoples of the Eastern nations. In safeguarding the integrity of China, in securing equality of commercial opportunity, in endeavoring to forestall efforts at exploitation and aggression, in seeking to remove suspicion and allay apprehensions, and in enlarging through assured tranquility the opportunities of peaceful commerce, we have been pursuing under different conditions the same aims of independence, security, and peace which determined the declaration of Monroe.

With respect to Europe, our policy has continued to be, in the phrase of Jefferson, "Peace, commerce, and honest friendship with all nations, entangling alliances with none. . . ."

The bitter controversy which followed World War I showed with what tenacity we still hold to the principle of not meddling in the political strife of Europe. . . .

The preponderant thought among us undoubtedly is that our influence would not be increased by pooling it. The influence that is due to our detachment and impartiality could not long be maintained if we should substitute the role of a partisan in European quarrels, and the constant efforts of propagandists have brought vividly before us the fact that where the direct American interest is not clearly perceived foreign controversies afford abundant opportunity for the play among us of intense racial feeling. . . . The difficulties which beset Europe have their causes within Europe and not in any act or policy of ours.

Generally, our policies toward Europe may thus be summarized: We are still opposed to alliances. We refuse to commit ourselves in advance with respect to the employment of the power of the United States in unknown contingencies. We reserve our judgment to act upon occasion as our sense of duty permits. . . .

There is plainly no inconsistency between these policies and the Monroe Doctrine. Our position as a world power has not affected it. The question is whether that Doctrine is still important under changed conditions. The answer must be in the affirmative. . . .

Our affirmative policies relating to our own conduct in relation to other American States, and not merely our policy with respect to the conduct of non-American powers, should be clearly envisaged. . . .

First—We recognize the equality of the American republics, their equal rights under the law of nations. . . .

Second—It follows that it is a part of our policy to respect the territorial integrity of the Latin American republics. We have no policy of aggression; we do not support aggression by others; we are opposed to aggression by any one of the Latin American republics upon any other. . . .

Third—States have duties as well as rights. Every State on being received into the family of nations accepts the obligations which are the essential conditions of international intercourse. Among these obligations is the duty of each State to respect the rights of citizens of other States which have been acquired within its jurisdiction in accordance with its laws. . . .

Fourth—It is the policy of this Government to make available its friendly assistance to promote stability in those of our sister republics which are especially afflicted with disturbed conditions involving their own peace and that of their neighbors. . . .

Fifth—The United States aims to facilitate the peaceful settlement of difficulties between the Governments in this hemisphere. . . .

Sixth—In seeking to promote peace, as well as to aid in the reduction of unproductive expenditures, this Government has sought to encourage the making of agreements for the limitation of armament. . . .

Seventh—The policies which have been described are not to secure peace as an end in itself, but to make available the opportunities of peace; that is, to open the way to a mutually helpful cooperation. This is the object of the Pan-American conferences. . . .

Eighth—It should also be observed that in our commercial relations the United States is seeking unconditional most-favored-nation treatment in customs matters. . . .

Ninth—We have certain special policies of the highest importance to the United States.

We have established a waterway between the Atlantic and Pacific Oceans—the Panama Canal. Apart from obvious commercial considerations, the adequate protection of this canal—its complete immunity from any adverse control—is essential to our peace and security. We intend in all circumstances to safeguard the Panama Canal. We could not afford to take any different position with respect to any other waterway that may be built between the Atlantic and the Pacific Oceans. Disturbances in the Caribbean region are therefore of special interest to us not for the purpose of seeking control over others but of being assured that our own safety is free from menace.

With respect to Cuba, we have the special interests arising from our treaty and our part in the securing of her independence. It is our desire to see her independence not weakened but safeguarded and her stability and prosperity assured. Our friendly advice and aid are always available to that end.

7

The Problems of a Creditor Nation

☆ *The payment of debts incurred by certain European nations during World War I and the reconstruction period was made difficult if not impossible by the continually favorable balance of trade held by the United States during the 1920's. Disagreement over the method of payment produced constant bickering and helped to perpetuate economic disequilibrium among nations.* * ☆

The war . . . transformed the United States from a debtor to a creditor nation. Where, on balance, the American debt to the world in 1914 had been $3,000,000,-000 in 1921 the world owed the United States $4,000,000,000, war debts aside. Since the American material circumstances had now been radically altered, its traditional policy was no longer consistent with its changed circumstances. For, if it were to collect what was owed it abroad, it could no longer maintain an export surplus or preserve the existing protective tariff. . . .

For convenience, foreign debts are measured in terms of money, but, in practice they represent goods, services and gold. Thus the $4,000,000,000 which the world owed the United States in 1920 apart from the war debts, represented the surplus of goods sold and services rendered abroad by America in the years between 1914 and 1920. To collect these debts, and to collect the interest due upon

* From Frank H. Simonds, *American Foreign Policy in the Post-War Years*, pp. 23-30. Copyright, 1935, The Johns Hopkins Press, Baltimore. Used by permission.

them annually, the United States had to take its payment in kind. And since, at the moment, the debtor states were holding on to their gold to support their currencies, payment had to be accepted in goods or services.

Before 1914, the countries which were America's creditors had, without exception, maintained an import surplus. Since, however, they had been unwilling to accept enough goods and services from the United States to meet the annual interest due them on past lendings to America, they had re-lent to the United States that part of the sums due for which they did not accept payment in goods and services. The United States was now bound to follow the same course. If, however, by insisting upon maintaining an export surplus, it refused to take any payment in kind and, in addition, further expanded the sum already owing it from abroad, by an annual excess in exports, then the amount due would mount steeply through the operation of compound interest until it attained unmanageable proportions.

That was what did actually happen. The United States refused to modify its traditional policy. As a result, between 1920 and 1930 its exports, goods, services and gold included, amounted to $66,500,000,000 and its imports to but $66,000,000,000 and the difference constituted an export surplus of $500,000,000. Merely through normal trade, therefore, $500,000,000 was added to the capital of its foreign loans. In the meantime nothing had been paid upon the principal and the annual interest charges were, therefore, pyramided upon the original obligation. Thus, had no other factor been involved, the world's debt to the United States must at least have doubled in the eleven years between 1920 and 1930.

But something else did happen. The United States resolved to collect the war debts, which were eventually to be capitalized at $12,000,000,000. Annual payments upon these were, moreover, to start at $250,000,000, rise shortly to $450,000,000 and remain at that peak level for upwards of half a century. But how was this further payment to be accepted? It, too, could be made only in goods, commodities and gold, and the gold supplies of the debtor countries were inadequate to meet any considerable fraction of their debts.

The accidents of war, together with the decision to collect the war debts had thrust the United States into the position of a creditor country upon a grand scale. On balance, the world now owed it $14,000,000,000, whereas in 1914 it had owed the world $3,000,000,000. Only one country had ever occupied a similar position and that was Great Britain. It had, moreover, taken the British the better part of a century to build up a foreign holding of $20,000,000,000 and the United States had acquired a foreign investment three-quarters as large in seven brief years.

If the American people were resolved to play the part of a creditor country, which had been the familiar role of the British for so long, then they were also bound to adopt the British technique, for none other was discoverable. . . .

The smallest examination of the British system, however, disclosed the significant fact that Great Britain had prepared the way for its later performance as a creditor country by a major surgical operation. By the repeal of the Corn Laws in 1846, England had sacrificed its agriculture. Thenceforth it could export the production of its factories and accept payment therefor in the form of foodstuffs and raw materials. Thus, before it became a creditor country, it had, by adopting free trade, opened its market to future debtors. . . .

[The British technique] was open to the United States only in theory and not in practice. No administration, whether Democratic or Republican, could even dream of following the British example of 1846 and scrapping American agriculture in order to expand foreign trade or to collect foreign debts. Not less absurd was the notion of reversing the process and sacrificing the factory while clinging to the farm. Actually, even before the war, the United States had become a country of a balanced economy. It had acquired a degree of economic self-sufficiency unapproached by any other nation. Between 1920 and 1930, moreover, a state of approximate balance existed between its imports and exports as in fact it had existed between 1896 and 1914. For, in the later years the excess of exports over imports, goods, services and gold included, was but $500,000,000.

When, however, the Harding administration, Congress and public opinion demanded first, that the war debts be collected, second, that the existing tariff schedules be not merely maintained but presently raised and, finally, when the private investors in foreign securities clamored for the payment of interest upon their investments, what could be done? Only one thing: the American investor, by still further purchases of foreign paper could supply the foreign debtors, governmental and private, with the means to meet the costs of their debts to the United States annually and to liquidate the costs of the American export surplus as well. If the United States refused to accept payment in goods and services, then, since the debtors lacked adequate gold reserves, Uncle Sam had to lend from one pocket what he presently put back into another.

Such was the process which was begun in 1921 and continued until 1930. Concerning these years, too, there has grown up a legend that the United States annually loaned abroad vast sums to finance its export surpluses and therefore, in effect, gave away its goods. In fact, however, during these eleven years there was a difference of but $500,000,000 between what the United States sold and what it bought in goods, services and gold and this disparity in total export trade of $66,500,000,000 was relatively insignificant, amounting to materially less than one-tenth of one per cent.

What actually occurred was that between 1920 and 1930 the interest charges upon the $14,000,000,000 owed us from abroad, $10,000,000,000 in war debts and $4,000,000,000 in private investments, aggregated approximately $6,500,000,000, while the total export surplus was $500,-000,000. The world, therefore, owed us $7,000,000,000 which it could not pay in gold, because it lacked the necessary amounts above what it needed to retain to protect its currency. The United States, on its part, refused to accept payment in goods or services. The deadlock was broken, however, by American citizens who invested $7,000,000,000 in foreign securities. And out of the proceeds of these purchases, foreign countries and corporations remitted the annual instalments due for goods, war debts and private investments.

Taken as a whole, the United States did not invest any fresh money in Europe in these years. But one group of American citizens paid the interest due to the American Treasury upon war debts and to another group of citizens upon their private investments and accepted foreign securities in return. When the crash ultimately came, as it was bound to come, the first group still held the $7,000,000,-000 of foreign securities and the total debt of the world to the United States had expanded from $14,000,000,000 to $21,-000,000,000 and was still increasing at the rate of more than $1,000,000,000 annually.

8

The Hawley-Smoot Tariff

☆ *Alarmed by the growing domestic economic crisis, Congress under the prodding of protectionists like Senator Joseph R. Grundy of Pennsylvania, increased the American tariff rates by enacting the Hawley-Smoot law in June, 1930.* * ☆

The Hawley-Smoot tariff has become law. The bill which has kept Congress in continuous and stormy session for almost fourteen months was passed by the Senate on June 13, 44 votes to 42, and by the House the following day, 222 votes to 153. As signed by the President, the new law levies duties on 3,218 articles imported by the United States. A total of 1,122 items in the former Fordney-McCumber tariff are altered: 887 revised upward, 235 downward. The average *ad valorem* rate or its equivalent is 41 per cent, an increase of 6.86 per cent over the average rate in the Fordney-McCumber act, or, on the basis of revenue collected, an increase of 20 per cent. This, in effect, is the outcome of the "limited revision" pledged in the campaign of 1928.

What are the international implications of the new tariff? First, the effect on international relations, both economic and political, probably has been emphasized to a greater extent during the past year than during the passage of any American tariff in recent history. As a result of the financial depression, indus-

* From William T. Stone, "The 'Grundy' Tariff Becomes Law," *News Bulletin* of the Foreign Policy Association, IX (June 20, 1930), p. 1. Used by permission.

trialists, bankers, and business men who in the past have accepted the protectionist doctrine as synonymous with "prosperity," have joined the academic economist in pointing to the dangers inherent in trade barriers. The statements of Henry Ford, Alfred P. Sloan, president of General Motors, and the president of the American Bankers Association have been heard where the voices of professors of economics have been unheeded in the past. The daily press, including a large proportion of Republican journals, has likewise sounded a strong note of warning. Of the many "polls" taken to show the trend of the press, none has shown a majority in favor of the present tariff law. A new and important section of opinion, it would appear, has recognized that trade beyond our borders, and the good will of foreign powers, tend to make the difference between good business and bad business, between prosperity and depression.

The possible consequences of the "Grundy" tariff have been foreshadowed for many months. During the period when the bill was under discussion, the United States received protests from no less than 42 foreign governments and dependencies, objecting to more than 300 items in the proposed law. Few of these protests received an impartial hearing.

More disturbing than protests have been the warnings of reprisal. Canada, best customer of the United States, has revised its tariff in anticipation of the American act, increasing the general rates and reducing the preferential duties applicable to Great Britain. Mexico has taken steps to place a protective duty on foodstuffs. European automobile interests have revived the agitation for a cartel directed against American manufacturers. Argentina has expressed its displeasure by a refusal to cooperate with the United States in many international conferences and conventions. Spain, Italy, France and Great Britain have indicated the serious consequences which might result from application of the new rates.

Reprisals are often as damaging to the country which applies them as to the country against whom they are directed, and all the warnings reported in the press may not actually materialize. But the basic fact remains that even without direct reprisals, the Hawley-Smoot Tariff must inevitably affect the purchases of foreign countries in the United States and may easily disturb the amicable relations of those countries with the United States.

9

The Case for Russian Recognition

☆ *The United States had persistently refused to recognize the Soviet regime established in Russia in 1917, in part due to its international revolutionary program and its failure to acknowledge the financial obligations of earlier governments. Senator William E. Borah of Idaho was a consistent critic of the American non-recognition policy.* * ☆

I can see no real peace in Europe until the Russian problem is settled. It is my belief there can be no disarmament of any moment, particularly land disarmament, until Russia is brought into the family of nations and amicable relations and clear understanding with all other powers are established; that there can be no economic health or stability in Europe, or the world, so long as this gigantic power, stupendous and incalculable in her natural wealth and her man-power, is writhing and struggling to escape her thralldom; and this will last so long as she is treated as an outlaw and denied an opportunity to enjoy the ordinary methods of credit and trade. I feel that all efforts toward peace and better understanding among nations must be indefinitely retarded so long as one-sixth of the earth's surface, occupied by the third largest population in the world, is estranged and afraid. . . .

I have listened over the radio to and read discussions on Russia much of late, and I have been interested in some of the

reasons for inveighing against Russia; some of the arguments which are advanced as to why we should refuse to recognize Russia or to even trade with Russia. It is urged in the first place that Russia is governed by a cruel dictator, that only a few ruthless rulers hold control. Suppose that is true. . . . the people of Russia are far better off under the present government than they have ever been in their history. They are undergoing great hardships and are undoubtedly suffering greatly. But they at least have a future, their face is toward better things. . . .

There can be no doubt, Mr. President, that a new life, a new existence has been given to the peasant of Russia. There can be no doubt that he is a different human being with a different outlook. They may inveigh and propagandize and falsify the facts, but the truth is, that the revolution has released the Russian people from the old, dead, hopeless past. . . .

It is also claimed that she has repudiated her debts and confiscated property. She did repudiate her debts and confiscate property. She has stood ready for eight

* From *Congressional Record*, 71st Congress, 3rd session, pp. 7037, 7041-7043.

years to pay her debts. She is willing to meet the United States at any time upon a basis of equality to compensate for the damages of confiscation if the United States will consider the damages of invasion. It is claimed also that Russia does not respect her contracts and her agreements. I have here upon my desk a list of some three or four hundred firms who have been, and still are, doing business in Russia. Has anyone heard of any violation of contract with these men? These firms have extended credit, they have made heavy contracts. Is not the very fact that they continue to do business with Russia a better evidence of Russia's keeping her contracts than the testimony of escapees and convicts and criminals and heated agitators . . .?

Mr. President, the three great and, I believe, imperishable instincts of the human race are religion, family, and property—something to believe, something to love, something to possess. Let us admit that those who now govern and dominate Russia, not the people of Russia, stand against them all. We stand for them all. Let us admit that it is an irreconcilable conflict. Let us concede that those who govern Russia, not the people of Russia, would uproot and destroy them all. Let us admit that they would summon them all to the bar of public opinion and would exile them from human affairs, if they had the power. We would foster and strengthen them all. Our whole civilization is built around them. But how deep and strong is our faith? Do we fear that capitalism will fail, will cave in, if brought in contact with communism . . .?

You can not put an embargo upon news or ideas in these days. The people do their own reading and their own thinking. I am glad it is so. The restlessness and the discontent in this country spring not at all from Russian literature or Russian teachings. We stand or fall not by what Russia does, but by what we do right here in our own country. We are slow about cleaning up our cities and making property safe and human life secure. We have failed to give work to those who are hungry and who would like to work. We have been unable to cleanse our system of corruption. We have tolerated a system which compels honest and clean business men to pay tribute to crooks and criminals for the protection which their government fails to give. These are the things which cause restlessness and discontent and discouragement among our own people. It is not Russian literature which is disturbing our people or which we need fear. It is not that which is happening in Russia nor what Russia is proposing that is bringing doubt and worry to our own people. It is the conditions here in our own land. These are the things which challenge the attention and arouse the anxiety of the American people.

Capitalism should turn its eyes inwardly and take an account of its own internal affairs. Capitalism must turn its eyes inwardly and take into consideration and solve its own internal problems. If we do not solve them, God only knows what will happen. If we do solve them, communism and all antagonistic "isms" will prove impotent in their tasks. We have in this country from five to seven million men and women unemployed, seeking something to do. What has communism to do with that, and what is our solution? There is in the capitalistic nations of the world some fifteen to sixteen million men and women unemployed. What has communism to do with that? The mechanization of modern industries has left millions of men and women in middle life, or later, to readjust their whole lives to wholly new conditions, to adapt themselves to wholly new environments. They want to know how. Capitalism has not answered. Communism has had nothing to do with that. Mass production, our boasted achievement, continues to pile up goods in the sight of those whose purchasing power is daily diminishing. What is capitalism's answer to that? And what had Communism to do with bringing on that condition? We can not answer such questions by assailing communism. We hear about a surplus of fuel, and yet we know there are millions who are unable to secure enough of this surplus to keep them from hunger and cold. What is capitalism's answer to that? Can we meet the problem by assailing communism? I am not in the least disturbed about communism of itself. I am, I confess, disturbed about the unsolved problems of capitalism, and I am almost equally disturbed over the fact that the time which we ought to devote to solving these questions and to bringing about conditions which would help to solve them, is devoted to attacking some other theory and agitating against some other government.

10

Intervention in Nicaragua

☆ *The outbreak of revolution in Nicaragua in 1926 was soon followed by American intervention to maintain law and order. This
action resulted in the holding of elections under American supervision in 1928, when a former rebel leader was elected president. In
a message of January 10, 1927, President Coolidge explained the reasons for American intervention.* ☆

I have the most conclusive evidence
that arms and munitions in large quantities have been on several occasions since
August, 1926, shipped to the revolutionists
in Nicaragua. Boats carrying these munitions have been fitted out in Mexican
ports, and some of the munitions bear evidence of having belonged to the Mexican
Government. It also appears that the
ships were fitted out with the full knowledge of and, in some cases, with the
encouragement of Mexican officials and
were in one instance, at least, commanded by a Mexican naval reserve officer. At the end of November, after
spending some time in Mexico City, Doctor Sacasa went back to Nicaragua, landing at Puerto Cabezas, near Bragmans
Bluff. He immediately placed himself at
the head of the insurrection and declared
himself President of Nicaragua. He has
never been recognized by any of the Central American Republics nor by any other
government, with the exception of Mexico, which recognized him immediately.
As arms and munitions in large quanti-

* From *Congressional Record*, 69th Congress, 2nd
session, pp. 1325-1326.

ties were reaching the revolutionists, I
deemed it unfair to prevent the recognized government from purchasing arms
abroad, and, accordingly, the Secretary
of State has notified the Diaz Government
that licenses would be issued for the export of arms and munitions purchased in
this country. It would be thoroughly inconsistent for this country not to support
the government recognized by it while the
revolutionists were receiving arms and
munitions from abroad.

During the last two months the Government of the United States has received
repeated requests from various American
citizens, both directly and through our
consuls and legation, for the protection of
their lives and property. The Government
of the United States has also received requests from the British charge at Mana-
gua and from the Italian ambassador at
Washington for the protection of their respective nationals. Pursuant to such requests, Admiral Latimer, in charge of the
special service squadron, has not only
maintained the neutral zone at Bluefields
under the agreement of both parties but
has landed forces at Puerto Cabezas and

Rio Grande, and established neutral zones at these points where considerable numbers of Americans live and are engaged in carrying on various industries. He has also been authorized to establish such other neutral zones as are necessary for the purposes above mentioned.

For many years numerous Americans have been living in Nicaragua, developing its industries and carrying on business. At the present time there are large investments in lumbering, mining, coffee growing, banana culture, shipping, and also in general mercantile and other collateral business. All these people and these industries have been encouraged by the Nicaraguan Government. That Government has at all times owed them protection, but the United States has occasionally been obliged to send naval forces for their proper protection. In the present crisis such forces are requested by the Nicaraguan Government, which protests to the United States its inability to protect these interests and states that any measures which the United States deems appropriate for their protection will be satisfactory to the Nicaraguan Government.

In addition to these industries now in existence, the Government of Nicaragua, by a treaty entered into on the 5th day of August, 1914, granted in perpetuity to the United States the exclusive proprietary rights necessary and convenient for the construction, operation, and maintenance of an oceanic canal. . . .

There is no question that if the revolution continues American investments and business interests in Nicaragua will be very seriously affected, if not destroyed. The currency, which is now at par, will be inflated. American as well as foreign bond holders will undoubtedly look to the United States for the protection of their interests. . . .

Manifestly the relation of this Government to the Nicaraguan situation, and its policy in the existing emergency, are determined by the facts which I have described. The proprietary rights of the United States in the Nicaraguan canal route, with the necessary implications growing out of it affecting the Panama Canal, together with the obligations flowing from the investments of all classes of our citizens in Nicaragua, place us in a position of peculiar responsibility. I am sure it is not the desire of the United States to intervene in the internal affairs of Nicaragua or of any other Central American Republic. Nevertheless it must be said that we have a very definite and special interest in the maintenance of order and good government in Nicaragua at the present time, and that the stability, prosperity, and independence of all Central American countries can never be a matter of indifference to us. The United States can not, therefore, fail to view with deep concern any serious threat to stability and constitutional government in Nicaragua tending toward anarchy and jeopardizing American interests, especially if such state of affairs is contributed to or brought about by outside influences or by any foreign power. It has always been and remains the policy of the United States in such circumstances to take the steps that may be necessary for the preservation and protection of the lives, the property, and the interests of its citizens and of this Government itself. In this respect I propose to follow the path of my predecessors.

Consequently, I have deemed it my duty to use the powers committed to me to insure the adequate protection of all American interests in Nicaragua, whether they be endangered by internal strife or by outside interference in the affairs of that Republic.

11

The Clark Memorandum on the Monroe Doctrine

☆ *This memorandum, written in late 1928 by Under Secretary of State J. Reuben Clark, interpreted the Monroe Doctrine in a way which repudiated the Roosevelt Corollary. It came to represent United States policy under Herbert Hoover upon its publication in 1930.* * ☆

It is of first importance to have in mind that Monroe's declaration in its terms, relates solely to the relationships between European states on the one side, and, on the other side, the American continents, the Western Hemisphere, and the Latin American Governments which on December 2, 1823, had declared and maintained their independence which we had acknowledged. . . .

In the normal case, the Latin American state against which aggression was aimed by a European power, would be the beneficiary of the Doctrine not its victim. This has been the history of its application. The Doctrine makes the United States a guarantor, in effect, of the independence of Latin American states, though without the obligations of a guarantor to those states, for the United States itself determines by its sovereign will when, where, and concerning what aggressions it will invoke the Doctrine, and by what measures, if any, it will apply a sanction. In none of these things has any other state any voice whatever.

* From J. Reuben Clark, *Memorandum on the Monroe Doctrine*, Washington, 1930, pp. ix-xxv.

Furthermore while the Monroe Doctrine as declared, has no relation in its terms to an aggression by any other state than a European state, yet the principle "self-preservation" which underlies the Doctrine—which principle, as we shall see, is as fully operative without the Doctrine as with it—would apply to any non-American state in whatever quarter of the globe it lay, or even to an American state, if the aggressions of such state against other Latin American states were "dangerous to our peace and safety," or were a "manifestation of an unfriendly disposition towards the United States," or were "endangering our peace and happiness"; that is, if such aggressions challenged our existence. . . .

In this view, the Monroe Doctrine as such might be wiped out and the United States would lose nothing of its broad, international right; it would still possess, in common with every other member of the family of nations, the internationally recognized right of self-preservation, and this right would fully attach to the matters specified by the Doctrine if and whenever they threatened our existence, just as the right would attach in relation to any other act carrying a like menace. . . .

It is evident from the foregoing that the Monroe Doctrine is not an equivalent for "self-preservation"; and therefore the Monroe Doctrine need not, indeed should not, be invoked in order to cover situations challenging our self-preservation but not within the terms defined by Monroe's declaration. These other situations may be handled, and more wisely so, as matters affecting the national security and self-preservation of the United States as a great power. . . .

The statement of the Doctrine itself that "with the existing colonies or dependencies of any European power we have not interfered and shall not interfere," has been more than once reiterated.

It has also been announced that the Monroe Doctrine is not a pledge by the United States to other American states requiring the United States to protect such states, at their behest, against real or fancied wrongs inflicted by European powers, nor does it create an obligation running from the United States to any American state to intervene for its protection. . . .

The so-called "Roosevelt corollary" was to the effect, as generally understood, that in case of financial or other difficulties in weak Latin American countries, the United States should attempt an adjustment thereof lest European Governments should intervene, and intervening should occupy territory—an act which would be contrary to the principles of the Monroe Doctrine. This view seems to have had its inception in some observations of President Buchanan in his message to Congress of December 3, 1860, and was somewhat amplified by Lord Salisbury in his note to Mr. Olney of November 6, 1895, regarding the Venezuelan boundary dispute.

As has already been indicated above, it is not believed that this corollary is justified by the terms of the Monroe Doctrine, however much it may be justified by the application of the doctrine of self-preservation.

These various expressions and statements, as made in connection with the situations which gave rise to them, detract not a little from the scope popularly attached to the Monroe Doctrine, and they relieve that Doctrine of many of the criticisms which have been aimed against it.

Finally, it should not be overlooked that the United States declined the overtures of Great Britain in 1823 to make a joint declaration regarding the principles covered by the Monroe Doctrine, or to enter into a conventional arrangement regarding them. Instead this Government determined to make the declaration of high national policy on its own responsibility and in its own behalf. The Doctrine is thus purely unilateral. The United States determines when and if the principles of the Doctrine are violated, and when and if violation is threatened. We alone determine what measures if any, shall be taken to vindicate the principles of the Doctrine, and we of necessity determine when the principles have been vindicated. No other power of the world has any relationship to, or voice in, the implementing of the principles which the Doctrine contains. It is our Doctrine, to be by us invoked and sustainèd, held in abeyance, or abandoned as our high international policy or vital national interests shall seem to us, and to us alone, to demand.

It may, in conclusion, be repeated: The Doctrine does not concern itself with purely inter-American relations; it has nothing to do with the relationship between the United States and other American nations, except where other American nations shall become involved with European governments in arrangements which threaten the security of the United States, and even in such cases, the Doctrine runs against the European country, not the American nation, and the United States would primarily deal thereunder with the European country and not with the American nation concerned. The Doctrine states a case of the United States *vs.* Europe, and not of the United States *vs.* Latin America. Furthermore, the fact should never be lost to view that in applying this Doctrine during the period of one hundred years since it was announced, our Government has over and over again driven it in as a shield between Europe and the Americas to protect Latin America from the political and territorial thrusts of Europe; and this was done at times when the American nations were weak and struggling for the establishment of stable, permanent governments; when the political morality of Europe sanc-tioned, indeed encouraged, the acquisition of territory by force; and when many of the great powers of Europe looked with eager, covetous eyes to the rich, undeveloped areas of the American hemisphere. Nor should another equally vital fact be lost sight of, that the United States has only been able to give this protection against designing European powers because of its known willingness and determination, if and whenever necessary, to expend its treasure and to sacrifice American life to maintain the principles of the Doctrine. So far as Latin America is concerned, the Doctrine is now, and always has been, not an instrument of violence and oppression, but an unbought, freely bestowed, and wholly effective guaranty of their freedom, independence, and territorial integrity against the imperialistic designs of Europe.

XI

the road to war (1931-1941)

THE 1930's BEGAN somewhat auspiciously with the signing of the London Naval Treaty, which promised peace among the world's leading sea powers. Yet the following year one of those powers, Japan, forcibly wrested Manchuria from China. Although the League of Nations proved ineffectual in the crisis, Secretary of State Henry L. Stimson declared that the United States would not recognize territorial changes made in violation of the Kellogg-Briand Pact. When Franklin Roosevelt became President his energies were concentrated on domestic economic issues, but he continued the policy of withdrawal from the internal affairs of Latin American nations by endorsing the policy of the Good Neighbor and supporting the abrogation of the Platt Amendment.

Congress continued the efforts of the 1920's to profit by the apparent lessons of American involvement in World War I. The Johnson Act prohibited loans to foreign governments that had defaulted on their obligations to the United States, and the Neutrality Acts of 1935, 1936, and 1937 were designed to prevent incidents that might lead to war. As Italy, Germany, and Japan embarked on expansionist ventures, the President in 1937 sounded a call for a collective "quarantine" of aggressor nations, only to have his appeal rejected by the nation. Determined to secure some degree of preparedness, Roosevelt took steps at least to secure the solidarity and protect the integrity of the Western Hemisphere by concluding agreements with the Latin American countries.

When war finally came in Europe the President proclaimed the neutrality of the United States and sought to repeal the embargo provisions of the Neutrality Act. The fall of France in the spring of 1940 provoked a Presidential request for a vast and accelerated build-up of the armed forces, and Roosevelt began his program of aiding embattled Britain by exchanging fifty old destroyers for the right to establish American bases on British territory in the Western Hemisphere. Convinced that the safety of the free world was at stake, the President sought to commit the nation to the destruction of Hitlerism. The "great debate" over America's course began in earnest with the Lend Lease Act, and it became hotter when Russia entered the war in June of 1941 and distinguished citizens protested actions which in their opinion could lead only to American involvement.

While the nation became more committed to the European conflict, negotiations continued with Japan in an effort to restrain her expansionist activities. Believing that war was unavoidable, the American authorities intended to propose a modus vivendi which would delay hostilities for at least three months and permit the further fortification of the Philippines. Upon receipt of strong protests from China and Great Britain, the modus vivendi was dropped and a more demanding note was sent instead. The Japanese government made the decision for war on December 1, and six days later the attack on Pearl Harbor put an end to the Great Debate.

1

The Stimson Doctrine

☆ *In September, 1931, Japanese troops began hostilities which led eventually to their occupation of South Manchuria. The United States interpreted this action as being a violation of the Kellogg-Briand Pact and declared that it would act accordingly.** ☆

Please deliver to the Foreign Office on behalf of your Government as soon as possible the following note:

"With the recent military operations about Chinchow, the last remaining administrative authority of the Government of the Chinese Republic in South Manchuria, as it existed prior to September 18th, 1931, has been destroyed. The American Government continues confident that the work of the neutral commission recently authorized by the Council of the League of Nations will facilitate an ultimate solution of the difficulties now existing between China and Japan. But in view of the present situation and of its own rights and obligations therein, the American Government deems it to be its duty to

* From Secretary of State Henry L. Stimson to the Ambassador in Japan, January 7, 1932, in *Peace and War, United States Foreign Policy, 1931-1941*, Washington, 1943, pp. 801-802.

notify both the Imperial Japanese Government and the Government of the Chinese Republic that it cannot admit the legality of any situation *de facto* nor does it intend to recognize any treaty or agreement entered into between those Governments, or agents thereof, which may impair the treaty rights of the United States or its citizens in China, including those which relate to the sovereignty, the independence, or the territorial and administrative integrity of the Republic of China, or to the international policy relative to China, commonly known as the open door policy; and that it does not intend to recognize any situation, treaty or agreement which may be brought about by means contrary to the covenants and obligations of the Pact of Paris of August 27, 1928, to which Treaty both China and Japan, as well as the United States, are parties."

2

The Good Neighbor

☆ *In his inaugural address, March 4, 1933, President Roosevelt dedicated the nation to play the role of the "Good Neighbor" in its foreign relations. He explored this concept at length in its application to Latin America in an address of the Governing Board of the Pan-American Union, April 12, 1933.* ☆

I rejoice in this opportunity to participate in the celebration of "Pan-American Day" and to extend on behalf of the people of the United States a fraternal greeting to our sister American Republics. The celebration of "Pan-American Day" in this building, dedicated to international good-will and cooperation, exemplifies a unity of thought and purpose among the peoples of this hemisphere. It is a manifestation of the common ideal of mutual helpfulness, sympathetic understanding and spiritual solidarity.

There is inspiration in the thought that on this day the attention of the citizens of the twenty-one Republics of America is focused on the common ties—historical, cultural, economic, and social—which bind them to one another. Common ideals and a community of interest, together with a spirit of cooperation, have led to the realization that the well-being of one Nation depends in large measure upon the well-being of its neighbors. It is upon these foundations that Pan Americanism has been built.

* From Samuel I. Rosenman, *The Public Papers and Addresses of Franklin D. Roosevelt, II*, pp. 129-131. Published by Random House, Inc., New York, 1938.

This celebration commemorates a movement based upon the policy of fraternal cooperation. In my Inaugural Address I stated that I would "dedicate this Nation to the policy of the good neighbor —the neighbor who resolutely respects himself and, because he does so, respects the rights of others—the neighbor who respects his obligations and respects the sanctity of his agreements in and with a world of neighbors." Never before has the significance of the words "good neighbor" been so manifest in international relations. Never have the need and benefit of neighborly cooperation in every form of human activity been so evident as they are today.

Friendship among Nations, as among individuals, calls for constructive efforts to muster the forces of humanity in order that an atmosphere of close understanding and cooperation may be cultivated. It involves mutual obligations and responsibilities, for it is only by sympathetic respect for the rights of others and a scrupulous fulfillment of the corresponding obligations by each member of the community that a true fraternity can be maintained.

The essential qualities of a true Pan Americanism must be the same as those which constitute a good neighbor, namely, mutual understanding, and, through such understanding, a sympathetic appreciation of the other's point of view. It is only in this manner that we can hope to build up a system of which confidence, friendship and good-will are the cornerstones.

In this spirit the people of every Republic on our continent are coming to a deep understanding of the fact that the Monroe Doctrine, of which so much has been written and spoken for more than a century, was and is directed at the maintenance of independence by the peoples of the continent. It was aimed and is aimed against the acquisition in any manner of the control of additional territory in this hemisphere by any non-American power.

Hand in hand with this Pan-American doctrine of continental self-defense, the peoples of the American Republics understand more clearly, with the passing years, that the independence of each Republic must recognize the independence of every other Republic. Each one of us must grow by an advancement of civilization and social well-being and not by the acquisition of territory at the expense of any neighbor.

In this spirit of mutual understanding and of cooperation on this continent you and I cannot fail to be disturbed by any armed strife between neighbors. I do not hesitate to say to you, the distinguished members of the Governing Board of the Pan-American Union, that I regard existing conflicts between four of our sister Republics as a backward step.

Your Americanism and mine must be a structure built of confidence, cemented by a sympathy which recognizes only equality and fraternity. It finds its source and being in the hearts of men and dwells in the temple of the intellect.

We all of us have peculiar problems, and, to speak frankly, the interest of our own citizens must, in each instance, come first. But it is equally true that it is of vital importance to every Nation of this Continent that the American Governments, individually, take, without further delay, such action as may be possible to abolish all unnecessary and artificial barriers and restrictions which now hamper the healthy flow of trade between the peoples of the American Republics.

3

Insulation from War

☆ *The prevailing American attitude toward European affairs and the desire to avoid further involvement were reflected in the passage of the Johnson Act of 1934 and the Neutrality Acts of 1935, 1936, and 1937. Some critics felt, however, that neutrality legislation not only would fail to keep the nation out of war but would actually facilitate its involvement.* ☆

(a) THE JOHNSON ACT*

An Act to prohibit financial transactions with any foreign government in default on its obligations to the United States.

Be it enacted, That hereafter it shall be unlawful within the United States or any place subject to the jurisdiction of the United States for any person to purchase or sell the bonds, securities, or other obligations of, any foreign government or political subdivision thereof or any organization of association acting for or on behalf of a foreign government or political subdivision thereof, issued after a passage of this Act, or to make any loan to such foreign government, political subdivision, organization, or association, except a renewal or adjustment of existing indebtedness while such government, political subdivision, organization, or association, is in default in the payment of its obligations, or any part thereof, to the Government of the United States. Any person violating the provisions of this Act shall upon conviction thereof be fined not more

than $10,000 or imprisoned for not more than five years, or both.

SEC. 2. As used in this Act the term "person" includes individual, partnership, corporation, or association other than a public corporation created by or pursuant to special authorization of Congress, or a corporation in which the Government of the United States has or exercises a controlling interest through stock ownership or otherwise.

(b) THE "NEUTRALITY ACT"*

SECTION 1. (a) Whenever the President shall find that there exists a state of war between, or among, two or more foreign states, the President shall proclaim such fact, and it shall thereafter be unlawful to export, or attempt to export, or cause to be exported, arms, ammunition, or implements of war from any place in the United States to any belligerent state named in such proclamation, or to any neutral state for transshipment to, or

* April 13, 1934. From 48 U.S. Stats. 574.

* May 1, 1937. From 50 U.S. Stats. 121.

for the use of, any such belligerent state.

(b) The President shall, from time to time, by proclamation, extend such embargo upon the export of arms, ammunition, or implements of war to other states as and when they may become involved in such war.

(c) Whenever the President shall find that a state of civil strife exists in a foreign state and that such civil strife is of a magnitude or is being conducted under such conditions that the export of arms, ammunition, or implements of war from the United States to such foreign state would threaten or endanger the peace of the United States, the President shall proclaim such fact, and it shall thereafter be unlawful to export, or attempt to export, or cause to be exported, arms, ammunition, or implements of war from any place in the United States to such foreign state, or to any neutral state for transshipment to, or for the use of, such foreign state.

(d) The President shall, from time to time by proclamation, definitely enumerate the arms, ammunitions, and implements of war, the export of which is prohibited by this section. . . .

(e) Whoever, in violation of any of the provisions of this Act, shall export, or attempt to export, or cause to be exported, arms, ammunition, or implements of war from the United States shall be fined not more than $10,000, or imprisoned not more than five years, or both. . . .

(f) In the case of the forfeiture of any arms, ammunition, or implements of war by reason of a violation of this Act, . . . such arms, ammunition, or implements of war shall be delivered to the Secretary of War for such use or disposal thereof as shall be approved by the President of the United States.

(g) Whenever, in the judgment of the President, the conditions which have caused him to issue any proclamation under the authority of this section have

ceased to exist, he shall revoke the same, and the provisions of this section shall thereupon cease to apply with respect to the state or states named in such proclamation, except with respect to offenses committed, or forfeitures incurred, prior to such revocation. . . .

SEC. 3. (a) Whenever the President shall have issued a proclamation under the authority of section 1 of this Act, it shall thereafter be unlawful for any person within the United States to purchase, sell, or exchange bonds, securities, or other obligations of the government of any belligerent state or of any state wherein civil strife exists, named in such proclamation, or of any political subdivision of any such state, or of any person acting for or on behalf of the government of any such state, or of any faction or asserted government within any such state wherein civil strife exists, or of any person acting for or on behalf of any faction or asserted government within any such state wherein civil strife exists, issued after the date of such proclamation, or to make any loan or extend any credit to any such government, political subdivision, faction, asserted government, or person, or to solicit or receive any contribution for any such government, political subdivision, faction, asserted government, or person: *Provided,* That if the President shall find that such action will serve to protect the commercial or other interests of the United States or its citizens, he may, in his discretion, and to such extent and under such regulations as he may prescribe, except from the operation of this section ordinary commercial credits and short-time obligations in aid of legal transactions and of a character customarily used in normal peacetime commercial transactions. Nothing in this subsection shall be construed to prohibit the solicitation or collection of funds to be used for medical aid and assistance, or for food and clothing to relieve human suffering, when such solicitation or collection of funds is made on behalf of and for use by any person or oganization which is not acting for or on behalf of any such government, political subdivision, faction, or asserted government. . . .

SEC. 4. This Act shall not apply to an American republic or republics engaged in war against a non-American state or states, provided the American republic is not cooperating with a non-American state or states in such war. . . .

SEC. 6. (a) Whenever the President shall have issued a proclamation under the authority of section 1 of this Act, it shall thereafter be unlawful, until such proclamation is revoked, for any American vessel to carry any arms, ammunition, or implements of war to any belligerent state, or to any state wherein civil strife exists, named in such proclamation, or to any neutral state for transshipment to, or for the use of, any such belligerent state or any such state wherein civil strife exists. . . .

SEC. 7. (a) Whenever, during any war in which the United States is neutral, the President, or any person thereunto authorized by him, shall have cause to believe that any vessel, domestic or foreign, whether requiring clearance or not, is about to carry out of a port of the United States, fuel, men, arms, ammunition, implements of war, or other supplies to any warship, tender, or supply ship of a belligerent state, but the evidence is not deemed sufficient to justify forbidding the departure of the vessel . . . he shall have the power and it shall be his duty to require the owner, master, or person in command thereof, before departing from a port of the United States, to give a bond to the United States, with sufficient sureties, in such amount as he shall deem proper, conditioned that the vessel will not deliver the men, or any part of the cargo, to any warship, tender, or supply ship of a belligerent state.

(b) If the President, or any person thereunto authorized by him, shall find that a vessel, domestic or foreign, in a port of the United States, has previously cleared from a port of the United States during such war and delivered its cargo or any part thereof to a warship, tender, or supply ship of a belligerent state, he may prohibit the departure of such vessel during the duration of the war.

SEC. 8. Whenever, during any war in which the United States is neutral, the President shall find that special restrictions placed on the use of the ports and territorial waters of the United States by the submarines or armed merchant vessels of a foreign state, will serve to maintain peace between the United States and foreign states, or to protect the commercial interests of the United States and its citizens, or to promote the security of the United States, and shall make proclamation thereof, it shall thereafter be unlawful for any such submarine or armed merchant vessel to enter a port or the territorial waters of the United States or to depart therefrom, except under such conditions and subject to such limitation as the President may prescribe. . . .

SEC. 9. Whenever the President shall have issued a proclamation under the authority of section 1 of this Act it shall thereafter be unlawful for any citizen of the United States to travel on any vessel of the state or states named in such proclamation, except in accordance with such rules and regulations as the President shall prescribe. . . .

SEC. 10. Whenever the President shall have issued a proclamation under the authority of section 1, it shall thereafter be unlawful, until such proclamation is revoked, for any American vessel engaged in commerce with any belligerent state, or any state wherein civil strife exists, named in such proclamation, to be armed or to carry any armament, arms, ammunition, or implements of war, except small arms and ammunition therefor which the President may deem necessary and shall publicly designate for the preservation of discipline aboard such vessels.

(c) THE UNNEUTRALITY OF NEUTRALITY LEGISLATION*

This record of American policy over the last generation has two aspects—the national and the international. Just as Great Britain turned from her traditions with the ill-fated entente with France and Russia of 1904, so the United States broke with its fundamental principles by the unprecedented decision to participate in a European war and send troops to cure Europe of nationalistic wars and autocratic governments. The results of that adventure, which have helped neither Europe nor the United States, are likely to be far-reaching. For not merely American neutrality, but American independence, may be "a thing of the past."

Our subjection began in August, 1914, and there has been little recovery from that depression. There are no longer many principles in American foreign policy. Having flouted the wisdom of those who charted America's course, we now respond easily to temptations to enforce policies formulated in other countries without our participation. The American people, having falsely been told that our effort to preserve our neutrality got us into the war, have been driven in their perplexity to heterodox measures, such as the 1937 Pittman Act, which are designed to insulate the United States from all contact with belligerent powers, but which are likely to have quite different effects.

It would have been more sensible simply to embargo arms and loans as did the 1935-36 legislation. For the rest, we should have maintained the freedom of the seas and the time-honored rights of neutrals which other nations, more confi-

* From Edwin Borchard and William Potter Lage, *Neutrality for the United States*, pp. 344-345, 348-350. Copyright, 1937, Yale University Press, New Haven. Used by permission.

dent of their capacity to stay out of wars when they wish, must now uphold. By resigning all opportunity to stand for American rights, we come close to insuring license for belligerents only.

The retreat from American traditions has been stimulated by the provocative interventionist policy of the League of Nations, whose devotees have continued to befuddle the American people with the argument that neutrality is immoral and that in a European war the United States cannot remain neutral. Without knowing the identity of the combatants or the issues of the war, we are blandly informed that the United States has no choice but to participate. The argument is humiliating to American independence which, indeed, is the inevitable victim of the assault. But it has encouraged European nations to seek to enlist us in the name of the Higher Morality in their perpetual feuds, and Kellogg Pacts open a ready door to involvement.

The attack on neutrality as a principle and a practice, so sedulously cultivated since the war, has, however, been based not only on the League cult of partisanship, but also on the contention that the law is now so uncertain that neutrals have no rights on which they can rely. It is argued that as neutrality failed to keep us out of war in 1917, unneutrality must perforce become the national policy. It has even been urged, entirely without justification, that insistence on our neutral rights brought us into the war and that escape lies in an abandonment of neutral rights. This belief is implicit in the 1937 legislation.

But the fact is that neutral rights were as clear in 1914 as was any other branch of public law, and while the law was grossly violated during the war, it has not thereby been ended or modified. America submissiveness may have temporarily weakened respect for law, but its permanent vitality is unimpaired—unless indeed unmitigated force has now become the sole arbiter of human affairs.

. . . there does not seem to be any short cut to peace. That is a condition which must be carefully nurtured in the soil of contentment, confidence, and mutual respect. The effort to organize collective armed intervention for peace can never achieve peace. To engender peace by the threat of force is inherently incongruous. World cooperation is to be found in ameliorating the underlying causes of friction and in the adoption of the time-honored, homely virtues of simple decency, fairness, and reconciliation of conflicting interests, in the adjustment of grievances, and in strengthening, not weakening, the rules of law. This is the type of world cooperation that is likely to produce measurable peace, and there is in it no threat to use force.

The 1919 "peace" doctrines and the machinery for carrying them into effect have been tried and found wanting. This ought now to be clear enough. There is danger in further relying upon a novel remedy conditioned upon a change in human and international relations which is nonexistent. That way can lead only to disappointment and despair. The Hague Conferences were closer to reality than the postwar machinery, and in their modest way achieved practical successes which the more ambitious demand for wholesale regeneration cannot record.

Carried away by enthusiasm for noble ends, the United States rushed to Europe in 1917 to make the world "safe for democracy," to fight a "war to end war." In that period the golden age of rhetoric and phantasy in these matters was inaugurated. But in the light of the results achieved, the enterprise must be regarded

as a ghastly failure. Europe is today less peaceful in time of peace than she has ever been. The "international government" which was established at Geneva has not brought unification or political cooperation, but on the contrary has widened the rifts between the countries of the continent. The concert of Europe has rarely been less harmonious. Democracy is not in high renown and dictatorships of a kind not dreamed of in the nineteenth century mar wide areas of the landscape. Collective and individual insecurity is nearly universal.

These phenomena are not accidental. They are the result of ill-considered policies which could not have lasted as long as they have without the cooperation of the United States in giving the countries of Europe the impression that we could be counted on to do again what we had just done. The least that can now be done is to avoid similar ineptitude in the future. By intervention in European quarrels we can make the situation worse, but never better. The road prepared for us by the coercive peace machinery of Geneva, which has proved so alluring to some of our statesmen, can lead only to deeper involvement. Europe must work out its own problems; it understands them better than we ever can.

It is inevitable that the temptations to "cooperate" with the "peace-loving" nations of Europe will destroy our objectivity and neutrality and by making the United States the particular friend of some Powers make us necessarily the enemies of others. The sound advice of George Washington . . . was based on a profound knowledge of human nature. By cultivating friendly relations with all nations, developing with each the highest possible degree of trade, by bargaining off the international debts as part of the terrible price paid for a bitter lesson, by using the great gifts and resources which nature has placed in our keeping to set the world an example of contented living, we may again demonstrate the American capacity to manage American affairs.

There is no improvised formula to insure abstention from war and yet maintain national dignity. Neither the taking of sides nor widespread embargoes mark the road to peace. Far more important are an honest intention to remain aloof from foreign conflict, a refusal to be stampeded by unneutral propaganda, a knowledge of the law and a capacity to stand upon it, meeting emergencies and problems not romantically but wisely. The cultivation of sagacity in these matters, of detachment, of moderation, of toleration, of the spirit of live and let live, and the renunciation of the psychology and policy of "enforcing peace" by hostile measures probably present the only tangible hope for preserving peace in broad areas of the world.

4

The Quarantine Address

☆ *In the middle 1930's, serious threats to world peace were posed by Mussolini's attack on Ethiopia, Hitler's violation of the Versailles Treaty, Japan's resumed invasion of China, and the intervention of Germany, Italy, and Russia in the Spanish Civil War. Alarmed by these developments, President Roosevelt urged in a speech in Chicago, October 5, 1937, a quarantine of aggressors by the peace-loving nations of the world.** ☆

On my trip across the continent and back . . . as I have seen with my own eyes, the prosperous farms, the thriving factories, and the busy railroads—as I have seen the happiness and security and peace which covers our wide land—almost inevitably I have been compelled to contrast our peace with very different scenes being enacted in other parts of the world.

It is because the people of the United States under modern conditions must, for the sake of their own future, give thought to the rest of the world, that I, as the responsible executive head of the Nation, have chosen this great inland city and this gala occasion to speak to you on a subject of definite national importance.

The political situation in the world, which of late has been growing progressively worse, is such as to cause grave concern and anxiety to all the peoples and nations who wish to live in peace and amity with their neighbors.

Some 15 years ago the hopes of man-

* From *Peace and War, United States Foreign Policy, 1931-1941*, Washington, 1943, pp. 383-387.

kind for a continuing era of international peace were raised to great heights when more than 60 nations solemnly pledged themselves not to resort to arms in furtherance of their national aims and policies. The high aspirations expressed in the Briand-Kellogg Peace Pact and the hopes for peace thus raised have of late given away to a haunting fear of calamity. The present reign of terror and international lawlessness began a few years ago.

It began through unjustified interference in the internal affairs of other nations or the invasion of alien territory in violation of treaties and has now reached a stage where the very foundations of civilization are seriously threatened. The landmarks and traditions which have marked the progress of civilization toward a condition of law, order, and justice are being wiped away.

Without a declaration of war and without warning or justification of any kind, civilians, including women and children, are being ruthlessly murdered with bombs from the air. In times of so-called peace ships are being attacked and sunk by submarines without cause or notice. Nations are fomenting and taking sides in civil warfare in nations that have never done them any harm. Nations claiming freedom for themselves deny it to others.

Innocent peoples and nations are being cruelly sacrificed to a greed for power and supremacy which is devoid of all sense of justice and humane consideration.

To paraphrase a recent author, "perhaps we foresee a time when men, exultant in the technique of homicide, will rage so hotly over the world that every precious thing will be in danger, every book and picture and harmony, every treasure garnered through two millenniums, the small, the delicate, the defenseless— all will be lost or wrecked or utterly destroyed."

If those things come to pass in other parts of the world let no one imagine that America will escape, that it may expect mercy, that this Western Hemisphere will not be attacked, and that it will continue tranquilly and peacefully to carry on the ethics and the arts of civilization.

If those days come "there will be no safety by arms, no help from authority, no answer in science. The storm will rage till every flower of culture is trampled and all human beings are leveled in a vast chaos."

If those days are not to come to pass— if we are to have a world in which we can breathe freely and live in amity without fear—the peace-loving nations must make a concerted effort to uphold laws and principles on which alone peace can rest secure.

The peace-loving nations must make a concerted effort in opposition to those violations of treaties and those ignorings of humane instincts which today are creating a state of international anarchy and instability from which there is no escape through mere isolation or neutrality. . . .

There is a solidarity and interdependence about the modern world, both technically and morally, which makes it impossible for any nation completely to isolate itself from economic and political upheavals in the rest of the world, especially when such upheavals appear to be spreading and not declining. There can be no stability or peace either within nations or between nations except under laws and moral standards adhered to by all. International anarchy destroys every foundation for peace. It jeopardizes either the immediate or the future security of every nation, large or small. It is, therefore, a matter of vital interest and concern to the people of the United States that the sanctity of international treaties and the maintenance of international morality be restored. . . .

The peace, the freedom, and the security of 90 percent of the population of the world is being jeopardized by the remaining 10 percent, who are threatening a breakdown of all international order and law. Surely the 90 percent who want to live in peace under law and in accordance with moral standards that have received almost universal acceptance through the centuries, can and must find some way to make their will prevail.

The situation is definitely of universal concern. The questions involved relate not merely to violations of specific provisions of particular treaties; they are questions of war and of peace, of international law, and especially of principles of humanity. It is true that they involve definite violations of agreements, and especially of the Covenant of the League of Nations, the Briand-Kellogg Pact, and the Nine Power Treaty. But they also involve problems of world economy, world security, and world humanity.

It is true that the moral consciousness of the world must recognize the importance of removing injustices and wellfounded grievances; but at the same time it must be aroused to the cardinal necessity of honoring sanctity of treaties, of respecting the rights and liberties of others, and of putting an end to acts of international aggression.

It seems to be unfortunately true that the epidemic of world lawlessness is spreading.

When an epidemic of physical disease starts to spread, the community approves and joins in a quarantine of the patients in order to protect the health of the community against the spread of the disease.

It is my determination to pursue a policy of peace and to adopt every practicable measure to avoid involvement in war. It ought to be inconceivable that in this modern era, and in the face of experience, any nation could be so foolish and ruthless as to run the risk of plunging the whole world into war by invading and violating in contravention of solemn treaties the territory of other nations that have done them no real harm and which are too weak to protect themselves adequately. Yet the peace of the world and the welfare and security of every nation is today being threatened by that very thing.

No nation which refuses to exercise forbearance and to respect the freedom and rights of others can long remain strong and retain the confidence and respect of other nations. No nation ever loses its dignity or good standing by conciliating its differences and by exercising great patience with and consideration for the rights of other nations.

War is a contagion, whether it be declared or undeclared. It can engulf states and peoples remote from the original scene of hostilities. We are determined to keep out of war, yet we cannot insure ourselves against the disastrous effects of war and the dangers of involvement. We are adopting such measures as will minimize our risk of involvement, but we cannot have complete protection in a world of disorder in which confidence and security have broken down.

If civilization is to survive the principles of the Prince of Peace must be restored. Shattered trust between nations must be revived.

Most important of all, the will for peace on the part of peace-loving nations must express itself to the end that nations that may be tempted to violate their agreements and the rights of others will desist from such a cause. There must be positive endeavors to preserve peace.

America hates war. America hopes for peace. Therefore, America actively engages in the search for peace.

5

Hemisphere Solidarity

☆ *The German annexation of Austria and the Sudetenland in 1938 and attempts to extend Nazi and Fascist influence to Latin America, stimulated efforts to coordinate Western Hemisphere defense. The first step in this direction was taken at the Inter-American Conference at Lima, Peru, in December 1938.** ☆

The Governments of the American States

DECLARE:

First. That they reaffirm their continental solidarity and their purpose to collaborate in the maintenance of the principles upon which the said solidarity is based.

Second. That faithful to the above-mentioned principles and to their absolute sovereignty, they reaffirm their decision to maintain them and to defend them against all foreign intervention or activity that may threaten them.

Third. And in case the peace, security or territorial integrity of any American Republic is thus threatened by acts of any nature that may impair them, they proclaim their common concern and their determination to make effective their

solidarity, coordinating their respective sovereign wills by means of the procedure of consultation, established by conventions in force and by declarations of the Inter-American Conferences, using the measures which in each case the circumstances may make advisable. It is understood that the Governments of the American Republics will act independently in their individual capacity, recognizing fully their juridical equality as sovereign states.

Fourth. That in order to facilitate the consultations established in this and other American peace instruments, the Ministers for Foreign Affairs of the American Republics, when deemed desirable and at the initiative of any one of them, will meet in their several capitals by rotation and without protocolary character. Each Government may, under special circumstances or for special reasons, designate a representative as a substitute for its Minister for Foreign Affairs.

Fifth. This Declaration shall be known as the "Declaration of Lima."

* The Declaration of Lima, approved December 24, 1938, in *Report of the Delegation of the United States of America to the Eighth International Conference of American States*, Washington, 1941, p. 190.

6

Repeal of the Embargo

☆ *World War II erupted on September 1, 1939, when German armies invaded Poland. On September 21, 1939, the President, convinced that the existing neutrality laws would operate to the advantage of Germany, requested Congress to repeal the embargo on the grounds that it was likely to lead to American involvement in the war.** ☆

Since 1931 the use of force instead of the council table has constantly increased in the settlement of disputes between nations—except in the Western Hemisphere, where there has been only one war, now happily terminated.

During these years also the building up of vast armies, navies, and storehouses of war has proceeded abroad with growing speed and intensity. But, during these years, and extending back even to the days of the Kellogg-Briand Pact, the United States has constantly, consistently, and conscientiously done all in its power to encourage peaceful settlements, to bring about reduction of armaments, and to avert threatened wars. We have done this not only because any war anywhere necessarily hurts American security and American prosperity, but because of the more important fact that any war anywhere retards the progress of morality and religion and impairs the security of civilization itself.

For many years the primary purpose

of our foreign policy has been that this Nation and this Government should strive to the utmost to aid in avoiding war among other nations. But if and when war unhappily comes, the Government and the Nation must exert every possible effort to avoid being drawn into the war.

The executive branch of the Government did its utmost, within our traditional policy of noninvolvement, to aid in averting the present appalling war. Having thus striven and failed, this Government must lose no time or effort to keep the Nation from being drawn into the war.

In my candid judgment we shall succeed in these efforts.

Beginning with the foundation of our constitutional government in the year 1789, the American policy in respect to belligerent nations, with one notable exception, has been based on international law. Be it remembered that what we call international law has had as its primary objectives the avoidance of causes of war and the prevention of the extension of war.

The single exception was the policy adopted by this Nation during the Napo-

* From *Peace and War, United States Foreign Policy, 1931-1941*, Washington, 1943, pp. 486-488.

REPEAL OF THE EMBARGO

leonic Wars, when, seeking to avoid

leonic Wars, when, seeking to avoid involvement, we acted for some years under the so-called Embargo and Non-Intercourse Acts. . . .

Our next deviation by statute from the sound principles of neutrality and peace through international law did not come for 130 years. It was the so-called Neutrality Act of 1935—only 4 years ago—an act continued in force by the joint resolution of May 1, 1937, despite grave doubts expressed as to its wisdom by many Senators and Representatives and by officials charged with the conduct of our foreign relations, including myself. I regret that the Congress passed that act. I regret equally that I signed that act.

On July fourteenth of this year I asked the Congress in the cause of peace and in the interest of real American neutrality and security to take action to change that act.

I now ask again that such action be taken in respect to that part of the act which is wholly inconsistent with ancient precepts of the law of nations—the embargo provisions. I ask it because they are, in my opinion, most vitally dangerous to American neutrality, American security, and American peace.

I seek a greater consistency through the repeal of the embargo provisions and a return to international law. I seek re-enactment of the historic and traditional American policy which, except for the disastrous interlude of the Embargo and Non-Intercourse Acts, has served us well for nearly a century and a half.

It has been erroneously said that return to that policy might bring us nearer to war. I give to you my deep and unalterable conviction, based on years of experience as a worker in the field of international peace, that by the repeal of the embargo the United States will more probably remain at peace than if the law remains as it stands today. I say this because with the repeal of the embargo this Government clearly and definitely will insist that American citizens and American ships keep away from the immediate perils of the actual zones of conflict.

Repeal of the embargo and a return to international law are the crux of this issue.

To those who say that this program would involve a step toward war on our part, I reply that it offers far greater safeguards than we now possess or have ever possessed to protect American lives and property from danger. It is a positive program for giving safety. This means less likelihood of incidents and controversies which tend to draw us into conflict, as they did in the last World War. There lies the road to peace!

7

Rearmament and Aid

☆ *After the German conquest of Poland and during the winter of 1939-1940 it appeared that the opposing German and British-French armies were stalemated. In April 1940, however, German forces quickly overran Norway and Denmark, and the following month they launched a massive attack on the Low Countries and France. President Roosevelt concluded that this blitzkrieg required that the United States drastically step up its defense program. After the fall of France in June and the attempts to crush Britain by air and submarine warfare, Roosevelt, in order to provide England with badly needed vessels and the United States with defense bases, executed the Destroyer-Bases agreement with England. As the war continued and England's resources approached exhaustion, the President sought and received authorization to give direct aid to any nations whose defense was considered vital to American security.* ☆

(a) PRESIDENT ROOSEVELT'S ADDRESS TO CONGRESS*

These are ominous days—days whose swift and shocking developments force every neutral nation to look to its defenses in the light of new factors. The brutal force of modern offensive war has been loosed in all its horror. New powers of destruction, incredibly swift and deadly have been developed; and those who wield them are ruthless and daring. No old defense is so strong that it requires no further strengthening, and no attack is so unlikely or impossible that it may be ignored.

Let us examine, without self-deception, the dangers which confront us. Let us

* May 16, 1940. From *Peace and War, United States Foreign Policy, 1931-1941*, Washington, 1943, pp. 527-530.

measure our strength and our defense without self-delusion.

The clear fact is that the American people must recast their thinking about national protection.

Motorized armies can now sweep through enemy territories at the rate of 200 miles a day. Parachute troops are dropped from airplanes in large numbers behind enemy lines. Troops are landed from planes in open fields, on wide highways, and at local civil airports.

We have seen the treacherous use of the "fifth column" by which persons supposed to be peaceful visitors were actually a part of an enemy unit of occupation. Lightning attacks, capable of destroying airplane factories and munition works hundreds of miles behind the lines, are part of the new technique of modern war.

The element of surprise which has ever been an important tactic in warfare has become the more dangerous because of the amazing speed with which modern equipment can reach and attack the enemy's country.

Our own vital interests are widespread. More than ever the protection of the whole American Hemisphere against invasion or control or domination by non-American nations has the united support of the 21 American republics, including the United States. More than ever this protection calls for ready-at-hand weapons capable of great mobility because of the potential speed of modern attack.

The Atlantic and Pacific Oceans were reasonably adequate defensive barriers when fleets under sail could move at an average speed of 5 miles an hour. Even then by a sudden foray it was possible for an opponent actually to burn our National Capitol. Later, the oceans still gave strength to our defense when fleets and convoys propelled by steam could sail the oceans at 15 or 20 miles an hour.

But the new element—air navigation—steps up the speed of possible attack to 200, to 300 miles an hour. . . .

Surely, the developments of the past few weeks have made it clear to all of our citizens that the possibility of attack on vital American zones ought to make it essential that we have the physical, the ready ability to meet those attacks and to prevent them from reaching their objectives.

This means military implements—not on paper—which are ready and available to meet any lightning offensive against our American interest. It means also that facilities for production must be ready to turn out munitions and equipment at top speed.

We have had the lesson before us over and over again—nations that were not ready and were unable to get ready found themselves overrun by the enemy. So-called impregnable fortifications no longer exist. A defense which allows an enemy to consolidate his approach without hindrance will lose. A defense which makes no effective effort to destroy the lines of supplies and communications of the enemy will lose.

An effective defense by its very nature requires the equipment to attack an aggressor on his route before he can establish strong bases within the territory of American vital interests. . . .

Our immediate problem is to superimpose on [our] production capacity a greatly increased additional production capacity. I should like to see this Nation geared up to the ability to turn out at least 50,000 planes a year. Furthermore, I believe that this Nation should plan at this time a program that would provide us with 50,000 military and naval planes.

The ground forces of the Army require the immediate speeding up of last winter's program to procure equipment of all kinds, including motor transport and artillery, including antiaircraft guns and full ammunition supplies. It has been planned to spread these requirements over the next 3 or 4 years. We should fill them at once. At this time I am asking the immediate appropriation by the Congress of a large sum of money for four primary purposes:

First, to procure the essential equipment of all kinds for a larger and thoroughly rounded-out Army;

Second, to replace or modernize all old Army and Navy equipment with the latest type of equipment;

Third, to increase production facilities for everything needed for the Army and Navy for national defense. We require the ability to turn out quickly infinitely greater supplies;

Fourth, to speed up to a 24-hour basis all existing Army and Navy contracts and all new contracts to be awarded.

(b) PRESIDENT ROOSEVELT'S MESSAGE TO CONGRESS*

I transmit herewith for the information of the Congress notes exchanged between the British Ambassador at Washington and the Secretary of State on September 2, 1940, under which this Government has acquired the right to lease naval and air bases in Newfoundland, and in the islands of Bermuda, the Bahamas, Jamaica, St. Lucia, Trinidad, and Antigua, and in British Guiana; also a copy of an opinion of the Attorney General dated August 27, 1940, regarding my authority to consummate this arrangement.

The right to bases in Newfoundland and Bermuda are gifts—generously given and gladly received. The other bases mentioned have been acquired in exchange for fifty of our over-age destroyers.

This is not inconsistent in any sense with our status of peace. Still less is it a threat against any nation. It is an epochal and far-reaching act of preparation for continental defense in the face of grave danger.

Preparation for defense is an inalienable prerogative of a sovereign state. Under present circumstances this exercise of sovereign right is essential to the maintenance of our peace and safety. This is the most important action in the reinforcement of our national defense that has been taken since the Louisiana Purchase. Then as now, considerations of safety from overseas attack were fundamental.

The value to the Western Hemisphere of these outposts of security is beyond calculation. Their need has long been recognized by our country, and especially by those primarily charged with the duty of charting and organizing our own naval and military defense. They are essential to the protection of the Panama Canal, Central America, the Northern portion of South America, The Antilles, Canada, Mexico, and our own Eastern and Gulf Seaboards. Their consequent importance in hemispheric defense is obvious. For these reasons I have taken advantage of the present opportunity to acquire them.

(c) LEND-LEASE ACT*

SEC. 3. (a) Notwithstanding the provisions of any other law, the President may, from time to time, when he deems it in the interest of national defense, authorize the Secretary of War, the Secretary of the Navy, or the head of any other department or agency of the Government—

(1) To manufacture in arsenals, factories, and shipyards under their jurisdiction, or otherwise procure, to the extent to which funds are made available therefor, or contracts are authorized from time to time by the Congress, or both, any defense article for the government of any country whose defense the President deems vital to the defense of the United States.

(2) To sell, transfer title to, exchange, lease, lend, or otherwise dispose of, to any such government any defense article, but no defense article not manufactured or procured under paragraph (1) shall in any way be disposed of under this paragraph, except after consultation with the Chief of Staff of the Army or the Chief of Naval Operations of the Navy, or both. The value of defense articles disposed of in any way under authority of this shall not exceed $1,300,000,000. The value of such defense articles shall be determined by the head of the department

---

* September 3, 1940. From *Peace and War, United States Foreign Policy, 1931-1941*, Washington, 1943, pp. 564-565.

* March 11, 1941. From *Peace and War, United States Foreign Policy, 1931-1941*, Washington, 1943, pp. 627-630.

or agency concerned or such other department, agency or officer as shall be designated in the manner provided in the rules and regulations issued hereunder. Defense articles procured from funds hereafter appropriated to any department or agency of the Government, other than from funds authorized to be appropriated under this Act, shall not be disposed of in any way under authority of this paragraph except to the extent hereafter authorized by the Congress in the Acts appropriating such funds or otherwise.

(3) To test, inspect, prove, repair, outfit, recondition, or otherwise to place in good working order, to the extent to which funds are made availble therefor, or contracts are authorized from time to time by the Congress, or both, any defense article for any such government, or to procure any or all such services by private contract.

(4) To communicate to any such government any defense information, pertaining to any defense article furnished to such government under paragraph (2) of this subsection.

(5) To release for export any defense article disposed of in any way under this subsection to any such government.

(b) The terms and conditions upon which any such foreign government receives any aid authorized under subsection (a) shall be those which the President deems satisfactory, and the benefit to the United States may be payment or repayment in kind or property, or any other direct or indirect benefit which the president deems satisfactory. . . .

(d) Nothing in this Act shall be construed to authorize or to permit the authorization of convoying vessels by naval vessels of the United States.

(e) Nothing in this Act shall be construed to authorize or to permit the authorization of the entry of any American vessel into a combat area in violation of section 3 of the Neutrality Act of 1939. . . .

SEC. 9. The President may, from time to time, promulgate such rules and regulations as may be necessary and proper to carry out any of the provisions of this Act; and he may exercise any power or authority conferred on him by this Act through such department, agency, or officer as he shall direct.

SEC. 10. Nothing in this Act shall be construed to change existing law relating to the use of the land and naval forces of the United States, except insofar as such use relates to the manufacture, procurement, and repair of defense articles, the communication of information and other noncombatant purposes enumerated in this Act.

8

The Four Freedoms

☆ *After Roosevelt's reelection in 1940, he declared that the United States had a responsibility not only to defend the nation but to contribute to the prevalence of principles consistent with American ideals. This was incorporated in a message to Congress, January 6, 1941.** ☆

In the future days, which we seek to make secure, we look forward to a world founded upon four essential human freedoms.

The first is freedom of speech and expression—everywhere in the world.

The second is freedom of every person to worship God in his own way—everywhere in the world.

The third is freedom from want—which translated into world terms, means economic understandings which will secure to every nation a healthy peacetime life for its inhabitants—everywhere in the world.

The fourth is freedom from fear—

* From *Peace and War, United States Foreign Policy, 1931-1941*, Washington, 1943, p. 611.

which, translated into world terms, means a world-wide reduction of armaments to such a point and in such a thorough fashion that no nation will be in a position to commit an act of physical aggression against any neighbor—anywhere in the world.

That is no vision of a distant millennium. It is a definite basis for a kind of world attainable in our own time and generation. That kind of world is the very antithesis of the so-called new order of tyranny which the dictators seek to create with the crash of a bomb.

To that new order we oppose the greater conception—the moral order. A good society is able to face schemes of world domination and foreign revolutions alike without fear.

9

The Stakes of War

☆ *In a radio address to the nation, May 27, 1941, President Roosevelt summarized the actions which the United States had taken to provide for its own defense and the defense of the embattled democracies. He then discussed at length the dangers that America would face in the event of an Axis victory.** ☆

The pressing problems that confront us are military problems. We cannot afford to approach them from the point of view of wishful thinkers or sentimentalists. What we face is cold, hard fact.

The first and fundamental fact is that what started as a European war has developed, as the Nazis always intended it should develop, into a world war for world-domination.

Adolf Hitler never considered the domination of Europe as an end in itself. European conquest was but a step toward ultimate goals in all the other continents. It is unmistakably apparent to all of us that, unless the advance of Hitlerism is forcibly checked now, the Western Hemisphere will be within range of the Nazi weapons of destruction.

For our own defense we have accordingly undertaken certain obviously necessary measures.

First, we joined in concluding a series of agreements with all the other American republics. This further solidified our hemisphere against the common danger.

And then, a year ago, we launched, and

* From *Peace and War, United States Foreign Policy, 1931-1941*, Washington, 1943, pp. 662-670.

are successfully carrying out, the largest armament-production program we have ever undertaken.

We have added substantially to our splendid Navy, and we have mustered our manpower to build up a new Army which is already worthy of the highest traditions of our military service.

We instituted a policy of aid for the democracies—the nations which have fought for the continuation of human liberties.

This policy had its origin in the first month of the war, when I urged upon the Congress repeal of the arms-embargo provisions in the Neutrality Law. In that message of September 1939, I said, "I should like to be able to offer the hope that the shadow over the world might swiftly pass. I cannot. The facts compel my stating, with candor, that darker periods may lie ahead."

In the subsequent months, the shadows deepened and lengthened. And the night spread over Poland, Denmark, Norway, Holland, Belgium, Luxemburg, and France.

In June 1940, Britain stood alone, faced by the same machine of terror which had overwhelmed her allies. Our Government rushed arms to meet her desperate needs.

In September 1940, an agreement was completed with Great Britain for the trade of 50 destroyers for 8 important off-shore bases.

In March 1941, the Congress passed the Lend-Lease Bill and an appropriation of seven billion dollars to implement it. This law realistically provided for material aid "for the government of any country whose defense the President deems vital to the defense of the United States".

Our whole program of aid for the democracies has been based on hard-headed concern for our own security and for the kind of safe and civilized world in which we wish to live. Every dollar of material we send helps to keep the dictators away from our own hemisphere. Every day that they are held off gives us time to build more guns and tanks and planes and ships.

We have made no pretense about our own self-interest in this aid. Great Britani understands it—and so does Nazi Germany.

And now—after a year—Britain still fights gallantly, on a "far-flung battle line." We have doubled and redoubled our vast production, increasing, month by month, our material supply of tools of war for ourselves and Britain and China—and eventually for all the democracies.

The supply of these tools will not fail—it will increase.

With greatly augmented strength, the United States and the other American republics now chart their course in the situation of today.

Your Government knows what terms Hitler, if victorious, would impose. They are, indeed, the only terms on which he would accept a so-called "negotiated" peace.

Under those terms, Germany would litterally parcel out the world—hoisting the swastika itself over vast territories and populations and setting up puppet governments of its own choosing, wholly subject to the will and the policy of a conqueror.

To the people of the Americas, a triumphant Hitler would say, as he said after the seizure of Austria, and after Munich, and after the seizure of Czechoslovakia: "I am now completely satisfied. This is the last territorial readjustment I will seek." And he would of course add: "All we want is peace, friendship, and profitable trade relations with you in the New World."

And were any of us in the Americas so incredibly simple and forgetful as to accept those honeyed words, what would then happen?

Those in the New World who were seeking profits would be urging that all that the dictatorships desired was "peace." They would oppose toil and taxes for more American armament. Meanwhile, the dictatorships would be forcing the enslaved peoples of their Old World conquests into a system they are even now organizing—to build a naval and air force intended to gain and hold and be master of the Atlantic and the Pacific as well.

They would fasten an economic stranglehold upon our several nations. Quislings would be found to subvert the governments in our republics; and the Nazis would back their fifth columns with invasion, if necessary.

I am not speculating about all this. I merely repeat what is already in the Nazi book of world-conquest. They plan to treat the Latin American nations as they are now treating the Balkans. They plan then to strangle the United States of America and the Dominion of Canada.

The American laborer would have to compete with slave labor in the rest of the world. Minimum wages, maximum hours? Nonsense! Wages and hours would be fixed by Hitler. The dignity and power and standard of living of the American worker and farmer would be gone. Trade unions would become historical relics and collective bargaining a joke.

Farm income? What happens to all farm surpluses without any foreign trade? The American farmer would get for his products exactly what Hitler wanted to give. He would face obvious disaster and complete regimentation.

Tariff walls—Chinese walls of isolation —would be futile. Freedom to trade is essential to our economic life. We do not eat all the food we can produce; we do not burn all the oil we can pump; we do not use all the goods we can manufacture. It would not be an American wall to keep Nazi goods out; it would be a Nazi wall to keep us in.

The whole fabric of working life as we know it—business, manufacturing, mining, agriculture—all would be mangled and crippled under such a system. Yet to maintain even that crippled independence would require permanent conscription of our manpower; it would curtail the funds we could spend on education, on housing, on public works, on flood control, on health. Instead, we should be permanently pouring our resources into armaments; and, year in and year out, standing day and night watch against the destruction of our cities.

Even our right to worship would be threatened. The Nazi world does not recognize any God except Hitler; for the Nazis are as ruthless as the Communists in the denial of God. What place has religion which preaches the dignity of the human being, of the majesty of the human soul, in a world where moral standards are measured by treachery and bribery and fifth columnists? Will our children, too, wander off, goose-stepping in search of new gods?

We do not accept, and will not permit, this Nazi "shape of things to come." It will never be forced upon us if we act in this present crisis with the wisdom and the courage which have distinguished our country in all the crises of the past. . . .

The war is approaching the brink of the Western Hemisphere itself. It is coming very close to home.

Control or occupation by Nazi forces of any of the islands of the Atlantic would jeopardize the immediate safety of portions of North and South America and of the island possessions of the United States and of the ultimate safety of the continental United States itself.

Hitler's plan of world-domination would be near its accomplishment today, were it not for two factors: One is the epic resistance of Britain, her Colonies, and the great Dominions, fighting not only to maintain the existence of the Island of Britain, but also to hold the Near East and Africa. The other is the magnificent defense of China, which will, I have reason to believe, increase in strength. All of these, together, prevent the Axis from winning control of the seas by ships and aircraft.

The Axis powers can never achieve their objective of world-domination unless they first obtain control of the seas. This is their supreme purpose today; and to achieve it, they must capture Great Britain.

They could then have the power to dictate to the Western Hemisphere. No spurious argument, no appeal to sentiment, and no false pledges like those given by Hitler at Munich, can deceive the American people into believing that he and his Axis partners would not, with Britain defeated, close in relentlessly on this hemisphere.

But if the Axis powers fail to gain control of the seas, they are certainly defeated. Their dreams of world-domination will then go by the board; and the criminal leaders who started this war will suffer inevitable disaster. . . .

The deadly facts of war compel nations, for simple self-preservation, to make stern choices. It does not make sense, for instance, to say, "I believe in the defense of all the Western Hemisphere," and in the next breath to say, "I will not fight for that defense until the enemy has landed on our shores." And if we believe in the independence and integrity of the Americas, we must be willing to fight to defend them just as much as we would fight for the safety of our own homes.

It is time for us to realize that the safety of American homes even in the center of our country has a definite relationship to the continued safety of homes in Nova Scotia or Trinidad or Brazil.

Our national policy today, therefore, is this:

First, we shall actively resist wherever necessary, and with all our resources, every attempt by Hitler to extend his Nazi domination to the Western Hemisphere, or to threaten it. We shall actively resist his every attempt to gain control of the seas. We insist upon the vital importance of keeping Hitlerism away from any point in the world which could be used and would be used as a base of attack against the Americas.

Second, from the point of view of strict naval and military necessity, we shall give every possible assistance to Britain and to all who, with Britain, are resisting Hitlerism or its equivalent with force of arms. Our patrols are helping now to in-sure delivery of the needed supplies to Britain. All additional measures necessary to deliver the goods will be taken. Any and all further methods or combination of methods, which can or should be utilized, are being devised by our military and naval technicians, who, with me, will work out and put into effect such new and additional safeguards as may be needed.

The delivery of needed supplies to Britain is imperative. This can be done; it must be done; it will be done.

To the other American nations—20 republics and the Dominion of Canada—I say this: The United States does not merely propose these purposes, but is actively engaged today in carrying them out.

I say to them further: You may disregard those few citizens of the United States who contend that we are disunited and cannot act.

There are some timid ones among us who say that we must preserve peace at any price—lest we lose our liberties forever. To them I say: Never in the history of the world has a nation lost its democracy by a successful struggle to defend its democracy. We must not be defeated by the fear of the very danger which we are preparing to resist. Our freedom has shown its ability to survive war, but it would never survive surrender. "The only thing we have to fear is fear itself."

10

The Anti-Interventionists

☆ *In 1941 the actions and statements of the President were heatedly debated. The opponents maintained that a continuance of the President's policies would contribute neither to peace nor to the solution of the world's problems.* ☆

(a) ADDRESS OF CHARLES A. LINDBERGH AT NEW YORK*

It is not only our right, but is our obligation as American citizens to look at this war objectively and to weigh our chances for success if we should enter it. I have attempted to do this, especially from the standpoint of aviation; and I have been forced to the conclusion that we cannot win this war for England, regardless of how much assistance we extend.

I ask you to look at the map of Europe today and see if you can suggest any way in which we could win this war if we entered it. Suppose we had a large army in America, trained and equipped. Where would we send it to fight? The campaigns of the war show only too clearly how difficult it is to force a landing, or to maintain an army, on a hostile coast.

Suppose we took our Navy from the Pacific, and used it to convoy British shipping. That would not win the war for England. It would, at best, permit her to exist under the constant bombing of the German air fleet. Suppose we had an air force that we could send to Europe. Where could it operate? Some of our squadrons

might be based in the British Isles; but it is physically impossible to base enough aircraft in the British Isles alone to equal in strength the aircraft that can be based on the Continent of Europe.

I have asked these questions on the supposition that we had in existence an Army and an air force large enough and well enough equipped to send to Europe; and that we would dare to remove our Navy from the Pacific. Even on this basis, I do not see how we could invade the Continent of Europe successfully as long as all of that Continent and most of Asia is under Axis domination. But the fact is that none of these suppositions are correct. We have only a one-ocean Navy. Our Army is still untrained and inadequately equipped for foreign war. Our air force is deplorably lacking in modern fighting planes.

When these facts are cited, the interventionists shout that we are defeatists, that we are undermining the principles of democracy, and that we are giving comfort to Germany by talking about our military weakness. But everything I mention here has been published in our newspa-

* April 23, 1941. From *The New York Times,* April 24, 1941.

pers, and in the reports of congressional hearings in Washington. Our military position is well known to the governments of Europe and Asia. Why, then, should it not be brought to the attention of our own people?

I say it is the interventionist in America, as it was in England and in France, who gives comfort to the enemy. I say it is they who are undermining the principles of democracy when they demand that we take a course to which more than 80 per cent of our citizens are opposed. I charge them with being the real defeatists, for their policy has led to the defeat of every country that followed their advice since this war began. There is no better way to give comfort to an enemy than to divide the people of a nation over the issue of foreign war. There is no shorter road to defeat than by entering a war with inadequate preparation. Every nation that has adopted the interventionist policy of depending on some one else for its own defense has met with nothing but defeat and failure.

When history is written, the responsibility for the downfall of the democracies of Europe will rest squarely upon the shoulders of the interventionists who led their nations into war uninformed and unprepared. With their shouts of defeatism, and their disdain of reality, they have already sent countless thousands of young men to death in Europe. From the campaign of Poland to that of Greece, their prophecies have been false and their policies have failed. Yet these are the people who are calling us defeatists in America today. And they have led this country, too, to the verge of war.

There are many such interventionists in America, but there are more people among us of a different type. That is why you and I are assembled here tonight. There is a policy open to this nation that will lead to success—a policy that leaves us free to follow our own way of life, and to develop our own civilization. It is not a new and untried idea. It was advocated by Washington. It was incorporated in the Monroe Doctrine. Under its guidance, the United States became the greatest nation in the world.

It is based upon the belief that the security of a nation lies in the strength and character of its own people. It recommends the maintenance of armed forces sufficient to defend this hemisphere from attack by any combination of foreign powers. It demands faith in an independent American destiny. This is the policy of the America First Committee today. It is a policy not of isolation, but of independence; not of defeat, but of courage. It is a policy that led this nation to success during the most trying years of our history, and it is a policy that will lead us to success again.

We have weakened ourselves for many months, and still worse, we have divided our own people by this dabbling in Europe's wars. While we should have been concentrating on American defense we have been forced to argue over foreign quarrels. We must turn our eyes and our faith back to our own country before it is too late. And when we do this, a different vista opens before us. Practically every difficulty we would face in invading Europe becomes an asset to us in defending America. Our enemy, and not we, would then have the problem of transporting millions of troops across the ocean and landing them on a hostile shore. They, and not we, would have to furnish the convoys to transport guns and trucks and munitions and fuel across three thousand miles of water. Our battleships and submarines would then be fighting close to their home bases. We would then do the bombing from the air and the torpedoing at sea. And if any part of an enemy convoy should ever pass our navy and our air force, they would still be faced with the guns of our coast artillery and behind them the divisions of our Army.

The United States is better situated from a military standpoint than any other nation in the world. Even in our present condition of unpreparedness no foreign power is in a position to invade us today. If we concentrate on our own defenses and build the strength that this nation should maintain, no foreign army will ever attempt to land on American shores.

War is not inevitable for this country. Such a claim is defeatism in the true sense. No one can make us fight abroad unless we ourselves are willing to do so. No one will attempt to fight us here if we arm ourselves as a great nation should be armed. Over a hundred million people in this nation are opposed to entering the war. If the principles of democracy mean anything at all, that is reason enough for us to stay out. If we are forced into a war against the wishes of an overwhelming majority of our people, we will have proved democracy such a failure at home that there will be little use fighting for it abroad.

(b) STATEMENT OF ALFRED M. LANDON, HERBERT HOOVER, JOHN L. LEWIS AND FOURTEEN OTHER REPUBLICAN LEADERS*

The American people should insistently demand that Congress put a stop to step by step projection of the United States in undeclared war. Congress has not only the sole power to declare war but also the power and responsibility to keep the country out of war unless and until both houses have otherwise decided. Exceeding its expressed purpose, the lend-lease bill has been followed by Naval action, by military occupation of bases outside the Western Hemisphere, by promise of unauthorized aid to Russia and by other belligerent moves.

Such warlike steps, in no case sanctioned by Congress, undermine its constitutional powers and the fundamental principles of democratic government. The representatives of the people, in passing the lend-lease bill, expressed the national conviction that preservation of the British Empire and China is desirable for us and for civilization. We hold that view but the intent of Congress was that lend-lease material should be transferred to belligerent ownership in the United States and utilized only to protect the independence of democracies.

We hold that in giving generous aid to these democracies at our seaboard we have gone as far as is consistent either with law, with sentiment or with security. Recent events raise doubts that this war is a clear-cut issue of liberty and democracy. It is not purely a world conflict between tyranny and freedom. The Anglo-Russian alliance has dissipated that illusion.

In so far as this is a war of power-politics, the American people want no part in it. American participation is far more likely to destroy democracy in this country and thus in the Western Hemisphere than to establish it in Europe. The hope of civilization now rests primarily upon the preservation of freedom and democracy in the United States.

That will be lost for a generation if we join in this war. We maintain that American lives should be sacrificed only for American independence or to prevent the invasion of the Western Hemisphere.

Few people honestly believe that the Axis is now or will in the future, be in a position to threaten the independence of any part of this hemisphere if our defenses are properly prepared.

Energies of this country should be concentrated on the defense of our own liberties. Freedom in America does not

* August 5, 1941. From *The Topeka Daily Capital*, August 6, 1941.

depend on the outcome of struggles for material power between other nations.

(c) ADDRESS OF NORMAN THOMAS*

Any legislative formula which will extend indefinitely the term of service of drafted men and increase indefinitely their number, will have the double effect of adversely affecting the morale of the army and of encouraging the President to disregard his solemn promises to the American people that not one of our sons shall be put into foreign wars. . . .

The only thing that can clear the War Department and the President himself from a charge of bad faith to the men and disloyalty to the purpose of the Conscription Law would be clear proof of a danger to our national defense even graver than that which existed when the law was adopted. The President himself recognized this truth when, in his message to Congress, he asserted with great emphasis "I do believe—I know—that the danger is infinitely greater." To that statement I reply, respectfully but earnestly "Mr. President, if what you say is true it is because of what you have done and what you expect to do contrary to the spirit of your promise to the American people not to put their sons into foreign wars.

"Let us look at the record. A year ago Stalin was Hitler's virtual ally; today he is his enemy and the German invasion of Russia proceeds far more slowly than the German timetable. Even military victory is not likely to abolish a Russian resistance which will greatly weaken Germany's power to strike elsewhere. A year ago we lived in momentary dread of a British collapse; today our fears are not for England, but for the British Empire, which has actually been expanded during the year by British conquest of Ital-

* July 29, 1941. From *Vital Speeches*, VII (August 15, 1941), pp. 671-672.

ian East Africa and Ethiopia and French Syria. A year ago Nazi air war threatened the devastation of the British Isles; today the RAF with comparative impunity carries the war into western Europe and the actual physical invasion of England seems less and less likely. A year ago our nearest neighbor, Mexico, was in an unsettled condition and it was at least possible that there might be civil war by which Nazis could profit; today Mexico is internally at peace and on more friendly terms with the American government than ever before. In general progress has been made with all South American countries. The Caribbean has become an American lake. A year ago our enormous armament program had hardly begun; today it has been pushed far, despite mistakes and failures which have cost us, and will cost us, dear. It is true that when the Conscription bill was passed Japan had not then occupied bases in Indo-China, but neither had her potential strength been weakened by another year of war.

"Where then, Mr. President, is the infinitely greater danger, unless you yourself have determined to preserve the British Empire, perhaps with us as senior or junior partner, at any cost; unless you yourself are willing if necessary to have our sons die in jungles and deserts in Asia and Africa as well as on the Continent of Europe?"

Neither Japan nor Germany, nor both combined can or will aggressively attack us in this hemisphere, or even in the Philippines unless first they are convinced that, come what may, we intend and we are ready aggressively to attack them.

The real danger lies simply in the Administration's aggression. Since the election the President no longer talks of steps short of war; since the occupation of Iceland in the eastern hemisphere he no longer talks of defense of the western hemisphere. The Administration's original demand for holding draftees in service was accompanied by demand for the removal of any restriction of the power of the President to send our sons anywhere in the wide world without declaration of war by Congress. Owing to the intensity of opposition this demand was temporarily withdrawn, but only temporarily. Indeed, Secretary Stimson's formula for the declaration of a national emergency would probably have evaded any restriction upon the power of the President and for that reason was rejected, even by the Administration's devoted followers in the Senate. If Congress now gives the President the power he wants, ways will easily be found to use that power in Africa, Siberia Indo-China, and the Dutch East Indies. Already two of Great Britain's leading Generals have confidently expressed their conviction that American boys can and must be used in Europe and Africa for complete victory over Hitler. Indeed strange rumors are afloat, to one of which Senator Wheeler referred in a letter to the Secretary of War—as yet unanswered—that 20,000 American soldiers are now in Egypt. . . .

Once more the basic issue in connection with the extension of the draft, as of our government policy toward Japan, boils down to the question, do we want war? More than ever I am opposed to American entry into total war which will inevitably destroy a democracy which we cannot give to others. Hence my opposition to this legislation which will increase the President's power to wage total war without even convincing the American people of its necessity. That danger is far graver than any danger of attack upon us. . . .

To the Administration and Congress I say: "Neither the American people nor the verdict of history will forgive you if you put us into total war or send our sons to decide which of two ruthless dictators shall dominate the European continent and which of two rival empires shall exploit the poor people of Indo-China or keep the Indian patriot Nehru in jail. The judgment of history and of the people may be delayed. It will be inescapable. For your failure, here on this blessed continent, to make our own democracy work for the conquest of our own poverty, for your sacrifice of it to armament economics, militarism, imperialism and war itself, generations will pay in blood and tears. Out of that conviction arises my plea; it is late, but not too late. America wants to be kept from total war; it can be kept from total war, but you will make the task of thus delivering our people vastly harder if you extend the draft. Act now to give us hope of peace."

11

Planning for War

☆ *Although America was not at war, the military leaders by September of 1941, had prepared a strategy that largely governed our operations in World War II.** ☆

10. It is believed that the overthrow of the Nazi regime by action of the people of Germany is unlikely in the near future, and will not occur until Germany is upon the point of military defeat. Even were a new regime to be established, it it not at all certain that such a regime would agree to peace terms acceptable to the United States.

11. Assuming the truth of the views expressed in the preceding paragraph, it is the opinion of the Joint Board that Germany and her European satellites can not be defeated by the European Powers now fighting against her. Therefore, if our European enemies are to be defeated, it will be necessary for the United States to enter the war, and to employ a part of its armed forces offensively in the Eastern Atlantic and in Europe or Africa.

12. The Joint Board also holds the view that, if, under present circumstances, Japan should advance against the British in Malaya and against the Dutch in the Netherlands East Indies, British and Dutch forces probably could not successfully withstand such an advance in the

absence of active military assistance by the United States. The result of an attack by Japan on the Eastern Siberian Soviet Republic cannot now be predicted.

13. In view of the preceding considerations, the Joint Board recommends that the over-all production and material objective of the United States be designed to meet United States needs while engaged simultaneously in war against Germany and Japan, under either of the following sets of circumstances:

a. While associated as a belligerent with the British Commonwealth, the Netherlands East Indies, Russia, and China.

b. While associated as a belligerent with Canada and some of the Latin American countries, other belligerent Powers having been defeated by Germany and Japan.

14. Due to inadequate industrial capacity and material resources, friendly Powers must look to the United States for a large part of the munitions and other materials which they will require for success. The munitions and other materials which may be produced or controlled by the United States should be divided between itself and friendly Powers in such a manner as to effectuate the success of the military strategy adopted by the

* From "Joint Board Estimate of United States Over-all Production Requirements," September 11, 1941, in Robert E. Sherwood, *Roosevelt and Hopkins, An Intimate History*, pp. 411-418. Copyright, 1948, by Robert E. Sherwood. Used by permission of Harper & Brothers.

United States as best calculated to defeat our common enemies. . . .

21. The Joint Board is convinced that the first major objective of the United States and its Associates ought to be the complete military defeat of Germany. If Germany were defeated, her entire European system would collapse, and it is probable that Japan could be forced to give up much of her territorial gains, unless she had already firmly established herself in such strength that the United States and its Associates could not afford the energy to continue the war against her.

22. An inconclusive peace between Germany and her present active military enemies would be likely to give Germany an opportunity to reorganize continental Europe and to replenish her strength. Even though the British Commonwealth and Russia were completely defeated, there would be important reasons for the United States to continue the war against Germany, in spite of the greatly increased difficulty of attaining final victory. From this it follows that *the principal strategic method employed by the United States in the immediate future should be the material support of present military operations against Germany, and their reenforcement by active participation in the war by the United States while holding Japan in check pending future developments.* Necessarily, only small Army contingents are now sufficiently equipped and trained for immediate participation in offensive operations. [The underscored words in the foregoing are General Marshall's and Admiral Stark's]

23. Except in the case of Russia, the principal strength of the Associated Powers is in naval and air categories. Naval and air power may prevent wars from being lost, and by weakening enemy strength may greatly contribute to victory. By themselves, however, naval and

air forces seldom, if ever, win important wars. It should be recognized as an almost invariable rule that only land armies can finally win wars.

24. It is out of the question to expect the United States and its Associates to undertake in the near future a sustained and successful land offensive against the center of the German power. It being obvious that the Associated Powers can not defeat Germany by defensive operations, effective strategic offensive methods other than by early land offensive in Europe must be employed. These methods may be found in a continuation of the economic blockade; the prosecution of land offensives in distant regions where German troops can exert only a fraction of their total strength; air and sea offensives against German military, economic and industrial resources; and the support of subversive activities in the conquered territories. Strategic methods to be employed against Japan (assuming her in the war) should be a strong defense of Siberia and Malaysia; an economic offensive through blockade; a reduction of Japanese military power by raids; and Chinese offensives against the Japanese forces of occupation.

25. The major strategic objectives which it is believed the United States and the Associated Powers should adopt are indicated below. . . .

a. *The security of the Western Hemisphere* against the extension into it of European or Asiatic political or military power is an essential of United States strategy. . . .

b. *The security of the United Kingdom* is essential to the prosecution in the Eastern Hemisphere of military operations against Germany and Japan. . . .

c. *Safety of the sea communications of the Associated Powers* throughout the world is essential to the continuance of their war effort. . . .

d. *The enforcement of economic block-*

ade is, for the time being, likely to be the most effective offensive method for use against Germany and Japan. . . .

e. *The retention by the British of the control of the Red Sea, Irak, and Iran* is necessary for preserving opportunities for decisive land action against Germany. . . .

f. *The maintenance of an active front in Russia* offers by far the best opportunity for a successful land offensive against Germany, because only Russia possesses adequate manpower, situated in favorable proximity to the center of German military power. . . .

g. *Prevention of Axis penetration into Northwest Africa and the Atlantic Islands* is very important, not only as a contribution to the defense of the Western Hemisphere, but also as security to British sea communications and as a potential base for a future land offensive. . . .

h. *Retention by the United States and its Associates of the Philippines, Malaya, the 'Netherlands East Indies, Australasia, Burma, and China* would have far-reaching effects. . . .

i. *Retention of Eastern Siberia by Russia* is necessary if Japan is to be checked. Only material assistance can be provided by the United States to Siberia. No materials can be sent to Siberia by water when Japan is at war with Russia, but deliveries of aircraft could continue by air.

26. The following principles have been taken into consideration in arriving at recommendations concerning the strengths of the armed forces which the United States should undertake to raise or support, in whole or in part:

a. The navy considers that, since the principal strength of the Associated Powers is at present in naval and air categories, the strategy which they should adopt should be based on the effective employment of these forces, and the employment of land forces in regions where Germany can not exert the full power of her land armies. The Army believes that the foregoing strategy may not accomplish the defeat of Germany and that it may be necessary to come to grips with the German armies on the continent of Europe. Consequently, the Army feels that the equipment of land armies necessary to meet this contingency should be provided as a part of the over-all production requirements.

b. Past experience of the United States and other Powers should condition estimates of the capability of the United States to support a war effort, with due regard to differences in over-all industrial capacity; differences in availability of materials; and an appropriate balance between the man-power to be employed in the armed forces, and the man-power to be employed in industry and essential civilian services. Because of the present high degree of mechanization, a greater proportion of man-power must be allocated to industry for the manufacture of equipment and munitions than was the case in former wars.

c. The sound use of diplomatic, economic, financial, and propaganda weapons, will serve to reduce the magnitude of the direct military effort.

d. The burdens of the war effort, even though continued by the United States over a long period of time, should be so adjusted as to maintain the morale and the will to fight of the civilian population.

12

Negotiations with Japan

☆ *While American attention was focused largely on events in Europe, relations with Japan, which had been tense for a decade, became progressively critical in the summer and fall of 1941. American global interests appeared to be increasingly jeopardized by Japanese aggrandizement. Japanese and American concern over the situation brought about a series of negotiations in an attempt to reconcile the differences between the two governments. In drafting a reply to the Japanese note of November 20, a proposed modus vivendi was ultimately rejected by American policy makers in favor of the sterner note sent November 26.* ☆

(a) JAPANESE PROPOSAL TO THE UNITED STATES*

1. Both the Governments of Japan and the United States undertake not to make any armed advancement into any of the regions in the South-eastern Asia and the Southern Pacific area excepting the part of French Indo-China where the Japanese troops are stationed at present.

2. The Japanese Government undertakes to withdraw its troops now stationed in French Indo-China upon either the restoration of peace between Japan and China or the establishment of an equitable peace in the Pacific area.

In the meantime the Government of Japan declares that it is prepared to remove its troops now stationed in the southern part of French Indo-China to the northern part of the said territory upon

the conclusion of the present arrangement which shall later be embodied in the final agreement.

3. The Government of Japan and the United States shall cooperate with a view to securing the acquisition of those goods and commodities which the two countries need in Netherlands East Indies.

4. The Governments of Japan and the United States mutually undertake to restore their commercial relations to those prevailing prior to the freezing of the assets.

The Government of the United States shall supply Japan a required quantity of oil.

5. The Government of the United States undertakes to refrain from such measures and actions as will be prejudicial to the endeavors for the restoration for general peace between Japan and China.

* November 20, 1941. From *Peace and War, United States Foreign Policy, 1931-1941*, Washington, 1943, pp. 801-802.

(b) AMERICAN MODUS VIVENDI*

1. The Government of the United States and the Government of Japan, both being solicitous for the peace of the Pacific, affirm that their national policies are directed toward lasting and extensive peace throughout the Pacific area and that they have no territorial designs therein. They undertake reciprocally not to make by force or threat of force, unless they are attacked, any advancement, from points at which they have military establishments, across any international border in the Pacific area.

2. The Japanese Government undertakes forthwith to withdraw its armed forces now stationed in southern French Indochina, not to engage in any further military activities there, including the construction of military facilities, and to limit Japanese military forces in northern French Indochina to the number there on July 26, 1941, which number in any case would not exceed 25,000 and which number would not be subject to replacement.

3. The Government of the United States undertakes forthwith to remove the freezing restrictions which were placed on Japanese assets in the United States on July 26 and the Japanese Government agrees simultaneously to remove the freezing measures which it imposed in regard to American assets in Japan. Exports from each country would thereafter remain subject to the respec-

* Drafted November 22, 1941. From *Pearl Harbor Attack. Hearings Before The Joint Committee on the Investigation of the Pearl Harbor Attack*, Part 14, 79th Congress, 1st session, pp. 1113-1115.

tive export control measures which each country may have in effect for reasons of national defense.

4. The Government of the United States undertakes forthwith to approach the British and the Dutch Governments with a view to those Goverments' taking, on a basis of reciprocity with Japan, measures similar to those provided for in paragraph three above.

5. The Government of the United States would not look with disfavor upon the inauguration of conversations between the Government of China and the Government of Japan directed toward a peaceful settlement of their differences nor would the Government of the United States look with disfavor upon an armistice during the period of any such discussions. The fundamental interest of the Government of the United States in reference to any such discussions is simply that they be based upon and exemplify the fundamental principles of peace which constitute the central spirit of the current conversations between the Government of Japan and the Government of the United States.

In case any such discussions are entered into between the Government of Japan and the Government of China, the Government of the United States is agreeable to such discussions taking place in the Philippine Islands, if so desired by both China and Japan.

6. It is understood that this *modus vivendi* is of a temporary nature and shall not remain in effect for a period longer than three months unless renewed by common agreement.

(c) AMERICAN PROPOSAL FOR AGREEMENT WITH JAPAN*

The Government of the United States and the Government of Japan propose to take steps as follows:

* November 26, 1941. From *Peace and War, United States Foreign Policy, 1931-1941*, Washington, 1943, pp. 811-812.

1. The Government of the United States and the Government of Japan will endeavor to conclude a multilateral non-aggression pact among the British Empire, China, Japan, the Netherlands, the

Soviet Union, Thailand and the United States.

2. Both Governments will endeavor to conclude among the American, British, Chinese, Japanese, the Netherland and Thai Governments an agreement whereunder each of the Governments would pledge itself to respect the territorial integrity of French Indochina and, in the event that there should develop a threat to the territorial integrity of Indochina, to enter into immediate consultation with a view to taking such measures as may be deemed necessary and advisable to meet the threat in question. Such agreement would provide also that each of the Governments party to the agreement would not seek or accept preferential treatment in its trade or economic relations with Indochina and would use its influence to obtain for each of the signatories equality of treatment in trade and commerce with French Indochina.

3. The Government of Japan will withdraw all military, naval, air and police forces from China and from Indochina.

4. The Government of the United States and the Government of Japan will not support—militarily, politically, economically—any government or regime in China other than the National Government of the Republic of China with capital temporarily at Chungking.

5. Both Governments will give up all extraterritorial rights in China, including rights and interests in and with regard to international settlements and concessions, and rights under the Boxer Protocol of 1901.

Both Governments will endeavor to obtain the agreement of the British and other governments to give up extraterritorial rights in China, including rights in international settlements and in concessions and under the Boxer Protocol of 1901.

6. The Government of the United States and the Government of Japan will enter into negotiations for the conclusion between the United States and Japan of a trade agreement, based upon reciprocal most-favored-nation treatment and reduction of trade barriers by both countries, including an undertaking by the United States to bind raw silk on the free list.

7. The Government of the United States and the Government of Japan will, respectively, remove the freezing restrictions on Japanese funds in the United States and on American funds in Japan.

8. Both Governments will agree upon a plan for the stabilization of the dollar-yen rate, with the allocation of funds adequate for this purpose, half to be supplied by Japan and half by the United States.

9. Both Governments will agree that no agreement which either has concluded with any third power or powers shall be interpreted by it in such a way as to conflict with the fundamental purpose of this agreement, the establishment and preservation of peace throughout the Pacific area.

10. Both Governments will use their influence to cause other governments to adhere to and to give practical application to the basic political and economic principles set forth in this agreement.

XII

world war II (1941-1945)

T HE ATTACK on Pearl Harbor united the nation for war, and indecision regarding Europe was resolved a few days later when Hitler declared war on the United States. The world conflict with Germany and Japan was a reality, and the President set about the formidable task of mobilizing the resources of the nation to wage a total war for survival.

The new methods of warfare which had evolved with technological advances demanded a greater coordination of the national effort, and the government was required to exercise a considerable amount of control over the total economy. To provide the ships, tanks, weapons, and supplies needed to wage war over the entire face of the globe, the government had to organize industry, manpower, and raw materials on a scale hitherto undreamed of. The difficulties were enormous, but the self-styled "arsenal of democracy" lived up to its promise in spite of a number of errors and false starts.

Military operations, of course, were decisive, for the enemy powers fought until they were soundly defeated. Waging a coalition war is difficult at best, but the most effective coordination was achieved by Great Britain and the United States. Naval strategy involved sea battles, the support of amphibious opertions, and the delivery of troops and supplies through waters often dominated by enemy submarines and planes. Military mistakes made by the Axis leaders contributed to the allied victory, a victory that often was far from certain.

Fighting, however, did not occupy the total energies of the nation. Though the Supreme Court upheld the government order for the relocation of people of Japanese descent on the grounds of military necessity, Justice Frank Murphy entered a vigorous dissent on the grounds of racial discrimination and the deprivation of constitutional liberties. Reinhold Niebuhr analyzed the philosophical and theological aspects of the conflict in terms which probed beneath the more obvious political issues. At the height of hostilities President Roosevelt announced

an "economic bill of rights" for the nation, which pledged a
resumption of the New Deal when peace was attained. And in
the presidential campaign of 1944 the Republican candidate,
Thomas E. Dewey, attacked the Democratic administration for
its faulty direction of the war effort and its apparent collectivist
tendencies.

But planning for war and peace are inseparable, and in a
series of momentous conferences from Casablanca to Potsdam
the allied leaders coordinated their strategy for victory and their
proposals for world settlement. An early Senate commitment to
support United States membership in an international organization aided the President in establishing the framework of the
United Nations. But certain agreements with Russia concerning
territorial readjustment and the plight of liberated nations
appeared inconsistent with the professed war aims of the allies.
The death of Franklin Roosevelt at the point of victory in Europe
passed these problems into the hands of a new and untested
national executive.

1

Industrial Mobilization

☆ *Among the immediate problems facing the nation following the outbreak of hostilities were those of determining the material needs of modern war and arranging for production in sufficient quantity to insure victory. Only with time and experience was the nation able to come to grips with these problems.* ☆*

Under the traditional American system, industry does not produce war munitions until there are Government orders; Government orders are not placed until there are appropriations; and appropriations are not made until requests based on estimates and supporting information are submitted to Congress for action. In fact, in peacetime, the control over the whole process centers in the appropriation by Congress. It was natural, therefore, for procurement officers not to take vigorous action to raise war production before appropriations were available. Not only was this against the whole tradition of the past, but it would, if carried far enough, have been a criminal offense. But any restriction, real or imagined, imposed by appropriations, disappeared after the declaration of war. Appropriations were made in lump sums, so that appropriation language no longer limited the military agencies in their war activities.

While Congress had slowed up the building of training camps only a few months earlier, it . . . acted [in 1942] with great dispatch. Within 6 months, almost

* From Bureau of the Budget, *The United States at War*, Washington, 1946, pp. 112-115.

$100,000,000,000 was appropriated, and in the next 4 months another $60,000,000,000 was added. . . . Of these stupendous authorizations, the Army received $95 billion, the Navy $50 billion, lend-lease $5 billion, and the Maritime Commission $3.5 billion. Never before or since, have such immense financial authorizations been given in so short a period.

By spring the floodgates were open. Equipped with virtually unlimited financial authorizations, the procurement agencies went to work to place their contracts with the industries of America. This was not too difficult. Industry was now eager to get into war work, especially as the WPB materials orders and limitation orders began to interfere with normal production of civilian items. The services were equipped with high priorities, which gave the contractors confidence that they would be able to get the materials and components they required, price arrangements were generous and elastic, and the manufacturers were not unwilling, under pressure, to sign additional contracts even when their plants were already full, hoping to expand, or find some other method of discharging their inflated obligations. With this combination of circumstances, over $100 billion of contracts were placed in the first 6 months of 1942. In other words, industry signed up to deliver for war more than the total production of the American economy in the Nation's most prosperous and productive prior year. At the time there were also some $20 billion of orders outstanding, mostly for munitions. The new orders included $68 billion for munitions, $12.6 billions for industrial expansion, and $6.9 billions for military construction.

Under this flood of war orders, a number of things were bound to happen, and did happen.

First, it became utterly impossible to produce everything ordered at any time in any near future. It was an industrial impossibility. The total called for was in excess of our industrial capacity.

Second, there was a resulting collision between the various production programs and between the men who were responsible for them. Merchant ships took steel from the Navy, and the landing craft cut into both. The Navy took aluminum from aircraft. Rubber took valves from escort vessels, from petroleum, and from the Navy. The pipe lines took steel from ships, new tools, and the railroads. And at every turn there were foreign demands to be met as well as requirements for new plants.

Third, all semblance of balance in the production program disappeared because of the different rates of contracting and of production that resulted from the scramble to place orders. If there ever had been a planned balance between men, ships, tanks, planes, supplies, weapons, ammunition, and new facilities, and there is no evidence that there was, that balance disappeared in the differential time required to develop the orders, the differential energies of the various procurement

officers, and the differential difficulties of getting production out.

Fourth, there was terrific waste in conversion. After a tragically slow start, many a plant was changed over to war production when its normal product was more needed than its new product. Locomotive plants went into tank production, when locomotives were more necessary—but the Tank Division did not know this. Truck plants began to produce airplanes, a change that caused shortages of trucks later on. In some cases, plants were converted at great cost of steel and copper, when a fraction of the precious metals involved would have brought a greater return at some other place in the economy. The scramble for a production we could not attain, brought us waste instead.

Fifth, we built many new factories, and expanded many others, which we could not use and did not need. Many of these factories we could not supply with labor or with raw materials, or if we had, we would not have been able to fly the planes or shoot the ammunition that would have come out of them. But in the process we used up critical materials and manpower which might better have gone into something else. In the light of the tremendous contracts outstanding especially in the early part of 1942, however, these plants seemed necessary to some people, and under the system they were given high priorities. In most cases they were also financed by the Government. The result was, however, an overconcentration of contracts in the larger corporations and a failure to fully utilize the facilities of many small manufacturers whose plants could have produced "bits and pieces." It did not escape the attention of Congress that better utilization of small plants could have reduced the necessary expansion of facilities.

Finally, the priority system broke down because of "priority inflation." People with military contracts had the right to take more scarce materials and components than there were, so that a priority or an allocation became nothing more than a "hunting license." In other words, these who were issuing priorities did not limit their high-ranking authorizations within the allocations given them by the Requirements Committee. In fact, there was very little connection between the two, partly because the allocations were based on a quarterly time schedule, while the priorities carried no terminal date and were good at any time.

2

The Labor Front

☆ *The demands of industry for workers increased sharply at a time when millons of men were being taken into the armed forces. The resulting strain on labor resources forced the government to provide for the efficient and fair utilization of manpower.* * ☆

Within the general context of labor's role in wartime industrial mobilization, the Federal government faced three tasks concerning labor itself: 1) to develop methods for handling labor-management disputes, 2) to establish a wage policy which would dovetail with efforts to hold down the cost-of-living, and 3) to maintain an adequate supply of industrial workers as well as assure their efficient distribution.

Of these three, the most persistent problem was the handling of labor-management disputes. Nine months prior to Pearl Harbor the Roosevelt administration had attempted to deal with this matter by creating a National Defense Mediation Board consisting of representatives from labor, management and the public. Specifically, the board shouldered the responsibility of settling disputes in defense industries, but because it could not enforce its decisions its efforts were not always successful. In at least three cases the War Department had to step in and seize strike-bound plants in order to prevent work stoppages from hampering

* From Robert K. Murray, "Government and Labor during World War I and II," *Current History*, XXXVII (September, 1959), pp. 148-151. Used by permission.

the defense program. Labor opposition to such mediation procedures was sporadic at first, but, finally, when the N.D.M.B. rendered an adverse decision in the Lewis-sponsored "captive mine" coal strike of November, 1941, and the pits were threatened with government seizure, C.I.O. members of the board resigned.

Pearl Harbor forced an immediate change in attitude. Acting upon a labor-management pledge that all disputes would be settled by peaceful means and that the rulings of a war labor board would be obeyed, the President created a National War Labor Board on January 21, 1942, thereby eliminating the N.D.M.B. Sometimes called "the Supreme Court for labor disputes," this new board was headed by William H. Davis, former head of the N.D.M.B., and consisted of twelve members—four representing the public, four representing employers and four representing employees. Operating through 12 regional offices, the N.W.L.B. assumed the dual responsibility of settling industrial disputes and achieving wage stabilization. Unlike the N.D.M.B., the N.W. L.B. possessed considerable power since refusal or failure to obey its decisions almost invariably resulted in plant seizure and government operation. Also, because the matters under its jurisdiction required the formulation of a general wartime labor policy, the N.W.L.B. emerged as a powerful policy-making as well as adjudicatory body.

From the beginning the road of the N.W.L.B. was rocky; yet the board not only survived the bumps but completed the journey with its influence considerably expanded. First, in order to reduce industrial tension, it successfully initiated a "maintenance-of-membership" agreement which disposed of the controversial closed-shop question by protecting organized labor's position in expanding war plants. Under this agreement existing unions were allowed to bargain for all workers during the life of the bargaining contract even though new workers entering the industry were not required to join the union as a condition of employment. This maintenance-of-membership plan obviously shielded unions from raids by employers, and, despite the concerted opposition of the management representatives on the N.W.L.B., the agreement was staunchly upheld during the remainder of the war.

If the maintenance-of-membership formula removed one area of conflict between labor and management, the problem of wage stabilziation remained to plague the N.W.L.B. It was clear from the outset that industrial peace, despite the post-Pearl Harbor pledges of both labor and capital, would depend to a large extent on the preservation of a balance between prices and wages. Taking its cue from a presidential "cost-of-living" message to Congress in April, 1942, the N.W.L.B. promulgated two months later a wage stabilization policy known as the "Little Steel formula."

This formula grew out of a dispute between the Steel Workers of America and Little Steel over the demand for a $1.00 per day wage increase. The N.W.L.B. fi-nally awarded a 44 cents per day increase on the basis that the cost-of-living had only risen to that extent between January, 1941, and May, 1942. Labor severely criticized this decision, arguing that the principle of collective bargaining had been undermined, that laborers had been prevented from improving their relative standard of living, and that wage earners had been singled out unfairly since similar controls were not imposed on farmers or high-income groups. Nevertheless, the Little Steel formula was thereafter applied in all wage disputes. This "hold-the-line" concept was further strengthened by the Anti-Inflation Act of October 2, 1942, on the basis of which Roosevelt gave the N.W.L.B. the task of stabilizing all wages and most salaries under $5,000 at their September 15, 1942, levels.

Labor bridled at this wage "freeze" and the result was a marked rise in the number of strikes. The year 1943 saw a three-fold increase in the amount of production time lost through work stoppages, with the most serious strike of that year occurring in May in the nation's coal fields. This latter dispute was referred to the N.W.L.B. but the United Mine Workers' Union, which was demanding, among other things, a $2.00 per day increase, refused to take part in N.W.L.B. hearings. The board therefore turned the matter over to the President who for six months thereafter engaged in a running fight with John L. Lewis over the refusal of the government to grant the union's full demands. Finally, a negotiated agreement was reached between Lewis and Secretary of Interior Harold Ickes, which, with the N.W.L.B.'s endorsement, authorized a $1.50 per day increase plus certain other benefits. Technically, the Little Steel formula was thus saved, since the stated increase was within the formula's range. Actually, however, because of the fringe benefits included, the formula was neatly by-passed.

THE SMITH-CONNALLY ACT

The success of the miners in thawing the hold-the-line wage freeze policy of the N.W.L.B. proved costly. Disturbed by labor's increasing belligerency, a worried Congress hastily passed the Smith-Connally, or War Labor Disputes Act, of June 25, 1943. This law gave statutory status to the N.W.L.B. for the duration of the war plus six months and authorized it to determine hours, wages and working conditions during that time. It also gave the President specific authority to seize and operate any strike-bound plant, mine or facilitiy which was necessary to the war effort. While such installations were under government operation, all strikes and lockouts were prohibited and conditions and terms of employment were frozen. Moreover, a 30-day "cooling-off" period was now required before *any* strike could be called. During this period the N.W.L.B. was authorized to conduct a secret strike ballot.

The Smith-Connally Act not only marked a clear shift in congressional attitudes toward labor, but also reflected a growing hostility on the part of the general public as well. This fact, together with an increasing flexibility in the application of the Little Steel formula and a more rigid price control policy, kept labor generally quiet for the remainder of the war. Yet most of the credit must go to the N.W.L.B. and the overwhelming majority of the nation's laboring men. From its creation to the war the N.W.L.B. handled 17,807 labor disputes and reduced the loss of production time from strikes to one-third the normal peacetime level. During the same period, while prices climbed 31.7 per cent above their pre-war average, the N.W.L.B. granted wage adjustments in 353,749 instances, involving 23 million workers, and amounting to a 40.5 per cent increase above pre-war levels. Labor, meanwhile, more than proved its faithfulness. Most wartime strikes were outlawed or of very short duration, and labor leaders, except for the irascible Lewis, kept the "no strike" pledge. Time lost from work stoppages in the peak war years of 1943 and 1944 amounted to only one-tenth of one per cent of the total work time—a better record than British labor achieved even under her strict labor conscription law.

MANPOWER ALLOCATION

The two-fold problem of maintaining an adequate labor supply and supervising its efficient distribution was in some respects the easiest, but in other respects the hardset, task facing the government. Because of the staggering loss of more than eleven million men and women to the armed forces, the supply had to be recruited from the formerly unemployed, the normally unemployable, women, farmers, the aged, and the young. Overtime wages, patriotism and escape from boredom were but a few of the factors which helped alleviate the labor supply problem. In this connection, the training-within-industry program, begun by Hillman under the old N.D.A.C. and continued throughout the war by other mobilization agencies, helped fill the gap.

Distribution was another matter. It was hoped that wage incentives might solve the problem of geographic labor shortages, and war plants in such areas were encouraged to increase their pay rates and offer overtime opportunities. However, such action created more problems than were solved—workers were drained off from other nearby war plants or from agriculture and inflationary tendencies were heightened.

To effect a more systematic approach to these matters, President Roosevelt established the War Manpower Commission on April 18, 1942. . . .

The W.M.C. quickly took under its wing the entire Selective Service structure and also absorbed the United States Employment Service. Under its aegis a system of priorities for skilled labor was established and a list of critical war occupations was drawn up. In February, 1943, when President Roosevelt put defense industries on a 48-hour week, the W.M.C. was directed to carry out the order. At the same time the W.M.C. classified labor shortage areas into four groups and tried every voluntary means at its disposal to direct labor into these regions.

Because of the lack of voluntary response, the W.M.C. was reduced by early 1943 to using force in order to solve the labor allocation problem. In April of that year the W.M.C., acting on a presidential "hold-the-line" order, "froze" workers to their jobs by forbidding those engaged in essential occupations to shift to jobs of higher pay without commission approval. Moreover, a policy of "essentiality of employment" rather than age or dependency became the basic criterion of Selective Service for draft deferment.

Even so, labor shortages in numerous areas continued throughout 1943. This fact, plus the anti-labor hostility engendered by the rebellious action of John L. Lewis and his coal miners, caused some officials to advocate a more stringent manpower policy. Using Britain and Australia as examples, both Donald Nelson and Paul McNutt urged the enactment of a national service law which would conscript for the farm and factory as well as for the armed forces. Roosevelt resisted such advice until, thoroughly angered by the antics of Lewis and disturbed by mounting labor unrest, he, too, succumbed. In his annual message to Congress on January 11, 1944, he endorsed the idea of a national service act which would prohibit all strikes and make available every able-bodied adult for war production.

Fortuitous circumstances forestalled any action on this request. For sound political reasons many congressmen were loathe to support the proposed law. Besides, the brightening military picture in the spring and summer of 1944 eliminated much of the urgency. The W.M.C. itself challenged the proposal on the ground that there was no longer need for such rigid controls since the army's goal of 7.7 million men had just been reached and no more men over 36 were to be drafted. But the most important factor was the violent union opposition which greeted the suggestion.

The war ended therefore without any truly practical solution having been found to the labor manpower problem. The training-within-industry program, wage incentives, priorities for skilled labor, the job "freeze," and the "essentiality of employment" draft policy had proved only mildly successful. For this reason, the closing days of the war still saw the spectre of a national service law looming ominously on the horizon.

3

The Agricultural Front

☆ *Agriculture was also called upon to meet increased production demands as a result of the war. The accomplishment of this task was accompanied by unprecedented prosperity for the farmer.** ☆

The wartime output of agricultural products was large by any standard, though by no means so remarkable as the increase in industrial output, nor was it so large as many assume it to have been. The base customarily used in computing increases is that of 1935-1939, a period of low demand when farmers were plagued by surpluses, and a period in which active efforts were being made to reduce acreages of the major farm crops. This level was approximately that of 1924-1929 and was 5 per cent below the high level of production in 1931. Wheat acreage in three of the base years stood at approximately 50 million (harvested) as compared to more than 60 million at the beginning of the decade. Cotton acreage was about 35 per cent below that of 1929 and 1930. Corn acreage, likewise, was some 6 to 8 per cent below the high levels of the period around 1930. Thus, with restrictions eased and rapidly rising prices, the stage was set for a major upsurge in production if the weather proved favorable.

The 1940 production was about 3 per cent above that of 1939. A further gain

* From Murray R. Benedict, *Farm Policies of the United States, 1790-1950*, pp. 440-442, 449-450, 452. Copyright, 1953, The Twentieth Century Fund, New York. Used by permission.

of 3 points was registered in 1941, and a big jump of 12 points in 1942. Thereafter, production increased more slowly. The amounts made available for human use gained still more strikingly, reaching approximately 130 per cent of prewar in 1944 and 1945. This difference is due mainly to the rapid replacement of horse and mule power with tractors, thus reducing the feed used in supplying animal power.

The gain was largest in oil crops, from an index of 165 (1935-1939 - 100) in 1940 to 274 in 1945 after having reached a peak of 300 in 1943. These crops, principally soybeans, had started to increase sharply as early as 1938. The stimulus given in the war years was thus an acceleration of a shift already well under way. Peanut acreage was nearly doubled during the war years, mainly in response to the drive for increased production of oilseeds after Pearl Harbor. The percentage increase in livestock production was next in magnitude, reaching a level in 1943, 1944 and 1945 about 30 per cent above that of prewar period. Food grains showed similar but less consistent gains, reaching a high of 142 in 1945, a record which was to be exceeded substantially in the three following years. Feed grains and truck crops increased about in line with the average for all crops, and fruits, nuts and vegetables (other than truck crops) at a slower rate. Cotton and the sugar crops fell off sharply, while tobacco remained about constant.

The total acreage of crops did not at any time reach the levels attained in the early 1930's—375 million in 1932. At the outbreak of war, total acreage in crops stood at 348 million. A joint report by the Bureau of Agricultural Economics and the Agricultural Research Administration recommended an increase in overall crop acreage of somewhat over 25 million acres. This, however, was not achieved. The acreage in crops reached its peak at 365 million in 1944, but fell off to 357 million in 1945.

The BAE-ARA report recommended increases in food crops for direct consumption, oilseeds, sweet potatoes, Irish potatoes, dry beans and peas, vegetables and soybeans. It suggested reductions of 10 per cent in hog production, 5 per cent in sheep and lambs, and 2 per cent in chickens and broilers. Cattle and calves, dairy products and eggs were to be increased. At that time it was estimated that maximum production for agriculture, at average yields, would be 19 per cent above that of 1940. The actual achievement, with a strong assist in the way of favorable weather, was about 14 per cent. . . .

The index of wholesale prices of farm products stood at 92 in 1939 (1910-1914-100), that of commodities other than farm products at 118. Recovery from the lows of 1932 had been faster for farm products than for other commodities but, having started from a lower level, the farm price index still was considerably below that of nonfarm commodities.

However, this comparison requires some qualification. The years 1938 and 1939 were marked by a slump in farm prices from the high level of 121 in 1937.

For the decade as a whole, farm prices were below the 1939 level only in 1931, 1932 and 1933. Also, the nature of farm products changes less than does that of nonfarm commodities. For example, the 1939 washing machine, refrigerator, automobile and tractor were quite different commodities from those of 1914. Such changes in content of commodities having the same name is, in fact, one of the major defects of a parity ratio extending over long periods.

Be that as it may, the start of the war period found agricultural prices at a level that farmers considered far from satisfactory, one which they were making vigorous efforts to improve. The war in Europe and the accompanying upsurge in United States industrial employment brought a quick improvement in United States farm prices. They stood at 116 in 1941. In the meantime, nonfarm prices moved up less sharply to 131. That is, farm prices in this period advanced at about twice the rate of nonfarm prices.

Farm prices continued their rapid increase in 1942 and 1943, reaching a level of 172 in the latter year. At this point the upsurge was checked, with the general level advancing only to 173 in 1944 and 180 in 1945. But an enormous further increase was to be recorded in 1946, 1947 and 1948, after the abandonment of price controls and rationing. Nonfarm commodities moved up much more slowly and modestly—to 144 in 1942, 146 in 1943, 148 in 1944 and 150 in 1945. Here, however, there was downgrading of quality in many items continuing to be sold under the same name. The over-all increase in wholesale prices of farm products from 1939 to 1945 was 95 per cent, that for non-farm commodities about 28 per cent. The increase in prices paid to farmers was even more striking—from 95 to 202, or 112 per cent.

The parity ratio, that is, the ratio of

prices received by farmers to prices paid by them, stood at 77 in 1939. By 1942 it had passed the 100 mark and stood at 106. It reached 119 in 1943 but dropped back slightly in 1944 and 1945 as farm prices became more stable while other prices continued to edge upward. The comparable price increase for farm products in World War I was about 115 per cent. Thus, the actual percentage increase in the two wars was similar. It is apparent, however, that the increase would have been considerably greater in World War II had there been no rationing and price control. . . .

Between 1939 and 1945, total national income rose from $71.5 billion to $164 billion, an advance of 129 per cent. Income from farming during the same period increased from $5.25 billion to approximately $14 billion or about 165 per cent. During this period, the population on farms declined significantly while the number of employed urban workers increased greatly. Consequently, the changes in per capita income reflect more accurately the changes in relative well-being of the two groups. The farm population numbered, in 1939, 30,480,000. By 1945 this was down to 25,190,000. The farm population consists normally of a larger proportion of children than does the nonfarm population. This tendency probably was accentuated during the war years by the heavy drainage of adults out of agriculture, both for military service and for work in the war industries.

Per capita income of persons on farms, from farming, rose from $173 in 1939 to $554 in 1945, an increase of 220 per cent.

Income per person not on farms rose in the same period from $663 to $1,320, an increase of 99 per cent. The parity income ratio on a 1910-1914 basis, and in per capita terms, stood at 95 in 1939, dropped to 88 in 1940, and then rose rapidly, reaching 151 in 1945. That is, by 1945 the average farm person's situation as compared to that of the average urban dweller was presumably some 50 per cent better than the comparable relationship in 1910-1914.

Aside from returns to labor and to agriculture, the major distributive share in national income was that of corporate profits. Corporate profits after taxes stood at the comparatively low level of $5 billion in 1939. They rose to $6.4 billion in 1940, to $9.4 billion in 1941, and increased gradually to a peak of $10.8 billion in 1944. There was a sharp drop in 1945 to $8.5 billion and thereafter a rapid and large increase. Corporate profits thus made a gain of 116 per cent between 1939 and 1944 but were only 70 per cent above prewar in 1945. The rise was less, percentagewise and in total, than that of agricultural net incomes which correspond roughly in total amount in dollars. The percentage gain in profits was approximately equal to the gain in average weekly earnings of factory workers up to 1944. For 1945 it was substantially lower.

Corporation dividend payments to individuals rose only 23.5 per cent between 1939 and 1945. A large part of the increased earnings of corporations was retained in undistributed profits to meet the expected difficulties of the reconversion period.

4

Military Operations

☆ *The complexities of home front mobilization were paralleled in the expanded dimensions of land, sea, and air operations carried out over the entire face of the globe. The faults of the adversaries were almost as important in determining victory as were Allied strengths. These factors were discussed at length by Chief of Naval Operations Ernest J. King and Army Chief of Staff George C. Marshall.* ☆

(a) REPORT OF FLEET ADMIRAL ERNEST J. KING*

The major strategic decision of the war provided first for the defeat of Germany and then for the defeat of Japan. Both of these tasks have now been accomplished and we can view in clearer perspective the two major campaigns which led to victory. The contrast between them is at once apparent. The war in Europe was primarily a ground and air war with naval support, while the war in the Pacific was primarily a naval war with ground and air support.

In the European war, sea power was an essential factor because of the necessity of transporting our entire military effort across the Atlantic and supporting it there. Without command of the sea, this could not have been done. Nevertheless, the surrender of the land, sea and air forces of the German Reich on 8 May 1945 was the direct result of the applica-

tion of air power over land and the power of the Allied ground forces.

In the Pacific war, the power of our ground and strategic air forces, like sea power in the Atlantic, was an essential factor. By contrast with Germany, however, Japan's armies were intact and undefeated and her air forces only weakened when she surrendered, but her Navy had been destroyed and her merchant fleet had been fatally crippled. Dependent upon imported food and raw materials and relying upon sea transport to supply her armies at home and overseas, Japan lost the war because she lost command of the sea, and in doing so lost—to us—the island bases from which her factories and cities could be destroyed by air.

From the earliest days of the war our submarines, operating offensively in the farthest reaches of the Pacific, exacted a heavy toll of Japanese shipping. At a conservative estimate, they sank, in addition to many combatant ships, nearly two thirds of the merchant shipping which Japan lost during the war.

* December 8, 1945. From *The War Reports of General of the Army George C. Marshall, General of the Army H. H. Arnold, Fleet Admiral Ernest J. King*, pp. 654-659. Published by J. B. Lippincott, Philadelphia, 1947.

Our surface forces—fast task forces composed of aircraft carriers, fast battleships, cruisers, and destroyers—carried the war to the enemy homeland and destroyed impressive numbers of naval vessels and merchant ships. Our amphibious forces, operating initially behind air offensives and under air cover launched from carriers, seized the island bases which made possible the achievements of land-based aircraft in cutting enemy lines of communications and in carrying devastation to the Japanese home islands.

Thus our sea power separated the enemy from vital resources on the Asiatic mainland and in the islands which he had seized early in the war, and furnished us the bases essential to the operations of shore-based aircraft from which the atomic bombs finally were despatched, and on which troops and supplies were being massed for the invasion of Kyushu and of Honshu. The defeat of Japan was directly due to our overwhelming power at sea.

The destruction of the Japanese Navy followed the Nelsonian doctrine that naval victory should be followed up until the enemy fleet is annihilated. Of 12 battleships, 11 were sunk; of 26 carriers, 20 were sunk; of 43 cruisers, 38 were destroyed; and so on through the various types of ships, which collectively constituted a fleet considerably larger than ours was before the war began. The few ships that remained afloat were for the most part so heavily damaged as to be of no military value.

In striking contrast is the record of our ships. Although 2 old battleships were lost at Pearl Harbor, 8 new battleships have since joined the fleet. Against 5 aircraft carriers and 6 escort carriers lost, we completed 27 carriers and 110 escort carriers. While we lost 10 cruisers, 48 new cruisers have been commissioned. We lost 52 submarines and built 203. The capacity of the United States to build warships, auxiliary ships and merchant ships, while supporting our forces and our Allies all over the world, exceeded all former records and surpassed our most sanguine hopes. . . .

In the successful application of our sea power, a prime factor has been the flexibility and balanced character of our naval forces. In the Atlantic the German Navy was virtually limited to the use of submarines, without surface and naval air support. In the Pacific, Japanese sea power was hampered by army control, and Japanese naval officers lacked the freedom of initiative so necessary to gain and exercise command of the seas. On the other hand, while ours was a vast fleet, it was also a highly flexible and well-balanced fleet, in which ships, planes, amphibious forces and service forces in due proportion were available for unified action whenever and wherever called upon.

It is of interest to note, in connection with formulation of plans for the future strength of our Navy, that our fleet in World War II was not solely engaged in fighting enemy fleets. On numerous occasions a large part of the fleet effort was devoted to operations against land objectives. A striking example is the capture of Okinawa. During the three months that this operation was in progress our Pacific Fleet—the greatest naval force ever assembled in the history of the world—was engaged in a continuous battle which for sustained intensity has never been equaled in naval history; yet at this time the Japanese Navy had virtually ceased to exist—we were fighting an island, not an enemy fleet.

With the possible exception of amphibious warfare, which covers a field of considerably broader scope, the outstanding development of the war in the field of naval strategy and tactics has been the convincing proof and general acceptance of the fact that, in accord with the basic concept of the United States Navy, a concept established some 25 years ago, naval aviation is and must always be an integral and primary component of the fleet.

Naval aviation has proved its worth not only in its basic purpose of destroying hostile air and naval forces, but also in amphibious warfare involving attacks in support of landing operations, in reconnaissance over the sea and in challenging and defeating hostile land-based planes over positions held in force by the enemy. . . .

The epic advance of our united forces across the vast Pacific, westward from Hawaii and northward from New Guinea, to the Philippines and to the shores of Japan, was spearheaded by naval aviation and closely supported by the power of our fleets. In these advances, some of the steps exceeded 2,000 miles and the assaulting troops often had to be transported for much greater distances. The Navy moved them over water, landed them and supported them in great force at the beaches, kept them supplied and, particularly at Okinawa, furnished air cover during weeks of the critical fighting ashore. . . .

In connection with the matter of command in the field, there is perhaps a popular misconception that the Army and the Navy were intermingled in a standard form of joint operational organization in every theater throughout the world. Actually, the situation was never the same in any two areas. For example, after General of the Army Dwight D. Eisenhower had completed his landing in Normandy, his operation became purely a land campaign. The Navy was responsible for maintaining the line of communications across the ocean and for certain supply operations in the ports of Europe, and small naval groups became part of the land army for certain special purposes, such as the boat groups which helped in the crossing of the Rhine. But the strategy and tactics of the great battles leading up to the surrender of Germany were primarily army affairs and no naval officer had anything directly to do with the command of this land campaign.

A different situation existed in the Pacific, where, in the process of capturing small atolls, the fighting was almost entirely within range of naval gunfire; that is to say, the whole operation of capturing an atoll was amphibious in nature, with artillery and air support primarily naval. This situation called for a mixed Army-Navy organization which was entrusted to the command of Fleet Admiral Nimitz. A still different situation existed in the early days of the war during the Solomon Islands campaign where Army and Navy became, of necessity, so thoroughly intermingled that they were, to all practical purposes, a single service directed by Admiral William F. Halsey, Jr. Under General of the Army Douglas MacArthur, Army, Army aviation, and the naval components of his command were separate entities tied together only at the top in the person of General MacArthur himself. In the Mediterranean the scheme of command differed somewhat from all the others.

All these systems of command were successful largely because each was placed in effect to meet a specific condition imposed by the characteristics of the current situation in the theater of operations.

(b) REPORT OF GENERAL OF THE ARMY GEORGE C. MARSHALL*

As evaluated by the War Department General Staff, the interrogations of the captured German commanders disclose the following:

The available evidence shows that Hitler's original intent was to create, by absorption of Germanic peoples in the areas contiguous to Germany and by the

* September 1, 1945. From *The War Reports of General of the Army George C. Marshall, General of the Army H. H. Arnold, Fleet Admiral Ernest J. King*, pp. 143-148. Published by J. B. Lippincott, Philadelphia, 1947.

strengthening of her new frontiers, a greater Reich which would dominate Europe. To this end Hitler pursued a policy of opportunism which achieved the occupation of the Rhineland, Austria, and Czechoslovakia without military opposition.

No evidence has yet been found that the German High Command had any over-all strategic plan. Although the High Command approved Hitler's policies in principle, his impetuous strategy outran German military capabilities and ultimately led to Germany's defeat. The history of the German High Command from 1938 on is one of constant conflict of personalities in which military judgment was increasingly subordinated to Hitler's personal dictates. . . .

The campaigns in Poland, Norway, France, and the Low Countries developed serious diversions between Hitler and the General Staff as to the details of execuion of strategic plans. In each case the General Staff favored the orthodox offensive, Hitler an unorthodox attack with objectives deep in enemy territory. In each case Hitler's views prevailed and the astounding success of each succeeding campaign raised Hitler's military prestige to the point where his opinions were no longer challenged. His military self-confidence became unassailable after the victory in France, and he began to disparage substantially the ideas of his generals even in the presence of junior officers. Thus no General Staff objection was expressed when Hitler made the fatal decision to invade Soviet Russia.

When Italy entered the war Mussolini's strategic aims contemplated the expansion of his empire under the cloak of German military success. Field Marshal Keitel reveals that Italy's declaration of war was contrary to her agreement with Germany. Both Keitel and Jodl agree that it was undesired. From the very beginning Italy was a burden on the German war potential. Dependent upon Germany and German-occupied territory for oil and coal Italy was a constant source of economic attrition. Mussolini's unilateral action in attacking Greece and Egypt forced the Germans into the Balkan and African campaigns, resulting in over-extension of the German armies which subsequently became one of the principal factors in Germany's defeat.

Nor is there evidence of close strategic coordination between Germany and Japan. The German General Staff recognized that Japan was bound by the neutrality pact with Russia but hoped that the Japanese would tie down strong British and American land, sea, and air forces in the Far East.

In the absence of any evidence so far to the contrary, it is believed that Japan also acted unilaterally and not in accordance with a unified strategic plan.

Here were three criminal nations eager for loot and seeking greedily to advance their own self-interest by war, yet unable to agree on a strategic over-all plan for accomplishing a common objective.

The steps in the German defeat, as described by captured members of the High Command, were:

1. Failure to Invade England. Hitler's first military setback occurred when, after the collapse of France, England did not capitulate. According to Colonal General Jodl, Chief of the Operations Staff of the German High Command, the campaign in France had been undertaken because it was estimated that with the fall of France, England would not continue to fight. The unexpectedly swift victory over France and Great Britain's continuation of the war found the General Staff unprepared for an invasion of England. Although the armistice with France was concluded on 22 June 1940, no orders to prepare for the invasion of Britain were issued prior to 2 July. Field Marshal Kesselring stated that he urged the invasion since it generally was believed in Germany that England was in a critical condition. Field Marshal Keitel, Chief of Staff of German Armed Forces, however, stated that the risk was thought to be the existence of the British fleet. He said the army was ready but the air force was limited by weather, the navy very dubious. Meanwhile, in the air blitz over England the German Air Force had suffered irreparable losses from which its bombardment arm never recovered.

2.   The Campaign of 1941 in the Soviet Union. In the autumn of 1941 after the battle of Vysma, the Germans stood exhausted but apparently victorious before Moscow. According to Jodl, the General Staff of the armed forces considered that one last energetic push would be sufficient to finish the Soviets. The German High Command had neither envisioned nor planned for a winter campaign. A sudden change in the weather brought disaster. The Red Army defense, a terrific snowstorm, and extremely unseasonable cold in the Christmas week of 1941 precipitated the strategic defeat of the German armed forces. Impatient of all restraint, Hitler publicly announced that he had more faith in his own intuition than in the judgment of his military advisers. He relieved the Commander in Chief of the Army, General von Brauschitsch. It was the turning point of the war.

3.   Stalingrad. Even after the reverse before Moscow in 1941, Germany might have avoided defeat had it not been for the campaign in 1942 which culminated in the disaster at Stalingrad. Disregarding the military lessons of history, Hitler, instead of attacking the Soviet armies massed in the north, personally planned and directed a campaign of which the immediate objectives were to deprive the Soviet Union of her vital industries and raw materials by cutting the Volga at Stalingrad and seizing the Caucasian oil fields. Beyond these concrete objectives

was evidently the Napoleonic dream of a conquest of the Middle East and India by a gigantic double envelopment with one pincer descending from the Caucasus through Tiflis and the other from North Africa across Egypt, Palestine, and the Arabian desert. The campaign collapsed before Stalingrad with the magnificent Russian defense of that city and in the northern foothills of the Caucasus, where a break-down of German transport to the front left the German armor stalled for 3 weeks for lack of fuel in the critical summer months of 1942. Field Marshal Keitel in reviewing this campaign remarks that Germany failed completely to estimate properly the reserve of Russian industrial and productive power east of the Urals. The statement of both Keitel and Jodl is that neither was in favor of the Stalingrad campaign, but that the recommendations of the High Command were overruled by Adolf Hitler.

4.   Invasion of North Africa. Allied landings in North Africa came as a surprise to the German High Command. Field Marshal Kesselring, who, at the time, was commanding all German forces in the Mediterranean except Rommel's desert task force, states that his headquarters did expect a landing and had requested reinforcement by a division. However, Kesselring's fears were not heeded by Hitler and Goering. Allied security and deception measures for the landing operations were found to have been highly effective. Only when the Allied fleets and convoys were streaming through the Straits of Gibralter did the Germans realize that something very special was under way, and even then false conclusions were drawn: either that the Allies intended to land in rear of Rommel in the Middle East, or that these were British reinforcements en route to the Far East, or supplies for starving Malta. Since no advance preparation had been made by the Germans to repel such an

Allied invasion of North Africa, all subsequent efforts to counter the Allies suffered from hasty improvisation. Defense continued, however, because, as Field Marshal Keitel now states, since evacuation was impossible, the Germans had only the choice of resisting or surrendering.

5. The Invasion of France. All German headquarters expected the Allied invasion of France. According to Colonel General Jodl, both the general direction and the strength of the initial assault in Normandy were correctly estimated; but Field Marshal Keitel states that the Germans were not sure exactly where the Allies would strike and considered Brittany as more probable because of the three major U-boat bases located in that region. Both agree that the belief of the German High Command that a second assault would be launched, probably by an army under General Patton, held large German forces in the Pas-de-Calais area. Both Keitel and Jodl believed that the invasion could be repulsed or at worst contained, and both named the Allied air arm as the decisive factor in the German failure.

Prior to the invasion, important divergencies of opinion developed between Field Marshal von Rundstedt, Commander in Chief West, and Rommel, commander of the threatened army group. Rundstedt desired to hold his armored forces in a group around Paris and in Eastern France; Rommel to push them forward to positions in readiness close to the cost. The Rommel view prevailed. Von Rundstedt was subsequently relieved by Colonel General von Kluge.

Soon after the Allied capture of Cherbourg, dissension again broke out in the High Command. Von Kluge and Rommel wished to evacuate all Southwestern France, blocking or destroying its usable ports. They believed that a continuation of the fight in Normandy could only end with the destruction of their Western armies

and that they should withdraw before disintegration began. Von Kluge recommended defense on the general line: lower Seine-Paris-Fontainebleau-Massif Central. Hitler refused to accept this recommendation, relieved Kluge from command, and reappointed Von Rundstedt as Commander in Chief West. Under direct instructions, Rundstedt continued the battle of Normandy to its final denouement. Hitler himself ordered the Avranches-Mortain counter-attack and was much surprised when it completely failed. Keitel expresses further surprise at the audacious exploitation of the American breakthrough at Avranches during this counterattack, and particularly of the thrust toward Brest.

6. The Ardennes Counterattack. The German offensive in December 1944 was Hitler's personal conception. According to Jodl, the objective of the attack was Antwerp. It was hoped that overcast weather would neutralize Allied air superiority, and that an exceptionally rapid initial break-through could be achieved. Other German officers believe that this operation was reckless in the extreme, in that it irreparably damaged the comparatively fresh armored divisions of the Sixth Panzer Army, the principal element of Germany's strategic reserve, at a moment when every available reserve was needed to repulse the expected Soviet attack in the east.

7. The Crossing of the Rhine. Even after the failure of the German counter-offensive in the Ardennes, the Germans believed that the Rhine line could be held. The loss of the Remagen bridge, however, exploded this hope. The entire Rhine defensive line had to be weakened in the attempt to contain the bridgehead, and the disorderly German retreat in the Saar and Palatinate rendered easy the subsequent drive eastward of the Allied armies toward Hamburg, Leipzig, and Munich.

Not only were the European partners of the Axis unable to coordinate their plans and resources and agree within their own nations how best to proceed, but the Eastern partner, Japan, was working in even greater discord. The Axis, as a matter of fact, existed on paper only. Eager to capitalize on the preoccupation of the Western Powers in Europe, Japan was so greedy for her own immediate conquests that she laid her strategy, not to help Germany defeat Russia and Great Britain, but to accumulate her own profit. Had the way been open Germany and Japan would have undoubtedly joined their armies in Central Asia, but to Japan this objective was secondary to looting the Far East while there was no real force to stop her.

5

Japanese-Americans

☆ *In 1942, the President authorized the Army to take steps to restrain people of Japanese descent as a security measure. This led to a series of orders providing for the removal and detention even of Japanese-Americans. In Korematsu v. United States, 1944, an American citizen of Japanese descent unsuccessfully challenged an exclusion order before the Supreme Court.** ☆

MR. JUSTICE BLACK delivered the opinion of the Court. . .

It is said that we are dealing here with the case of imprisonment of a citizen in a concentration camp solely because of his ancestry, without evidence of inquiry concerning his loyalty and good disposition towards the United States. Our task would be simple, our duty clear, were this a case involving the imprisonment of a loyal citizen in a concentration camp because of racial prejudice. Regardless of the true nature of the assembly and relocation centers—and we deem it unjustifiable to call them concentration camps with all the ugly connotations that term implies—we are dealing specifically with nothing but an exclusion order. To cast this case into outlines of racial prejudice, without reference to the real military dangers which were presented, merely confuses the issue. Korematsu was not excluded from the Military Area because of hostility to him or his race. He *was* excluded because we are at war with the Japanese Empire, because the properly

constituted military authorities feared an invasion of our West Coast and felt constrained to take proper security measures, because they decided that the military urgency of the situation demanded that all citizens of Japanese ancestry be segregated from the West Coast temporarily, and finally because Congress, reposing its confidence in this time of war in our military leaders—as inevitably it must—determined that they should have the power to do just this. There was evidence of disloyalty on the part of some, the military authorities considered that the need for action was great, and time was short. We cannot—by availing ourselves of the calm perspective of hindsight—now say that at that time these actions were unjustified.

Affirmed

MR. JUSTICE MURPHY, dissenting.

The exclusion of "all persons of Japanese ancestry, both alien and non-alien," from the Pacific Coast area on a plea of military necessity in the absence of martial law ought not to be approved. Such exclusion goes over "the very brink of

* 323 U.S. 214.

constitutional power" and falls into the ugly abyss of racism.

In dealing with matters relating to the prosecution and progress of war, we must accord great respect and consideration to the judgments of the military authorities who are on the scene and who have full knowledge of the military facts. The scope of their discretion must, as a matter of necessity and common sense, be wide. And their judgments ought not to be overruled lightly by those whose training and duties ill-equip them to deal intelligently with matters so vital to the physical security of the nation.

At the same time, however, it is essential that there be definite limits to military discretion, especially where martial law has not been declared. Individuals must not be left improverished of their constitutional rights on a plea of military necessity that has neither substance nor support. Thus, like other claims conflicting with the asserted constitutional rights of the individual, the military claim must subject itself to the judicial process of having its reasonableness determined and its conflicts with other interests reconciled. "What are the allowable limits of military discretion, and whether or not they have been overstepped in a particular case, are judicial questions." *Sterling v. Constantin,* 287 U.S. 378,401.

The judicial test of whether the Government, on a plea of military necessity, can validly deprive an individual of any of his constitutional rights is whether the deprivation is reasonably related to a public danger that is so "immediate, imminent, and impending" as not to admit of delay and not to permit the intervention of ordinary constitutional processes to alleviate the danger. *United States v. Russell,* 13 Wall. 623, 627-8; *Mitchell v. Harmony,* 13 How. 115, 134-5; *Raymond v. Thomas,* 91, U.S. 712,716. Civilian Exclusion Order No. 34, banishing from a prescribed area of the Pacific Coast "all persons of Japanese ancestry, both alien and non-alien," clearly does not meet that test. Being an obvious racial discrimination, the order deprives all those within its scope of the equal protection of the laws as guaranteed by the Fifth Amendment. It further deprives these individuals of their constitutional rights to live and work where they will, to establish a home where they choose and to move about freely. In excommunicating them without benefit of hearings, this order also deprives them of all their constitutional rights to procedural due process. Yet no reasonable relation to an "immediate, imminent, and impending" public danger is evident to support this racial restriction which is one of the most sweeping and complete deprivations of constitutional rights in the history of this nation in the absence of martial law. . . .

I dissent, therefore, from this legalization of racism. Racial discrimination in any form and in any degree has no justifiable part whatever in our democratic way of life. It is unattractive in any setting but it is utterly revolting among a free people who have embraced the principles set forth in the Constitution of the United States. All residents of this nation are kin in some way by blood or culture to a foreign land. Yet they are primarily and necessarily a part of the new and distinct civilization of the United States. They must accordingly be treated at all times as the heirs of the American experiment and as entitled to all the rights and freedoms guaranteed by the Constitution.

6

The Moral Issue

☆ *Reinhold Niebuhr (1892-   ), clergyman and theologian, has for four decades played a significant role in American religion and thought. He early interpreted the threats of totalitarian dictatorships as warnings against the dangers which might befall those addicted to the comfortable life and optimistic viewpoints.* ☆

Almost every version of modern culture has some futile and fatuous scheme for lifting men from selfish purposes as painlessly as possible. The simplest idea of all is that which underlies the laissez faire social philosophies of the eighteenth and nineteenth centuries. According to these philosophies all conflicting interests in human society, and all competing egoistic drives, would result in harmony rather than conflict if they were only left alone. If political society did not interfere with economic process, economic life would achieve a natural harmony. This idea, which obviates the necessity of either moral or political control upon selfish impulses, was a nice device for eating your cake and having it too. It justified unrestrained selfishness without justifying egoism morally; for it gave the assurance that "each man seeking his own would serve the commonweal." The only difficulty with the idea is that it is not true. The one element of truth in it is that there are indeed certain automatic harmonies in the economic process, and it is

* From Reinhold Niebuhr, "A Faith for History's Greatest Crisis," *Fortune*, XXIV (July, 1942), pp. 122, 125-126, 128, 131. Courtesy of *Fortune* Magazine.

wise to maintain them. But on the whole, history, unlike nature, has no natural balance of power. Where power is disproportionate, power dominates weakness and injustice results. A technical civilization actually accentuates previous disproportions of power, so that the theory was less true for the growing technical society to which it was applied than for a more static agrarian society, to which it had not been applied.

The theory of the harmlessness of natural man, if only he is not controlled and regulated, is usually compounded with another theory, which is a little more profound. It is the theory that ignorant selfishness is dangerous to society, but that a wise and prudent selfishness knows how to relate the interests of the self to the interests of the whole; so that a wise egoist, while seeking his own pleasure, will finally serve "the greatest good of the greatest number." The confidence in the essential virtue of the intelligent man takes various forms. Sometimes intelligence supposedly restrains egoism in its narrow form and broadens it to include the interests of others. Sometimes it is assumed that the intelligence preserves a nice balance between egoistic and altruistic impulses. And sometimes reason throws the weight of its authority on the side of altruism as against egoism.

In the philosophy of Hegel, reason overcomes the narrow interests of the individual self by creating the state, as an expression of the broader interests of the collective self. Hegelian philosophy fails to consider, however, that human society is engulfed in conflict more frequently by competing collective wills than by conflicting individual wills and interests. The most tragic conflicts of history are between states, nations, classes, and races, and not between individuals.

The trust of the modern man in reason thus takes many forms. In all of them it assumes that reason is an organ of the universal and that in some way or other increasing reason will progressively remove conflict from human society and produce an ultimately perfect coincidence of interest with interest and a finally perfect conformity of will to will. Even Marxism, which is presumably a revolt against this trust in reason, is another version of the same faith. It assumes that nothing but the "class organization" of society tempts men to subordinate their reason to their passions and interest; and that the conflicts in human society will result in an ultimate catastrophe from which a new society will emerge in which there will be perfect harmony.

This trust in reason, as the organ of human virtue and as the guarantor of social peace and justice, underlies modern man's faith in history. For he conceives of history as a movement in which reason is progressively coming into control of all the vitalities, interests, and passions of life. If we are involved in conflict today we may therefore attribute it to the ignorance and the superstitition of men; and look forward hopefully to the day when increasing education and advancing intelligence will have dispelled the bigotries of ignorant men and destroyed the parochialism of backward races and nations.

If the revolt against our civilization is to be understood profoundly and not merely attributed to the conspiracies of "bad" men, we must realize that totalitarian philosophy has in every case taken neglected portions of the total truth about man and history and fashioned them into perverse but potent instruments against a civilization that did not understand the nature and history of man. For the liberal faith in reason, Nazism substituted the romantic faith in vitality and force. For the simple faith that right creates its own might, it substituted the idea that might makes right. For the hope of liberal democracy that history was in the process of eliminating all partial, national, and racial loyalties and creating a universal community of mankind, it substituted a primitive loyalty to race and nation as the final end of life. In place of the sentimental idea that men could easily combine devotion to their own interests with loyalty to universal justice, it proclaimed the cynical idea that there is no justice but that which serves "my" or "our" purpose and interest.

It is wrong to worship force and to make power self-justifying. But such an error could not have arisen in a civilization that had not made the opposite mistake and assumed that men were in the process of becoming purely rational. It is perverse to make the interests of our nation the final end of life. But this error could not have achieved such monstrous proportions if our culture had not foolishly dreamed and hoped for the development of "universal" men, who were bereft of all loyalties to family, race, and nation. It is monstrous to glorify war as the final good. But that error could not have brought us so close to disaster if a comfortable civilization had not meanwhile regarded peace as a final good; and had not expected perfect peace to be an attainable goal of history. It is terrible to conduct the diplomacy and military strategy of nations upon the basis of "all or nothing" policies. But the fury expressed in such policies would have not come so close to success if it had not been met by the illusions of comfortable and fat nations in which the love of ease had been compounded with the caution of prudence, and the two together had resulted in an inability to act. If the lies embodied in the Nazi creed did not contain a modicum of truth and if that modicum of truth had not been directed against our weakness and our illusions, we would not have come so close to disaster.

We have defined the error that underlies all the optimistic illusions of our culture as a too-simple confidence in man, particularly in rational man, and as a too-simple hope in the progressive achievement of virtue in history, by reason of the progressive extension of intelligence. This confidence that human history ultimately answers all its unsolved problems and overcomes all its earlier insecurities, that history is itself a kind of process of redemption, has gained such a strong hold upon modern man because it is actually partly true and because all the tremendous advances of science, technology, and inteligence seemed to justify the belief. The Renaissance, which trusted in history, triumphed over the Reformation, which had serious questions about history, because we were actually making progress in so many directions that it seemed plausible to assume that all these advances could be summed up as moral progress. But this final conclusion represents a grievous error. There is always progress in history in the sense that it cumulates wisdom, perfects technics, increases the areas of human cooperation, and extends the human control over nature. But this cannot be regarded as moral progress. There are morally

ambiguous elements in human history on every new level of achievement. We ought to have known that. A person progresses from childhood to maturity, but it is not easy to compare the virtue of maturity with the innocency of a child, because mature life achieves higher unities and is subject to greater complexities than child life. It is in fact irrelevant to measure mature virtue with childish innocency because they are incommensurate. So it is with the history of mankind.

The advancement of knowledge may mitigate social conflict, but intelligence may also be the servant of imperial ambition. The applied sciences and technics may multiply human power and increase comfort. But the Nazis may use the power for destructive ends; and the democratic world may be beguiled by the comforts of bourgeois society into a false security. Modern means of communication may increase the breadth and extent of human communities, but they also enlarge areas of human conflict. Reason may serve as an arbitrator betwen my interest and those of my fellowmen. In that case, reason is a servant of justice. But reason may, as Bergson observed, also break the communities of primitive life by giving the egoistic urge a new instrument.

Whether one analyzes the advances of history in terms of technics or of intelligence, it is quite apparent that history is not so simple as we have believed. The morally ambiguous note remains in it on every level. The securities of its maturity save us from the insecurities of childhood; but they do not save us from the new insecurities of maturity. The wisdom of maturity is a cure for the ignorance of childhood; but it is no cure for the ignorance of maturity. It is because we have trusted history too much that we understand neither life nor history. History cannot be the answer to our problems, for history is itself our problems. History is in short, an inadequate god. We have failed to gauge every contemporary problem in its true depth because of this false faith in history. Previous civilizations only made the mistake of misjudging their own history and estimating their own security too highly. We went one step beyond them in pride and pretension. We thought no evil could befall us because we trusted not "Roman civilization" nor medieval culture, but history itself. Yet our error was greater than previous errors, precisely because we believed that history's development of all human potencies also guaranteed the elimination of all human insecurities. The very opposite is the truth. A highly dynamic technical society is more destructive in its decay than a simple agrarian society. The destruction dumped from the skies by modern airplanes is more awful than the lethal power of a bow and arrow.

And neither the further advance of science nor the mere return to religion will give us the perspective required. Neither return to a simpler piety nor advance from piety to a sophisticated scientific culture can solve our problem. Religious and scientific leaders may have been fighting each other, but they have shared the same common and erroneous faith. Neither were driven beyond the characteristic complacency of modern man in regard to history. The scientists may have regarded themselves as very sophisticated and thought of the religious people as very sentimental. But these superficial differences were insignificant. Scientists and pietists agreed in regarding human history as the answer to all human problems rather than as itself the great human problem.

If we seek for a cultural reconstruction in our day, we must look for something more fundamental than the mere extension of scientific knowledge, for science gives no answer to the ultimate problem of the meaning of life. Nor can we be satisfied with the conventional advice to return to religion. There must indeed be a return to religion in the sense that all final answers to ultimate problems are religious answers, whether clothed in the language and pretensions of science, philosophy, or religion. But a religious answer, per se, is no more adequate than a scientific answer. The Nazi answer to the problem of life is a religious answer; but Nazi religion is a primitive religion, which declares that the triumph of "my" nation fulfills the meaning of life and history. The Buddhist answer to the problem of life is a religious answer. But it declares that life is fulfilled by escape from history.

The primary significance of the Hebraic-Christian tradition, which underlies our Western culture, is that it regards historical existence as meaningful, but it sees no fulfillment of life's meaning in history, because it recognizes that history, on every level of achievement, contains ambiguities, problems, and insecurities that demand an answer. The answer to these problems given by the Christian faith is that history is borne by a divine reality that completes what remains incomplete in history and purges what is evil in history. This answer can be taken seriously only by those who recognize the seriousness of the problem to which it is an answer.

Our modern culture since the Renaissance has not taken the Christian faith seriously because it had a simpler answer to the problems of life. It agreed with Christianity in regarding human history as meaningful, but it assigned a simple meaning to history. The Reformation was meanwhile overwhelmed because it was too pessimistic about the possibilities of history.

An adequate faith for our day must again combine these broken fragments of the Christian tradition. Any culture or any religion that is deficient in the "tragic sense of life" is certainly inadequate to give us light and guidance in a day in which the very securities of a technical society have been transmuted into evil. We need a faith that throws light upon the importance of every historical task and responsibility. But it must on the other hand reveal the limits of all historical striving. Without such a faith, the modern man remains an inveterate utopian, disavowing all religious ultimates in one breath and in the next breath affirming his faith in some incredible utopia, some impossible heaven on earth.

An adequate religious culture must transcend the stabilities, securities, achievements of any given civilization. If faith is bound up with these too completely, life becomes meaningless when they break down. It must give people the resource to rebuild a civilization without illusions and yet without despair. We must, for instance, achieve a higher level of international organization after the war or our civilization will sink even lower. If we engage in the task of world reconstruction without a disavowal of the utopian illusion, which has informed our culture particularly since the eighteenth century, we shall ask for the impossible by way of world federation or some world superstate; we shall not get it, and then we shall be tempted again to despair and disillusionment. Furthermore, the utopians will always tempt the realists among us to become cynical in their reaction to utopianism. These cynics will be inclined to assert that history contains no new possibilities for good. They will seek to reconstruct the world on the basis of the precarious balance of power, and they will not find a new level of international community compatible with our new economic interdependence.

All political and economic achievements must be informed by a religion and a culture, which know that history is a realm of infinite possibilities, and that each new level of maturity places new responsibilities upon us. But it must also be understood that all historic achievements are limited and precarious; that human egoism, individual and collective, can be transmuted and sublimated on many new levels, but that it cannot be eliminated from history. The faith that man as a particular force in history, contending against other particular forces, is in the process of becoming a universal force, has no historical evidence to justify it. The modern man regards himself as so sophisticated and is nevertheless incredibly credulous. Human existence is precarious and will remain so to the end of history. Human achievement contains a tragic element of frustration and corruption and will contain it to the end of history. There is an ultimate answer to these tragic aspects of human existence, but that answer can be known only to those who have stopped looking for some easy escape from tragedy.

The Christian religion regards history as meaningful but as having no fulfillment of its meaning within itself. In that sense Christianity is "otherworldly." For this reason all modern substitutes for the Christian faith, in which history is fulfilled in some kind of utopia, naturally find the Christian faith incredible because they have a simpler answer to the problems of life. The Christian faith becomes credible only when those simpler answers are refuted by history, as indeed they are bound to be.

According to the Christian faith all finite and historical existence points to a ground and an end beyond itself. This divine end and ground is paradoxically defined as having a double relation to history. God judges the world because there are violations of the law of life on every level of human achievement. God "saves" the world because he has resources of mercy beyond this judgment. But mercy cannot express itself without taking justice seriously. Thus God is pictured as being able to be merciful only by taking the consequences of his judgment upon and into himself. These paradoxes of the Christian faith have sometimes been stated in terms of a wooden literalism that has made them offensive to human intelligence. But it is well to remember that they are a "stumbling block" and "foolishness" even when stated profoundly. The reason for this is that all men would like to believe that they have the power within themselves to complete their lives and their history. But this is exactly what all men lack.

A faith that is able to transcend the catastophes of history must therefore be able to define both the possibilities of human creativity in history and the limits of human possibilities. It must also be able to clarify the fact that the evils of fanaticism, conflict, imperialism, and tyranny have their source in man's ambition to overleap his limitations and to seek unconditional power, virtue, and security for his existence.

For this reason historical catastrophe seems to be nothing but chaos, which drives men to despair without the profundities of the Christian faith. And Christian faith becomes vapid and sentimental in periods of stability and peace. It recovers its own profoundest insights precisely in those periods of social chaos when all simpler interpretations of life break down and force men to seek for a profounder interpretation of existence.

7

A Program for Victory and Security

☆ *By the beginning of 1944, although the Allies had won some military victories, the President was convinced that the United States was not sufficiently mobilized for the war effort or prepared for the peace to follow. In his State of the Union message to Congress on January 11, Roosevelt presented a controversial blueprint for action on these problems.* ☆*

The one supreme objective for the future . . . can be summed up in one word: Security.

And that means not only physical security which provides safety from attacks by aggressors. It means also economic security, social security, moral security— in a family of nations. . . .

If ever there was a time to subordinate individual or group selfishness to the national good, that time is now. Disunity at home—bickerings, self-seeking partisanship, stoppages of work, inflation, business as usual, politics as usual, luxury as usual —these are the influences which can undermine the morale of the brave men ready to die at the front for us here. . . .

Therefore, in order to concentrate all our energies and resources on winning the war, and to maintain a fair and stable economy at home, I recommend that the Congress adopt:

(1) A realistic tax law—which will tax all unreasonable profits, both individual and corporate, and reduce the ultimate cost of the war to our sons and daughters.

* From *Congressional Record*, 78th Congress, 2nd session, pp. 55-56.

The tax bill now under consideration by the Congress does not begin to meet this test.

(2) A continuation of the law for the renegotiation of war contracts—which will prevent exorbitant profits and assure fair prices to the Government. For 2 long years I have pleaded with the Congress to take undue profits out of war.

(3) A cost of food law—which will enable the Government (a) to place a reasonable floor under the prices the farmer may expect for his production; and (b) to place a ceiling on the prices of consumer will have to pay for the food he buys. This should apply to necessities only; and will require public funds to carry out. It will cost in appropriations about one percent of the present annual cost of the war.

(4) Early reenactment of the stabilization statute of October, 1942. This expires June 30, 1944, and if it is not extended well in advance, the country might just as well expect price chaos by summer. We cannot have stabilization by wishful thinking. We must take positive action to maintain the integrity of the American dollar.

(5) A national service law—which, for the duration of the war, will prevent strikes, and, with certain appropriate exceptions, will make available for war production or for any other essential services every able-bodied adult in this Nation. . . .

It is our duty now to begin to lay the plans and determine the strategy for the winning of a lasting peace and the establishment of an American standard of living higher than ever before known. We cannot be content, no matter how high that general standard of living may be, if some fraction of our people—whether it be one-third or one-fifth or one-tenth—is ill-fed, ill-clothed, ill-housed, and insecure. . . .

In our day these economic truths have become accepted as self-evident. We have accepted, so to speak, a second Bill of Rights under which a new basis of security and prosperity can be established for all—regardless of station, race, or creed.

Among these are:

The right to a useful and remunerative job in the industries or shops or farms or mines of the Nation;

The right to earn enough to provide adequate food and clothing and recreation;

The right of every farmer to raise and sell his products at a return which will give him and his family a decent living;

The right of every businessman, large and small, to trade in an atmosphere of freedom from unfair competition and domination by monopolies at home or abroad;

The right of every family to a decent home;

The right to adequate medical care and the opportunity to achieve and enjoy good health;

The right to adequate protection from the economic fears of old age, sickness, accident, and unemployment;

The right to a good education.

All of these rights spell security. And after this war is won we must be prepared to move forward, in the implementation of these rights, to new goals of human happiness and well-being.

America's own rightful place in the world depends in large part upon how fully these and similar rights have been carried into practice for our citizens. For unless there is security here at home there cannot be lasting peace in the world. . . .

I ask the Congress to explore the means for implementing this economic bill of rights—for it is definitely the responsibility of the Congress so to do. Many of these problems are already before committees of the Congress in the form of proposed legislation. I shall from time to time communicate with the Congress with respect to these and further proposals. In the event that no adequate program of progress is evolved, I am certain that the Nation will be conscious of the fact.

Our fighting men abroad—and their families at home—expect such a program and have the right to insist upon it. It is to their demands that this Government should pay heed rather than to the whining demands of selfish pressure groups who seek to feather their nests while young Americans are dying.

8

Politics as Usual

☆ *In June of 1944, the young governor of New York, Thomas E. Dewey, was nominated for president by the Republicans on a platform that was internationalist and progressive in tone. Running at the height of the war, Governor Dewey waged a vigorous campaign, as reflected in his speech of October 7, 1944.** ☆

We have a fateful decision to make, but that decision must be made not on vague and irresponsible political discussion but on the facts. On Thursday night of this week my opponent repeated his charge that "there are politicians and others who quite openly worked to restrict the use of the ballot in this election." Now I do not know whom Mr. Roosevelt means, because he seems to lack the courage to name names and say what he means. So let's look at the facts.

He sadly complained that not enough people vote. But he pointed with pride to the fact that in 1940 62½ per cent of the eligible voters of this nation went to the polls. Well, in the State of New York not 62½ per cent but 77 per cent of the eligible soldiers and sailors of our State have had ballots mailed to them already. Despite my opponent's attempt to play politics with the soldier vote every evidence indicates that as a nation we will have an even larger percentage of soldier votes than we will of civilians.

Let's have no more of this political pre-

* From *Vital Speeches,* XI (October 15, 1944), pp. 13-15.

tense on a matter of importance to us all. Now we know where the truth is. And let me point out my opponent is relying for his main support upon a solid block of votes in States where millions of American citizens are deprived of their right to vote by the poll tax and by intimidation. Not once in twelve years has my opponent lifted a finger to correct this and his platform is cynically silent on the subject.

In his speech of Thursday night my opponent softly denies that he welcomes "the support of any person or group committed to communism or fascism."

Now, that is news. But doesn't this soft disclaimer come a trifle late? Only last week in Madison Square Garden Earl Browder, the head of the Communist party in America, proclaimed to 15,000 cheering adherents that the election of my opponent was essential to his aims. This is the same Earl Browder, now such a patriot, who was convicted as a draft dodger in the last war, convicted again as a perjurer and pardoned by Franklin Roosevelt in time to organize the campaign for his fourth term. The soft disclaimer does come a little late.

Now, why is my opponent's election so

essential to the aims of the Communists? The answer is right in the record of this Administration. The aims of the New Dealers were stated on May 23, 1939, by Adolf Berle in a carefully written memorandum submitted to the Temporary National Economic Committee, an official agency set up to decide upon our future for us. There he said: "Over a period of years the Government will gradually come to own most of the productive plants in the United States."

Now, who is this Adolf Berle? He is one of the original brain trusters and today he holds the office of Assistant Secretary of State.

What does he mean by the Government owning "most of the productive plants in the United States." That means, of course, a system where Government would tell each of us where we could work, at what, and for how much.

Now, I do not know whether my opponent calls that system communism or national socialism, or fascism. He can take it any way he likes it. It's his program, not mine. But I do know it is not an American system and it's not a free system.

Let's just see how far we have traveled down that New Deal road. A report just released by a Congressional committee headed by a Democratic United States Senator shows there are fifty-five Government corporations and credit agencies with net assets of twenty-seven billions. The Federal Government now owns or operates one-fifth of the manufacturing plants in the country.

Little by little, the New Deal is developing its own form of corporate State. It becomes clear why the twice convicted Comrade Browder and his friends are so eager for the re-election of my opponent. There is another reason. They love to fish in troubled waters. Their aims can best be served by unemployment and discontent. They remember that the New Deal

in all its seven peace-time years never cured unemployment. They remember that in the spring of 1940 we still had 10,-000,000 unemployed. They remember that under the New Deal we had to have a war to get jobs. That's why they want a fourth term and sixteen years of the New Deal. That is one of the very good reasons why it's time for a change.

Just for a moment let's look at the way this tired Administration bungled its way into conversion for war production. Then we will know how well they can convert for peace and for jobs. In August, 1939, more than six years after Hitler came to power, Mr. Roosevelt finally created a War Resources Board under Edward R. Stettinius. It worked for three months and brought in a report, but the report was buried and the board quietly died. The report is still a secret after five years. Like so many other things, we will never know about it until a new Administration opens the record of these past twelve years.

With Poland conquered, Hitler took Norway and invaded the Lowlands. At last, in response to public pressure on May 25, 1940, Mr. Roosevelt acted. He created the Office for Emergency Management under Executive Order No. 8,248.

But just four days later he piled on top of this one a seven-man advisory commission. In doing this he was repeating with exact fidelity the most notorious blunder of the first World War. Of course it failed.

So next we are handed the prize monstrosity of all, the Office of Production Management under two different heads, William Knudsen and Sidney Hillman. . . .

Of course that agency was a failure, too. So Mr. Roosevelt piled on still another one, the Supply Priorities and Allocations Board. That was on Aug. 28, 1941, and of course that failed too. It was not until five weeks after Pearl Harbor that Mr.

444   WORLD WAR II (1941-1945)

Roosevelt did what should have been done at the beginning. At last we got a War Production Board with a single responsible administrator at the head of it.

But that was not the end. By way of coordinating all this confusion, and, as he said, "to resolve and determine controversies," my opponent created a sixth agency, the Office of War Mobilization. That was on May 27, 1943, eighteen months after Pearl Harbor. Still conflicting orders, overlapping responsibilities, backbiting and character assassination handicapped the war effort.

So the inevitable happened again, a little over a month ago. The War Production Board itself, fell apart. One official after another resigned in a torrent of recrimination and the head of the board was given a ticket to China.

Now, during all these months that the war effort was being hampered by open warfare in Washington, the responsible head of our Government was doing nothing about it. For weeks our daily papers carried stories of internal dissensions within the board. After it finally blew up, Mr. Roosevelt's only comment was that he had, of course, been aware of dissension but he had "hoped it would disappear." Judging by the words of my opponent it has become dreadfully clear that his Administration is too tired even to do the job at hand. It is obviously too tired for the job ahead.

We need a house cleaning in Washington. We need clear lines of authority with competent men to carry out their jobs. We need team work in our Government. That's why it's time for a change.

9

Coalition Strategy

☆ *Great efforts were made during the war to integrate the strategies of the Allied powers. The most dramatic of these efforts took the form of periodic meetings between the chiefs of government of the leading countries in the fighting coalition called the United Nations.* ☆

(a) PRESIDENT ROOSEVELT'S RADIO REPORT TO THE NATION*

The decisions reached and the actual plans made at Casablanca were not confined to any one theater of war or to any one continent or ocean or sea. Before this year is out, it will be made known to the world—in actions rather than in words—that the Casablanca Conference produced plenty of news; and it will be bad news for the Germans and Italians—and the Japanese. . . .

In an attempt to ward off the inevitable disaster, the Axis propagandists are trying all of their old tricks in order to divide the United Nations. They seek to create the idea that if we win this war, Russia, England, China, and the United States are going to get into a cat-and-dog fight.

This is their final effort to turn one nation against another, in the vain hope that they may settle with one or two at a time—that any of us may be so gullible and so forgetful as to be duped into making "deals" at the expense of our Allies.

* February 12, 1943, on the Casablanca Conference with Prime Minister Winston Churchill. From *War Messages of Franklin D. Roosevelt, December 8, 1941-October 12, 1945*, Washington, 1945, pp. 70-71.

To these panicky attempts to escape the consequences of their crimes we say —all the United Nations say—that the only terms on which we shall deal with an Axis government or any Axis factions are the terms proclaimed at Casablanca: "Unconditional Surrender." In our uncompromising policy we mean no harm to the common people of the Axis nations. But we do mean to impose punishment and retribution in full upon their guilty, barbaric leaders. . . .

In the years of the American and French revolutions the fundamental principle guiding our democracies was established. The cornerstone of our whole democratic edifice was the principle that from the people and the people alone flows the authority of government.

It is one of our war aims, as expressed in the Atlantic Charter, that the conquered populations of today be again the masters of their destiny. There must be no doubt anywhere that it is the unalterable purpose of the United Nations to restore to conquered peoples their sacred rights.

(b) STATEMENT ISSUED BY PRESIDENT ROOSEVELT, GENERALIS-SIMO CHIANG KAI-SHEK, AND PRIME MINISTER WINSTON CHURCHILL*

The several military missions have agreed upon future military operations against Japan. The Three Great Allies expressed their resolve to bring unrelenting pressure against their brutal enemies by sea, land, and air. This pressure is already rising.

The Three Great Allies are fighting this war to restrain and punish the aggression of Japan. They covet no gain for themselves and have no thought of territorial expansion. It is their purpose that Japan shall be stripped of all the islands in the Pacific which she has seized or occupied since the beginning of the first World War

in 1914, and that all the territories Japan has stolen from the Chinese, such as Manchuria, Formosa, and the Pescadores, shall be restored to the Republic of China. Japan will also be expelled from all other territories which she has taken by violence and greed. The aforesaid three great powers, mindful of the enslavement of the people of Korea, are determined that in due course Korea shall become free and independent.

With these objects in view the three Allies, in harmony with those of the United Nations at war with Japan, will continue to persevere in the serious and prolonged operations necessary to procure the unconditional surrender of Japan.

* Following the Cairo Conference of November 22-26, 1943. From *Department of State Bulletin*, IX, p. 393.

(c) STATEMENT ISSUED REGARDING THE TEHERAN CONFERENCE BY PRESIDENT ROOSEVELT, MARSHAL JOSEPH STALIN, AND PRIME MINISTER CHURCHILL*

We—the President of the United States, the Prime Minister of Great Britain, and the Premier of the Soviet Union, have met these four days past, in this, the Capital of our Ally, Iran, and have shaped and confirmed our common policy.

We express our determination that our nations shall work together in war and in the peace that will follow.

As to war—our military staffs have joined in our round table discussions, and we have concerted our plans for the destruction of the German forces. We have reached complete agreement as to the scope and timing of the operations to be undertaken from the east, west and south.

The common understanding which we have here reached guarantees that victory will be ours.

* December 1, 1943. From *Department of State Bulletin*, IX, p. 409.

And as to peace—we are sure that our concord will win an enduring Peace. We recognize fully the supreme responsibility resting upon us and all the United Nations to make a peace which will command the goodwill of the overwhelming mass of the peoples of the world and banish the scourge and terror of war for many generations.

With our Diplomatic advisors we have surveyed the problems of the future. We shall seek the cooperation and active participation of all nations, large and small, whose peoples in heart and mind are dedicated, as are our own peoples, to the elimination of tyranny and slavery, oppression and intolerance. We will welcome them, as they may choose to come, into a world family of Democratic Nations.

No power on earth can prevent our destroying the German armies by land, their U Boats by sea, and their war plants from the air.

Our attack will be relentless and increasing.

Emerging from these cordial conferences we look with confidence to the day when all peoples of the world may live free lives, untouched by tyranny, and according to their varying desires and their own consciences.

We came here with hope and determination. We leave here, friends in fact, in spirit and in purpose.

(d) PROCLAMATION SIGNED AT POTSDAM*

(1) We—the President of the United States, the President of the National Government of the Republic of China, and the Prime Minister of Great Britain, representing the hundreds of millions of our countrymen, have conferred and agree that Japan shall be given an opportunity to end this war.

(2) The prodigious land, sea and air forces of the United States, the British Empire and of China, many times reinforced by their armies and air fleets from the west, are poised to strike the final blows upon Japan. This military power is sustained and inspired by the determination of all the Allied Nations to prosecute the war against Japan until she ceases to resist.

(3) The result of the futile and senseless German resistance to the might of the aroused free peoples of the world stands forth in awful clarity as an example to the people of Japan. The might that now converges on Japan is immeasurably greater than that which, when applied to the resisting Nazis, necessarily laid waste to the lands, the industry and the method of life of the whole German people. The full application of our military power, backed by our resolve, *will* mean the inevitable and complete destruction of the Japanese armed forces and just as inevitably the utter devastation of the Japanese homeland.

(4) The time has come for Japan to

*July 26, 1945, by President Harry S. Truman and Prime Minister Churchill with the concurrence of Generalissimo Chiang Kai-shek. From *Department of State Bulletin*, XII, pp. 137-138.

decide whether she will continue to be controlled by those self-willed militaristic advisers whose unintelligent calculations have brought the Empire of Japan to the threshold of annihilation, or whether she will follow the path of reason.

(5) Following are our terms. We will not deviate from them. There are no alternatives. We shall brook no delay.

(6) There must be eliminated for all time the authority and influence of those who have deceived and misled the people of Japan into embarking on world conquest, for we insist that a new order of peace, security and justice will be impossible until irresponsible militarism is driven from the world.

(7) Until such a new order is established *and* until there is convincing proof that Japan's war-making power is destroyed, points in Japanese territory to be designated by the Allies shall be occupied to secure the achievement of the basic objectives we are here setting forth.

(8) The terms of the Cairo Declaration shall be carried out and Japanese sovereignty shall be limited to the islands of Honshu, Hokkaido, Kyushu, Shikoku and such minor islands as we determine.

(9) The Japanese military forces, after being completely disarmed, shall be permitted to return to their homes with the opportunity to lead peaceful and productive lives.

(10) We do not intend that the Japanese shall be enslaved as a race or destroyed as a nation, but stern justice shall be meted out to all war criminals, includ-

ing those who have visited cruelties upon our prisoners. The Japanese Government shall remove all obstacles to the revival and strengthening of democratic tendencies among the Japanese people. Freedom of speech, of religion, and of thought, as well as respect for the fundamental human rights shall be established.

(11) Japan shall be permitted to maintain such industries as will sustain her economy and permit the exaction of just reparations in kind, but not those which would enable her to re-arm for war. To this end, access to, as distinguished from control of, raw materials shall be permitted. Eventual Japanese participation in world trade relations shall be permitted.

(12) The occupying forces of the Allies shall be withdrawn from Japan as soon as these objectives have been accomplished and there has been established in accordance with the freely expressed will of the Japanese people a peacefully inclined and responsible government.

(13) We call upon the government of Japan to proclaim now the unconditional surrender of all Japanese armed forces, and to provide proper and adequate assurances of their good faith in such action. The alternative for Japan is prompt and utter destruction.

10

The Morgenthau Plan

☆ *The Allied plans for the postwar administration of Germany were influenced by a proposal of Secretary of the Treasury Henry Morgenthau, Jr., in the summer of 1944, which called for the demilitarization, partitioning, de-industrialization, and control of Germany. The Morgenthau plan represented the widespread sentiment to prevent a resurgent Germany from starting another war.** ☆

PROGRAM TO PREVENT GERMANY FROM STARTING A WORLD WAR III

1. Demilitarization of Germany

It should be the aim of the Allied Forces to accomplish the complete demilitarization of Germany in the shortest possible period of time after surrender. This means completely disarming the German Army and people (including the removal or destruction of all war material), the total destruction of the whole German armament industry, and the removal or destruction of other key industries which are basic to military strength.

2. New Boundaries of Germany

(a) Poland should get that part of East Prussia which doesn't go to the U.S.S.R. and the southern portion of Silesia.

(b) France should get the Saar and the adjacent territories bounded by the Rhine and the Moselle Rivers.

* "Program to Prevent Germany from Starting a World War III," from special insert in Henry Morgenthau, Jr., *Germany Is Our Problem.* Copyright, Harper & Brothers, New York, 1945. Used by permission.

(c) As indicated in 4 below an International Zone should be created containing the Ruhr and the surrounding industrial areas.

3. Partitioning of New Germany

The remaining portion of Germany should be divided into two autonomous, independent states, (1) a South German state comprising Bavaria, Wuerttemberg, Baden and some smaller areas and (2) a North German state comprising a large part of the old state of Prussia, Saxony, Thuringia and several smaller states.

There shall be a custom union between the new South German state and Austria, which will be restored to her pre-1938 political borders.

4. The Ruhr Area

(The Ruhr, surrounding industrial areas . . . including the Rhineland, the Kiel Canal, and all German territory north of the Kiel Canal.)

Here lies the heart of German industrial power. This area should not only be stripped of all presently existing industries but so weakened and controlled that it can not in the foreseeable future become an industrial area. The following steps will accomplish this:

(a) Within a short period, if possible not longer than 6 months after the cessation of hostilities, all industrial plants and equipment not destroyed by military action shall be completely dismantled and transported to Allied Nations as restitution. All equipment shall be removed from the mines and the mines closed.

(b) The area should be made an international zone to be governed by an international security organization to be established by the United Nations. In governing the area the international organization should be guided by policies designed to further the above stated objective.

5. Restitution and Reparation

Reparations, in the form of future payments and deliveries, should not be demanded. Restitution and reparation shall be effected by the transfer of existing German resources and territories, e.g.,

(a) by restitution of property looted by the Germans in territories occupied by them;

(b) by transfer of German territory and German private rights in industrial property situated in such territory to invaded countries and the international organization under the program of partition;

(c) by the removal and distribution among devastated countries of industrial plants and equipment situated within the International Zone and the North and South German states delimited in the section on partition;

(d) by forced German labor outside Germany; and

(e) by confiscation of all German assets of any character whatsoever outside of Germany.

6. Education and Propaganda

(a) All schools and universities will be closed until an Allied Commission of Education has formulated an effective reorganization program. It is contemplated that it may require a considerable period of time before any institutions of higher education are reopened. Meanwhile the education of German students in foreign universities will not be prohibited. Elementary schools will be reopened as quickly as appropriate teachers and textbooks are available.

(b) All German radio stations and newspapers, magazines, weeklies, etc. shall be discontinued until adequate controls are established and an appropriate program formulated.

7. Political Decentralization

The military administration in Germany in the initial period should be carried out with a view toward the eventual partitioning of Germany. To facilitate partitioning and to assure its permanence the military authorities should be guided by the following principles:

(a) Dismiss all policy-making officials of the Reich government and deal primarily with local governments.

(b) Encourage the reestablishment of state governments in each of the states (Lander) corresponding to 18 states into which Germany is presently divided and in addition make the Prussian provinces separate states.

(c) Upon the partition of Germany, the various state governments should be encouraged to organize a federal government for each of the newly partitioned areas. Such new governments should be in the form of a confederation of states, with emphasis on states' rights and a large degree of local autonomy.

8. Responsibility of Military for Local German Economy

The sole purpose of the military in control of the German economy shall be to facilitate military operations and military occupation. The Allied Military Government shall not assume responsibility for such economic problems as price controls, rationing, unemployment, production, reconstruction, distribution, consumption, housing, or transportation, or take any measures designed to maintain or strengthen the German economy, except those which are essential to military operations. The responsibility for sustaining the German economy and people rests with the German people with such facilities as may be available under the circumstances.

9. Controls over Development of German Economy

During a period of at least twenty years after surrender adequate controls, including controls over foreign trade and tight restrictions on capital imports, shall be maintained by the United Nations designed to prevent in the newly-established states the establishment or expansion of key industries basic to the German military potential and to control other key industries.

10. Agrarian Program

All large estates should be broken up and divided among the peasants and the system of primogeniture and entail should be abolished.

11. Punishment of War Crimes and Treatment of Special Groups

A program for the punishment of certain war crimes and for the treatment of Nazi organizations and other special groups is contained in section 11 [of a separate document].

12. Uniforms and Parades

(a) No German shall be permitted to wear, after an appropriate period of time following the cessation of hostilities, any military uniform or any uniform of any quasi military organizations.

(b) No military parades shall be permitted anywhere in Germany and all military bands shall be disbanded.

13. Aircraft

All aircraft (including gliders), whether military or commercial, will be confiscated for later disposition. No German shall be permitted to operate or to help operate any aircraft, including those owned by foreign interests.

14. United States Responsibility

Although the United States would have full military and civilian representation on whatever international commission or commissions may be established for the execution of the whole German program, the primary responsibility for the policing of Germany and for civil administration in Germany should be assumed by the military forces of Germany's continental neighbors. Specifically, these should include Russian, French, Polish, Czech, Greek, Yugoslav, Norwegian, Dutch and Belgian soldiers.

Under this program United States troops could be withdrawn within a relatively short time.

11

Preparation for World Peace

☆ *By 1943, the Congress had committed itself to the support of United States membership in an international organization to maintain world peace. Preparations were made at the Yalta Conference in February, 1945, for the establishment of a world organization. At least of equal importance were the Yalta Conference provisions for the treatment of Germany and the countries liberated in Europe, Russia's entry into the war against Japan, and Russian territorial gains after the war.* ☆

(a) RESOLUTION BY REPRESENTATIVE J. WILLIAM FULBRIGHT OF ARKANSAS*

RESOLVED *by the House of Representatives* (*the Senate concurring*), That the Congress hereby expresses itself as favoring the creation of appropriate international machinery with power adequate to establish and to maintain a just and lasting peace, among the nations of the world, and as favoring participation by the United States therein through its constitutional processes.

(b) RESOLUTION OF SENATOR TOM CONNALLY OF TEXAS†

Resolved, That the war against all our enemies be waged until complete victory is achieved.

That the United States cooperate with its comrades-in-arms in securing a just and honorable peace.

That the United States, acting through its constitutional processes, join with free and sovereign nations in the establishment and maintenance of international authority with power to prevent aggression and to preserve the peace of the world.

That the Senate recognizes the necessity of there being established at the earliest practicable date a general international organization, based on the principle of the sovereign equality of all peace-loving states, and open to membership by all such states, large and small, for the maintenance of international peace and security.

That, pursuant to the Constitution of the United States, any treaty made to effect the purpose of this resolution, on

* Passed by the House September 21, 1943. From *Congressional Record,* 78th Congress, 1st session, p. 7729.
† Passed by the Senate November 5, 1943. From *Congressional Record,* 78th Congress, 1st session, p. 9222.

behalf of the Government of the United States with any other nation or any associations of nations, shall be made only by and with the advice and consent of the Senate of the United States, provided two-thirds of the Senators present concur.

(c) AGREEMENT SIGNED BY PRESIDENT ROOSEVELT, MARSHAL STALIN, AND PRIME MINISTER CHURCHILL AT YALTA*

I. WORLD ORGANIZATION

It was decided:

(1) that a United Nations Conference on the proposed world organizations should be summoned for Wednesday, 25th April, 1945, and should be held in the United States of America.

(2) the Nations to be invited to this Conference should be:

(a) the United Nations as they existed on the 8th February, 1945; and

(b) such of the Associated Nations as have declared war on the common enemy by 1st March, 1945. . . .

"C" VOTING

1. Each member of the Security Council should have one vote.

2. Decisions of the Security Council on procedural matters should be made by an affirmative vote of seven members.

3. Decisions of the Security Council on all other matters should be made by an affirmative vote of seven members including the concurring votes of the permanent members; provided that, in decisions under Chapter VIII, Section A and under the second sentence of paragraph 1 of Chapter VIII, Section C, a party to a dispute should abstain from voting. . . .

TERRITORIAL TRUSTEESHIP

It was agreed that the five Nations which will have permanent seats on the Security Council should consult each other prior to the United Nations Conference on the question of territorial trusteeship. . . .

* February 11, 1945. From *Senate Document* No. 123, 81st Congress, 1st session, pp. 27-34.

II. DECLARATION ON LIBERATED EUROPE

The following declaration has been approved:

"The Premier of the Union of Soviet Socialist Republics, the Prime Minister of the United Kingdom and the President of the United States of America have consulted with each other in the common interest of the peoples of their countries and those of liberated Europe. They jointly declare their mutual agreement to concert during the temporary period of instability in liberated Europe the policies of their three governments in assisting the peoples liberated from the domination of Nazi Germany and the peoples of the former Axis satellite states of Europe to solve by democratic means their pressing political and economic problems.

"The establishment of order in Europe and the re-building of national economic life must be achieved by processes which will enable the liberated peoples to destroy the last vestiges of Nazism and Fascism and to create democratic institutions of their own choice. . . ."

III. DISMEMBERMENT OF GERMANY

It was agreed that Article 12 (a) of the Surrender Terms for Germany should be amended to read as follows:

"The United Kingdom, the United States of America and the Union of Soviet Socialist Republics shall possess supreme authority with respect to Germany. In the exercise of such authority they will take such steps, including the complete disarmament, demilitarisation and dismemberment of Germany as they deem requisite for future peace and security. . . ."

VII. POLAND

The following declaration on Poland was agreed to by the Conference:

"A new situation has been created in Poland as a result of her complete liberation by the Red Army. This calls for the establishment of a Polish Provisional Government which can be more broadly based than was possible before the recent liberation of Western Poland. The Provisional Government which is now functioning in Poland should therefore be reorganised on a broader democratic basis with the inclusion of democratic leaders from Poland itself and from Poles abroad. This new Government should then be called the Polish Provisional Government of National Unity.

"M. Molotov, Mr. Harriman and Sir A. Clark Kerr are authorized as a commission to consult in the first instance in Moscow with members of the present Provisional Government and with other Polish democratic leaders from within Poland and from abroad, with a view to the reorganization of the present Government along the above lines. This Polish Provisional Government of National Unity shall be pledged to the holding of free and unfettered elections as soon as possible on the basis of universal suffrage and secret ballot. In these elections all democratic and anti-Nazi parties shall have the right to take part and to put forward candidates.

"When a Polish Provisional Government of National Unity has been properly formed in conformity with the above, the Government of the U.S.S.R., which now maintains diplomatic relations with the present Provisional Government of Poland, and the Government of the United Kingdom and the Government of the United States of America will establish diplomatic relations with the new Polish Provisional Government of National Unity, and will exchange Ambassadors by whose reports the respective Governments will be kept informed about the situation in Poland.

"The three Heads of Government consider that the Eastern frontier of Poland should follow the Curzon Line with digressions from it in some regions of five to eight kilometers in favour of Poland. They recognise that Poland must receive substantial accessions of territory in the North and West. They feel that the opinion of the new Polish Provisional Government of National Unity should be sought in due course on the extent of these accessions and that the final delimitation of the Western frontier of Poland should thereafter await the Peace Conference. . . ."

(b)   *Protocol on German Reparations*
The Heads of the three governments agreed as follows:

1. Germany must pay in kind for the losses caused by her to the Allied nations in the course of the war. Reparations are to be received in the first instance by those countries which have borne the main burden of the war, have suffered the heaviest losses and have organized victory over the enemy.

2. Reparations in kind are to be exacted from Germany in three following forms:

(a) Removals within 2 years from the surrender of Germany or the cessation of organised resistance from the national wealth of Germany located on the territory of Germany herself as well as outside her territory (equipment, machine-tools, ships, rolling stock, German investments abroad, shares of industrial, transport and other enterprises in Germany, etc.), these removals to be carried out chiefly for purpose of destroying the war potential of Germany.

(b) Annual deliveries of goods from current production for a period to be fixed.

(c) Use of German labour.

3. For the working out on the above principles of a detailed plan for exaction of reparation from Germany an Allied Reparation Commission will be set up in Moscow. It will consist of three representatives—one from the Union of Soviet Socialist Republics, one from the United Kingdom and one from the United States of America.

4. With regard to the fixing of the total sum of the reparation as well as the distribution of it among the countries which suffered from the German aggression the Soviet and American delegations agreed as follows:

"The Moscow Reparation Commission should take in its initial studies as a basis for discussion the suggestion of the Soviet Government that the total sum of the reparation in accordance with the points (a) and (b) of the paragraph 2 should be 20 billion dollars and that 50% of it should go to the Union of the Soviet Socialist Republics."

The British delegation was of the opinion that pending consideration of the reparation question by the Moscow Reparation Commission no figures of reparation should be mentioned.

The above Soviet-American proposal has been passed to the Moscow Reparation Commission as one of the proposals to be considered by the Commission. . . .

(c) *Agreement Regarding Japan*

The leaders of the three Great Powers —the Soviet Union, the United States of America and Great Britain—have agreed that in two or three months after Germany has surrendered and the war in Europe has terminated the Soviet Union shall enter into the war against Japan on the side of the Allies on condition that:

1. The status quo in Outer-Mongolia (The Mongolian People's Republic) shall be preserved;

2. The former rights of Russia violated by the treacherous attack of Japan in 1904 shall be restored, viz:

(a) the southern part of Sakhalin as well as all the islands adjacent to it shall be returned to the Soviet Union,

(b) the commercial port of Dairen shall be internationalized, the preeminent interests of the Soviet Union in this port being safeguarded and the lease of Port Arthur as a naval base of the U.S.S.R. restored,

(c) the Chinese-Eastern Railroad and the South-Manchurian Railroad which provides an outlet to Dairen shall be jointly operated by the establishment of a joint Soviet-Chinese Company it being understood that the preeminent interests of the Soviet Union shall be safeguarded and that China shall retain full sovereignty in Manchuria;

3. The Kuril islands shall be handed over to the Soviet Union.

It is understood, that the agreement concerning Outer-Mongolia and the ports and the railroads referred to above will require concurrence of Generalissimo Chiang Kai-shek. The President will take measures in order to obtain this concurrence on advice from Marshal Stalin.

The Heads of the three Great Powers have agreed that these claims of the Soviet Union shall be unquestionably fulfilled after Japan has been defeated.

For its part the Soviet Union expresses its readiness to conclude with the National Government of China a pact of friendship and alliance between the U.S.S.R. and China in order to render assistance to China with its armed forces for the purpose of liberating China from the Japanese yoke.

XIII

leader of the free world (1946-1961)

BY THE end of World War II it was obvious that a great shift had taken place in American foreign policy. A nation which traditionally held itself aloof from European affairs and foreign entanglements had overwhelmingly endorsed membership in an international organization to maintain the peace. But it soon became evident that a new aggressor, the Soviet Union, was attempting to extend its system to other nations by means of subversion, intimidation, and guerilla warfare. In 1947 President Truman responded to this threat by asking Congress to authorize economic and military aid for Greece and Turkey to help them resist Communism. Soon afterward, Secretary of State George C. Marshall announced that the United States was willing to assist other nations in restoring their economy, and a vigorous program was soon launched that helped Western Europe to overcome the after effects of war. Money and supplies, however, were not sufficient to meet the Communist challenge, and in 1949 the United States joined the North Atlantic Treaty Organization, the country's first formal military alliance in 150 years.

The Far Eastern situation remained critical because of internal dissension in China, where, in spite of American aid, the Nationalist government of Chiang Kai-shek was finally driven from the continent by the Communist elements under Mao Tse-tung. Another great debate occurred as the administration was blamed for the disappearance of 600,000,000 people behind the Iron Curtain. Then in 1950 the Communist North Koreans launched an attack on the Republic of Korea, and President Truman quickly acceded to the appeal of the United Nations Security Council for military assistance to repel the invasion. As the limited conflict continued in Korea, a "preventive war" against Soviet Russia was advocated by those who believed that the heart of the world conspiracy should be destroyed.

To some, the Korean experience demonstrated the inadequacies of conventional methods of warfare, and a new

Republican administration adopted a military policy stressing
the deterring of armed attack by the threat of massive retaliation
with nuclear weapons. While the possibility of peaceful coexistence with communist nations was debated and disarmament proposals were offered, in 1956 a series of revolts in Poland
and Hungary stirred the hope that Russia's satellite nations were
going to win their freedom. But the Poles gained only a degree
of autonomy, and Soviet tanks ended the aims of Hungarian
patriots. At the same time a rift opened between the United States
and its allies when Great Britain, France, and Israel invaded
Egypt.

Major foreign policy issues faced the nation as the sixties
began. Should Communist China be recognized or admitted to
the United Nations? Would summit conferences between the
heads of state bring solutions which failed to develop through
the traditional channels of diplomacy? What military posture
should be adopted by the government? As a new administration
took office in 1961, the United States, leader of the Free World,
sought to meet its responsibilities in the struggle with
Communism.

1

Post-War Foreign Policy Attitudes

☆ *Reversing the position taken following World War I, the United States in the post-World War II period continued to exercise the world leadership which it had won during the war. Not only did the nation endorse collective security but, when circumstances demanded, bipartisan legislative support for this policy was readily available.** ☆

"Our forces will never be used to initiate war against any nation; they will be used only for the defense of the free world."

These words, uttered by President Eisenhower in the midst of last Fall's bitter congressional elections, went unchallenged, almost unnoticed. Here lies proof of the monumental change that has occurred during the past 15 years in the American public's view of foreign policy. . . .

[In June, 1941,] short of a direct attack on our possessions, we were unwilling to go to war. Nine years later there was overwhelming support for President Truman's decision to send American forces into combat in Korea. Even Senator Taft hailed the presidential decision and termed the action a complete refutation of Secretary Acheson's policies.

As the Korean war became increasingly complicated, criticism mounted, but few at the time or later challenged the original decision. In the recesses be-

tween elections even those adhering to the doctrines of "Truman's war" and "Twenty Years of Treason" have registered their approval of the commitment of American troops. Said Vice President Nixon in 1953:

". . . let's recognize right now that the decision to go into Korea was right. It was right because the Communists had to be stopped. And let me say that in the past I have had occasion to disagree with the former President of the United States, Mr. Truman, on some issues, but on this issue President Truman was right, and he deserves credit for making that decision. . . ."

It was during World War II that the United States accepted its new position and the Free World accepted the United States as its leader. But the United States was only one of five major powers engaged in defeating Germany and Japan. Beyond the common aims of victory and unconditional surrender, each member of the grand alliance desired something different from the final outcome. This was to be our next hard lesson in international politics. An earlier appreciation of this key fact might have spared later disillu-

* From Mary K. Hammond, "Revolution in Foreign Policy: 1932-1952," *Current History*, XXVIII (January, 1955), pp. 1, 5-6. Used by permission.

sionment and angry charges of "sell-out"; it is unlikely that it would have changed the power relationships emerging with the war's end.

Major wars always begin with one balance of international strengths and weaknesses and end with another. Subconsciously Americans have always expected the termination of hostilities to witness a return to the *status quo ante bellum*. Wars beget new powers, new relationships, but this is not to say that the war was in vain. The war accomplished its purpose of destroying German hegemony over the continent of Europe and Japanese mastery of the Pacific. That it left two titans sparring for dominant power in Europe and Asia was inevitable. Inevitable, but not clearly recognized by American planners.

President Roosevelt pinned his major hopes for the post-war world on the United Nations. He expounded his concept of the Four Policemen—the United States, Britain, the U.S.S.R., and China—joined in harmonious unison to maintain peace. He conceived his major problem to be selling Marshal Stalin on the concept of the United Nations and the Four Policemen. The "sale" was the great triumph he thought had been won at Yalta. Apparently F.D.R. never pondered the answer to the old Latin question: *"Quis custodiet ipsos custodes. . . ?*

Seldom has an agreement been attacked as bitterly as the Yalta agreement. Basically, the European side of the agreement merely stated an existing military fact. Russian troops were in possession of Eastern Europe and showed no signs of imminent departure, unless British and American troops forced the issue. The Western Allies did what they could to alleviate a bad situation. The Declaration on Liberated Europe stated that the Allies would "jointly assist" those freed from Nazi tyranny "to form interim governmental authorities broadly represen-

tative of all democratic elements in the population and pledged to the earliest possible establishment, through free elections, of governments responsive to the will of the people." The terms "free elections" and "democratic elements" obviously meant different things to the East and West, and the West was not prepared forcibly to gain acceptance of its definition.

The Soviet Union also flagrantly violated the provisions of the peace treaties for the Eastern European countries. Simultaneously, the United States was rushing pell mell into demobilization and normalcy. The fault for the complexion of Eastern Europe today lies not with Yalta; it goes as deep as Russia's centuries-old paramount interest in the region and America's light-hearted assumption that the end of hostilities ended the necessity for strength.

Much the same reasoning applies to the Asiatic provisions of Yalta. Certainly, a lack of understanding of Russia's long-term interests in Manchuria was responsible for the naive assumption that the U.S.S.R. would willingly deliver Manchuria into Chinese hands. But there is every indication that agreement or no, Russia would have moved into the area, and the American public in 1945 was no more prepared to fight Russia in Manchuria than it is in 1955 to assist Chiang Kai-shek's "unleashed" armies regain the Chinese mainland.

It took two full years after the war's end for the United States government fully to appreciate the nature of the new threat to the nation's security. But this time the challenge was not met with neutrality legislation. There followed in rapid order the Truman Doctrine of military and financial assistance to countries threatened by Russia, the Marshall Plan to strengthen Western Europe economically, the policy of containment, the Berlin airlift, the Korean War, the North

Atlantic Treaty, and the Southeast Asia Defense Treaty.

It was a major misfortune of American foreign policy that the great revolution was carried on under the aegis of one political party. In fourteen years a multitude of petty grievances accumulate, speculations turn sour and there are major miscalculations. This left one party particularly vulnerable to criticism for everything that went wrong—and in the domestic struggle for power the errors were played up to the exclusion of the many positive accomplishments. In reality, there is every reason to believe that after 1940 our foreign policy would have remained basically unchanged regardless of which party was in power.

It was President Truman's "terrible, do-nothing" Republican Eightieth Congress which passed the Marshall Plan, Greek-Turkish aid and military help to the Chinese Nationalists. It extended the Trade Agreements Act, passed the Voice of America Act, approved the Inter-American Treaty of Reciprocal Assistance and a Displaced Persons Act.

But only in the past two years, under the Eisenhower administration, has it become clear how fundamentally and permanently altered is the international outlook of the United States. The emphasis may be placed slightly differently, and there will have to be a major effort made to disabuse present leaders of the hollow shibboleths involved in charges of Democratic treason. But since the 1951 great debates on troops for Europe and MacArthur's "go-it-alone" Asian policy, the major segments of both political parties and the great bulk of the public are agreed on broad general terms on policy.

2

Resisting Soviet Aggression

☆ *In 1945 it became apparent that the imperfect American-Russian harmony achieved during the war was not going to continue. Serious disagreements between the United States and the Soviet Union arose over the organization of the United Nations and treaties with the defeated nations. Moreover, evidence that Russia had not abandoned the concept of world revolution was revealed by her efforts to establish Communist governments throughout Eastern Europe and even in Asia. President Truman, deciding that negotiations alone were inadequate, early in 1947 initiated a more forceful approaching dealing with Communist aggression. Later in 1947, acting on a plan advocated by Secretary of State George C. Marshall, Congress approved a large scale aid program which bolstered the economic defenses of Western Europe. Increasing tensions led to United States participation in the creation of a military alliance in 1949—the North Atlantic Treaty Organization.* ☆

(a) TRUMAN DOCTRINE: MESSAGE OF THE PRESIDENT TO CONGRESS*

The gravity of the situation which confronts the world today necessitates my appearance before a joint session of the Congress.

The foreign policy and the national security of this country are involved.

One aspect of the present situation, which I wish to present to you at this time for your consideration and decision, concerns Greece and Turkey.

The United States has received from the Greek Government an urgent appeal for financial and economic assistance. Preliminary reports from the American Ambassador in Greece corroborate the

* March 12, 1947. From *Department of State Bulletin,* XVI, pp. 534-537.

statement of the Greek Government that assistance is imperative if Greece is to survive as a free nation. . . .

Greece must have assistance if it is to become a self-supporting and self-respecting democracy.

The United States must supply that assistance. We have already extended to Greece certain types of relief and economic aid, but these are inadequate.

There is no other country to which democratic Greece can turn.

No other nation is willing and able to provide the necessary support for a democratic Greek Government.

The British Government, which has been helping Greece, can give no further financial or economic aid after March 31. Great Britain finds itself under the necessity of reducing or liquidating its commitments in several parts of the world, including Greece.

We have considered how the United Nations might assist in this crisis. But the situation is an urgent one requiring immediate action, and the United Nations and its related organizations are not in a position to extend help of the kind that is required.

It is important to note that the Greek Government has asked for our aid in utilizing effectively the financial and other assistance we may give to Greece, and in improving its public administration. It is of the utmost importance that we supervise the use of any funds made available to Greece, in such a manner that each dollar spent will count toward making Greece self-supporting, and will help to build an economy in which a healthy democracy can flourish.

No government is perfect. One of the chief virtues of a democracy, however, is that its defects are always visible and under democratic processes can be pointed out and corrected. The Government of Greece is not perfect. Nevertheless it represents 85 percent of the members of the Greek Parliament who were chosen in an election last year. Foreign observers, including 692 Americans, considered this election to be a fair expression of the views of the Greek people.

The Greek Government has been operating in an atmosphere of chaos and extremism. It has made mistakes. The extension of aid by this country does not mean that the United States condones everything that the Greek Government has done or will do. We have condemned in the past, and we condemn now, extremist measures of the right or the left. We have in the past advised tolerance, and we advise tolerance now.

Greece's neighbor, Turkey, also deserves our attention.

The future of Turkey as an independent and economically sound state is clearly no less important to the freedom-loving peoples of the world than the future of Greece. The circumstances in which Turkey finds itself today are considerably different from those of Greece. Turkey has been spared the disasters that have beset Greece. And during the war the United States and Great Britain furnished Turkey with material aid.

Nevertheless, Turkey now needs our support.

Since the war Turkey has sought additional financial assistance from Great Britain and the United States for the purpose of effecting that modernization necessary for the maintenance of its national integrity.

That integrity is essential to the preservation of order in the Middle East.

The British Government has informed us that, owing to its own difficulties, it can no longer extend financial or economic aid to Turkey.

As in the case of Greece, if Turkey is to have the assistance it needs, the United States must supply it. We are the only country able to provide that help.

I am fully aware of the broad implications involved if the United States extends assistance to Greece and Turkey, and I shall discuss these implications with you at this time.

One of the primary objectives of the foreign policy of the United States is the creation of conditions in which we and other nations will be able to work out a way of life free from coercion. This was a fundamental issue in the war with Germany and Japan. Our victory was won over countries which sought to impose their will, and their way of life, upon other nations.

To insure the peaceful development of nations, free from coercion, the United

States has taken a leading part in establishing the United Nations. The United Nations is designed to make possible lasting freedom and independence for all its members. We shall not realize our objectives, however, unless we are willing to help free peoples to maintain their free institutions and their national integrity against aggressive movements that seek to impose upon them totalitarian regimes. This is no more than a frank recognition that totalitarian regimes imposed upon free peoples, by direct or indirect aggression, undermine the foundations of international peace and hence the security of the United States.

The peoples of a number of countries of the world have recently had totalitarian regimes forced upon them against their will. The Government of the United States has made frequent protests against coercion and intimidation, in violation of the Yalta agreement, in Poland, Rumania, and Bulgaria. I must also state that in a number of other countries there have been similar developments.

At the present moment in world history nearly every nation must choose between alternative ways of life. The choice is too often not a free one.

One way of life is based upon the will of the majority, and is distinguished by free institutions, representative government, free elections, guaranties of individual liberty, freedom of speech and religion, and freedom from political oppression.

The second way of life is based upon the will of a minority forcibly imposed upon the majority. It relies upon terror and oppresion, a controlled press and radio, fixed elections, and the suppression of personal freedoms.

I believe that it must be the policy of the United States to support free peoples who are resisting attempted subjugation by armed minorities or by outside pressures.

I believe that we must assist free peoples to work out their own destinies in their own way.

I believe that our help should be primarily through economic and financial aid which is essential to economic stability and orderly political processes.

The world is not static, and the *status quo* is not sacred. But we cannot allow changes in the *status quo* in violation of the Charter of the United Nations by such methods as coercion, or by such subterfuges as political infiltration. In helping free and independent nations to maintain their freedom, the United States will be giving effect to the principles of the Charter of the United Nations.

It is necessary only to glance at a map to realize that the survival and integrity of the Greek nation are of grave importance in a much wider situation. If Greece should fall under the control of an armed minority, the effect upon its neighbor, Turkey, would be immediate and serious. Confusion and disorder might well spread throughout the entire Middle East.

Moreover, the disappearance of Greece as an independent state would have a profound effect upon those countries in Europe whose peoples are struggling against great difficulties to maintain their freedoms and their independence while they repair the damages of war.

It would be an unspeakable tragedy if these countries, which have struggled so long against overwhelming odds, should lose that victory for which they sacrificed so much. Collapse of free institutions and loss of independence would be disastrous not only for them but for the world. Discouragement and possibly failure would quickly be the lot of neighboring peoples striving to maintain their freedom and independence.

Should we fail to aid Greece and Turkey in this fateful hour, the effect will be far reaching to the West as well as to the East.

We must take immediate and resolute action.

I therefore ask the Congress to provide authority for assistance to Greece and Turkey in the amount of $400,000,000 for the period ending June 30, 1948. In requesting these funds, I have taken into consideration the maximum amount of relief assistance which would be furnished to Greece out of the $350,000,000 which I recently requested that the Congress authorize for the prevention of starvation and suffering in countries devastated by the war.

In addition to funds, I ask the Congress to authorize the detail of American civilian and military personnel to Greece and Turkey, at the request of those countries, to assist in the tasks of reconstruction, and for the purpose of supervising the use of such financial and material assistance as may be furnished. I recommend that authority also be provided for the instruction and training of selected Greek and Turkish personnel.

Finally, I ask that the Congress provide authority which will permit the speediest and most effective use, in terms of needed commodities, supplies, and equipment, of such funds as may be authorized.

If further funds, or further authority, should be needed for purposes indicated in this message, I shall not hesitate to bring the situation before the Congress.

On this subject the Executive and Legislative branches of the Government must work together.

This is a serious course upon which we embark.

I would not recommend it except that the alternative is much more serious.

The United States contributed $341,-000,000,000 toward winning World War II. This is an investment in world freedom and world peace.

The assistance that I am recommending for Greece and Turkey amounts to little more than one-tenth of one percent of this investment. It is only common sense that we should safeguard this investment and make sure that it was not in vain.

The seeds of totalitarian regimes are nurtured by misery and want. They spread and grow in the evil soul of poverty and strife. They reach their full growth when the hope of a people for a better life has died.

We must keep that hope alive.

The free peoples of the world look to us for support in maintaining their freedoms.

If we falter in our leadership, we may endanger the peace of the world—and we shall surely endanger the welfare of our own nation.

Great responsibilities have been placed upon us by the swift movement of events.

I am confident that the Congress will face these responsibilities squarely.

(b) MARSHALL PLAN: ADDRESS BY SECRETARY OF STATE GEORGE C. MARSHALL AT HARVARD UNIVERSITY*

I need not tell you gentlemen that the world situation is very serious. That must be apparent to all intelligent people. I think one difficulty is that the problem is one of such enormous complexity that the very mass of facts presented to the public by press and radio make it exceedingly

* June 5, 1947. From *Department of State Bulletin*, XVI, pp. 159-160.

difficult for the man in the street to reach a clear appraisement of the situation. Furthermore, the people of this country are distant from the troubled areas of the earth and it is hard for them to comprehend the plight and consequent reactions of the long-suffering peoples, and the effect of those reactions on their governments in connection with our efforts to promote peace in the world.

In considering the requirements for the rehabilitation of Europe, the physical loss of life, the visible destruction of cities, factories, mines, and railroads was correctly estimated, but it has become obvious during recent months that this visible destruction was probably less serious than the dislocation of the entire fabric of European economy. For the past ten years conditions have been highly abnormal. The feverish preparation for war and the more feverish maintenance of the war effort engulfed all aspects of national economies. Machinery has fallen into disrepair or is entirely obsolete. Under the arbitrary and destructive Nazi rule, virtually every possible enterprise was geared into the German war machine. Long-standing commercial ties, private institutions, banks, insurance companies, and shipping companies disappeared, through loss of capital, absorption through nationalization, or by simple destruction. In many countries, confidence in the local currency has been severely shaken. The breakdown of the business structure of Europe during the war was complete. Recovery has been seriously retarded by the fact that two years after the close of hostilities a peace settlement with Germany and Austria has not been agreed upon. But even given a more prompt solution of these difficult problems, the rehabilitation of the economic structure of Europe quite evidently will require a much longer time and greater effort than had been foreseen.

There is a phase of this matter which is both interesting and serious. The farmer has always produced the foodstuffs to exchange with the city dweller for the other necessities of life. This division of labour is the basis of modern civilization. At the present time it is threatened with breakdown. The town and city industries are not producing adequate goods to exchange with the food-producing farmer. Raw materials and fuel are in short supply. Machinery is lacking or worn out. The farmer or the peasant cannot find the goods for sale which he desires to purchase. So the sale of his farm produce for money which he cannot use seems to him an unprofitable transaction. He, therefore, has withdrawn many fields from crop cultivation and is using them for grazing. He feeds more grain to stock and finds for himself and his family an ample supply of food, however short he may be on clothing and the other ordinary gadgets of civilization. Meanwhile people in the cities are short of food and fuel. So the governments are forced to use their foreign money and credits to procure these necessities abroad. This process exhausts funds which are urgently needed for reconstruction. Thus a very serious situation is rapidly developing which bodes no good for the world. The modern system of the division of labour upon which the exchange of products is based is in danger of breaking down.

The truth of the matter is that Europe's requirements for the next three or four years of foreign food and other essential products—principally from America—are so much greater than her present ability to pay that she must have substantial additional help or face economic, social, and political deterioration of a very grave character.

The remedy lies in breaking the vicious circle and restoring the confidence of the European people in the economic future of their own countries and of Europe as a whole. The manufacturer and the farmer throughout wide areas must be able and willing to exchange their products for currencies the continuing value of which is not open to question.

Aside from the demoralizing effect on the world at large and the possibilities of disturbances arising as a result of the desperation of the people concerned, the consequences to the economy of the United

States should be apparent to all. It is logical that the United States should do whatever it is able to do to assist in the return of normal economic health in the world, without which there can be no political stability and no assured peace. Our policy is directed not against any country or doctrine but against hunger, poverty, desperation, and chaos. Its purpose should be the revival of a working economy in the world so as to permit the emergence of political and social conditions in which free institutions can exist. Such assistance, I am convinced, must not be on a piecemeal basis as crises develop. Any assistance that this Government may render in the future should provide a cure rather than a mere palliative. Any government that is willing to assist in the task of recovery will find full co-operation, I am sure, on the part of the United States Government. Any government which maneuvers to block the recovery of other countries cannot expect help from us. Furthermore, governments, political parties, or groups which seek to perpetuate human misery in order to profit therefrom politically or otherwise will encounter the opposition of the United States.

It is already evident that, before the United States Government can proceed much further in its efforts to alleviate the situation and help start the European world on its way to recovery, there must be some agreement among the countries of Europe as to the requirements of the situation and the part those countries themselves will take in order to give proper effect to whatever action might be undertaken by this Government. It would be neither fitting or efficacious for this Government to undertake to draw up unilaterally a programme designed to place Europe on its feet economically. This is the business of the Europeans. The initiative, I think, must come from Europe. The role of this country should consist of friendly aid in the drafting of a European programme and of later support of such a programme so far as it may be practical for us to do so. The programme should be a joint one, agreed to by a number of, if not all, European nations.

An essential part of any successful action on the part of the United States is an understanding on the part of the people of America of the character of the problem and the remedies to be applied. Political passion and prejudice should have no part. With foresight, and a willingness on the part of our people to face up to the vast responsibility which history has clearly placed upon our country, the difficulties I have outlined can and will be overcome.

(c) NORTH ATLANTIC TREATY*

The Parties to this Treaty reaffirm their faith in the purposes and principles of the Charter of the United Nations and their desire to live in peace with all peoples and all governments.

They are determined to safeguard the freedom, common heritage and civilization of their peoples, founded on the principles of democracy, individual liberty and the rule of law.

They seek to promote stability and well-being in the North Atlantic area.

They are resolved to unite their efforts for collective defense and for the preservation of peace and security.

They therefore agree to this North Atlantic Treaty:

Article 1. The Parties undertake, as set forth in the Charter of the United Nations, to settle any international disputes in which they may be involved by peaceful means in such a manner that international peace and security, and justice, are not endangered, and to refrain in their international relations from the threat or use of force in any manner inconsistent with the purposes of the United Nations.

Art. 2. The Parties will contribute toward the further development of peaceful and friendly international relations by strengthening their free institutions, by bringing about a better understanding of the principles upon which these institutions are founded, and by promoting conditions of stability and well-being. They will seek to eliminate conflict in their international economic policies and will encourage economic collaboration between any or all of them.

Art. 3. In order more effectively to achieve the objectives of this Treaty, the Parties, separately and jointly, by means of continuous and effective self-help and mutual aid, will maintain and develop their individual and collective capacity to resist armed attack.

Art. 4. The Parties will consult together whenever, in the opinion of any of them, the territorial integrity, political independence or security of any of the Parties is threatened.

Art. 5. The Parties agree that an armed attack against one or more of them in Europe or North America shall be considered an attack against them all; and consequently they agree that, if such an armed attack occurs, each of them, in exercise of the right of individual or collective self-defense recognized by Article 51 of the Charter of the United Nations, will assist the Party or Parties so attacked by taking forthwith, individually and in concert with the other Parties, such action as it deems necessary, including the use of armed force, to restore and maintain the security of the North Atlantic area.

Any such armed attack and all measures taken as a result thereof shall immediately be reported to the Security Council. Such measures shall be terminated when the Security Council has taken the measures necessary to restore and maintain international peace and security.

Art. 6. For the purpose of Article 5 an armed attack on one or more of the Parties is deemed to include an armed attack on the territory of any of the Parties in Europe or North America, on the Algerian departments of France, on the occupation forces of any Party in Europe, on the islands under the jurisdiction of any Party in the North Atlantic area north of the Tropic of Cancer or on the vessels or aircraft in this area of any of the Parties.

Art. 7. This treaty does not affect, and shall not be interpreted as affecting, in any way the rights and obligations under the Charter of the Parties which are

* Signed April 4, 1949, by the United States, Great Britain, Canada, France, Belgium, the Netherlands, Luxembourg, Italy, Denmark, Norway, Iceland, and Portugal. From 63 U.S. Stats. 2242.

members of the United Nations, or the primary responsibility of the Security Council for the maintenance of international peace and security.

Art. 8. Each Party declares that none of the international engagements now in force between it and any other of the Parties or any third state is in conflict with the provisions of this Treaty, and undertakes not to enter into any international engagement in conflict with this Treaty.

Art. 9. The Parties hereby establish a council, on which each of them shall be represented, to consider matters concerning the implementation of this Treaty. The council shall be so organized as to be able to meet promptly at any time. The council shall set up such subsidiary bodies as may be necessary; in particular it shall establish immediately a defense committee which shall recommend measures for the implementation of Articles 3 and 5.

Art. 10. The Parties may, by unanimous agreement, invite any other European state in a position to further the principles of this Treaty and to contribute to the security of the North Atlantic area to accede to this Treaty. Any state so invited may become a party to the Treaty by depositing its instrument of accession with the Government of the United States of America. The Government of the United States of America will inform each of the Parties of the deposit of each such instrument of accession.

Art. 11. This Treaty shall be ratified and its provisions carried out by the Parties in accordance with their respective constitutional processes. The instruments of ratification shall be deposited as soon as possible with the Government of the United States of America, which will notify all the other signatories of each deposit. The Treaty shall enter into force between the states which have ratified it as soon as the ratifications of the majority of the signatories, including the ratifications of Belgium, Canada, France, Luxembourg, the Netherlands, the United Kingdom and the United States, have been deposited and shall come into effect with respect to other states on the date of the deposit of their ratifications.

Art. 12. After the Treaty has been in force for ten years, or at any time thereafter, the Parties shall, if any of them so requests, consult together for the purpose of reviewing the Treaty, having regard for the factors then affecting peace and security in the North Atlantic area, including the development of universal as well as regional arrangements under the Charter of the United Nations for the maintenance of international peace and security.

Art. 13. After the Treaty has been in force for twenty years, any Party may cease to be a party one year after its notice of denunciation has been given to the Government of the United States of America, which will inform the Governments of the other Parties of the deposit of each notice of denunciation.

3

The Loss of China

☆　*Civil war had raged in China for a generation except for a brief period during World War II. In 1945, the fighting between Chiang Kai-shek's forces and Communist elements was resumed, much to the dismay of the United States. Despite American attempts to settle the conflict and support of the Kuomintang government, the Communists finally emerged victorious on the mainland of China. In a letter to President Truman of July 30, 1949, Secretary of State Dean Acheson reviewed recent American relations with China.**　☆

THE PRESIDENT: In accordance with your wish, I have had compiled a record of our relations with China, special emphasis being placed on the last five years. . . .

The record shows that the United States has consistently maintained and still maintains those fundamental principles of our foreign policy toward China which include the doctrine of the Open Door, respect for the administrative and territorial integrity of China, and opposition to any foreign domination of China. . . .

The reports of United States military and diplomatic officers reveal a growing conviction through 1943 and 1944 that the Government and the Kuomintang had apparently lost the crusading spirit that won them the people's loyalty during the early years of the war. In the opinion of many observers they had sunk into corruption, into a scramble for place and power, and into reliance on the United States to win the war for them and to preserve their

own domestic supremacy. The Government of China, of course, had always been a one-party rather than a democratic government in the Western sense. The stresses and strains of war were now rapidly weakening such liberal elements as it did possess and strengthening the grip of the reactionaries who were indistinguishable from the war lords of the past. The mass of the Chinese people were coming more and more to lose confidence in the Government.

It was evident to us that only a rejuvenated and progressive Chinese Government which could recapture the enthusiastic loyalty of the people could and would wage an effective war against Japan. American officials repeatedly brought their concern with this situation to the attention of the Generalissimo and he repeatedly assured them that it would be corrected. He made, however, little or no effective effort to correct it and tended to shut himself off from Chinese officials who gave unpalatable advice. In addition to a concern over the effect which this

* From *United States Relations with China*, Washington, 1949, pp. III-XVI.

atrophy of the central Chinese administration must have upon the conduct of the war, some American observers, whose reports are also quoted in the attached record, were concerned over the effect which this deterioration of the Kuomintang must have on its eventual struggle, whether political or military, with the Chinese Communists. These observers were already fearful in 1943 and 1944 that the National Government might be so isolating itself from the people that in the postwar competition for power it would prove itself impotent to maintain its authority. Nevertheless, we continued for obvious reasons to direct all our aid to the National Government. . . .

When peace came the United States was confronted with three possible alternatives in China: (1) it could have pulled out lock, stock and barrel; (2) it could have intervened militarily on a major scale to assist the Nationalists to destroy the Communists; (3) it could, while assisting the Nationalists to assert their authority over as much of China as possible, endeavor to avoid a civil war by working for a compromise between the two sides.

The first alternative would, and I believe American public opinion at the time so felt, have represented an abandonment of our international responsibilities and of our traditional policy of friendship for China before we had made a determined effort to be of assistance. The second alternative policy, while it may look attractive theoretically and in retrospect, was wholly impracticable. The Nationalists had been unable to destroy the Communists during the 10 years before the war. Now after the war the Nationalists were, as indicated above, weakened, demoralized, and unpopular. They had quickly dissipated their popular support and prestige in the areas liberated from the Japanese by the conduct of their civil and military officials. The Communists on the other hand were much stronger than they

had ever been and were in control of most of North China. Because of the ineffectiveness of the Nationalist forces which was later to be tragically demonstrated, the Communists probably could have been dislodged only by American arms. It is obvious that the American people would not have sanctioned such a colossal commitment of our armies in 1945 or later. We therefore came to the third alternative policy whereunder we faced the facts of the situation and attempted to assist in working out a *modus vivendi* which would avert civil war but nevertheless preserve and even increase the influence of the National Government.

. . . our policy at [the time of the Marshall mission in 1945] was inspired by the two objectives of bringing peace to China under conditions which would permit stable government and progress along democratic lines, and of assisting the National Government to establish its authority over as wide areas of China as possible. As the event proved, the first objective was unrealizable because neither side desired it to succeed: the Communists because they refused to accept conditions which would weaken their freedom to proceed with what remained consistently their aim, the communization of all China; the Nationalists because they cherished the illusion, in spite of repeated advice to the contrary from our military representatives, that they could destroy the Communists by force of arms.

The second objective of assisting the National Government, however, we pursued vigorously from 1945 to 1949. The National Government was the recognized government of a friendly power. Our friendship, and our right under international law alike, called for aid to the Government instead of to the Communists who were seeking to subvert and overthrow it. . . . The National Government had in 1945, and maintained until the early fall of 1948, a marked superiority in man power and armament over their rivals. Indeed during that period, thanks very largely to our aid in transporting, arming and supplying their forces, they extended their control over a large part of North China and Manchuria. By the time General Marshall left China at the beginning of 1947, the Nationalists were apparently at the very peak of their military successes and territorial expansion. The following year and a half revealed, however, that their seeming strength was illusory and that their victories were built on sand. . . .

The reasons for the failures of the Chinese National Government . . . do not stem from any inadequacy of American aid. Our military observers on the spot have reported that the Nationalist armies did not lose a single battle during the crucial year of 1948 through lack of arms or ammunition. The fact was that the decay which our observers had detected in Chungking early in the war had fatally sapped the powers of resistance of the Kuomintang. Its leaders had proved incapable of meeting the crisis confronting them, its troops had lost the will to fight, and its Government had lost popular support. The Communists, on the other hand, through a ruthless discipline and fanatical zeal, attempted to sell themselves as guardians and liberators of the people. The Nationalist armies did not have to be defeated; they disintegrated. History has proved again and again that a regime without faith in itself and an army without morale cannot survive the test of battle. . . .

Fully recognizing that the heads of the Chinese Communist Party were ideologically affiliated with Moscow, our Government nevertheless took the view, in the light of the existing balance of forces in China, that peace could be established only if certain conditions were met. The Kuomintang would have to set its own house in order and both sides would have to make concessions so that the Government of China might become, in fact as well as in name, the Government of all China and so that all parties might function within the constitutional system of the Government. Both internal peace and constitutional development required that the progress should be rapid from one party government with a large opposition party in armed rebellion, to the participation of all parties, including the moderate non-communist elements, in a truly national system of government.

None of these conditions has been realized. The distrust of the leaders of the leaders of both the Nationalist and Communist Parties for each other proved too deep-seated to permit final agreement, notwithstanding temporary truces and apparently promising negotiations. The Nationalists, furthermore, embarked in 1946 on an over-ambitious military campaign in the face of warnings by General Marshall that it not only would fail but would plunge China into economic chaos and eventually destroy the National Government. General Marshall pointed out that though Nationalist armies could, for a period, capture Communist-held cities, they could not destroy the Communist armies. Thus every Nationalist advance would expose their communications to attack by Communist guerrillas and compel them to retreat or to surrender their armies together with the munitions which the United States has furnished them. No estimate of a military situation has ever been more completely confirmed by the resulting facts.

The historic policy of the United States of friendship and aid toward the people of China was, however, maintained in both peace and war. Since V-J Day, the United States Government has authorized aid to Nationalist China in the form of grants and credits totaling approximately 2 billion dollars, an amount equivalent in value to more than 50 percent of the monetary expenditures of the Chinese

Government and of proportionately greater magnitude in relation to the budget of that Government than the United States has provided to any nation of Western Europe since the end of the war. In addition to these grants and credits, the United States Government has sold the Chinese Government large quantities of military and civilian war surplus property with a total procurement cost of over 1 billion dollars, for which the agreed realization to the United States was 232 million dollars. A large proportion of the military supplies furnished the Chinese armies by the United States since V-J Day has, however, fallen into the hands of the Chinese Communists through the military ineptitude of the Nationalist leaders, their defections and surrenders, and the absence among their forces of the will to fight.

It has been urged that relatively small amounts of additional aid—military and economic—to the National Government would have enabled it to destroy communism in China. The most trustworthy military, economic, and political information available to our Government does not bear out this view.

A realistic appraisal of conditions in China, past and present, leads to the conclusion that the only alternative open to the United States was full-scale intervention in behalf of a Government which had lost the confidence of its own troops and its own people. Such intervention would have required the expenditure of even greater sums than have been fruitlessly spent thus far, the command of Nationalist armies by American officers, and the probable participation of American armed forces—land, sea, and air—in the resulting war. Intervention of such a scope and magnitude would have been resented by the mass of the Chinese people, would have diametrically reversed our historic policy, and would have been condemned by the American people. . . .

The unfortunate but inescapable fact is that the ominous result of the civil war in China was beyond the control of the government of the United States. Nothing that this country did or could have done within the reasonable limits of its capabilities could have changed that result; nothing that was left undone by this country has contributed to it. It was the product of internal Chinese forces, forces which this country tried to influence but could not. A decision was arrived at within China, if only a decision by default.

4

Aggression in Korea

☆ *In 1945, the northern portion of Korea was occupied by Soviet forces and the southern part by United States troops. Efforts to unite the two sections proved unsuccessful, and two mutually antagonistic governments were formed which came to war with the invasion of South Korea on June 25, 1950. The United Nations Security Council immediately called for a cessation of hostilities, and when this was not forthcoming it recommended that steps be taken to repel the invasion.* ☆

(a) THE UNITED NATIONS SECURITY COUNCIL RESOLUTION*

The Security Council

Recalling the finding of the General Assembly in its resolution of 21 October 1949 that the Government of the Republic of Korea is a lawfully established government "having effective control and jurisdiction over that part of Korea where the United Nations Temporary Commission on Korea was able to observe and consult and in which the great majority of the people of Korea reside; and that this Government is based on elections which were a valid expression of the free will of the electorate of that part of Korea and which were observed by the Temporary Commission; and that this is the only such Government in Korea";

Mindful of the concern expressed by the General Assembly in its resolutions of 12 December 1948 and 21 October 1949 of the consequences which might follow

* Of June 25, 1950. From United Nations, Security Council, *Official Records,* Fifth Year, #15, p. 18.

unless Member States refrained from acts derogatory to the results sought to be achieved by the United Nations in bringing about the complete independence and unity of Korea; and the concern expressed that the situation described by the United Nations Commission on Korea in its report menaces the safety and well being of the Republic of Korea and of the people of Korea and might lead to open military conflict there;

Noting with grave concern the armed attack upon the Republic of Korea by forces from North Korea,

Determines that this action constitutes a breach of the peace,

I.   *Calls* for the immediate cessation of hostilities; and

Calls upon the authorities of North Korea to withdraw forthwith their armed forces to the thirty-eighth parallel;

II.   *Requests* the United Nations Commission on Korea

(a)   To communicate its fully considered recommendations on the situation with the least possible delay;

(b) To observe the withdrawal of the North Korean forces to the thirty-eighth parallel; and

(c) To keep the Security Council in-

formed on the execution of this resolution;

III. *Calls upon* all Members to render every assistance to the United Nations in the execution of this resolution and to refrain from giving assistance to the North Korean authorities.

(b) THE UNITED NATIONS SECURITY COUNCIL RESOLUTION*

The Security Council,

Having determined that the armed attack upon the Republic of Korea by forces from North Korea constitutes a breach of the peace, having called for an immediate cessation of hostilities, and having called upon the authorities of North Korea to withdraw forthwith their armed forces to the 38th parallel, and having noted from the report of the United Nations Commission for Korea that the authorities in North Korea have neither ceased hostili-

* Of June 27, 1950. From United Nations, Security Council, *Official Records*, Fifth Year, #16, p. 4.

ties nor withdrawn their armed forces to the 38th parallel and that urgent military measures are required to restore international peace and security, and having noted the appeal from the Republic of Korea to the United Nations for immediate and effective steps to secure peace and security,

Recommends that the Members of the United Nations furnish such assistance to the Republic of Korea as may be necessary to repel the armed attack and to restore international peace and security in the area.

5

Preventive War Talk

☆ *Frustration over the course of the war in Korea, where the United Nations forces had been driven into a corner of southeastern Korea by late summer, 1950, led to demands for more effective American action. Among the more extreme demands were those which advocated that the United States use force directly against Russia to prevent Soviet expansion. The following selection is reprinted from* U. S. News & World Report, *published at Washington.** ☆

Talk of a preventive war, cropping up in several forms, is raising new questions for U. S. policy planners now, at a time when relations with the Russian world are touch and go.

New proposals for some form of preventive action, with or without an ultimatum to Russia, are appearing in statements of some public figures as well as in more and more locker-room talk by private citizens. As typical examples:

A Cabinet member, Navy Secretary Francis P. Matthews, expressed his unofficial views in a recent speech like this: "To have peace we should be willing, and declare our intention, to pay any price, even the price of instituting a war, to compel co-operation for peace."

An influential Congressman, in recent private conversation, put it this way: "If a man who has been threatening your life suddenly starts building a machine gun across the street from your house, do you

* " 'Preventive War' Talk—Why: Fear of A-Bombs on U.S. Cities," XXIX (September 8, 1950), pp. 11-12.

wait until he finishes it and starts to shoot before you do something about it? Russia is that man."

A university president, Harold E. Stassen, is urging that Russia be warned that any further aggression by either Soviet or satellite forces will mean a declaration of war by the United Nations on the Soviet Union. He asks: "Should we not make it clear that an attack in Indo-China, or Burma, or Greece, or Turkey, or Germany, or Austria will mean that war will come to Moscow, to the Urals and to the Ukraine?"

An Army general, now retired, thinks that U.N. forces in Korea should be greatly increased, then used to "strike at the heart of the trouble, the Communist Government in Moscow." The combined forces of the West, he says in private conversation, should be used immediately to "remove the rotten apples in the Kremlin."

An Air Force general goes even further. Maj. Gen. Orvil Anderson stated last week that the doctrine of waiting until you're hit first "doesn't come from Americans. Americans believe in taking the initiative." He added: "Give me the order to do it and I can break up Russia's five A-bomb nests in a week." General Anderson was immediately suspended from command of the Air War College as a result of these comments.

The head of a big veterans' group, Harold Russell of Amvets, is urging that Congress "make it clear to Russia that another military aggression by a satellite power will be considered an act of war."

These proposals, all involving some form of preventive military action, show the range of ideas in a growing mass of unofficial talk. This talk is in direct opposition to official policy, as expressed by President Truman last week when he said, "We do not believe in aggressive or preventive war." But unofficial talk persists, and can be multiplied many times in conversations of private citizens. To a large degree they represent a revival of the "30-day preventive war" idea advanced in 1948 by individual Air Force officers. . . .

Widespread talk of preventive military action against Russia if Communist aggression does not cease . . . is stemming from a growing fear of sudden attack on U. S. cities and on Western Europe. But, to date, that talk is being effectively countered by the cold military fact that, in the opinion of U.S. defense planners, the West is not strong enough to make such an attack even if it wanted to.

6

The "New Look" in Military Policy

☆ *The Republican administration installed in 1953, was determined to avoid a recurrence of the Korean experience. Secretary of State John Foster Dulles, in a speech of January* VB, VTED, *announced a new security policy which stressed the deterrence of aggression by threatening the use of "massive retaliatory power."* ☆

We live in a world where emergencies are always possible, and our survival may depend upon our capacity to meet emergencies. Let us pray that we shall always have that capacity. But, having said that, it is necessary also to say that emergency measures—however good for the emergency—do not necessarily make good permanent policies. Emergency measures are costly; they are superficial; and they imply that the enemy has the initiative. They cannot be depended on to serve our long-time interests.

This "long time" factor is of critical importance. . . .

We need allies and collective security. Our purpose is to make these relations more effective, less costly. This can be done by placing more reliance on deterrent power and less dependence on local defensive power.

This is accepted practice so far as local communities are concerned. We keep locks on our doors, but we do not have an armed guard in every home. We rely principally on a community security system so well equipped to punish any who

* From *Department of State Bulletin*, XXX, pp. 107-108.

break in and steal that, in fact, would-be aggressors are generally deterred. That is the modern way of getting maximum protection at a bearable cost. . . .

Local defense will always be important. But there is no local defense which alone will contain the mighty landpower of the Communist world. Local defenses must be reinforced by the further deterrent of massive retaliatory power. A potential aggressor must know that he cannot always prescribe battle conditions that suit him. Otherwise, for example, a potential aggressor, who is glutted with manpower, might be tempted to attack in confidence that resistance would be confined to manpower. He might be tempted to attack in places where his superiority was decisive.

The way to deter aggression is for the free community to be willing and able to respond vigorously at places and with means of its own choosing.

So long as our basic policy concepts were unclear, our military leaders could not be selective in building our military power. If an enemy could pick his time and place and method of warfare—and if our policy was to remain the traditional one of meeting aggression by direct and local opposition—then we needed to be ready to fight in the Arctic and in the Tropics; in Asia, the Near East, and in Europe; by sea, by land, and by air; with old weapons and with new weapons.

The total cost of our security efforts, at home and abroad, was over $50 billion per annum, and involved, for 1953, a projected budgetary deficit of $9 billion; and $11 billion for 1954. This was on top of taxes comparable to wartime taxes; and the dollar was depreciating in effective value. Our allies were similarly weighed down. This could not be continued for long without grave budgetary, economic and social consequences.

But before military planning could be changed, the President and his advisers, as represented by the National Security Council, had to take some basic policy decisions. This has been done. The basic decision was to depend primarily upon a great capacity to retaliate, instantly, by means and at places of our choosing. Now the Department of Defense and the Joint Chiefs of Staff can shape our military establishment to fit what is *our* policy, instead of having to try to be ready to meet the enemy's many choices. That permits of a selection of military means instead of a multiplication of means. As a result, it is now possible to get, and share, more basic security at less cost.

7

The Soft Sell

☆ *While attempting to impress the Russians with American determination to ersist aggression by whatever means necessary, the Eisenhower administration also indicated its willingness to arrive at a peaceful accommodation between the Free World and the Communist Bloc. At Geneva, Switzerland, in 1955, the President met with the Soviet leaders in an attempt to resolve pressing international issues. At the conference the President revealed his proposal for arms reduction and limitation.* ☆

(a) EISENHOWER ON COEXISTENCE*

[Question.] Chalmers M. Roberts, Washington Post and Times Herald: ... what are the possibilities for peaceful coexistence between Soviet Russia and Communist China, on the one hand, and the non-Communist nations on the other?

THE PRESIDENT. Of course, that almost calls for a very long explanation; I will try to limit my comments to a very few.

For a long, long time everybody in the United States has urged that we attempt to reach a proper basis for peaceful coexistence. We have found, though, an aggressive attitude on the part of the other

side that has made such an accomplishment or consummation not easy to reach. In other words, there must be good faith on both sides. Moreover, let us make certain that peaceful coexistence does not mean appeasement in the sense that we are willing to see any nation in the world, against its will, subordinated to an outside nation. ...

So, I would say that within the limits I have just so briefly alluded to, why, I say the hope of the world would be that kind of an existence, because, certainly, we don't expect to be eliminated; and certainly, I think, it would be silly to say you can eliminate the other instantly. We have got to find ways of living together.

* News Conference of June 30, 1954. From *Public Papers of the President of the United States Dwight D. Eisenhower 1954,* Washington, 1960, pp. 603-604.

(b) "OPEN SKIES" PROPOSAL: STATEMENT BY PRESIDENT EISENHOWER AT THE GENEVA CONFERENCE OF HEADS OF GOVERNMENT*

Disarmament is one of the most important subjects on our agenda. It is also extremely difficult. In recent years the scientists have discovered methods of mak-

* July 21, 1955. From *Documents on Disarmament, 1945-1959,* I, Washington, 1960. pp. 486-488.

ing weapons many, many times more destructive of opposing armed forces—but also of homes, and industries and lives—than ever known or even imagined before. These same scientific discoveries have made much more complex the problems of limitation and control and reduction of armament.

After our victory as Allies in World War II, my country rapidly disarmed. Within a few years our armament was at a very low level. Then events occurred beyond our borders which caused us to realize that we had disarmed too much. For our own security and to safeguard peace we needed greater strength. Therefore we proceeded to rearm and to associate with others in a partnership for peace and for mutual security.

The American people are determined to maintain and if necessary increase this armed strength for as long a period as is necessary to safeguard peace and to maintain our security.

But we know that a mutually dependable system for less armament on the part of all nations would be a better way to safeguard peace and to maintain our security.

It would ease the fears of war in the anxious hearts of people everywhere. It would lighten the burdens upon the backs of the people. It would make it possible for every nation, great and small, developed and less developed, to advance the standards of living of its people, to attain better food, and clothing, and shelter, more of education and larger enjoyments of life.

Therefore the United States Government is prepared to enter into a sound and reliable agreement making possible the reduction of armament. . . .

No sound and reliable agreement can be made unless it is completely covered by an inspection and reporting system adequate to support every portion of the agreement.

The lessons of history teach us that disarmament agreements without adequate reciprocal inspection increase the dangers of war and do not brighten the prospects of peace.

Thus it is my view that the priority attention of our combined study of disarmament should be upon the subject of inspection and reporting.

Questions suggest themselves.

How effective an inspection system can be designed which would be mutually and reciprocally acceptable within our countries and the other nations of the world? How would such a system operate? What could it accomplish?

Is certainty against surprise aggression attainable by inspection? Could violations be discovered promptly and effectively counteracted?

We have not as yet been able to discover any scientific or other inspection method which would make certain of the elimination of nuclear weapons. So far as we are aware no other nation has made such a discovery. Our study of this problem is continuing. We have not as yet been able to discover any accounting or other inspection method of being certain of the true budgetary facts of total expenditures for armament. Our study of this problem is continuing. We by no means exclude the possibility of finding useful checks in these fields.

As you can see from these statements, it is our impression that many past proposals of disarmament are more sweeping than can be insured by effective inspection.

Gentlemen, since I have been working on this memorandum to present to this Conference, I have been searching my heart and mind for something that I could say here that could convince everyone of the great sincerity of the United States in approaching this problem of disarmament.

I should address myself for a moment

principally to the Delegates from the Soviet Union, because our two great countries admittedly possess new and terrible weapons in quantities which do give rise in other parts of the world, or reciprocally, to the fears and dangers of surprise attack.

I propose, therefore, that we take a practical step, that we begin an arrangement, very quickly, as between ourselves—immediately. These steps would include:

To give to each other a complete blueprint of our military establishments, from beginning to end, from one end of our countries to the other; lay out the establishments and provide the blueprints to each other.

Next, to provide within our countries facilities for aerial photography to the other country—we to provide you the facilities within our country, ample facilities for aerial reconnaissance, where you can make all the pictures you choose and take them to your own country to study, you to provide exactly the same facilities for us and we to make these examinations, and by this step to convince the world that we are providing as between ourselves against the possibility of great surprise attack, thus lessening danger and relaxing tension. Likewise we will make more easily attainable a comprehensive and effective system of inspection and disarmament, because what I propose, I assure you, would be but a beginning.

Now from my statements I believe you will anticipate my suggestion. It is that we instruct our representatives in the Subcommittee on Disarmament in discharge of their mandate from the United Nations to give priority effort to the study of inspection and reporting. Such a study could well include a step by step testing of inspection and reporting methods.

The United States is ready to proceed in the study and testing of a reliable system of inspections and reporting, and when that system is proved, then to reduce armaments with all others to the extent that the system will provide assured results.

The successful working out of such a system would do much to develop the mutual confidence which will open wide the avenues of progress for all our peoples.

The quest for peace is the statesman's most exacting duty. Security of the nation entrusted to his care is his greatest responsibility. Practical progress to lasting peace is his fondest hope. Yet in pursuit of his hope he must not betray the trust placed in him as guardian of the people's security. A sound peace—with security, justice, well-being, and freedom for the people of the world—*can* be achieved, but only by patiently and thoughtfully following a hard and sure and tested road.

8

Crisis of 1956

☆ *The apparent easing of world tensions at Geneva continued for more than a year. This so-called "spirit of Geneva" was dashed in October, 1956, by the brutal suppression of the successful Hungarian revolution by Soviet armed forces. The Free World reaction to the Hungarian situation was complicated by the Franco-British-Israeli attack on Egypt, October 31, 1956.* ☆

(a) LETTER OF PRESIDENT DWIGHT D. EISENHOWER TO NIKOLAI BULGANIN, CHAIRMAN OF THE COUNCIL OF MINISTERS, U.S.S.R.*

I have noted with profound distress the reports which have reached me today from Hungary.

The Declaration of the Soviet Government of October 30, 1956, which restated the policy of non-intervention in internal affairs of other states, was generally understood as promising the early withdrawal of Soviet forces from Hungary. Indeed, in that statement, the Soviet Union said that (quote) it considered the further presence of Soviet Army units in Hungary can serve as a cause for an even greater deterioration of the situation (unquote). This pronouncement was regarded by the United States Government and myself as an act of high statesmanship. It was followed by the express request of the Hungarian Government for the withdrawal of Soviet forces.

Consequently, we have been inexpressibly shocked by the apparent reversal of

* November 4, 1956. From *American Foreign Policy, Current Documents, 1956*, Washington, 1959, pp. 467-468.

this policy. It is especially shocking that this renewed application of force against the Hungarian Government and people took place while negotiations were going on between your representatives and those of the Hungarian Government for the withdrawal of Soviet forces.

As you know, the Security Council of the United Nations has been engaged in an emergency examination of this problem. As late as yesterday afternoon the Council was led to believe by your representative that the negotiations then in progress in Budapest were leading to agreement which would result in the withdrawal of Soviet forces from Hungary as requested by the government of that country. It was on that basis that the Security Council recessed its consideration of this matter.

I urge in the name of humanity and in the cause of peace that the Soviet Union take action to withdraw Soviet forces from Hungary immediately and to permit the Hungarian people to enjoy and exercise the human rights and fundamental freedoms affirmed for all peoples in the United Nations Charter.

The General Assembly of the United Nations is meeting in emergency session this afternoon in New York to consider this tragic situation. It is my hope that your representative will be in a position to announce at the session today that the Soviet Union is preparing to withdraw its forces from that country and to allow the Hungarian people to enjoy the right to a government of their own choice.

(b) ADDRESS TO THE PEOPLE BY PRESIDENT EISENHOWER ON THE MIDDLE EAST SITUATION*

The United States—through all the years since the close of World War II—has labored tirelessly to bring peace and stability to [the Middle East].

We have considered it a basic matter of United States policy to support the new State of Israel and—at the same time—to strengthen our bonds both with Israel and with the Arab countries. But, unfortunately through all these years, passion in the area threatened to prevail over peaceful purposes, and in one form or another, there has been almost continuous fighting.

This situation recently was aggravated by Egyptian policy including rearmament with Communist weapons. We felt this to be a misguided policy on the part of the Government of Egypt. The State of Israel, at the same time, felt increasing anxiety for its safety. And Great Britain and France feared more and more that Egyptian policies threatened their "life line" of the Suez Canal.

These matters came to a crisis on July 26th of this year, when the Egyptian Government seized the Universal Suez Canal Company. For 90 years—ever since the inauguration of the canal—that company has operated the canal, largely under British and French technical supervision.

Now there were some among our allies who urged an immediate reaction to this event by use of force. We insistently urged otherwise, and our wish prevailed

—through a long succession of conferences and negotiations for weeks—even months—with participation by the United Nations. And there, in the United Nations, only a short while ago, on the basis of agreed principles, it seemed that an acceptable accord was within our reach.

But the direct relations of Egypt with both Israel and France kept worsening to a point at which first Israel—then France—and Great Britain also—determined that, in their judgment, there could be no protection of their vital interests without resort to force.

Upon this decision, events followed swiftly. On Sunday [Oct. 28] the Israeli Government ordered total mobilization. On Monday, their armed forces penetrated deeply into Egypt and to the vicinity of the Suez Canal, nearly 100 miles away. And on Tuesday, the British and French Governments delivered a 12-hour ultimatum to Israel and Egypt—now followed up by armed attack against Egypt.

The United States was not consulted in any way about any phase of these actions. Nor were we informed of them in advance.

As it is the manifest right of any of these nations to take such decisions and actions, it is likewise our right—if our judgment so dictates—to dissent. We believe these actions to have been taken in error. For we do not accept the use of force as a wise or proper instrument for the settlement of international disputes.

To say this, in this particular instance,

* October 31, 1956. From *American Foreign Policy, Current Documents, 1956*, Washington, 1959, pp. 648-650.

is in no way to minimize our friendship with these nations nor our determination to maintain those friendships.

And we are fully aware of the grave anxieties of Israel, of Britain, and of France. We know that they have been subjected to grave and repeated provocations.

The present fact, nonetheless, seems clear: The action taken can scarcely be reconciled with the principles and purposes of the United Nations to which we have all subscribed. And, beyond this, we are forced to doubt that resort to force and war will for long serve the permanent interest of the attacking nations. . . .

. . . it will remain the dedicated purpose of your government to do all in its power to localize the fighting and to end the conflict.

We took our first measure in this action yesterday. We went to the United Nations with a request that the forces of Israel return to their own land and that hostilities in the area be brought to a close. This proposal was not adopted, because it was vetoed by Great Britain and by France.

The processes of the United Nations, however, are not exhausted. It is our hope and intent that this matter will be brought before the United Nations General Assembly. There, with no veto operating, the opinion of the world can be brought to bear in our quest for a just end to this tormenting problem. In the past the United Nations has proved able to find a way to end bloodshed. We believe

it can and that it will do so again.

My fellow citizens, as I review the march of world events in recent years, I am ever more deeply convinced that the processes of the United Nations represent the soundest hope for peace in the world. For this very reason, I believe that the processes of the United Nations need further to be developed and strengthened. I speak particularly of increasing its ability to secure justice under international law.

In all the recent troubles in the Middle East, there have indeed been injustices suffered by all nations involved. But I do not believe that another instrument of injustice—war—is the remedy for these wrongs.

There can be no peace without law. And there can be no law if we were to invoke one code of international conduct for those who oppose us and another for our friends.

The society of nations has been slow in developing means to apply this truth.

But the passionate longing for peace on the part of all peoples of the earth compels us to speed our search for new and more effective instruments of justice.

The peace we seek and need means much more than mere absence of war. It means the acceptance of law, and the fostering of justice, in all the world.

To our principles guiding us in this quest we must stand fast. In so doing we can honor the hopes of all men for a world in which peace will truly and justly reign.

9

Non-Recognition of Communist China

☆ *Since the establishment of a Communist government in mainland China in 1949, the questions of its recognition by the United States and admission to the United Nations have often arisen. In an address at San Francisco on June 28, 1957, Secretary of State John Foster Dulles vigorously defended the American refusal to extend to Communist China the privileges enjoyed by lawful governments.* ☆

On the China mainland 600 million people are ruled by the Chinese Communist Party. That party came to power by violence and, so far, has lived by violence.

It retains power not by will of the Chinese people but by massive, forcible repression. It fought the United Nations in Korea; it supported the Communist war in Indochina; it took Tibet by force. It fomented the Communist Huk rebellion in the Philippines and the Communists' insurrection in Malaya. It does not disguise its expansionist ambitions. It is bitterly hateful of the United States, which it considers a principal obstacle in the way of its path of conquest.

In the face of this condition the United States has supported, morally and materially, the free nations of the Western Pacific and Southeast Asia. Our security treaties make clear that the violation of these nations by international communism would be considered as endangering our own peace and safety and that we would act accordingly.

Together we constitute a goodly company and a stout bulwark against aggression.

As regards China, we have abstained from any act to encourage the Communist regime—morally, politically, or materially. Thus:

We have not extended diplomatic recognition to the Chinese Communist regime;

We have opposed its seating in the United Nations;

We have not traded with Communist China or sanctioned cultural interchanges with it. . . .

United States diplomatic recognition of Communist China would have the following consequences:

(1) The many mainland Chinese, who by Mao Tse-tung's own recent admission seek to change the nature of their government, would be immensely discouraged.

(2) The millions of overseas Chinese would feel that they had no Free China to which to look. Today increasing numbers of these overseas Chinese go to Free China to study. Six years ago there were less than 100 Chinese students from Southeast Asia and Hong Kong studying in

* From *American Foreign Policy, Current Documents, 1957,* Washington, 1961, pp. 1124-1130.

Taiwan. Now there are nearly 5,000.

The number of Chinese students from overseas communities coming to Free China has increased year by year; the number going to Communist China has declined, and hundreds of disillusioned students have made their way out of mainland China in the past 2 years.

If the United States recognized the Chinese Communist regime, many of the millions of overseas Chinese in free Asian countries would, reluctantly, turn to acceptance of the guiding direction of the Communist regime. This would be a tragedy for them; and it would imperil friendly governments already menaced by Chinese Communist subversion.

(3) The Republic of China, now on Taiwan, would feel betrayed by its friend. That Government was our ally in the Second World War and for long bore alone the main burden of the Far Eastern war. It had many tempting opportunities to compromise with the Japanese on terms which would have been gravely detrimental to the United States. It never did so. We condemn the Soviets for having dishonored their 20-year treaty pledge of 1945 to support the Chinese National Government as the central government of China. We are honorbound to give our ally, to whom we are pledged by a mutual defense treaty, a full measure of loyalty.

(4) The free Asian governments of the Pacific and Southeast Asia would be gravely perplexed. They are not only close to the vast Chinese land mass, but geographically and, to some extent, politically, they are separated as among themselves. The unifying and fortifying influence is, above all, the spirit and resolution of the United States. If we seemed to waver and to compromise with communism in China, that would in turn weaken free Asia resistance to the Chinese Communist regime and assist international communism to score a great success in its program to encircle us.

United States recognition of Communist China would make it probable that the Communist regime would obtain the seat of China in the United Nations. That would not be in the interest either of the United States or of the United Nations.

The United Nations is not a reformatory for bad governments. It is supposedly an association of those who are already "peaceloving" and who are "able and willing to carry out" the charter obligations. The basic obligation is not to use force, except in defense against armed attack.

The Chinese Communist regime has a record of successive armed aggressions, including war against the United Nations itself, a war not yet politically settled but discontinued by an armistice. The regime asserts not only its right but its purpose to use force if need be to bring Taiwan under its rule.

The Republic of China is entitled to a permanent seat and veto power in the Security Council. Should a regime which in 7 years has promoted five foreign or civil wars—Korea, Indochina, Tibet, the Philippines, and Malaya; which itself has fought the United Nations and which today stands condemned by the United Nations as an aggressor; which defies the United Nations' decision to reunify Korea; and which openly proclaims its continuing purpose to use force—should that regime be given a permanent seat, with veto power, in the body which under the charter has "primary responsibility for the maintenance of international peace and security"?

Communist Russia, with its veto power, already seriously limits the ability of the United Nations to serve its intended purposes. Were Communist China also to become a permanent, veto-wielding member of the Security Council, that would, I fear, implant in the United Nations the seeds of its own destruction.

Let me turn now to the matter of trade and cultural relations, which could exist, to a limited degree, without recognition.

Normal peacetime trade with China, from which the American and Chinese peoples would benefit, could be in the common interest. But it seems that that kind of trade is not to be had in any appreciable volume.

Trade with Communist China is not a normal trade. It does not provide one country with what its people want but cannot well produce for themselves, in exchange for what other people want but cannot well produce for themselves. Trade with Communist China is wholly controlled by an official apparatus, and its limited amounts of foreign exchange are used to develop as rapidly as possible a formidable military establishment and a heavy industry to support it. The primary desire of that regime is for machine tools, electronic equipment, and, in general, what will help it produce tanks, trucks, planes, ammunition, and such military items.

Whatever others may do, surely the United States, which has heavy security commitments in the China area, ought not to build up the military power of its potential enemy.

We also doubt the value of cultural exchanges, which the Chinese Communists are eager to develop. They want this relationship with the United States primarily because, once that example were given, it would be difficult for China's close neighbors not to follow it. These free nations, already exposed to intense Communist subversive activities, could not have the cultural exchanges that the Communists want without adding greatly to their danger.

These are considerations which argue for a continuance of our present policies. What are the arguments on the other side?

There are some who say that we should accord diplomatic recognition to the Communist regime because it has now been in power so long that it has won the *right* to that.

That is not sound international law. Diplomatic recognition is always a privilege, never a right.

Of course, the United States knows that the Chinese Communist regime exists. We know that very well, for it has fought us in Korea. Also, we admit of dealing with the Chinese Communists in particular cases where that may serve our interests. We have dealt with it in relation to the Korean and Indochina armistices. For nearly 2 years we have been, and still are, dealing with it in an effort to free our citizens and to obtain reciprocal renunciations of force.

But diplomatic recognition gives the recognized regime valuable rights and privileges, and, in the world of today, recognition by the United States gives the recipient much added prestige and influence at home and abroad.

Of course, diplomatic recognition is not to be withheld capriciously. In this matter, as others, the United States seeks to act in accordance with principles which contribute to a world society of order under law.

A test often applied is the ability of a regime actually to govern. But that is by no means a controlling factor. Nations often maintain diplomatic relations with governments-in-exile. And they frequently deny recognition to those in actual power.

Other customary tests are whether, as Thomas Jefferson put it, the recognized government reflects "the will of the nation, substantially declared"; whether the government conforms to the code of civilized nations, lives peacefully, and honors its international obligations.

Always, however, recognition is admitted to be an instrument of national policy, to serve enlightened self-interest.

One thing is established beyond a doubt.

There is nothing automatic about recognition. It is never compelled by the mere lapse of time.

Another argument beginning to be heard is that diplomatic recognition is inevitable, so why not now?

First, let me say emphatically that the United States need never succumb to the argument of "inevitability." We, with our friends, can fashion our own destiny. We do not accept the mastery of Communist forces.

And let me go on to say: Communist-type despotisms are not so immutable as they sometimes appear. Time and circumstances work also upon them. . . .

There are some who suggest that, if we assist the Chinese Communists to wax strong, then they will eventually break with Soviet Russia and that that is our best hope for the future.

No doubt there are basic power rivalries between Russia and China in Asia. But also the Russian and Chinese Communist parties are bound together by close ideological ties.

Perhaps, if the ambitions of the Chinese Communists are inflated by successes, they might eventually clash with Soviet Russia. Perhaps, too, if the Axis Powers had won the Second World War, they would have fallen out among themselves. But no one suggested that we should tolerate and even assist an Axis victory because in the end they would quarrel over the booty—of which we would be part.

10

Summitry

☆ *In 1959 and 1960, the United States again attempted to use "summit" conferences between heads of governments not only to determine Free World strategy but to resolve conflicts that might lead to war. While considerable pessimism was expressed about the efficacy of summitry, the widespread disquietude over the possibility of international nuclear war seemed to warrant these extraordinary diplomatic methods.** ☆

Secretary of State Herter's admission that the summit conference is "uncertain as to outcome" raises again the question whether this extraordinary negotiating technique is really necessary. If, as Mr. Herter said last week, the Big Four heads of government are not likely to agree on Berlin, and nothing can be anticipated on disarmament beyond a directive to their foreign ministers which may produce a limited agreement, it would seem that they could save themselves the trouble of meeting.

Certainly there are fewer tangible signs of an improvement in Soviet behavior than there were before the summit conference of 1955. At that time the thaw following the death of Stalin, which produced the armistice in Korea and permitted the conclusion of a state treaty with Austria, inspired plausible hopes that the cold war could be brought to a stop.

The results five years ago, however, were "very discouraging," as Mr. Herter conceded when he met with the Senate

* From Thomas J. Hamilton, "Summit's Usefulness," in "News Of The Week in Review," *The New York Times,* March 27, 1960. Used by permission.

Foreign Relations Committee last week. Mr. Herter's remarks together with the stiffer line now being taken by the United States regarding both disarmament and Berlin, seem to indicate that second thoughts have developed in the State Department and the Pentagon about the advantages to be gained from the summit meeting. Prime Minister Macmillan's hurried visit to Washington is nominally concerned with the Western position on nuclear tests. It is known that his Government is equally concerned over basic positions to be taken by the West at the summit.

Until last year the Western powers, and the United States in particular, had taken the position that the heads of government should not meet again unless and until negotiations at a lower level had reduced the area of disagreement to two or three issues.

As a corollary, the United States said repeatedly during the Foreign Ministers' conference in Geneva last spring that there could be no summit meeting unless the foreign ministers had made satisfactory progress on Berlin.

No such progress was made, but at Camp David Mr. Khrushchev gave General Eisenhower to understand that he would not impose a time limit for a settlement of the Berlin question.

Sources close to the Soviet delegation at the United Nations are not much more optimistic than Mr. Herter about the outcome of the summit meeting. They emphasize, however, that the conversations during General Eisenhower's visit to the Soviet Union are those which offer the real hope of an agreement.

This prediction, of course, is in accordance with the inveterate Soviet position that in affairs of great moment it is only the two super-powers that count. If it is correct, everything could be left over until President Eisenhower goes to Moscow.

Obviously, however, only physical force could keep either Mr. Macmillan or General de Gaulle from joining Mr. Khruschev at the summit. General de Gaulle is of the same mind as Dean Acheson and Chancellor Adenauer, and feels that no change in the status of West Berlin should even be discussed. But his concept of France's place in the nuclear world compels him to attend and play the role of host.

Mr. Macmillan also will have to be there. His Government has been under such pressure from the British Labor party to negotiate at the summit that he took the lead in the effort to arrange the meeting.

General Eisenhower's acceptance of the summit meeting, despite the stand previously taken by his Administration, no doubt reflects his hope of improving relations with the Soviet Union during his final year in office, an election year.

But aside from these special considerations, the three Western heads of government agreed to the summit for the overriding reason that public opinion in their countries and elswhere compelled them to do so.

Although some of Mr. Khrushchev's peace proposals, such as his demand for total disarmament, seem to be mere propaganda, the belief that they must be seriously considered is so wide-spread that they cannot be ignored. Moreover, Mr. Khrushchev had spread the word that his Foreign Minister is a mere technician, and that it was useless to negotiate with anyone except himself.

Not merely this argument, but the whole concept of summitry, has been attacked by Dean Rusk, president of the Rockefeller Foundation, who was Assistant Secretary of State under Mr. Acheson. If Mr. Khrushchev "insists upon having a Foreign Minister to whom he does not wish to give his confidence," Mr. Rusk writes in the April issue of the quarterly Foreign Affairs, "is he to impose the same ignominious status upon the Secretary of State of the United States?"

Certainly no one can quarrel with Mr. Rusk's argument that negotiations require "time, patience and precision, three resources which are not found in abundance at the highest political level," and that a summit meeting is a court of last resort where "the costs of error or misunderstanding are multiplied by the seriousness of the issues and the power of those present."

Mr. Rusk, moreover, is apprehensive about a climactic meeting between two men, one "impulsive in manner, supremely confident as only a closed mind can be . . . possibly subject to high blood pressure," and the other "weighted down by a sense of responsibility for the hundreds of millions who have freely given him their confidence . . . a man with a quick temper and a weak heart."

Clearly the popularity of summit meetings derives from the growing sense of panic created by the nuclear arms race and the belief that only heroic methods can prevent a war. But the result, unless one side or the other is prepared to make costly concessions, may be to make things worse.

11

Defense Policies Appraised

☆ *While the need for a correlation of diplomacy and force was recognized, some contended that our military potential was inadequate to support our diplomatic objectives. One of the most distinguished critics was the former Army Chief of Staff, General Maxwell D. Taylor, who, in a statement of June 14, 1960, questioned both the organization and the policies guiding our national defense.* ☆

The formulation of national policy, to include security policy, may be said to be the first responsibility of the fountainhead of government. There follows immediately thereafter the requirement for a national strategy which combines in proper proportion all available ways and means to implement the national policy. These ways and means include political, economic, and psychological elements as well as military. Thus, military strategy in proper perspective is but a part of national strategy, and is formulated at a third level in the echelons of national planning.

At all three of these levels—national policy, national strategy and military strategy—there is need for clearly fixed responsibility for planning, execution, and followup. Often the stress is placed upon planning but execution is the payoff and the adequacy of execution requires verification. Under our present system, the responsibility for these functions at

* From *Organizing for National Security,* Hearings Before the Subcommittee on National Policy Machinery of Committee on Government Operations, United States Senate, 86th Congress, 2nd session, Part V, pp. 768-771.

the level of national policy and strategy rests with the President assisted by his civilian advisers and advisory agencies. For military strategy, the President bears the responsibility as Commander in Chief but in practice delegates direct responsibility to the Secretary of Defense assisted by the Joint Chiefs of Staff. It is the adequacy of this total organizational structure which I understand concerns this subcommittee.

In my observation, the existing organizational system is inadequate in certain respects for the complex task set before it. Viewed from the position of a service Chief of Staff, the system is most visibly defective in its failure to provide clear guidance for the formulation of military strategy and for the generation of the military forces to implement that strategy. As a result, the Joint Chiefs of Staff have often been at odds over what is expected of the Armed Forces and have been unable to agree on the size and kinds of forces needed to provide the military component of the national strategy.

In the absence of agreement by the military chiefs, economic and budgetary factors have come to play an overriding part in determining military posture. Each year the services receive rigid budget guidelines which control the growth, direction, and evolution of the Armed Forces. These guidelines are often set with little knowledge of their strategic implications.

As a matter of fact, it is very difficult to determine their implications because of the way in which the defense budget is constructed. In spite of the fact that modern war is no longer fought in terms of a separate Army, Navy, and Air Force, nonetheless we still budget vertically in these service terms. Yet, if we are called upon to fight, we will not be interested in the services as such. We will be interested rather in task forces, these combinations of Army, Navy, and Air Force which are functional in nature, such as the atomic retaliatory forces, overseas deployments, continental air defense forces, limited war expeditionary forces, and the like. But the point is that we do not keep our budget in these terms. Hence it is not an exaggeration to say that we do not know what kind and how much defense we are buying with any specific budget. This kind of budgeting makes it hard to determine what our military posture will be at any given time in the future. It would not, however, prevent the determination of actual strength in being at any present moment, provided the forces in being are viewed in functional categories. Some such recurrent appraisal is particularly necessary in view of our worldwide political commitments to some 48 nations. Although these commitments carry serious military implications, there is no standard procedure to my knowledge for comparing military strength and political obligations. We lack a system of politico-military bookkeeping to assure that commitments and capabilities are kept in balance. I suggest that this is an area worthy of the attention of this subcommittee.

As a result of the foregoing conditions, we have the strange phenomenon of the partial loss of control of the military in a Government where all parties, including the military, are dedicated to the principle of civilian control. The implementation of the principle has been too often confused with the need for layers of civilians between the responsible military chiefs and the seats of decisionmaking authority. Actually such layering often contributes to the opacity of guidance reaching the military as well as to the filtering out of responsible military advice needed in formulating high policy. True civilian control, on the other hand, should be such as to assure that the military build forces of a size and kind consistent with the approved national policy and capable of providing the President and the Secretary of State with a flexible tool for defense and maneuver. The lack of a clearly defined national strategy, the resulting vagueness of guidance—other than fiscal—provided the military, and the obsolete method of budgetmaking combine to make difficult if not impossible this meaningful kind of civilian control.

If certain defects are found in our present policymaking machinery, it would be fair to ask for suggestions as to improvement. I would suggest the need for five improvements or changes:

(a) A more clearly defined national policy to include a national security policy.

(b) A better staff organization for planning and implementing national strategy and for verifying its execution. The revised procedure should include a tie-in between national strategy and the national budget, a tie-in which does not presently exist.

(c) A defense budget based on operational functions rather than on the military services.

(d) A division of the functions of the

present Joint Chiefs of Staff between a Defense Chief of Staff and a Supreme Military Council.

(e) Clearer guidance for the development of military strategy and the generation of military forces.

As these points are broad generalities, I will illustrate specifically the kind of clearer guidance which I view as badly needed by the Military Establishment to assure a flexible military strategy appropriate to the threat confronting the United States. Such guidance flowing from the Commander in Chief to the Department of Defense and the military services might read as follows:

The objective of the military preparations of the United States is to create respect for the strength of the United States without arousing fear of its misuse. That respect should be sufficient to deter military attack on the United States and to discourage aggression in any area of U.S. interest. If deterrence fails, our strength should be sufficient to impose appropriate punishment upon the aggressor.

In short, U.S. military strength should be such as to impress possible enemies and encourage friends and neutrals but should not inspire fear arising from the nature of its weapons or from the character of the strategy which directs its use.

To achieve this kind of military strength, the Department of Defense will conform to the following guidance:

(a) The Armed Forces of the United States will be so organized and trained as to have the capability of deterring a general atomic attack on the United States and of dealing a crippling second strike against the aggressor if deterrence fails. The weapons system for retaliation will consist primarily of long-range missiles with atomic warheads, firing from mobile or concealed positions removed from important friendly targets. To add to its deterrent effect as well as to its capability of survival, the system will be provided with an active air and antimissile defense.

(b) Concurrently and with equal priority of effort, the Armed Forces of the United States will be so organized and trained as to have the capability of sustained combat on the ground and at sea, placing primary reliance on the use of nonatomic weapons but having tactical atomic weapons in reserve. These forces will have strategic and tactical mobility to permit prompt and timely intervention in any area of vital U.S. interest.

(c) The role and missions of the military services will be redefined to fix clearly service responsibility for the organization and training of the forces required under subparagraphs a and b above.

(d) To support the foregoing forces the Department of Defense may plan upon receiving an annual sum approximating 10 percent of the gross national product. For midrange fiscal planning it will submit to the President annually a 5-year military program for overall approval. This program will define and justify goals for all categories of operational forces required in this period. These goals will be based upon the estimated military threat and the extent of the political commitments of the United States which have military implications. The Department of Defense will justify its annual budget in terms of operational forces required to meet the approved force goals.

(e) The Secretary of State and the Secretary of Defense will make an annual report to the President on the adequacy of the military forces in being in relation to the current military threat and to the current commitments which may require the use of military forces for their fulfillment.

12

The Berlin Crisis, 1961

☆ *In his address to the people of July 25, 1961, President Kennedy emphatically reaffirmed previous American commitments to maintain the freedom and accessibility of West Berlin and called upon the American people to ready themselves for war if that be necessary to fulfill our obligation.* * ☆

Seven weeks ago tonight I returned from Europe to report to you on my meeting with Soviet Premier Krushchev and others. His grim warnings about the future of the world, the aide-memoire he presented me on Berlin, the subsequent speeches and threats which he and his agents have launched, and the increase in the Soviet Military Budget he announced, have all prompted a series of decisions by this Administration and consultations within the Atlantic Community. In Berlin, as you recall, he intends to bring to an end, through a stroke of his pen, first our legal rights to be in West Berlin—and secondly our ability to make good on our commitment to the two million free people of that city. That we cannot permit.

We are clear about what must be done —and we intend to do it. I want to talk frankly with you tonight about the first steps we shall take. These actions will require sacrifice on the part of many citizens. More will be required in the future. They will require, for all of us, courage and perseverance for many years to come. But if we and our allies act out of

* From *The Washington Post*, July 26, 1961.

the strength and unity of our purpose— with calm determination and steady nerves—using restraint in our words as well as our weapons—I am hopeful that both peace and freedom will be sustained.

The immediate threat to free men is in West Berlin. But that isolated outpost is not an isolated problem. The threat is world-wide. Our effort must be equally wide and strong, and not be obsessed by a single manufactured crisis. We face a challenge in Berlin, but there is also, for example a challenge in Southeast Asia, where the borders are less guarded, the enemy harder to find, and the danger of communism often less apparent to the local population. We face a challenge in our own hemisphere, and wherever else the freedom of human beings is at stake.

Let me remind you that the fortunes of war and diplomacy left the free people of West Berlin 110 miles behind the Iron Curtain. We are there as a result of our victory over Nazi Germany—and our basic rights deriving from that victory include both our presence in Berlin and the enjoyment of access across East Germany. These rights have been repeatedly confirmed and recognized in special agreements with the Soviet Union. Berlin is not a part of East Germany, but a separate territory under the control of the allied powers. Thus our rights there are clear and firmly rooted. But in addition to those rights is our commitment to sustain—and defend, if need be—the opportunity for more than two million people to determine their own future and choose their own way of life.

Thus, our presence in West Berlin, and our access thereto, cannot be ended by any act of the Soviet Government. The NATO shield was long ago extended to cover West Berlin—and we have given our word that an attack in that city will be regarded as an attack upon us all. . . .

So long as the Communists insist that they are preparing to end unilaterally our rights in West Berlin and our commitments to its people, we must be prepared to defend those rights and commitments. We will at all times be ready to talk, if talk will help. But we must also be ready to resist with force, if force is used. Either alone would fail. Together, they can serve the cause of peace and freedom.

The new preparations that we shall make to defend the peace are part of the long-term build-up in our strength which has been under way since January. They are based on our needs to meet a worldwide threat, on a basis which stretches far beyond the present Berlin crisis. Our primary purpose is neither propaganda nor provocation—but preparation.

A first need is to hasten progress toward the military goals which the North Atlantic allies have set for themselves. In Europe today nothing less will suffice. We will put even greater resources into fulfilling those goals, and look to our allies to do the same.

The supplementary defense build-ups that I asked from the Congress in March and May have already started us moving toward these and our other defense goals. They included an increase in the size of the Marine Corps, improved readiness of our reserves, expansion of our air and sea lift, and stepped-up procurement of needed weapons, ammunition, and other items. To insure a continuing invulnerable capacity to deter or destroy any aggressor, they provided for the strengthening of our missile power and for putting 50 per cent of our B-52 and B-47 bombers on a ground alert which would send them on their way within 15 minutes of warning.

These measures must be speeded up, and still others must now be taken. We must have sea and airlift capable of moving our forces quickly and in large numbers to any part of the world.

But even more importantly, we need the capability of placing in any critical area at the appropriate time a force, which, combined with that of our allies, is large enough to make clear our determination and ability to defend our rights at all costs—and to meet all levels of aggressor pressure with whatever levels of force are required. We intend to have a wider choice than humiliation or all-out nuclear action.

While it is unwise either to call up or to send abroad excessive numbers of these troops before they are needed, let me make it clear that I intend to take as time goes on whatever steps are necessary to make certain that such forces can be deployed at the appropriate time without lessening our ability to meet other military needs.

Thus, in the days and months ahead, I shall not hesitate to ask for additional measures from the Congress, or exercise any of the executive powers I possess to meet this threat to peace. Everything essential to the security of freedom will be done; and if that should require more men, taxes, controls or other new powers, I shall not hesitate to request them. The measures proposed today will be constantly studied, and altered as necessary. But while we will not let panic shape our policy, neither will we permit timidity to direct our program.

Accordingly, I am now taking the following steps:

(1) I am tomorrow requesting of the Congress for the current fiscal year an additional $3,247,000,000 of appropriations for the military forces.

(2) To fill out our present Army Divisions, and to make more men available for prompt deployment, I am requesting an increase in the Army's total authorized strength from 875,000 to approximately one million men.

(3) I am requesting an increase of 29,000 and 63,000 men respectively in the active duty strength of the Navy and Air Force.

(4) To fulfill these manpower needs, I am ordering that our draft calls be doubled and tripled in the coming months; I am asking the Congress for authority to order to active duty certain ready reserve units and individual reservists, and to extend tours of duty; and, under that authority, I am planning to order to active duty a number of air transport squadrons and Air National Guard tactical air squadrons, to give us the airlift capacity and protection we may need. Other reserve forces will be called up if needed.

(5) Many ships and planes once headed for retirement are to be retained or reactivated, increasing our tactical airpower and our sea lift, airlift, and anti-submarine warfare capability. In addition, our strategic air power will be increased by delaying the deactivation of B-47 bombers.

(6) Finally, some $1.8 billion—about half of the total sum—is needed for the procurement of non-nuclear weapons, ammunition and equipment.

XIV

the fair deal (1945-1953)

WORLD WAR II had placed more than 15,000,000 Americans in uniform, and the sudden surrender of Japan set in motion the greatest demobilization in the nation's history. Many veterans, eager to resume their interrupted civilian life, returned to a world they never knew. Ingratitude, discrimination, and high costs often made the road back a tougher obstacle course than any encountered in the service. But an economy starved for consumer goods, along with financial assistance furnished by the government, sped the absorption of the displaced veterans.

The abrupt termination of the huge orders for war materiel brought the fear of a recession similar to that following World War I. The National Association of Manufacturers, presenting its case for industry, claimed that the federal tax system must be revised to permit greater capital investment. The farmer appeared to accept the principle of price supports for his product while disagreeing on how they should be applied, but he was insistent on a stable dollar in purchasing power. Labor sought greater security, more social benefits, and control of the cost of living. Clearly, each of these groups was demanding some action of the Federal government to implement its program.

The record of the Republican-controlled 80th Congress on these and other problems provided the basic issue for the 1948 political campaign. While President Truman castigated what he called the "do-nothing" Congress for blocking social legislation, others pointed out that though the Congress had been thwarted by numerous Presidential vetoes, it had enacted vital foreign aid bills, a badly needed labor statute, and authorization to implement the Hoover Commission's findings on a reorganization of the Federal government.

Harry Truman's reelection was ascribed in part to his vigorous campaign and his espousal of social legislation, which he urged Congress to adopt in his State of the Union message in 1949. The President's second term was generally one of disap-

pointment on the domestic scene. Truman suffered a significant
setback when the Supreme Court declared unconstitutional his
seizure of steel mills closed by strikes, and his criticism of the
Taft-Hartley Act was dulled by evidence that it often operated
to labor's advantage. Nevertheless, the administration, at its
conclusion, proudly pointed to an American economy which,
in the period 1929-1952, had doubled industrial production and
increased agricultural output by fifty per cent, though it was not
explained whether this growth could be attributed to the New
Deal program or the enormous demands of world conflict and
rehabilitation.

The question of civil rights became increasingly important in
the years following the war as minority groups sought the freedoms guaranteed by the Constitution. The issue was clouded by a
growing awareness of the Communist threat, and efforts were
made to protect the nation from the subversive activities which
characterized the tactics and marked the success of this international revolutionary movement. As the search for Communists
in the Federal government was highlighted by the probes and
pronouncements of Senator Joseph McCarthy of Wisconsin,
some feared that the United States, in its zeal to eliminate sus-
picious elements, might win a skirmish but lose the war.

1

The Veteran's Return

☆ *One of the more difficult problems facing the nation after World War II was the reabsorption of the veteran into civilian life. Bill Mauldin wrote a classic account which reflected the attitudes of many veterans toward what they found "Back Home." Some excerpts from his book are given below.** ☆

In the Fort Dix separation center I ran into a newly-returned 3rd Division man whose first day back on home soil gave him a couple of experiences that seemed pretty typical of the reception many thousands of others were getting in the summer of 1945.

He told me that after he had been checked through customs and all the assorted receiving points, he took a train to Trenton, New Jersey, where he stood on a corner waiting for the bus to Fort Dix. A lady of hefty build came up to him and asked him if he had been overseas. The soldier, who was wearing the Silver Star, the Purple Heart with a cluster, the Combat Infantry Badge, and six gold bars on his sleeve to denote three years of foreign service, allowed as how he was just back from across the water.

"I can't understand it," the lady said, "All you boys coming back like this. You must have pull somewhere. My boy has been in Europe for months and months, and he writes that it may be a long time before he gets back."

* From *Back Home* by Bill Mauldin, pp. 21-22, 50-52, 61-63, 65-68, 133-135, 168-170. © 1947 by Bill Mauldin, by permission of William Sloane Associates

He told me he was back in Trenton a few days later on a pass, and he went to a drugstore to get a package of cigarettes. He asked the man behind the cigar counter for a popular brand, whereupon the man got huffy and spoke as follows, "In case you haven't heard, young man, there is a cigarette shortage. Also for your information, the reason for the shortage is that all cigarettes are in the army. Why don't you buy cigarettes in your post exchange and leave me alone?"

* * * * * *

A number of employers, who had filled with overage men and draft-board rejectees the jobs left by men who had received greetings from the president, had trained their new men at the expense of considerable effort and money. They didn't take to the idea of putting the veterans back on the old jobs, especially since they would have to be retrained because their long absence had made them rusty. Although the law said they had to take the veterans back, many employers were not above using ruses to get around the law. They were patriotic fellows, all right, and they had bought their share of war bonds, but they were also business-

men who consider wastefulness a sacri-
lege. The trick of playing on the veteran's
sympathy . . . was fairly widespread. Particularly if the veteran was young and
single, he couldn't help feeling a pang of
regret when his boss informed him that
of course he could have his old position,
but he felt the veteran should realize that
the man who now held his job was supporting a family and had bought a house
and would find it catastrophic to pack his
dependents and go seeking a new job—
while young men, especially war heroes,
would find no trouble at all getting new
jobs, and probably better-paying ones at
that.

During the sudden slump that followed
the closing of war factories, there was a
real problem facing young ex-soldiers who
hadn't held a pre-war job. If they had been
lucky enough to attend specialist schools in
the army and were trained in mechanical work, or radio, or engineering, or any
such skilled trade, they were often able
to place themselves. The guys who got it
in the neck, of course, were the infantry-
men whose wartime training and experience didn't exactly fit them for peacetime
work. I did a drawing overseas about a
paddlefoot, stooped under a load consisting of a mortar tripod, grenades, rifles,
trench knife, bandoleers, and other implements of destruction, who was watching
a grimy engineer place logs in a muddy
road. "Yer lucky," said the infantryman.
"Yer learnin' a trade." This turned out
to be rather prophetic.

* * * * * *

It will be interesting for some historian
to review the great American housing
famine some decades hence. He will see
a real study in paradoxes. Real-estate
people talk about our country's great
traditions and history and record of
free enterprise, yet by refusing to allow
children in many of their buildings they
are raising untold hell with the birth rate
of their beloved country, depriving the na-

tion of future men and women to uphold its great traditions. Broken families
are often the result of forcing young cou-
ples to crowd in with their in-laws. This
creates chaos, and everybody knows that
chaos breeds revolution. The historian
will probably scratch his head and conclude that real-estate people were in secret league with the communists during
that phase of American history.

While some senators were making a lot
of noise in Congress in 1946 about the vicious OPA, many people who were on the
suffering end of the postwar housing shortage got a sardonic laugh from the news
story about a certain senator's son. When
OPA temporarily expired, and before rent
ceilings were re-established, he cashed in
on his old man's noble efforts by boosting
the rent of a piece of his property, which
was occupied by a veteran and his family,
to a fantastic sum several hundred per
cent greater than it had been.

* * * * * *

I have been privileged to hear many intelligent and successful citizens argue
against the evils of rent control, and they
are very convincing. They talk about supply and demand, about free enterprise and
the American tradition. Their best argument is about how the housing situation
would be greatly relieved if all rent controls were lifted so that people could invest in real estate and build new units
with some assurance that their investment
would make a profit—an assurance and
incentive that are lacking while the lid is
on. They admit that the unscrupulous element among the landlord clique would
take advantage of the situation for a while,
but they say in a few years everything
would level off and landlords would come
begging their old tenants to return. This
sounds awfully logical, but my thinking is
sometimes governed more by emotion
than logic, and I sometimes wonder if several thousand families, evicted because
they couldn't pay a skyrocketing rent,

sitting on the sidewalks with their worldly goods decomposing in the rain, waiting for a few years to pass for things to level off, form a suitable sacrifice to lay on the altar of the great god Free Enterprise.

It would be very unfair to make a blanket condemnation of landlords and call them all unscrupulous. Many of them have a legitimate beef about the way bureaucracy has treated them, and they have as much right as anybody else to send men to Washington to join the swollen ranks of lobbyists for special interests and pour sweet somethings into our legislators' ears. Having been in the army and had my fill of pompous little men in position of authority, and having seen a few examples of the more distasteful brand of government official, I am as anti-bureaucrat as the next guy. But it would be nice if somebody could find a solution to the housing problem short of letting the relatives of congressmen walk all over the rest of the citizenry.

* * * * * *

The term "highway robbery" was never used in a more literal sense than when applied to America's present-day used-car shysters, and within a few hours after I started shopping I became painfully aware of it. The OPA was supposed to be functioning in that department, but as far as cars were concerned the OPA might never have existed. I saw 1937 Pontiacs —cars that had cost around a thousand dollars when new and were now eight-year-old jalopies—priced at $1500. The familiar gimmick was the radio. The car was priced legally, but it had a "special" radio worth almost $1000. The prize package in the first establishment I visited was a 1942 Cadillac convertible that had cost about $2000 when new, and had nearly fifty thousand miles registered on the speedometer. It was a handsome number in gray, with white side-wall tires that still showed a little tread here and there from their second recapping job. This

Cadillac had a chain attached to the ignition key, and engraved on a little tab at the end of the chain was the name of a well-known movie character. The salesman said the car was available for $5000 (more than twice its OPA price), and pointed out that among its other virtues was the fact that its new owner could brag in an offhand way that "this buggy used to belong to .... You've heard of him, of course."

* * * * * *

The Nisei came home loaded with medals and covered with scars and minus limbs and eyes, and they found themselves getting kicked out of Arizona barbershops and San Francisco restaurants just as if they had never left home. Even some prejudiced people were appalled by the sight of a one-legged soldier with a Purple Heart getting a physical knocking-around by a pot-bellied, sound-limbed merchant or doorman, so there was a flurry of public indignation, but it didn't last. William Randolph Hearst, whose papers appear all over the country, . . . had never stopped beating the drum about the Yellow Peril. Indeed he was one of those who agitated for the relocation plan, which took advantage of the war and rid the West Coast of its Japanese-American population. When the Nisei veterans and their families trickled back after the war they found that their homes, farms, and businesses had been taken over by lazy white trash whose prejudices were based largely on commercialism, and who naturally had no desire to move out. They could never have built the homes and businesses or developed the farms themselves, because that took sacrifice, thrift, and back-breaking labor. Inspired by the Hearst papers and their own selfish motives, these usurpers found it easier to scare the Nisei away than to return the property or to pay for it.

In a commendable effort to help the situation, the War Department sent several white officers, who had served with the Nisei units in Italy and France, around the West Coast on lecture tours, so they could tell the farmers and businessmen about the job the Nisei had done in the war and appeal to their instincts for fair-mindedness. It wasn't much use. In Los Angeles I talked to a first lieutenant who had just finished one of the tours late in 1945. He had been with one of the regiments in Italy, and had seen hundreds of the Nisei boys, whom he had learned to love and respect, killed in action. He told me about paying a visit to a vegetable-packing shed in the northern part of California, where a lanky farmer asked him, "How many of them Japs in your company got killed?" "All but two of the men who started in my platoon were killed by the end of the war," the lieutenant replied. "Too goddam bad they didn't get the last two," said the farmer.

2

The "Interests" Speak

☆ *The post-war period witnessed an open scramble for political and economic power among the three major economic groups, business, agriculture, and labor. Security appeared to be the watchword— for the National Association of Manufacturers, security for free enterprise; for the Farm Bureau, security of farm income; for the Congress of Industrial Organizations, security for life.* ☆

(a) A NATIONAL ASSOCIATION OF MANUFACTURERS SPOKESMAN*

As we see it, the critical alternatives which confront us today are the American individual competitive enterprise system or the dictated or managed economy —under whatever label.

The difference, fundamentally, is this:

American economic practice insists first of all upon the production of goods, in order to have goods to distribute. Distribution is equitable, through the natural interplay of supply-demand, freedom of choice, opportunity, incentive, and initiative.

Managed economy is preoccupied, first of all, with how it will distribute goods which may or may not be produced under the direction of a central planning board. Freedom of choice, opportunity, incentive, and initiative are restricted if not eliminated; an economy cannot be controlled unless the lives of the individuals which form the economy are controlled.

The NAM's purpose in supplying the

* 1948. From Morris Sayre. "The Stake of Industry," *Annals of the American Academy of Political and Social Science,* CCLIX (September, 1948), pp. 114-116. Used by permission.

American public with this clear understanding of how our free economy works pervades its numerous informative and co-operative services to members, and its publication and advertising activities.

The present inflation with its wage-price spiral superimposed upon the basic cause of too great a money supply and too few goods, our program to aid European recovery, and the requirements of our military security involve economic questions which the American people must resolve.

Building upon the conviction that only through the high productivity of a free economy can our present-day challenges be met, the NAM committees and staff have done a vast amount of fact-finding and analysis in regard to our major current problems. To present to the public these facts and the viewpoints of the best thinking of American industrial management, is the continuing task of the association.

We believe that capital formation is absolutely basic to America's productive strength. "Capital formation" is an economist's term, but it can be very simply illustrated. One of our primitive ancestors, many centuries ago, had what his brother savages probably considered a streak of laziness. Instead of going out hunting small game with bare hands or stones, he pottered about with a length of lively wood and a strip of hide. Finally he succeeded in fashioning a rude device which would send a sharpened stick through the air to its mark much faster and truer than he could throw a stone.

He had invented the first bow and arrow. But more important—although he did not suspect it—he was one of the first links in the chain of capital formation upon which all economic progress, and modern civilization itself, are built. By diverting his efforts from the immediate task of hunting food for the day, he was providing himself with the tools to make his future hunting far more effective.

Today it requires a great deal of real wealth to replace the machines, tools, buildings, and other plant equipment which wear out. It requires a vast amount of investment to launch new industries, new inventions, new processes—all of which mean more goods, new and better goods, more jobs, more opportunities for the thousands of young persons who look for occupations each year as our population grows.

Capital formation has gone on in all ages and under all forms of economy. No matter what kind of economy may be in operation, capital equipment has to be supplied to make future high production possible. Under our American free economy, capital formation has reached its highest levels, providing the highest standards of living and of real wages the world has ever known. This has been done under the American way of fair rewards, which makes savings and venture investments attractive.

But for almost two decades, capital formation has been far below the level it had reached during the sixty years of America's greatest industrial progress. From 1869 through 1928 we Americans, instead of living up to the hilt of our total production, set aside just about one-fifth of the value of our production to plow back as investment in our facilities for future production.

We have not been doing that since about 1930. As a result—using our historic 20 per cent of total production as the highwater mark—we have been accumulating a serious deficit in capital formation.

In the sixty-year period of high capital formation, the growth in the rate of creation of real wealth—goods and services—was spectacular. Through every decade of those times there surged an ever widening stream of the necessities and comforts of life. In 1919-28 the gross national product was almost twelve times as great as in 1869-78. The Nation grew in real wealth at the rate of nearly 4 per cent a year. Real hourly earnings in manufacturing have more than doubled in the past fifty years.

Today our national and international responsibilities are far greater than ever before. Yet the investment needed for the country's economic health is being diverted from productive purposes by our present system of taxation. No longer is America plowing back one-fifth of the wealth produced into the machine tools and industrial plant needed to create more prosperity and more jobs.

Using this time-tested mark, this country is falling short of the supply of private saving and investment necessary to our economic strength by some eight billion dollars a year.

The cause of the deficit in capital formation—the lack of individual saving in general, and of individual venture saving (the saving that can be risked in business investment) in particular—lies in the Federal tax system.

Our present individual tax system has

the effect of placing the heaviest burden on precisely the income classes who otherwise would provide the largest percentage of venture savings. We believe the present tax structure should be overhauled to prevent the incentives necessary for economic strength from being destroyed and to keep the sources of investment in America's progress from being dried up.

It is thoroughly recognized by the NAM that there are compelling reasons for expenditures to safeguard national defense and to achieve the objectives of this country's program to aid European recovery.

However, these are additional reasons for maintaining and expanding our productive power. Government expenditures come from the funds of the people. If a tax system which does not regard the economic strength of the Nation as a whole is to drain away the fair rewards that make men save and invest in the tools of production, we shall be in no case to provide for military security, to assist Europe to recover, or to maintain the American family's standard of living.

When faced by unusual additional expenses, an individual or a business does not need to be persuaded that economies in other directions should be made. By the same simple logic it is apparent that in this period more than in all past periods, the people of this country cannot afford governmental waste, extravagance, or nonessential activities. We believe it is imperative for Congress to follow continuously a program of trimming down or eliminating unproductive or unnecessary Government agencies and activities.

Considerations of government expenditures naturally bring the military budget into focus. We in the NAM believe that present and proposed military spending should be reviewed, to accomplish three purposes:

1. To assure adequate funds for the military safety of the United States.

2. To eliminate military spending which does not contribute to America's immediate or long-term strength.

3. To keep the total of military and other governmental spending from sapping America's strength to produce. Without this productive power, no military security program will be able to maintain this Nation's freedom.

Any review of the Nation's economic problems must include the public debt, which of course is just what the term indicates. It is the debt of all the individuals who make up the American public. It amounts to nearly seven thousand dollars for every American family of four.

Proposals have been made to use an anticipated Federal surplus to lop off some seven billion dollars of the public debt. Economists are not in complete agreement as to what might happen if so large a portion of the debt were to be retired suddenly; but it may be expected that its deflationary effect would be the cause of credit dislocations which, once under way, might seriously constrict business activity.

It is the NAM's conviction that the public debt should be reduced in a systematic way, by an orderly plan which will avoid needless inflationary or deflationary spurts and spasms. We believe it would be entirely practicable to retire the debt within about one generation by paying it off at the rate of $2.5 billion a year.

(b) AN AMERICAN FARM BUREAU SPOKESMAN*

First of all, farmers want a fair opportunity to earn enough to enable their families to live comfortably, to enjoy in

* 1948. From Allan B. Kline, "What the Farmers Want," *Annals of the American Academy of Political and Social Science*, CCLIX (September, 1948), pp. 122-126. Used by permission.

moderate degree the better things of life, to become educated according to modern standards, and to attain a measure of security for their old age. . . .

The Roosevelt administration was responsible for several precedent-breaking farm laws. Surviving the Supreme Court decision of 1936, and still on the statute books, are measures which permit farmers to regulate production of basic farm commodities in the name of soil conservation; to store surpluses in the ever-normal granary and to secure nonrecourse loans on the stored commodities; and to market certain perishable commodities such as milk under collective bargaining arrangements with processors under the Marketing Agreement Act of 1938. There is other legislation also, but we are concerned here principally with the legislation I have mentioned.

Regional hearings all over the United States have definitely established that farmers generally favor the principles underlying this legislation. There is great difference of opinion among farmers as to the price levels which should be assured under these laws. Producers of certain commodities want very high loan levels for stored commodities, while others want loan levels primarily as a stop-loss device. In the legislation referred to is a provision for giving each producer of basic commodities a marketing quota which limits the amount of the commodity that he is permitted to place on the market. Such quotas are operative only when more than two-thirds of the farmers participating in the program vote affirmatively for them. Some groups in agriculture want to be able to vote for marketing quotas whenever supply is in fair balance with demand and when the ever-normal granary is full enough to secure the consumer public against shortages. Other groups would like to vote on marketing quotas only when supplies are considerably in excess of demand.

While we do have this difference of opinion, it is clear that farmers want some sort of price assurance based upon the parity principle. It may be said also that the bulk of farmers do not want fixed prices or rigid price structures. They want to leave a substantial area for the operation of free markets. For example, they do not want to maintain corn prices at a rigidly high level which would unduly disturb the ratios between feed grains and livestock prices. Too rigid formulas in these things might freeze production in an uneconomic pattern and prevent the shifting of farm production to meet changes in consumer demand. For instance, with vastly increased incomes, consumers have indicated that they like to eat more meat, more dairy products, more fruits and vegetables than they consumed in pre-war days. Shifts in production to meet such changes should be relatively easy to make, and any legislation which would hinder such shifts would certainly not be desirable.

Farmers want as large a market as possible, and therefore they are in favor of improving foreign relations, which will lead to increased trade. It is true that there are forty million more people to feed and clothe in the United States than there were after World War I, which leads some to believe that the foreign market is not nearly so important as it once was. However, it should be remembered that the shift to mechanical power on farms has eliminated some seventeen or eighteen million horses and mules from our farms; and each of these animals required just about the same acreage for subsistence as a human being requires.

The trend, of course, is toward still further mechanization. Furthermore, the productive capacity of the United States is so great that our farmers could supply a very much larger volume of commodities for export purposes than they customarily have supplied. For example, we have grown as much as forty million acres of cotton in the past. Now we grow only about half that amount. Tobacco production could also be enormously increased.

So we see that farmers are acutely aware of the importance of foreign trade. It must be admitted that producers of certain commodities in agriculture exhibit the desire to have their cake and eat it too when it comes to foreign trade. They want to let in imports which will compete with someone else rather than with them. These inconsistencies are probably fundamental in human nature and we should not be surprised at them. The hope is that as time goes on, improved understanding of the whole question of imports and exports will lead to the backing of rational and constructive policies.

In spite of the inconsistencies that I have noted, farmers have backed the reciprocal-trade idea rather consistently and they have demonstrated in other ways their appreciation of the importance of better trade relations. They have always insisted that they be fairly treated in formulating trade policies. They appreciate the fact that adverse effects on rather large groups may result from sudden shifts in policy. They have favored gradual shifts in established policies, so that industries affected may have opportunity to adjust their operations to new conditions. They are truly interested in any program designed to advance foreign trade, but before approving any such program they want to be sure that it is sound. . . .

A word should be said about what farmers do not want. In contacts with thousands of farmers each year, I am amazed at the number to whom 1933 is still a bitter memory. They are convinced that there is no good reason why we should permit conditions to develop which will bring on another period such as that which culminated in 1933. Farmers believe that wealth can come only from production. When they produce a bushel of wheat or a bale of cotton, they cannot understand why either unit should not buy as much in goods and services one year as another. They believe that the Nation itself would be better off if something approximating such a condition could be attained.

The farmer's interest in stablized prices is due largely to the fact that changes in the general price level affect him to a greater extent than almost any other group. When the general price level declines, prices of farm products, along with prices of raw materials generally, decline more rapidly than most. Prices of goods used in farm production decline more slowly, resulting in disparity for farmers.

The farmers are the only major group which has addressed itself seriously to the problem of creating a dollar of fairly constant purchasing power. The farmers believe that something could be done with money and credit to iron out the more violent swings in the purchasing power of the current dollar. They do not quite understand a credit system that makes borrowing easy when you need not borrow, but hard or impossible when you need credit to save your business. The great popularity of the Federal Land Bank loans has been due largely to the fact that they provide for long-time loans on land. Farming is usually a slow turnover, and a credit system patterned after our commercial credit system did not begin to meet agriculture's needs.

(c) CONGRESS OF INDUSTRIAL ORGANIZATIONS' PROPOSALS*

Basic Security: The vital factor in an organized, orderly society is the basic security of the individual. If this basic security is absent, there can be no such thing as the common good or the general welfare.

Each individual must be free to exercise his human rights—economic, political, and civil.

Collective Bargaining: If our economy and institutions are to remain free, genuine collective bargaining must be safeguarded and extended.

The Taft-Hartley Law has undermined the national policy established during the Roosevelt administration. This law attempts to take us back in the direction of the old evils of individual bargaining.

The T-H Law has been directly responsible for the revival of government by injunction. The Act constitutes a dangerous challenge to the right of free speech and to our free press. It has increased industrial strife, upset union security provisions in thousands of existing agreements and opened up opportunities for endless lawsuits by unscrupulous employers against unions.

This convention should forthrightly demand the repeal of the Taft-Hartley Act. The experience under the law has demonstrated the truth of President Truman's statement when he vetoed the law and said, "It is a bad bill. It is bad for labor, bad for management, and bad for the country."

Fair Labor Standards: To assure workers and employers alike of fair treatment, our laws governing minimum wages and maximum hours must be considerably strengthened. The principle of equal pay

* 1948. From Congress of Industrial Organizations' Proposals to the Platform Committee of the Democratic National Convention, 1948, reprinted in *Annals of the American Academy of Political and Social Science*, CCLIX (September, 1948), pp. 150-151. Used by permission of American Federation of Labor and Congress of Industrial Organizations.

for equal work regardless of race or sex must be generally applied throughout American industry.

Production and Distribution: Between June of 1946, the effective end of OPA, and the beginning of 1948, the cost of living has gone up more than one-fourth. This rise unfortunately still continues. As a result, families are hard put to buy food and clothes, let alone anything beyond. The high cost of living is a household reality.

The 80th Congress has ignored realities and in so doing has contributed to the inflationary spiral.

We reiterate the need for an effective program of control over prices and for immediate and effective legislation by the Congress to restore price controls over the basic necessities of life.

The best preventive of inflation and exploitation through shortages of goods, is the exercise of proper price controls by the government.

Housing: The lack of housing requires no detailed analysis. It is real; it is here; and there presently exists no detailed orderly plan for its alleviation. The government must give effective leadership to the private building construction industry. It must apply systems of allocation and price control in distribution of building materials.

We must, however, recognize the void in our housing requirements that cannot be met by private industry. This void must be filled by the government with publicly financed and operated housing projects available to persons in the low-income brackets at reasonable rents.

In view of the delay in providing adequate housing, we urge that effective rent controls be restored.

Health: The health of the people is an integral part of their security. We must admit frankly that our technological advances in the field of industrial production have not been matched in other related fields such as that of health and medical care.

The present system of financing medical care and its related fields must be greatly improved and expanded. We can no longer accept invalid arguments against national health insurance plans which will afford both members of the medical profession and its consumers of medical care, free choice in the rendition of acceptance of medical care. We must give to the health of the people at least as much regard as we give the education of the people.

Education: Our educational system must be greatly expanded and improved.

Specifically we urge adequate federal aid for all education, and enactment of the Labor-Education Extension Service to provide for adult workers.

Social Security: A minimum program should embody:

1. A substantial rise in the present level of old-age benefits and a reduction in retirement age. This level has been unchanged for 9 years, during which time the cost of living has moved upward.

2. An extension of the entire social security program, including unemployment insurance and old-age, sickness and death and survivors' benefits to make its benefits available to the many under-privileged groups who are now denied protection.

3. A nationwide system of unemployment insurance, paying adequate benefits for a decent period of time.

4. The institution of sickness and disability insurance to provide a complete program (on a federal level) of health protection and disability payments.

3

Postwar Politics

☆ *In the November 1946 elections the Republicans won a majority of the seats in the House and Senate under the slogan "Had Enough?" The Democratic President, Harry S. Truman, and the Republican-controlled 80th Congress frequently found themselves in bitter disagreement. President Truman successfully exploited the record of this Congress in the 1948 election.* ☆

(a) THE 80TH CONGRESS*

The European nations, in response to Secretary Marshall's Harvard speech of June 5, 1947, were meeting in Paris to see what they could do collectively to rebuild their economies. At home the Administration had initiated a series of studies to see to what extent the U. S. could aid without depleting its own resources. In Europe, traveling Congressmen were to make their own appraisals. At the instance of Speaker Martin, one committee under Christian Herter of Massachusetts was charged with making a special study of foreign aid. In November, even before the Administration had detailed its blueprint of the European Recovery Program, the Herter committee had come to the independent conclusion that the U. S. must take Europe off relief and put it back to work.

By Christmas there was general agreement in the Administration, in Congress, and in the country at large that a European recovery program was necessary.

The differences to be worked out concerned how much Congress should appropriate and how the plan should be administered. A breach threatened over the mechanics of aid. The Secretary of State saw E.R.P. as an extension of State Department operations and announced his adamant opposition to the idea of "two secretaries of state." In neither house could this position be sustained since Congress had no confidence in the State Department as an operating body or in its personnel as managers. A stubborn refusal to arbitrate could have wrecked the program. On his own initiative, Senator Vandenberg called in the Brookings Institution to make an independent report on the management of foreign aid. The formula that the institution suggested was accepted and written into the law as the Economic Cooperation Administration. The European Recovery Program became law on April 3, 1948, fifteen days before the critical Italian election. It was an act of prudent, generous, inter-nation dealing without precedent in history, passed with-

* From "Congress Comes Through," *Fortune,* XXXVII (June, 1948), pp. 79-80. Courtesy of Fortune Magazine.

out major dissension and with unparalleled speed.

The Congress took the initiative in another phase of foreign policy: China. The problem was complicated by the personal attitude of General Marshall. His own failure to fulfill an impossible assignment in China — a coalition between the Communists and the Kuomintang—inhibited him from taking a rational or objective view of the struggle for power there. A Congress that had provided aid to fight Communists in Greece and Turkey became increasingly critical of our China policy. It could not see the difference between Communists in Greece and Communists in China. Largely at the urgent insistence of Speaker Martin, aid to the Nationalist Government of China became part of U. S. policy and was included as a part of the European Recovery Program. Certainly in meeting the challenge of foreign policy the Eightieth Congress had proved its ability to work without partisanship in the national interest.

The major postwar domestic issue before Congress was labor. In the depression, when the balance between labor and management had been weighted against labor, Congress had redressed it by the Wagner Act. By 1946 the balance had swung overwhelmingly in favor of labor. A series of paralyzing postwar strikes had delivered dangerous shocks to the economy. The 113-day strike at G.M., the steel impasse, and the coal tie-ups had proved that the existing machinery was inadequate. Even the President, friendly as he was to labor, had been exasperated by union tactics, and in the brief railway strike of 1946 had proposed the desperate remedy of drafting strikers into the Army. This Draconian measure was blocked in the Senate by a Republican, Senator Taft. But later Taft and the Republican leaders were to make reform of the labor laws a campaign issue in the 1946 elections.

When the Eightieth Congress assembled, the Republicans appeared to have little chance to redeem this election promise. Nearly everyone wanted a new labor law; most people were sure that no satisfactory measure could be drawn and passed. The difficulties were formidable because the Republicans did not have the necessary two-thirds majority. Since the Administration—and the unions—wanted no real reform, support of some Democrats was necessary if the anticipated presidential veto was to be overridden. There were also important differences within the Republican party itself to be overcome, still further differences in approach and concept between the House and Senate. The House was for much more drastic action; it put its views into a bill that forbade industry-wide bargaining and abolished the NLRB. It was in the Senate that statesmanship asserted itself.

There the *de facto* leader of the majority, Taft, had put himself into an exposed and politically dangerous post as chairman of the Labor Committee in order to force through a new labor policy. Undoubtedly his own inclinations were to write a more stringent bill than that which emerged from the committee. But within the committee there were Senators like Morse of Oregon and Pepper of Florida who were opposed to fundamental reforms. The balance was finally achieved through the astute and skillful negotiation of a freshman Senator from New York, Irving M. Ives. As chairman of the New York State Joint Legislative Committee on Industrial and Labor Conditions he had as much practical experience in the arbitration of labor disputes as anyone in the country. The end result was the Taft-Hartley Act, the bill that critics said could not be written.

The President vetoed the bill, using in his message extreme terms that echoed the most extreme criticism of the left wing of the C.I.O. He was overridden and the bill he so bitterly assailed as "dangerous" and "unworkable" was to be invoked by him less than a year later to bring John L. Lewis to heel. The unions continued to make an issue of the Taft-Hartley Act by calling it a "slave-labor bill" but the truth was that it rescinded few of the basic rights granted by the earlier Wagner Act and curtailed only those privilges that many felt had degenerated into abuses.

Perhaps the most enduring contribution to good government that the Eightieth Congress made was the Lodge-Brown bill. This established a commission, under the chairmanship of former President Hoover, to study the reorganization of the executive branch of the government. Congress itself had tried without success over a number of years to reorganize the government. The government branches proliferated, growing like some tropical plant until the pattern of administration became more and more tangled. The new commission was authorized to draft disinterested authorities in administration and business practice to study government operations. The commission was also instructed to make its report not to the Eightieth but the Eighty-first Congress. This wise provision put the commission's findings above and beyond current political debate. It meant that the commission's recommendations would be received by the next Congress and the next President and could become a true charter for businesslike management of the nation's affairs.

The controversies of the Eightieth Congress turned largely on the coming struggle for the presidency. Although the White House and the Hill worked together on foreign policy the divisions on domestic policy were bitter. In the last two years Mr. Truman has vetoed 125 bills. The longest and bitterest of the quarrels between President and Congress resulted from Republican determination to reduce taxes and incidentally to fulfill a politically profitable promise. In the 1947 session Mr. Truman twice vetoed Republican tax bills and had his veto sustained.

Mr. Truman's opposition to tax reduction was anchored in his repeated assertion that tax reduction was in itself inflationary. As the political storm rose, his anchor chain slipped and the politician in Mr. Truman overcame the economist. He himself proposed tax reduction—of a kind. Every taxpayer was to receive for himself and each dependent a flat $40 credit to be paid for by an increased tax on corporation profits. Mr. Truman knew in advance, of course, his proposal had no chance for acceptance. His political gesture provoked a political reaction. Old Harold Knutson, whose bills the President had twice vetoed, exclaimed: "My God! I didn't know inflation had gone that far. Tom Pendergast paid only $2 a vote and now Truman proposes to pay $40." In the end, eighty-two Democrats in the House and twenty-seven in the Senate voted with the Republicans to override Mr. Truman's third veto of a Republican tax bill.

(b) ADDRESS OF PRESIDENT HARRY S. TRUMAN IN ACCEPTING THE DEMOCRATIC PRESIDENTIAL NOMINATION*

I accept the nomination, and I want to thank this Convention for its unanimous

* July 14, 1948. From *Democracy At Work, Being The Official Report of the Democratic National Convention*, pp. 300-306. Published by the Local Democratic Political Committee of Pennsylvania, Philadelphia, 1948.

nomination of my good friend and colleague, Senator Barkley, of Kentucky. He is a great man and a great public servant. Senator Barkley and I will win this election and make those Republicans like it. Don't you forget that. We will do that because they are wrong and we are right, and I will prove it to you in a few minutes. . . .

We will be working together for victory in a great cause. Victory has become a habit of our Party, and it has been elected four times in succession; and I am convinced that it will be elected a fifth time next November.

The reason is that the people know the Democratic Party is the people's party, and the Republican Party is the party of special interests and it always has been and always will be. . . .

Confidence and security have been brought to the American people by the Democratic Party. Farm income has increased from less than $2.5 billion in 1932 to more than $18 billion in 1947. Never in the world were the farmers of any Republic or any Kingdom, or any other country as prosperous as the farmer of the United States and if they don't do their duty by the Democratic Party, they are the most ungrateful people in the world.

And what I have said to the farmer I will say again: They are the most ungrateful people in the world if they pass the Democratic Party by this year.

The wages and salaries in this country were $29 billion in 1933, and more than $128 billion in 1947. That is labor, and labor never had but one friend in politics, and that is the Democratic Party, and Franklin D. Roosevelt.

The total national income has increased from less than $40 billion in 1933 to $203 billion in 1947, the greatest in all of the history of the world.

These benefits have been spread to all of the people because it is the business of the Democratic Party to see that the people get a fair share of these things. This last worst 80th Congress proved just the opposite for the Republicans. The record on foreign policy of the Democratic Party is that the United States has been turned away permanently from isolationism and we have converted the greatest and best of the Republicans to our viewpoint on that subject.

The United States has to accept its full responsibility for leadership in international affairs. . . .

We have removed the trade barriers in the world which is the best asset we can have for peace. Those trade barriers must not be put back into operation again. We have started a foreign aid program which means the recovery of Europe and China and the Far East. We instituted the program for Greece and Turkey, and I will say to you that all of these things were done in a cooperative bi-partisan manner.

The Foreign Relations Committees of the Senate and House were taken into the full confidence of the President in every one of these moves, and don't let anybody tell you anything else. . . .

I would like to say a word or two now about what I think the Republicans did here, and I will speak from actions and from history and from experience. The situation in 1932 was due to the policies of the Republican Party in control of the Government of the United States. The Republican Party, as I said a while ago, favors the privileged few and not the common, every-day man. Ever since its inception that Party has been under the control of special privilege, and they concretely proved it in the 80th Congress. They proved it by the things they did to the people and not for them. They proved it by the things they failed to do.

Now let us look at some of them, just a few. Time and again I demanded the extension of price control before it expired on June 30, 1946. I asked for that extension in September of 1945, in November 1945, in the message on the State of the Union in 1946, and that price control legislation did not come to my desk until June 30, 1946, on the day on which it was supposed to expire, and it was such a rotten bill that I could not sign it; and after that they sent me one just as bad, and I had to sign it because they quit and went home.

It was said when OPA died that prices would adjust themselves for the benefit of the country. They have adjusted themselves all right. They have gone all of the way off the chart in adjusting themselves at the expense of the consumer and for the benefit of the people that hold the goods.

I called a special session of Congress in November of 1947—November 17, 1947—and I set out a ten-point program for the welfare and benefit of this country, among other things stand-by price control.

I got nothing. Congress has still done nothing. Away back four and a half years ago, while I was in the Senate, we passed a housing bill in the Senate known as the Wagner-Ellender-Taft Bill. It was a bill to clear the slums in the big cities and to help erect low-rent housing.

That bill, as I said, passed the Senate four years ago. It died in the House. That bill was reintroduced in the 80th Congress as the Taft-Ellender-Wagner Bill,—the name was slightly changed—but it was practically the same bill and it passed the Senate. It was allowed to die in the House of Representatives. . . .

In the field of labor, we needed moderate legislation to promote labor-management harmony, but Congress instead passed that so-called Taft-Hartley Act, which has disrupted labor-management relations, and will cause strife and bitterness for years to come, if it is not repealed, as the Democratic Platform says it ought to be repealed.

I tried to strengthen the Labor Department. The Republican platform of 1944 said if they were in power they would build up a strong Labor Department, and you know what they did to the Labor Department. They have simply torn it up. There is one bureau left that is func-

tioning, and they cut the appropriation on that so it cannot function properly. I recommended an increase in the minimum wage and what did I get? Nothing—absolutely nothing. I suggested that the schools in this country were crowded, with teachers underpaid, and that there was a shortage of teachers.

One of the greatest national needs is more and better schools. I urged Congress to provide $300 million to aid the states in relieving the present educational crisis.

Congress studied the matter for two again I have recommended improvements in the Social Security Law, including extending protection to those not now covered, increasing the benefits, reducing the eligible age of women from 65 to 60.

Congress studied the matter for two years and could not get time to extend benefits, but did get time to take Social Security benefits away from 750,000 people. They passed that over my veto. I have repeatedly asked the Congress to pass a health program. The nation suffers from lack of medical care. That situation can be remedied any time the Congress wants to act upon it.

Everybody knows that I recommended to the Congress a civil rights program. I did so because I believe it to be my duty under the Constitution.

Some of the members of my own Party disagree violently on this matter, but they stand up and do it openly. People can say where they stand, but the Republicans all tell where we stand, but the Republicans all profess to be for these measures but the 80th Congress failed to act. They had enough men, and they had cloture. There were enough people that would vote for cloture.

Everybody likes to have low taxes, but we must reduce the national debt in time of prosperity, and when tax relief can be given, it ought to go to those who need it most and not go to those who need it least, as the Republican rich-man tax bill did, as they did when they passed it over my veto on the third try.

The first one of these tax bills that they sent me was so rotten that they could not stomach it themselves. They finally did send one that was somewhat improved, but it still helps the rich and sticks the knife into the backs of the poor. . . .

My duty as President requires that I use every means within my power to get the laws the people need on such important matters, and I am therefore calling this Congress back into session on the 26th of July. That is on the 26th day of July, which out in Missouri we call Turnip Day.

I am going to call that Congress back, and I am going to ask them to pass laws halting rising prices and to lower the housing prices, which they say that they are for in their platform. At the same time, I shall ask them to act upon other vitally needed measures, such as aid to education, which they say that they are for; a National Health Program; Civil Rights legislation, which they say that they are for; and increase in the minimum wage, which I doubt very much they are for; an extension of Social Security coverage and increased benefits, which they say they are for; the projects needed in our program to provide public power and cheap electricity. . . .

[The Republicans] are going to try to dodge their responsibilities, and they are going to drag all of the red herrings they can across this campaign, but I am here to say to you that Senator Barkley and I are not going to let them get away with it.

Now, what that worst 80th Congress does in this special session will be the test. The American people will not decide by listening to mere words or by reading a mere platform. They will decide on the record, the record as it has been written, and in the record is the stark truth that the battle lines of 1948 are the same as they were back in 1932 when the Nation lay helpless and prostrate as a result of the Republican inaction. . . .

I must have your help, you must get in and push and win this election. The country can't afford another Republican Congress.

4

The Fair Deal Program, 1949

☆ *Mr. Truman, by the beginning of his second term as President, had developed into a fighting advocate of the positive use of government power for social and economic welfare. The body of his proposals which were presented in his State of the Union message in January, 1949, excerpted below, was generally blocked in the Democratic controlled 81st and 82nd Congresses.** ☆

During the last 16 years the American people have been creating a society which offers new opportunities for every man to enjoy his share of the good things of life.

In this society we are conservative about the values and principles which we cherish; but we are forward-looking in protecting those values and principles and in extending their benefits. We have rejected the discredited theory that the fortunes of the Nation should be in the hands of a privileged few. We have abandoned the "trickle down" concept of national prosperity. Instead, we believe that our economic system should rest on a democratic foundation and that wealth should be created for the benefit of all.

The recent election shows that the American people are in favor of this kind of society and want to go on improving it.

The American people have decided that poverty is just as wasteful and just as unnecessary as preventable disease. We have pledged our common resources to

* From *Congressional Record*, 81st Congress, 1st session, pp. 66-69.

help one another in the hazards and struggles of individual life. We believe that no unfair prejudice or artificial distinction should bar any citizen of the United States from an education, or from good health, or from a job that he is capable of performing.

Reinforced by these policies, our private enterprise system has reached new heights of production. Since the boom year of 1929, while our population has increased by only 20 percent, our agricultural production has increased by 45 percent, and our industrial production has increased by 75 percent. We are turning out far more goods and more wealth per worker than we have ever done before.

But, great as our progress has been, we still have a long way to go....

The Employment Act of 1946 pledges the Government to use all its resources to promote maximum employment, production, and purchasing power. This means that the Government is firmly committed to protect business and the people against the dangers of recession and against the evils of inflation. This means that the Government must adapt its plans and policies to meet changing circumstances. . . .

We should strengthen our anti-trust laws by closing those loopholes that permit monopolistic mergers and consolidations.

Our national farm program should be improved—not only in the interest of the farmers but for the lasting prosperity of the whole Nation. Our goals should be abundant farm production and parity of income for agriculture. Standards of living on the farm should be just as good as anywhere else in the country.

Farm price supports are an essential part of our program to achieve these ends. Price supports should be used to prevent farm price declines which are out of line with general price levels, to facilitate adjustments in production to consumer demands and to promote good land use. . . .

We must push forward with the development of our rivers for power, irrigation, navigation, and flood control. We should apply the lessons of our Tennessee Valley experience to our other great river basins.

I again recommend that action be taken by the Congress to approve the St. Lawrence seaway and power project. . . .

The present coverage of the social-security laws is altogether inadequate, and benefit payments are too low. One-third of our workers are not covered. Those who receive old age and survivors insurance benefits receive an average payment of only $25 a month. Many others

who cannot work because they are physically disabled are left to the mercy of charity. We should expand our social-security program, both as to size of benefits and extent of coverage, against the economic hazards due to unemployment, old age, sickness, and disability.

We must spare no effort to raise the general level of health in this country. In a nation as rich as ours, it is a shocking fact that tens of millions lack adequate medical care. We are short of doctors, hospitals, and nurses. We must remedy these shortages. Moreover, we need—and we must have without further delay—a system of prepaid medical insurance which will enable every American to afford good medical care.

The housing shortage continues to be acute. As an immediate step, the Congress should enact the provisions for low-rent public housing, slum clearance, farm housing, and housing research which I have repeatedly recommended. The number of low-rent public housing units provided for in the legislation should be increased to 1,000,000 units in the next 7 years. Even this number of units will not begin to meet our need for new housing. . . .

The fulfillment of this promise is among the highest purposes of government. The civil rights proposals I made to the Eightieth Congress, I now repeat to the Eighty-first Congress. They should be enacted in order that the Federal Government may assume the leadership and discharge the obligations clearly placed upon it by the Constitution.

5

Executive Authority Denied

☆ *Truman ran into trouble in 1952, when, broadly interpreting his powers as Commander-in-Chief during the Korean war, he ordered government seizure and operation of struck steel mills without statutory authority. In Youngstown Co. v. Sawyer, decided June 2, 1952, the Supreme Court ruled 6 to 3 that the President's action was without foundation in law.* ☆

MR. JUSTICE BLACK delivered the opinion of the Court.

We are asked to decide whether the the President was acting within his constitutional power when he issued an order directing the Secretary of Commerce to take possession of and operate most of the Nation's steel mills. The mill owners argue that the President's order amounts to law-making, a legislative function which the Constitution has expressly confided to the Congress and not to the President. The Government's position is that the order was made on findings of the President that his action was necessary to avert a national catastrophe which would inevitably result from a stoppage of steel production, and that in meeting this grave emergency the President was acting within the aggregate of his constitutional powers as the Nation's Chief Executive and the Commander in Chief of the Armed Forces of the United States. The issue emerges here from the following series of events:

In the latter part of 1951, a dispute arose between the steel companies and

* From 343 U.S. 579.

their employees over terms and conditions that should be included in new collective bargaining agreements. Long-continued conferences failed to resolve the dispute. On December 18, 1951, the employees' representative, United Steelworkers of America, C.I.O., gave notice of an intention to strike when the existing bargaining agreements expired on December 31. The Federal Mediation and Conciliation Service then intervened in an effort to get labor and management to agree. This failing, the President on December 22, 1951, referred the dispute to the Federal Wage Stabilization Board to investigate and make recommendations for fair and equitable terms of settlement. This Board's report resulted in no settlement. On April 4, 1952, the Union gave notice of a nationwide strike called to begin at 12:01 A.M. April 9. The indispensability of steel as a component of substantially all weapons and other war materials led the President to believe that the proposed work stoppage would immediately jeopardize our national defense and that governmental seizure of the steel mills was necessary in order to assure the continued availability of steel. Reciting these considerations for his action, the President, a few hours before the strike was to begin, issued Executive Order 10340. . . . The Order directed the Secretary of Commerce to take possession of most of the steel mills and keep them running. . . .

The President's power, if any, to issue the order must stem either from an act of Congress or from the Constitution itself. There is no statute that expressly authorizes the President to take possession of property as he did here. Nor is there any act of Congress to which our attention has been directed from which such a power can fairly be implied. Indeed, we do not understand the Government to rely on statutory authorization for this seizure. There are two statues which do authorize the President to take both personal and real property under certain conditions. However, the Government admits that these conditions were not met and that the President's order was not rooted in either of the statutes. The Government refers to the seizure provisions of one of these statutes (sec. 201 (b) of the Defense Production Act) as "much too cumbersome, involved, and time-consuming for the crisis which was at hand."

Moreover, the use of the seizure technique to solve labor disputes in order to prevent work stoppages was not only unauthorized by any congressional enactment; prior to this controversy, Congress had refused to adopt that method of settling labor disputes. When the Taft-Hartley Act was under consideration in 1947, Congress rejected an amendment which would have authorized such governmental seizures in cases of emergency. Apparently it was thought that the technique of seizure, like that of compulsory arbitration, would interfere with the process of collective bargaining. . . .

It is clear that if the President had authority to issue the order he did, it must be found in some provisions of the Consti-

tution. And it is not claimed that express constitutional language grants this power to the President. The contention is that presidential power should be implied from the aggregate of his powers under the Constitution. Particular reliance is placed on provisions in Article II which say that "the executive Power shall be vested in a President" . . .; that "he shall take Care that the Laws be faithfully executed"; and that he "shall be Commander in Chief of the Army and Navy of the United States."

The order cannot properly be sustained as an exercise of the President's military power as Commander in Chief of the Armed Forces. The Government attempts to do so by citing a number of cases upholding broad powers in military commanders engaged in day-to-day fighting in a theater of war. Such cases need not concern us here. Even though "theater of war" be an expanding concept, we cannot with faithfulness to our constitutional system hold that the Commander in Chief of the Armed Forces has the ultimate power as such to take possession of private property in order to keep labor disputes from stopping production. This is a job for the Nation's lawmakers, not for its military authorities.

Nor can the seizure order be sustained because of the several constitutional provisions that grant executive power to the President. In the framework of our Constitution, the President's power to see that the laws are faithfully executed refutes the idea that he is to be a law maker. The Constitution limits his functions in the law-making process to the recommending of laws he thinks wise and the vetoing of laws he thinks bad. And the Constitution is neither silent nor equivocal about who shall make laws which the President is to execute. The first section of the first article says that "All legislative Powers herein granted shall be vested in a Congress of the United States. . . ." After granting many powers to the Congress, Article I goes on to provide that Congress may" make all Laws which shall be necessary and proper for carrying into Execution the foregoing Powers and all other Powers vested by this Constitution in the Government of the United States, or in any Department or Officer thereof."

The President's order does not direct that a congressional policy be executed in a manner prescribed by the President. The preamble of the order itself, like that of many statutes, sets out reasons why the President believes certain policies should be adopted, proclaims these policies as rules of conduct to be followed, and again, like a statute, authorizes a government official to promulgate additional rules and regulations consistent with the policy proclaimed and needed to carry that policy into execution. The power of Congress to adopt such public policies as those proclaimed by the order is beyond question. It can authorize the taking of private property for public use. It can make laws regulating the relationships between employers and employees,

prescribing rules designed to settle labor disputes, and fixing wages and working conditions in certain fields of our economy. The Constitution does not subject this law-making power of Congress to presidential or military supervision or control.

It is said that other Presidents without congressional authority have taken possession of private business enterprises in order to settle labor disputes. But even if this be true, Congress has not thereby lost its exclusive constitutional authority to make laws necessary and proper to carry out the powers vested by the Constitution "in the Government of the United States, or any Department or Officer thereof."

The Founders of this Nation entrusted the law-making power to the Congress alone in both good and bad times. It would do no good to recall the historical events, the fears of power and the hopes for freedom that lay behind their choice. Such a review would but confirm our holding that this seizure order cannot stand.

6

Taft-Hartley Act Appraised

☆ *The National Labor Relations Act of 1947 continued to be controversial throughout the Truman and into the Eisenhower administrations. A dozen years after its passage, however, the evidence indicated that the law was neither as severe as labor had feared nor as successful as business had hoped.** ☆

Twelve years have elapsed since Congress enacted the Labor Management Relations Act in 1947. This law, popularly known as the Taft-Hartley Act, replaced the Wagner Act of 1935, one of the corner stones of the New Deal legislation. . . .

The Wagner Act kept the government out of active regulation of collective bargaining. It was assumed that if workers were guaranteed the right to organize and to engage in collective bargaining through their representatives, unions and management would resolve the problems of industrial relations. In contrast, the authors of the Taft-Hartley Act held that government regulation of collective bargaining was needed to protect the interests of individual workers, management and the public. In 1947, the Eightieth Congress replaced the Wagner Act with the Taft-Hartley Act.

The new act retained the Wagner Act provisions pertaining to the right of workers to organize and to engage in collective bargaining under government protection. But in order to protect the various inter-

* From Sar A. Levitan, "Labor under the Taft-Hartley Act," *Current History*, XXXVII (September, 1959), pp. 160-164. Used by permission.

ests of the parties concerned with collective bargaining, Congress added numerous new provisions regulating the content and procedures of labor-management relations. Underlying these new provisions were the following three assumptions:

(1) Workers need the protection of the law against abuse of power by labor leaders.

(2) The business community needs governmental assistance to equalize the alleged excessive powers that unions possess in collective bargaining.

(3) The public at large needs protection against work stoppages which may threaten the very health and safety of the community.

In line with the first assumption, the Taft-Hartley Act contains a number of provisions regulating the internal affairs and administration of unions. The aim of these provisions is presumably to guarantee the rights of workers in relation to their unions.

In order to protect the right of a worker to secure new employment, the Act banned closed shop agreements, which limited hiring to union members only. However, union shop agreement remained legal. Under this type of agreement an employer may hire any worker, but the new employee is required to join the union within a specified period of time, usually 30 days after hiring. To secure a union shop a majority of employees had in the first place to select the union to represent them in collective bargaining. A special provision of the Act (Section 14b) permitted states to outlaw union shops or any other form of union security. . . .

The Taft-Hartley Act specifically guarantees the rights of a labor organization to prescribe its own rules with respect to the acquisition or retention of membership [Sec. 8b (1) (A)]. But within this framework, the Act sets forth certain limitations and restrictions upon union activities designed to protect the rights of individual workers from union coercion or restraint. Congress qualified the rights of unions to determine eligibility for membership where a union shop is in effect. The union may not force an employer to discriminate against an employee on any "ground other than his failure to tender the periodic dues and the initiation fees uniformly required as a condition of acquiring or retaining membership" [Sec. 8 (b) (2)].

The Act also prohibits unions from charging excessive or discriminatory initiation fees or dues. By paying his initiation fee and dues an employee fulfills his obligations to a union under the provisions of the Act, which prohibits discrimination by an employer against an employee for nonmembership in a union when a union shop is in effect.

Before a union becomes eligible for protection by the National Labor Relations Board, a local union and the national or international organization with which it is affiliated must register and file certain reports. The union must file with the United States Secretary of Labor detailed statements showing the names of its officers, procedures by which they were elected and the compensation of the principal officers, the minimum and maximum initiation fees and dues, and a detailed financial statement of union receipts and disbursements. These reports must be filed annually and all the members of the union must be furnished copies of the financial statement. . . .

About a third of the 72,000 labor organizations in the nation currently file financial reports under the Taft-Hartley Act, and altogether about 41,000 organizations have filed at least one report since 1947. Many local or national unions that have refrained from filing reports do not have any cause to resort to the N.L.R.B. This applies particularly to government employees' unions. In addition, the United Mine Workers and the Typographical Union have chosen to carry on without the assistance of the N.L.R.B.

In 1957 the Department of Labor revised the financial forms that unions are required to file. The new forms requiring more detailed information resulted from the McClellan Committee disclosures. Union spokesmen have asserted that the filing requirements, as required by the recent revisions, impose an undue and largely unnecessary burden. The problem is particularly apparent in the case of smaller locals with no officials technically competent to supply information requested in the forms. Consequently, they are forced to spend part of their funds for specialized aid. . . .

Only time will tell whether in the future the new detailed financial reports required of unions that use the services of the N.L.R.B. will eliminate or reduce the misappropriation or misuse of union funds, such as has been disclosed by the McClellan Committee. The fact is that the Teamsters, Engineers and Bakers did comply with the earlier Taft-Hartley reporting requirements, but this did not prevent the misuse of union funds.

In addition, each officer of the union and of the parent body must file annually an affidavit declaring that he is not a member of the Communist party and that he does not believe in and is not a member or supporter of an organization that believes in or teaches the overthrow of the United States government by force or any illegal methods.

The intent of this provision was to aid members in Communist-dominated unions to clean their organizations of Communist leaders and to eliminate political strikes. Opponents of the measure felt that it offered a gratuitous insult to American labor leaders to compel them to sign affidavits which impugn their loyalty and that the filing of affidavits would not achieve the objective of driving Communists (or pro-Communists) out of union office. In the application of the provision, the N.L.R.B. took the position that a union fulfills the non-Communist affidavit requirement when all the officers of the union sign the form even if there is cause to question the veracity of some signatories. Fraudulent cases are handled by the Department of Justice.

The effectiveness of the non-Communist affidavit has been open to question. Certainly Communist influence in unions has been appreciably weakened since the passage of the Taft-Hartley Act. But it is doubtful whether the requirement to file an affidavit has materially contributed to this development. Possibly in a number of cases Communist union leaders have had to relinquish their positions, but in some instances, it has been claimed, they continued to dominate unions, while other members "fronted" for them. The fact that known Communist leaders could not continue in a position of leadership in unions must have helped other unions take over locals from Communist-dominated organizations. But most of the ten Communist-dominated unions that the C.I.O. expelled in 1949 and 1950 had filed non-Communist affidavits. It is doubtful, therefore, whether the Act has been instrumental in helping unions rid themselves of Communist domination where such leadership had succeeded in infiltrating American unions.

Finally, the Taft-Hartley Act regulates the internal affairs of unions by curbing their political activities. The act prohibits unions from making contributions or expenditures in connection with federal elections, political conventions or party caucuses. The restrictions upon union financial contributions for political purposes have been justified on the basis that American labor has refused to express allegiance to any political party, and the expenditures of union funds for political purposes is not a proper area of union activity. According to this view, union contributions for political purposes constitute an abridgement of the rights of those members who oppose these expenditures. Business corporations also are prohibited from making political contributions.

It appears questionable whether the prohibition has appreciably prevented the use of union funds for political activities. The courts have chosen to construe the section rather narrowly. Moreover, the Taft-Hartley Act imposes no limitations upon educational activities, which many unions have interpreted rather broadly. The distinction between political education and union contributions for political purposes is rather a hazy one. So, although unions cannot contribute to political campaigns, they conduct educational activities which may be of considerable political significance.

The major provisions aimed at protecting management against unfair labor practices deal with restrictions upon secondary boycotts, picketing, featherbedding and jurisdictional disputes.

A secondary boycott is an attempt by a union to influence an employer to exert economic pressure upon another employer with whom the union has a dispute. The Taft-Hartley Act contains a blanket prohibition against this type of boycott. But in actual industrial relations it has been frequently very difficult to differentiate between a primary and a secondary boycott.

The United States Supreme Court has found that to ban all secondary boycotts would prevent unions from exerting pressure on employers with whom the unions have primary disputes. Consequently a number of secondary boycotts have been held legal under Supreme Court rulings. Whether additional and more precise prohibition of secondary boycotts is desirable has remained a bone of contention. Moreover, the justification for secondary boycotts is that the employer against whom the union exercises pressure is not necessarily an innocent bystander in the conflict between the union and the other employer. . . .

Another issue deals with the right of a union to picket an establishment where the union does not represent the employees. The Taft-Hartley Act and National Labor Relations Board interpretations provide for specific procedures under which a union can establish the claim that it represents a majority of employees in a given establishment. Once a union establishes that it represents a majority of the employees it wins the right to bargain for them and to picket the premises, if an amicable settlement is not reached. . . .

Whether unions should be allowed to picket the premises of an employer when the employees have not shown prior interest in being represented by the union has been debated for years. Frequently this is the only means by which a union can organize non-union employees. . . .

Opponents of this type of picketing maintain that it should be outlawed. They assert that the law provides for an orderly procedure by which the union can organize employees and establish the right to represent them. . . .

Featherbedding refers to the practice of some unions to require employers to pay for unnecessary work or to hire an excessive number of employees. The Taft-Hartley Act prohibits featherbedding devices by unions. But this provision has rarely been enforced since this is a highly technical subject. In most cases it is difficult for an outsider to determine what constitutes featherbedding devices and the courts have usually refused to determine the number of employees needed to perform a given task and what constitutes useful or needed work.

Another Taft-Hartley provision, aimed at protecting employers, bans jurisdictional strikes. This type of strike occurs when two different unions attempt to organize the same group of employees or claim the right to perform the same work. In such cases the employer is frequently an innocent victim in a strife between unions. When the dispute is between two unions over the claim to perform a certain type of work, the National Labor Relations Board is authorized to determine to what union the work is to be assigned, unless the unions can settle their differences without governmental interference.

Jurisdictional disputes have been common in the construction industry. The ban on jurisdictional disputes and the authority given to the N.L.R.B. to resolve these disputes have stimulated unions to set up private machinery to settle jurisdictional differences.

The Taft-Hartley Act recognizes the public interest in strike stoppages by establishing a special procedure for regulating work stoppages which threaten the "national health and safety." The Act authorizes the President of the United States to determine when a national emergency dispute exists. He then appoints a special board of inquiry, which makes a preliminary report to the President. Upon receiving the board's report, the President may instruct the Attorney General to seek an injunction which would prohibit the work stoppage for 80 days.

If the dispute is not settled within 60 days, the special board of inquiry reports to the President the issues involved in the dispute and the employer's last offer. During the succeeding 15 days, the National Labor Relations Board polls the workers involved in the dispute as to whether the employer's offer is acceptable to them. After a total of 80 days the injunction is dissolved and the work stoppage may be renewed. The President then may report to Congress the outcome of the procedings with or without his recommendations as to the action needed to resolve the dispute.

In the 12 years since the enactment of the Taft-Hartley Act the emergency procedure has been invoked 15 times; ten times by President Truman and five times by President Eisenhower. In 4 of the 15 cases strikes occurred after the 80-day injunction had expired and several other cases were not settled during the mandatory cooling-off period. . . .

Conclusion

A dozen years have elapsed since the passage of the Labor Management Relations Act. It was enacted in a charged atmosphere, full of recriminations. Labor spokesmen referred to the law as the "slave labor act." Experience has shown that the fears of labor leaders about the impact of the act were exaggerated. Labor has dropped its adamant insistence that the act must be repealed and has suggested that it be amended. On the other hand, even the sponsors of Taft-Hartley have conceded that many of its provisions were poorly conceived and that the act needs revision.

7

American Economic Progress

☆ *During the 1952 presidential campaign the Democratic slogan was "you never had it so good." The final Economic Report of President Truman of January 14, 1953, revealed the basis for this contention. While the report did indicate that the nation had found its way back to prosperity, there was some dispute as to what was responsible.* * ☆

The Nation's progress during this past quarter-century is evident in the figures which sum up total economic activity.

In 1929, the output of all goods and services was 172 billion dollars; in 1952, total output amounted to 345 billion dollars—measured in both cases in uniform 1952 prices. Industrial production has doubled, and agricultural output has risen about 50 percent.

Last year, on the average, more than 61 million workers had civilian jobs, compared with almost 48 million in 1929. Both were good years for employment. In 1952, however, the average individual worked fewer hours—and produced more goods. From 1929 to 1952, the length of the workweek for all types of activity dropped from about 48 to 40 hours, but each worker turned out on the average 80 percent more goods and services. This greater yield reflects more and better equipment, and higher skills, than existed 25 years ago. Invention and business initiative have more than kept up with the

* From *The Economic Report of the President, Transmitted To The Congress, January 14, 1953,* Washington, 1953, pp. 1-7.

rise in the number of men and women seeking work, and have made it possible for them to find better jobs.

While we have been producing more for consumers, we have at the same time been adding to equipment on farms and in factories. In 1952, for example, we spent about 26 billion dollars for machines and other kinds of durable equipment, compared with a little more than 11 billion dollars in 1929, both measured in 1952 prices.

Vast resource development projects and conservation programs have been undertaken in the past quarter-century, some public, some private, and many a mixture of the two. Public construction expenditures for flood control, navigation improvements, agricultural land reclamation, hydro-electric power facilities, and soil and forest conservation have increased more than 300 percent in real terms. Multiple-purpose development of the Tennessee, Columbia, and other rivers has been far advanced. Huge additional amounts are being invested in atomic energy. Private mining, timber, and other concerns have increasingly adopted conservation practices, and have invested heavily in research and development. Individual farmers, frequently aided by the Government, have greatly enlarged their investment in their own land. Production and consumption of nearly all raw materials have increased since 1929. These developments have enormously enlarged the productive power of our factories and farms, helped to power and equip the American home with the most modern conveniences, and correspondingly lifted the standard of living.

The Nation's progress is shown also in greatly increased earnings and improved living standards. In 1929, average annual income after taxes was a little more than $1,000 per capita, while last year the average was about $1,500—again measured in 1952 prices. It should be noted that, while the real buying power of individuals was rising, the population of the United States increased by about 35 million. Our economy now provides much more for many more people.

The greatly improved living standards which have been achieved during the past quarter-century are evident in more tangible data than the number of dollars earned or spent.

In 1929, there were 23 million automobiles in use, and in 1952 there were 44 million. In the same span of time, the number of homes with a mechanical refrigerator increased from about 10 to 80 percent. The number with radios increased from 40 to 96 percent, and 40 percent now have television sets. Compared with 10 percent in 1929, nearly 90 percent of all farm are now electrified.

During the era as a whole, we have built 12 million new nonfarm homes, most of them since World War II. Home ownership increased from 48 percent of all families in 1930 to 55 percent in 1950. Terms of housing finance have improved greatly, bringing home ownership within the reach of lower income groups, and also facilitat-

ing construction of apartments and other houses for rent. In the blighted sections of cities, a hopeful number of slum clearance and redevelopment projects both public and private have been undertaken, though far from enough.

And the record has not been written in total quantities alone, whether of dollars, automobiles, or houses. The products of our economy are now far better distributed than they used to be. Adequate statistics do not go back to 1929. But since 1935-36, the real incomes of families and single persons in the lowest two-fifths of the income range have increased 90 percent, while the increase in the top fifth has been about 40 percent. This improved distribution is not only a mark of social progress and increasing human contentment; it is also a vital underpinning of sustained and advancing general prosperity for all sectors of the economy.

Improved and more widely available education, medical care, and economic security are among the cherished features of the American way of life. So are the basic freedoms, full enjoyment of which depends upon progressive removal of discriminatory practices in the market place and elsewhere. . . .

Total educational expenditures, in constant prices, have about doubled since 1929. Capital outlays for public schools, again in constant prices, have gone up 63 percent in the same period. Teachers are better trained, curriculums have improved, and schools are designed for more effective learning.

Total per capita expenditures for health and medical services have nearly doubled during this era, after adjusting for price change. Outlays for hospital construction, both public and private, have risen about 83 percent. There is one doctor for every 740 persons now, compared with one for every 800 in 1929. Expenditures for medical research mounted to nearly 200 million dollars in 1952. The quality of medical care has improved with the development of new drugs, better techniques of surgery and hospital treatment, and the extension of preventive medicine.

It has been essential to do justice to those who have fought to defend us against enemies. Since 1929, the number of veterans has increased from 4.7 million to 19.7 million. Veterans and their families now comprise 40 percent of the total civilian population. Some 7.8 million veterans have received education and training aid since World War II, and an additional 600,000 have received vocational rehabilitation training. Increasing numbers of Korean war veterans will be receiving similar help. Unemployment insurance has been paid to about 9 million veterans. Farm and business loans, and housing mortgage guarantees and loans, have also helped veterans.

Progress in social security has been significant, with the advent in the mid-1930's of old-age insurance, unemployment insurance, and new and improved public assistance programs. The Federal old-age and survivors insurance program covers 45 million persons, while Federal-State public assistance is available for dependent children, the blind, needy old persons, and the permanently and totally disabled. The Federal-State unemployment insurance system now covers about 35 million jobs.

The eventual elimination of discrimination based on race, religion, economic status, or section of the country is a continuing objective of national policy. Discrimination is in part economic in origin, and can be reduced by economic measures. Throughout the past quarter-century, particularly as part of the economic and social reforms of the thirties, great though insufficient gains have been made.

Workers have been guaranteed the right to organize and bargain collectively. The Fair Labor Standards Act established the principle of minimum wages and maximum hours. Fair employment practices acts have been passed in some 12 States.

Economic justice for American agriculture has advanced tremendously since the period just before the great depression. Vast conservation programs, intensified agricultural research, loans and assistance to farm families, especially low income families, price supports to reduce instability, and rural electrification have combined to improve rural life. Since 1929, per capita farm income in constant dollars has increased about 80 percent. The gain here has been relatively large, because the farmer had been left so far behind during the uneven prosperity of the late 1920's.

Opportunities for business have also widened, particularly as a result of the unprecedented period of prosperity since around 1940. There were only a third as many business failures in 1952 as in 1929, even though the number of business firms in operation has increased by one-third. In this quarter-century, while wholesale prices rose 80 percent and consumers' prices 55 percent, corporate profits rose more than 300 percent before taxes and more than 100 percent after taxes.

Working conditions have benefited enormously under the joint impact of union efforts, business policies of sharing productivity gains, and government programs. For factory workers with three dependents, the increase in average weekly take-home pay (after allowing for the taxes paid by a family of this size) has been from $39 to about $63, measured in 1952 prices.

8

The Civil Rights Committee

☆ *During the New Deal and especially during World War II, minority groups were encouraged in the struggle to secure their civil rights. President Truman proved to be sympathetic to the movement for racial equality under law. A fundamental program for civil rights progress was outlined in the report of the President's Committee on Civil Rights in 1947.* * ☆

"Man is endowed by his Creator with certain inalienable rights. Among these are life, liberty, and the pursuit of happiness. To secure these rights, *governments are instituted among men.*"

THE ESSENTIAL RIGHTS

The rights essential to the citizen in a free society can be described in different words and in varying orders. The three great rights of the Declaration of Independence have just been mentioned. Another noble statement is made in the Bill of Rights of our Constitution. A more recent formulation is found in the Four Freedoms.

Four basic rights have seemed important to this Committee and have influenced its labors. We believe that each of these rights is essential to the well-being of the individual and to the progress of society.

1. **The Right to Safety and Security of the Person.** Freedom can exist only where the citizen is assured that his person is

* From *To Secure These Rights, The Report of The President's Committee On Civil Rights*, pp. 5-9, 20, 23, 53, 55, 57-58. Published by Simon & Schuster, New York, 1947.

secure against bondage, lawless violence, and arbitrary arrest and punishment. Freedom from slavery in all its forms is clearly necessary if all men are to have equal opportunity to use their talents and to lead worthwhile lives. Moreover, to be free, men must be subject to discipline by society only for commission of offenses clearly defined by law and only after trial by due process of law. Where the administration of justice is discriminatory, no man can be sure of security. Where the threat of violence by private persons or mobs exists, a cruel inhibition of the sense of freedom of activity and security of the person inevitably results. Where a society permits private and arbitrary violence to be done to its members, its own integrity is inevitably corrupted. It cannot permit human beings to be imprisoned or killed in the absence of due process of law without degrading its entire fabric.

2. **The Right of Citizenship and its Privileges.** Since it is a purpose of government in a democracy to regulate the activity of each man in the interest of all men, it follows that every mature and

responsible person must be able to enjoy full citizenship and have an equal voice in his government. Because the right to participate in the political process is customarily limited to citizens there can be no denial of access to citizenship based upon race, color, creed, or national origin. Denial of citizenship for these reasons cheapens the personality of those who are confined to this inferior status and endangers the whole concept of a democratic society.

To deny qualified citizens the right to vote while others exercise it is to do violence to the principle of freedom and equality. Without the right to vote, the individual loses his voice in the group effort and is subjected to rule by a body from which he has been excluded. Likewise, the right of the individual to vote is important to the group itself. Democracy assumes that the majority is more likely as a general rule to make decisions which are wise and desirable from the point of view of the interests of the whole society than is any minority. Every time a qualified person is denied a voice in public affairs, one of the components of a potential majority is lost, and the formation of a sound public policy is endangered.

To the citizen in a democracy, freedom is a precious possession. Accordingly, all able-bodied citizens must enjoy the right to serve the nation and the cause of freedom in time of war. Any attempt to curb the right to fight in its defense can only lead the citizen to question the worth of the society in which he lives. A sense of frustration is created which is wholly alien to the normal emotions of a free man. In particular, any discrimination which, while imposing an obligation, prevents members of minority groups from rendering full military service in defense of their country is for them a peculiarly humiliating badge of inferiority. The nation also suffers a loss of manpower and is unable to marshal maximum strength at a moment when such strength is most needed.

3. The Right to Freedom of Conscience and Expression. In a free society there is faith in the ability of the people to make sound, rational judgments. But such judgments are possible only where the people have access to all relevant facts and to all prevailing interpretations of the facts. How can such judgments be formed on a sound basis if arguments, viewpoints, or opinions are arbitrarily suppressed? How can the concept of the marketplace of thought in which truth ultimately prevails retain its validity if the thought of certain individuals is denied the right of circulation? The Committee reaffirms our tradition that freedom of expression may be curbed by law only where the danger to the well-being of society is clear and present.

Our forefathers fought bloody wars and suffered torture and death for the right to worship God according to the varied dictates of conscience. Complete religious liberty has been accepted as an unquestioned personal freedom since our Bill of Rights was adopted. We have insisted only that religious freedom may not be pleaded as an excuse for criminal or clearly antisocial conduct.

4. The Right to Equality of Opportunity. It is not enough that full and equal membership in society entitles the individual to an equal voice in the control of his government; it must also give him the right to enjoy the benefits of society and to contribute to its progress. The opportunity of each individual to obtain useful employment, and to have access to services in the fields of education, housing, health, recreation and transportation, whether available free or at a price, must be provided with complete disregard for race, color, creed, and national origin. Without this equality of opportunity the individual is deprived of the chance to develop his potentialities and to share the fruits of society. The group also suffers through the loss of the contributions which might have been made by persons excluded from the main channels of social and economic activity. . . .

THE CONDITION OF OUR RIGHTS

1. The Right to Safety and Security of the Person. . . . The [lynching] record for 1947 is incomplete. There has been one lynching, one case in which the victim escaped, and other instances where mobs have been unable to accomplish their purpose. On February 17, 1947, a Negro youth named Willie Earle, accused of fatally stabbing a taxi driver in the small city of Greenville, South Carolina, was removed from jail by a mob, viciously beaten and finally shot to death. In an unusual and impressive instance of state prosecution, 31 men were tried for this crime. All were acquitted on the evening of May 21, 1947. Early the next morning, in Jackson, North Carolina, another Negro youth, Godwin Bush, arrested on a charge of approaching a white woman, was removed from a local jail by a mob, after having been exhibited through the town by the sheriff. Bush succeeded in escaping from his abductors, and, after hiding for two days in nearby woods, was able to surrender himself safely into the custody of FBI agents and officers of the state. The Committee finds it encouraging to note that the Governor of North Carolina has made vigorous efforts to bring to justice those reponsible for this attempted lynching.

While available statistics show that, decade by decade, lynchings have decreased, this Committee has found that in the year 1947 lynching remains one of the most serious threats to the civil rights of Americans. It is still possible for a mob to abduct and murder a person in some sections of the country with almost certain assurance of escaping punishment for the crime. The decade from 1936 through 1946 saw at least 43 lynchings. No person

received the death penalty, and the majority of the guilty persons were not even prosecuted. . . .

4. The Right to Equality of Opportunity. . . . In private business, in government, and in labor unions, the war years saw a marked advance both in hiring policies and in the removal of on-the-job discriminatory practices. Several factors contributed to this progress. The short labor market, the sense of unity among the people, and the leadership provided by the government all helped bring about a lessening of unfair employment pracices. Yet we did not eliminate discrimination in employment. The Final Report of the federal Fair Employment Practice Committee, established in 1941 by President Roosevelt to eliminate discrimination in both government and private employment related to the war effort, makes this clear.

Four out of five cases which arose during the life of the Committee, concerned Negroes. However, many other minorities have suffered from discriminatory employment practices. The FEPC reports show that eight percent of the Committee's docket involved complaints of discrimination because of creed, and 70 percent of these concerned Jews. It should be noted that FEPC jurisdiction did not extend to financial institutions and the professions, where discrimination against Jews is especially prevalent. Witnesses before this Committee, representing still other minority groups, testified as follows:

The Japanese Americans: "We know, too, what discrimination in employment is. We know what it means to be unacceptable to union membership; what it means to be the last hired and first fired; what it means to have to work harder and longer for less wages. We know these things because we have been forced to experience them."

The Mexican Americans: "We opened an employment bureau (to help Mexican

Americans) in our office last year for San Antonio. We wrote to business firms throughout the city, most of whom didn't answer. We would call certain firms and say that we heard they had an opening for a person in a stock room or some other type of work; or I would go myself. But thinking I was the same in prejudice as they, they would say, 'You know we never hire Mexicans.' "

The American Indians: "As with the Negroes, Indians are employed readily when there is a shortage of labor and they can't get anyone else. When times get better, they are the first ones to be released. . . ."

If he can get himself hired, the minority worker often finds that he is being paid less than other workers. This wage discrimination is sharply evident in studies made of individual cities and is especially exaggerated in the South. A survey, conducted by the Research and Information Department of the American Federation of Labor shows that the average weekly income of white veterans ranges from 30 to 78 percent above the average income of Negro veterans in 26 commu-

nities, 25 of them in the South. In Houston, for example, 36,000 white veterans had a weekly income of $49 and 4,000 Negro veterans had average incomes of $30 —a difference of 63 percent. These differences are not caused solely by the relegation of the Negroes to lower types of work, but reflect wage discriminations between whites and Negroes for the same type of work. The Final Report of the FEPC states that the hourly wage rates for Negro common laborer averaged 47.4 cents in July, 1942, as compared with 65.3 cents for white laborers.

Nor can the disparity be blamed entirely on differences in education and training. The 1940 census reveals that the median annual income of Negro high school graduates was only $775 as compared with $1,454 for the white high school graduate; that the median Negro college graduate received $1,074 while his white counterpart was earning $2,046; that while 23.3 percent of white high school graduates had wage or salary incomes over $2,000, but four percent of Negro graduates achieved that level. . . .

9

The Danger Within

☆ *The concern over internal subversion increased progressively following revelations of Communist espionage after World War II. This concern reached a high plateau during the period 1950-1955 as the Cold War intensified. The ideas of the more rabid anti-Communists were reflected in the activities of Senator Joseph R. McCarthy of Wisconsin and in part put into law in the McCarran Internal Security Act, which was passed over President Truman's veto in the fall of 1950.* ☆

(a) INTERNAL SECURITY ACT OF 1950*

Section 1. (a) This title may be cited as the "Subversive Activities Control Act of 1950".

(b) Nothing in this Act shall be construed to authorize, require, or establish military or civilian censorship or in any way to limit or infringe upon freedom of the press or of speech as guaranteed by the Constitution of the United States and no regulation shall be promulgated hereunder having that effect. . . .

Sec. 3. For the purposes of this title—. . . .

(3) The term "Communist-action organization" means—

(a) any organization in the United States (other than a diplomatic representative or mission of a foreign government accredited as such by the Department of State) which (i) is substantially directed, dominated, or controlled by the foreign government or foreign organization controlling the world Communist movement

referred to in section 2 of this title, and (ii) operates primarily to advance the objectives of such world Communist movement as referred to in section 2 of this title; and

(b) any section, branch, fraction, or cell of any organization defined in subparagraph (a) of this paragraph which has not complied with the registration requirements of this title.

(4) The term "Communist-front organization" means any organization in the United States (other than a Communist-action organization as defined in paragraph (3) of this section) which (A) is substantially directed, dominated, or controlled by a Communist-action organization, and (B) is primarily operated for the purpose of giving aid and support to a Communist-action organization, a Communist foreign government, or the world Communist movement referred to in section 2 of this title.

(5) The term "Communist organization" means a Communist-action organi-

* From 64 U.S. Stats. 987.

zation or a Communist-front organization. . . .

Sec. 4. (a) It shall be unlawful for any person knowingly to combine, conspire, or agree with any other person to perform any act which would substantially contribute to the establishment within the United States of a totalitarian dictatorship, as defined in paragraph (15) of section 3 of this title, the direction and control of which is to be vested in, or exercised by or under the domination or control of, any foreign government, foreign organization, or foreign individual: *Provided, however,* That this subsection shall not apply to the proposal of a constitutional amendment. . . .

(d) Any person who violates any provision of this section shall, upon conviction thereof, be punished by a fine of not more than $10,000, or imprisonment for not more than ten years, or by both such fine and such imprisonment, and shall, moreover, be thereafter ineligible to hold any office, or place of honor, profit, or trust created by the Constitution or laws of the United States. . . .

(f) Neither the holding of office nor membership in any Communist organization by any person shall constitute per se a violation of subsection (a) or subsection (c) of this section or of any other criminal statute. The fact of the registration of any person under section 7 or section 8 of this title as an officer or member of any Communist organization shall not be received in evidence against such person in any prosecution for any alleged violation of subsection (a) or subsection (c) of this section or for any alleged violation of any other criminal statute.

Sec. 5. (a) When a Communist organization, as defined in paragraph (5) of section 3 of this title, is registered or there is in effect a final order of the Board requiring such organization to register, it shall be unlawful—

(1) For any member of such organization, with knowledge or notice that such organization is so registered or that such order has become final—

(A) in seeking, accepting, or holding any nonelective office or employment under the United States, to conceal or fail to disclose the fact that he is a member of such organization; or

(B) to hold any nonelective office or employment under the United States; or

(C) in seeking, accepting, or holding employment in any defense facility, to conceal or fail to disclose the fact that he is a member of such organization; or

(D) if such organization is a Communist-action organization, to engage in any employment in any defense facility.

(2) For any officer or employee of the United States or of any defense facility, with knowledge or notice that such organization is so registered or that such order has become final—

(A) to contribute funds or services to such organization; or

(B) to advise, counsel or urge any person, with knowledge or notice that such person is a member of such organization, to perform, or to omit to perform, any act if such act or omission would constitute a violation of any provision of subparagraph (1) of this subsection. . . .

Sec. 6. (a) When a Communist organization as defined in paragraph (5) of section 3 of this title is registered, or there is in effect a final order of the Board requiring such organization to register, it shall be unlawful for any member of such organization, with knowledge or notice that such organization is so registered or that such order has become final—

(1) to make application for a passport, or the renewal of a passport, to be issued or renewed by or under the authority of the United States; or

(2) to use or attempt to use any such passport. . . .

Sec. 7. (a) Each Communist-action organization (including any organization required, by a final order of the Board, to register as a Communist-action organization) shall . . . register with the Attorney General, on a form prescribed by him by regulations, as a Communist-action organization. . . .

(c) The registration required by subsection (a) or (b) shall be made—

(1) in the case of an organization which is a Communist-action organization or a Communist-front organization on the date of enactment of this title, within thirty days after such date;

(2) in the case of an organization becoming a Communist-action organization or a Communist-front organization after the date of the enactment of this title, within thirty days after such organization becomes a Communist-action organizaion or a Communist-front organization, as the case may be; and

(3) in the case of an organization which by a final order of the Board is required to register, within thirty days after such order becomes final . . . .

Sec. 8. (a) Any individual who is or becomes a member of any organization concerning which (1) there is in effect a final order of the Board requiring such organization to register under section 7 (a) of this title as a Communist-action organization, (2) more than thirty days have elapsed since such order has become final, and (3) such organization is not registered under section 7 of this title as a Communist-action organization, shall within sixty days after said order has become final, or within thirty days after becoming a member of such organization, whichever is later, register with the Attorney General as a member of such organization. . . .

Sec. 10. It shall be unlawful for any organization which is registered under section 7, or for any organization with respect to which there is in effect a final order of the Board requiring it to register under section 7, or for any person acting for or on behalf of any such organization—

(1) to transmit or cause to be transmitted, through the United States mails or by any means or instrumentality of interstate or foreign commerce, any publication which is intended to be, or which it is reasonable to believe is intended to be, circulated or disseminated among two or more persons, unless such publication, and any envelope, wrapper, or other container in which it is mailed or otherwise circulated or transmitted, bears the following, printed in such manner as may be provided in regulations prescribed by the Attorney General, with the name of the organization appearing in lieu of the blank: "Disseminated by —————, a Communist organization" or

(2) to broadcast or cause to be broadcast any matter over any radio or television station in the United States, unless such matter is preceded by the following statement, with the name of the organization being stated in place of the blank: "The following program is sponsored by —————, a Communist organization."

Sec. 11. (a) Notwithstanding any other provision of law, no deduction for Federal income-tax purposes shall be allowed in the case of a contribution to or for the use of any organization if at the time of the making of such contribution (1) such organization is registered under section 7, or (2) there is in effect a final order of the Board requiring such organization to register under section 7.

(b) No organization shall be entitled to exemption from Federal income tax, under section 101 of the Internal Revenue Code, for any taxable year if at any time during such taxable year (1) such organization is registered under section 7, or (2) there is in effect a final order of the Board requiring such organization to register under section 7.

Sec. 12. (a) There is hereby established a board, to be known as the Subversive Activities Control Board, which shall be composed of five members, who shall be appointed by the President, by and with the advice and consent of the Senate. . . .

(e) It shall be the duty of the Board—

(1) Upon application made by the Attorney General under section 13 (a) of this title, or by any organization under section 13 (b) of this title, to determine whether any organization is a "Communist-action organization" within the meaning of paragraph (3) of section 3 of this title, or a "Communist-front organization" within the meaning of paragraph (4) of section 3 of this title; and

(2) upon application made by the Attorney General under section 13 (a) of this title, or by any individual under section 13 (b) of this title, to determine whether any individual is a member of any Communist-action organization registered, or by final order of the Board required to be registered, under section 7 (a) of this title. . . .

Sec. 102. (a) In the event of any one of the following:

(1) Invasion of the territory of the United States or its possessions,

(2) Declaration of war by Congress, or

(3) Insurrection within the United States in aid of a foreign enemy,

and if, upon the occurrence of one or more of the above, the President shall find that the proclamation of an emergency pursuant to this section is essential to the preservation, protection and defense of the Constitution, and to the common defense and safety of the territory and people of the United States, the President is authorized to make public proclamation of the existence of an "Internal Security Emergency. . . ."

Sec. 103. (a) Whenever there shall be in existence such an emergency, the President, acting through the Attorney General, is hereby authorized to apprehend and by order detain, pursuant to the provisions of this title, each person as to whom there is reasonable ground to believe that such person probably will engage in, or probably will conspire with others to engage in, acts of espionage or of sabotage.

(b) Any person detained hereunder (hereinafter referred to as "the detainee") shall be released from such emergency detention upon—

(1) the termination of such emergency by proclamation of the President or by concurrent resolution of the Congress;

(2) an order of release issued by the Attorney General;

(3) a final order of release after hearing by the Board of Detention Review, hereinafter established;

(4) a final order of release by a United States court, after review of the action of the Board of Detention Review, or upon a writ of habeas corpus. . . .

Sec. 104. (a) The Attorney General, or such officer or officers of the Department of Justice as he may from time to time designate, are authorized during such emergency to execute in writing and to issue—

(1) a warrant for the apprehension of each person as to whom there is reasonable ground to believe that such person probably will engage in, or probably will conspire with others to engage in, acts of espionage or sabotage; and

(2) an application for an order to be issued pursuant to subsection (d) of this section for the detention of such person for the duration of such emergency.

Each such warrant shall issue only upon probable cause, supported by oath or affirmation, and shall particularly describe the person to be apprehended or detained.

(b) RADIO ADDRESS OF SENATOR JOSEPH R. McCARTHY*

There is no reason on earth why this fight to expose and remove Communists and traitors from positions of power should be a contest between America's two great political parties. Certainly the millions of loyal American Democrats love America and despise Communist spies and saboteurs just as much as the average Republican. Certainly there is no division along party lines among the mothers and fathers and wives of the 140,000 Korean casualties whose miseries have come to them from the trickeries and betrayals of an administration whose foreign policy was so carefully shaped by the Alger Hisses, the Harry Dexter Whites, the Owen Lattimores, the Dean Achesons, the John Carter Vincents.

We should keep in mind that as of tonight we are engaged in a war which was declared against us 105 years ago—declared by Karl Marx, redeclared in 1914 by Lenin, repeatedly reaffirmed by Joseph Stalin, and approved two and a half weeks ago by high officials of the Kremlin. It is the Communist war against free men. The issue was not created by McCarthy. It was with us long before I came to Washington. It will be with us until our civilization either wins this war or is destroyed.

We should bear in mind that when that first Communist declaration of war was made 105 years ago, you could number the active Communist leaders on the fingers of both hands. At the time Truman took over the Presidency of this nation, the number of people under Communist domination was 180 million. During his term as President, the figure increased from 180 million to 800 million people. This represents the greatest victory of any brutalitarian dictatorship since time first commenced to run. Why? Is it because

Communist slavery is more attractive than the clean fresh air of freedom? Certainly not. Does the human race welcome chains? Certainly not. Then why?

The pattern of Communist conquest has been the same in every country over which the Stygian blackness of Communist night has descended. Always first the infiltration of key posts in government by Communist traitors and then the creeping paralysis of fear to speak out and expose the traitors. This fear in each country which was taken over has been engendered and nurtured not only by Communists, but also by the phoney, deluded, fuzzy-minded and egg-headed "liberals" in whose book it is a mortal sin ever to expose or criticize a Communist. Of course, it is perfectly proper for the Communist to scream lies and vituperation at anyone who hurts the Communist cause. Thus the picture has been in Hungary, Czechoslovakia, Rumania, and every other nation taken over by the black death of Communism. Thus it is in our country today. . . .

It is all a matter of cold record. The most amazing and disturbing thing about this incredibly unbelievable picture is that as the danger to this nation is slowly and laboriously exposed, instead of an admission of guilt or stupidity, Democrats from coast to coast join the chorus of the Communist *Daily Worker* and shout, "Oh, isn't this McCarthyism an awful thing?"

How many American young men have died and how many will die because of this stupidity, blindness and treason no one will ever know. But what answer do we get when it is exposed? The leader of the Democrat Party—Harry Truman—in the most intemperate language condemns the Attorney General for giving the American people the facts. He then proceeds to damn McCarthy, drawing heavily upon his repertoire of dirty names

* November 24, 1953. From *The New York Times*, November 25, 1953.

because I took some part in the exposure of the Communist infiltration of his administration.

I would not be concerned about what a defeated and discredited politician has to say, except that his leadership—if you can call it that—on the Communist issue is being followed by so many Democrats. . . .

Democrat office seekers from the Atlantic to the Pacific have been proclaiming that McCarthyism is an issue in this campaign. In a way, I guess, it is, because my position as Chairman of the Investigating Committee where I can continue to expose and dig out Communists depends upon Republican Senators being retained in office.

Therefore, if the American people agree with Truman that what he calls McCarthyism is bad, that it is wrong to dig out and expose traitors, they have a chance to get rid of me as chairman of the Investigating Committee next fall by defeating any Republican up for election.

If the American people, on the other hand, believe in the necessity of digging out and getting rid of the type of people who have been before our committee—for example, those who refuse to say whether they would sabotage our defense plants if ordered to do so by the Communist Party on the ground that the truth might send them to jail—if they believe, as I do that treason, dishonesty and stupidity, should be exposed wherever and whenever found, then their answer is to keep the Republicans in power so we may continue to clean out the Augean stables.

But now let us take a look at the Republican Party. Now that we are in office, if we are to keep faith with the American people, we must keep our own house clean. During last year's campaign and during the 1950 campaign, I perhaps spent as much time as any other man talking to the people of this nation, urging them to defeat certain Senators who were

untrue to their country—not because they were evil men, but because of the mistaken idea which they developed in the Washington atmosphere of smog that their first loyalty was to keep their party in power and then if there was any loyalty left over, they could give that to their country.

Over the past few months, I have been becoming somewhat disturbed that my party might also fall victim to the same evil which beset the Democrat Party, and did so much toward destroying this nation. I realize full well that what I am about to say will disturb some of my Republican friends—in fact, some of them have strongly urged that I avoid this matter. If I did so, however, then I could never in good faith come before the American people again. Tonight I remind those Republican friends of mine that no political party can be perfect. Your batting average cannot be 100 percent. The test in the eyes of the American people should be—are you trying to do a good job, are you honest with us, and when you make mistakes are you willing to admit those mistakes? And finally—do those in control of your party have sufficient intelligence and courage so that their batting average is high? If we do that, we are a good party; in another respect we must differ from the Truman Democrat Party which followed the theory that it was a favor to give the people an accounting of what was being done. The Republican theory must be that a detailed accounting is an absolute irrevocable right of the American people.

Before looking at some of the cases in which our batting average is zero, let me make it clear that I think the new Administration is doing a job so infinitely better than the Truman-Acheson regime that there is absolutely no comparison.

For example, while almost daily from the time I mentioned the 57 Communists and 205 security risks in government, until the time the Truman-Acheson regime was removed from office—almost daily some leader of the Democrat Party would proclaim to the country that there were no Communists in government, and that my attempt to dig them out was dishonest and a hoax. The new Administration has now gotten rid of 1456, all of whom were security risks and practically all of whom were removed because of Communist connections and activities or perversion. An excellent record for the time President Eisenhower has been in office.

However, let us glance at a few cases where our batting average is zero—where we struck out. For example, we still have John Patton Davies on the payroll after 11 months of the Eisenhower Administration. And who is John Patton Davies? John Patton Davies was . . . part and parcel of the old Acheson-Lattimore-Vincent-White-Hiss group which did so much toward delivering our Chinese Friends into Communist hands. . . . Why is this man still a high official in our government?

Now let us examine the failure of my party to liquidate the foulest bankruptcy of the Democrat Administration. On September 12, 1953, the Chinese Communists announced that they would not treat as prisoners of war American fliers who were shot down during the Korean War over Manchuria. On September 10, 1953, the Army announced that some 900 American young men known to have been prisoners of the Communists in Korea were unaccounted for. . . .

How brave are we—how brave are we when we do not use all the power of this nation to rescue those airmen and the 900 other military men who have been unaccounted for for months? I realize, of course, the low ebb to which our honor has sunk over the past 20 years. But it is time that we, the Republican Party, liquidate this blood-stained blunder of the Acheson-Truman regime. We promised

the American people something different. Let us deliver—not next year or next month—let us deliver now.

(c) LOYALTY CRUSADE: A CRITIQUE*

In the United States by mid-century, the tensions generated by the cold war and the accompanying militarization of the American economy were bringing a new series of attacks upon traditional civil liberties. With the outbreak of an actual shooting war against the Red armies in Korea, public hysteria in the United States over the danger of communism and the accompanying fear of disloyal or subversive activities reached a new high point. The American temper seemed dangerously close to the type of fanaticism from which totalitarian movements derived their chief strength. An official campaign of organized hatred toward an unpopular minority group could also be interpreted as a sign of loss of faith in American institutions. Meanwhile, on all sides there was evidence, as Supreme Court Justice Robert H. Jackson pointed out, that "Of late years the Government is using its power as never before to pry into . . . lives and thoughts upon the slightest suspicion of less than complete trustworthiness. It demands not only probity, but unquestioning ideological loyalty."

Underlying the whole structure of postwar American concern with security and loyalty was the fact of atomic energy. After the explosion of the first atomic bombs over Japan, the awestruck popular expectation of a new world era gave way to widespread horror over the destructive nature of the new weapon, and an even more pressing fear lest an atomic war be unleashed against mankind. In the rapid deterioration of the wartime spirit

* From Arthur A. Ekirch, Jr., *The Decline of American Liberalism*, pp. 336-347. Copyright © 1955 by Arthur A. Ekirch, Jr. Used by permission of David McKay Company, Inc., publishers.

of Interallied cooperation, this latter concern was directed mainly against the possibility of war between Russia and the United States. For its part Russia feared further American use of the bomb, while the United States sought to keep Russia from gaining an understanding of the technique of its production.

The decision of the Truman administration to keep atomic energy as a "sacred trust" had fateful international and domestic implications. Signifying distrust of Russia, it also quite naturally intensified Soviet fears of American power. The decision likewise largely ignored the counter-recommendation of Secretary of War Stimson, that the United States enter at once into direct negotiation with Russia for the purpose of working out some method for the international control of atomic energy. Stimson, who had played an important role in encouraging the research that had led to the bomb and who had also advocated its use against Japan, was, without regretting those decisions, nevertheless most anxious that the United States try every possible means to reach an agreement with Russia in the whole area of nuclear energy. Stimson knew that reputable scientists discounted the possibility that America's exclusive knowledge of the bomb could long be kept secret. However, even temporary sole possession of the bomb greatly increased American fears of espionage. The exposure of a Russian spy ring operating in Canada, followed by revelations of similar espionage activity in the United States, naturally reinforced the public's anxiety.

While spying, or intelligence and counterintelligence work, was an obvious corollary of the pursuit of power politics, American concern over atomic secrets plus the presence of an active communist group in the United States intensified the problem. Not all American Communists were potential espionage agents of the Soviet, but their essential loyalty to the

United States was certainly open to question, and it was in no sense desirable that they should work in sensitive or important positions in the Government. The dilemma facing the American people, and a matter of vital concern to liberals, was how to handle the communist problem without destroying fundamental American liberties. The general solution that was worked out—involving the Federal loyalty program, the prosecution of Communist party leaders, and the McCarran Internal Security Act virtually outlawing the party—was, however, neither liberal nor legally defensible from the standpoint of traditional American values and constitutional law. . . .

The evident American intention to go beyond a rational approach to the communist problem indicated a desire not only to punish criminal and seditious acts on the part of Communists but also to suppress all communist or radical speech and thought. This determination, shared even by some liberals, rested on the assumption that communism was a conspiracy and an ideological threat that could not be governed by traditional American conceptions of due process and clear and present danger. Militant liberals of the New Deal and World War II period, who had revised these historic concepts and had also added the doctrine of guilt by association as a means of combating American Nazis and of finding some advance point for security, now saw the same technique invoked against left-wing and communist elements. . . .

The question of communism as a conspiracy came before the Federal court in New York in 1949 in the trial of eleven leading American Communists on charges of violating the Smith Act by organizing to teach or advocate the overthrow of the government of the United States by force and violence. Their conviction on grounds of what might be called intellectual conspiracy, without any overt revolutionary act on their part, seemed to many American liberals to reverse the standard for free speech offered by Justice Holmes after World War I—"whether the words used are used in such circumstances and are of such a nature as to create a clear and present danger that they will bring about the substantive evils that Congress has a right to prevent." Although the Supreme Court in 1951 upheld the Communists' conviction, Justices Black and Douglas in their dissenting opinions reaffirmed Holmes's argument for free speech and denied that there was any evidence of the defendants' urging a specific overt act of terror or violence. Uneasy over a conviction that hinted at thought control, some liberals also pointed to the additional practical difficulty that now the Communists would be driven underground and would thus be less subject to either prosecution or persuasion. On the other hand, many liberals accepted the contention that communism was a conspiracy of such magnitude that, even without overt action on its part, it represented the clear and present danger referred to by Justice Holmes.

The definition of sedition in terms of a person's words instead of his deeds still did not go far enough to satisfy those who demanded complete national unity and unswerving loyalty, in thought as well as in speech and action, on the part of all Americans. This illiberal pressure for one hundred per cent conformity gained extraordinary success in the postwar era through the use of what has been called "the simple stratagem of charging a man with disloyalty, instead of with treason or espionage or sabotage." This device evaded all the constitutional safeguards and requirements surrounding a charge of treason and confronted an individual with accusations often difficult to disprove if only because of their vague and secret nature.

Since it was not easy to read a man's mind or to probe the depths of his innermost thoughts, the enforcement of so unprecise a value as loyalty came to depend largely on the use of the doctrine of guilt or innocence by association. The organizations a man belonged to, his friends, what he read, or how he spent his leisure time, all became indices of his loyalty or disloyalty. For this there was, of course, a certain logic that was at once both primitive and highly sophisticated. Obviously almost everyone was likely to draw conclusions about people on the basis of their associations; and relevant associations, not torn from their proper context, had always been a stock in trade of historical writing and criticism. The danger was not in drawing inferences from associations—an often necessary feature of exercising judgment and making decisions—but it was rather the growing practice of determining guilt by association that was out of harmony with the American tradition that crime must be personal and proved before an individual stand condemned. . . .

With Congress and the country apparently convinced that communism was a conspiracy that automatically involved its disciples in crime, and with their growing acceptance of the doctrine of guilt by association, the only remaining task was to formalize the procedures for uncovering persons suspected of disloyalty or subversion. This exercise in thought control, which reflected too the growing nationalism and centralization of all values, was achieved through such devices as Congressional investigations, loyalty-security programs, and the official registration or listing of organizations deemed subversive. These steps were reinforced by state laws governing criminal syndicalism and excluding Communist party candidates from a place on the ballot. The argument of some liberals that political purges or tests of this type were justified if confined to Communists overlooked the problem of how Communists could be discovered

without also probing the views and associations of those suspected of being
Communists, or fellow travelers, or individuals who secretly sympathized with
the party. It was simple logic in looking
for "Reds" to direct a passing glance at
some of the other colors in the left-wing
political spectrum. Thus even socialists
and certain varieties of liberals could be,
and were, placed under attack.

What many anticommunist liberals
overlooked, in the zeal of their often new-
found faith, was that a society could create a class of political untouchables only
at the peril of being itself affected by
the very virus it sought to isolate. The
danger in the antiradical and anticommunist crusade after World War II did
not stem primarily from the irresponsible tactics of the various Congressional
investigating committees or individuals
like Senator Joseph McCarthy, reprehensible though their methods were. "Mc-
Carthyism," after all, was a result or a
symptom, not a cause. The danger rather
lay in the assumption that there was a
minority class or group of political lepers
guilty of so-called wrong thinking. The
contention, popular with some liberals,
that communism was not heresy but conspiracy, even if true, overlooked the fact
that all heresy which went beyond mere
academic protest contained the seeds of
possible conspiracy and subversion. Expressed in action, by sedition or revolution, such heresy or conspiracy could and
undoubtedly would be met by a vigorous
and rightful counteraction. But the censorship of ideas was different from resistance to rebellion. No matter how radical
or subversive an idea or ideology, the attempt to eradicate it by force or suppression was purely and simply the application
of methods of thought control traditionally practiced by totalitarian regimes.

The way in which the campaign against
communism could be broadened, under
the doctrine of guilt by association, into
a general onslaught against all those whose
patriotism was questioned was best illustrated by the Federal loyalty-security
program. Some of the procedures in this
program were not unlike the normal investigation conducted by the Civil Service
Commission of all applicants for government jobs. The vital differences, of
course, were the damage to the reputation
of an individual whose loyalty was questioned, and the program's reliance on a
whole web of circumstantial evidence furnished by secret informers. President Truman supported the FBI's contention that
its function was investigatory and that it
could not reveal its sources of information or attempt to usurp judical and administrative responsibility by evaluating
the materials in its files. Though the FBI
position was justifiable, the dismissal of
an employee on the basis of the testimony
of informers whom he could not cross-
examine was obviously susceptible of injustice. A heavy burden was placed on the
Loyalty Review Board charged with
evaluating the uneven, and often mali-
cious or trivial, materials in a person's
file. And the question also arose of how
valid or reliable an FBI report actually
was.

There was a growing danger that the
use of the FBI to investigate loyalty and
to uncover evidence of subversive activities would result in the creation of the
type of Federal police force long regarded
as the badge of a totalitarian state. These
functions, which had been taken away
from the Bureau after its unsavory role
in the antiradical campaign of 1919 and
1920, were restored to it in 1939 by order
of President Roosevelt, who requested the
Bureau "to take charge of the investigatory work in matters relating to espionage,
sabotage, and violations of the neutrality
regulations." Increasingly therefore the
FBI was being changed from a normal
investigatory and law-enforcement agency into an instrument of counterespionage,

using the techniques of paid informers, *agents provocateurs,* and wiretapping. These methods, together with the tremendous expansion in the personnel and budget of the Bureau that necessarily accompanied its added tasks, aroused fears on the part of many liberals that the United States was coming under the sway of a Federal police force.

Nevertheless, despite all the problems that the loyalty program gave rise to, certainly no fair-minded citizen could maintain that the government should give employment to individuals disloyal to the United States. Criticism of the loyalty program therefore rested chiefly on the question of whether government workers received sufficient guarantees against improper accusations, and of whether jeopardizing the reputations of a large number of individuals was worth the tremendous cost, direct and indirect, of exposing a small minority of subversive or disloyal persons. By March 1952, out of four million individuals whose loyalty was checked, only one out of two hundred required a thorough field investigation and one out of two thousand needed to be removed from government service. These removals, it had to be remembered, were for alleged disloyalty and presumably not for any misdeeds that could be prosecuted by the courts. Indeed, the whole intent of the loyalty program was to dismiss those individuals whose activities, though suspect, were not such as to subject them to normal legal and judicial procedures.

Many liberals, on the assumption that some sort of governmental machinery was necessary to stamp out disloyalty, devoted their major efforts to setting up additional administrative safeguards to help prevent the unjust dismissal of government workers innocent of any disloyalty. What these liberals failed to perceive, however, was that the more numerous the safeguards the greater the potential damage to the reputation of anyone finally adjudged disloyal in a secret hearing before an administrative tribunal. No program, no matter how circumspect, could expect to achieve perfection in measuring such intangibles as loyalty and disloyalty. Basically the question to be decided was not factual or legal, but motivational, with all the subjectivity which that implied. . . .

Unfortunately, most liberals, wedded to the historic fetish of civil service reform, failed to perceive that their preoccupation with job security had led them into the most monstrous insecurity of all—the plight of the individual denied a position, not through the workings of the business cycle or the whims of an employer but through the systematic tyranny of an official administrative body. "Men might as well be imprisoned," John Stuart Mill observed, "as excluded from the means of earning their bread." Disloyalty, to be sure, was not a crime, but the findings indelibly recorded on an individual's civil service personnel file were tantamount to conviction by a court.

XV

the Eisenhower years (1953-1961)

T HE ELECTION of 1952 was eagerly anticipated by the Republican Party, which had been denied control of the national government for twenty years. It chose as standard bearer the popular General of the Army Dwight D. Eisenhower. His opponent, Governor Adlai E. Stevenson of Illinois, was not so widely known. The campaign was highlighted by Republican criticism of welfare statism, corruption and "communism" in government, and the failure to end the war in Korea. The Democrats stressed the role of government in promoting prosperity and security, and displayed their record of forthright resistance to Communist aggression. The election resulted in victory for the Republican Party, which gained control of the White House and, by small margins, the Senate and the House of Representatives.

Promising a clean sweep, the new administration sought to remove government from business activities and eliminate unwelcome officeholders. Little was done, however, to modify key New Deal and Fair Deal measures, and President Eisenhower acknowledged that it was the responsibility of government to see that prosperity was maintained and to prevent "any real injustice in the business of living." The candidates of 1952 resumed their contest in 1956, and while the President claimed credit for social legislation his opponent protested that it had been passed by Democrats in the face of Republican opposition. Eisenhower's second victory was even more impressive than his first, though both houses of Congress were won by the Democrats.

Notable advances in the field of civil rights were made during these years. In Brown v. Topeka, the Supreme Court held that "separate but equal" educational facilities were in violation of the Constitution, and schools were enjoined to integrate their student bodies. Many states and communities openly defied judicial commands, and in 1957 the President ordered federal troops into Little Rock, Arkansas, to protect from mobs Negro children attending a formerly all white high school. The rights of individuals to refuse to answer certain questions asked by

Congressional investigating committees were confirmed by the Supreme Court in 1957, when it held that "there is no congressional power to expose for the sake of exposure." It appeared to some that the United States was beginning to practice what it had been preaching for so long.

The Eisenhower years were characterized by a general prosperity blemished by occasional recessions. The President never denied that the government had a responsibility to act during these periods of unemployment and reduced output, but he resisted the pressure for huge federal expenditures to "prime the pump." As the administration announced in 1960 that new levels of economic growth had been reached, the nation was again plagued by a recession that found almost 5,000,000 out of work. Some urged the United States to readjust its foreign trade policies to meet changes in the world economy or suffer a deterioration of its financial position at home and in its affairs abroad.

1

The Republican Party Platform, 1952

☆ *After a spirited convention fight, Dwight D. Eisenhower was nominated as the Republican candidate for president in July, 1952. The Republicans also adopted an outspoken platform to back up their call to the people to rid the nation of the problems of "corruption, Communism, and Korea."* ☆

FOREIGN POLICY

We charge that the leaders of the Administration in power lost the peace so dearly earned by World War II.

The moral incentives and hopes for a better world which sustained us through World War II were betrayed, and this has given Communist Russia a military and propaganda initiative which, if unstayed, will destroy us.

They abandoned friendly nations such as Latvia, Lithuania, Esthonia, Poland and Czechoslovakia to fend for themselves against the Communist aggression which soon swallowed them.

They required the National Government of China to surrender Manchuria with its strategic ports and railroads to the control of Communist Russia. They urged that Communists be taken into the Chinese Government and its military forces. And finally they denied the military aid that had been authorized by Congress and which was crucially needed if China was to be saved. Thus they sub-

stituted on our Pacific flank a murderous enemy for an ally and friend.

In all these respects they flouted our peace-assuring pledges such as the Atlantic Charter, and did so in favor of despots, who, it was well known, consider that murder, terror, slavery, concentration camps and the ruthless and brutal denial of human rights are legitimate means to their desired ends.

Teheran, Yalta, and Potsdam were the scenes of those tragic blunders with others to follow. The leaders of the Administration in power acted without the knowledge or consent of Congress or of the American people. They traded our overwhelming victory for a new enemy and for new oppressions and new wars which were quick to come.

In South Korea, they withdrew our occupation troops in the face of the aggressive, poised-for-action, Communist military strength on its nothern border. They publicly announced that Korea was of no concern to us. Then when the Communist forces acted to take what seemed to have been invited, they committed this nation to fight back under the most unfavorable conditions. Already the tragic

* From *Republican Party Platform, 1952*.

cost is over 110,000 American casualties.

With foresight, the Korean war would never have happened.

In going back into Korea, they evoked the patriotic and sacrificial support of the American people. But by their hampering orders they produced stalemates and ignominious bartering with our enemies, and they offer no hope of victory.

They have effectively ignored many vital areas in the face of a global threat requiring balanced handling.

The people of the other American republics are resentful of our neglect of their legitimate aspirations and cooperative friendship.

The Middle East and much of Africa seethe with anti-American sentiment.

The peoples of the Far East who are not under Communist control find it difficult to sustain their morale as they contrast Russia's "Asia first" policy with the "Asia last" policy of those in control of the Administration now in power. . . .

They profess to be following a defensive policy of "containment" of Russian communism which has not contained it.

Those in control of the party in power have, in reality, no foreign policy. They swing erratically from timid appeasement to reckless bluster.

The good in our foreign policies has been accomplished with Republican cooperation, such as the organization of the United Nations, the establishment of the trusteeship principle for dependent peoples, the making of peace with Japan and Germany and the building of more solid security in Europe. But in the main the Republican party has been ignored and its participation has not been invited.

The American people must now decide whether to continue in office the party which has presided over the disastrous reversal of our fortunes and the loss of our hopes for a peaceful world.

The Republican party offers, in contrast to the performance of those now running

our foreign affairs, policies and actions based on enlightened self-interest and animated by courage, self-respect, steadfastness, vision, purpose, competence and spiritual faith.

The supreme goal of our foreign policy will be an honorable and just peace. We dedicate ourselves to wage peace and to win it.

We shall eliminate from the State Department and from every Federal office all, wherever they may be found, who share responsibilities for the needless predicaments and perils in which we find ourselves. We shall also sever from the public payroll the hordes of loafers, incompetents and unnecessary employees who clutter the Administration of our foreign affairs. The confusions, overlappings and extravagance of our agencies abroad hold us up to the ridicule of peoples whose friendship we seek.

We shall substitute a compact and efficient organization where men of proven loyalty and ability shall have responsibility for reaching our objectives. They will reflect a dynamic initiative. Thus we can win the support and confidence which go only to those who demonstrate a capacity to define and get results.

We shall have positive peace-building objectives wherever this will serve the enlightened self-interest of our nation and help to frustrate the enemy's designs against us.

In Western Europe we shall use our friendly influence without meddling or imperialistic attitudes, for ending the political and economic divisions which alone prevent that vital area from being strong in its own right.

We shall encourage and aid the development of collective security forces there, as elsewhere, so as to end the Soviet power to intimidate directly or by satellites and so that the free governments will be sturdy to resist Communist inroads.

In the balanced consideration of our

problems, we shall end neglect of the Far East which Stalin has long identified as the road to victory over the West. We shall make it clear that we have no intention to sacrifice the East to gain time for the West. . . .

The Government of the United States, under Republican leadership, will repudiate all commitments contained in secret understandings such as those of Yalta which aid Communist enslavements. It will be made clear, on the highest authority of the President and the Congress, that United States policy, as one of its peaceful purposes, looks happily forward to the genuine independence of those captive peoples.

We shall again make liberty into a beacon light of hope that will penetrate the dark places. That program will give the Voice of America a real function. It will mark the end of the negative, futile and immoral policy of "containment" which abandons countless human beings to a despotism and Godless terrorism which in turn enables the rulers to forge the captives into a weapon for our destruction.

We shall support the United Nations and loyally help it to become what it was designed to be, a place where differences would be harmonized by honest discussion and a means of collective security under agreed concepts of justice. We shall seek real meaning and value for our regional security treaties, which implies that all parties shall contribute their loyal support and fair shares.

We shall see to it that no treaty or agreement with other countries deprives our citizens of the rights guaranteed them by the Federal Constitution.

We shall always measure our foreign commitments so that they can be borne without endangering the economic health or sound finances of the United States. Stalin said that "the moment for the decisive blow" would be when the free nations were isolated and were in a state of "practical bankruptcy." We shall not allow ourselves to be isolated and economically strangled, and we shall not let ourselves go bankrupt.

Sums available by this test, if competently used, will be more effective than vastly larger sums incompetently spent for vague and endless purposes. We shall not try to buy goodwill. We shall earn it by sound, constructive self-respecting policies and actions. . . .

The policies we espouse will revive the contagious, liberating influences which are inherent in freedom. They will inevitably set up strains and stresses within the captive world which will make the rulers impotent to continue in their monstrous ways and mark the beginning of their end.

Our nation will become again the dynamic, moral and spiritual force which was the despair of despots and the hope of the oppressed. As we resume this historic role, we ourselves will come to enjoy again the reality of peace, security and solvency, not the shabby and fleeting counterfeit which is the gift of the Administration in power. . . .

COMMUNISM

By the Administration's appeasement of communism at home and abroad it has permitted Communists and their fellow travelers to serve in many key agencies and to infiltrate our American life. When such infiltration becomes notorious through the revelations of Republicans in Congress, the Executive Department stubbornly refused to deal with it openly and vigorously. It raised the false cry of "red herring" and took other measures to block and discredit investigations. It denied files and information to Congress. It set up boards of its own to keep information secret and to deal lightly with security risks and persons of doubtful loyalty. It only undertook prosecution of the most notorious Communists after public opinion forced action.

The result of these policies is the needless sacrifice of American lives, a crushing cost in dollars for defense, possession by Russia of the atomic bomb, the lowering of the Iron Curtain, and the present threats to world peace. Our people have been mired in fear and distrust and employees of integrity in the Government service have been cruelly maligned by the Administration's tolerance of people of doubtful loyalty.

There are no Communists in the Republican party. We have always recognized communism to be a world conspiracy against freedom and religion. We never compromised with communism and we have fought to expose it and to eliminate it in government and American life.

A Republican President will appoint only persons of unquestioned loyalty. We will overhaul loyalty and security programs. In achieving these purposes a Republican President will cooperate with Congress. . . .

SMALL BUSINESS IN A FREE ECONOMY

For twenty years the Administration has praised free enterprise while actually wrecking it. Here a little, there a little, year by year, it has sought to curb, regulate, harass, restrain and punish. There is scarcely a phase of our economic and social life today in which government does not attempt to interfere.

Such hostility deadens initiative, discourages invention and experiment and weakens the self-reliance indispensable to the nation's vitality. Merciless taxation, senseless use of controls and ceaseless effort to enter business on its own account, have led the present Government to unrestrained waste and extravagance in spending, irresponsibility in decision and corruption in administration.

The anti-monopoly laws have been em-ployed, not to preserve and foster competition but to further the political ambitions of the men in power. Wage and price controls have been utilized, not to maintain economic stability, but to reward the friends and punish the enemies of leaders of the party in power.

Neither small nor large business can flourish in such an atmosphere. The Republican party will end this hostility to initiative and enterprise.

We will aid small business in every practicable way. We shall remove tax abuses and injurious price and wage controls. Efforts to plan and regulate every phase of small business activity will cease. We will maintain special committees in Congress whose chief function will be to study and review continuously the problems of small business and recommend legislation for their relief. . . .

Our goal is a balanced budget, a reduced national debt, an economical administration and a cut in taxes. We believe in combatting inflation by encouraging full production of goods and food and not through a program of restrictions. . . .

CORRUPTION

The present Administration's sordid record of corruption has shocked and sickened the American people. Its leaders have forfeited any right to public faith by the way they transact the Federal Government's business.

Fraud, bribery, graft, favoritism and influence-peddling have come to light. Immorality and unethical behavior have been found to exist among some who were entrusted with high policy-making positions, and there have been disclosures of close alliances between the present Government and underworld characters.

Republicans exposed cases of questionable and criminal conduct and relentlessly pressed for full investigations into the cancerlike spread of corruption in the Administration. These investigations uncovered a double standard in Federal tax law enforcement—lenient treatment to political favorites including even some gangsters and crooks but harassment and threats of prosecution for many honest taxpayers over minor discrepancies.

Besides tax fixes and scandals in the Internal Revenue Bureau, investigations have disclosed links between high officials and crime, favoritism and influence in the R. F. C., profiteering in grain, sale of postmasterships, tanker ship deals in the Maritime Commission, ballot-box stuffing and thievery, and bribes and payoffs in contract awards by officials in agencies exercising extraordinary powers and disbursing billions of dollars. . . .

The Republican party pledges to put an end to corruption, to oust the crooks and grafters, to administer tax laws fairly and impartially and to restore honest government to the people.

2

The Democratic Side, 1952

☆ *Although there were a number of eager aspirants for the Democratic presidential nomination in 1952, the reluctant Adlai E. Stevenson, Governor of Illinois, was finally selected. In his unsuccessful bid for election, Stevenson found his campaign complicated by the need to defend the Truman administration and yet present a constructive program of his own. Portions of Governor Stevenson's speech at St. Louis on October 9, 1952, are given below.** ☆

Twenty-five years from now there will be thirty-five million more of us than there are now. At every dinner table set for four people today there is an invisible fifth plate. In 1975 the land which has always answered our increasing needs will have to fill that plate as well as the other four. It will have to provide joists and rafters, flooring and roofing, for the now invisible fifth house. This is the measure of the task cut out for us—and of the opportunity the future holds for men of vision and daring.

I would speak to you tonight about our opportunities. I would speak to you of America's new frontier.

Before exploring this frontier, however, before suggesting what lies ahead in the next twenty-five years, let us for a moment glance backward twenty-five years. America in 1927 lived in a fool's paradise. It ended rudely. We came to a stop in 1930. The whole mighty engine flew apart. Numerous thoughtful men actually questioned whether the system of American capitalism could survive.

Well, it is one of history's odd ironies that today the Republicans are accusing us Democrats of being enemies of free capitalistic enterprise—when the plain truth is that it was Democrats that saved the American capitalistic system under the leadership of Franklin Roosevelt.

Today America is more prosperous than any other nation in history....

Today not everyone in this country is sharing fairly in our national prosperity. Schoolteachers, pensioners, old people living on savings, widows living on the proceeds of life insurance—these people often cannot make ends meet today because prices have outrun their incomes. We must stop the price rise—and we know how to do it if only the Republican Old Guard will give us a chance.

Others among us are in a still more serious plight. How can we talk about prosperity to the sick who cannot afford proper medical care, to the mentally ill for whom there is no room in our overcrowded institutions? How can we talk about prosperity to the hundreds of thousands who can find no decent place to

* From *The New York Times,* October 10, 1952.

live at prices they can afford? And how can we talk prosperity to a sharecropper living on worn-out land, or to city dwellers packed six to a room in an unlit tenement with a garbage-strewn alley for their children's playground?

To these people, national prosperity is a mockery—to the eleven million familes in this nation with incomes of less than $2,000 a year.

Do these facts shock you? They shock me. What can we do to improve this situation? There will always be the foolish and improvident. But we are concerned here with much more than that. And what is the proper role of government?

This is one of the great questions on which our two political parties divide.

It seems to me that the answer is this: Government has three duties.

First, government is an umpire, denying special privilege, ensuring equal rights, restraining monopoly and greed and bigotry, making sure that the game is played according to the rules. On this point, the Republicans agree—so long as they write the rules.

Second, government has the duty of creating an economic climate in which creative men can take risks and reap rewards, so that our economic life will have a continuous flow of fresh ideas and fresh leadership; and, of course, it means the building of solid defenses against the greatest threat to that flow—depression.

This, perhaps above all others, has been the great contribution of the Democratic Party in the last twenty years. In taking the nation out of the worst depression in its history, we reformed the economy so effectively that, under continuing wise leadership, there never need be another disastrous depression such as we have known in the past.

The way you stay out of depressions is by stability and maintaining the buying power of the people. In the last twenty years—through price supports for the farmers, minimum-wage and collective-bargaining laws for the workers, social-security measures for the unemployed and the elderly—we have built foundations under the national economy.

The Republicans are against depression just as much as we Democrats are—and especially during September and October of election years! But the rest of the time they are busy opposing and denouncing most of these defenses against depression as "socialistic."

Third, government has the duty of helping the people develop their country.

The Federal Government made the Louisiana Purchase, and on that land a nation grew to greatness. No private corporation would have built Grand Coulee Dam, yet in the Grand Coulee country people are building their homes and establishing their private businesses, and farmers are converting desert into garden.

And this is only one of the frontiers that government has helped the people open in recent years. The Republicans disagree on this. They say that such activity is interference with private enterprise. But the fact is that it is this very activity of government which enables private enterprise to flourish.

Have any great frontiers in human history ever been opened without the help of government? Christopher Columbus discovered the New World, but it was the Queen of Spain who provided his ships. The American Government not only bought the Louisiana Territory but subsidized the railroads that spanned it, opened government lands to homesteaders, built TVA so the Middle South could lift itself out of the quagmire of want. Government achieved the miracle of atomic power which is the new dimension for both good and evil in the world of tomorrow.

It is this partnership of government with free and daring men that we need today. . . .

We can make America the land for all of us what we want it to be for each of us. We need more hospitals, more schools, more housing, more electric power, more soil conservation.

And we can achieve these things—if we but have faith in ourselves, in our heritage of freedom and in our limitless future.

In the first six weeks of the campaign I set forth—as clearly as I could—the policies which I think are best calculated to keep our frontiers ever widening and which will enable all the people to share fairly in the new age of abundance.

Let me remind you of these Democratic policies:

One. To repeal and replace the Taft-Hartley law with a new law which promotes the private settlement of disputes, and to work in other ways for an orderly and fair balancing of the interests between labor and management. Production postponed is production lost, and in our industrial society production losses are coffin nails for workers and owners and consumers alike.

Two. Price supports for agriculture; continuing search for practicable methods of supporting the prices of perishables; continuation and improvement of such other programs as rural electrification and soil conservation.

Three. To widen the coverage and expand the benefits available under our social-security system and to honor our obligations to the veteran.

Four. To continue our efforts through private, local, state and Federal action to eradicate discrimination based on race, religion, or national origin.

Five. To move ahead on our well-established housing programs.

Six. To meet our most pressing educational needs.

Seven. To combat relentlessly the inflation which strikes so heavily at family budgets.

Eight. To review our tax policy with an eye to the effect of taxes on incentives to produce and invest, on the ability to consume the full output of the economy, and on the need for a balanced budget.

Nine. To encourage small business and enforce our anti-monopoly laws.

Ten. To continue the progressive development and sound conservation of the nation's land and water resources. . . .

That is our program. We take our stand upon the fundamental principle that the role of government is, to sum up, just this: To remove the roadblocks put in the way of the people by nature and by greedy men; to release the energies of the people, so that free men may work the miracles of the future as they have worked the miracles of the past. . . .

A new day is dawning. I do not say all problems are solved. Far from it. But we have dared to try to solve them. We have courage to dare the new, the compassion to help the wretched and the vision to see what men can really be in the society of our dreams.

3

The Republican Temper

☆ *The return to power of the Republicans did not mean a repudiation of the concepts of government responsibility for the national welfare which had developed during the previous generation, as President Eisenhower pointed out in 1954. The changes were in striving for greater economy and efficiency in the Federal government and the encouragement of a greater sense of responsibility by state and local governments.* ☆

(a) ADDRESS OF PRESIDENT EISENHOWER TO THE PEOPLE*

This Administration believes that no American—no one group of Americans—can truly prosper unless all Americans prosper. We are one family made up of millions of Americans with the same hopes for a full and happy life. We must not become a nation divided into factions, or special groups and hostile cliques.

We believe that the slum, the out-dated highway, the poor school system—deficiencies in health protection, the loss of a job, and the fear of poverty in old age—in fact, any real injustice in the business of living—penalizes us all. And this Administration is committed to help you prevent them.

Ground work has been laid by this Administration in the strong belief that the Federal government should be prepared at all times—ready, at a moment's notice —to use every proper means to sustain the basic prosperity of our people.

I therefore give you this assurance:

Every legitimate means available to the Federal government that can be used to sustain that prosperity is being used and will continue to be used as necessary.

This Administration believes that we must not and need not tolerate a boom-and-bust America. We believe that America's prosperity does not and need not depend upon war or the preparation for war. We know that this great country can make the adjustments necessary to meet changing circumstances without encouraging disaster and without bringing about the economic chaos for which the Communists hope. Our system is the greatest wealth producer in the world—in terms of the life and the well-being of every citizen.

(b) AGRICULTURAL PROBLEMS †

Occasionally there are people who look wistfully for a solution to what is called

* January 4, 1954. From *The New York Times*, January 5, 1954.

† 1954. From Ezra Taft Benson, "A Workable Farm Policy," *The Atlantic Monthly*, CLXXXXIV (July, 1954), pp. 53-56. Used by permission of Ezra Taft Benson.

the "farm problem." Actually there is no single over-all problem. Neither is there a single solution.

The problems of agriculture are changing ones. They are numerous. They vary from year to year in complexity and severity. In meeting these problems it is important that we keep our eye at all times on the goal of a stronger and better America. Solutions must strengthen the cause of freedom. They must deal fairly with farmers and other economic groups of our society. . . .

Our problems today center in the necessity of shifting from an agricultural economy of practically unlimited wartime demands to the more moderate demands of peacetime, while providing reasonable protection for farm income. The present farm program employing emergency, wartime, rigid price supports for a few important commodities is impeding such a transition. To a marked degree it is making an *orderly* transition impossible.

The present program has a number of flaws:—

It results in unbalanced production through rigid supports on some commodities for which demands are decreasing.

It encourages a build-up of surpluses which in turn depress prices.

It discourages sound soil conservation practices by maintaining artificial demands for some soil-depleting crops.

It tends to price certain commodities out of both domestic and foreign markets and thus stimulates use of less expensive substitutes.

It destroys the function of price as a brake on overproduction.

It fails to provide reasonable protection for 60 per cent of our annual farm marketings which are not under price supports.

It provides the greatest help to those who need it least—the low-cost, big-volume producers—the least help to small marginal producers.

It creates the complex problem of what to do with land taken out of production because of severe acreage controls.

It provides for such drastic production restrictions that even with high price supports income is seriously jeopardized.

On top of all these disadvantages, the present program has not prevented a decline in net farm income for five out of the past six years. Under this program the government now has between 6 and 7 billion dollars invested in commodities whose prices are being supported. More than 2.5 billion of this amount is represented by commodities actually held in government storage. The balance has been loaned on commodities a large part of which will eventually wind up in government hands. These surpluses hang over the market. They depress prices. They drain off taxpayers' dollars day in and day out. The cost of storage alone is running more than half a million dollars a day.

Let us visualize for a moment what this means. If we were to load on a single train all of the wheat which the government has under loan and in storage, such a train would extend from San Francisco to New York and then back to St. Louis, a total of 4222 miles. If we loaded all of the corn tied up in price-support operations on a single train, the caboose would be in Los Angeles and the locomotive in Newark, N.J. This train would be 3052 miles long.

Other major commodities either under loan or in government storage include more than 8 million bales of cotton, nearly 1.5 billion pounds of dairy products, and almost a billion pounds of vegetable oils. . . .

Altogether, four commodities—wheat, corn, dairy products, and cotton and cottonseed oil, which comprise only 23 per cent of farm marketings—account for roughly nine tenths of our investments in all price-support operations. More than half of the nation's 5.5 million farmers either do not produce these four commodities or market such small amounts that they derive little in the way of price-support benefits.

To show in the extreme the consequences of high price supports, a caller at my office recently suggested that if this principle had been applied to the harness industry a number of years ago we still might have a thriving harness business in this country. That might be true, but it is certain our storehouses would be filled with harnesses. . . .

Most of the *permanent* progress of agriculture has stemmed from research, education, scientific development, improved marketing, and better production methods. Through these processes we have produced food and fiber when they have been needed. With these same processes we can achieve permanent gains through the use and adjustment of an abundant production.

We are looking to science to play a major role in cushioning the impact of our present agricultural shift. . . .

Scientists are finding valuable new uses for other farm products. But science cannot carry the entire load of changing to a peacetime agriculture. Nor can it do the job fast enough.

To assist in this shift, the Administration early this year presented a new farm program to Congress. It is designed to bring about orderly adjustments before production distortions of a few commodities demoralize our markets, further overtax our storage facilities, and threaten a breakdown of our entire farm price-support system.

This program centers on the following five interrelated points:—

Great Flexibility. This would be achieved through adoption of flexible price supports and a modernized parity formula applicable to all commodities. These flexible supports would help bring

about shifts to keep production more in line with consumer needs.

Increased Domestic Consumption. To accomplish this, we are placing greater emphasis on agricultural marketing services, assisting the food industry with promotion programs and fostering more intensive research.

Increased Foreign Consumption. To achieve this goal and reverse the recent downswing in exports, we sent foreign trade missions to Europe, Latin America, and the Far East. We also are improving our service to foreign exporters, finding markets outside the normal trade channels through barter and acceptance of local currencies, seeking authority to dispose of a billion dollars' worth of surpluses over three years to help carry out the objectives of American foreign policy.

Insulated Emergency Reserves. We are proposing to set aside up to 2.5 billion dollars' worth of surplus commodities to implement the adjustment from the old program to the new. These reserves would be removed from regular market channels and held for emergency and relief purposes at home and abroad.

Wisely Used Diverted Acreage. We are working on plans to see that acreage not needed for major crop production is transferred into new soil-building crops. At present about 25 million acres are being taken out of production of wheat, corn, and cotton. The government will give financial assistance in putting at least a portion of these acres to different uses.

The heart of this five-point program is the flexibility of price supports and adoption of modernized parity for wheat, cotton, corn, and peanuts—the only commodities still on an old parity basis. Unfortunately, these features are also the most controversial.

Modernized parity takes into account increased production efficiency and changes in consumer demand in calculating the cost-price position of the farmer. For wheat, old parity is about 15 points higher than modernized parity. This is because significant changes have occurred in the demand for wheat and in the cost of wheat production during the past forty years.

Our people now consume about 130 pounds of wheat a year per capita. Four decades ago they consumed 200 pounds. In 1910-1914, the base period on which old parity is figured, it took an average of 106 man-hours to produce 100 bushels of wheat. In 1950 it took 26 man-hours. The result of these changes is that when wheat is supported by the government at price relationships which were appropriate forty years ago, overproduction is encouraged in all other areas as well as in the wheat belt. To calculate prices of some items on the old basis and the remainder on the new creates serious disparities and maladjustments. Under existing law, modernized parity is scheduled to go into effect on January 1, 1956. . . .

Flexible supports provide for some price fluctuation to keep supply and demand in better balance, while at the same time placing a strong floor ranging between 75 and 90 per cent of parity under the prices of basic commodities.

They produce greater stability in farming operations and in farm markets.

They encourage sound farm management practices.

They create better price equality in relation to other commodities.

They assure abundant food supplies for consumers at reasonable prices.

They stimulate expansion of market outlets at home and abroad.

They hold production controls to a minimum.

They give added incentive for conservation and soil improvement.

They encourage efficient use of agricultural resources.

Flexible price supports will promote these goals with a maximum of reliance on the cooperative and competitive efforts of free men and a minimum of dependence on government control.

(c) REPORT OF THE COMMISSION ON INTERGOVERNMENTAL RELATIONS*

THE COMMISSION ON INTERGOVERNMENTAL RELATIONS

In recent years, the almost continous presence of a crisis, either economic or military, has accounted for vast expansions of National activities. Many of these programs have been of an emergency nature; a great many others, however, have lastingly influenced the division of governmental responsibilities between the National Government and the States.

Profound as their impact has been, war and economic crisis have not been the

only major causes of the growing pressure for National action. Equally insistent pressures have been brought about by intensified industrialization and population shifts from rural to urban areas; new advances in transportation and communications; and, flowing from these developments, greatly accelerated mobility of people and interchange of ideas.

These changes have been reflected in part in a growing governmental concern with the economic and social welfare of the individual. And many individuals who once looked no further than their city hall or State capitol now turn toward Washington when problems arise. We are doing today as a Nation many things that we

* 1955. From The Commission on Intergovernmental Relations, *A Report To The President for Transmittal To The Congress*, Washington, 1955, pp. 1-6.

once did as individuals, as local communities, or as States. . . .

To many, the expanding powers of the National Government seemed destined to reduce the States to mere administrative provinces. This prospect was sharpened by Supreme Court decisions which appeared to have the effect of removing almost all significant constitutional limitations on the expansion of National activities. It was often aggravated by the conviction that many of the newer activities constituted invasions of individual freedom and ought not to be undertaken by any level of government. Thus the fear of usurpation of State rights was frequently combined with the fear of undue paternalism.

On the other hand, many who had welcomed the expansion of National authority began to wonder if our system of federalism had become an obstacle to effective government. Their fear was that our form of government would prove too slow-moving and cumbersome to deal with the intricate social and economic problems of an increasingly interdependent society and to cope with authoritarian regimes of the Fascist, Nazi, and Communist varieties. Our governmental system must be remodeled, many thought, if it is to be adjusted properly to 20th-century conditions.

The Commission views both positions as extremes. The National Government and the States should be regarded not as competitors for authority but as two levels of government co-operating with or complementing each other in meeting the growing demands on both. Chiefly because of war and the recuring threat of war, the expenditures of the National Government have grown much larger than those of the States and localities. But State and local activities also continue to expand. Equally significant is the increased interest in and recognition of the importance of State and local Governments as essential elements in an effective federal structure.

The continuing vitality of State and local government affords the most solid evidence that our federal system is still an asset and not a liability. To be sure, it is not a neat system, and not an easy one to operate. It makes large demands on our sense of responsibility, our patience, our self-restraint. It requires toleration of diversity with respect to taxes, roads, schools, law enforcement, and many other important matters. Those who have a passion for streamlining can easily point to awkward features.

Nevertheless, the federal principle, along with the principle of checks and balances, remains one of the great institutional embodiments of our traditional distrust of too much concentrated authority in government or, to state it positively, of our traditional belief in distribution of authority among relatively independent governing bodies. . . .

Living in an age of peril, we could perhaps not afford the extra margin of individual freedom which our federal system makes possible if the price were the weakening of national security. We should not think of government only in terms of the scope it leaves for the individual; we must think equally of its capacity to govern. Individual freedom depends on preserving representative government. If division of authority between the National Government and the States should impede our efforts to preserve our Nation and the rest of the free world, it would jeopardize the freedom of the individual.

But experience amply justifies the view that our federal system, with the degree of flexibility that it permits, can be adapted to crises of the present and future as successfully as it has been to those of the past. As an instrument of positive government, it possesses—at least for a nation as large and diverse as ours—a clear advantage over a strongly centralized government. In helping to bolster the principle of consent; in facilitating wide participation in government; in furnishing training grounds for leaders; in maintaining the habit of local initiative; in providing laboratories for research and experimentation in the art of government; in fostering competition among lower levels of government; in serving as outlets for local grievances and for political aspirations—in all these and many other ways, the existence of many relatively independent and responsible governments strengthens rather than weakens our capacity for government. . . .

Responsibility implies restraint as well as action. The States have responsibilities not only to do efficiently what lies within their competence, but also to refrain from action injurious to the Nation; the National Government has responsibilities not only to perform, within the limits of its constitutional authority, those public functions the States cannot perform, but also to refrain from doing those things the States and their subdivisions are willing and able to do. . . .

Far from weakening the National Government, the strengthening of State and local government would increase its effectiveness. The responsibilities that unavoidably must fall on the National Government are formidable. The fullest possible utilization of the resources of the State and local governments is desirable both to supplement National action where National action is necessary, and to relieve the National Government of having to divert its resources and energies to activities that could be handled as well or better by the States and their subdivisions. . . .

The degree and limits of National participation must therefore be determined by the exercise of balanced judgment. In addition to appraising carefully in each instance the need for National participa-

tion, the National Government should hold essential participation to the minimum required for attaining its objective. In all of its actions the National Government should be concerned with their effects on State and local governments.

The preservation and strengthening of our federal system depend in the last analysis on the self-restraint and responsibility, as well as the wisdom, of our actions as citizens. If we are not willing to leave some room for diversity of policy, to tolerate some lack of uniformity in standards, even in many matters which are of national concern and about which we may feel strongly, the essence of federalism, even if not the legal fiction, will have been lost. We must also realize that it can be lost, or its vitality sapped, by nonuse of State and local initiative as well as by overuse of National authority. We have therefore as citizens a responsibility to see to it that those legitimate needs of society that could be met by timely State and local action do not by default have to be met by the National Government. . . .

Assuming efficient and responsible government at all levels—National, State, and local—we should seek to divide our civic responsibilities so that we:

Leave to private initiative all the functions that citizens can perform privately; use the level of government closest to the community for all public functions it can handle; utilize co-operative intergovernmental arrangements where appropriate to attain economical performance and popular approval; reserve National action for residual participation where State and local governments are not fully adequate, and for the continuing responsibilities that only the National Government can undertake.

4

Modern Republicanism's Appeal, 1956

☆ *Though in 1955 the President had suffered a heart attack and as late as June, 1956, had been hospitalized for abdominal surgery, he declared his intention to run for reelection. The Republican convention renominated Eisenhower without opposition on the first ballot. During the campaign the President took a moderate position on social and economic matters, as was reflected in his address at Lexington, Kentucky, October 1, 1956.** ☆

Now, I wish tonight to answer three basic questions: What is the job to be done? How much of that job has already been done? How do we get the rest done?

So we begin, really, with this question: What do we want this country to be like as the next four years unfold?

Let me give you some highlights of the picture that I keep constantly before me.

I see an America in which every man can eat his own bread in peace, raise his own family in security and strengthen his own spirit and mind in dignity.

This will be an America where there are more than seventy million jobs at good wages.

An America where the schoolroom shortage is erased, where every child can go to a good school and every young talent can be developed to the full.

An America in which farm surpluses no longer crush down farm prices and the farmer.

And this, incidentally, means an Amer-

* From *Vital Speeches*, XXIII (October 15, 1956), pp. 2-4.

ica where no politician any longer can treat the farmer himself as a product to be bid for in the political marketplace.

I see an America where intensive medical research has conquered some of our most killing and crippling diseases.

An America where every family can afford and find a decent home.

An America where a mighty network of highways spreads across our country, and where ocean ships sail into the ports of the Great Lakes, bringing a fresh surge of progress and growth.

An America where long and costly strikes will be rare, where older workers will be hired entirely on the basis of ability, and where local unemployment problems will be attacked by special programs of financial and technical aid.

An America where we shall see the benefits of our recent action to conserve our soil and water resources, where abundant new supplies of power will be unleashed for our surging industrial growth.

An America where the greatest possible government efficiency allows the lowest possible government cost—and hence lower taxes.

And this, incidentally, will mean an America whose government is not run by politicians who think that the way to lower taxes is to increase expenditures. Our way to reduce expenditures is very old fashioned, but it has one important advantage—it works.

An America where special laws will have improved and protected the competitive position of small business, so vital to our free economy.

And an America where our troubled period of adjustments to the practical meaning of equal opportunity without regard to race will have largely given way to a new spirit of understanding and harmony.

All of this means, finally, an America fully armed—materially and spiritually—to lead the free nations of the world, for our prosperity and our strength are necessary to serve not only our own comforts and securities but the hopes and needs of free men everywhere.

Now we come to our second key question: How much of this job already has been done?

Now I shall be very blunt and very truthful. I am proud of the record to date.

And permit me please to explain why I speak of such pride. It is not to make a political boast—or to ask praise for the performance of duty.

I speak of it because our past performance is the evidence that we can and will do the job that remains to be done.

There is one simple proof of this point.

Most of the items I have just listed in our hopes and plans for the years ahead are already backed up by specific laws enacted or bills in Congress—based on my last three messages on the State of the Union.

This, then, is not a set of glittering phrases coined in the frenzied weeks of a political campaign. This is a working plan of action.

Let us look at a few examples.

Before all else—in our hearts and in our deeds—comes our quest for peace.

In Korea, long since, the guns have been stilled—and in America the casualty lists have ended. The road to secure world peace, obviously, merely began with the Korean armistice. But it did begin. And there have been no more Koreas anywhere in the world.

What about our progress at home?

As to jobs: I have just received the figures for the month of September just since I've arrived in your city. There were more people employed throughout our country than in any other September in our history. The figure is 66,100,000. There were 700,000 more people employed in August. And I suppose the opposition will try to make something of this point. But the fact is that those 700,000 were almost entirely made up of young people who gave up their temporary summer employment to return to school.

What is even more encouraging—unemployment for September dropped to a rate lower than in peacetime September during the twenty-year rule of the opposition party.

So there's the record—more employment than any September in our history and less unemployment than any peacetime September during the entire twenty-year rule of the opposition.

Now as to wages: I realize that averages do not mean much to any one individual. But the fact is that the worker in our factories today is making an average of $12 a week more than he did in August, 1952. Most of this is clear gain because taxes have been reduced, while the cost of living has increased less than 3 per cent.

As to farm prices: Except for the Korean War years, this will be the first year since 1947 when farm prices have gone up.

As to homes: More homes have been built in the last three years than in any previous three-year period.

As to transportation: The huge, new interstate highway network is already under construction. And so is the St. Lawrence Seaway—after about thirty years of talk and delay.

As to older workers: We have been carrying on a new Federal-state project to help older workers get jobs. We have launched a whole new array of special housing, health and other programs for retired or aging persons.

As to small business: We created the Small Business Administration. And we have substantially increased the share of defense contracts going to small business.

As to Government efficiency: Our Federal civilian payroll in June, 1956, was 167,300 less than at the end of the preceding Administration. We have cut taxes by $7,400,000,000, with about two-thirds of the cut going directly to individuals. And, we have balanced the budget.

A great cooperative effort was launched to improve earning opportunities in low income rural areas. A special campaign is in force now to improve the working conditions and regularity of income of migrant farm laborers. The rate of rehabilitating handicapped workers—and finding useful employment for them—has reached an all-time high.

And assistance to the aged—in such forms as increased medical aid—has been improved beyond any programs known in the past.

Now as to social security: We made coverage virtually complete by bringing in 10,000,000 more people—and we put through the biggest real increase in benefits in the program's history.

As to civil rights: Genuine progress has been made in eliminating racial segregation and inequality of opportunity—in all areas of direct Federal responsibility. This has applied in the District of Colum-

bia, in Government departments, in the armed forces and Government contracts with private industry.

These are a few of the actions taken that clearly mark our new direction.

They also give a background of clear fact to enable us to judge some of the political oratory heard these days. This oratory, at its most reckless, has plunged to the wild extremes of charging this Administration with such fabulous failings as not guarding the peace—and not caring for the welfare of any humble citizen or any needy family in our land.

We should not, perhaps, be too much surprised at such talk.

We all know that there are people who suffer from living in a world of words and phrases for so long that they can no longer recognize action when they see it.

And when it comes to a really critical matter like political leadership, we recall a fact that all of us have seen in our daily lives; the longest lectures almost always come from those with least experience.

Our third and final question is: How do we get on with the rest of the job?

The first thing to do is clear. It is for the people to elect a Republican administration and to send to Washington men like John Sherman Cooper and Thruston B. Morton. . . .

With the help of such men, we can then begin by going to work on some of our unfinished business in our program which has been blocked by the opposition in Congress.

One or two examples. Most urgent of all is the problem of our schools. Here let us get a few simple facts straight.

Our serious schoolroom shortage has actually been somewhat reduced in these last years—with the building of more classrooms in these four years than in the preceding twelve. This local and state action, however, has not been enough. I therefore called upon the last Congress to enact a $2,000,000,000 program of Federal grants and other aids for school construction over a five-year period.

I insisted that Federal aid be distributed to states on the basis of need. Moreover, I insisted this aid be over and above what the states are now doing, and that the states themselves match the Federal funds. These requirements are essential if we are realistically to take up the critical lag already existing, rather than merely to keep step with new and growing needs.

As for the opposition: not one of its proposals met these simple, vital requirements. Now, within the last week, we see the strange spectacle of an apparently confused candidate of the opposition supporting the principles of the bills that we proposed, and that his party defeated.

There was only one clear vote, my friends, on my call for action. In the House, the opposition voted against it by 215 to 9—while three-fourths of the Republicans voted for it. In the Senate, the opposition never allowed it to get to a vote.

As a result, we have now lost one out of five precious years. To meet this, I see only one answer—to stick to our determination to get the schools we need —on schedule.

I shall accordingly call upon the next session of Congress to enact legislation that will do the job—not in five years— but in four.

There is other unfinished business to which I shall return.

I shall call again for financial and technical aid to areas suffering chronic local unemployment.

I shall call again for extension of the Federal Minimum Wage Law to great numbers of working men and women who today do not have its protection.

I shall again call for grants to states to expand and strengthen their programs for occupational safety. I called for this action by the last session of Congress. And the opposition Congress refused even to hold a hearing.

And I shall call for further help to small business with some dozen specific recommendations for action.

These are just a few examples of the specific tasks ahead.

But most important of all in getting on with the job is our understanding of one general principle: The need always to encourage the full and free energies of labor and industry, of private organizations and individual citizens. These are the energies that make America prosper and grow.

My friends, to turn back now to the unsound, inflationary, anti-business, heavy-tax, heavy-spending, Government-interference, centralized control polices from which this country has so recently been rescued could reverse all the progress we have made. Surely this is a risk that it would be foolish to run.

Let me, at the same time, make one thing absolutely clear. Where the job before us, or any part of it, is one that only the Federal Government can do effectively, this Government must and will act promptly.

When I spoke to you from San Francisco, I said there was within our reach a new world of good life, goodwill, and good hope. We have made real progress toward such a world, for we have found, and are following, the new direction of our nation.

We still have a distance to go. It can be an exciting journey, a satisfying journey, a confident journey, for we know where we are going, and we know how to get there.

Four years ago, four years ago, my friends, we set out to do a job together. When I think of the America that we would like to see by 1960, I say, let us get on with the rest of the job.

5

Stevenson Runs Again

☆ *After a strenuous pre-convention campaign for delegate support, Adlai Stevenson was renominated as the Democratic presidential candidate. Stevenson charged the Republican administration with being slow in grappling with pressing issues and credited the Democrats with many of the accomplishments claimed by the Eisenhower administration. This approach was well seen in Stevenson's Pittsburgh address of October 3, 1956, which, incidentally, was a reply to Eisenhower's Lexington address.** ☆

On Monday of this week, the real issue in this 1956 election campaign was joined—and I felt it was important to get before you—squarely and promptly—the Democratic position on this issue.

The Republican candidate for the Presidency said on Monday that this election will hinge on the question, as he put it, of "which party, in these recent years, has done more to help all citizens meet the problems of their daily lives."

This is a proper statement of the issue. Of course, what matters is which party will do more in the future to help people meet the always new problems of their daily lives. But I'm sure that is what the Republican candidate meant. And he is right that each party's past record offers the best test of its future performance.

So, if the record is to be the test, let's get the record straight!

I think it is too bad that the President indulged in such gross misstatements of the record. He is an honorable man and could hardly have deliberately intended such misrepresentations.

Fortunately, the facts to set the record straight are at hand. Now let's look at them.

The President's speech referred to our Social Security program, and he claimed credit on behalf of the Republican party for its enlargement.

The fact is that this program—which so vitally helps almost all our older citizens and others in need meet the problems of their daily lives—was developed by Democrats against bitter Republican oppositon.

The fact is that in this very year in Congress the Democrats proposed that Social Security benefits be paid to employees fifty years old or older, who become permanently disabled, and to reduce the age of eligibility for Social Security for women to sixty-two. The fact is that 85 per cent of the Democratic Senators voted for the change on disability and 84 per cent of the Republicans voted against it.

* From *The New York Times*, October 4, 1956.

The President reported in his listing of what he called Republican progress, that —and I quote him—"the minimum wage was increased."

The fact is that he himself, as well as his Congressional leaders, ardently opposed the successful Democratic effort to raise the minimum wage to $1.

The President even took credit in his speech for seeking a program to help distressed areas suffering from chronic local unemployment.

The fact is that the only adequate bill to help these areas was introduced in Congress by Democrats, was passed by the Senate over strong Republican opposition, and was killed in the House by the President's own leaders.

The President tried to claim that this Republican administration was the first to take up the cause of the needy farmer.

The fact is that the Democrats initiated the program of federal aid to the family farm with the Farm Security Administration nearly twenty years ago.

The President even listed farm prices in his summary of Republican progress. The fact is that farm income declined by one-fifth during his term of office.

"The cost of living," the President went on to say, "has been remarkably stabilized."

The fact is that, by the statistics of the Department of Labor, the cost of living reached, this July, the highest point in history.

The President gave the Republican party credit for helping small business. The fact is that last year the rate of small business failures was higher than at any time since 1941. The further fact is that the Eisenhower administration proposed no program for the relief of small business until this year, on the eve of the election, and even then after Congress adjourned.

The President gave the Republican administration credit for progress in civil rights—and the areas of progress he enumerated were all areas of federal responsibility and were all initiated by Democratic administrations.

The fact is that the President has taken no clear position and exercised no leadership in connection with the pressing present problem of school desegregation.

The President gave the Republican administration credit for a $12 a week increase in wages since August, 1952. The fact is that a substantial part of that increase took place under the Truman administration.

The President implied that the Republican tax cut of 1954 benefited everybody. The fact is that 91 cents of every dollar of that tax cut went to corporations and to families with incomes above $5,000 a year.

The President even claimed that the Republican party had ended "special favoritism and laxity" in Washington—but the facts are written otherwise in the record of the Dixon-Yates contract, the natural resources giveaway, and the resignations under fire of his Secretary of the Air Force and other top level officials of his administration. And I won't mention the numerous loopholes in the tax law sponsored by his administration.

The President said that he and the Republicans wanted federal aid to education —and that the Democrats defeated it. The facts are:

First, that the only bill that came up for passage and which would have provided $400 million a year for school construction was defeated by the Republicans in the House, and

Second, that during the first two years of his administration, when he had a Republican Congress, he proposed no legislation for federal aid for public schools other than in relation to defense areas.

These are the facts!

I have no way of knowing whether the President knew them when he spoke, or whether he didn't. But someone did.

Yes, and the American people knew these facts—from their own lives.

Are you a crippled miner, totally disabled, fifty years old, with children to feed and no way to do it—until the Democrats in Congress this year made you eligible for social security benefits?

Are you a working woman of sixty-two who can now retire—because of the action of this Democratic Congress?

Are you a man who almost lost his home in the depression—until the Home Owners Loan Corporation saved it?

Do you work in a steel mill here around Pittsburgh? Do you remember what the corporations did to your union—until the Democrats passed the Wagner Labor Act?

Are you a storekeeper, a businessman, who would have lost your business in the depression if it hadn't been for Franklin Roosevelt and a Democratic policy?

Are you an auto worker in Detroit who worried about temporary unemployment —until the Democrats established unemployment compensation?

Did you almost lose your Iowa farm twenty years ago—and did the Democratic farm program help you to save it? This made a difference in your life—and so does this administration's attitude toward agriculture.

Do you live in a part of the country where REA power lines, brought in during Democratic administrations and against Republican opposition, have transformed life's whole pattern?

Or are you a veteran from Minneapolis raising a family in a house in the suburbs —because we Democrats made it possible for you to buy a home with a GI loan?

I won't ask tonight if you are a mother with a five-year old wondering what kind of school he'll go to next year, or a housewife worrying about high prices.

Run down the list of the measures which in what the President calls "these recent years" have strengthened the framework of economic security, social welfare and personal freedom. Ask yourself which of these measures originated with the Republicans, which with the Democrats. And I haven't even mentioned TVA or the great industrial development in our great river valleys.

I rest my case confidently on your answer.

I say in all soberness that nearly every governmental program in our time—in this generation—which has helped citizens meet the problems of their daily lives more effectively, which has enriched, enlarged and brightened their daily lives has been a Democratic program.

And I further say that this is no accident.

There is a deep and continuing difference between our parties—a difference in composition, in tradition and in ideals.

This is as it should be; this is why we believe in the two-party system. But let us not exaggerate these differences. Both parties share a profound belief in our nation, in our Constitution, in our legacy of political freedom and economic enterprise, in our commitment to the dignity of the individual, in our passion for peace, in our faith in divine Providence.

Let us never forget, even in the heat of a political campaign, that the things which unite us are still far more important than the things which divide us.

Yet within the framework of agreement there exists notable differences—differences which have existed since the founding of the Republic.

Thomas Jefferson defined the fundamental difference nearly a century and a half ago when he said that men are divided into two parties: "those who fear and distrust the people" and "those who identify themselves with the people." And Alexander Hamilton replied for the opposite tradition that the nation should be governed by the "rich and well-born."

President Eisenhower's administration

has reflected the philosophy of his party.

But the Democratic party has had different values and a different tradition.

Our faith has always been in the people —that their welfare is the paramount obligation.

Our hope is to build a society—a New America—where the ideals we inherited from our forefathers will find a new fulfillment in a land of freedom and justice; where our abundance will serve, not just a few—not just what Hamilton called the "rich and well-born," but all of us.

6

The Desegregation Issue

☆ *In the case of Brown v. Board of Education, the Supreme Court overturned by unanimous decision on May 17, 1954, the "separate but equal" doctrine, leaving the way open to public school integration by judicial order. Resistance to integration persisted in many areas and occasionally led to intervention by federal authorities, even to the use of federal troops at Little Rock, Arkansas, in 1957.* ☆

(a) BROWN V. BOARD OF EDUCATION OF TOPEKA ET AL*

MR. CHIEF JUSTICE WARREN delivered the opinion of the Court.

These cases come to us from the States of Kansas, South Carolina, Virginia, and Delaware. They are premised on different facts and different local conditions, but a common legal question justifies their consideration together in this consolidated opinion.

In each of the cases, minors of the Negro race, through their legal representatives, seek the aid of the courts in obtaining admission to the public schools of their community on a nonsegregated basis. In each instance, they had been denied admission to schools attended by white children under laws requiring or permitting segregation according to race. This segregation was alleged to deprive the plaintiffs of the equal protection of the laws under the Fourteenth Amendment. In each of the cases other than the Delaware case, a three-judge federal district court denied relief to the plaintiffs on the so-called "separate but equal" doctrine an-

* 1954. 347 U.S. 483.

nounced by this Court in *Plessy* v. *Ferguson*, 163 U.S. 537. Under that doctrine, equality of treatment is accorded when the races are provided substantially equal facilities, even though these facilities be separate. In the Delaware case, the Supreme Court of Delaware adhered to that doctrine, but ordered that the plaintiffs be admitted to the white schools because of their superiority to the Negro schools.

The plaintiffs contend that segregated public schools are not "equal" and cannot be made "equal," and that hence they are deprived of the equal protection of the laws. Because of the obvious importance of the question presented, the Court took jurisdiction. Argument was heard in the 1952 Term, and reargument was heard this Term on certain questions propounded by the Court.

Reargument was largely devoted to the circumstances surrounding the adoption of the Fourteenth Amendment in 1868. It covered exhaustively consideration of the Amendment in Congress, ratification by the states, then existing practices in racial segregation, and the views of proponents and opponents of the Amendment. This discussion and our own investigation convince us that, although these sources cast some light, it is not enough to resolve the problem with which we are faced. At best, they are inconclusive. The most avid proponents of the post-War Amendments undoubtedly intended them to remove all legal distinctions among "all persons born or naturalized in the United States." Their opponents, just as certainly, were antagonistic to both the letter and the spirit of the Amendments and wished them to have the most limited effect. What others in Congress and the state legislatures had in mind cannot be determined with any degree of certainty.

An additional reason for the inconclusive nature of the Amendment's history, with respect to segregated schools, is the status of public education at that time. In the South, the movement toward free common schools, supported by general taxation, had not yet taken hold. Education of white children was largely in the hands of private groups. Education of Negroes was almost nonexistent, and practically all of the race were illiterate. In fact, any education of Negroes was forbidden by law in some states. Today, in contrast, many Negroes have achieved outstanding success in the arts and sciences as well as in the business and professional world. It is true that public school education at the time of the Amendment had advanced further in the North, but the effect of the Amendment on Northern States was generally ignored in the congressional debates. Even in the North, the conditions of public education did not approximate those existing today. The curriculum was usually rudimentary; ungraded schools were common in rural areas; the school term was but three months a year in many states; and compulsory school attendance was virtually unknown. As a consequence, it is not surprising that there should be so little in the history of the Fourteenth Amendment relating to its intended effect on public education.

In the first cases in this Court construing the Fourteenth Amendment, decided shortly after its adoption, the Court interpreted its as proscribing all state-imposed discriminations against the Negro race. The doctrine of "separate but equal" did not make its appearance in this Court until 1896 in the case of *Plessy* v. *Ferguson, supra,* involving not education but transportation. American courts have since labored with the doctrine for over half a century. In this Court, there have been six cases involving the "separate but equal" doctrine in the field of public education. In *Cumming* v. *County Board of Education*, 175 U.S. 528, and *Gong Lum* v. *Rice*, 275 U.S. 78, the validity of the doctrine itself was not challenged. In more recent cases, all on the graduate school level, inequality was found in that specific benefits enjoyed by white students were denied to Negro students of the same educational qualifications. *Missouri ex rel. Gaines* v. *Canada*, 305 U.S. 337; *Sipuel* v. *Oklahoma,* 332 U.S. 631; *Sweatt* v. *Painter,* 339 U.S. 629; *McLaurin* v. *Oklahoma State Regents*, 339 U.S. 637. In none of these cases was it necessary to re-examine the doctrine to grant relief to the Negro plaintiff. And in *Sweatt* v. *Painter, supra,* the Court expressly reserved decision on the question whether *Plessy* v. *Ferguson* should be held inapplicable to public education.

In the instant cases, that question is directly presented. Here, unlike *Sweatt* v. *Painter*, there are findings below that the Negro and white schools involved have been equalized, or are being equalized, with respect to buildings, curricula, qualifications and salaries of teachers, and other "tangible" factors. Our decision, therefore, cannot turn on merely a comparison of these tangible factors in the

Negro and white schools involved in each of the cases. We must look instead to the effect of segregation itself on public education.

In approaching this problem, we cannot turn the clock back to 1868 when the Amendment was adopted, or even to 1896 when *Plessy* v. *Ferguson* was written. We must consider public education in the light of its full development and its present place in American life throughout the Nation. Only in this way can it be determined if segregation in public schools deprives these plaintiffs of the equal protection of the laws.

Today, education is perhaps the most important function of state and local governments. Compulsory school attendance laws and the great expenditures for education both demonstrate our recognition of the importance of education to our democratic society. It is required in the performance of our most basic public responsibilities, even service in the armed forces. It is the very foundation of good citizenship. Today it is a principal instrument in awakening the child to cultural values, in preparing him for later professional training, and in helping him to adjust normally to his environment. In these days, it is doubtful that any child may reasonably be expected to succeed in life if he is denied the opportunity of an education. Such an opportunity, where the state has undertaken to provide it, is a right which must be made available to all on equal terms.

We come then to the question presented: Does segregation of children in public schools solely on the basis of race, even though the physical facilities and other "tangible" factors may be equal, deprive the children of the minority group of equal educational opportunities? We believe that it does.

In *Sweatt* v. *Painter, supra,* in finding that a segregated law school for Negroes could not provide them equal educational opportunities, this Court relied in large part on "those qualities which are incapable of objective measurement but which make for greatness in a law school." In *McLaurin* v. *Oklahoma State Regents, supra,* the Court, in requiring that a Negro admitted to a white graduate school be treated like all other students, again resorted to intangible considerations: ". . . his ability to study, to engage in discussions and exchange views with other students, and, in general, to learn his profession." Such considerations apply with added force to children in grade and high schools. To separate them from others of similar age and qualifications solely because of their race generates a feeling of inferiority as to their status in the community that may affect their hearts and minds in a way unlikely ever to be undone. The effect of this separation on their educational opportunities was well stated by a finding in the Kansas case by a court which nevertheless felt compelled to rule against the Negro plaintiffs: "Segregation of white and colored children in public schools has a detrimental effect upon the colored children. The impact is greater when it has the sanction of the law; for the policy of separating the races is usually interpreted as denoting the inferiority of the Negro group. A sense of inferiority affects the motivation of a child to learn. Segregation with the sanction of law, therefore, has a tendency to [retard] the educational and mental development of Negro children and to deprive them of some of the benefits they would receive in a racial[ly] integrated school system." Whatever may have been the extent of psychological knowledge at the time of *Plessy* v. *Ferguson,* this finding is amply supported by modern authority. Any language in *Plessy* v. *Ferguson* contrary to this finding is rejected.

We conclude that in the field of public education the doctrine of "separate but equal" has no place. Separate educational facilities are inherently unequal. Therefore, we hold that the plaintiffs and others similarly situated for whom the actions have been brought are, by reason of the segregation complained of, deprived of

the equal protection of the laws guaranteed by the Fourteenth Amendment. This disposition makes unnecessary any discussion whether such segregation also violates the Due Process Clause of the Fourteenth Amendment.

(b) PRESIDENT EISENHOWER'S ADDRESS TO THE PEOPLE ON THE LITTLE ROCK SITUATION*

For a few minutes this evening I want to speak to you about the serious situation that has arisen in Little Rock. To make this talk I have come to the President's office in the White House. I could have spoken from Rhode Island, where I have been staying recently, but I felt that, in speaking from the house of Lincoln, of Jackson and of Wilson, my words would better convey both the sadness I feel in the action I was compelled today to take and the firmness with which I intend to pursue this course until the orders of the Federal Court at Little Rock can be executed without unlawful interference.

In that city, under the leadership of demagogic extremists, disorderly mobs have deliberately prevented the carrying out of proper orders from a Federal Court. Local authorities have not eliminated that violent opposition and, under the law, I yesterday issued a Proclamation calling upon the mob to disperse.

This morning the mob again gathered in front of the Central High School of Little Rock, obviously for the purpose of again preventing the carrying out of the Court's order relating to the admission of Negro children to that school.

Whenever normal agencies prove inadequate to the task and it becomes necessary for the Executive Branch of the Federal Goverment to use its powers and authority to uphold Federal Courts, the President's responsibility is inescapable.

In accordance with that responsibility, I have today issued an Executive Order directing the use of troops under Federal authority to aid in the execution of Federal law at Little Rock, Arkansas. This became necessary when my Proclamation of yesterday was not observed, and the obstruction of justice still continues. . . .

As you know, the Supreme Court of the United States has decided that separate public educational facilities for the races are inherently unequal and therefore compulsory school segregation laws are unconstitutional.

Our personal opinions about the decision have no bearing on the matter of enforcement; the responsibility and authority of the Supreme Court to interpret the Constitution are very clear. Local Federal Courts were instructed by the Supreme Court to issue such orders and decrees as might be necessary to achieve admission to public schools without regard to race—and with all deliberate speed.

During the past several years, many communities in our Southern States have instituted public school plans for gradual progress in the enrollment and attendance of school children of all races in order to bring themselves into compliance with the law of the land.

They thus demonstrated to the world that we are a nation in which laws, not men, are supreme.

I regret to say that this truth—the cornerstone of our liberties—was not observed in this instance.

* September 24, 1957. From *Public Papers of the Presidents of the United States, Dwight D. Eisenhower, 1957*, Washington, 1958, pp. 689-691, 694.

It was my hope that this localized situation would be brought under control by city and State authorities. If the use of local police powers had been sufficient, our traditional method of leaving the problems in those hands would have been pursued. But when large gatherings of obstructionists made it impossible for the decrees of the Court to be carried out, both the law and the national interest demanded that the President take action. . . .

At a time when we face grave situations abroad because of the hatred that Communism bears toward a system of government based on human rights, it would be difficult to exaggerate the harm that is being done to the prestige and influence, and indeed to the safety, of our nation and the world.

Our enemies are gloating over this incident and using it everywhere to misrepresent our whole nation. We are portrayed as a violator of those standards of conduct which the peoples of the world united to proclaim in the Charter of the United Nations. There they affirmed "faith in fundamental human rights" and "in the dignity and worth of the human person" and they did so "without distinction as to race, sex, language or religion."

And so, with deep confidence, I call upon the citizens of the State of Arkansas to assist in bringing to an immediate end all interference with the law and its processes. If resistance to the Federal Court orders ceases at once, the further presence of Federal troops will be unnecessary and the City of Little Rock will return to its normal habits of peace and order and a blot upon the fair name and high honor of our nation in the world will be removed.

7

Judicial Control of Congress

☆ *After World War II the investigative activities of the Congressional committees broadened to the point where their propriety and legality were sharply questioned. In Watkins v. United States the petitioner, who had been found guilty of contempt of Congress, maintained that the House Committee on Un-American Activities could not legally compel him to disclose information merely for the sake of disclosure. The Supreme Court, in effect, upheld this contention in an 8 to 1 decision on May 17, 1957.** ☆

In the decade following World War II, there appeared a new kind of congressional inquiry unknown in prior periods of American history. Principally this was the result of the various investigations into the threat of subversion of the United States Government, but other subjects of congressional interests also contributed to the changed scene. This new phase of legislative inquiry involved a broad-scale intrusion into the lives and affairs of private citizens. It brought before the courts novel questions of the appropriate limits of congressional inquiry. Prior cases, like *Kilbourn,* *McGrain* and *Sinclair,* had defined the scope of investigative power in terms of the inherent limitations of the sources of that power. In the more recent cases, the emphasis shifted to problems of accommodating the interest of the Government with the rights and privileges of individuals. The central scheme was the application of the Bill of Rights as a restraint upon the as-

sertion of governmental power in this form.

It was during this period that the Fifth Amendment privilege against self-incrimination was frequently invoked and recognized as a legal limit upon the authority of a committee to require that a witness answer its questions. Some early doubts as to the applicability of that privilege before a legislative committee never matured. When the matter reached this Court, the Government did not challenge in any way that the Fifth Amendment protection was available to the witness, and such a challenge could not have prevailed. It confined its argument to the character of the answers sought and to the adequacy of the claim of privilege. . . .

A far more difficult task evolved from the claim by witnesses that the committees' interrogations were infringements upon the freedoms of the First Amendment. Clearly, an investigation is subject to the command that the Congress shall make no law abridging freedom of speech or press or assembly. While it is true that

* From 354 U.S. 178.

there is no statute to be reviewed, and that an investigation is not a law, nevertheless an investigation is part of lawmaking. It is justified solely as an adjunct to the legislative process. The First Amendment may be invoked against infringement of the protected freedoms by law or by lawmaking.

Abuses of the investigative process may imperceptibly lead to abridgment of protected freedoms. The mere summoning of a witness and compelling him to testify, against his will, about his beliefs, expressions or associations is a measure of governmental interference. And when those forced revelations concern matters that are unorthodox, unpopular, or even hateful to the general public, the reaction in the life of the witness may be disastrous. This effect is even more harsh when it is past beliefs, expressions or associations that are disclosed and judged by current standards rather than those contemporary with the matters exposed. Nor does the witness alone suffer the consequences. Those who are indentified by witnesses and thereby placed in the same glare of publicity are equally subject to public stigma, scorn and obloquy. Beyond that, there is the more subtle and immeasurable effect upon those who tend to adhere to the most orthodox and uncontroversial views and associations in order to avoid a similar fate at some future time. That this impact is partly the result of non-governmental activity by private persons cannot relieve the investigators of their responsibility for initiating the reaction. . . .

Accommodation of the congressional need for particular information with the individual and personal interest in privacy is an arduous and delicate task for any court. We do not underestimate the difficulties that would attend such an undertaking. It is manifest that despite the adverse effects which follow upon compelled disclosure of private matters,

not all such inquires are barred. *Kilbourn v. Thompson* teaches that such an investigation into individual affairs is invalid if unrelated to any legislative purpose. That is beyond the powers conferred upon the Congress in the Constitution. *United States v. Rumely* makes it plain that the mere semblance of legislative purpose would not justify an inquiry in the face of the Bill of Rights. The critical element is the existence of, and the weight to be ascribed to, the interest of the Congress in demanding disclosures from an unwilling witness. We cannot simply assume, however, that every congressional investigation is justified by a public need that overbalances any private rights affected. To do so would be to abdicate the responsibility placed by the Constitution upon the judiciary to insure that the Congress does not unjustifiably encroach upon an individual's right to privacy nor abridge his liberty of speech, press, religion or assembly.

Petitioner has earnestly suggested that the difficult questions of protecting these rights from infringement by legislative inquiries can be surmounted in this case because there was no public purpose served in his interrogation. His conclusion is based upon the thesis that the Subcommittee was engaged in a program of exposure for the sake of exposure. The sole purpose of the inquiry, he contends, was to bring down upon himself and others the violence of public reaction because of their past beliefs, expressions and associations. In support of this argument, petitioner has marshalled an impressive array of evidence that some Congressmen have believed that such was their duty, or part of it.

We have no doubt that there is no congressional power to expose for the sake of exposure. The public is, of course, entitled to be informed concerning the workings of its government. That cannot be inflated into a general power to expose where the predominant result can only be an invasion of the private rights of individuals. But a solution to our problem is not to be found in testing the motives of committee members for this purpose. Such is not our function. Their motives alone would not vitiate an investigation which had been instituted by a House of Congress if that assembly's legislative purpose is being served.

Petitioner's contentions do point to a situation of particular significance from the standpoint of the constitutional limitations upon congressional investigations. The theory of a committee inquiry is that the committee members are serving as the representatives of the parent assembly in collecting information for a legislative purpose. Their function is to act as the eyes and ears of the Congress in obtaining facts upon which the full legislature can act. To carry out this mission, committees and subcommittees, sometimes one Congressman, are endowed with the full power of the Congress to compel testimony. In this case, only two

men exercised that authority in demanding information over petitioner's protest.

An essential premise in this situation is that the House or Senate shall have instructed the committee members on what they are to do with the power delegated to them. It is the responsibility of the Congress, in the first instance, to insure that compulsory process is used only in furtherance of a legislative purpose. That requires that the instructions to an investigating committee spell out that group's jurisdiction and purpose with sufficient particularity. Those instructions are embodied in the authorizing resolution. That document is the committee's charter. Broadly drafted and loosely worded, however, such resolutions can leave tremendous latitude to the discretion of the investigators. The more vague the committee's charter is, the greater becomes the possibility that the committee's specific actions are not in conformity with the will of the parent House of Congress.

8

The Economy of the Eisenhower Years

☆ *While most Americans enjoyed unprecedented prosperity during the Eisenhower years, the nation experienced several economic setbacks characterized by decreases in production and profits and increases in unemployment and inventories. President Eisenhower commented on economic problems and appropriate government action in his 1958 Chicago address.* ☆

(a) GENERAL PROSPERITY, ECONOMIC REPORT OF THE PRESIDENT*

The vigor of the underlying forces that make for growth in the American economy was clearly evident in 1959. Employment, production, and income at the end of the year were substantially above the levels reached at the end of 1958, despite the prolonged strike in the steel industry. As this Economic Report is transmitted to the Congress, the outlook is good for an extension of growth through 1960 and beyond. . . .

A few facts illustrate the ability of the American economy to continue raising what has long been the highest living scale in the world, while carrying a heavy defense burden and meeting broad international obligations.

In the 14 years since the passage of the Employment Act, employment has advanced, on the average, by nearly 800,000 a year. In real terms, the Nation's output of goods and services, as well as its personal income, has increased by more than

50 percent, or at a rate of 3.2 percent per year; and the output of the private sector of the economy has advanced at a slightly higher rate, 3.5 percent. For industrial production, the rate of increase has been 4.5 percent. The annual increase of 3.2 percent in total national output, which corresponds to a doubling every 22 years, is roughly equivalent to the long-term average reached in our previous history. Thus, the American economy has sustained its long-term record of growth, despite the high level of industrial development already achieved and despite temporary setbacks.

The increase in national output has made possible very great gains in the well-being of American families. . . . Real income per capita has increased by nearly 20 percent since 1946, and the increase per family has been 16 percent. As incomes have risen and as paid vacations have become longer and more common, leisure time has increased and recreational activities have become more widely enjoyed. The shortage of housing so evident

* 1960. From *Economic Report of the President, Transmitted to the Congress, January 20, 1960*, Washington, 1960, pp. 1-3.

immediately after World War II has been virtually eliminated. Since 1946, the housing supply has been increased by the construction of 15 million private nonfarm dwelling units, and there have been marked improvements in the quality of housing. At the same time, there has been a general increase in home ownership; some 60 percent of all nonfarm dwelling units are owned by the occupant families.

Attention to such material advances should not obscure the accompanying gains made with respect to other components of our well-being, some of which are less tangible. In health, there has been remarkable progress in the reduction of infant and maternal mortality, in the prevention, mitigation, and treatment of many diseases, in restoring the physically handicapped, in making available a better balanced diet at lower cost, and in creating other conditions conducive to longer years of life and greater efficiency. Health services are more and more widely available, and the great majority of Americans now have some protection under voluntary plans of hospital, surgical, and medical insurance.

Notable gains have been made in education and other cultural areas. School enrollment has risen in the last 12 years from 50 percent to about 65 percent of all persons in the age group of 5 to 29 years. From 1946 to 1959, the number of Bachelor's and first professional degrees conferred annually almost trebled, and the number of Master's and second professional degrees showed a still greater relative increase. To some extent, these advances represent the resumption of academic work interrupted by war, but the large gains made in the past few years indicate a rising trend that will accelerate in the years ahead. The number of earned Doctorates conferred rose sharply after the war, reaching in 1954 a new high, which has been maintained for several years. In the past decade, more

than 83,000 Doctorates have been conferred, compared with some 27,000 during the 1930's and about 31,000 in the 1940's. Marked increases are expected also in the next several years. Another source of satisfaction is the record of scientific achievement. Since 1946, close to half of the Nobel awards for contributions to medicine, chemistry, and physics have been bestowed on American citizens.

The economic security of American families has been advanced significantly in the years since World War II. About 58 million persons—87 percent of all those in paid employment—are now covered by the Federal Government's old-age, survivors, and disability insurance system and related programs. More than 19 million persons are covered by privately financed pension plans. The Federal-State Unemployment Compensation System, which has proved its worth as a defense against loss of income during periods of economic adversity, now provides protection for nearly 85 percent of all persons on nonfarm payrolls.

But the progress made under Government programs should not divert attention from the extensive provisions made independently by Americans for personal and family security. The number of life insurance policyholders, for example, has increased by about 60 percent since 1946; about 115 million persons were insured through legal reserve companies in 1959. The volume of time and savings deposits of individuals has increased by nearly $35 billion, or more than 50 percent, since 1952. Share accounts in savings and loan associations have also risen by $35 billion in this period—by nearly 200 percent.

And it is not too much to say that we have made good progress in moderating fluctuations in our economy. Although economic recessions, however minor, must remain a matter of concern to all Americans, the relative mildness and short duration of the three since the war have to be reckoned as a major factor in the strengthening of personal security.

(b) PRESIDENT EISENHOWER'S ADDRESS AT CHICAGO*

This autumn we are reaching new peaks in living and producing. . . .

Last month unemployment dropped by 600,000.

Housing is booming.

Labor's share of the national income is now 71 percent, 6 percent higher than in 1952.

Last month the average weekly earnings of production workers hit a record of over $85.

More important, family purchasing power is up 7 percent.

Agricultural exports totaled over $8.5 billion in the two years ending last June —the highest ever.

Gross farm income, per capita income of farm people, land values, farm ownership—all these are up or stand at record highs.

Now, in weighing these encouraging advances, it is important to realize that they are firmly anchored in a fiscal policy that is sane, sensible, and trustworthy. That policy is but the reflection of an abiding Republican faith—faith in the vitality of our free economy, and faith in its strength. That policy and that faith concern each one of us directly and personally.

Here is an example.

All of us know that, in a free economy, periodically the business cycle will temporarily turn down. This happened in our country a year ago. What then did those of little faith do?

At once they rushed to the wailing wall. Frantically merchandising doubt and fear, they forecast disaster with every decimal decline in the nation's economic indices. To meet their own forecasts, they cried out for massive public works and an avalanche of Federal spending.

What a myth!

The most deceptive notion taught by self-styled liberals is that when the economy starts to slow up, only a vast outpouring of your tax dollars will pump us out of trouble. That just means trying to live on new debts. It means diluting the dollar to fool the public into believing the economy is booming. It is cheating your children. This is a counterfeit logic. No sound-thinking American can possibly accept that philosophy.

We did not accept it, the radicals in Congress notwithstanding. Early this year we launched an orderly program to promote confidence and to help renew economic growth. These measures were not massive and heavy-handed. They did not founder the economy. Huge programs would have only enfeebled the economy.

Instead, the Administration last winter gave the private citizen and private enterprise a helping hand, not a Federal wheel-chair. In this, we kept faith with America. In this we again demonstrated our belief in the incentive system under which this nation has flourished beyond all others on the earth.

At some future time the business cycle may again show signs of slowing up. Should that occur, let us pray and hope that steadiness of faith and action, rather than hysterical fear, will be our government's guide.

Already the nation has repudiated those who panicked, those who prophesied that only huge Federal spending would save us from ruin. Already we are climbing to new levels of national income whose upper limits are not yet measureable.

* October 22, 1958. From *Public Papers of the Presidents of the United States, Dwight Eisenhower, 1958,* Washington, 1959, pp. 787-790.

Fellow Americans, Republican faith in the regenerative powers of our economy has been well placed.

Now in the years ahead our economic growth must be real productive gains not measured in the puffed up statistics of inflation.

Unlike certain economists influential in the opposition party, thoughtful Americans know that inflation is neither necessary nor desirable for sound economic growth. Unbridled inflation leads only to the dismal cycle of boom or bust. It robs us of our savings. It shrinks our pensions and insurance policies by paying back dollars worth less than when they were earned.

By now the farmer, the wage-earner, the businessman have all discovered the tragic effect of inflation. It is this: a pocketbook, though bulging more and more, buying ever less at the corner store. That is why all of us—regardless of party —must be hard-headed in our fight against inflation.

That's why Government must itself set an example to the nation. Government must keep its spending down.

And that, too, is Republicanism.

You and I know the irresistible impulse of the political radical. It is to squander money—your money. The result, another spurt of inflation.

In the last Congress the spendthrifts authorized the spending of billions more than sound government management required. Only aggressive Republican action stopped the authorization of still more billions.

Fellow citizens, every governmental economy is a block against inflation, inflation that picks the pockets of everyone, inflation that deals most harshly with the aged and with the poor.

I cannot too strongly emphasize that if we are to keep our economy vigorous and healthy, we must never cease our fight against reckless spending—and its offspring, inflation.

9

International Trade

☆ *For several generations the United States had maintained a favorable balance of international trade. Therefore, the nation was surprised to find by the end of the 1950's that it was incurring a deficit on its balance of payments. Sir Oliver Franks, former British ambassador to the United States, comments on the relation of this development to the formation first of the European Common Market composed of the "Inner Six," and later the trade alliance led by Great Britain called the "Outer Seven."** ☆

It seems to me that the economic objectives to which we have been accustomed in Europe and the United States since the Second World War paralleled the attempt to answer the dominant political and strategic problem, that of East-West tension polarized in Washington and Moscow. The two aims we tried to realize were, first, the recovery of Western Europe and, secondly, the strengthening of world liquidity so that the international exchanges of trade would not break down through lack of the means of payment.

Throw your mind back to the second half of 1947, when concentrated work first began on the Marshall Plan. Who can forget how doubtful any real recovery of Western Europe seemed, how easily the collapse of Western Europe might have tilted the world balance decisively in favor of the East and Communism? When I was at the Paris Conference in the late

* From Sir Oliver Franks, "The New International Balance: Challenge to the Western World," *Saturday Review*, XLIII (January 16, 1960), pp. 20, 22-24. Used by permission of Committee for Economic Development.

summer of 1947 it was only a matter of weeks before France and Italy ran out of dollars with which to pay for bread grains—and this in a world in which there were no surplus bread grains outside North America. Only twelve years ago Europe was on the threshold of catastrophe, while lack of gold or inadequate reserves of acceptable currencies in many countries made any lasting revival of international trade a dim and distant prospect. At this point you will allow me, as a citizen of Britain, to observe that while these two great aims—the recovery of Europe and the building up of reserves and liquidity in most of the Western world— were common objectives of the peoples on both sides of the Atlantic and while cooperation between them was genuine and strong, nothing at all could have been achieved without the broad, imaginative, constructive initiatives of American policy. The Marshall Plan itself, the whole story of aid and assistance, the steady liberalization of the international trading policies of the United States during the period, are historical evidence of this truth.

But why do I dig back twelve years into the past? To remind you how greatly things have changed. In the late 1940s and through most of the 1950s we were quite clear about these international economic objectives in the Western world and worked steadily towards them: there was no problem of identification. But now Europe has recovered. Think, too, how much the problems of world liquidity have been eased. No doubt it would be foolish to talk of ultimate or enduring solutions or hope that no further difficulties will arise. But consider how international trade has revived, how the manufacturing industries of Western Europe have been rebuilt, how the reserves of their central banks have been increased, and how the gold stocks of the free world are better distributed. When we add to all this the increase in the resources of the International Monetary Fund and the increased strength of sterling, one of the two great international trading currencies, surely the contrast between now and the late 1940s is absolute. We have moved into a different sort of world. . . .

Just as twelve years ago the balance of the world depended upon the fate of Western Europe, so in these coming years it will surely turn on the destiny of the newly developing countries.

We all know that many of them intend to develop at all costs. It is no use wondering whether it is wise. We developed ourselves earlier and they are now going to develop themselves in turn. They face a vicious circle. Low living standards and free, broadly democratic societies cannot produce sufficient savings for the rapid economic development they will not forego. They need more capital to increase output; low output prevents sufficient saving for capital.

This circle can be broken in one of two ways. It can be broken by tyranny which, by enforcing hardships on the people and holding down their standard of living, forces the savings for rapid development. Or it can be broken by capital from outside which gives a free society the chance both to develop and to remain free. This vicious circle for country after country will be broken one way or the other in coming years.

We have already had evidence in the Middle East of how real and how urgent these problems are. I do not understate when I say that the world balance will shift decisively against us if we fail to devise adequate means to realize the twin objectives I have identified. . . .

I now come to the next problem. You in the United States have been giving a good deal of thought to the groupings that are emerging in Western Europe. People sometimes speak of the emergence of economic blocs. I should not use the term "bloc" myself. It implies a permanence and a defensive attitude which do not exist in the present situation. I regard it as premature and unreasonably pessimistic to think of Western Europe as split into economic blocs. . . .

My observations are these: I do not think it realistic to suppose that there will not be regional economic groupings somewhere between the single nation-states of today and the universality of all the nations. After all, we have done it ourseves on the political front in NATO.

The plain fact is that the world is too big, the individual nation is too small. Regional groupings are a natural occurrence nowadays. You in the United States sometimes tend to forget that you are both one nation and a large regional group.

I regard the idea of the unity of Western Europe as the one great creative political idea that has emerged since the Second World War. If the idea of one community, one society in Europe, is to have any validity, it must gradually clothe itself with economic meaning. I think that any country, yours or mine, which failed to recognize this would certainly put itself in the wrong.

I should admit that we in Britain have been slow to appreciate and understand the political idea and its driving force which underlie the institutions of the Six. I regard it as a misfortune, and I am sure that almost all of us in Britain do so, that we have had to devise the Seven. Given our difficulties for the time being with the Six, I think the Seven became inevitable as a stage of development. But it is our task to see that these are temporary phases in the adjustment of Western Europe to the European idea.

The interest of the United States, I suggest, is not to try to break down these groupings, still less to favor one against the other. Its true interest is twofold: first, to see the two groupings ultimately merge so that the dream of the free movement of men, goods, and ideas comes true in Western Europe; secondly, to work with these groupings, or the group that may emerge, so that together we progressively lower economic discrimination in the free world. . . .

I should also like to mention your growing concern about the adverse balance of payments of the United States. Here I have to speak about your own affairs and, if what I have to say is not suitably hedged about with qualifications, I hope you will remember that the qualifications are at any rate in my mind. I shall take the two economic objectives of the Western world as my guide.

The fact is that the United States, after incurring a deficit on its balance of payments for some years of the order of $1.5 billion a year on the average, suddenly found, in 1958 and 1959, that the deficit had increased sharply. It appears that in the two years together the United States has lost about $7 billion in gold and dollars. The United States cannot, and of course will not, live with a deficit on this

scale for a long period. But compared with the rest of us, you still have very comfortable reserves, and the advantage of this is that you have time to determine and apply a sensible course of action. The methods by which this deficit is reduced and brought within reasonable limits are all-important for the rest of the free world, both the industrialized countries of the Atlantic Community and the developing regions. Some methods are consistent with the guiding objectives of us all, and some are not.

I think it is clear that the one method of dealing with this problem which would be disastrous is if the United States attempted to rid itself of a deficit on the balance of payments by one drastic surgical operation.

I need not elaborate on why the consequences of this would be disastrous for all the neighbors of the United States in the free world. But it would also be disastrous for the United States because it would mean risking, and probably losing a great deal of, that large area of the world won for freedom since the end of the World War II. It is of vital importance that you do not try to shake off these difficulties by a large and violent lurch of policy. I do not think you will make such a decision.

The means by which it is sought to reduce the deficit on your balance of payments must be numerous. Something of everything that is relevant must be done: no one line must be pressed too hard. How can we spell this out?

One measure you have already adopted is to maintain a steady campaign for more manufactured exports from your own country to other industrialized countries. . . .

Next, it is clearly the job of recovered Europe to dismantle dollar discriminations in trade which had their justification in an earlier period. This has already happened on a considerable scale and can go further. Convertibility of European currencies against the dollar has gone a long way. . . .

But let me say one thing here: it is important that you do not expect too much. You cannot escape the size of your own economy, the vast power of your productive machine, and your wealth. You are so disproportionate to the rest of us that what in fact is fair can easily seem the reverse to you. It is our job in Europe to do more: we shall help but can never stand in your shoes.

Beyond this, I am aware that all countries faced with dfficulties in the balance of payments are subject to internal political pressures. I will say only this: In the period since the Second World War you have, by economic aid and expenditure abroad on a very large scale, created conditions in which international trade has expanded freely. You have provided a growing market for imported goods, free from quantitative control except for a few exceptions. You have progressively reduced the level of the tariff under the Reciprocal Trade Agreements program. I know that on occasion the straight line of policy has to become a little wavy in places to accommodate the existing political situation. But there is all the difference in the world between a rare concession and a breaking of the line. This last would be to deny that leadership of the free world which history in this half-century has given the American nation.

In conclusion it remains for me to express one conviction. We shall run into real difficulties about the new economic problems which confront us in the broad relationship between Western Europe and the United States unless we are prepared to look at these issues and resolve them in the light of the wider objectives which we must pursue together.

XVI

our generation and our future

T HE DECADE of the 1960's faced the nation with a series of challenges that demanded a reappraisal of existing institutions, practices, and values. Many Americans discerned a trend toward "conformity," whereby the individual sought to be as little different from others as possible. This tendency to allow others to determine one's habits and tastes was attributed to many factors, including modern advertising and generally higher incomes, but it seemed to reflect a sense of insecurity and an abdication of personal responsibility in favor of group decisions. Conventional class lines were replaced by new status classifications based on symbols created by standardized patterns of work and community living. Added leisure time, higher income, and increased education helped equate culture with social acceptability, though ostentation rather than sincere appreciation often resulted. The age of material abundance revealed anew that man did not live by bread alone and led to a questioning of the American conception of the "good life." A nation that had finally won the age-old struggle for food and shelter groped anxiously for a solution to its new dissatisfactions and lack of fulfillment.

In the economic arena, the concentration of wealth brought varied reactions from observers. Professor Galbraith contented that "countervailing powers," such as chain retail organizations and large unions, had emerged to exercise restraint on the activities of large corporations and create a equilibrium of power. Adolf Berle maintained that corporate power carries with it an obligation to the society, and that controls must be developed to insure that this obligation is met. Of great concern was the introduction of automatic control devices in business and industry which threatened to replace all industrial workers except the technician who serviced the machine. Automation was a double-edged sword, which promised greater efficiency and lower costs as well as hardship on displaced workers.

The harnessing of the atom appeared to offer the greatest possibilities for good and evil since man devised the fist hatchet. As a new source of industrial power it provided a solution to the dilemma of the exhaustion of nature's supply of gas, coal, and oil. But nuclear energy had been first employed by man as a weapon of war, and the horrifying prospect of its future use in this capacity cast a pall of gloom over all the peoples of the earth. Some questioned the validity of a conflict that would destroy civilization and render the planet virtually uninhabitable.

The complex nature of the problems and the crucial importance of their outcome posed the question whether the nation could any longer afford the luxury of a government based on compromise and the whims of an ill-informed electorate. As uncertainty and fear came to dominate national and human aspirations, a new President reaffirmed his faith in basic American principles and announced his blueprint for the future.

1

The "Pleasing" Society

☆ *In 1950 a fresh analysis of American motivation appeared in* The Lonely Crowd. *Soon intellectuals were discussing its controversial ideas, especially the assertion that behavior was now patterned on securing the approval of others rather than being motivated by one's own opinion.* * ☆

In America middle-class children have allowances of their own at four or five; they have, as opinion leaders in the home, some say in the family budget. The allowances are expected to be spent, whereas in the earlier era they were often used as cudgels of thrift. Moreover, the monopolistic competition characteristic of this era can afford, and is interested in, building up in the child habits of consumption he will employ as an adult. For he will live long, and so will the monopoly. . . .

For all these reasons, then, it has become worth while for professional storytellers to concentrate on the child market; and as the mass media can afford specialists and market research on the particular age cultures and class cultures involved, the children are more heavily cultivated in their own terms than ever before. But while the educator in earlier eras might use the child's language to put across an adult message, today the child's

language may be used to put across the advertiser's and storyteller's idea of what children are like. No longer is it thought to be the child's job to understand the adult world as the adult sees it; for one thing, the world as the adult sees it today is perhaps a more complicated one. Instead, the mass media ask the child to see the world as "the" child—that is, the *other* child—sees it. This is partly the result of the technical advances that make it possible for the movies to create the child world of Margaret O'Brien and her compeers, for the radio to have its array of Hardys, Aldriches, and other juveniles, and for advertising and cover art to make use of professional child models. The media have created a picture of what boyhood and girlhood are like (as during the war they created the picture of the GI, again using the considerably edited language of the soldier) and they force children either to accept or aggressively to resist this picture of themselves.

The child begins to be bombarded by radio and comics from the moment he can listen and just barely read. The bombardment—which of course inevitably over- and under-shoots—hits specifically at

* From David Riesman with Nathan Glazer and Reuel Denney, *The Lonely Crowd—A Study of The Changing American Character*, pp. 120-122, 251-255. Published by Doubleday Anchor Books, Doubleday & Company, Inc., Garden City, 1953. Copyright 1950, 1953 Yale University Press. Used by permission of Yale University Press.

very narrow age-grades. For example, there seems to be for many children a regular gradation of comic-reading stages: from the animal stories like *Bugs Bunny* to invincible heroes like *Superman,* and from there to heroes like *Batman* who, human in make-up, are vulnerable, though of course they always win. . . .

To be sure, the change from the preceding era of inner-direction in America is not abrupt; such changes never are. Formerly the mass media catered to the child market in at least three fields; school texts or homilies, magazines designed for children, and penny dreadfuls. But when these are compared with the contemporary media we are at once aware of differences. The appraisal of the market by the writers of this earlier literature was amateurish in comparison with market research today. Moreover, they aimed generally to spur work drives and stimulate nobility rather than to effect any socialization of taste. The English boys' weeklies, as Orwell describes them, usually opposed liquor and tobacco—as did the clergyman authors of school and church readers. Such admonitions remind us of the "crime doesn't pay" lesson of the comics, a facade for messages of more importance. The boys' weeklies and their American counterparts were involved with training the young for the frontiers of production (including warfare), and as an incident of that training the embryo athlete might eschew smoke and drink. The comparable media today train the young for the frontiers of consumption— to tell the difference between Pepsi-Cola and Coca-Cola, as later between Old Golds and Chesterfields.

We may mark the change by citing an old nursery rhyme:

> "This little pig went to market;
> This little pig stayed at home.
> This little pig had roast beef;
> This little pig had none.
> This little pig went wee-wee-wee

> All the way home."

The rhyme may be taken as a paradigm of individuation and unsocialized behavior among children of an earlier era. Today, however, all little pigs go to market; none stay home; all have roast beef, if any do; and all say "we-we". . . .

IS THERE A RULING CLASS LEFT?

. . . people go on acting as if there still were a decisive ruling class in contemporary America. In the post-war years, businessmen thought labor leaders and politicians ran the country, while labor and the left thought that "Wall Street" ran it, or the "sixty families." Wall Street, confused perhaps by its dethronement as a telling barometer of capital-formation weather, may have thought that the midwestern industrial barons, cushioned on plant expansion money in the form of heavy depreciation reserves and undivided profits, ran the country. They might have had some evidence for this in the fact that the New Deal was much tougher with finance capital—e.g., the SEC and the Holding Company Act—than with industrial capital and that when, in the undistributed profits tax, it tried to subject the latter to a stockholder and money-market control, the tax was quickly repealed.

But these barons of Pittsburgh, Weirton, Akron, and Detroit, though certainly a tougher crowd than the Wall Streeters, are . . . coming more and more to think of themselves as trustees for their beneficiaries. And whereas, from the point of view of labor and the left, these men ran the War Production Board in the interest of their respective companies, one could argue just as easily that the WPB experience was one of the congeries of factors that have tamed the barons. It put them in a situation where they had to view their company from the point of view of "the others."

Despite the absence of intensive studies of business power and of what happens in a business negotiation, one can readily get an impressionistic sense of the change in business behavior in the last generation. In the pages of *Fortune*, that excellent chronicler of business, one can see that there are few survivals of the kinds of dealings—with other businessmen, with labor, with the government—that were standard operating practice for the pre-World War I tycoons. Moreover, in its twenty-year history, *Fortune* itself has shown, and perhaps it may be considered not too unrepresentative of its audience, a steady decline of interest in business as such and a growing interest in once peripheral matters, such as international relations, social science, and other accoutrements of the modern executive.

But it is of course more difficult to know whether character has changed as well as behavior—whether, as some contend, businessmen simply rule today in a more subtle, more "managerial" way. In "Manager Meets Union" Joseph M. Goldsen and Lillian Low have depicted the psychological dependence of a contemporary sales manager on the approval of the men under him, his willingness to go to great lengths, in terms of concessions, to maintain interpersonal warmth in his relations with them, and his fierce resentment of the union as a barrier to this emotional exchange. As against this, one must set the attitude of some of the auto-supply companies whose leadership still seems much more craft-oriented than people-oriented and therefore unwilling to make concessions and none too concerned with the emotional atmosphere of negotiations. Likewise, the General Motors—UAW negotiations of 1946, as reported in print, sound more like a cockfight than a Platonic symposium, although in Peter Drucker's *Concept of the Corporation*, a study of General Motors published in the same year, there is much evidence of

management eagerness to build a big, happy family.

Power, indeed, is founded, in a large measure, on interpersonal expectations and attitudes. If businessmen *feel* weak and dependent, they do in actuality *become* weaker and more dependent, no matter what material resources may be ascribed to them. My impression, based mainly on experiences of my own in business and law practice, is that businessmen from large manufacturing companies, though they often talk big, are easily frightened by the threat of others' hostility; they may pound the table, but they look to others for leadership and do not care to get out of line with their peer-groupers. . . .

Businessmen, moreover, are not the only people who fail to exploit the power position they are supposed, in the eyes of many observers, to have. Army officers are also astonishingly timid about exercising their leadership. During the war one would have thought that the army would be relatively impervious to criticism. But frequently the generals went to great lengths to refrain from doing something about which a congressman might make an unfriendly speech. They did so even at times when they might have brushed the congressman off like an angry fly. When dealing with businessmen or labor leaders, army officers were, it seemed to me, astonishingly deferential; and this was as true of the West Pointers as of the reservists. Of course, there were exceptions, but in many of the situations where the armed services made concessions to propitiate some veto group, they rationalized the concessions in terms of morale or of postwar public relations needs or, frequently, simply were not aware of their power position.

To be sure, some came to the same result by the route of a democratic tradition of civilian dominance. Very likely, it was a good thing for the country that the services were so self-restrained. I do not here deal with the matter on the merits but use it as an illustration of changing character and changing social structure.

All this may lead to the question: well, who *really* runs things? What people fail to see is that, while it may take leadership to start things running, or to stop them, very little leadership is needed once things are under way—that, indeed, things can get terribly snarled up and still go on running. If one studies a factory, an army group, or other large organization, one wonders how things get done at all, with the lack of leadership and with all the featherbedding. Perhaps they get done because we are still trading on our reserves of inner-direction, especially in the lower ranks. At any rate, the fact they do get done is no proof that there is someone in charge.

2
Taste and Status in America

☆ *In 1959* Fortune *magazine ran a series of perceptive articles on American life. Reprinted below are excerpts from these articles, one dealing with changes in taste, the other with shifts from conventional class to new status lines.* ☆

(a) "HOW AMERICAN TASTE IS CHANGING"*

But is it possible to talk about absolute standards of taste? A lot of cagey thinkers, from the dawn of civilization, have maintained that anybody laying down such standards is simply describing his personal inclinations. It is certainly true that taste cannot be analyzed and graded to close standards, like aluminum alloys, or internal-combustion engines. Moreover, taste is often the cloak of the intellectual snob who automatically defines as bad anything that is popular. Yet there appear to be some fundamentals of fitness, proportion, and beauty. Give a group of people a series of pictures of objects and tell them to pick the best and the worst, and they agree remarkably on the extremes of both good and bad. What is more, a nation's taste is the measure of its culture, and to deny the reality of qualitative differences in taste is to slam the door on all inherited cultural values. If those values mean anything at all, there is an important difference between J. D. Salinger and Mickey Spillane, between the *Eroica*

and *Pink Shoe Laces*, between O'Neill and soap opera, between the Parthenon and a hot-dog stand.

Perhaps the most practical approach to taste values is simply to observe that "good" taste is usually the taste of the "upper" classes, the artistically proficient, or the learned. But the arbiters or makers of taste are not only educators, the *avant-garde*, the intellectuals, the writers, the designers. They are also, as we shall see, often manufacturers and merchandisers. These arbiters, of course, don't always agree among themselves, but whether they agree or not, they do set standards. So let us say that "good" taste in the U.S. is represented by the preferences of its tastemakers.

Four major forces are working to elevate American taste: (1) rising real income; (2) more education, both formal and informal; (3) the efforts of the tastemakers to spread their own gospel; and (4) the old American striving for self-betterment.

The effect of rising real income on U.S. taste is not merely that it enables people to buy more. It usually enables business

---

* By Gilbert Burck. From *Fortune*, LX *(July 1959)* pp. 115-116, 196. Courtesy of *Fortune* Magazine.

to provide consumers with a steadily wider range of choices, thus making mass production the agent not of uniformity but of constantly widening variety. And along with more money, Americans are getting more leisure in which to develop their taste.

But income and leisure without education are like force without direction. As the excesses of America's own newly rich suggest, more leisure and more money for masses of Americans without more and better education could produce a temporary decline in public taste. Immediately after World War II, for example, warplant workers splurged on the elaborate, overstuffed "borax" furniture they had set their hearts on years before.

Not that formal education necessarily improves anyone's taste. But it does help; in fact it is probably the most powerful single factor in the improvement process. And never in American history has education expanded so fast as it is now expanding. The number of adult Americans who have completed high school rose from 27 million, or 33 per cent of the adult population, in 1947 to 39 million, or 40 per cent of the adult population, in 1957; during the 1960's it will surely rise to about 55 million, or 50 per cent of the adult population. During the past decade the number of youths attending college has risen around 50 per cent; during the decade ahead it is expected to double, reaching perhaps seven million. According to the U.S. Office of Education, 35 million to 40 million adults are "interested" in after-hours study programs, and some nine million are actually enrolled in organized courses.

Surely not far behind the formal educators as molders of taste are the informal educators or tastemakers. They have always existed, but never in such quantity. In the past they consisted of a tiny aristocracy, who so to speak administered a nation's culture; today America probably supports the largest taste-conscious *haute bourgeoisie* in history, expressing itself through an extraordinary variety of communications. People who think they possess good taste, like people who believe they possess the one true religion, often harbor a missionary's urge to convert others; and the American people, for the good of their taste, are being subjected to a constant drumfire of instruction, persuasion, and information. The so-called shelter or home-service magazines, for example, play an enormous role in creating the demand for houses and furnishings gratifying to behold. The mass magazines have made such subjects as America's Arts and Skills and Adventures of the Mind interesting to millions of people without talking down or unduly oversimplifying.

And it is merely recording the obvious to say that high culture in the U.S is not only very much alive but is growing fast. The American artistic output, as the whole world testifies, is both sizable and respectable. American writing, painting, sculpture, architecture, and music were once merely imitations and extensions of European culture; today they influence the culture of the rest of the world as much as it influences them.

If, as Walt Whitman once observed, it takes great audiences to produce great art, the U.S. should very soon be launching a great new era of musical composition. There are today forty-two major American symphony orchestras, against six in 1905 and thirty-two in 1956. Counting those in colleges and smaller communities, the total is more than 1,100, and at least 275 of them were formed between 1951 and 1957.

A growing number of Americans are not put off by "difficult" listening. Alban Berg's atonal opera *Wozzeck*, which was expected to be a flop when introduced at the Metropolitan Opera last year, played to sold-out houses. When it was put on the air on a Saturday afternoon, several out-of-town newspapers assigned their music critics to review the broadcast. One reason for this broadening of U.S. musical taste is that the sale of serious music on records has been increasing at least as fast as the sale of all records. The fact is that many Americans with a record player today listen to more musical works in a year than even professional musicians once could in dozens of years.

Although Americans may not read as many books per capita as the British, Scandinavians, and French, the astonishing fact, considering the competition of other diversions such as radio and television, is that they read as many as they do, and that many of them are as good as they are. Americans are buying some 630 million books a year (including paperbacks and juveniles but not textbooks), up from 330 million ten years ago. The success of the paperbacks, which are selling several hundred million copies a year, is enormously significant. A large percentage of the total is trash, but paperback versions of *The Iliad* and *The Odyssey* have together sold more than a million copies. So has J. D. Salinger's *The Catcher in the Rye* and George Orwell's *1984* (which argues, ironically, that the mass media of today will pave the way for the "double-think" of 1984). "The paperbacks," as Clifton Fadiman has noted, "are democratizing reading. They are conferring upon it the simple, healthy status of a normal habit."

What is also relevant, one of the most successful newspaper columns of recent origin is Mortimer Adler's feature dealing with philosophical questions suggested by readers. Inaugurated October 19, 1958 (in Chicago *Sun-Times*), it has been syndicated in newspapers from one end of the country to the other.

Radio and television, which have received their share of criticism, cannot be excluded from any inventory of American cultural media. Although they thrive on mass production, they also cater to special audiences. One can sometimes see or hear on them works one might never have seen or heard in a country with an aristocratic high culture and no mass media, such as Britain and Germany fifty years ago.

All this, of course, does not mean that the masses, for the first time in history, are rushing to embrace high culture. What is significant is that millions of the kind of Americans who make the nation's tastes have clung to or taken up the values of high culture *voluntarily*, uncoerced by state or other cultural authority, in a tolerably free market, and in the face of powerful competition from a multitude of mundane leisure activities. What millions have thus found good, millions more, if past behavior means anything, will almost surely find good.

(b) "THE NEW MASSES"*

In several interesting respects the blue and white collars still play different roles in the suburbs, and still have different reasons for moving there. There have always been some blue-collar families in suburbia, of course, but until recently they tended to be the local service and construction workers who, in middle-class communities, lived on the other side of the tracks. The newer blue-collar suburbanites are characteristically the skilled production workers who man the new industrial plants on the outskirts of metropolitan areas. (Between 1952 and 1957, the suburbs accounted for 80 per cent of all new jobs in the New York metropolitan area.) Unlike the white-collar man, who characteristically moves *away* from his job when he migrates to the suburbs, the blue-collar man is usually moving closer to his job, and is much preoccupied with traffic conditions and driving time between his suburban home and his suburban factory.

* By Daniel Seligman. From *Fortune*, (May 1959), pp. 109-111. Courtesy of *Fortune* Magazine.

The white collar is often acutely conscious of the prestige thought to attach to some particular suburban town or neighborhood. He may load an extra commuting burden on himself to live in such a place—indeed, he may feel that commuting itself is invested with a kind of upper-middle-class prestige value. The blue collar, however, tends to see commuting time simply as an extension of his working day.

The young white collar usually regards his first suburban home as a temporary lodgment on the way to a better one. The blue collar sees it as security for his old age, and for this reason, perhaps, is much more concerned with getting a durable physical property than the white collar is.

But the significant fact is that, while these differences persist, the living habits of the blue and white collars have been converging in many respects; indeed, one might regard the suburbs today as the new American melting pot. A community leader in Royal Oak, a Detroit suburb, notes that the auto workers who followed the plants out of town were "swallowed up" when they lived in Detroit. "When they come out here, they seem hungry for community affairs." Indeed, the fact that they regard their first suburban homes as permanent living places often gives the blue collars a stake in local government that the more transient white collars do not feel they have. A real-estate developer who built a community of $16,000-to-$17,000 houses northwest of Chicago says that about half the community is blue collar, and that he has been "amazed and pleased to see how they've taken hold and run the community. I've sat in on some committees they have, and I'll tell you they make a hell of a lot more sense than some of the junior-executive types I've seen." Even in Park Forest, the Chicago suburb that has been much discussed . . . as a prototypical junior-executive community, there is now a

blue-collar minority verging on 10 per cent, and in two recent years the Little League baseball chairmen have been blue collars. With a few exceptions, the people surveyed by *Fortune* reported that the new blue-collar suburbanites are *not* segregated socially. . . .

While the older class lines are losing their meaning, it would be wildly unrealistic to argue that the U.S. is developing into a society of equals. Instead of having a fairly clear position in an oversimplified but still identifiable "class," the American of the 1960's is seen by the sociologists as a man with a "status." There are dozens of shadings of status—of a man's standing in the eyes of others. Status is more easily changed, obviously, than class. A family's status may jump a notch not only with the father's promotion at the office, but with the mother's election to the chairmanship of a suburban charity drive, or the son's enrollment at the state university.

Spending and status are still intimately related, of course, but in such diverse and sometimes paradoxical ways that novel opportunities and hazards are continually cropping up in the consumer markets. On the one hand, as more and more Americans have been enabled to adopt some form of the middle-class style of life, they have also become increasingly aware of, and more finely attuned to, the nuances that can disclose "the difference"—the difference between those with more and with less income and responsibility. In an age when millions of Americans live in superficially similar suburban developments, the flagstone walk the developer has given his more expensive houses is attentively noted.

The nuances involve much more than displays of income and raw purchasing power, however, since status is importantly bound up with education— which implies, among other things, the exercise of good taste in consumption. In an age when millions can travel abroad, the difference between a three-week economy trip to London-Paris-Rome and a six-week trip taking in Athens and Istanbul is not just the difference in cost but also in sophistication of the itinerary. Then there is the "keeping-down-with-the-Joneses" phenomenon so often seen in modern suburbia, which is not so much a pressure against heavy spending as a pressure to spend money as educated men are supposed to spend it—i.e., on fine high-fidelity sets and good wines rather than expensive fur coats and cars. And yet—just to complicate things still more—there has been such a proliferation of interesting, sophisticated, or chic things to spend money on that it is increasingly difficult to say that any two or three of these things are *the* badges of status.

The preoccupation with status is a phenomenon whose origins are interesting—especially, perhaps, to marketing and advertising men who are increasingly obliged to think of products as status symbols. The preoccupation is related in part to the fact that since 1940 over 20 million adult Americans have spent a good deal of time in the armed forces, where one is obliged constantly to think about "rank." It is also related to the fact that more and more Americans work for large organizations: something like 38 per cent of the labor force is employed in organizations that have over 500 employees. The figure (which includes all government employees) was only 28 per cent in 1940. In the nature of the case, large organizations are status-ridden: titles and responsibilities are carefully defined in job descriptions, and relationships are carefully plotted on organization charts.

3

A French View of Contemporary America

☆   *Jean-Paul Sartre (1905-   ), the popular French existentialist
writer, viewed Americans as people living under many myths. He
saw Americans confronted by the dilemma of wanting to live up to
certain national images while trying to preserve their own individ-
ualities.* *   ☆

There are the great myths, the myths
of happiness, of progress, of liberty, of
triumphant maternity; there is realism
and optimism—and then there are the
Americans, who, nothing at first, grow
up among these colossal statues and find
their way as best they can among them.
There is this myth of happiness: black-
magic slogans warn you to be happy at
once; films that "end well" show a life
of rosy ease to the exhausted crowds; the
language is charged with optimistic and
unrestrained expressions—"have a good
time," "life is fun," and the like. But there
are also those people, who, though conventionally happy, suffer from an obscure
malaise to which no name can be given,
who are tragic through fear of being so,
through that total absence of the tragic in
them and around them.

There is this collectivity which prides
itself on being the least "historical" in the
world, on never complicating its problems
with inherited customs and acquired
rights, on facing as a virgin a virgin future in which everything is possible—and

there are these blind gropings of bewil-
dered people who seek to lean on a tradition, on a folklore. There are the films
that write American history for the
masses and, unable to offer them a Kentucky Jeanne d'Arc or a Kansas Charle-
magne, exalt them with the history of the
jazz singer, Al Jolson, or the composer,
Gershwin. Along with the Monroe doctrine, isolationism, scorn for Europe, there
is the sentimental attachment of each
American for his country of origin, the inferiority complex of the intellectuals before the culture of the old Continent, of
the critics who say, "How can you admire
our novelists, you who have Flaubert?" of
the painters who say, "I shall never be
able to paint as long as I stay in the
United States"; and there is the obscure,
slow effort of an entire nation to seize
universal history and assimilate it as its
patrimony.

There is the myth of equality—and
there is the myth of segregation, with
those big beach-front hotels that post
signs reading "Jews and dogs not allowed,"
those lakes in Connecticut where Jews
may not bathe, and that racial *tchin*, in
which the lowest degree is assigned to the

* From Jean-Paul Sartre, "Americans and Their
Myths," *The Nation*, CLXV (October 18, 1947), pp.
402-403. Used by permission.

Slavs, the highest to the Dutch immigrants of 1680. There is the myth of liberty—and the dictatorship of public opinion; the myth of economic liberalism—and the big companies extending over the whole country which, in the final analysis, belong to no one and in which the employees, from top to bottom, are like functionaries in a state industry. There is respect for science and industry, positivism, an insane love of "gadgets"—and there is the somber humor of the *New Yorker,* which pokes bitter fun at the mechanical civilization of America and the hundred million Americans who satisfy their craving for the marvelous by reading every day in the "comics" the incredible adventures of Superman, or Wonderman, or Mandrake the Magician.

There are the thousand taboos which proscribe love outside of marriage—and there is the litter of used contraceptives in the backyards of coeducational colleges; there are all those men and women who drink before making love in order to transgress in drunkenness and not remember. There are the neat, coquettish houses, the pure-white apartments with radio, armchair, pipe, and stand—little para-

dises; and there are the tenants of those apartments who, after dinner, leave their chairs, radios, wives, pipes, and children, and go to the bar across the street to get drunk alone.

Perhaps nowhere else will you find such a discrepancy between people and myth, between life and the representation of life. An American said to me at Berne: "The trouble is that we are all eaten by the fear of being less American than our neighbor." I accept this explanation: it shows that Americanism is not merely a myth that clever propaganda stuffs into people's heads but something every American continually reinvents in his gropings. It is at one and the same time a great external reality rising up at the entrance to the port of New York across from the Statue of Liberty, and the daily product of anxious liberties. The anguish of the American confronted with Americanism is an ambivalent anguish, as if he were asking, "Am I American enough?" and at the same time, "How can I escape from Americanism?" In America a man's simultaneous answers to these two questions make him what he is, and each man must find his own answers.

4

Reflections on the Fifties

☆ *Joseph Wood Krutch saw the decade of the 1950's as a battle ground between the humanistic and the scientific approaches to the nature of man. This conflict, in his opinion, demanded a reappraisal of the basic assumptions concerning the "good life."** ☆

If we assume that the boasted alienation of the intellectual and the artist does not mean simply (as the alienated themselves seem sometimes to think) the end of everything, then it may foreshadow either of two opposite developments. It may mean that the artist and the philosopher are indeed on the way out as significant elements in the life of mankind and that what the Fifties witnessed was simply their death agony and the final failure of an approach to life which will be completely forgotten in the purely rational, material, and scientific "culture" now evolving. Conceivably, on the other hand, it may mean just the opposite, namely that the world of science and engineering, of Madison Avenue and the usual ideas of progress, is coming to an end either by self-destruction or in response to the protest of an outraged humanity whose despair will vanish when the world ceases to violate it. The Fifties have given no clear indication which outcome is the more likely to occur.

If the technician and the existentialist seem to have been living in worlds so com-

pletely discontinuous that no communication between them was possible, the less esoteric "social critics" did succeed in making some contact with those who directed the institutions under attack. Thus Madison Avenue took the critics of advertising seriously enough to answer them, and the dominant school of "educators" was, for the first time in a generation, compelled to defend rather than merely to take for granted the neglect of "basic education" in the interests of "life adjustment," "the normal child," etc. At the same time, criticism of "conformity" became so prevalent that nonconformists were, with some show of reason, accused of merely practicing a new conformity of their own.

Obviously, then, the accomplishments, the methods, and the ideals of those ruling our society did not go entirely unchallenged. The Fifties was an ideological battle ground. But the outcome is still dubious and the question whether or not the attacks will have any large permanent effect remains open. How deep will the proposed reforms in education go? Was the "hate Detroit" movement (as one automobile manufacturer called it) significant as at least a symbol of a real revolt

* From Joseph Wood Krutch, "Reflections on the Fifties," *Saturday Review*, XLIII (January 2, 1960), pp. 7, 9-11. Used by permission.

against the whole insane tendency to regard "bigger" (also "faster," "costlier," etc.) as necessarily "better" or was it merely one of fashion's trivial shifts and no more significant than the rise and fall of hemlines and waists? Though Madison Avenue did deign to take notice of its critics it was not apparent that advertising either changed its methods or lost any of its power. Television was so little affected that it elaborated during the decade the most grandiose and unequivocal swindle ever perpetrated in the whole history of the medicine show—of which institution, rather than the theatre, it is an extension. At the same time "popular culture" got so much (often favorable) attention from one section of the intelligentsia that it seemed as likely to convert the highbrow as to be reformed by him.

As juvenile delinquency continued to rise it was more and more discussed. Here and there individuals timidly raised the question whether the increasing lawlessness and violence of teen-agers did not cast some doubts upon the attempts to deal with it by "modern" methods based upon "understanding" and the assumption that since "society" was responsible, the individual could not justifiably be held to account. Juveniles themselves were prompt to proclaim themselves merely the product of their environment and even to remind law enforcement officers that, as juveniles, they were specifically exempt from the normal legal penalties no matter how "adult" the crimes themselves seemed to be. But in the case of this particular problem also, it is still uncertain whether any fundamental change in the approach will actually be made or whether the majority will continue to agree that (as one of a band of teen-agers arrested for vandalizing a grave "just for kicks" recently complained): "Adults don't understand the problems of the juvenile."

Obviously (to put all this in another way) the decade of the Fifties was aware of many unanswered questions, both detailed and more inclusive, but it gave no clear answer to any of them. Despite its almost obsessive concern with "security" it felt desperately insecure. The decade seemed to bring no nearer any new Age of Confidence like that to which it looked back incredulously, but which had seemed to those who lived in it before World War I the natural and permanent result of the answers—scientific, moral, and political—which the nineteenth century had given. Not a few of the most searching minds of the Fifties were uncertain whether our world was, in fact, poised between two worlds, one dying and the other only temporarily powerless to be born, or whether it had reached an impasse beyond which no new civilization could even be hoped for. If the most notable achievements of the decade turn out to be merely bigger bombs and smaller automobiles, then history (again supposing that there is to be any) will not consider its contributions very great.

"Agonizing reappraisal," a phrase first applied to a specific situation, was found so generally apt that it became among intellectuals a cliche which by itself reveals a state of mind. But there are at least some who believe that if the Fifties seem to have accomplished comparatively little it is because too few who believed that they were asking fundamental questions went on to ask others still more fundamental, but continued instead to accept premises which made searching inquiry impossible.

Most people supposed, for example, that they were raising an ultimate question when they debated Communism vs. liberal democracy as it exists in the United States. Yet, however important certain differences between the two systems may be and however preferable one may be to the other, the fact remains that the kinds of Good Life which each promises have a great deal in common. Both accept power, wealth, and the standard of living as the chief tangible evidences of success or failure and both accept much the same theories of human nature (the chief difference lying in the greater clarity and rigidity with which the Communists formulate them). Both tend, that is to say, to assume that man is the product of society, that his nature and his condition can both be improved only through the improvement of social conditions, and that, given material welfare, men will inevitably become more intelligent, more moral, and more cultured. The dispute between them tends to become merely a dispute over the question of which system is most likely to produce the kind of society both aim at.

If you believe that there is something more than mere sentimentality in the charge that American life (indeed, the life in all "developed" countries) is materialistic, conformist, and increasingly barbaric in its indifference to any culture except that of TV, the movies, and jazz; if you believe that all the money spent on schools has not provided a good education and that juvenile delinquency is by no means confined to "the underprivileged"; if you believe all that, then you can hardly avoid asking, not only whether democracy or Communism will in the end be most successful in providing a high standard of living for all, but also whether the pursuit of a high standard of living is actually the chief end of man. Even if it is a *sine qua non* of the Good Life it may not be the one thing necessary.

Perhaps the "agonizing reappraisal" so often recommended has not been profound enough, however agonizing it may have been. And perhaps it would be worth while to look at some of the most fundamental questions of our times, and see whether there is any sign that anyone began to ask them during the Fifties.

The fundamental answers which we

have on the whole made, and which we continue to accept, were first given in the seventeenth century by Francis Bacon, Thomas Hobbes and Rene Descartes, and were later elaborated and modernized by Marx and the Darwinians. These basic tenets of our civilization (in chronological but not quite logical order) are: 1) the most important task to which the human mind may devote itself is the "control of nature" through technology (Bacon); 2) man may be completely understood if he is considered to be an animal, making predictable reactions to that desire for pleasure and power to which all his other desires may by analysis be reduced (Hobbes); 3) all animals (man excepted) are pure machines (Descartes); 4) man, Descartes notwithstanding, is also an animal and therefore also a machine (Darwin); 5) the human condition is not determined by philosophy, religion, or moral ideas because all of these are actually only by-products of social and technological developments which take place independent of man's will and uninfluenced by the "ideologies" which they generate (Marx).

Perhaps none of these answers to fundamental questions was given in quite so simple a form by the thinker to whom it is here attributed. Perhaps the assent given to them is more explicit and unqualified among Communists than among even left-wing liberals of the West. But at the very minimum they haunted the imagination and influenced the thinking even of those most disturbed by their implications.

To insist that these commonly accepted answers should be re-examined is not necessarily to deny that some of them served for a time as useful working principles. Marxism led to a recognition of the social factors which do indeed influence moral ideas and conduct. The assumption that all living creatures are machines did lead to a better understanding of the human mechanism. Darwinism did furnish the key to many secrets. Baconianism is responsible for all that is good as well as most that is evil in a technologically advanced civilization. But useful working principles outlive their usefulness. And just as the time came when a complete acceptance of Newtonian physics would have made further understanding of the physical world impossible, so a refusal to question Baconianism, Hobbism, Darwinism, and the rest makes it impossible to deal with the problems to which an uncritical acceptance of them has led.

Nevertheless a majority, even of the thoughtful, refuse to recognize (to take specific examples) that still greater production will not guarantee a better life; that a refusal to recognize the moral responsibility of the individual cannot solve the problem of juvenile delinquency; and, perhaps most important of all, that the invention of a device which may annihilate the human race proves that our boasted "control of nature" is so much an illusion that we have no idea how to control a phenomenon far more dangerous than any previous threats.

We have reached the end of an epoch because the accepted answers to the most fundamental questions created a situation bristling with problems which cannot be solved in the terms those answers prescribe. Unless we can to some extent modify them the end of an epoch may also be the end of a world.

To what extent, if any, did the decade of the Fifties recognize the possibility of modifying the answers upon the basis of which the good and bad of our world have been constructed? Paradoxically enough, the most radical revisions were those that continued to be made by the physicists who explicitly rejected the whole concept of a rigidly and mechanically predictable universe. While they were doing so, sociologists, psychologists, and

even biologists often seemed unaware that by doing so the physicists had knocked the props from under the now old-fashioned premises of the science of life and the science of man which had rested largely upon the picture of the physical universe now abandoned by those whose special fields of competence it is.

The extent to which these latter were willing either to draw conclusions outside the field of physics or even to admit that such conclusions might legitimately be drawn varied from individual to individual. But it is surely of great possible significance that during the closing year of the decade Harvard's P. W. Bridgman, a Nobel Prizewinner and one of the most distinguished of living physicists, should have published a long, closely reasoned, and difficult book ("The Way Things Are") in which he renounced his previous convictions to declare that he no longer believed sociology, ethics, esthetics, or even biology to be subjects which can be profitably studied by the "positive" methods borrowed from the physical sciences. Thus he reaffirmed precisely what three centuries had tended increasingly to doubt—namely our mysterious, incommensurable humanness.

Though sociologists and psychologists may on the whole have tended to cling most stubbornly to traditional attitudes, not all of either did so and some biologists and anthropologists quite explicitly rejected century-old orthodoxies in such popular books as "The Universe and You," by McGill's geneticist N. T. Berrill, and "The Immense Journey," by Pennsylvania's anthropologist Loren Eiseley.

Looking about for a single brief statement which would illustrate what may possibly be the most significant tendency of the Fifties I choose the following from Sir Julian Huxley, partly because it opens a wide chink in the armor of the mechanist, the positivist, and the determinist, partly because no one questions the scientific competence of Sir Julian or could accuse him of having been, in general, anything but orthodox in his convictions. Writing a preface to a work by the somewhat mystical French biologist de Chardin, he says: "Some biologists, indeed, would claim that mind is generated solely by the complexification of certain types of organization, namely brains. However, such logic appears to me narrow. The brain alone is not responsible for mind, even though it is a necessary organ for its manifestation."

To anyone who will let those sentences and their implications sink in, it will be evident that once the independence of the mind as separate from the brain is granted, once mind is regarded as an independent creator, then every one of the five basic assumptions upon which the modern world rests (or perhaps one should now say totters) is, happily, open to question.

5

American Capitalism

☆ *A concern over the use of the enormous power developed by our economic institutions continued undiminished. The question most discussed was whether this power—with its ability to benefit or harm society—was adequately restrained. One of the leading American economists, John Kenneth Galbraith, contended that a force called "countervailing power" tended to effect this restraint. The profound analyst of corporate structure, Adolf Berle, held that existing controls were inadequate.* ☆

(a) COUNTERVAILING POWER*

The comparative importance of a small number of great corporations in the American economy cannot be denied except by those who have a singular immunity to statistical evidence or striking capacity to manipulate it. In principle the American is controlled, livelihood and soul, by the large corporation; in practice he seems not to be completely enslaved. Once again the danger is in the future; the present seems still tolerable. Once again there may be lessons from the present which, if learned, will save us in the future. . . .

. . . with the widespread disappearance of competition in its classical form and it replacement by the small group of firms if not in overt, at least in conventional or tacit collusion, it was easy to suppose that

* The selections from John Kenneth Galbraith, *American Capitalism, the Concept of Countervailing Power*, pp. 109, 111-123, 126-128, 136-137, copyright © 1952, 1956 by John Kenneth Galbraith, are reprinted by permission of and arrangement with Houghton Mifflin Company and Hamish Hamilton Ltd., the authorized publishers.

since competition had disappeared, all effective restraint on private power had disappeared. Indeed this conclusion was all but inevitable if no search was made for other restraints and so complete was the preoccupation with competition that none was made.

In fact, new restraints on private power did appear to replace competition. They were nurtured by the same process of concentration which impaired or destroyed competition. But they appeared not on the same side of the market but on the opposite side, not with competitors but with customers or suppliers. It will be convenient to have a name for this counterpart of competition and I shall call it *countervailing power.*

To begin with a broad and somewhat too dogmatically stated proposition, private economic power is held in check by the countervailing power of those who are subject to it. The first begets the second. The long trend toward concentration of industrial enterprise in the hands of a relatively few firms has brought into existence not only strong sellers, as economists have supposed, but also strong buyers as they have failed to see. The two develop together, not in precise step but in such manner that there can be no doubt that the one is in response to the other.

The fact that a seller enjoys a measure of monopoly power, and is reaping a measure of monopoly return as a result, means that there is an inducement to those firms from whom he buys or those to whom he sells to develop the power with which they can defend themselves against exploitation. It means also that there is a reward to them, in the form of a share of the gains of their opponents' market power, if they are able to do so. In this way the existence of market power creates an incentive to the organization of another position of power that neutralizes it. . . .

It was always one of the basic presuppositions of competition that market power exercised in its absence would invite the competitors who would eliminate such exercise of power. The profits of a monopoly position inspired competitors to try for a share. In other words competition was regarded as a *self-generating* regulatory force. The doubt whether this was in fact so after a market had been pre-empted by a few large sellers, after entry of new firms had become difficult and after existing firms had accepted a convention against price competition, was what destroyed the faith in competition as a regulatory mechanism. Countervailing power is also a self-generating force and this is a matter of great importance. . . .

The operation of countervailing power is to be seen with the greatest clarity in the labor market where it is also most fully developed. Because of his comparative immobility, the individual worker has long been highly vulnerable to private

economic power. The customer of any particular steel mill, at the turn of the century, could always take himself elsewhere if he felt he was being overcharged. Or he could exercise his sovereign privilege of not buying steel at all. The worker had no comparable freedom if he felt he was being underpaid. Normally he could not move and he had to have work. Not often has the power of one man over another been used more callously than in the American labor market after the rise of the large corporation. As late as the early twenties, the steel industry worked a twelve-hour day and seventy-two-hour week with an incredible twenty-four-hour stint every fortnight when the shift changed.

No such power is exercised today and for the reason that its earlier exercise stimulated the counteraction that brought it to an end. In the ultimate sense it was the power of the steel industry, not the organizing abilities of John L. Lewis and Philip Murray, that brought the United Steel Workers into being. The economic power that the worker faced in the sale of his labor—the competition of many sellers dealing with few buyers—made it necessary that he organize for his own protection. There were rewards to the power of the steel companies in which, when he had successfully developed countervailing power, he could share. . . .

Countervailing power in the retail business is indentified with the large and powerful retail enterprises. Its practical manifestation, over the last half-century, has been the rise of the food chains, the variety chains, the mail-order houses (now graduated into chain stores), the department-store chains, and the co-operative buying organizations of the surviving independent department and food stores. . . .

The buyers of all these firms deal directly with the manufacturer and there are few of the latter who, in setting prices, do not have to reckon with the attitude and reaction of their powerful customers. The retail buyers have a variety of weapons at their disposal to use against the market power of their suppliers. Their ultimate sanction is to develop their own source of supply as the food chains, Sears, Roebuck and Montgomery Ward have extensively done. They can also concentrate their entire patronage on a single supplier and, in return for a lower price, give him security in his volume and relieve him of selling and advertising costs. This policy has been widely followed and there have also been numerous complaints of the leverage it gives the retailer on his source of supply. . . .

Countervailing power also manifests itself, although less visibly, in producers' goods markets. For many years the power of the automobile companies, as purchasers of steel, has sharply curbed the power of the steel mills as sellers. Detroit is the only city where the historic basing-point system was not used to price steel. Under the basing-point system, all producers regardless of location quoted the same price at any particular point of delivery. This obviously minimized the opportunity of a strong buyer to play one seller off against the other. The large firms in the automobile industry had developed the countervailing power which enabled them to do precisely this. They were not disposed to tolerate any limitations on their exercise of such power. . . .

The development of countervailing power requires a certain minimum opportunity and capacity for organization, corporate or otherwise. If the large retail buying organizations had not developed the countervailing power which they have used, by proxy, on behalf of the individual consumer, consumers would have been faced with the need to organize the equivalent of the retailer's power. This would have been a formidable task but it has

been accomplished in Scandinavia where the consumer's co-operative, instead of the chain store, is the dominant instrument of countervailing power in consumers' goods markets. There has been a similar though less comprehensive development in England and Scotland. In the Scandinavian countries the co-operatives have long been regarded explicitly as instruments for bringing power to bear on the cartels; i.e., for exercise of countervailing power. This is readily conceded by many who have the greatest difficulty in seeing private mass buyers in the same role. But the fact that consumer co-operatives are not of any great importance in the United States is to be explained, not by any inherent incapacity of the American for such organization, but because the chain stores pre-empted the gains of countervailing power first. . . .

In the light of the difficulty in organizing countervailing power, it is not surprising that the assistance of government has repeatedly been sought in this task. Without the phenomenon itself being fully recognized, the provision of state assistance to the development of countervailing power has become a major function of government—perhaps the major domestic function of government. Much of the domestic legislation of the last twenty years, that of the New Deal episode in particular, only becomes fully comprehensible when it is viewed in this light. . . .

Labor sought and received it in the protection and assistance which the Wagner Act provided to union organization. Farmers sought and received it in the form of federal price supports to their markets— a direct subsidy of market power. Unorganized workers have sought and received it in the form of minimum wage legislation. The bituminous-coal mines sought and received it in the Bituminous Coal Conservation Act of 1935 and the National Bituminous Coal Act of 1937. These measures, all designed to give a group a market power it did not have before, comprised the most important legislative acts of the New Deal. They fueled the sharpest domestic controversies of the New and Fair Deals.

There should be no problem as to why this legislation, and the administrations that sponsored it, were keenly controversial. The groups that sought the assistance of government in building countervailing power sought that power in order to use it against market authority to which they had previously been subordinate. Those whose power was thereby inhibited could hardly be expected to welcome this development or the intervention of the government to abet it.

Because the nature of countervailing power has not been firmly grasped, the government's role in relation to it has not only been imperfectly understood but also imperfectly played. One is permitted to hope that a better understanding of countervailing power will contribute to better administration in the future.

(b) "FREEDOM AND THE CORPORATION"*

Today approximately 50 per cent of American manufacturing—that is everything other than financial and transportation—is held by about 150 corporations, reckoned, at least, by asset values. If finance and transportation are included, the total increases. If a rather larger group is taken, the statistics would probably show that about two-thirds of the economically productive assets of the United States, excluding agriculture, are owned by a group of not more than 500 corporations. This is actual asset ownership. (Some further statistical analysis is called for if financial corporations be included, for these, of course, double up. One of the largest and most plainly oligar-

* By Adolf A. Berle, Jr. From *Saturday Review*, XLI (January 18, 1958), pp. 42, 44, 62-63. Used by permission.

chically controlled corporations in the United States, the Metropolitan Life Insurance Company, duplicates assets because it holds securities of other corporations.) But in terms of power, without regard to asset positions, not only do 500 corporations control two-thirds of the nonfarm economy but within each of that 500 a still smaller group has the ultimate decision-making power. This is, I think, the highest concentration of economic power in recorded history.

We can talk about the various alleged legal controls which somehow or other, when the chips are down, neither control nor even seek to control. We can point out the fear of "monopoly" and "restraint of trade" and say that from time to time this fear has checked the process. True, our law has prevented any one of these power groups from becoming a monopoly, but it has not seriously prevented the concentration of power as power, though it has prevented certain ultimate results. The question is then: Why has concentrated economic power in America not got completely out of hand? Many of these corporations have budgets, and some of them have payrolls, which, with their customers, affect a greater number of people than most of the ninety-odd sovereign countries of the world. American Telephone and Telegraph, for example, based on combined population and wealth, would be somewhere around the thirteenth state of the union in terms of budget, and certainly larger than many of the countries of South America. Some of these corporations are units which can be thought of only in somewhat the way we have heretofore thought of nations.

Whether we like it or not, this is what has happened. As noted, it is not the product of evil-minded men. I believe that we must try to work with the system. The dangers are obvious. But history cannot usually be reversed. Until engineers and economic forces give us a way by which a man can manufacture an automobile in his back yard we will continue to have organizations the size of General Motors or Ford—as long as people want Chevrolets or Fords. We will have railroads the length of the Union Pacific as long as people want to go across the continent by railroad. In other words, until a combination of technique and organization can be invented permitting *individuals* to do the job, we are bound to try to make the best we can out of the situation. To my mind most of the results are rather surprisingly good.

This does not mean, however, that I am not afraid. I am. I believe it is the *content* of these systems rather than their *form* that matters. Their power can enslave us beyond present belief, or perhaps set us free beyond present imagination. The choice lies with the men who operate the pyramids, and with the men affected who can demand what they really want. Our Anglo-Saxon democratic liberties, after all, were beaten out, not against the framework of the personal possessory property regime, but against the background of two of the most brutal despotisms in Western history; the Angevin dynasty in Normandy and the Tudor dynasty in England.

We have to accept this power situation as, let us call it, a neutral mechanism subject to the control of the body politic as long as we *keep* it subject to that control. That control, I believe, will be essentially intellectual and philosophical, capable of being translated into legal rules when necessity arises. In that respect I make three points in summary:

1. The first is that whenever there is a question of power there is a question of legitimacy. As things stand now, these instrumentalities of tremendous power have the slenderest claim of legitimacy. This is probably a transitory period. They must find some claim of legitimacy, which also means finding a field of responsibility

and a field of accountability. Legitimacy, responsibility and accountability are essential to any power system if it is to endure. They correspond to a deep human instinct. A man desires beyond anything else to have someone give him the accolade of "Well done, thou good and faithful servant," thereby risking the condemnation of "You have been no good—get out." If he has to say it to himself, or hear it from a string of people whom he himself has hired or controls, he is apt to die a cynical and embittered man.

The medieval feudal power system set the "lords spiritual" over and against the "lords temporal." These were the men of learning and of the church who in theory were able to say to the greatest power in the world: "You have committed a sin; therefore either you are excommunicate or you must mend your ways." The "lords temporal" could reply: "I can kill you." But the "lords spiritual" could retort: "Yes, that you can, but you cannot change the philosophical fact."

In a sense this is the great lacuna in the economic power system today. In theory the stockholders can act as the "lords spiritual" through their vote. In fact they cannot, and they know they cannot. Are the pension trustees or their equivalent slowly emerging as the men who can? They had not thought so—nobody had thought so. They have been essentially a method of transmission of choice and not much else. We are looking for the kind of thing that C. Wright Mills in his recent book on the American power elite rightly said did not exist. He wrongly concluded, therefore, that the system was a mess, which it obviously is not. But every time we have had the chance to construct this kind of elite we seem to have abandoned it, and chucked in an administrator instead.

2. My second summary point is that the sheer power of invading personality is great and that a doctrine is already at

work which plays a second joke on our constitutional system. The United States began by saying that its Federal government could not construct corporations and apparently by assuming that the states would not. Both have done so. It also said that corporations should be kept apart from governmental power. *De facto,* they have not been. We are now, in fact, beginning to converge on a doctrine which may well push right over the line when the next case comes up. This doctrine is that where a corporation has power to affect a great many lives (differing from the little enterprise which can be balanced out by the market) it should be subject to the same restraints under the Constitution that apply to an agency of the Federal or state government. In that case, the Bill of Rights and the Fourteenth and Fifteenth Amendments would apply. At the moment this is one jump ahead of current law. Yet it seems probable that this will be the next phase—just as we already have the constitutional doctrine that under the First Amendment you may not by private contract prohibit a Negro from buying land.

3. My third point is destined to be in infinitely greater controversy, and I do not know what the end of the controversy will be. Great corporate power is exercised in relation to certain obligations:

1. It should supply the want in the area of its production. Where the community has come to rely on a corporation for steel, oil, automobiles or cigarettes, the corporation is obliged reasonably to meet that demand.
2. The price must not be considered extortionate. It must be "acceptable"—which doesn't necessarily mean fair or just.
3. It must provide at least some continuity of employment.
4. It must give a continuing attention to the technical progress of the art.

At every point in the individual history of large corporations there has been some moment of impact on the community when either the community felt the corporation was not fufilling its obligations or, alternatively, the corporation realized it was up against a situation it could not handle. In every case the result has been either a friendly and orderly, or unfriendly and disorderly, hassle out of which a piece of planned economy emerged. Roughly two-thirds of American industry or much of American finance is now controlled by a formal or informal Federal industrial plan. Here are two illustrations at each end of the cycle.

The oil industry claims to be the most non-socialist, free-wheeling, private business that ever was. But the fact is that after many vicissitudes it sought control by, and is controlled by, various Acts of Congress. After orderly discussion certain laws were passed. Under these laws, first, the Bureau of Mines of the Department of Interior estimates the probable consumption month by month of gasoline and the chief oil products. Second, an interstate treaty exists among the oil-producing states, ratified by the Congress. Third, a Congressional Act makes it illegal to transport oil in interstate commerce which has been produced in excess of a state allowance. This legislation might break down if it were not for the fact that because there is a relatively concentrated system in the oil industry the refineries will not buy "non-certified" oil anyway. As a result, the big companies do not violate the Act; the little ones cannot; and the result is a planned oil economy by which supply is equated to demand and the oil industry from well to refinery to gas station is more or less geared to meet it.

Here is a disorderly example: Aluminum was manufactured by a monopoly which was ordered to be split up under an anti-trust decree. By a combination of administrative orders entirely without administrative rationale but all working toward the same end the Federal government used the aluminum plants it had itself created during World War II in order to set up two competitors to Alcoa. It likewise required Alcoa to sell its Aluminum of Canada shares. This was not enough by itself, so the government for a period of years handled its defense orders in such a way that the new companies had adequate assurance of a market until they could get properly under way. The policy still is to make certain that the new companies, which can stay in business only by being assured a reasonable market, will get the extent of market they need. There was a stockpiling arrangement at one time, followed later by the release of part of the stockpiled aluminum. In a wholly disorderly way which only the American system could ever conceive, there arose the equivalent of a *de facto* planned economy in aluminum. At the moment this industry now sails away, free-wheeling. But there is not the slightest doubt that if conditions required transition back into a planned economy it would happen.

Obviously a system like this is just as good as the ideas and strength of the body politic behind it. The same system in the hands, for example, of a Latin American dictator could produce terrible oppression.

There is a gradually growing feeling that pension trusts, for examples, must be controlled. A pension trust ring could be something to bind a man beyond belief. It could bind him to his job. He could not change it without losing a substantial part of his life savings. He might be controlled in all sorts of ways. We are beginning to think even that the pension trust right which cannot be transferred to some other pension trust is suspect.

As men think, so they are. We are really seeking now a body of doctrine which will control power. I close by returning to my first point, which related to the desperate search for a field of responsibility and accountability referent to some point of view outside the system: that is, to some modern "lords spiritual."

6

The Challenge of Automation

☆ *Labor was alarmed, and business and industry intrigued, by the implications of the automatic control of machinery. Walter P. Reuther, president of the United Auto Workers, asserted in a statement of October 17, 1955, that the revolutionary aspect of automation was that unlike previous technological changes, in addition to increasing the productivity of labor it also replaced the worker.* * ☆

We have been told so often that automation is going to bring on the second industrial revolution that there is, perhaps, a danger we may dismiss the warning as a catch-phrase, and lose sight of the fact that, not only the technique, but the philosophy of automation is revolutionary, in the truest sense of the word. Automation does not only produce changes in the methods of manufacturing, distribution, many clerical operations, and in the structure of business organization, but the impact of those changes on our economy and our whole society bids fair to prove quite as revolutionary as were those of the first industrial revolution.

Through the application of mechanical power to machinery, and the development of new machinery to use this power, the first industrial revolution made possible a vast increase in the volume of goods produced for each man-hour of work. Succeeding technological improvements —such as the development of interchange-

able parts and the creation of the assembly line which were essential to the growth of mass production industries— have led to continuous increases in labor productivity. But however much these machines were improved, they still required workers to operate and control them. In some operations, the worker's function was little more than to feed the material in, set the machine in operation and remove the finished product. In others, proper control of the machine required the exercise of the highest conceivable skills. But whether the required skill was little or great, the presence of a human being, using human judgment, was essential to the operation of the machine.

The revolutionary change produced by automation is its tendency to displace the worker entirely from the direct operation of the machine, through the use of automatic control devices. No one, as far as I know, has yet produced a fully satisfactory definition of automation, but I think John Diebold came close to expressing its essential quality when he described automation as "the integration of machines with each other into fully auto-

* From *Automation and Technological Change.* Hearings Before the Subcommittee on Economic Stabilization of the Joint Committee on the Economic Report, Congress of the United States, 84th Congress, 1st session, Washington, 1955, pp. 98-102.

matic, and, in some cases, self-regulating systems. . . ."

The revolutionary implications of this new technology can best be understood by looking at a few examples of what is actually being done through automation today, in scattered parts of the economy.

The application of automation ranges all the way from individual automatic machines to virtually automatic factories.

An example of the first is an automatic lathe, produced by the Sundstrand Machine Tool Co., described in *American Machinist,* March 14, 1955, page 117, which gages each part as it is produced and automatically resets the cutting tools to compensate for tool wear. In addition, when the cutting tools have been worn down to a certain predetermined limit, the machine automatically replaces them with sharp tools. The parts are automatically loaded onto the machine and are automatically unloaded as they are finished. These lathes can be operated for 5 to 8 hours without attention, except for an occasional check to make sure that parts are being delivered to the loading mechanism.

A completely automatic plant is now producing mixed and ready-to-use concrete for the Cleveland Builders Supply Co. (*Business Week,* Apr. 16, 1955, p.80). Operated from an electronic control panel, the plant can produce and load into ready-mix trucks any one of some 1,500 different mixing formulas that may be demanded. This plant uses no manual labor at any point in the process.

By a combination of teletype and radio, the control operator is informed as to the particular formula to be loaded into each truck as it arrives. He gets out a punched card, coded for that formula, and the automatic mechanisms take over. Specified amounts of the required materials are delivered by conveyors, in precisely the right quantities, to a mixing bin where they are automatically mixed and then loaded into the waiting truck. The control mechanisms even measure and compensate for any deficiency or excess of water in the aggregate (sand, coarse rock, slag, etc.) which goes into the mixer, and if the order calls for a dry mix, the materials are automatically routed through a dry spout.

This automatic plant has a capacity of 200 cubic yards of concrete per hour, as against 100 cubic yards per hour in the company's conventional plants. . . .

One of the factors which has been responsible for the steadily increasing rate of productivity since World War II has been the enormous increase in research expenditures both by industry and by Government. Alfred North Whitehead, the British philospher, once said, "The greatest invention of the 19th century was the invention of the art of inventing." We might add that one of the great developments of the 20th century has been to change inventing from an art to a standard business procedure. The research department is now a fixture in every important corporation, while the needs of government, especially in national defense, have added to the numbers of research workers, many of whose discoveries are readily applied to industry.

As a result, the flow of what may be considered routine technological innovations—new production methods, new materials and machines applicable only to specific processes or industries, and improvements in work flow—has been greatly accelerated. Harlow Curtice, president of General Motors, noted recently that "new products, new processes are coming off the drawing boards of the engineers and out of the laboratories of the scientists at ever faster pace."

This great expansion of industrial research, and the flood of routine technological innovations it produces, have been sufficient, alone, in recent years, to boost the rate of rising productivity to the extent that past notions of what were normal productivity increases are already obsolete. Technological improvements of this sort, and on an increasing scale, can be expected to continue. By themselves, they would pose serious problems of adjusting our economy so as to provide sufficient purchasing power to absorb the steadily accelerating flow of goods which can be produced with every man-hour of labor. . . .

What is the attitude of the trade-union movement, and specifically of the CIO, to this new technology of automation?

First of all, we fully realize that the potential benefits of automation are great, if properly handled. If only a fraction of what technologists promise for the future is true, within a very few years automation can and should make possible a 4-day workweek, longer vacation periods, opportunities for earlier retirement, as well as a vast increase in our material standards of living.

At the same time, automation can bring freedom from the monotonous drudgery of many jobs in which the worker today is no more than a servant of the machine. It can free workers from routine, repetitious tasks which the new machines can be taught to do, and can give to the workers who toil at those tasks the opportunity of developing higher skills.

But in looking ahead to the many benefits which automation can produce, we must not overlook or minimize the many problems which will inevitably arise in making the adjustment to the new technology—problems for individual workers and individual companies, problems for entire communities and regions, problems for the economy as a whole.

What should be done to help the worker who will be displaced from his job, or the worker who will find that his highly specialized skill has been taken over by a machine? What about the businessman who lacks sufficient capital to automate his plant, yet has to face the competition of firms whose resources enable them to build whole new automatic factories? Will automation mean the creation of whole new communities in some areas, while others are turned into ghost towns? How can we increase the market for goods and services sufficiently, and quickly enough, to match greatly accelerated increases in productivity?

Finding the answers to these questions, and many others like them, will not be an easy process, and certainly not an automatic one. Even if the greatest care is taken to forsee and meet these problems, adjustments for many people will prove difficult and even painful. If there is no care and no foresight, if we subscribe to the laissez-faire belief that "these things will work themselves out," untold harm can be done to millions of innocent people and to the whole structure of our economy and our free society.

The CIO insists that we must recognize these problems and face up to them. But our recognition that there will be problems, and serious problems, to be solved, does not mean that we are opposed to automation. We are not. We fully recognize the desirability, as well as the inevitability of technological progress. But we oppose those who would introduce automation blindly and irresponsibly, with no concern for any result except the achievement of the largest possible quick profit for themselves.

7

The Atomic Future

☆ *The release of the atom stimulated efforts to harness atomic energy for peaceful purposes. The results of these endeavors presaged world-wide, revolutionary technological and economic changes.* ☆*

Although the extent of uranium and thorium reserves is not known, it has been estimated by a consultant of the Atomic Energy Commission, Palmer Putnam, that the recoverable heat content of the world's supply of uranium and thorium is twenty-five times that of existing coal reserves and one hundred times that of oil and gas.

If we assume that an efficiency of even 10 per cent could be achieved in releasing usable energy by the fusion process, one cubic mile of sea water would supply enough energy to do the world's work for three hundred centuries—at the 1950 rate of consumption. Higher rates of consumption are likely in the future, but they could be met almost indefinitely without any noticeable diminution of the immense volume of sea water on earth. This possibility may be contrasted vividly with the rapid encroachments made on currently used types of fuel.

If in the future the people of the United States should use no more petroleum and natural gas than in the decade 1940-50, their domestic resources of oil would give

out in thirty-four years and of natural gas in fifty-nine years. These figures are from recent estimates of the United States Geological Survey. We probably shall consume more per person than in the past. The reserves will be used up more quickly if we do so, unless new deposits are discovered in the meantime—as they may be.

Coal is next in order as the prevalent source of heat, light, and power. The Geological Survey estimates that there are enough assured reserves in the United States to last 484 years at the 1940-50 level of output. So perhaps there will be enough to keep us going for two hundred years or so at the higher level of consumption that is sure to come with a larger population, the need for more energy in more mechanized production, and the imminent scarcity of petroleum and natural gas.

In addition, there are reserves about four times as large as the assured ones, that may ultimately be recoverable—at higher cost.

Water power now supplies only a small fraction of energy used in the United States. More of it could be developed, but even so it would not add greatly to the total supply of power. The prospect for further economical use of winds and tides

* George Soule, *The Shape of Tomororw*, pp. 99-102. Published by The New American Library, New York, 1958. Copyright © 1958 The Twentieth Century Fund. By permission of the Twentieth Century Fund.

for production of energy is not bright. Wood and other vegetation can be directly burned—an inefficient way of obtaining heat—or converted into fuel alcohol. Forests would be quickly eradicated if we returned to the old custom of burning wood for heat to drive locomotives and steamboats or to fire stationary steam boilers.

There are still extensive deposits of oil and coal in other parts of the world. Many regions, however, including some of the most densely populated, are without them. With the world-wide spread of industry, the competition for these remaining sources of industrial power will be fierce.

The chances are that as atomic energy is developed for industrial purposes, it will be the principal source of energy for large or stationary power installations, while the much scarcer deposits of oil, gas, and coal—all of which may be converted into motor fuel—will be reserved for small and mobile units like gasoline and diesel engines—and of course also for the many valuable chemical by-products. Should mineral fuels give out, products, such as alcohol, distilled from wood or other vegetation could serve the same purpose.

Civilization, therefore, is not likely to perish because of any shortage of energy resources, now that we are entering the atomic age.

As soon as nuclear energy becomes cheap enough, existing electric power stations will of course substitute atomic fuel for coal and oil. But even if the fuel were to be had for nothing, the cost of electricity to the consumer per kilowatt hour could not be much reduced on that account. The reason is that the cost of fuel itself is a very small part of the expense incurred in generating electricity by any method, transmitting it, often over considerable distances, and distributing it to consumers. A large part of this expense consists of the carrying charges on the costly capital equipment which is required. When rates are reduced, it is usually a consequence mainly of more efficient equipment or fuller use of existing capacity, sometimes brought about by interconnection of systems. One might infer that these factors would not be much changed by the use of nuclear fuel.

It is necessary, however, to consider not merely the cost of the fuel at its source, but the cost of transporting it to the furnaces where it is burned. Coal, the world's chief industrial fuel, is heavy and bulky; consequently industries and plants which use it are usually found not too far from the source of supply or in places to which it can be carried by cheap water transportation.

This has much to do with the location of industry, both in the United States and throughout the world. Most of the noted iron and steel regions, for example, exist where coal and iron are available in proximity—western Pennsylvania, the vicinity of Birmingham, England, the Ruhr in Germany, Silesia, the Don Basin in Russia. Regions which do not have easy access to coal, oil, or waterpower usually have little industry, especially heavy industry.

But a small shipment of uranium, or a few gallons of the hydrogen isotopes out of which fusion heat is derived, would be enough to supply a power plant for a very long time—perhaps for years. Such quantities could be carried anywhere, by land, sea, or air, at a negligible cost per unit of the heat which may be obtained from them. It would be possible, as far as fuel costs are concerned, to locate an industry anywhere.

Italy has long been at an industrial disadvantage because she has no coal and, at least until recently, little petroleum. Britain, where modern industry was first to arise based on coal deposits for industrial fuel, now has to go miles deep for it, and must follow the veins far out to sea. Britain has almost no petroleum deposits. Atomic energy will be a lifesaver for both Italy and Britain. Little coal exists in South America, and the South American deposits of petroleum are not widely distributed. This is one important reason why South American nations have not been noted for industrial centers. Atomic energy may change all that. The peasants of India now burn cow dung, having little wood and no coal. Some day they may use electrical power, generated from nuclear fuel.

Nuclear fuel, carried by plane to the vast antarctic regions, could supply power for any use that might be found for it. Indeed, hydrogen fuel might be produced on the spot from the immense wastes of snow and ice.

It is impossible to predict the momentous consequences to the world that might flow from these atomic discoveries, now in their infancy.

8

Atomic Peril

☆ *The continued development of atomic energy for military purposes led to grave and universal concern about the disastrous potential of nuclear weapons. A graphic account of the awesome results of atomic war, based on the hypothetical bombing of St. Louis, was prepared for use by the Greater St. Louis Citizens' Committee for Nuclear Information.** ☆

Tomorrow it will be just one year since That Day—the day that ended the world we used to live in, and reduced our lives to an elemental struggle against hunger, sickness, grief, and despair. Here in this camp outside Vermillion, 17,000 of us who managed to pull through, more or less, are living in huts, tents, and sod houses. Among the St. Louisans here, by some ironical chance, are three of us who were active in CNI. Yesterday we decided to mark this grim anniversary by writing down the history of this terrible year, as we know it.

My name is George Scott. I'm a physicist—or at least, I was. My being alive today is just chance. I was preparing a paper that had to be finished on That Day, so I stayed home to work on it in the little study I had built for myself in the basement of my new house out beyond Creve Coeur. On the campus, hardly anybody survived.

It has been pretty hard to separate sound information from the rumors that

fill the air, but it's now generally agreed that the continental U.S. was hit by nearly 1500 megatons on the one day that the war lasted. Seventy cities were hit, as well as major defense installations and atomic facilities. About 23 million people were killed that first day. More than that have died since, but nobody agrees about the exact figure.

I remember that when the Holifield Committee held hearings on the subject, back in 1959 I think, one expert estimated that a massive attack would injure about 43 million people, of whom more than a third would survive. That's not the way it was, though; the injured didn't have much chance, with the hospitals gone and medical supplies burned up and the doctors mostly dead. As for the uninjured —well, there was starvation, and there was typhus, and then there were a lot of people who just went out of their minds and either killed themselves or died because they couldn't make the effort to survive.

St. Louis was hit by two weapons, of eight and ten megatons equivalence. The bombs exploded at 11th and Pine. They

* From Part I of "Nuclear War In St. Louis: One Year Later," *Nuclear Information*, II (September 1959), pp. 1-2. Used by permission.

say there's a crater there now, almost a mile across and several hundred feet deep. The force of the blast, and the enormous heat, destroyed everything in a circle extending north and south to the city limits, and westward as far as Big Bend. East of Grand almost everybody was wiped out at once. From Grand to Big Bend some people survived the attack itself, but not many are still alive.

The ferocious heat of the explosion caused the worst havoc. Fires were started instantaneously as far away as Weldon Spring. People who were out in the open suffered third-degree burns even in Ellisville. Second-degree burns were common several miles beyond that. And many people were burned by fires started by the explosion.

The destruction of major firehouses, an the panic following the explosion, made fire control impossible. The many small blazes ignited by the explosion joined to form bigger blazes, and these finally flowed together to become one huge "firestorm" that enveloped most of the city and raged for hours. Terrific winds traveled radially inward toward the center of the conflagration, from all directions. An enormous column of smoke rose rapidly over the burning area. The loss of oxygen and the outpouring of acrid fumes in the region of the fire seem to have accounted for the deaths of many who might otherwise have been able to reach safety.

The forests and fields caught fire too. The prevailing west of southwest wind swept these fires along, denuding vast areas of Illinois and southern Missouri. Throughout the entire country forest fires raged for weeks. The eastern Ozarks burned for two weeks, until heavy rains put out the blaze.

Ironically enough, radiation caused little harm immediately—first the heat and fire and flying debris got in their deadly blows. But the fallout came soon enough. It is now calculated that an amount of fission products equivalent to a nine megaton all-fission explosion was produced by the two weapons used on St. Louis. Of this staggering amount, about seven megatons of energy equivalent came down as local fallout; the other two megatons have been dispersed in the stratosphere and will come down as world-wide fallout. The local fallout was distributed down-wind over an elongated area about eighty miles wide at the widest point, and about 200 miles long —approximately 9000 square miles altogether, stretching across southern Illinois towards Evansville, Indiana.

Casualties from local fallout were heaviest around East St. Louis. In Belleville, persons in the open or in adequate shelters received radiation doses of over 1000 rads during the second hour after the attack. During the first twenty-four hours after the attack the total radiation to such persons was about 5000 rads. Since about 700 rads of radiation received in one dose, will kill half the people exposed to it, those who received 5000 rads didn't live through the second day. Although many people stayed indoors in an attempt to avoid the fallout hazard, some were in buildings that reduced the radiation to one-tenth, so that 500 rads were absorbed within a day. All who received as much as 1000 rads within a few hours were dead by the end of the week. For those who received 500 rads in a short interval, mortality was about 90 per cent; mostly they were dead by the middle of November.

In the whole 9000-square-mile area of appreciable local fallout, people who couldn't or didn't find shelter received doses up to 5000 rads the second day after the attack, 250 the third day, 150 the fourth day, and 100 on the fifth day. They didn't live much longer than that.

The region of local fallout is still radioactive. The persistence of high radioactivity was one of the factors that led to the decision, later in December, to avacuate most of the area. Another factor was the probability that no crops could be raised on the heavily contaminated soil for a long time, and then there was also the fear that the denuded land, with its water-holding cover gone, would be subject to severe flooding in the spring.

It turns out that the decision was well taken. We hear that over hundreds of square miles of southern Illinois there is still nothing to be seen but the scarred, eroded earth—nothing was planted, and nothing has sprouted. West of St. Louis conditions are said to be somewhat better, but the ground is so badly contaminated that there is no possibility of using food grown on it. The worst of it is that the peak of accumulation of the long-lived isotopes is still in the future. In about two years we expect that the Strontium 90 concentration in the local fallout region will range from 10,000 to 300,000 millicuries per square mile, and Cesium 137 from 20,000 to 600,000.

On a world-wide scale, the explosion of 4000 megatons of weapons released 2000 megatons of energy equivalent of fission products. This means that a total of 200 million curies of Strontium 90 was produced. (Remember that a "curie" is a thousand millicuries.) Four-fifths of this came down as local fallout, but the remaining 40 million curies will come down gradually from the stratosphere. In two to five years, when the Strontium 90 concentration will be greatest, the average Strontium 90 concentration in the north temperate zone will be about 1000 millicuries per square mile. Back in the late Fifties we were concerned because the soil around St. Louis had forty-six millicuries per square mile because of fallout from testing! And yet it is expected that ten to twenty per cent of the area of the United States will have concentrations up to 500 times greater than the north temperate zone average of 100 millicuries per square mile. Right now it doesn't seem possible that food crops could be grown in such areas for a century at least.

9

The People in Power

☆ *The prominent political analyst and commentator, Walter Lippmann (1889-   ), has for a half century examined the relationship between the people and the government. In the following selection Lippmann makes the controversial assertion that mass opinion has too greatly influenced the government with resultant harmful effects.** ☆

. . . there has developed in this century a functional derangement of the relationship between the mass of the people and the government. The people have acquired power which they are incapable of exercising, and the governments they elect have lost powers which they must recover if they are to govern. What then are the true boundaries of the people's power? The answer cannot be simple. But for a rough beginning let us say that the people are able to give and to withhold their consent to being governed—their consent to what the government asks of them, proposes to them, and has done in the conduct of their affairs. They can elect the government. They can remove it. They can approve or disapprove its performance. But they cannot administer the government. They cannot themselves perform. They cannot normally initiate and propose the necessary legislation. A mass cannot govern. The people, as Jefferson said, are not "qualified to exercise them-

* From *Essays in the Public Philosophy* by Walter Lippmann, pp. 14-15, 19-20, 24-27, by permission of Little, Brown & Co. Copyright, 1955, by Walter Lippmann. Published by Little, Brown—Atlantic Monthly Press.

selves the Executive Department; but they are qualified to name the person who shall exercise it . . . They are not qualified to legislate; with us therefore they only choose the legislators."

Where mass opinion dominates the government, there is a morbid derangement of the true functions of power. The derangement brings about the enfeeblement, verging on paralysis, of the capacity to govern. This breakdown in the constitutional order is the cause of the precipitate and catastrophic decline of Western society. It may, if it cannot be arrested and reversed, bring about the fall of the West.

The propensity to this derangement and the vulnerability of our society to it have a long and complex history. Yet the more I have brooded upon the events which I have lived through myself, the more astounding and significant does it seem that the decline of the power and influence and self-confidence of the Western democracies has been so steep and so sudden. We have fallen far in a short span of time. However long the underlying erosion had been going on, we were still a great and powerful and flourishing community when the First World War began. What we have seen is not only decay—though much of the old structure was dissolving—but something which can be called an historic catastrophe. . . .

Experience since 1917 indicates that in matters of war and peace the popular answer in the democracies is likely to be No. For everything connected with war has become dangerous, painful, disagreeable and exhausting to very nearly everyone. The rule to which there are few exceptions—the acceptance of the Marshall Plan is one of them—is that at the critical junctures, when the stakes are high, the prevailing mass opinion will impose what amounts to a veto upon changing the course on which the government is at the time proceeding. Prepare for war in time of peace? No. It is bad to raise taxes, to unbalance the budget, to take men away from their schools or their jobs, to provoke the enemy. Intervene in a developing conflict? No. Avoid the risk of war. Withdraw from the area of the conflict? No. The adversary must not be appeased. Reduce your claims on the area? No. Righteousness cannot be compromised. Negotiate a compromise peace as soon as the opportunity presents itself? No. The aggressor must be punished. Remain armed to enforce the dictated settlement? No. The war is over.

The unhappy truth is that the prevailing public opinion has been destructively wrong at the critical junctures. The people have imposed a veto upon the judgments of informed and responsible officials. They have compelled the governments, which usually knew what would have been wiser, or was necessary, or was more expedient, to be too late with too little, or too long with too much, too pacifist in peace and too bellicose in war, too neutralist or appeasing in negotiation or too intransigent. Mass opinion has acquired mounting power in this century. It has shown itself to be a dangerous master of decisions when the stakes are life and death. . . .

The record shows that the people of the democracies, having become sovereign in this century, have made it increasingly difficult for their governments to prepare properly for war or to make peace. Their responsible officials have been like the ministers of an opinionated and willful despot. Between the critical junctures, when public opinion has been inattentive or not vehemently aroused, responsible officials have often been able to circumvent extremist popular opinions and to wheedle their way towards moderation and good sense. In the crises, however, democratic officials—over and above their own human propensity to err—have been compelled to make the big mistakes that public opinion has insisted upon. Even the greatest men have not been able to turn back the massive tides of opinion and of sentiment.

There is no mystery about why there is such a tendency for popular opinion to be wrong in judging war and peace. Strategic and diplomatic decisions call for a kind of knowledge—not to speak of an experience and a seasoned judgment—which cannot be had by glancing at newspapers, listening to snatches of radio comment, watching politicians perform on television, hearing occasional lectures, and reading a few books. It would not be enough to make a man competent to decide whether to amputate a leg, and it is not enough to qualify him to choose war or peace, to arm or not to arm, to intervene or to withdraw, to fight on or to negotiate.

Usually, moreover, when the decision is critical and urgent, the public will not be told the whole truth. What can be told to the great public it will not hear in the complicated and qualified concreteness that is needed for a practical decision. When distant and unfamiliar and complex things are communicated to great masses of people, the truth suffers a considerable and often a radical distortion. The complex is made over into the simple, the hypothetical into the dogmatic, and the relative into an absolute. Even when there is no deliberate distortion by censorship and propaganda, which is unlikely in time of war, the public opinion of masses cannot be counted upon to apprehend regularly and promptly the reality of things. There is an inherent tendency in opinion to feed upon rumors excited by our own wishes and fears. . . .

In government offices which are sensitive to the vehemence and passion of mass sentiment public men have no sure tenure. They are in effect perpetual office seekers, always on trial for their political lives, always required to court their restless constituents. They are deprived of their independence. Democratic politicians rarely feel they can afford the luxury of telling the whole truth to the people. And since not telling it, though prudent, is uncomfortable, they find it easier if they themselves do not have to hear too often too much of the sour truth. The men under them who report and collect the news come to realize in their turn that it is safer to be wrong before it has become fashionable to be right.

With exceptions so rare that they are regarded as miracles and freaks of nature, successful democratic politicians are insecure and intimidated men. They advance politically only as they placate, appease, bribe, seduce, bamboozle, or otherwise manage to manipulate the demanding and threatening elements in their constituencies. The decisive consideration is not whether the proposition is good but whether it is popular—not whether it will work well and prove itself but whether the active talking constituents like it immediately. Politicians rationalize this servitude by saying that in a democracy public men are the servants of the people.

This devitalization of the governing power is the malady of democratic states. As the malady grows the executives become highly susceptible to encroachment and usurpation by elected assemblies; they are pressed and harassed by the higgling of parties, by the agents of organized interests, and by the spokesmen of sectarians and ideologues. The malady can be fatal. It can be deadly to the very survival of the state as a free society if, when the great and hard issues of war and peace, of security and solvency, of revolution and order are up for decision, the executive and judicial departments, with their civil servants and technicians, have lost their power to decide.

10

Union and Compromise

☆ *Herbert Agar (1897-   ), editor and observer, has taken issue with the contention that partisan consistency is necessary for the strength of the nation. Agar argues that continued political compromise has been responsible for the maintenance of national unity.* ☆

During Grover Cleveland's first term in the White House, James Bryce published his remarkable book, *The American Commonwealth*. Surveying the party system from the English point of view, and with quiet surprise, he made the classic statement of the difference between the Republicans and the Democrats.

"What are their principles [he wrote], their distinctive tenets, their tendencies? Which of them is for free trade, for civil-service reform, for a spirited foreign policy . . . for changes in the currency, for any other of the twenty issues which one hears discussed in the country as seriously involving its welfare? This is what a European is always asking of intelligent Republicans and intelligent Democrats. He is always asking because he never gets an answer. The replies leave him in deeper perplexity. After some months the truth begins to dawn on him. Neither party has anything definite to say on these issues; neither party has any principles, any distinctive tenets. Both have traditions. Both claim to have tendencies. Both have

certainly war cries, organizations, interests, enlisted in their support. But those interests are in the main the interests of getting or keeping the patronage of the government. Tenets and policies, points of political doctrine and points of political practice, have all but vanished. They have not been thrown away but have been stripped away by Time and the progress of events, fulfilling some policies, blotting out others. All has been lost, except office or the hope of it."

This is a true description of the parties as they were, and as they still are; but Bryce's explanation of how they came to be that way is misleading. He assumes that if the American parties were healthy they would resemble the parties of Great Britain. They would have "principles" and "tenets," and would thus be forced to take sides on all "the twenty issues that one hears discussed." And he assumes that "Time and the progress of events" have deprived the parties of their principles, leaving them with nothing but "office or the hope of it." But this is too short a view; Lord Bryce was confused by the brief history of the Republican Party, which possessed principles in 1856 and none in 1886. He thought this was a sign of failure and decay; but in fact it was a sign of health; 1856 had been the exception and the danger; 1886 was the reassuring norm.

The purpose—the important and healthy purpose—of an American party is to be exactly what Lord Bryce describes, and by implication deplores. The party is intended to be an organization for "getting or keeping the patronage of government." Instead of seeking "principles," or "distinctive tenets," which can only divide a federal union, the party is intended to seek bargains between the regions, the classes, and the other interest groups. It is intended to bring men and women of all beliefs, occupations, sections, racial backgrounds, into a combination for the pursuit of power. The combination is too various to possess firm convictions. The members may have nothing in common except a desire for office. Unless driven by a forceful President they tend to do as little as possible. They tend to provide some small favor for each noisy group, and to call that a policy. They tend to ignore any issue that rouses deep passion. And by so doing they strengthen the Union.

The decisive American experience—the warning against politics based on principles—took place between 1850 and 1860. A subtle and healing compromise had been effected in 1850; yet year by year, whether through fate or through human folly, it slowly disintegrated. The best men watched in anguish but could not halt the ruin. In the name of principles and distinctive tenets the Whig Party was ground to bits. A new party was born which met Lord Bryce's requirements. The Republicans knew exactly where they stood on the major issue and would not give an inch. Finally, the same "principles" broke the Democratic Party, and the Union of 1789 perished.

The lesson which America learned was useful: in a large federal nation, when a problem is passionately felt, and is dis-

cussed in terms of morals, each party may divide within itself, against itself. And if the parties divide, the nation may divide; for the parties, with their enjoyable pursuit of power, are a unifying influence. Wise men, therefore, may seek to dodge such problems as long as possible. And the easiest way to dodge them is for both parties to take both sides. This is normal American practice, whether the issue turns section against section, like "cheap money"; or town against country, like Prohibition; or class against class like the use of injunctions in labor disputes. It is a sign of health when the Democrats choose a "sound-money" candidate for the presidency and a "cheap-money" platform, as they did in 1868; or when they choose a "wet" Eastern candidate for the presidency and a "dry" Western candidate for the vice-presidency, as they did in 1924. It is a sign of health when the Republicans choose a "sound-money" platform but cheerfully repudiate it throughout the "cheap-money" states, as they did in 1868.

A federal nation is safe so long as the parties are undogmatic and contain members with many contradictory views. But when the people begin to divide according to reason, with all the voters in one party who believe one way, the federal structure is strained. We saw this in 1896, during the last great fight for "free silver." To be sure, there remained some "gold Democrats" and some "silver Republicans" in 1896; yet the campaign produced the sharpest alignment on principle since the Civil War. And the fierce sectional passions racked the nation. Luckily, the silver issue soon settled itself, and removed itself from politics, so the parties could relapse into their saving illogicality.

The faults of such irrational parties are obvious. Brains and energy are lavished, not on the search for truth, but on the search for bargains, for concessions which will soothe well-organized minorities, for excuses to justify delay and denial. Unofficially, and in spite of any constitution, successful federal politics will tend to follow Calhoun's rule of concurrent majorities. Every interest which is strong enough to make trouble must usually be satisfied before anything can be done. This means great caution in attempting new policies, so that a whole ungainly continent may keep in step. Obstruction, evasion, well-nigh intolerable slowness— these are the costs of America's federal union. And the endless bartering of minor favors which we saw at its silliest in President Arthur's Congress is also part of the price. And so is the absence of a clear purpose whenever the President is weak or self-effacing, since the sum of sectional and class interests is not equal to the national interest, and the exchange of favors between blocs or pressure groups does not make a policy.

Yet no matter how high one puts the price of federal union, it is small compared to the price which other continents have paid for disunion, and for the little national states in which parties of principle can live (or more often die) for their clearly defined causes. And the price is small compared to what America paid for her own years of disunion. The United States, of course, may some day attain such uniformity (or have it thrust upon her) that she will abandon her federal structure; but until that happens she will be governed by concurrent majorities, by vetoes and filibusters, by parties which take both sides of every dangerous question, which are held together by the amusements and rewards of office-seeking, and which can only win an election by bringing many incompatible groups to accept a token triumph in the name of unity, instead of demanding their full "rights" at the cost of a fight.

11

The New Frontier

☆ *In 1960, Vice President Richard M. Nixon and United States Senator John F. Kennedy of Massachusetts were nominated, respectively, for president by the Republican and Democratic parties. By a narrow margin, Kennedy was elected. President Kennedy, in his State of the Union address to Congress of January 30, 1961, indicated the problems facing the nation, as he saw them, and the action he considered desirable to meet these problems.* * ☆

The present state of the economy is disturbing. We take office in the wake of seven months of recession, three and a half years of slack, seven years of diminished economic growth, and nine years of falling farm income. . . .

We cannot afford to waste idle hours and empty plants while awaiting the end of the recession. We must show the world what a free economy can do—to reduce unemployment, to put unused capacity to work, to spur new productivity, and to foster higher economic growth within a range of sound fiscal policies and relative price stability.

I will propose to the Congress within the next fourteen days measures to improve unemployment compensation through temporary increases in duration on a self-supporting basis—to provide more food for the families of the unemployed, and to aid their needy children—to redevelop our areas of chronic labor surplus—to expand the services of the United States employment offices—to stimulate housing

and construction—to secure more purchasing power for our lowest paid workers by raising and expanding the minimum wage—to offer tax incentives for sound plant investment—to increase the development of our natural resources—to encourage price stability—and to take other steps aimed at insuring a prompt recovery and paving the way for increased long-range growth. This is not a partisan program concentrating on our weaknesses—it is, I hope, a national program to realize our national strength.

Efficient expansion at home, stimulating the new plant and technology that can make our goods more competitive, is also the key to the international balance of payments problem. Laying aside all alarmist talk and panicky solutions, let us put that knotty problem in its proper perspective.

It is true that, since 1958, the gap between the dollars we spend or invest abroad and the dollars returned to us has substantially widened. This over-all deficit in our balance of payments increased by nearly $11,000,000,000 in the last three

* From *Vital Speeches*, XXVII (February 15, 1961), pp. 258-262.

years—and holders of dollars abroad converted them to gold in such a quantity as to cause a total outflow of nearly $5,000,-000,000 of gold from our reserve. The total deficit was caused in large part by our failure of our exports to penetrate foreign markets—the result both of restrictions on our goods and our own uncompetitive prices. The 1960 deficit, on the other hand, was more the result of an increase in private capital outflow seeking new opportunity, higher return or speculative advantage abroad. . . .

Prudence and good sense do require, however, that new steps be taken to ease the payment deficits and prevent any gold crises. Our success in world affairs has long depended in part upon foreign confidence in our ability to pay. A series of executive orders, legislative remedies and cooperative efforts with our allies will get under way immediately—aimed at attracting foreign investment and travel to this country—promoting American exports, at stable prices and with more liberal Government guarantees and financing—curbing tax and customs loopholes that encourage undue spending of private dollars abroad—and (through O.E.C.D., NATO and otherwise) sharing with our allies all efforts to provide for the common defense of the free world and the hopes for growth of the less developed lands. . . .

But more than our exchange of international payments is out of balance. The current Federal budget for fiscal 1961 is almost certain to show a net deficit. The budget already submitted for fiscal 1962 will remain in balance only if the Congress enacts all the revenue measures requested—and only if an earlier and sharper upturn in the economy than my economic advisers now think likely produces the tax revenues estimated.

Nevertheless, a new Administration must of necessity build on the spending and revenue estimates already submitted. Within that framework, barring the development of urgent national defense needs or a worsening of the economy, it is my current intention to advocate a program of expenditures which, including revenue from a stimulation of the economy, will not of and by themselves unbalance the earlier budget.

However, we will do what must be done. For our national household is cluttered with unfinished and neglected tasks. Our cities are being engulfed in squalor. Twelve long years after Congress declared our goal to be "a decent home and a suitable environment for every American family," we still have 25,-000,000 Americans living in substandard homes. A new housing program under a new housing and urban affairs department will be needed this year.

Our classrooms contain 2,000,000 more children than they can properly have room for, taught by 90,000 teachers not properly qualified to teach. One-third of our most promising high school graduates are financially unable to continue the development of their talents.

The war babies of the Nineteen Forties, who overcrowded our schools in the Nineteen Fifties, are now descending in the Nineteen Sixties upon our colleges—with two college students for every one ten years from now—and our colleges are ill prepared. . . .

Medical research has achieved new wonders—but these wonders are too often beyond the reach of too many people, owing to a lack of income (particularly among the aged), a lack of hospital beds, a lack of nursing homes and a lack of doctors and dentists. Measures to provide health care for the aged under Social Security, and to increase the supply of both facilities and personnel, must be undertaken this year.

Our supply of clean water is dwindling. Organized and juvenile crimes cost the taxpayers millions of dollars every year, making it essential that we have improved enforcement and new legislative safeguards. The denial of constitutional rights to some of our fellow Americans on account of race—at the ballot box and elsewhere—disturbs the national conscience, and subjects us to the charge of world opinion that our democracy is not equal to the high promise of our heritage. . . .

But all these problems pale when placed beside those which confront us around the world. . . .

Each day the crises multiply. Each day their solution grows more difficult. Each day we draw nearer the hour of maximum danger, as weapons spread and hostile forces grow stronger. I feel I must inform the Congress that our analyses over the last ten days make it clear that —in each of the principal areas of crisis —the tide of events has been running out and time has not been our friend. . . .

To meet this array of challenges—to fulfill the role we cannot avoid on the world scene—we must re-examine and revise our whole arsenal of tools. . . .

First, we must strengthen our military tools. We are moving into a period of uncertain risk and great commitments in which both the military and diplomatic possibilities require a free world force so powerful as to make any aggression clearly futile. . . .

. . . I have asked the Defense Secretary to initiate immediately three steps most clearly needed now:

A.—First, I have directed prompt action to increase our airlift capacity. Obtaining additional air transport mobility —and obtaining it now—will better assure the ability of our conventional forces to respond, with discrimination and speed, to any problem at any spot on the globe at any moment's notice. . . .

B.—I have directed prompt action to step up our Polaris submarine program. Using unobligated ship-building funds now (to let contracts originally scheduled for the next fiscal year) will build and place on station—at least nine months earlier than planned—substantially more units of a crucial deterrent. . . .

C.—I have directed prompt action to accelerate our entire missile program. . . .

If we are to keep the peace, we need an invulnerable missile force powerful enough to deter any aggressor from even threatening an attack that he would know could not destroy enough of our own forces to prevent his own destruction. . . .

Secondly, we must improve our economic tools. Our role is essential and unavoidable in the construction of a sound and expanding economy for the entire non-Communist world, helping other nations build the strength to meet their own problems, to satisfy their own aspirations, to surmount their own dangers. . . .

A.—I intend to ask the Congress for authority to establish a new and more effective program for assisting the economic, educational and social development of other countries and continents. That program must stimulate and take more effectively into account the contributions of our allies, and provide central policy direction for all our own programs that now so often overlap, conflict or diffuse our energies and resources. Such a program, compared to past programs, will require:

More flexibility for short-run emergencies.

More commitment to long-term development.

New attention to education at all levels. . . .

B.—I hope the Senate will take early action approving the convention establishing the Organization for Economic Cooperation and Development. This will be an important instrument in sharing with our allies this development effort—working toward the time when each nation will contribute in proportion to its ability to pay. For, while we are prepared to assume our full share of these huge burdens, we cannot and must not be expected to bear them alone.

C.—To our sister republics of the south, we have pledged a new alliance for progress—alianza para progreso. . . . To start this nation's role at this time in that alliance of neighbors, I am recommending the following:

That the Congress appropriate in full the $500,000,000 fund pledged by the act of Bogota, to be used not as an instrument of the "cold war," but as a first step in the sound development of the Americas. . . .

That our delegates to the O.A.S., working with those of other members, strengthen that body as an instrument to preserve the peace and to prevent foreign domination anywhere in the hemisphere.

That, in cooperation with other nations, we launch a new hemisphere attack on illiteracy and inadequate educational opportunities at all levels; and, finally,

That a food-for-peace mission be sent immediately to Latin America to explore ways in which our vast food abundance can be used to help end hunger and malnutrition in certain areas of suffering in our own hemisphere.

D.—This Administration is expanding its new food-for-peace program in every possible way. The product of our abundance must be used more effectively to relieve hunger and help economic growth in all corners of the globe. . . .

E.—An even more valuable national asset is our reservoir of dedicated men and women—not only at our college campuses but in every age group—who have indicated their desire to contribute their skills, their efforts, and a part of their lives to the fight for world order. We can mobilize this talent through the formation of a national Peace Corps, enlisting the services of all those with the desire and capacity to help foreign lands meet their urgent needs for trained personnel.

Finally, while our attention is centered on the development of the non-Communist world, we must never forget our hopes for the ultimate freedom and welfare of the Eastern European people. In order to be prepared to help re-establishing historic ties of friendship, I am asking the Congress for increased discretion to use economic tools in this area whenever this is found to be clearly in the national interest. . . .

Third, we must sharpen our political and diplomatic tools—the means of cooperation and agreement on which an enforceable world order must ultimately rest.

A.—I have already taken steps to coordinate and expand our disarmament effort—to increase our programs of research and study—and to make arms control a central goal of our national policy under my direction. The deadly arms race, and the huge resources it absorbs, have too long overshadowed all else we must do. . . .

B.—We must increase our support of the United Nations as an instrument to end the "cold war" instead of an arena in which to fight it. In recognition of its increasing importance and the doubling of its membership:

We are enlarging and strengthening our own mission to the U. N.

We shall help insure that it is properly financed.

We shall work to see that the integrity of the office of the Secretary General is maintained.

And I would address a special plea to the smaller nations of the world—to join with us in strengthening this organization, which is far more essential to their security than it is to ours. . . .

C.—Finally, this Administration intends to explore promptly all possible areas of cooperation with the Soviet Union and other nations "to invoke the wonders of science instead of its terrors." Specifically, I now invite all nations—including the Soviet Union—to join with us in developing a weather prediction program, in a new communications satellite program and in preparation for probing the distant planets of Mars and Venus, probes which may some day unlock the deepest secrets of the universe.